The Mirror Test

THE MIRROR TEST

America at War in Iraq and Afghanistan

J. KAEL WESTON

ALFRED A. KNOPF   NEW YORK   2016

THIS IS A BORZOI BOOK
PUBLISHED BY ALFRED A. KNOPF

Grateful acknowledgment is made to the following for permission
to reprint previously published material: *Richmond Times-Dispatch:*
Excerpt from "Those Who Know Vietnam Hero Still Pondering
His Whereabouts," published in *Richmond Times-Dispatch* (May 15,
2000). Reprinted by permission of *Richmond Times-Dispatch*. Rodale:
Excerpt from "What is a Father? The Hero Figure" by Aaron Mankin,
published in *Best Life* (June 2007). Copyright © 2015 by Rodale.
Reprinted by permission of Rodale, via Wright's Media.

All photos are courtesy of the author, with the exception of the
following: UCLA Operation Mend photos by Michelle Van Vliet,
courtesy of the UCLA Division of Plastic & Reconstructive Surgery;
photo of Waleed and Colin McNease, courtesy of Colin McNease;
and three photos from the U.S. Department of Defense
(www.defense.gov).

Library of Congress Cataloging-in-Publication Data
Names: Weston, J. Kael, author.
Title: The mirror test : America at war in Iraq and Afghanistan / by J. Kael Weston.
Description: First edition. | New York : Alfred A. Knopf, 2016. | "A Borzoi Book."
Identifiers: LCCN 2015047993 (print) | LCCN 2016011224 (ebook) |
ISBN 9780385351126 (hardcover) | ISBN 9780385351133 (ebook)
Subjects: LCSH: Iraq War, 2003–2011. | Afghan War, 2001– | Iraq War, 2003–
2011—Personal narratives, American. | Afghan War, 2001—Personal narratives,
American. | Weston, J. Kael. | United States. Department of State—Officials and
employees—Biography.
Classification: LCC DS79.76 w464 2016 (print) | LCC DS79.76 (ebook) |
DDC 956.7044/345092—dc23
LC record available at http://lccn.loc.gov/2015047993

Front-of-jacket photograph © George Baier IV
Jacket design by Oliver Munday

Manufactured in the United States of America
First Edition

In gratitude to my twin brother, Kyle, the first and last editor. And to my parents, Brad and Linda, and the whole Weston family, who welcomed me back home to the white peaks and red canyons and Orion skies of the American West after a long time away.

And to Lieutenant General Larry Nicholson, WIA, a leader in both wars.

In memory of Abbas, Hamza, Najm, Kamal, Khudairi, Sami, Ibraheem, Qadir, Fassal, Jamal, Ryan, Nick, Trevor, Rick, Bill, RCH, and each of the 31 Angels, among so many, many others.

*

For all who "do" in times of war, including U.S. Army medic PFC Thomas (Tommie) L. Cole.

For all the teachers and students, over there and over here.

And especially for all the Iraqis, Afghans, and U.S. Marines along the way and through the years.

No better friends.
No greater sacrifice.

This book is not about heroes. . . . Nor is it about deeds, or lands, nor anything about glory, honour, might, majesty, dominion, or power, except War. Above all I am not concerned with Poetry. My subject is War, and the pity of War. The Poetry is in the pity.

WILFRED OWEN

The War Goes On

Life MAGAZINE COVER, FEBRUARY 11, 1966

The Last of the Light Brigade

There were thirty million English who talked of England's might,
There were twenty broken troopers who lacked a bed for the night.
They had neither food nor money, they had neither service nor trade;
They were only shiftless soldiers, the last of the Light Brigade.

They felt that life was fleeting; they knew not that art was long,
That though they were dying of famine, they lived in deathless song.
They asked for a little money to keep the wolf from the door;
And the thirty million English sent twenty pounds and four!

They laid their heads together that were scarred and lined and grey;
Keen were the Russian sabres, but want was keener than they;
And an old Troop-Sergeant muttered, "Let us go to the man who writes
The things on Balaclava the kiddies at school recites."

They went without bands or colours, a regiment ten-file strong,
To look for the Master-singer who had crowned them all in his song;
And, waiting his servant's order, by the garden gate they stayed,
A desolate little cluster, the last of the Light Brigade.

They strove to stand to attention, to straighten the toil-bowed back;
They drilled on an empty stomach, the loose-knit files fell slack;
With stooping of weary shoulders, in garments tattered and frayed,
They shambled into his presence, the last of the Light Brigade.

The old Troop-Sergeant was spokesman, and "Beggin' your pardon," he said,
"You wrote o' the Light Brigade, sir. Here's all that isn't dead.
An' it's all come true what you wrote, sir, regardin' the mouth of hell;
For we're all of us nigh to the workhouse, an' we thought we'd call an' tell.

"No, thank you, we don't want food, sir; but couldn't you take an' write
A sort of 'to be continued' and 'see next page' o' the fight?
We think that someone has blundered, an' couldn't you tell 'em how?
You wrote we were heroes once, sir. Please, write we are starving now."

The poor little army departed, limping and lean and forlorn.
And the heart of the Master-singer grew hot with "the scorn of scorn."
And he wrote for them wonderful verses that swept the land like flame,
Till the fatted souls of the English were scourged with the thing called Shame.

O thirty million English that babble of England's might,
Behold there are twenty heroes who lack their food to-night;
Our children's children are lisping to "honour the charge they made"
And we leave to the streets and the workhouse the charge of the Light Brigade!

RUDYARD KIPLING, 1890*

*In 1915, Rudyard Kipling's only son, Second Lieutenant John Kipling, was killed in France during World War I at age eighteen.

Contents

PART III
Home

EPILOGUE
New York City

After War

I just ask Americans to stop and pause after they make
their first stare.

RONNY "TONY" PORTA, U.S. MARINE, WIA
ANBAR PROVINCE, IRAQ, 2007

Preface

I first met Marine Corporal Aaron Mankin in Fallujah in early 2005,
just before he lost most of his face in the Iraq War. The State Department had assigned me the prior summer to be the political adviser to
the three-star Marine commanding general based there and to oversee
the U.S. government's strategy in the city and Anbar province. Aaron, a
native of Rogers, Arkansas (home to the first Wal-Mart Discount City
store, which opened in 1962), professional in bearing, with cobalt eyes,
square jaw, high-and-tight haircut, showed maturity and possessed an
eloquence that belied his youthful age.

A few months later, Aaron and a unit of Marines were traveling in a
convoy when one of the largest roadside bombs to date detonated—an
explosion killing four, wounding eleven, and disfiguring Aaron in an
instant. His bones cracked and skin scorched. Ears, nose, and mouth
ravaged. Only Aaron's eyes were left unchanged, shielded by protective
goggles as fire roared through his vehicle's cramped rear compartment

and ignited the Marines' grenades, bullets, and flares. The blast lifted the twenty-six-ton transport vehicle nearly a dozen feet into the air, leaving a deep crater below. Aaron suffered severe burns to a quarter of his body, lost his right thumb and index finger. Doctors placed him on a ventilator in the intensive care unit at San Antonio's Military Medical Center. Ultimately, he underwent over sixty surgeries to reconstruct his face and help heal his wounded body.

Marine Corporal Tony Porta was also badly wounded in Iraq's Anbar province at age twenty. In a television interview, he described what happened after an IED blasted his convoy in 2007. "I saw my body just burned. I saw my skin melting. It was like a hot candle." His two best friends were killed in the explosion.

Both are brutal stories, but Aaron's and Tony's are not the only ones. The wars in Iraq and Afghanistan have resulted in more than 1,100 major burn victims and 1,700 amputees among the 50,000-plus combat casualties—the total killed or injured among U.S. troops. In December 2014 the Congressional Budget Office reported 3,482 hostile deaths, plus another thousand from nonbattle injuries or accidents, and 31,947 U.S. military personnel wounded in the Iraq War, with over 2,300 dead and 20,000 wounded in Afghanistan. An additional estimated 400,000 have been diagnosed with post-traumatic stress, mild traumatic brain injury, or both. These numbers continue to rise for those with visible and invisible wounds, not to mention the cumulative toll on veterans' families.

Iraqi and Afghan civilians have suffered on an even greater scale. Hundreds of thousands left dead and wounded, along with untold cases of psychological damage from unending warfare. Towns turned into battle zones and family compounds made of mud raided in darkness. Unlike U.S. troops and me, they could not redeploy. As we returned home, Iraqis and Afghans had no option but to remain amid persistent violence, caught in a truly forever war.

Some of the most grievously wounded veterans who survived the bombs and the bullets are cared for at Walter Reed National Military Medical Center, located just outside Washington, D.C. Where politicians commute to office suites in marble buildings and raise campaign money at invitation-only events far from the war fronts.

Staff Sergeant Brown of Sugar Land, Texas, lost three and a half limbs—both legs and much of his right arm—on his fourth combat tour. His genitals were shredded in the blast. "The new protective underwear came three weeks too late for me," he said. And all of it recorded by his buddy's headcam. During one visit, the Marine nonchalantly shared with me the images of his body disappearing in a cloud of Afghan dust and mist of his own blood, with his mom, Barbara, watchfully standing nearby in a Semper Fi Fund jacket.

"She likes to treat me like I am still a kid here."

But his comment did not sound like a complaint. For some reason that day in Helmand province's rutted valleys, the Marine added, he had not swept the ground with his metal detector as he had been trained to do, religiously, before starting out on another foot patrol. Staff Sergeant Brown had no idea it would be his last time standing, unaided.

Across the hall on the floor wounded Marines shared at Walter Reed, Corporal Lopez, a Californian, only remembered that a bomb had propelled him several feet into the air. In midflight, he turned and met the eyes of a fellow Marine crouched on the rooftop of an adjacent mud compound. He recalled floating, falling, landing, before passing out. Days later Lopez woke up after arriving in Germany's Landstuhl Regional Medical Center—the halfway point home. I noticed the blanket on his bed had a two-foot section sunken in just below the knee. The blast had destroyed one of his legs, and badly damaged the other. Lopez said he wanted to get back to Afghanistan and rejoin his squad. Marines always said as much, and as I had learned over the years I spent with them, Marines always meant it.

Captain Brad Fultz, a friend of mine wounded by a child suicide bomber in Afghanistan's Uruzgan province, met First Lady Michelle Obama on the fourth floor. Unlike other famous visitors and busy politicians, she lingered—before offering words of her own.

"We need to bring all of you back home from over there."

"I think a lot of Americans would agree with you," said Brad, one native Chicagoan to another. Michelle Obama soon departed, surrounded by a black-suited shell of Secret Service agents. Her husband, the commander in chief, began to draw down troops midway through his second term—before realities in Afghanistan, alongside a deteriorating security situation in Iraq, forced the timeline to be pushed back.

America's longest wars would go on.

A Navy nurse at Bethesda described one Marine's condition, her hardest case ever, she said, in a hospital ward built for pain. After stepping on a fertilizer-based bomb that severed both legs, the patient's subsequent invasive fungal infection had spread so quickly, so stubbornly, that surgeons could not keep ahead of it with their scalpels. And antibiotics only destroy bacteria, not fungi, the nurse explained. Doctors term the diagnosis "gross contamination of wounds."

Running out of places to cut, the medical team told the wounded young Marine and his parents that the decision to do more, to cut more—or not—was theirs: either remove portions at the waist, the highest bisection they had ever attempted, or he would certainly die. And even if they did perform the operation, the prognosis was very bad. Afghanistan's dirt had become entombed in the Marine's gut, invading and occupying his body at the cellular level. No medicine in the world could kill the foreign bugs with foreign names (zygomycetes such as *Rhizopus* spp., *Apophysomyces* spp., *Mucor* spp., *Saksenaea* spp., and *Absidia* spp.) killing him inside out. The Marine and his family had a final conversation. They decided not to go ahead with the surgery and instead to let go. Within days, he died.

For those fortunate enough to survive war like Aaron Mankin, Tony Porta, and other Bethesda patients, medical doctors in military burn care units who treat wounded veterans describe a key part in the recovery process. They call it "the mirror test." In this defining moment, morphine is no longer necessary as treatment has progressed. IVs and catheters are removed. Bandages are peeled back. The disfigured patients must then contemplate a first look into a mirror at his or her new self. The most familiar image that once greeted them morning and night over a toothbrush or under a razor—their own face—is gone. Doctors pay close attention to this critical juncture. Will the patient's gaze into the mirror signal one of recognition—horror, sadness, pity, surprise, resolve—or will the patient instead turn away? Will he or she begin to accept the same, but different, person now inhabiting the glass?

Medical staff let patients decide on their own when the time is right, as skin can be grafted but acceptance cannot. Days, weeks, months can pass.

Many wounded veterans delay this day for as long as possible. They might only choose to face the test before young family members arrive for their first hospital visit, fearful that a child's reaction might be more difficult than their own.

In an interview with *Best Life* magazine, Mankin describes his own experience:

> It was a month and a half before I was ready to look at myself in the mirror. Then one day I got out of my hospital bed to go to physical therapy, and I saw the mirror I'd passed countless times, refusing to see the truth about how hurt I was. I looked over my left shoulder, and there I was—this torn up, frail, thin individual with open wounds on his face that I barely recognized, and my worst imagination became my reality. I cried.
>
> Being a Marine, you want to tell yourself you're fine, just walk it off. But I couldn't walk this one off. I covered the bottom half of my face with my elbow, and looking at my eyes and my forehead, I didn't look any different. I knew inside I was still the same man. But not everyone would see that, and I was very concerned when Jake and Maggie, my little brother and sister, then eight and seven, came to see me in the hospital. I was their big brother. I was in the Marine Corps. I was invincible. That's how they saw me, but I didn't know if they would see me that way anymore.

Tony Porta, who would eventually undergo 128 surgeries, has recounted his own mirror moment: "I couldn't recognize myself. I saw scars. I saw blood. I didn't have any lips, my nose was missing, my ears were gone. That day I felt, 'how can I live like this?'"

Fifteen years have passed since September 11, 2001. Like Aaron's and Tony's, a disfigured veteran's mirror test should become our own: individual Americans reflecting on what it means when a country, but not a nation, goes to war—and is still at war.

It is past time for this kind of shared reckoning. More of us beginning to act conscientiously, indeed responsibly, as citizens—engaged citizens—seeking to better understand and learn from these 9/11 wars.

When we look into that mirror, let's not turn away.

The Mirror Test

Bugles are calling from prairie to shore,
Sign up and fall in and march off to war.

ENNIO MORRICONE
"THE STORY OF A SOLDIER"

PROLOGUE

Twentynine Palms, California

Toward the end of a long two-lane highway that joins Interstate 10, also
named Sonny Bono Memorial Freeway, a massive wind farm becomes
a whirring blur of bone-white blades. The sculpted mechanical arms,
dozens deep and in the same arid valley as Cathedral City, are engineered to grab and transfer energy from the sky. When San Gorgonio
Pass is quiet, they stand as a forest of giant, bent crosses suspended
aloft against the Southern California horizon. These steel structures
slice through the air in wide sweeps 300 days a year on average as high-
pressure systems dominate. When viewed on a windless day from the
San Jacinto Mountains that ring the Los Angeles Basin, the turbines,
made for movement but left still, resemble a vast cemetery.

It is about as far away from the U.S. capital and its Establishment
one can get without a passport or under sail. And where 2,650 miles
to the east, New York City's towering skyline, cut deepest on Septem-

ber 11, 2001, has been remade in lower Manhattan above a solemn memorial.

In this westernmost part of America, Marine Corps Base Twentynine Palms, all 590,000 acres, sits in California's high desert next to Joshua Tree National Park. Gnarled cacti border run-down motels, backlit in deepening reds at dusk. Only infrequent tourists count the palm trees on Main Street, but they never can get them to add up to the right number. (I too tried.)

Marines have nicknamed the base "29 Stumps." It is lunar and as remote as a town can feel despite being only an hour's drive from Palm Springs. That recreational oasis started as a stagecoach stop well before becoming a geriatric golfing mecca and home to Bob Hope of USO fame and America's first official "honorary veteran." Hope's last tour would be to Saudi Arabia and Kuwait in December 1990, visiting troops ordered to Operation Desert Shield—but not ordered all the way to Baghdad.

Extended cab 4x4 trucks steered by buff, tattooed, teenage Marines traverse the five-street military village. Corporals straddling chrome bullet bikes streak by—one-way blurs against asphalt and sagebrush. They challenge speed limits, or ignore them altogether, on the way in and out. Most people around 29 Stumps understand these adrenaline junkies.

Speed is a buzz, a deceptive and dangerous high, like war can be. For some, it is an escape. Perhaps the physics and physicality of motion enable Marines to put distance between them and their raw past in places named Ramadi, Fallujah, Rutbah, Hit, Now Zad, Marjah, Sangin, Kajaki, Taghaz. But it never lasts long. Or long enough.

Across Twentynine Palms, patriotism is overtly displayed as friends and brothers and fathers and mothers continually are ordered to the front lines. Marines sent to places like Helmand and back to Iraq's Anbar province, which means "granaries" in Arabic but is now far more known for its violence. "Support Our Troops" and "Proud USMC Wife" stickers and yellow ribbon magnets adorn bumpers and the front windows of the base's only grocery store. The Underground tattoo parlor and 29 Smoke Shop welcome customers next to the Potter's House Christian Fellowship Church, all aligned along a small strip mall.

Barbershops open early, keep their lights on late, and remain the best, recession-proof industry in town. Standard fade haircuts are a bargain at $10, a weekly Marine ritual. The most junior Marines, not the bull colonels, leave the biggest tips. Across counters and in lines, conversations tend to begin and end with "sir" and "ma'am," especially at the Warrior Club—an all-ranks dining facility that serves up "the finest in fast food," including double cheeseburgers, chicken strips, fish sticks, fries, nachos, "and much more!"

This land is the Marines' anchor, around which they train endlessly before being sent to battle. As America's foremost legion and with the youngest recruits, the United States Marine Corps orders its tanks, infantrymen, helicopters, and fighter jets to "war-game" across the base's 935 square miles in a mock operation first named Mojave Viper, then Enhanced Mojave Viper. Before 9/11 they were simply called CAX (pronounced "cacks"), Combined Arms Exercise.

If the business of the town and its combat training ranges were not so serious and deadly, and casualty counts on the real battlefields not so commonplace, one could imagine seeing Wile E. Coyote and the Road Runner zigzagging in their looping chases in the rearview mirror. Bugs Bunny himself once took on Hermann Göring (*Herr Meets Hare*) in World War II comic strips, prompting the Marine Corps to promote the rabbit to the rank of master sergeant. The two qualities innate among most Marines, strength and smart-ass humor, endure.

But Twentynine Palms is not a place of desert mirages or cartoon characters. It is where war's realities sink in, what it means when a country finds itself stuck at war, year after year.

Their boys killing our boys killing their boys.

During one road trip into town, I noticed a billboard along Highway 62—a route three times as deadly as others in the state—that read: "FREE Reconstructive Surgery for Battle-Scarred Warriors of the Iraq and Afghanistan Wars." Below was listed a phone number. In smaller print, it advertised a string of jarring postwar medical procedures:

Shrapnel Removal. Scar Revision. Laser for Facial Sandblast.

A decade and a half after September 11, 2001, Twentynine Palms remains one of the U.S. military's main springboards into war. It is among the most trodden Marine bases to which worn-down veterans return to breathe, train, do an about-face, and then repeat the cycle. Deployment. Redeployment. Deployment. Redeployment. As such

Twentynine Palms has a wartime conscience. It is forced to, with families waiting out yet another combat tour until their Marines come back home. Most do.

But for some U.S. troops, the return is as silent as it is final—KIA numbering in the thousands buried in communities, coast to coast, hundreds of miles away from the sunbaked yellow deserts of California. These other towns are well removed from Arlington National Cemetery as well, where the United States of America officially honors its war dead. And where commanders in chief dutifully cross the Potomac River each May over Memorial Day Weekend to pay respects to the men and women ordered to distant war fronts. These veterans include those interred in Section 60—called "America's Saddest Acre"—and not far from Arlington's Tomb of the Unknown Soldier: "Here rests in honored glory an American soldier known but to God."

Newcastle, Wyoming, located far from Washington, D.C., is one such hometown, a Marine kind of town and my kind of town, where the local war dead from Iraq and Afghanistan, all known, are still mourned.

It took me eleven hours to get to the plains of eastern Wyoming by way of Denver and Fort Collins, winding my way north on I-70 and I-25 across a rugged state line shared by Colorado and Utah, hypnotic highways, half-paved county roads, and dirt ones. NPR affiliate signals—no better companion for a bumpy road trip complemented by Billy Idol and Johnny Cash tracks and Dairy Queen drive-thrus—had mostly faded out.

I passed one lonesome town, Lost Springs, with a sign declaring: "POP 4, ELEV 4,996." Probably a single stubborn family. My aging Toyota Tacoma's odometer hit just over 75,100 miles when I stopped to fill up in Newcastle, an hour or so beyond the 3 Sisters Truck Stop in Manville (pop. 97). As I pumped four-buck-a-gallon gas, a hawk circled overhead between low clouds. It reminded me of those that soared between terraced valleys in Afghanistan's Qalandar District. Lots of hawks there, but never in Iraq. Above Fallujah's forest of minarets, the only birds of prey were our surveillance drones, known as ScanEagles back then—before newer, more quiet, more expensive, and lethal models, called Predators and Reapers, peered with metallic eyes from the sky.

This was tough, historic terrain. Just over the border in Montana the brash and theatrical George Armstrong Custer had been killed in June 1876 atop a green hill, surrounded by a joint fighting force of Lakota, Northern Cheyenne, and Arapahoe. Newspaper headlines at the time exclaimed "Terrible Butchery by the Indians!" and "Poor Custer" while avoiding his real epitaph: the inveterate gambler and Civil War hero, no less by age twenty-three at Gettysburg, had gone to America's frontier for gold, glory, and gore. In other words, Lieutenant Colonel Custer had ventured west as a veteran of one war seeking more war—and sure got it.

I myself learned in Iraq and Afghanistan that invasions and insurgencies—who did what, why, first, and to whom—differed in their historical details and settings. But the outcomes were the same. Revenge recycled, with no storybook ever-after endings.

No mythic last stands.

I arrived in Newcastle with almost 600 miles behind me and another 600 more to be retraced. The following morning while driving through the town, nestled along the rolling fringes of the Black Hills and Thunder Basin Grassland, I noticed folks getting up early for church. More than a few steeples rose above this burg of only 3,500 people. Theirs was a weekly ritual I found comforting, even though it had been a long time since I set foot into a chapel. Foxholes might or might not produce atheists, but agnostics aplenty.

Manhattan-born President Teddy Roosevelt—a cavalryman and veteran himself, Progressive movement leader, and protector of American wilderness—had visited this small Western prairie community during a whistle-stop tour in 1903, after camping in Yellowstone National Park. I could understand why. Newcastle still felt like the frontier.

It seemed fitting on this visit to the Cowboy State in late May that I was so close to the 900-foot-high Devils Tower in neighboring Crook County, where Lakota warriors fasted and prayed. They considered the serrated black volcanic formation to be the birthplace of wisdom, their place of renewal. Shamans led rituals there, including the sacred Sun Dance—a painful (pierced bodies and ripped flesh) but prized rite of passage among braves who would be expected to fight through more hostile encounters with more white men on horseback.

Custer's "Last Stand" aside, native tribes lost more of these battles than they won, including against new diseases that spread with the arrival of new neighbors. Throughout the West, once fence-less lands shrank into fenced-in reservations, the legacy of more broken promises in Washington. One of them now marked Crow Agency on maps, headquarters of the Crow Reservation, is home to the Little Bighorn Battlefield National Monument. The National Park Service calls it "a place of reflection."

A place where row upon row of headstones are etched with the names of U.S. Army dead from the "Indian Wars," with one centrally located stone memorial, the Bear Paw Monument of 1881, declaring: TO THE OFFICERS AND SOLDIERS KILLED, OR WHO DIED OF WOUNDS RECEIVED IN ACTION IN THE TERRITORY OF MONTANA, WHILE CLEARING THE DISTRICT OF THE YELLOWSTONE OF HOSTILE INDIANS. Below which, a much smaller and much newer sign is posted in the soil: PLEASE NOTE: "HOSTILE INDIANS" IS IN HISTORICAL CONTEXT WITH A TERM USED FOR NATIVE AMERICAN ENEMIES OF THE UNITED STATES DURING THE 19TH CENTURY. THE HISTORIC STRUCTURE IS PROTECTED BY THE 1966 HISTORIC PRESERVATION ACT AND CANNOT BE CHANGED TO REFLECT MODERN SOCIAL NORMS.

Nearby, a separate Indian Memorial was dedicated in 2003, one full century and twenty-seven years after the U.S. cavalry's unwise expedition on behalf of the unwise U.S. War Department. Its message: "In memory of all the tribes defending their way of life at the Battle."

A red granite headstone amid prairie grass reads A'KAVEHE' ONAHE, LIMBER BONES, A CHEYENNE WARRIOR FELL HERE ON JUNE 25, 1876 WHILE DEFENDING THE CHEYENNE WAY OF LIFE. A short downhill walk away, there is a separate quote inscribed on a gray granite wall: I WILL NEVER HARM THE CHEYENNE AGAIN. I WILL NEVER POINT MY GUN AT A CHEYENNE AGAIN. I WILL NEVER KILL ANOTHER CHEYENNE. A promise made by Custer (aka "Long Hair") seven years before his final battle.

These war monuments, older and newer, memorializing each side forced me to reflect on my own hard days, and years, among proud and war-hardened peoples. Many of them had fought us in defense of their own ways, their own lands.

In defense of their own tribes.

In defense of their own nations.

Now on native soil in wind-whipped Wyoming, I missed Afghanistan, but I did not miss Iraq. I never wanted to leave one, while the other I did not think I would survive. Two wars, seven years . . . a long list of Iraqi, Afghan, and American wounded and dead, including many friends.

How would we memorialize these wars?

When would we?

And which side, of the many in both wars, could claim any kind of victory in conflicts that had yet to end?

While I stirred Quaker Instant Oatmeal in the family-owned Sundowner Inn ("Convenience, Hospitality and Service with a smile") filled with plastic plants and a front porch framed by wagon wheels, the photographer Richard Avedon came to mind. He captured the real West in his lauded collection of unforgiving portraits, *In the American West*. Drunks, drifters, Mormons, ranchers, oil field workers, waitresses, coal miners, hay haulers, the homeless. Outsiders all, with one outcast in Utah telling him, "A train whistle is the loneliest sound you'll ever hear." Avedon knew this kind of townspeople and so did I. They are family.

Two months before Avedon's death at age eighty-one of a blood clot in the brain during a photo shoot in Texas of America's war wounded, he told me in Boston, "I can see Iraq in your eyes." I still think about his comment. His verdict. He must have seen the truth. How I knew from firsthand experience that war could orphan entire communities and take from adventurous U.S. Marines, many still teenagers, their lives or limbs in an instant—and by the hundreds.

The renowned photographer's project for *The New Yorker* had been titled "Democracy." It was left unfinished. Avedon's final photographs chronicled war recruits and war survivors being treated in the burn unit at San Antonio's Brooke Army Medical Center. Perhaps even his legendary eyes had finally seen too much as well. American soldiers of all people were Richard Avedon's last testament. Not the famous, including the politicians, most often framed in his striking black-and-white pictures.

This somehow seemed the right postscript to his life and work, culminating in the storied literary magazine's special November 2004 edition about the soul—at election time for a commander in chief—of a democratic nation, a constitutional republic that had rushed its troops, the few, to fight across two war fronts, over and over, on behalf of the many they left back home . . . and then mostly forgot about them, forgot about us, forgot about my friends, forgot about me.

Not to mention the countless Iraqi and Afghan families whose home fronts had become our war fronts. Both sides left scarred. But their wounds, those of Fallujans, Khostis, Helmandis, gouged deepest. Those "others" who had experienced America's latest wars without relief and whose stories were largely unknown: Baghdad truckers, Fallujah police and city council members, Sunni tribal sheikhs and imams throughout Anbar province, Afghan madrassa, college, and girl students in Khost province, Pashtun tribal elders, provincial governors, even former Taliban fighters and Guantánamo prison detainees, as well as a young taxi driver in Afghanistan named Dilawar.

Across seven consecutive years, summer 2003 to summer 2010, I saw countries and cultures collide—Iraqi, Afghan, American. I witnessed the devastating human costs of both wars on all sides. Caught in a sort of no-man's-land, the deaths of my Iraqi and Afghan friends meant just as much to me, hurt just as much, as when my Marine friends died. No distinction between "us" and "them" as the casualties mounted.

I had made my way to Wyoming to remember Marine Staff Sergeant Brian Bland, to keep a promise not to others but to myself. On January 26, 2005, he and thirty other American troops died in a helicopter crash in the middle of a remote and cold Anbar desert during a nighttime operation in support of an Iraqi election. Their deaths would remain the single largest casualty incident of both wars. I had basically ordered them on that mission.

At Newcastle's Greenwood Cemetery, which overlooks the town's U.S. 16 truck route and two rail lines, I stood next to Staff Sergeant Bland's granite headstone. It is shaped like a mountain peak. Engraved on one side, "Semper Fidelis," and on the other, a bullet bike and the words, "Beloved Son and Brother."

And so with something to say and something to leave behind, I stepped forward to introduce myself to this dead Marine. Introduce myself to Brian. Thirty more introductions lay ahead, thirty more KIA, thirty more reckonings. Road trips to Cherokee, Iowa (pop. 5,253), and Menard, Texas (pop. 1,471), would follow, as well as to Leadville, Colorado (pop. 2,580).

Before sunrise I had set out from the Sundowner Inn and driven past Donna's Main Street Diner, the Howdy Drive In, and a Pizza Hut, where I arrived on a hilltop. The eastern horizon beyond the South Dakota state line had begun to turn red, a wide crimson ribbon, above Newcastle's Corpus Christi Church. Exiting my truck, I saw cottontail rabbits scampering amid damp grass in front of me, startled, while a dark bird (a crow? a raven?) watchfully sat overhead on the branch of an old tree, unperturbed. It was a fitting scene, almost surreal.

But everything before me, everything behind me, everything to come was real. Not imagined or to be imagined. That would have made the morning easier. Days easier. Nights easier. It would have made everything about the wars so much easier.

Wars, however, are anything but easy—and anything but easy to end.

By the time church doors in Newcastle opened, I had already left town.

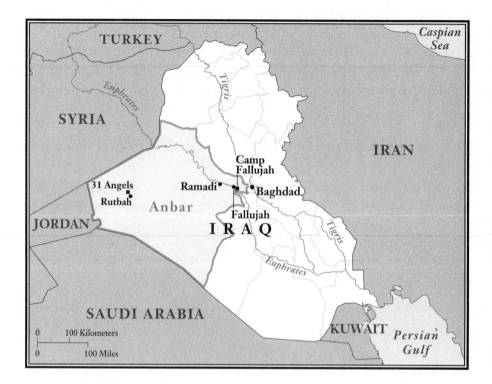

TURKEY

Caspian
Sea

SYRIA

Euphrates

IRAN

Camp
Fallujah

31 Angels   Ramadi • • Baghdad
Rutbah

Anbar

JORDAN

Fallujah

I R A Q

Tigris

Euphrates

Tigris

SAUDI ARABIA

KUWAIT   *Persian*
Gulf

0   100 Kilometers

0   100 Miles

PART I

The Wrong War

Could this be my own face, I wondered. My heart pounded at the idea, and the face in the mirror grew more and more unfamiliar.

MASUJI IBUSE, *Black Rain*

Think of the going out before you enter.

ARAB PROVERB

Quagmire

It was a smooth flight.

By summer 2003, massive and ongoing troop movements had outstripped the Pentagon's ability to fly U.S. service members to Iraq using only military aircraft. Lucrative contracts were awarded for commercial and charter airlines to fill the gap. Soon Boeing 757s helped transport battalions of Marines and soldiers to Kuwait. From there the Pentagon's workhorse C-130 flown by uniformed pilots—many National Guard units in effect federalized—made the final, corkscrew landing into Baghdad.

I was age thirty-one and headed to Iraq, to war, for the first time—not as a soldier but on behalf of the State Department. I had left the U.S. Mission to the United Nations in New York after diplomacy there failed, by design. The unnecessary war a commander in chief and the neoconservatives in Washington wanted, Iraqis got . . . and would keep getting for years to come. So did all of us who went over there, year after year after year.

Hearing that I worked for the State Department, the pilot guiding our flight invited me into the back part of the cockpit to observe our descent into the Middle East. The deserts below were dark, as was the sky. I did not see any stars. It was as if we were flying into a void, somewhere above us was Mars, the Red Planet, named, of course, after the Roman god of war. Compact, calm, and yet talkative, the pilot noted he was nearing retirement, but had volunteered for these special flights because he considered it to be an honor to fly troops to their last point before continuing into Baghdad, into the war. He said he was certain the U.S. needed to invade Iraq. The pilot believed Saddam Hussein was a threat and had hidden weapons of mass destruction.

Toward the end of our time in the air, with the copilot now flying the plane, the chief pilot gave me one of his business cards, embossed with his special designation as American Airlines' "senior pilot." I had no idea airlines had Number One pilots, rank ordered in seniority, but what an American notion: Top Dogs, even in commercial fleets.

With my first of two wars just beginning, it felt like an adventure. I was, oddly enough in retrospect, excited. I was also naive.

As I left the cockpit, he said he wanted to land in Baghdad one day. At Saddam's old airport before any other commercial U.S. pilot, once civilian flights were cleared to fly beyond Kuwaiti skies.

"We're American Airlines. We should be the first."

I kept to myself that I doubted any passengers would be collecting frequent flier miles on their way to and from Iraq anytime soon.

A few days later I arrived in Baghdad from Kuwait via a sweltering C-130, then by armored convoy into the center of Iraq's now occupied capital city. I suddenly represented the "Occupying Power" in the middle of Mesopotamia. I did not feel victorious. But I knew I wanted to show a less ugly or arrogant America, the kind that had lectured world leaders in the run-up to the war.

Few civilians had yet arrived in Iraq to staff the U.S.-led Coalition Provisional Authority (CPA). Part of the first wave in—and probably the most anti–Iraq War member of the group—I recognized in myself a degree of self-congratulatory pride in that fact: being against the war, but volunteering for it. This stand had cachet tied to it, but also conviction. I was not the kind to complain about Iraq in another "March of

Folly" fashion. That self-righteous phase of mine lasted about a week among friends, over many cups of coffee and a few beers. It got old fast, and they conveyed as much. Better to be in Baghdad, among Iraqis who could tell me what they thought—not what I might think they thought from thousands of safe miles away.

Everything about the place, the Coalition Provisional Authority, indeed felt provisional. Only about fifty State Department personnel had been assigned to help oversee Iraq's occupation and none of us had an at-war roadmap handy. We were hugely outnumbered.

Based on sheer size, the U.S. military basically ran the country despite Ambassador L. Paul Bremer III's being named by President George W. Bush as top envoy, or Iraq's "administrator." With such an anodyne-sounding title, he kept his pinstriped, dark suit attire, often adorned with red ties and white handkerchief. But Bremer also incorporated a different fashion protocol, soon mimicked by his inner circle: instead of State Department wingtips, he wore sand-colored canvas military boots. Granted, in a war zone, this sartorial combination looked odd yet seemed practical. It did not come across that way, however, to Iraqis. To them, boots were only made for stomping, not liberating.

We all were in way over our heads from the very beginning—a gut truth I felt from day one lasting all the way until I departed years later. All of us confronted the same dilemma. No matter what the reasons or the partisan insider connections that had brought us to Iraq as imperialists exported from America, we were linked by ignorance, unrealistic expectations (earnest idealism in some), and growing dangers. A Mission: Impossible.

I felt stir-crazy after just a week. To escape the palace intrigue and my more Machiavellian-minded colleagues, I ventured out as often and as far as I could, past towering date palm trees (a once famous Iraqi agricultural export) to explore Iraq beyond Saddam's former home—its manicured lawns and yellow flowers could be mistaken for a Palm Springs resort, alongside a deep blue Olympic-sized swimming pool with two diving boards, and a barbecue pit. Despite the "shock and awe" bombing of Baghdad by U.S. warplanes, it somehow retained its dictatorially opulent look and feel.

When stuck in the palace I would seek out some of the cleaners hired to sweep the ever-present sand from our white marbled floors, who made sure our shoes did not crunch as we navigated the vast floor space. They commuted from Baghdad's poorest Shia neighborhoods into the Green Zone, the ten-square-kilometer, heavily guarded enclave inhabited by coalition officials and military personnel that served as CPA headquarters. I tried to talk with them almost daily, their elementary English far surpassing my virtually nonexistent Arabic. The cleaning crew helped provide me with insights into life beyond the gates. At first, they were wary when I asked them questions, but eventually several opened up. One of the lead custodians, never seen inside without his broom or outside without cigarettes, offered memorable advice.

"Iraqis only respect and fear strength. Democracy won't work in Iraq."

He probably thought I would whisper his words into Bremer's ear, but I thankfully was not part of the administrator's closed inner circle. But what he said rang true. Iraqis knew all about survival, not voting booths.

The custodian asked me at one point why we had moved into Saddam's grand palace. I said because it was easiest to secure and convenient. He seemed like he wanted to say something in response, challenge me perhaps, but did not. I guessed what must have been on his mind. Just what kind of message did America intend to send to the Iraqi people as we moved into countless ex-dictator palaces virtually in the first week of our arrival?

It took between two and three hours each morning for the custodian and other palace cleaning staff to pass through multiple checkpoints, barriers that said everything about our relationship with the Iraqis we professed to know and sought to help. Concrete blast walls. Rings of razor wire. Armed security contractors with black shades and big rifles.

And badges. Lots of badges, different colors and codes to differentiate us from them. Haves, have-nots—those of us inside our climate-controlled bubble versus those who had to sweat out the invasion and growing insurgency.

Over the next year, dozens of Iraqi day laborers would die from car bombs exploding at the front gates as they waited to enter the Green Zone for another day of work. Theirs was arguably the most deadly, daily commute in Iraq. While at night American expatriates would hold "Baghdad Idol" contests and "Pirate Day" poolside parties.

·   ·   ·

That same first week, I asked my new boss what part of Iraq's impe-rial supervision would be mine. I did not want to have anything to do with oil. CPA life morphed into a power trip, temporarily infecting me as well. I confidently believed that I would be given a high-visibility assignment on a pressing political challenge—we had so many and all at once—given my prior work in New York in the Political Section at the U.S. Mission to the U.N.

Unexpectedly, however, top CPA management informed me that my new job would be as point man on a very different set of issues and characters: Iraq's truckers. I was not excited. I was not reassured. The only truckers I knew in the U.S. were from movies, and they did not seem to be the most diplomatic of groups. Or friendly.

This would prove to be the best kind of assignment. I could not have known it then, but Iraq's truckers would quickly become my first true link to the real Iraq. In many ways they comprised the lifeblood of a country in mounting disarray. If any goods needed to be transported from point A to B or all the way to Z, it was the truckers who would get them there. But they were on the verge of starting a mini-revolt over pay levels and requested an urgent meeting with me.

The truckers' argument lay in a gray area. They claimed Saddam's senior officials had promised them the funds prior to the invasion. As the new de facto government, teamster leaders argued that we were obligated to honor this commitment. So far Ambassador Bremer had vetoed any payout. Before the meeting, I did a bit of homework with our legal team and learned that our authorities under the guiding U.N. Security Council resolution were sweeping, but with limits—not all changes had to be made unilaterally by Ambassador Bremer via his signed orders. This gave me some degree of flexibility should I need it.

I had been warned that the head teamster, Mr. Bassam, was one of the most charismatic and intimidating Iraqis my colleagues had so far engaged in Baghdad. I thought he could not be a harder challenge than the Russian, Chinese, or French diplomats in New York, who sat along-side me on the U.N.'s Al Qaeda and Taliban Sanctions Committee. I had negotiated Security Council resolutions with these delegations and sparred over words that were binding upon governments under inter-national law.

Bassam proved me wrong. Upon finally meeting him, I almost expected to hear a Jersey accent. He was pudgy, bearded, with thick baseball-mitt-sized hands. Tony Soprano would have found a kindred spirit. He smelled of cigarette smoke and liked eating three-foot-long Tigris River carp, the key ingredient in a traditional dish called Masgouf—a local bony delicacy also favored by Saddam and, it was rumored, enjoyed by former French president Jacques Chirac, who had the fish flown to Paris and prepared by his personal chefs.

A trained mechanic, Bassam had risen to be a chief representative of Iraq's hundred-strong teamster high command, a group that controlled massive Volvo truck fleets crucial for stability in the country. He and his men moved food—tons of it, daily. Wheat flour, rice, sugar, beans, salt, cooking oil, tea. The staples a majority of Iraqis depended on to feed their families: any breakdown in Iraq's food distribution network could lead to riots and political paralysis. And the teamsters, I realized, had the most leverage. Not us.

Over that afternoon, with the staid deputy trade minister in suit and tie seated next to me, we listened to the teamsters' arguments. It turned out that Saddam functionaries had indeed promised them money. Some truckers were on the verge of revolting as a result of the lack of pay. We simply could not afford any disruption to the supply network, however brief. Finally, Bassam told me that the coalition needed more friends, not enemies, and truckers made good friends.

Touché, I thought.

The balding, elderly minister with his professor-like demeanor looked to me at the end of our session, but said nothing. I sat as an underdressed, decades-younger imperialist. His awkward silence signaled the decision was mine, not his. He handed me two official-looking memos in Arabic, noting one indicated approval, the other rejection. I signed the approval. Bassam reached out and shook my hand, his two-handed grip leaving indentations on my wrist. We both knew who was in charge.

I began to think how I would explain this unilateral decision of my own, contrary to Bremer's guidance, back at the palace. But in a few days, growing instability across the country became the overriding focus. And Iraqi media reports that the food basket entitlement might be reduced or eliminated by the Americans had led to a growing public outcry—"introduction of free market forces" had been a CPA mantra among some hard-core capitalists while anathema to the more measured British contingent. We needed the truckers on our side, which we had now. I never heard from Ambassador Bremer on the matter.

The deputy trade minister estimated my deal with Bassam would cost the Iraqi treasury, which we controlled, several million dollars. Their money spent in our, the Occupying Power's, interest—a pattern that would be replicated across other portfolios and amount to many hundreds of millions of dollars in expenditures with little oversight and even less transparency. An Australian colleague described arriving at Baghdad's Central Bank just after the invasion and withdrawing tens of millions of dollars in currency on behalf of Iraqi farmers. He received a handwritten receipt before loading the stacked bills into the back of an SUV.

This first meeting with Bassam would lead to more before long. I enjoyed the truckers' company, and they seemed to enjoy getting to know an American up close. So much so, bonding with Iraq's teamsters soon morphed into the most important, and most rewarding, part of my job during Iraq's official year-long occupation under the Coalition Provisional Authority. They became my rationale for regular trips outside the Green Zone and my link to the more vibrant and gritty Iraq. I visited their mechanic shops, ministry food warehouses, even a Sadr City slum truck lot in order to ensure that food movements proceeded despite mounting insurgent attacks across the country.

On one visit, mechanics showed me how they had learned during the decade-plus Iraq economic embargo to fix just about anything that had four or more wheels and a steering column. In those days, spare parts were very hard to get. All around me sat pieces of half-rebuilt trucks, vans, plus a few sedans arranged in jumbles. Bassam had managed to take advantage of his entrepreneurial side, post-invasion, likely pocketing significant sums. Who could blame him? I never asked where he found the parts or what he did with them as long as the food kept moving. And it did, even as the bombs proliferated along Iraq's highways.

I had experienced a bit of the teamsters' world, so I wanted to invite them to experience a bit of mine. I decided I would host Bassam and a half dozen mechanics in the Green Zone for dinner. With the palace tour date set, I was able to preapprove them for expedited entry. They arrived on time. As we passed through the last gate, with the manicured palatial splendor before us under unusually cloudy skies, one turned to me and said, under his breath, "This is not Iraq."

Over the next hour, we walked the grounds, past the swimming pool where suntanned CPA staffers lounged about. Some attempted, badly, backflips off the diving board. Embarrassed but not surprised by the life of leisure displayed around us, I hurried my guests into the palace cafeteria for the meal. Many eyes looked our way. These were not the usual variety of Iraqis who visited. The visit was clearly not going well, so I cut it short. None of the other Americans acknowledged them. The truckers felt like aliens in their own country. Our abbreviated tour seemed to register their collective disbelief about the decadent lifestyle of the former regime—and the current one.

In a final conversation, I tried to convince one of the mechanics (who had worked hard to become a midlevel manager) that our commitment to Iraq would see us all through the growing violence. My case by then had become rote but remained sincere: There is no better long-term partner than the United States; just look at Japan and Germany. We went to war with both. We defeated both—granted, one with two nuclear bombs. "They are now two of the largest economies in the world and our allies," I would say.

This logic worked at U.N. headquarters and in front of college students. It did not work in Iraq. The junior manager, an intense young man in his mid-twenties who always wore white button-down shirts and slacks even in the grimy truck repair shops, would have none of it. He reminded me that Americans had left southern Iraq unprotected after the Gulf War, even while encouraging the Shia population there to rise up against Saddam. Tens of thousands had been slaughtered by Iraqi government gunships following the U.S. troop withdrawal. His family. His tribe. President George Herbert Walker Bush and his secretary of defense, Dick Cheney, wanted no part in ordering the First Marine Division to march all the way to Baghdad, hence Bob Hope of the USO would only get as far as Kuwait on his final troop entertainment tour.

The young Iraqi's final words to me: "I'm Shia." Implicit message: we do not trust you.

Unwittingly, through the hollow palace tour, I had only reinforced his doubts—and my own. Bassam, uncharacteristically, looked dejected the entire time.

Only then did I begin to register that a growing Shia-Sunni divide, post our invasion, might unravel the country. These Iraqi truckers were not optimistic about Iraq's future even in 2003 and 2004. They knew the sentiment of the streets best because they lived amid them, full-time, far from our gated palace and its ice cream bar. This imperious disconnect would never change. Five years later, for example, an American ambassador to Iraq—who conveyed to Iraqis that he disliked them—would approve a $150,000 carved mahogany bar (well stocked and well used) in the new billion-dollar U.S. embassy compound.

It too had a swimming pool—an indoor one, Olympic-size.

By the end of 2003 and into 2004, Iraq was completely coming apart. The Green Zone had been under direct attack from mortar fire and regular explosions at our checkpoints. We hunkered down. Blast waves from massive car bombs shook the palace. Insurgent munitions landed next to our housing trailers (called "pods"), in our parking lots, even in the swimming pool at one point. Sirens blared. Life inside our bubble had forever altered, leading some colleagues to leave Baghdad early out of fear for their personal safety even if other excuses for sudden departures were given. Staffing the Iraq War was no longer such an adventure, no matter the résumé distinction.

I had been issued a stiff green and black camouflage Vietnam-era flak jacket, in storage since Richard Nixon's era as commander in chief. It was the exact model my dad said he had worn in Vietnam. While I needed a large, the only size they had left in stock was a medium. It did not even reach my belly button. This was the first indication of how under-equipped we all were, my one-size-too-small body armor matching the door-less Humvees we traveled in, feet dangling out and hands pressed to iron frames in order to prevent falling out.

Washington already believed "Mission Accomplished" even as the roadside bombs got bigger and more common and more deadly. A group of Marines I knew were among the first whose Humvee was blown up just outside Baghdad. All survived, mainly because insurgents were still learning their trade in how best to kill us. It did not take long, however, for them to perfect their violence.

Eventually, I did manage to escape the palace gates again for a final farewell lunch with Bassam at his favorite fish restaurant, located on the banks of the Tigris. A U.S. Army colonel from Indiana and good friend accompanied me with his pistol, because no Iraqi could be trusted one hundred percent in his view. Masgouf would be the featured dish, and as a seafood lover I could not wait to sample Iraq's famous delicacy, even if it was, well, carp.

Bassam escorted us to a small cement container at the outdoor restaurant's entrance. In it, several-meter-long greenish specimens sloshed about, aggressively competing for space. By tradition, we were asked by the chef to pick the one we wanted. I pointed to an especially lively carp, and we took our seats outside.

In half an hour it came out, flayed and roasted, black oily skin peeled from both sides. Charcoal permeated the air, mixed with the sweet smell of the whitish fish meat—covered completely by flies. Hundreds. The colonel, gastronomically wimping out, claimed that he had already eaten and was not feeling well. Bassam handed a large piece to me, with no attempt to wave away the swirl of black insects dive-bombing from all directions. It was my turn to smile. I graciously accepted and swallowed repeated mouthfuls.

He later said that I could depend on Iraq's truckers for anything, in effect as my own mini-militia. I thought he was joking. He was not. Bassam explained that the official memo I had signed months earlier had enabled thousands of truckers to feed their families. Despite being charged with moving Iraq's food basket, they had been suffering themselves, but most were too proud to admit just how much. His comments reinforced how distant the real Iraq remained from my own world of gated-community expats, still isolated in our self-imposed bubble a full twelve months into the war.

And yet there was a far bigger sort of charade under way at the same time than the posturing and partying in the Green Zone. It had its own twisted dynamic, centered in Washington, D.C.

From Baghdad, I watched a replay of President George W. Bush opening the annual black-tie Radio and Television Correspondents Association Dinner held March 24, 2004. Comedian A. J. Jamal, described in an introduction as the "entertainer of the evening," hosted the event at the U.S. capital's Hilton Hotel.

Bush had his own comedic role as the dinner's guest of honor.

Narrating a slide show spoof, he said aloud: "Those weapons of mass destruction have gotta be somewhere . . ."

Projected images showed him hunched over, arm outstretched, looking under a cabinet in the Oval Office. More footage depicted him ambling about his historic office, as the president continued to narrate. "Nope, no weapons over there. Maybe under here."

The gathering's high-profile media representatives and top politicians, appearing and acting like self-important D.C. glitterati, visibly loved the performance. Republican and Democratic congressional leaders (Senator Mitch McConnell, Congresswoman Nancy Pelosi) laughed aloud at the commander in chief's futile search for WMD inside the White House. They further guffawed as the president made more jokes about having his dog, Barney, neutered and getting his own facial profile measured for Mount Rushmore.

While viewing the dinner video clip, I noticed President Bush concluded his prepared laugh-along-with-me remarks with "a few serious photos" and a tribute to a deployed Special Forces unit. He said they had sent him a group picture and wrote they carried with them a piece of World Trade Center rubble from Ground Zero—all the way to Afghanistan, where the soldiers buried it.

In Iraq earlier that day, far from the Hilton ballroom full of tuxedos and sequins, and far from the Hindu Kush Mountains of Afghanistan and Pakistan—Osama bin Laden and Al Qaeda terrain—U.S. Army Staff Sergeant Wentz Jerome Henry Shanaberger, age thirty-three, from Zephyrhills, Florida (pop. 13,288), died, the Sunshine State's twenty-first KIA. The former Boy Scout and married father of five had been killed after being struck with three bullets. The next day, March 25, 2004, as Washingtonians went about their business, more service members died, alongside many more Iraqi civilians.

More dying followed the next week. And the next month. And the next year. And the next decade.

We of course, in Iraq, had yet to find any new stockpiles of WMD either.

Days later an all-hands urgent email message from the security office flashed across my computer screen, asking if anyone had recently traveled to Fallujah.

Fallujah?

I had barely heard of the place.

Hey there army,
Get in your tanks and follow me,
I am Marine Corps infantry.
Hey there navy,
Get in your ships and follow me,
I am Marine Corps infantry.
Hey there air force,
Get in your planes and follow me,
I am Marine Corps infantry.
Hey civilians,
Get off your butts and follow me,
We are the Marine Corps infantry.

MARINE CADENCE

Friends and Enemies

Scott Helvenston, Jerry Zovko, Wes Batalona, and Mike Teague were ambushed in two unarmored SUVs in the center of Fallujah a week after Washington's elite gathered amid laughs and entertainment and good food at their invitation-only multi-course dinner. Shot dead and set aflame, the men's charred remains were dragged through the streets and strung up on a bridge across the Euphrates River. Their mission that day? Escort a convoy to pick up kitchen equipment for a European food company doing work in Iraq.

Anbar was already Iraq's most violent province, but now Fallujah filled television screens worldwide. With approximately 38,000 coalition troops stationed there, mostly Marines, the embassy wanted civilian "commissars" seated alongside generals to ensure military tactics matched policy and overall political strategy in key provinces. That was the intent, anyway. I volunteered for the job. The problem: it was just me and I soon would be the sole State Department official in the expanse of 53,000 square miles inhabited by a million and half angry, largely anti-U.S. Sunnis. We had, after all, removed them from power and without much of a "here is what's next" plan.

It was more like "what do we do next?" with a collective head scratch.

Before leaving Baghdad, the recently arrived ambassador to Iraq (my new boss but the same one I had worked for in New York as well) John D. Negroponte, the future deputy secretary of state and first director of national intelligence, offered uncharacteristically blunt advice.

"Get out and do what you need to do, but be careful. When I was posted in Vietnam, we could walk around. Diplomats cannot do that here."

I wanted to mention to him, but did not, that I had already told Marines I would recommend the Blackwater team assigned to protect me in Anbar be recalled or sent somewhere else. They worked for the large U.S.-based private security company, founded by a wealthy former U.S. Navy SEAL, and had been hired by the State Department in Iraq. After the attack, their fleets of armored, tinted-windowed BMW sedans only drew more attention. Plus, Blackwater's attitude often alienated infantry corporals—not to mention Iraqis. Marines made a twentieth of the hired guns' salaries, contracted at as much as a thousand dollars a day including weekends, and were getting shot at more frequently. Fights had broken out between them in gyms in Ramadi. An embassy colleague told me the Anbar-based Blackwater team cost over $10 million per year to maintain. Too much taxpayer money, way too much in my view, and not the introduction I wanted with Marines or Anbaris—an imposing steel shield and wrong first impression.

Negroponte continued with his second point.

"And when you get to Fallujah, make sure the Marine generals understand you work for me." In other words, do not go rogue.

I was not in the military. I served in the State Department and knew my civilian chain of command, which went from me through the embassy's political counselor to the ambassador, that is, Negroponte himself. I did not salute or shoot a rifle to kill. I did not answer to Marines or generals. I wrote diplomatic cables and negotiated U.N. Security Council resolutions—a profession all about preventing wars, not managing preemptive ones.

And yet, one part of the U.S. military stood out in Iraq for all the right reasons. Early on in Baghdad I met an Air Force officer, uniform always pressed, who said he was midway through a four-month "combat" tour—in the Green Zone. I did not know military stints in Iraq could be so short. The State Department minimum was one year. Marines, in contrast, were the grimiest, covered in Anbar sand. They also appeared to be the happiest of America's service members. Though in the Marine way of war, and where they were sent, no one was ever really happy or for long, even amid some pranks and laughs. Confident and cocky, their strut stemmed from deployment in Iraq's most dangerous areas and associated reputation as being the most aggressive U.S. military branch. I was beginning to realize they made the best company in the real combat zones, the bomb- and insurgent-filled western desert precincts well beyond the elaborate palace grounds along the Tigris River in the Iraqi capital.

By the time I arrived in Anbar province in a massive, dual rotor CH-47 Chinook helicopter well after midnight in early July 2004, insurgents had been targeting our forces almost every day. I was flying west on the so-called milk run, the regularly scheduled flights across the region. Unlike the U.S. Army's sleek Black Hawk helicopter fleet (the ones our military always transported VIP senators in), Marines still proudly flew these lumbering, Vietnam-era workhorse Chinooks, which looked liked flying buses but were painted elephant gray and engineered to hover in the air hundreds of feet.

The morning after my arrival, a quick-paced young Marine escorted me around Camp Fallujah. Situated a mile east of the city of Fallujah, the expansive Marine base had originally been built by Saddam Hussein for the anti-Iran militia, the People's Mujahedin of Iran (or MEK), during Iraq's war with Iran (1980–88, a million dead). The MEK base, renamed Camp Fallujah on Pentagon maps, retained its military feel: physical separation from paved roads, perimeter fencing and thick walls, organized grid patterns, all amid pockets of palm trees. Following the Marines' arrival, vast tent encampments had been set up. Infantry battalions and supporting units had congregated on the base's outskirts, along with their war-making equipment, including howitzers and tanks. A dust cloud seemed to permanently hang above everything.

My sun-freckled and sunburnt Marine guide looked to be still a teenager, as so many deployed Marines were. He stopped to show me the official State Department SUV. Chunks of shrapnel from one of the many incoming mortar and rocket attacks had shredded the parked vehicle. Its windows were shattered, and the driver's seat's tan cushions had holes ripped into them, several inches wide. Its metal doors were punctured as well, like BB gun pellets—but much bigger—through a Coke can. The Marine said matter-of-factly, "Sir, I think you're going to need a new one." I sure did.

Due to its long-standing ties to the Islamic faith—and many mosques to prove as much—Fallujah had become known as Iraq's "City of Mosques." It lies almost midway between Baghdad (about forty miles from the capital) and Ramadi, along the winding Euphrates River. The city and its immediate surroundings comprised almost twenty-five square kilometers, the northern boundary marked by a nonfunctioning railway, with Fallujah's southern edge bordered by open desert. In its tightly packed neighborhoods lived between 250,000 and 350,000 residents. In summer it is scorching hot. In winter, it can be cold with some intermittent rain. I would experience both, preferring the heat to the cold, but the rain to the dust.

Before the invasion Fallujah was a secure city, long known as a principal stopping point on a major trade route along the road between Baghdad and Amman in Jordan (a city of "traders and raiders" is how one Iraqi described it, or as another explained, a city of "mosques, mechanics and Saddam's generals"). Most of the structures were single- or two-story, and its main street home to a row of mechanic shops, causing an omnipresent fog of diesel fumes to pollute the air. Baghdadis, I was told, considered Fallujans to have the best engine repair specialists. Their labor and parts offered at cheaper prices too compared to the capital. I would soon learn that Fallujans, like many Iraqis, made good capitalists. And not just after our arrival with a lot of our money distributed for them to spend.

Towering mosque domes and minarets filled Fallujah's skyline. The winding greenish, brownish, and pungent Euphrates River borders the western edge of the city, with two bridges connecting it to verdant farmland and the city's original hospital. One is old (the steel-girded "Blackwater Bridge" painted green was first built by the British during their imperial era) and a newer one, a concrete span that survived a laser-guided missile strike during the First Gulf War. The city's markets were well stocked. Many students attended classes, while others commuted to Baghdad to attend university courses. Fallujah was a sizable and bustling town—the second largest in Anbar—surrounded by more rural communities.

That was then. Before we Americans arrived via our ground and air military invasion. Now U.S. tanks were parked at the edge of the city's main street, providing ironclad over-watch. Massive, dirt-filled wire mesh containers stamped HESCO, sold by the Dubai-based conglomerate Hercules Engineering Solutions Consortium, comprised frontline berms. Rudimentary drones—unarmed in those days—flew overhead, with one particular model, named ScanEagle, buzzing like a flying lawn mower. Marine infantrymen, many still pimply, twitchy teenagers, positioned themselves nearby, chewing rainbow-colored MRE Skittles in between cleaning their rifles. (Superstitious, they avoided chalky Charms-brand candies.) To stay awake, grunts went through can after can of tobacco and drank gallon after gallon of coffee. Contrary to myth, none put Tabasco sauce in their eyes, which would have made them half blind and combat ineffective in an instant. The aged pepper-vinegar-mash concoction provided in MRE mini-bottles, however, did make the blandest food in any Anbar combat outpost taste better. A lot better.

Less known about Fallujah was its place in Jewish history. A Marine intelligence officer described how it had once been home to a temple, as well as a Jewish Academy centuries ago. Much of the Talmud had supposedly been written there in the Babylonian era. He said the last Jews reportedly left around 1948, but that in some ancient structures near the city, Hebrew writing could still be seen. I figured if Muslims and Jews could get along like they had long ago, perhaps Fallujah could regain some of its more harmonious past—not between Muslims and Jews but rather between Sunnis and Shia. Even by 2004, the frictions had begun to appear between national-level politicians and, ominously though quietly, within Iraqi security forces infected by sectarian leaders and agendas.

In this volatile environment filled with ancient history, Lieutenant General James T. Conway commanded a legion of Marines and soldiers. He had already attained legendary status in Marine circles. The Walnut Ridge, Arkansas, native was public-school-educated (Roosevelt High, Southeast Missouri State), like I had been, and said few but powerful words. He stood six-foot-five with a close-cropped haircut Marine style and had the square build and easy movement of a professional athlete. I had heard the general liked kayaking and fly-fishing in the Rocky Mountains—we just might get along, I thought. His deep voice, with the slight twang of his birthplace still present, seemed perfectly matched to a military man used to giving a lot of orders over many years. And then getting salutes and "yes, sir" and not the "let me think about it" reactions more typical in the U.S. government's civilian agencies. He defined the notion of "command presence." I was to be his adviser. Maybe even his confidant—that is, if he deemed me worthy of wartime confidences.

Conway had two sons also serving in the Marine Corps and a daughter married to a Marine Cobra helicopter pilot. The general had held several key positions prior to assuming charge of the San Diego–based 1st Marine Expeditionary Force (aka the Mighty MEF). I had been told by almost everyone on base that Conway would be Marine commandant one day.

The State Department had sent me to be his principal adviser on Iraqi political matters, though I did not answer to him. On questions of overall U.S. policy and strategy, I would have the final say among Marines, whatever their rank. This is what Ambassador Negroponte had meant when he reminded me that I worked for him, the top U.S. official in the country, not any U.S. military branch. In meetings, I spoke for Negroponte. All that said, I knew it would be far better to find ways to agree than to disagree with Marines whenever possible, particularly when seated next to Marine general officers. That was my goal, anyway, but unrealistic in practice on every occasion or in every internal political-military debate.

My main concern going in: the State Department representative before me had pissed off the commanding general. There was no ignoring it. Unbeknownst to General Conway, the diplomat had written a cable criticizing the Marine plan to establish a "Fallujah Brigade"—a force of Iraqis charged with quelling violence after the killing of the Blackwater security contractors. The cable then got leaked to *The Washington Post*, which put the general and Marines overall in an awkward position.

The White House wanted revenge for the killings. Marines, led by Conway, preferred to pursue a more measured response. They did not get the opportunity. President Bush ordered an attack in spring 2004, named Operation Vigilant Resolve. As civilians fled Fallujah, images on Al Jazeera both highlighted and exaggerated casualties. After a few days, the White House national security team reversed course. Iraqi leaders as well had told Ambassador Bremer in Baghdad they would quit their positions in the interim Iraqi government if the Fallujah offensive continued. Marines were thus first ordered to attack and then ordered to pull back within days—the worst combination, resulting in the untextbook outcome. The hornet's nest was shaken, not smashed. Not a course of action taught at the two Marine Schools of Infantry, either in North Carolina or the other in California. Conway and the Marines were left with only bad options now made worse, and the junior diplomat's leaked cable left them exposed, even if it had raised legitimate policy questions.

This was the context when I walked into the Marine command deck for my inaugural State Department–Marine Corps meeting. Civilian-military relations were strained to say the least. As the general's green political adviser, both to Marine ways and to the ways of the province, I preferred to be direct, telling his chief of staff, Colonel John Coleman, before my session with Conway: "I will not hit send on any reporting cable to the embassy and Washington that you and the generals have not seen first. We might agree to disagree in the end, but I will not go around anyone's back."

The chief—an intense Georgia native, with a severe haircut even by Marine standards, and thick gold ring marking him as a Virginia Military Institute man—replied swiftly, "You sure about that? If so, good, let's go see the general."

As I walked into Conway's office, the plywood walls shook behind the general. We fired our outgoing artillery rounds, which insurgents followed with their own incoming, like mad clockwork. Boom! Boom!

The room vibrated, as did his office back door in its flimsy aluminum frame.

"Welcome to Fallujah," Conway said, hardly looking up from his desk.

"Thanks, I think. It is a lot louder here than in the Green Zone. The security situation is getting bad in Baghdad too."

"You know Marines prefer it this way. They call Anbar the Wild West of Iraq for good reason."

I replied that I came from the western part of the U.S., adding, "Well, General, you'll like to hear then that my great-great-uncle was friends with Robert LeRoy Parker."

"Who?" Conway asked.

"That's Butch Cassidy's real name. My long-dead relative was a member of his gang that robbed plenty of banks and trains in Utah, Wyoming, and Colorado. Iraqi outlaws can't be that different, but probably are better armed than with just a Colt .45."

"I'm from a small town in Arkansas. We have some pretty tough folks there too, and Marines are pretty well armed, so don't worry."

So far, so good, the three-star commanding general seemed to be in a talking mood. No one else was in the room.

"Ambassador Negroponte gave me some advice before arriving. Seems everyone in Baghdad and some in Washington think that I am going to go native with you guys. But I know who protects me out here. It is not the State Department."

"We probably have enough firepower to cover a civilian or two. We are glad you're here. You might have heard about the State guy who just left," he added.

"Yeah, your chief of staff briefed me on that. I promised him and promise you that all my cables and policy recommendations will go to you first to review and comment on. I will not backchannel anything to Baghdad or Washington. If we disagree on any issue, and we might, I will make that clear to the ambassador."

Conway extended a handshake. "I think you will get along fine with us here."

On my way out, I noticed a Marine's desk in a small alcove. Above it, he had posted a quotation from Eleanor Roosevelt: "The Marines I have seen around the world have the cleanest bodies, the filthiest minds, the highest morale, and the lowest morals of any group of animals I have ever seen. Thank God for the United States Marine Corps."

Now that was a character reference to brag about—even placed on an office wall in Fallujah, Iraq. The partner of a wartime commander in chief, niece of another U.S. president, mother of six children, and author of her own newspaper column, she had also written the foreword to an important but little-known book. One about another war and the scars it would leave on the American home front at the time—by Allen

Eaton, published in 1952: *Beauty Behind Barbed Wire: The Arts of the Japanese in Our War Relocation Camps.*

The former first lady's tribute reminded me of another U.S. leader's loyalty to his USMC tribe. Senate majority leader from Montana and ambassador to Japan Mike Mansfield had only one title listed as his tombstone epitaph: "PVT U.S. Marine Corps."

As I left the command deck, a member of the general's staff asked me how the meeting had gone.

"Pretty good, I think. The CG did not boot me back to Baghdad."

"General Conway wouldn't do that, but speaking of which," the Marine went on, "did you actually volunteer to come out here? I didn't think the State Department would send someone else after that last guy who wrote that cable."

"Well, I might be the last," keeping to myself what I thought of the bad arithmetic of survival in Iraq's westernmost desert badlands—the worst odds in Iraq.

Marine egos and war-fighting abilities would be further tested in Anbar, and soon. The USMC was about to begin round two of a battle that would be as intense as those they had endured in Vietnam. No Southeast Asia jungles this time, but rather dense urban combat in a maze-like warren of city streets inhabited by well-armed and well-bunkered insurgents. Al Qaeda terrorists had made Iraq's City of Mosques their home. And they were ready to fight, not from a distance, but house-to-house and face-to-face.

In this violent and Richter scale environment, "calm" never lasted long. Two months after my arrival, the swooshing sound of a rocket overhead startled me. It passed so closely I ducked my head even though I was indoors. In only a second, a large explosion filled the dry desert air. I knew it had impacted not far away, and the blast wave meant it had to be a big one—not the usual mortars or other insurgent-launched ordnance that had been regularly landing on base. We had gotten used to those impacts, as much as one could. This impact sounded different, and a lot closer.

Contrary to my training—and knowing full well where I should not go—I hurried the short distance, less than 150 meters, to the regimental command building. I was tight with many Marines who worked there. While assigned to advise the generals, I spent a lot of time with the regiment and battalions because they were the units nearest to the street-level tactical fight and, more important, to the Iraqi people.

Just around the corner from my office, I could see waves of billowing smoke. It looked like a direct hit, and it looked bad. Several Marines gathered nearby. The new regimental commander had been badly injured. His name was Colonel Larry Nicholson. He had been rushed to the base hospital on the back of the military version of a John Deere Gator utility vehicle, along with Major Kevin Shea, who had been seated at Nicholson's desk while trying to solve a computer password login problem. Right after Nicholson stepped away and reached down to put a plug into its socket, the room exploded, with jagged pieces of shrapnel spread in all directions instantaneously. Major Shea was killed right away.

A Marine who had been in an adjacent corridor described the immediate aftermath: "I got around to the doors that used to lead to the CO's office, and all I could see was a gaping black hole, darkness and smoke. A female lieutenant was working on Colonel Nicholson like she really knew her business so everyone thought she was a corpsman and kept calling her 'Doc' . . . they got him patched up and hustled on out while he was having a lot of serious difficulty breathing, very hoarse raspy breathing and was covered in blood."

If there were an "X" on Camp Fallujah, insurgents had hit it. Dead-on. Only a few hours before, Nicholson had taken command of 1st Marines (RCT-1). Unbelievably, a rocket blasted right through his window into the middle of his office and on his first day as the regiment's top officer.

The colonel was a "grunt's grunt" with an addiction to instant coffee and hard candy. A compact Marine leader built like a fullback, he was already famous among Marines for his comment about the work ahead. "Full-spectrum counterinsurgency means we issue 5.56 rounds, Jolly Ranchers, and humanitarian assistance with equal enthusiasm and accuracy."

After passing through medical facilities in Germany, Nicholson checked into Bethesda. He later recounted how following four weeks of stateside recovery and more surgeries, he walked for the first time. Catheters and bandages removed, a Navy nurse helped keep him steady. In the hallways, he limped, resembling the slow shuffle of a geriatric ravaged by decades of arthritis, not a Marine regimental commander and infantry officer decades younger.

He noticed an old-timer in a red USMC baseball cap sitting nearby with a few other Marine Vietnam veterans. They stared as he passed. He overheard one of them telling his buddies, in a poor and rather unmuted attempt at a whisper: "See that fehhllarrr? He was the commanding officer of First Marines in Fallujah. We must sure as hell be losing this damn war if they are starting to shoot our colonels."

Nicholson went on to say, "That was the first time I laughed in a long, long time. It was a deep, honest laugh—guess they call it a belly laugh, as your gut starts to hurt—and it felt amazing, cleansing, and cathartic."

After almost being killed by the rocket that landed in his office, he unexpectedly showed up in Anbar three and a half months later, on Christmas Eve 2004. Nicholson had not asked his doctors for permission. He arranged his own transportation on military aircraft after getting new gear. As a full-bird Marine colonel, no one ever inquired about his health record.

Once back in Iraq, several of us noticed a pool of blood that regularly accumulated on his uniform, near his left shoulder.

His wounds had yet to heal.

In the practical art of war, the best thing of all is to take the enemy's country whole and intact; to shatter and destroy is not so good.

SUN TZU, *The Art of War*

Phantom Fury or New Dawn?

All of us who lived at Camp Fallujah through summer and early fall 2004 knew what was ahead: a lot more war.

Operation Vigilant Resolve had accomplished little, just more dangerous complications for frontline troops across Anbar amid Iraqi civilian casualties. It was intense fighting, but due to lack of coordination and short-lived resolve in the White House and in Baghdad, Marines were about to go back into Fallujah proper—this time for good.

The upcoming Iraqi election, set for January 2005, was one factor. The Bush administration hoped to show purple finger voters—indicating they had cast their ballots—in polling lines in Anbar, not just in the safer parts of Baghdad and elsewhere. That preferred picture would be an easier sell to the American public and Marines' and soldiers' parents—ballot boxes, not more bullets, in a war that seemed only to be getting worse and lasting longer than predicted. Than promised.

Secretary of Defense Donald Rumsfeld had offered his own calculation before the invasion: "I can't tell you if the use of force in Iraq today will last five days, five weeks, or five months, but it won't last any longer than that." This would be one of many wrong and misleading and flip statements he would make throughout the course of the wars in Iraq and Afghanistan. And unlike his equally controversial predecessor during the Vietnam War, Defense Secretary Robert McNamara—who had a real crisis of conscience eventually and said *mea culpa* to the families of American KIA, the Vietnamese people, and the world—Donald Rumsfeld would take nothing back in his public commentary.

With each passing day, I heard signs of the U.S. war machine ramping up: the thump above of helicopters and occasional sonic booms of jets; the mortar thuds and blasts of outgoing howitzer rounds that rang across our living areas. In our chow halls, we were eating MREs only, and limited portions at that because insurgents had attacked so many of our food convoys. Some of the most prized menus from this "MRE XXIV" era among Marines were Chicken with Salsa (my favorite), Beef Stew (mixed with jalapeño cheese), and Spaghetti with Meat Sauce. Pork Rib did not go over so well with anyone, on top of being a forbidden food among Muslims. We had stocked halal meals for them. Among other items, they contained raisins, sunflower seeds, a granola bar, and a small box of cereal, such as "they're gr-r-eat!" Frosted Flakes. Marines often raided (aka "rat-fucked")—as did I—those first, alongside other favorites (M&M's, pound cake, fudge brownies) inside various MREs.

Wartime diet restrictions aside, I sensed the days for diplomacy had ended, and rather abruptly. A message reinforced by the silence I received from State Department counterparts in Baghdad about longer-term, post-battle U.S. strategy. If we had to destroy Fallujah in order to save it, well, I would be left to help oversee the city's rebuilding. Where was our detailed, civilian-led plan? Marines had developed their own, to their credit, with promised coordination through Iraqi government ministries. The generals appeared more in charge in those days than the ambassadors. Perhaps because the embassy had mortars landing on its roof and car bombs blasting through perimeter gates, imagery that fit our nation-building predicament and counterinsurgency reality. The Iraq War was far from over.

How could Washington not see this, let alone not admit as much internally?

The American public was increasingly seeing the post-invasion "shock and awe" facade crumble.

When I received word to prepare for a VIP arriving via Black Hawk helicopter, I was not surprised. Ambassador Ronald Neumann's October 2004 trip to Fallujah from Baghdad meant we were in final countdown-to-battle mode. A circumspect, soft-spoken senior Foreign Service Officer made Arab-wise from multiple tours in the region (former U.S. ambassador in Algeria and Bahrain, as well as earlier tours in Senegal, Yemen, and Iran—before the hostage taking), he represented the best tradition of career diplomacy.

Listen. Listen some more. Then talk—in Arabic. In Baghdad, Neumann acted as a chief deputy to Negroponte, focusing specifically on political-military matters.

John Sattler, an energetic native of Monroeville, Pennsylvania, with three stars on his shoulder, had replaced Conway. He was gregarious and politically savvy, and had once been the Marine Corps' Senate liaison on Capitol Hill. In other words, he was a good fit for the critical job at a critical time. He and I met Neumann at the helicopter landing zone. We got into a Humvee and headed toward a final Hail Mary gathering with a delegation of leaders from Fallujah, led by a senior sheikh and the police chief. If the impending battle were to be avoided, that would depend on the outcome of this meeting.

The ambassador had one question for me.

"Do we need to do this, do we need to attack Fallujah?"

Truth was I believed we did—after the outright failure of Vigilant Resolve, the city was on the brink of falling even deeper into Al Qaeda's tentacled grip. We could not let that happen, at least in the period when our military's instinctive twitch muscles still dominated.

"Yes," I replied, while thinking we should not even be at war in Iraq in the first place.

Still, my honest answer bothered me. A lot of Marines were about to make huge sacrifices, losing limbs and, in many instances, their lives. I also knew Iraqi friends and their families would also be injured, or die, including one I had grown very close to in the preceding weeks.

Waleed was a son of Anbar who grew up amid date palm trees on the outskirts of Fallujah and swimming in the meandering muddy Euphrates River. We were about the same age, our early thirties. He was a charismatic lieutenant and officer in the local highway patrol whose powder blue uniform matched his eyes and the Anbar sky. Waleed could make a joke as quick and cutting as his political analysis. Like the teamsters in Baghdad, he did not hold a high-powered position in Iraqi society. As such, he had not lost touch with his community and everyday Iraqi society. He knew what was really going on in Anbar, unlike senior Iraqi officials who lived near senior U.S. officials in the luxurious Green Zone.

We spent hours discussing Iraq, the region, and what was ahead. Fluent in English, he liked to quiz me on American music, while I inquired about Iraqi history, particularly the British colonial era. In one of our first meetings, Waleed offered me memorable advice.

"This battle will come, Mr. Kael, but will not end when you Americans want it to. I know my people and they will fight as long as it takes to regain respect."

"Our respect?"

"Well, yes, but it is more about the new government you are bringing with you. We do not trust them. Iran has already won the war, not your government."

Waleed used to repeat a mantra in meetings and in email messages: "Remember, force and money equal a safe Iraq. It is not an easy mission, but it is not impossible"—pointedly and cleverly referencing President Bush's aircraft carrier "Mission Accomplished" landing and overhead banner.

Once I had asked Waleed a blunt question. "How do you survive Fallujah?"

He smiled and replied right away, "My God, my Glock, and my Galant."

Allah. His pistol. His car.

Despite this trifecta of protection, there was no way to be sure he could survive the coming battle.

With Waleed, Fallujans in general, and our Marines on my mind, Ambassador Neumann and I continued our short drive to a small compound right in the middle of the no-man's-land between Fallujah proper and Camp Fallujah. This was "the neutral zone." After our Humvee parked, we walked past massive HESCO barriers and razor wire along with several guard towers that formed the outermost perimeter of the compound. The courtyard was draped with giant spiderweb-like camouflage netting in various shades of tan, and the hum of diesel generators ensured a steady flow of power and sanity-saving air-conditioning as temperatures topped 110 degrees. Marines had hired local Iraqi contractors to build a fountain, which they painted light blue, and imported sod grass following an order by the 1st Marine Division commanding general, Jim Mattis. He wanted the welcoming center for Fallujans "to look better than Yosemite's Visitor Center." Not quite, but the general understood that even this small effort at greening one building's courtyard would show Iraqis the Americans had at least tried to make the setting a bit more inviting. Particularly given the hard discussions that happened there, like the one about to begin.

Marine staff officers informed us the opposing delegation would arrive within minutes to this micro-oasis. Sheikh Khaled al-Jumaili of the influential Jumaili tribe, a religious leader known to speak for thousands of Fallujans, would head it. He would be joined by the local police chief, who represented the reconstituted—but failing—Fallujah police force. They were, impossibly, trying to police a city that was run by insurgents and Al Qaeda and not the rule of law, even Iraqi style.

We had an ultimatum to deliver, and they knew it. If we were to avoid an assault by almost 15,000 coalition troops into Fallujah, a mass of iron armor and wall of grunts, something big and something unexpected needed to happen, fast, and with nothing lost in translation between us.

Ambassador Neumann, in khakis, a sports jacket, and a tie (but not Bremer-style boots), huddled with General Sattler and Colonel Mike Shupp, the regimental commander who had replaced Larry Nicholson. The plain, fluorescent-lit room had a small contingent of senior Marine officers and a spirited embassy political section officer who had joined the trip from Baghdad. She was the only woman in the room. There was little eye contact between those who wore Marine uniforms and those who wore Iraqi tribal dress. We drank coffee in mugs. They drank lukewarm tea served in small glass cups. Few Marines knew that Neumann had served in Vietnam as an infantry officer, earning a Bronze Star and Combat Infantry Badge. The Iraqis we were about to meet had no idea whatsoever that the ambassador himself had seen war before, up close, and was not going to be a pushover. He spoke softly but knew how to deliver a hard message.

Glass ashtrays and large Aquafina water bottles lined the middle of the table, though no one smoked. Sheikh Khaled sat in the middle of their side of the table, first among unequals and thereby announcing his lead spokesperson role. If anyone had received talking points from Al Qaeda operatives it was he. Khaled had large black eyes under thick brows that constantly darted around the room and exuded charisma. In his hands, multicolored and ornate prayer beads glinted as he passed them between thick fingers. Dressed all in white, the senior sheikh drew a stark contrast with the suited Ambassador Neumann and row of Marine officers surrounding the three-star Sattler, who would speak first for our side, while I took notes that would be transmitted in a diplomatic cable to Washington.

The drama played out quickly, each of us seated in hard chairs to match hard stares.

Sattler opened, insisting the Iraqis do one thing right away. He grabbed a Coke can, placing it next to his coffee mug.

"Hand over all your weapons. You know that's our request."

Sheikh Khaled (who had opted for Sprite over tea by then) and the police chief handed over two weapons: a rusted old pistol and a rusted old machine gun.

"That's it? That's all you intend to turn in?"

"That's everything," said Khaled.

"What kind of fool do you take me for?" asked Sattler in a rising voice. "This is our last chance to avoid a big fight. The next time we see each other one of us will be dead, and I will be looking at you."

The room fell silent. Sattler was voicing long-held Marine frustrations at the stalemated situation and spoke out as forcefully as I had ever heard him. Even I was taken aback by his comments, though justified.

After a while, Ambassador Neumann spoke and emphasized the political nature of events unfolding in Baghdad. Sunni citizens, including in insurgent- and terrorist-controlled Fallujah, could only be given the chance to vote in the upcoming election if the city became a lot safer. Polling day, as promised and promoted by President Bush—that anticipated purple finger moment—was set to occur across the province in only three months.

Sheikh Khaled acknowledged security challenges within Fallujah but offered no commitment to work toward a compromise and verifiable solution. He ignored any talk of Iraqi politics. Sunnis, by then, had announced their intention to boycott the upcoming American-imposed Election Day—rebelling against one-man, one-vote democracy forced upon them by Washington. The general and ambassador had tried with their words. Even so, I sensed that terrorists within Fallujah had ordered and intimidated the assembled Iraqis to hold firm. They were not there to negotiate with us. They were there to be defiant. And defiant they were.

"We have nothing more to say," Khaled concluded.

"Neither do we," replied Sattler, not usually a man, or general, of few words. He had delivered the ultimatum. Still, Neumann reached across the table to shake the hands of one of the silent members of the city delegation, a local engineer. And, to his credit, Sattler crossed his right arm over his chest, a sign of respect in Iraq. Khaled did not return the gesture.

The meeting broke up, and Sattler reported to his immediate boss, Lieutenant General Thomas Metz: "No deal." The whole meeting must have lasted less than thirty minutes. I escorted Ambassador Neumann back to the convoy. He would report the same message to Ambassador Negroponte, who certainly would relay it to the secretary of state and White House.

In only days we would be fighting the biggest battle of the Iraq War. More Marines dead. More Iraqis dead.

And what about Waleed and his family? I knew they would be caught between both sides with nowhere safe to go.

Nowhere to run.

Upon my return to Camp Fallujah, Marines of all ranks did not hesitate to interrogate me. Some of the best interrogators were the PSD (personal security detail) who moved the generals around the battle space, and often me as well. These Marines had a wood sign painted green, with skulls on it, in front of their shared quarters that included thick black lettering:

ACHTUNG: P.S.D. ONLY. Violators will be killed, shot, murdered, stabbed, beaten, gassed, disemboweled, burned, hung, spanked, eviscerated, castrated, impaled, whipped, drowned, tarred and feathered, shanked, drawn and quartered, sodomized. And DEVIL-DOGGED.

Their questions were both telling and tough to answer:
"What's our strategy here, Mr. Weston?"
"Do you think Iraqis give a rat's ass about democracy or elections?"
"What do I tell my parents, sir—my best friend just got blown up?"
"We don't do this, do we? Just invade another country because we can?"
"Why not let Basher waste this place and be done with it all?"
The "Basher" referred to was an AC-130 gunship. Its 20mm Vulcan cannon can fire up to 6,000 rounds a minute. The flying warship has bigger guns too: 40mm Bofors auto-cannon blasting forth copper-colored projectiles, elbow-to-fingertip in length. The modified plane even has a 105mm howitzer installed inside its metal belly. These largest of munitions measure arm length and are reloaded by hand. Once targeted, buildings implode, turning into rubble in seconds.

The first time I heard Basher above, it sounded as if demons had escaped from a deep hole in the Iraqi desert into the night sky over Fallujah. Thuds marked impacts in the industrial section of town, behind a row of mechanic shops and under a large water tower. The Basher airborne platform attacks from the left side of its fuselage, banking counterclockwise at an advantageous angle. Its trajectory piloted and pitched for killing. Thermal imaging enables the crew to see the fluorescent and warm 98.6-degree outlines of the "enemy" below—soon dead and turning cold, and only then disappearing from sight.

But Fallujah proved to be a battle of wills, not technology. And Iraqi will, Waleed had convinced me, should never be underestimated. Sheikh Khaled had made the same point in his defiant stand. And we would be fighting in their neighborhood, a longtime rebellious city of traders and raiders. Fallujah had seen war before.

Those good and fair questions among many more from other Marines did not result in satisfactory answers from me in the Marine infantry grunts' view. Even so, we were friends and I escaped being devil-dogged.

. . .

Not long after Ambassador Neumann departed and only hours before the multi-prong Fallujah assault was to commence, an unusually wet cold front moved across the city. The weather matched the mood. The rain turned dust to mud. Virga cloud formations hung delicately, drape-like, over the skyline, affecting our infrared vision.

Some Marines would have to go in semiblind.

Just before kickoff, as Marines like to call it, an infantry platoon and I, along with a Fox News reporter, Greg Palkot, camped out a hundred meters away from Entry Control Point One (ECP-1), a barricaded rectangular fortress located just beyond the cloverleaf highway intersection. It was considered the most dangerous single location in Iraq, a place I would have preferred to avoid in a State Department career that had begun in more sedate surroundings.

Despite the violent setting, there was time for Marines to read. I noticed one had a pile of paperback books stacked near his cot, carefully placed around his rifle. He said he hoped his family did not watch the news, including any on-site reports from our guest reporter.

"They don't need to see where I live and how dangerous it is. I lie to them when they ask about what it's like over here. Don't you?"

"I don't send many emails, never talk to them by phone," I replied. "But I do talk into a tape recorder and keep the tapes for my parents. They convinced me to send them, just like I had when I went away to college near Seattle."

"Cool, but how honest are you about what's going on here?"

I hesitated a bit. "Well, honest enough. I am not sure I will ever listen to them given everything we are seeing and what's about to happen."

In the city, a few muezzins began their calls to prayer, while the sounds of war ricocheted around us and dominated Fallujah's audioscape.

The Marine picked up his used book.

"I kinda like the way those mosques sound, sir. I'm sorta used to it. And I don't believe in anything."

And with that he moved back onto his green, dirt-covered cot, crossed his legs, and opened his novel by Mary Higgins Clark—not a title on junior Marines' recommended reading list per the commandant that has, at various times, included: *Ender's Game, Starship Troopers, The Ugly American, All Quiet on the Western Front, Rifleman Dodd, Marines in the Garden of Eden, The Forgotten Soldier . . .* and the U.S. Constitution. If he stayed in the Corps and became an officer and made colonel or general rank, the list of to-read titles would be different, such as: *Pentagon—How to Excel in a Bureaucracy, Decoding Clausewitz, Dereliction of Duty, Diplomacy, The Revenge of Geography, Another Bloody Century, How Wars End* . . . and *The Federalist Papers.*

Below him was an open MRE labeled Menu No. 17, Beef Teriyaki. I was tempted to suggest he add another title in his Fallujah reading pile, *Lord of the Flies,* but instead only asked him if there were any Chicken and Salsa MREs left that I could steal.

"Doubt it, sir."

Perhaps I should have mentioned to the bookish Marine rifleman that only by experiencing the Iraq War did I now truly understand why, in the final scene of William Golding's classic book, my favorite character, Ralph, wept. ("Ralph wept for the end of innocence, the darkness of man's heart, and the fall through the air of a true, wise friend called Piggy." My English teacher in high school had assigned *Lord of the Flies,* the first war book I ever read.)

And why so many families across Iraq already were weeping—many having lost their innocence and seen the darkness of man's heart as well—with more and more American families soon to follow. Perhaps this Marine's own family too if he were to be in the wrong place at the wrong time in the fighting to follow.

Instead I kept these thoughts to myself, turned around, and walked away.

Fox's Palkot embedded with us to broadcast live feature stories on the eve of battle. Fallujah made for great theater in a nation back home not yet weary of Iraq. We did not know it then, but *Time* magazine would soon put on its cover (November 22, 2004) one of the Marines who lived at ECP-1, under the heading "Street Fight: Inside the Battle for Fallujah." (The Marine would later send me an autographed copy, which showed him yelling with an intense expression under the imposing overhang of a dun-colored Fallujah home compound. The cover story began with a staff sergeant screaming, "We are not going to die!")

Former Marine Lieutenant Colonel Oliver North himself would show up soon enough, narrating a Fox program titled *War Stories with*

Ollie North. My mission was different. Unlike both Fox television reporters, my audience was the U.S. government. I had gone to ECP-1 to write a cable as a window into Fallujah for Washington before the battle.

Inside the State Department, this job function serves a dual purpose: to inform Washington but also to influence Washington. The best political officers and diplomats weave a story line beyond he-said, she-said transcripts. This was my goal, so I focused in my writing on what Fallujah looked like from outside, with the main voice being that of Waleed. In most cables, the only time my voice came through— signed off by the embassy and ambassador—occurred in a "comment" section. Some colleagues opted to avoid commentary. I believed the comment section remained important, particularly when reporting for the government in a war zone. Besides, Washington remained half a world away from the front lines and needed an honest take, which I worked hard to provide.

In some ways my cable content wrote itself in those days. So much visceral stuff was happening, huge events with lasting strategic significance. Fallujah formed a political officer's dream job albeit in a nightmarish setting. Days earlier, for example, the Iraqi prime minister ordered civilians to leave Fallujah. Marine Civil Affairs officers had been updating the generals and me about the steady flow of people leaving the city. Dozens and dozens fled daily. We received reports that certain neighborhoods in Baghdad had become "Little Fallujahs" as displaced families crammed themselves into relatives' homes. During some convoys outside Camp Fallujah, I looked out on the roads and saw long lines of civilian vehicles headed in one direction: away from Fallujah.

Yet over earthen HESCO barriers beyond ECP-1, I could see a few kids walking in the distance. They did not look like insurgents to me. Farther down the street, I saw what looked like a toddler, wandering alone—quite a place to get lost, with dozens of Marines watching the child's every move. I wondered how many other little kids had remained in the city. How many of them would soon be caught in our onslaught. The Marines around me were not much older than the two teens I first spotted, maybe by two or three years at most.

They would be trying to kill each other before long—war's red cycle, once started, very hard to stop.

These firsthand observations became the basis for a cable titled "A Window into Fallujah"—never mind that my "windows" were largely limited to observations from atop HESCO barriers turned parapets behind Marine tanks.

As a degree of consolation, I took State Department challenge coins with me to this same barricaded checkpoint. They had our government's eagle symbol on one side and a map of Iraq on the back. Troops collect them and, when at a bar, the coin from the highest-ranking officer trumps; the loser buys the beer. Marines liked the State Department version because they were rare—reflective of just how rare a sight a civilian was in the company of infantry Marines in Anbar, let alone Fallujah on the eve of battle. I told the corporals they were good luck coins, though I had no basis for that claim. While hardly superstitious myself, it felt good to give them out, since all of us knew the odds were that some would die in the days ahead. It was going to be bloody. It was going to be violent and loud. You could sense it in the air. You could see it in everyone's eyes.

Then nothing happened.

The move into Fallujah would be pushed back, again.

Why?

I took a short trip to Baghdad where I saw Ambassador Negroponte eating dinner in the marble palace dining facility in the Green Zone, just around the corner from where the twin towers of the World Trade Center had been drawn and prominently displayed during Ambassador Bremer's prior reign. A security detail stood close. Negroponte motioned me over, asking for an update on Fallujah. I provided him with what little I knew. He then remarked: "Not that I have any inside information, but I don't think the White House wants Fallujah on the front pages before Election Day."

There it was, nothing lost in translation whatsoever from the top American official in Iraq. The ultimate political maneuver in Washington that would keep an entire operation and thousands of U.S. troops in a deadly kind of limbo.

I began to realize then that U.S. elections, not Iraqi or Afghan ones, mattered most in both wars.

Meanwhile, Iraq's prime minister, Ayad Allawi, said Operation Phantom Fury would not be a welcome name to Iraqi ears. He ordered a new one: Al Fajr, which means "new dawn" in Arabic.

We used to wonder where war lived, what it was that made it so vile. And now we realize that we know where it lives . . . inside ourselves.

ALBERT CAMUS

Happy Birthday

Mosques and kebabs had once made Fallujah famous. Now it was the violence between the United States Marine Corps and thousands of insurgents and Al Qaeda terrorists. During the long lull before the battle, Fallujah's stockade of minarets, radiating outward from the largest mosque's turquoise dome, broadcast calls to prayer morning, noon, night. Stereo-like from all angles, it was beautiful and eerie. Insurgents had become unforgiving choirmasters. They intimidated and exiled moderate religious leaders and issued different messages. The American infidels occupied Iraq and had to be resisted, fought, and killed.

We replied, taunting, with our own music: heavy metal blaring from speakers atop Marine Humvees on the outskirts of the city. "Back in Black" by AC/DC echoed throughout Fallujah's streets, an updated version of *Apocalypse Now*'s "The Ride of the Valkyries" and a different sort of "Good Morning, Iraq" callout. Muezzins must have taken particular notice of the new audio brought by the Americans. The propaganda war had been well established by then on both sides, with insurgent flyers distributed in town declaring "Fallujah, the cemetery of the Americans." U.S. military leaflets urged all civilians to vacate without delay, echoing the official line of the Iraqi government.

Insurgents provoked us with other sounds too—thudding mortars and whistling rockets. We responded in kind with our own clamorous military hardware, destroying Fallujans' favorite kebab shop, Haji Hussein, with a laser-guided missile. We told ourselves we killed bad guys in the strike. Probably some.

I wished Ambassador Negroponte could have seen, felt, heard this period in Fallujah up close, and then picked up the phone to give the White House a personal sitrep (military parlance for situation report). Perhaps that would have reduced the degree of political gamesmanship under way. Probably not.

On Tuesday, November 2, 2004, George W. Bush defeated John Kerry and was reelected president and commander in chief (50.7 percent to 48.3 percent of the popular vote, 286 vs. 251 electoral votes). The Iraq file moved, mostly at least, from Karl Rove (Bush's beardless Rasputin, nicknamed Turd Blossom by the president) back to the White House national security team.

What awaited Marines in the days ahead was unlike anything that had confronted the U.S. military since the Iraq invasion in March 2003. Marine intelligence officers briefed the command team and me on the details: an estimated 3,000 to 4,000 insurgents had dug in deep, using houses and alleyways as bunkers, and mosques to store weapons. Throughout the city there were at least 300 "defensive sites," too many sniper positions to count, berms, and daisy-chained IEDs everywhere from the streets to kitchen walls. Amid all of this several hundred civilians were still in the city. Marines were ordered to spare them, but of course that would never be completely possible.

General Sattler himself had a meeting with the Iraqi prime minister to discuss the stakes and get the green light from Iraq's commander in chief. While seated in his office, the same office I had met General Conway in when I first arrived, one thing was becoming all too apparent. While countless Marines were deploying and redeploying, I would remain in Anbar. Still the only American government official based full-time in the province, and ultimately, still the only one having to oversee the rebuilding of whatever destruction we were about to deliver and in vast amounts.

Sattler told me how the session with the prime minister had gone.

"Can't say I want to have to do that again, but I said what I needed to."

"I bet you did. Without the Iraqi government in the lead on this, we won't get very far once the fighting stops. And who knows when it will. This war has gone on a lot longer than Rumsfeld or anyone predicted."

"No kidding," the general replied.

Knowing that Sattler had spent a lot of time on Capitol Hill, I figured there were probably not many other senior officers better suited to the task. He knew how politics worked, how politicians could trump generals—if they cared enough to provide strategic guidance. Few, it seemed, did.

Sattler recapped his exchange with Prime Minister Allawi to Marine historians in more detail years later, which would be part of an official Marine Corps history of the battle. He recalled the loaded conversation this way:

> You know, Mr. Prime Minister, don't tell us to go and expect us to stop. When you have exhausted all the political, all the opportunities to solve this problem, and that we can no longer let them export their ideas, their VBIEDs [car bombs], their IEDs, their raids. . . . When you reach that point, I actually said, "just tear your phone out of the wall. Don't think about calling us and telling us to stop because once we get going, we're going to have to go all the way. We're not gonna stop 'til we hit the southern end of the town. . . ." He said, "I understand. When I tell you go, we will accomplish the mission, we will complete the mission."

And so with the PM's blessing, Fallujah's New Dawn commenced late on November 7, 2004, and while Iraqi government–approved, this was a Marine-led fight. We all hoped it would have more resolve than the failed Vigilant Resolve operation half a year earlier.

The 1st Marine Division headquartered in Ramadi retained tactical command of the fight, but Sattler believed our infantry battalions could "clear" Fallujah faster. And as the highest-ranking Marine general in

Anbar and Iraq, for that matter, his decisions trumped the two-star division command. The overall top U.S. commander in Iraq, General George Casey, previously challenged him about his willingness to follow through with the attack.

"Getting cold feet, John?"

The half joke between top brass had a serious subtext.

There would be no turning back; instead there would be sequenced military maneuvers complete with a full-on "pincer" strategy and "blocking" positions. War 101 morphed into War 501, given the complexity Fallujah and Anbar represented. Impatient Marines matched against a patient enemy schooled in graduate-level warfare.

As banking Basher gunships began their work on Iraq's City of Mosques, Ambassador Negroponte asked me to consider leaving Fallujah to go work for him directly in Baghdad as his primary aide. Though I appreciated the offer, I chose to stay in Anbar with the Marines.

I had gone native—with the tribe initialed U.S.M.C. in place of the tribe initialed D.O.S.

Not a good State Department career move, but I knew where I was most needed. Besides the Marines had kept me safe, or safe enough—so far.

With the fighting now under way—with daily headlines across much of the world confirming as much—our Humvee crossed into the city on November 10, 2004, the Marine Corps' 229th birthday. It is a date never forgotten and the most important day of the year for the then nearly 200,000 Marines and their proud alums stationed around the world. By way of background: in 1775, the Second Continental Congress commissioned Samuel Nicholas as a "Captain of Marines." Marines made effective insurgents against the British Crown, wearing almost four-inch-high "leatherneck" collars to protect against sword blows, a nickname that stuck.

But this particular Marine birthday in this particular place, in this particular war, merited no celebration. Six Marines and a Navy Corpsman died before midnight this November 10 in Iraq: Cpl Romulo J. Jimenez II (21, of Bellington, West Virginia, pop. 1,929); LCpl Wesley

J. Canning (21, of Friendswood, Texas, pop. 37,5887); LCpl Aaron C. Pickering (20, of Marion, Illinois, pop. 17,413); LCpl Erick J. Hodges (21, of Bay Point, California, pop. 21,349); PO3 Julian Woods (22, of Jacksonville, Florida, pop. 842,583); Lt Dan T. Malcolm, Jr. (25, of Brinson, Georgia, pop. 213); SSgt Gene Ramirez (28, of San Antonio, Texas, pop. 1,409,000).

All told, November 2004 marked the month in which the U.S. suffered its most casualties during the Iraq War. The ferocity of the bloody street-to-street fight in Fallujah had no equal in the rest of the country, even in Baghdad.

Fallujah's KIA list grew quickly.

Lance Corporal Greg Rund would be one casualty. I had met him briefly. As a high school freshman, he survived the Columbine massacre in his native Littleton, Colorado (pop. 44,275), when two students killed twelve others and a teacher in the school's library and halls. But Lance Corporal Rund would not survive Fallujah. He lay dead at twenty-one, on his second tour, the Mile High State's eighteenth KIA. The Rund family would later ask that any donations be sent to Columbine High School in Littleton for the Greg Rund Memorial Scholarship Fund to "carry on Greg's spirit of leadership, patriotism, and his love of Columbine High School football."

As I thought of Rund and other Marine friends battling in the streets not far away, Lieutenant General Abdul Qadr Mohammad Jassim Obeidi al-Mifarji took the seat next to me in the Humvee. To the credit of Negroponte and the State Department security office in Baghdad, I was not restricted to stay on base. They wanted me out with infantry Marines at all levels, the only way I could do my job right.

Prime Minister Allawi had asked my Humvee seatmate, Abdul Qadr, to be the military governor of Fallujah, the top Iraqi official responsible for the city, the battle, and its aftermath. Bespectacled and slightly hunched, his demeanor seemed more academic than martial. He hid his steel spine well. Saddam Hussein had demoted and incarcerated the Ramadi native, a fellow Sunni, for seven years after he opposed Iraq's 1990 invasion of Kuwait.

"I am not a political man, but sent here to be the political military governor," he said while reaching for a bottle of water.

"I am not a military man, but I have been sent here to be a Marine commanding general's political adviser," I replied.

While not entirely fluent in English, he had understood enough and smiled.

"Trade places then?"

I smiled this time. "General, Fallujans will respect you. You are a military man, and from what my Fallujah contacts tell me, they want someone strong but fair."

"*Inshallah*," he said.

Outside our Humvee smoke filled the air, and we could hear a steady flow of small arms fire. I noticed some of the tallest mosque minarets had holes in them or were missing the top half. It helped that Abdul Qadr was Sunni, I thought, and had been a general during Saddam's time—particularly one who had been punished. Scars from Saddam equaled *wasta*, the Arabic word for influence. Like many Iraqis, he wore the exterior of a survivor. Across sectarian groups, they endured much during the era of the vicious dictator and his vengeful sons and subsequent international economic sanctions, only to be followed by the American–Al Qaeda era—and, eventually, life under the Islamic State.

General Sattler sat up front. He decided to visit the battlefield barely three days in, an unusual hands-on decision for a three-star commanding general. He passed us a map of our route, grids and corners I already knew well having seen the battle map for much of the prior three months. It looked like the Risk board game of my youth, though overwhelmingly covered in coalition pieces. A total force of 13,500 comprised of two Marine regiments, a Naval Mobile Construction Battalion (Seabees), U.S. Army battalions, British forces (the Black Watch), in addition to about 2,000 Iraqi troops. These were not plastic Marines and soldiers, however, but troops of blood and bone, all with pasts back home and, if lucky, with futures back home as well.

Fallujah's streets, oddly yet revealingly, had been assigned American names, many female. I was told the division's operations officer had reportedly picked them from among his family members, but this Marine lieutenant colonel later admitted to me most were the names of "past girlfriends." He explained a French general in Dien Bien Phu had done the same thing in Vietnam. So as our tanks and grunts cleared Iraq's City of Mosques of insurgents, their movement followed harmless-sounding routes. These female names and grid coordinates included "phase lines" and "objectives" marked:

Fran
Isabella
Jenna
Virginia

One of the main streets was also named Henry, perhaps after a dad or grandfather.

Abdul Qadr's earlier comment had gotten me thinking, and as our armored convoy continued on I told Sattler I would "rather be a general than an ambassador."

"Generals always stand up when an ambassador enters the room," Sattler said.

"Well," I replied, "it is all about implementation. Marines follow orders."

"Ha, true. State has a lot of talkers."

I thought of a variation of one of my favorite quotes: war might be too important to leave to military men, as French premier Georges Clemenceau remarked, but politicians, well, were politicians. Hearing my comment, Abdul Qadr nodded. Being a general-turned-military-governor, he knew both sides of both worlds. He would later become Iraq's minister of defense and thereby have to maneuver a political minefield as complex as the physical one we faced together in Anbar province.

As our driver guided us to the eastern edge of Fallujah, war's ever-ugly face showed itself. We saw a series of houses had been obliterated the prior day as our battalions penetrated from north to south, in an iron wave. Incinerated cars left as metal skeletons. Holes from the barrage of our munitions deeply pockmarked once private family gardens. Collapsed shops crumbled next to collapsed mosques. Three-hundred-sixty-degree devastation, as dogs darted between piles of rubble.

Abdul Qadr turned to Sattler and me.

"How many weapons to take these neighborhoods?"

His question, in broken English, sounded to me like a measured indictment. It appeared, he believed, our overuse of firepower far outdid the actual threat, or in Marine lingo "a display of disproportionate use of force." He had a point. Marines had spent weeks building an "iron mountain" before the battle. And they damn-well-thank-you-very-much had used it: 256,000 .50 caliber machine gun rounds, 4,600 fragmentary grenades, among other piles and crates of imported ordnance "Made in USA."

Abdul Qadr knew the more difficult part of the fight would be what followed. The rebuilding. The return of civilians. All the broken pieces to be put back together. This war would not end with this battle, that much was already clear. Stamina would have to replace the adrenaline rush. And endurance trump impatience.

A few minutes later, our Humvee entered the northeastern part of Fallujah, not far from Jolan Park. An Iraqi colonel with an impressively sculpted black mustache, seemingly right off a Cuban cigar box, briefed us. *A hard fight, still not over or won. The soldiers in his commando unit had been brave. The weather remained wet but manageable.* Though diminutive, the officer carried the room, gesticulating wildly and ensuring his interpreter got the story exactly right. No battlefield detail was to be lost in translation. He made only one request: "All I need is more ammo and cigarettes for my men."

On the way back to the base—after an insurgent rocket sailed five meters or so over our heads during a stop just north of the city—Governor-General Abdul Qadr gazed out of the Humvee's two-inch-thick windows into the smoldering city. He said nothing. I gazed out my side, noticing a few Iraqi soldiers amid dozens of Marines.

I too said nothing.

Along the city skyline, the images reflected the intensity of the ongoing fight. Oil columns of black smoke circled above minarets. Tanks positioned themselves at key junctions. Marine sniper teams could be seen atop some of the tallest compounds, scanning for Iraqi sniper teams—the ultimate contest of will and skill and luck.

As the sun sank over the Euphrates amid a cool November breeze, we made our way back to Camp Fallujah. As if on cue, our 155mm howitzers launched several rounds into the city we had just left. I did not feel reassured, knowing that it would be Abdul Qadr (though he would be transferred back to Baghdad before long), Civil Affairs Marines, and other local leaders, and me, who would have to deal with the mourning families who had a family member just blown up in their back kitchen or upstairs bedroom. I wanted to think we only killed terrorists, but had been in Iraq long enough to know otherwise. Our intelligence officers had been right. More than a few civilians had remained in the city. And more than a few were being killed—alongside a lot more terrorists, right? That is what I told myself. That is what we told ourselves. That is what we told Baghdad and Washington. I wanted to believe it.

Days later, in the Shurta (Arabic for "police") neighborhood a few hundred meters into the city, I viewed my first dead Iraqi body. Many more would follow. I had gone into the city to assess how big the rebuilding challenge would be. The corpse was flattened and in the middle of the road. Almost unrecognizable as a human body, it must have been run over a dozen times. I could not tell age, gender, cause of death, or whether the person had a weapon. Unlike war movies, death does not look heroic. It looks painful and not always sudden.

Gory. Random.

An eerie setting emptied of any sense of soul, Fallujah looked and sounded dead. Marines had reached the middle of the city and objective they were assigned, called "Phase Line Fran." The weather had cleared. Drifting columns of gray smoke turned a light blue sky hazy. I did not hear any muezzins' calls to prayer. Their voices were replaced with ours, mechanical and human—the crunch of tank tracks, the hum of Humvees, and jangle of Light Armored Vehicles punctuated by testosterone-drenched infantry yells, including the common refrain of "Get Some"—as in get some more war.

But I noticed even more Marines sat quietly, in corners, inside vehicles, and in makeshift command posts. Few words. Heavy eyes. Cigarette butts scattered around nicked boots. War is mostly about silences, lull after lull after lull, filled with absences, and alone time. Hidden battles already internalized. Emotional drawbridges up. Exhaustion, first physical and mental and then spiritual.

Then what, for all the years to follow?

Post-traumatic stress, for sure, and perhaps, if lucky, some post-traumatic growth. War equaling plenty of pain but also potential resilience.

Near the wrecked Fallujah fire station, I saw three Marine names in a row scraped on a wall: WARPIGS—Burns, Holder, and Magaoay. Followed by "Gave Their Lives Not For A Cause Or For Their Country But For Their Brothers!" Marines found comfort in that. Understandably. But to me, that kind of brotherly sacrifice did not excuse the policy malfeasance out of Washington that I was just beginning to understand the full extent of, with more Washington-to-Iraq disconnects to follow. The same malfeasance Marines were just beginning to understand as well—and inquire about.

Most of the houses' metal gates we passed had been blown up, tank rounds having gone right through some. I estimated around half of the city's neighborhoods were destroyed. The reconstruction needs were huge. No diplomatic cable of mine could capture the setting or mood of the leveled city, lunarlike in places. An embedded British journalist, James Hider, described the place this way in a dispatch back to London: "At midnight Fallujah looked like a scene from Stalingrad." Stalingrad did not end so well for the attacking Germans. The main Russian general in the besieged city urged his men to implement a new tactic: "hugging the enemy." They did, to devastating effect. In the most destroyed parts of Fallujah, such a World War II comparison almost seemed like an understatement.

In just a few hours, I had seen it all: the ripped sign of jagged metal torn in two above ECP-1, its traffic arrows warped and pointed skyward, with "Habaniya Lake" letters cut in half; another twisted one that read "Ar Rutbah"; water lines broken, turning street corners into two-to-three-foot swamps of gray-green muck; concrete dividers smashed under the weight of tanks; two-story houses sheared into blocks; palm trees bent at unnatural angles; massive walls of dirt piled in defensive positions—first by insurgents, later by Marine engineers; mosques filled with terrorists' weapons piled in high stacks and bundles of AK-47s and ordnance rounds protected by piles of imported tile from India.

And in one house I was called over to, Marines found the passport (number H0234224) of Sheikh Abdullah al-Janabi, a senior cleric and key insurgent leader. Holding it in my hands, I wondered if or when we would ever find him, or kill him. The travel document had an imprint in blue ink of Janabi's thumb and had been lying alongside, of all things, a Bronze Star, still in its case. Marines were unsure how the terrorists had gotten it—maybe from a convoy they had attacked and looted. I could not help but wonder which Marine's medal this had been, or would have been.

Throughout those days in Fallujah, new nouns had to be invented. Adjectives too. I began to see why war produced poets and their dark poems—even if we had cut through Fallujah via the knifelike and unadorned vocabulary of infantry grunts. Sharp, uncouth but practiced, and all edge—the camaraderie of the front line.

I realized the war we were living in those days would be hard to talk about, hard to write about. Iraq's bullet-ridden City of Mosques was awarding us all a different kind of educational degree—a mastery of fighting, a mastery of surviving.

A mastery of pain.

The Fallujans who remained had it even harder. Near the al-Hadra mosque, I saw women and children, plus a few teenagers. They clumped together, seeking refuge. I wondered how many more there were, and how many were innocent. Or if they were playing us for time before hidden brothers and uncles plotted to kill more corporals and captains. Or me.

A Humvee was parked nearby, with a large sign on the back of it that read: CAUTION STAY 100 METERS BACK OR YOU WILL BE SHOT with the same message in Arabic below. Another Humvee had a plastic yellow "Taxi" sign attached above it. And a third, I noticed, had a Santa and pinecone wreath attached to the front grille. "Happy Holidays" it read, an early bit of Christmas cheer for that Marine Civil Affairs crew, which seemed out of place, for sure, but welcome.

It paid to be paranoid in those days, even in supposed neutral territory. We found weapons inside mosques, considered to be off-limits Islamic sanctuaries. And towering minarets made good cover for insurgent sniper positions, so no ground in this city stayed hallowed for long.

My introduction to war's horror proved intense, but some Marines encountered worse. One friend, a captain and early test pilot for Ospreys, told me about his most jarring and surreal, but real, moment.

From the second floor of a building above, he saw a torn body, the freeze frame he said he would see "for the rest of my life." He described it to me in bursts of disconnected words. In such scenes there was no narrative, no flow and no poetry either. Just disconnect. A starving dog pulled at one end of the corpse, while a starving cat tugged on the other. In between, gray birds hovered, a feathered squall mixing overhead. It was like we were all living through Iraq's version of Picasso's *Guernica*, if not also a hellish Hieronymus Bosch–like *Last Judgment* scene, Fallujah-style.

Marines found the driver's license of one of the butchered and burned Blackwater contractors in the city. The generals asked that I make sure it got to our embassy in Baghdad, in addition to the identification documents of a twenty-four-year-old Japanese backpacker, Shosei Koda, whose decapitated body had been found in Baghdad, rolled up in an American flag. Intel officers believed his killers had used Fallujah as their home base, just as they had when American Nicholas Berg had been beheaded while wearing an orange jumpsuit. We would also locate a nameless "white woman's body" (as reported by Marines in internal emails) or what was left of it—not much—amid the torture rooms hidden inside walled compounds.

Each of us had images we wanted to forget, but could not, would not, and maybe even should not. Some battlefields in Iraq etched deeper into American psyches than others. Fallujah warranted its own terrible category, unmatched in other trying places like Mosul, Basra, or Tal Afar. Only its sister city of Ramadi came close and, later, Sadr City. Almost immediately after the initial war cries, we preferred to be anywhere else. I promised myself I would not repeat some war stories, but then did.

I witnessed one reporter back at base, shaking, at the very safe Marine Public Affairs Office, insisting she be "un-embedded" right away and flown back to Baghdad. She said something along the lines of, "This is worse than I ever imagined it could be." In that assessment, she was right. Troops had died and been wounded around her. Insurgents had tunneled below streets, unexpectedly popping up behind our lines. They were crafty killers, often loaded up on narcotics, berserker-like, and able to ingest too many rounds before dying.

But it was a young Iraqi survivor I talked to that first week who left the deepest impact on me. Marines had partially secured the city, and I was anxious to begin to get direct views from Fallujans. The embassy had received requests from senior Sunni leaders for nonmilitary updates. That was my job. The Iraqi kid must have been no older than fifteen, with black hair, black eyes, and blackened hands. Showing little fear but much intensity, he walked up to me outside the mosque. Perhaps he felt safer because I was a civilian without a weapon, even though I was surrounded by a platoon of Marines with rifles arrayed all around, sweeping back and forth in constant motion. I found a linguist to interpret for me. Amid all of ours, this is his story, one among many, with most still left untold.

Grandpa was old, too old to leave. He wanted to stay in our home even after the government told everyone to evacuate. Mother asked me to remain in the city to watch over him. She and my brothers and sisters left. When the Marines attacked, we stayed. The sounds scared us. We thought the house would collapse. Grandpa did not leave his room. A bullet, from one of your Marine snipers I think, shattered a window. Grandpa fell, dying. Maybe he looked out the window and you thought he was a terrorist. I don't know. I was scared, I moved his body outside, hoping someone might see us, help us. His body needed to be buried but where and how? I came to this mosque, looking for someone I knew. Instead, Marines. And more Marines. They wouldn't let me leave. Grandpa is still in front of our house. The gate is open. Marines don't need to break it to get inside.

Moved and open to his plea, I said I would try to help, not knowing where to start. Fallujah remained a war zone, with active clearing operations under way. But I discussed his situation with Marines to see whether we could locate the compound and assist in retrieving and burying the body. I said I would also raise the matter with members of the newly formed Fallujah reconstruction committee. This group of Iraqis had just begun to meet at Camp Fallujah in preparation for the return of tens of thousands of displaced residents.

But even weeks later, after searching several districts, we never located the grandfather's body. I believed the Iraqi kid's story.

"Will this all be worth it?"

Of all the questions Marines asked, this one stayed with me longest. I would not lie to them, but wanted to badly.

The truth: policy never matched the sacrifice. It never would, really, in Iraq. I lacked the ability to convey as much in a way that would alleviate past and present pain and all that was to come. More suffering than any of us could foresee in those early days when ego and adrenaline got the better of us all. Before cycles of revenge took hold, between Occupier and Occupied (the Kurds alone felt liberated)—USMC vs. IED—between two sides not yet bloodied enough, if that ever seemed possible in retrospect. Lance Corporal, United States Marine Corps, had become the most dangerous job title in Iraq. They comprised more KIA than any other part of the U.S. military. And we classified Iraqi men as "military-aged males" (or MAMs). Enemies and "fair" targets, even when some had shovels in hand—not to dig roadside bombs but rather to farm their fields.

And while our AC-130 air armada saved American lives, Bashers had largely obliterated the place, obliterated Iraq's City of Mosques—flattened terrain we would be tasked with rebuilding over the next five years. Terrorists left dead, but civilians killed and wounded too.

Another city destroyed in order to save it?

A rubbled Fallujah now home to phantoms and fury—Iraqi and American.

I had not seen Waleed since our last meeting. I could only hope his God, Glock, and Galant got him through this last battle. And perhaps a hell of a lot of luck.

Fallujah was his hometown, after all.

Waleed would survive, but just barely. He called me to say that he would not be returning to work for a while. He and his family had wisely relocated to a more rural part of Anbar. Where towering date palm trees far outnumbered towering minarets, where the Euphrates River was fished for carp unlike the deep bend of the river near Fallujah.

Where instead Marines fished its reedy edges for hidden insurgents or dead ones.

I will just say this, that as we go through the mortuary affairs, which is a very humanitarian process—a little gruesome, as you can imagine; a Marine who fought and might have lost a buddy is now aiding by picking up the terrorists and helping in the Islamic tradition of putting them with the right respect a combatant deserves on the battlefield.

COLONEL MIKE REGNER
PENTAGON BRIEFING, NOVEMBER 15, 2004

The Potato Factory

Before Anbar, before Fallujah, the Marine Corps in Iraq did not have to think that much about how to manage a large number of bodies—whether insurgents or KIA from within the USMC tribe. Processing dead insurgents was one thing. Processing dead Marines something else.

While America's fallen were sent home in flag-draped coffins, there were strict rules for burial in the Islamic faith. (1) It is obligatory to bury a dead body in the ground, so deep as to hide any smell from decomposition that might attract beasts of prey, and, if there is a danger of animals digging up remains, then the grave should be made solid with bricks. (2) If it is not possible to bury a dead body in the ground, it may be kept in a vault or a coffin instead. (3) The dead body should be laid in the grave on its right side so that the face remains toward the Qibla (toward Mecca).

While it may seem counter to war, we tried to make sure insurgents whom Marines had killed in battle were buried properly. It was a key part of regaining the trust of the civilians. Honoring your dead enemy, however, is not so simple in practice.

With bodies filling Fallujah's streets, I had been asked a specific question by Robert Ford, the political counselor at the embassy and a top State Department Arabist: how were we handling Iraqi remains? Senior Sunni politicians and religious scholars had pressed him on the matter. He and Ambassador Negroponte hoped to reassure Iraqi leaders that Muslim burial rites were being followed, at least as much as they could be.

Robert was a polyglot diplomat. In addition to being fluent in Arabic, he spoke French, German, and Turkish. Hence never needing an interpreter, which makes all the difference in diplomacy—a lot less lost in translation. Before joining the Foreign Service he had been a Peace Corps volunteer for four years in Morocco (self-described "long hair, huge mustache" days). What was less known about him? Iraqi television viewers had voted him as the "most attractive American"—and they meant in every way, given his frequent appearances on-screen and his way with Arabic. And he had been kidnapped in Najaf during the Coalition Provisional Authority era, an experience he downplayed despite undoubtedly being a terrifying one.

General Sattler pulled me aside and said, "Kael, tell the embassy we're on it. We are going to do this right."

"I will. Robert likes you, and knows we don't hide any problems from each other or play State Department versus Marine Corps games."

Sattler then acted fast, and asked Cheryl Ites, an innovative chief warrant officer from Bethlehem, Pennsylvania, to come up with a plan. And with that the Mortuary Affairs team was formed. Their base of operations would be a building for storing and processing food.

This location, a potato factory on the outskirts of Fallujah, was about to become an ad hoc mortuary. Situated halfway between Camp Fallujah and the eastern edge of the city, we passed the facility almost daily. It was a low building, surrounded by a wall. It had been a business that employed dozens. Now it was filling up with bodies. Hundreds. Why there? The cooling reefers (designed for potatoes) allowed the bodies to be stored longer. There they could be sorted and checked for non-Iraqi nationalities and anyone else with ties to the insurgency. I do not know how we differentiated which Arab was which, but I knew Washington wanted to find foreign fighters in Fallujah. Badly.

For the outside world, the narrative looked better that way: Marines fighting against hard-core, well-trained terrorists of the Al Qaeda variety, not the locals—that is, Fallujans lacking any ties whatsoever to the network responsible for 9/11 and instead revolting against an occupying U.S. Army and U.S. Marine Corps. I sensed there were a lot more insurgents of the native variety than any who had crossed the Syrian or Jordanian borders, plotting under Al Qaeda guidance to kill us in Fallujah. A homegrown insurgency, in other words, comprised mainly of rebellious Sunni homeboys. Outmatched, outgunned by our United States Marine Corps. Killed by U.S. Marines in great number.

Soon enough, I got word from Robert that "more information on the bodies would be helpful"—his diplomatic way of encouraging me to spend some time with the Mortuary Affairs unit. I told Robert I would do some firsthand reporting, not because I wanted to, but because I knew I should. He and Negroponte would only be getting more questions from top Iraqi leaders on the matter. Plus, Robert was an ideal boss, demanding with high expectations but fair. I owed him for giving me a long leash in Fallujah, perhaps the longest one in the entire State Department at the time. We trusted each other, and I definitely trusted his judgment.

Paul Wolfowitz, I thought, should take on this hellish assignment. The deputy defense secretary's demeanor was mortician-like in my view, and, Lord knows, he was responsible for many deaths.

I recalled how in April 2004 during Capitol Hill testimony, a member of Congress asked Wolfowitz about the U.S. troop casualty count.

"It's approximately 500, of which—I can get the exact numbers—approximately 350 are combat deaths."

The true figure? At the time, deaths totaled 722, with 521 from combat—the Pentagon's number two official off by more than 200 American lives.

A spokesman later added: "He misspoke. That's all."

That's all?

No one asked him about Iraqi lives. And I knew that Wolfowitz, like so many of the war's cheerleaders, would remain far away from a place like Anbar. Despite getting America into—but not yet out of—the wrong war they so much wanted.

On several occasions at Camp Fallujah, I sought out the Mortuary Affairs team in the chow halls, sitting next to the crew, even if most

Marines avoided MA at all costs. A friend warned I would be "jinxed" if I spent time with them, however short. Figuring we were all jinxed in Fallujah from the get-go anyway, the warnings did not persuade me to stay away.

Once in the main dining facility, I brought my tray over and sat down next to them.

"Sir, you sure? You know we bring bad juju."

"Well, I'm here because I'll be spending some time with you at the Potato Factory, not because I plan to trade jobs with you anytime soon."

"Yeah, I don't think anyone wants our job."

I went on to explain, "There are some questions from bigwigs in Baghdad about how we are handling the bodies in the city."

"Well, there's plenty of those still, but the cold weather is helping preserve them, helps with the smell a bit too."

As I reached for another bottle of water, I said I would be seeing them before long.

One of the Mortuary Affairs crew volunteered to educate me a bit before my arrival. He told me two things I did not know before the war and two things I will now never forget: it usually takes about three weeks for fingernails to fall off after death, and faces will be left unrecognizable by week four.

Looking up at a seven-ton truck, he said, "That'll be your transport from the Potato Factory to the city and back again. No Humvees. You'll be sharing space with dead insurgents.

"Okay with that?" he asked.

"I suppose so," I replied.

These massive vehicles were painted green on the outside, some with their floor beds now stained by crimson and even darker, curdled colors.

"Are you sure you want to go over there?" he asked again, implying it seemed that I might want to reconsider.

"No, but I've got two bosses asking me to."

"Okay. We'll get you there."

"A guaranteed return trip too? That'd sure be nice," I said before going to pack a few things. As creepy as it was going to be, right out of a Stephen King book I imagined, I would be spending a couple days there. At least one night, I knew, maybe two if I could handle the place.

The smell hit me first, even though I sat dozens of meters from entering the facility. The stench permeated the air, sinking into my clothing before I opened the Humvee door to get out. No wall can be made high enough to keep out certain odors—especially the odor of death.

Many of the toughest Marines, those who could bench-press 300 pounds, also avoided the facility. General Sattler himself did too. I could see why and sniff why as our vehicle pulled up outside the front gate. About twenty meters from the road, the building had a warehouse look, but was now guarded. A few trees bordered it, but they too looked overwhelmed with the stench, branches drooping, coated in omnipresent dust. Perhaps the plant kingdom responded to a place of death as much as the animal kingdom did. Life-giving oxygen itself seemed to be in shorter supply around the Potato Factory, as if the Grim Reaper had already secured a forever lease on the structure in order to personally oversee the black business under way within.

"Welcome, sir," said a junior Marine. "We have been expecting you. I hear you'll be with us for a while. Let me walk you over and introduce you to everyone."

The first MA member I saw was turned away from me. The dark-haired sergeant had inscribed on the back of his green hospital surgeonlike gown a few choice job description lines in black marker. They got my attention quickly—and not in an inviting way:

"I see smell and lick dead people"
"People are dying to see me" (with a tombstone and "RIP" drawn underneath)
"I need help"
And the kicker: "I love my job"

I noticed his white rubber gloves had turned reddish brown.

The rest of the Mortuary Affairs team acted friendly and welcoming enough, but a few seemed perhaps too comfortable with laughs about the morbid business they were in. A default coping mechanism, most likely, and who could blame them—theirs was a job no one else wanted.

"Here, sir, see the difference between being on ice and not? Ha, ha," he said a little too casually. I suppose he viewed me as a "civilian at war" guinea pig, one of those "State Department guys" who quaked when thinking about leaving the wire and did not know the difference between a U.S. Marine and a U.S. soldier, or between a noncommissioned officer (NCO) and a boot lieutenant (LT) commissioned after Officer Candidate School (OCS) at Quantico. Though tempted, I did not tell him my dad had been a sergeant in Vietnam in 1969 and had seen plenty of bodies and human wreckage. And that war, unfortunately, ran in the Weston family across generations.

A second Marine was hunched close to a set of remains, a blackened lump of indistinguishable biological body matter, scissors in hand and wearing a surgical mask. Another Marine leaned over both, observing (maybe the MA supervisor?) while smoking a cigar. The strong smell of a cigar far preferable, I thought, to the far stronger smell of death.

I focused my eyes in their direction and saw that the only body not decayed was that of a person U.S. military HQ had flown stateside to Dover, at FedEx speed, and back in a few days. He had been killed in a mosque during the battle. The incident received worldwide media attention after an NBC reporter, Kevin Sites, filmed a Marine shooting an Iraqi. Stateside specialists had attempted to determine more about this dead man, hence the VIP treatment, despite being DOA. Had he been a legitimate target? Or not? Gray degrees of rights and wrongs, open to different interpretations, none of which was settled as "facts" in the end, as was so often (too often) the case in both *Rashomon*-like wars.

War was like a kaleidoscope of truths and lies, I was fast learning, who or which side saw or did what, and why.

As I walked even farther into the building, I had second thoughts. The lime green corrugated walls looked sickly above the floor space dotted with tables held in place by sandbags, all surrounded by piles of black body bags. Some had full bodies. Others had only partial remains. I saw more than a few Purell bottles around.

The smell was even more brutal inside. General Sattler was right to stay far away. I asked the nearest Marine: "Where's the Mentholatum or something very strong? Quick, I need some to stuff up my nostrils, whatever it is you guys use here."

"You don't want to do that."

"Yes, I do. And fast."

"No, sir, you don't. Trust me."

"Why not? This smell is going to kill me."

"We all thought that at first, but let me tell you a story. I have tissue here you can jam up your nose."

"Tissue, really?"

"Here's the deal. We had a Marine who used to handle the bodies. He was big on cherry ChapStick. So he put that up his nose to cover the smell. Well, he was in Kuwait on his way home, and guess what he happened to smell as he was walking along, minding his own business, happy to be out of Iraq. Yup, cherry ChapStick. He had a major flashback tied to this place, the death smell. He totally freaked out."

"You still want that Mentholatum?"

I accepted the tissue he handed me and stuffed more than I thought possible up each nostril. It mostly worked. The crew then began to educate me on the processing. The "I lick dead people" sergeant handed me the standard form they had been required to fill out for each set of remains. It read at the top: "Record of Identification Processing Anatomical Chart." The document had the outlines of a male body, front and back. On this one, I noticed the entire lower half had been shaded completely black.

"What's does that mean?" I asked, even though I already had guessed what it meant.

"Well, that guy had mashed-up legs when he was brought in. Maybe got run over by a tank or had them crushed when a building fell on him."

In the clothing items section, someone had written, "1 sock, black" and "1 jacket, cargo, green." Further details listed were more graphic:

Severely decomposed upper torso
Traumatic amputation left leg
Traumatic amputation right leg (Note: still in bag)
Traumatic amputation left hand
Equipment on remains showed left hip replacement

(An old man maybe? . . . A grandfather perhaps? I thought to myself while reading the form.)

Age, height, name all listed as "und" and "unidentified."

"Thanks," I said. "Interesting case. How can you tell if he was an insurgent?"

"It's hard, unless we find things in their pockets or clothes. We really could only assess half of this guy's story because half of him is pretty much gone."

Over the next two days, I joined the MA Marines as they went out into Fallujah to retrieve and transport bodies. Mornings had cooled enough by then so their work was a bit easier. This was one advantage of doing it in November and December and not in the middle of summer, when temperatures top 110-plus degrees for days on end. I sat next to two Marines. Both were young, a male and a female. He was at least six-foot-four and she no more than five-foot-two. They had been on duty at the factory for a couple of weeks and seemed to be holding up well, or at least doing a good job of faking like they were, the more likely reality.

The first compound we visited was in an abandoned neighborhood. Even the surviving dogs and cats and birds stayed away. The front gate had been blown up. Our infantry units marked houses with Xs on their maps, flagging the structures with bodies found in them, now ready for pickup. But depending on whether you were Iraqi or American meant a different interpretation. Marines claimed they were using harmless Xs. Fallujans claimed Christian crosses had been spray-painted on their homes. (Before long, we would hear complaints of some Marines trying to convert Fallujans to Christianity at city checkpoints. These were isolated cases but did not go over well with city leaders or Marine leaders—or with me.)

As I entered the main hallway, I saw that Marines had grappling hooks in their hands. It reminded me of REI or Black Diamond climbing gear. Since insurgents booby-trapped bodies, often with hidden grenades, the remains first had to be dislodged as a precaution and from a distance. If they did not explode, black body bags were brought out from the trucks and the bodies put inside.

I almost turned around before entering any farther—into what I knew would be a house of horror. I noticed the rugs had been rolled up. On the walls were a few posters with mosques on them and some small tapestries. Half a dozen Marines had begun to attach the hooks and straps to bodies in a bedroom about a dozen feet in front of me. I stepped back. One leaned in, tugging hard, his left knee recoiled and rifle still slung over his back. Only one of them wore a surgical mask, and I suddenly wished I had one too—or half a dozen, which I would have put on all at once.

He tugged, and the body slid a few feet. He tugged again, and this time it rolled a few times. Several Marine arms reached out, robotic almost, and placed the remains into a bag, and then began work on the next body. And the next . . .

I noticed a staff sergeant outside, just beyond the door, refusing to go inside the house. He looked about my age, thirtysomething and entering his fourth decade of life, though Iraqi years should count times seven each—at least. Wondering if there was a problem, I asked why.

"I don't want to see my Marines doing this."

I felt bad that he had to make that statement. I wish he had just glared at me, when no explanation was needed. He knew his own limits, what his own psyche could handle, and would not cross that line, though his Marines did not have the same option. Sanity amid insanity—it made sense to me. Maybe I should have followed his lead and stayed outside. I wish I had.

With the grappling hook test passed—no hidden bombs on the bodies—we stepped even deeper into this house of death. Once inside what looked to be the kitchen area, my boots began to slide on the floor. Below me were maggots. Hundreds. Smeared under each foot. In the bedroom a few meters away, Marines were still pulling out half-decomposed bodies. Bloated. Soft. Purple. One lay under a bed. It was impossible to tell if this was an insurgent or civilian. This is something I often think about. Was he hiding out of fear and had no weapon? Or was he holding an AK, or a pistol, and in the process of shooting a Marine from below? Our Rules of Engagement prioritized American lives—and never again would be as unrestricted as they were during the battles of Fallujah.

On the bedroom wall was a small mirror. I saw my own reflection in it briefly, and the blurred motion of Marines doing their work behind me.

I wondered who the owners of this home were. Maybe I had already met them. Or what was left of them and now inserted into the black bags at my feet.

The next house, in Fallujah's southernmost quadrant, had a body near a stairwell without railings in a half-built dilapidated structure. Gray cinder block walls. Weapons, stacked AKs, were close. This dead man's skin was dried out, looking like brown leather on a sunken, worn-out couch.

The day was done. Several sets of remains had been recovered. We piled into the back of the seven-ton for a silent ride back to the Potato Factory before sundown and passed several mosques. Their minarets were silent, no muezzins to call for prayer time. They had fled.

As the convoy lurched forward, one of the Marines said, "Just heard we have more to pick up tomorrow."

The embassy got its first preliminary report from me via classified email, but I had one final trip to make. I needed to find out what happened to the bodies after they had been processed in the Potato Factory. Last rites for "the enemy," you could say. Their burial, after Marines recorded what they had found on them, in their clothes, called "pocket litter." Some, they said, had Syrian features. Others looked Saudi.

To the credit of Colonel Mike Regner, when asked during the briefing for Pentagon-based press, he conveyed the numbers that some politicians in Washington did not want to hear: "The next question, before I continue on to the tactical laydown because I brought up detainees, is yes, there are some foreign fighters in that element. Predominantly, however, most of the 1,052 are in fact Iraqis. But there are individuals that are from different countries, and I don't really have that right in front of me at this time . . . but out of 1,052 most likely about 1,040—or 1,030—are Iraqis."

So the foreign fighter body count based on firsthand Marine reports, the best anyone had? Twelve or a max of twenty, according to Regner, out of over a thousand counted and processed up to that point.

At the end of the following day, our Humvee stopped north of the city, near an abandoned railroad station that had been out of use for decades. I had hitched a ride with a Marine officer from one of the battalions. This was our destination, located maybe half a mile from the Potato Factory. The sun was setting, casting an orange glow across trenches. A Marine backhoe had graded perpendicular lines, several feet deep. The grid had a mathematical quality to it, the product of engineers laying out an impromptu cemetery for hundreds of dead.

I watched as black body bags were lowered into the ground. I did not consider verifying that they were all turned toward Mecca—even if I had the Muslim holy site's GPS coordinates. It would have been impossible, and I did not want any of the soft and lumpy bags opened. Neither did the Marines. The operation had a brutal and methodical efficiency to it. It was essentially a mass grave.

Marines were in a hurry, in a race with the sinking sun. They worked in teams of three. One held the front of the stretcher with remains on top, two at the back. A row of large, green dust-covered seven-ton trucks lined up behind them.

Once the body bags were lowered, another Marine signaled the backhoe operator to drop the soil. With a loud mechanical grind, piles of earth and sand fell, creating big swirls of dust in the air. Big enough, I imagined, they could be seen by Fallujans inside the city. Our shadows grew long as the sun set and temperatures dropped. Metal poles about five feet high, sticking up from the ground like a giant iron rectangular pincushion, became the only gravesite markers. Two Marines, shoulder-high in the ground, finished their work situating the day's final remains in each trench. They jumped up and said nothing.

One of the last bags I saw had a single white piece of tape across it that read "Joleen Dist" (signifying "Jolan/Joleen District" inside Fallujah) before it too was lowered into a trench, one of the anonymous, nameless, faceless, story-less dozens.

The sun had disappeared, so we made our way back to the Potato Factory. The gravesite was not a place anyone wanted to spend the night, no matter how well armed or armored. I opted not to have any dinner. Around midnight, I noticed the lights had been left on inside several of the large rooms, but no Marines were near. An unattended laptop blinked, strobelike, atop a card table. I peered through a heavy metal door into a reefer on one side of the hallway. It was filled with bags of potatoes and a conveyor belt. On the other side, through a door numbered 10 in bright red paint, was a room filled with bodies in body bags. Both sides of the hallway creeped me out, and I was glad to leave and find a live human being sitting in another part of the Potato Factory. We sat close but did not talk.

The MA crew still had a lot of work to do. The next morning they posed for a group photo, most with blank expressions. Two held a cardboard sign:

CAMP IDAHO
Fallujah, Iraq
You kill 'em, We chill 'em
MORTUARY AFFAIRS

In the center someone had drawn a Mr. Potato Head wearing a helmet, with a shovel in his right hand and a bucket in his left.

Soon things would get a lot more complicated because the questions about the bodies began coming from Iraqis themselves. The bodies. What was being done with the bodies? There were rumors on the streets. The dead discarded. The dead carried away by dogs. Hundreds missing.

All these things were true. All of it was hard. Dogs had tried to dig up the bodies. The first packs I saw were as large as a dozen, strength in numbers, but more often in groups of three or four. I am not sure when the order was given to shoot, but it was, and as the grunts became more comfortable with their orders, the city got quieter, a lot less barking. Some of the Marines said they were dog owners back home, as I had been. They hated the extermination job, as I would have.

Killing dogs was at least in line with Muslim tradition. No desecration of bodies by beasts of prey—it was what humans had managed to do to each other by then that proved to be the most disturbing.

Where were the bodies? Fallujah's leaders also wanted to know.

They made their case: "The people plan to go north of the city and find their dead family members. Can you make sure the Marines allow them to do that?

"In our religion, we believe their bodies will be pure. They can be buried again in the Muslim way. This is our home, our city. Our right."

Their right, I thought. Would I allow a mass disinterment to commence just outside city limits? Fallujans basically planned to bring shovels with them to dig up bodies and try to find family members among the hundreds of corpses. Those odds were not good. Neither were the visuals.

The last thing we needed in Fallujah was an impromptu excavation of the battle's unofficial graveyard, scraped into the dry yellow soil by a Marine backhoe.

We had to have a counter-plan, and fast.

Only one man could settle the matter, and I decided to ask him for help—even when I knew he had many reasons to walk away: Sheikh Hamza Abbas al-Isaawi, Fallujah's grand mufti. White-robed, gray-bearded, soft-spoken, he carried himself as I imagined a biblical wise man would. Like a pope in Rome, his words moved the masses. Like a pope in Rome, he was deemed untouchable—by us and by Al Qaeda in Iraq, the affiliated offshoot of the Osama bin Laden organization. Short in stature, with a white-gray beard, he had the largest following in the city. The senior religious leader possessed a quiet charisma and that most rare of qualities found in a combat zone: moral authority. Unlike us, he did not negotiate or caveat away his core beliefs. He safeguarded them. *Hamza the Pure*, I thought, pure being the word that matched him most, even in a city full of impurities, destruction, and danger-ous political liaisons among insurgents and between our collaborating partners and us.

When the mufti walked into the CMOC, I asked for the favor right away.

"Sheikh Hamza, can you prevent the people from pursuing the matter of the bodies with us? I know this will be hard for even you, but if they start to move north with shovels, only bad things will follow."

He paused for a long time, as powerful leaders can and not have anyone interrupt their thoughts.

"I should consult the other imams first."

"We don't have time for that. Ordinarily, I'd agree. But the Marines have already moved many of the buried just north of the city, near the railway tracks. They are doing their best," I explained.

"Many families are asking me about the missing. What should I tell them?"

"Please tell them we are treating the remains with respect, and we will keep records that will be handed over to the government. Right now, that is the best we can do."

"Our religion has specific rules about the bodies of the dead," Hamza went on.

"I know them, or at least most of them. We are not letting dogs get close."

And with that remark, I realized I had misspoke. The last image the grand mufti of Fallujah needed to enter his mind was a pack of dogs roaming the streets of his city, hungry and with few options.

"I will tell the people to stay away. I trust you."

"Shukran. We will not disappoint you. We will keep our promise."

After my meeting with Hamza, I submitted my final report to the embassy the next day in the form of a cable. They opted not to send it, to "kill it" in State Department–speak. Some in Baghdad considered it "too gory" for Washington readers. War is very much that, but I did not press the matter. It took me a week to be able to refocus on other issues after my time at the Potato Factory. I cut my food intake in half if not more, and all I wanted to do was drink a lot of water. I found myself washing my hands more than usual, scouring them with soap, and running a lot longer on my usual route around base. And I had only spent a few days there, not weeks. Like those corporals had, along with so many other Marines.

General Sattler asked how my visit had gone.

"You survive the place?"

"Well, let's just say I won't be going back anytime soon. And the smell of that place won't be leaving me anytime soon."

Some aspects of the Iraq War could never be washed off, or washed away, or forgotten, no matter how hard one tried or wished.

Remarkably, with Hamza's direct intervention, we did not hear about the bodies from most residents. Some Marine Civil Affairs units were questioned, but the mufti had done what he said he would do. Given the quiet, I was sure he had asked, in effect ordered, the rest of the imams also to cooperate. His *wasta* or influence was such that they did not use the mass grave to inflame residents. The ambassador and Robert Ford in Baghdad also received calls from senior Sunni politicians that the situation had "improved" in Fallujah.

I knew the deeper truth. Truths buried a few feet underground. Relations between returning residents and us had improved a little, but not a lot, or nearly enough. I had seen dogs that had made their way north, following the scent of death, even if the people had not yet. Some of Fallujah's families inevitably would see the same thing—a trail of canines leading to the dead.

Sheikh Hamza requested a follow-up meeting to finalize our under-standing about what message he would convey to Fallujans regarding our handling of the bodies. I told him about my time at the Potato Factory, as well as near the trenches. He thanked me for the additional information and said he would honor our request. Within days, he made it official: formally discouraging Fallujans from digging in the American-made cemetery for Iraqi dead. Coming from the top reli-gious leader in the city, his was an order. Everyone complied and did not pursue the issue any longer. He and I agreed that while Fallujah's difficult past must be acknowledged, our focus had to be on its present and future.

After meeting this brief second time in the center of the city, behind barricades to protect Americans only, the mufti started to prepare to return to his mosque. He preferred to walk there, among his people, unarmed and unprotected.

Above him, I could see on one side a large hole in a minaret, on the other, a ripped metal gouge in the city's main water tank.

The new Fallujah framed.

I again promised Sheikh Hamza we would transfer the Marine archive of dead bodies collected at the Potato Factory, all our records, to the Iraqi government. This way, families would have some infor-mation. Perhaps even a bit of consolation. He nodded, grateful and relieved, it seemed.

The grand mufti had done his part, and he trusted me to do mine.

As Hamza walked slowly away, appearing as if he had a cane in his right hand but did not, I began to hear a few muezzins begin their cho-rus. Calls to prayer echoed in the city. I knew the mufti himself would soon be leading prayers in his mosque. What he prayed about most certainly would include us, the Americans. Each week, I was gaining a fuller measure of this man. If he had wanted to whisper more rebellion he could have, turning city blocks against every Marine on patrol. He did not. He worked with us.

He collaborated.

Sheikh Hamza soon disappeared behind a HESCO barrier as Marines on post radioed each other to "watch that guy," followed by the standard Marine-speak between messages of "send it." I began to realize our arrangement, however, would not hold. Could not hold. The Potato Factory archive had too many hard and politically explosive questions associated with what had gone on there . . . just how many of the dead were verified as insurgents versus "unknown/unidentified." That category would mean "civilians" to Iraqi officials in Baghdad— and to worldwide media and to some Americans paying attention back home. How many other "terrorists" had hip replacement surgery? Not so indicative of the young foreign fighter type.

We did not keep our promise to the grand mufti of Fallujah as far as I know, and I was his main American contact. I believe the records of the city's dead, whether insurgent or local, never made it into the hands of Fallujah leaders. The bodies held too many secrets to share.

And so did we, the Americans.

Death has a tendency to encourage a depressing view of war.

DONALD RUMSFELD

Clear, Hold, Build

Shortly before I would witness the horror-show conditions at the Potato Factory, Secretary of Defense Donald Rumsfeld received a document in Washington, D.C., stamped 12 Nov 04 10:15 AM and titled: "Fact Sheet: Defining Victory in Fallujah."

It listed as "accomplished" (a popular word those days) various high-priority U.S. policy objectives—even as Fallujah was crumbling under the weight and velocity and ferocity of American artillery and ammo, amid war cries on both sides and intermittent rain. This already checked checklist included:

- deny Fallujah as a sanctuary for terrorist elements;
- disrupt and damage terrorist organizations;
- kill or capture large number of terrorists;
- build confidence of Iraqi security forces ("they have distinguished themselves");
- demonstrate determination of Iraqi Interim Government;

- liberate people of Fallujah from terrorist control and intimidation;
- enable people of Fallujah to participate in January elections;
- enable people of Fallujah to participate in Iraq's reconstruction ("reconstruction projects ready to go; follow-up is key")

That was the plan, anyway. How Fallujah had been summarized via simplified bullet points—all by *day five* of the street-to-street battle—to a top member of the American war cabinet. A very, very optimistic assessment offered by those deployed in U.S. government interagency conference rooms.

Meanwhile, on the ground, our list of accomplishments looked a lot different than everything being trumpeted in our country's capital. It would stay that way for a long time. And follow-up certainly was key. We were the ones doing it.

Much to their credit, while the fighting was still under way and bodies were being cleared, Marines had also established a Civil Military Operations Center (CMOC) just off Route Fran in the middle of the city. I relocated there as well. I felt that in order to better understand the people of Fallujah, I should live as close to their world as possible. Ours was not a fancy place or comfy living space.

A dingy, dusty compound, the CMOC had served as the central sports facility in town during Saddam's era. Now it would be the place where everyday Fallujans, our Iraqi collaborators, and the U.S. military would commingle. Fallujans needed things from us. We needed things from them. It would be the meeting place of two worlds, one housing Civil Affairs officers charged with reconstruction and a contingent of Marines assigned security duties. And there was me too, a State Department regiment, battalion, company, platoon, and squad of . . . one. Marines had reengineered the structure into a Marine combat outpost (that did nation building and city building on the side), sandbagged and razor-wired around the perimeter, with high HESCO barriers snaking north, south, east, and west. The remnants of a boxing ring formed our central "courtyard." It had seen better big-bout days, but did make for a good big-drag smoke pit.

We slept on standard-issue green cots, half a dozen or more to a room. Shelves stocked with canned food, lots of mac-and-cheese packets, Top Ramen noodles, Mister Salty pretzels, and protein powder. Windowpanes had been blown out during the battle, some now covered in plywood and plastic. The three shower stalls rarely had hot water—great when summer temps reached furnace levels, not so great when they dropped to around freezing in winter. Our lunches consisted of MREs, with the occasional "tray rat" (tray rations) borrowed from rifle company cooks who lived on the other side of our downtown compound, also shared by the local police.

Our new Fallujah home, which included about two dozen Marines and me, had a radius of no more than 100 or so meters. Anywhere beyond that required everyone to wear body armor and a Kevlar helmet, and to keep a quick pace as snipers began to move back into town. During the day, we heard Muslim calls to prayer (*adhan*): "Allahu akbar," Allah is the greatest, with the morning Islamic refrain translating as "Prayer is better than sleep." Across the nights, we heard war: mortars, bullets, RPGs. Thuds. Whizzes. Blasts. Needless to say, few Americans or few Fallujans, faithful and otherwise, got much sleep.

A big sign hung outside, red letters on yellow background, which announced to all: "Fallujah Help Center." On our CMOC walls listed under "logistics" we had reminders of what it required to rebuild and attempt to "hold" a city like Fallujah. This would not be about guns, tanks, and battlefield adrenaline, but about un-Marine-like patience, as well as a whole array of nonmilitary items: 200 Turkish Port-a-Johns, 20,000 mats, 10,000 heaters, 5,000 stoves, 10,000 gas lanterns, 10 to 12 trucks of canned food, 5 trucks of medical supplies, 20,000 blankets, and a lot more.

We would also receive regular calls from Marines or returning Fallujans, who were finding bodies in homes, in front or back yards, or in their gardens. Their reports almost staccato and soon predictable: *Another body. Jolan Park. Two more. Industrial section. Fox Company. Get MA there. Blue mosque. More remains. House marked. Near Route Henry. QRF standing by.* And so on. We did not put these stats on our dry erase board, but Mortuary Affairs stayed busy, still commuting to and from the Potato Factory.

While Rumsfeld was being briefed inside the Beltway that everything not yet accomplished had been accomplished, Fallujans, thankfully, were starting to show up to help get stuff done.

Fawzi Mohammad, a city engineer and deputy head of the local reconstruction committee, represented this hands-on partnering. Despite losing much in the battle, we sought out collaborators like him to stand with us in rebuilding their destroyed hometown. Iraqi security forces would increasingly be expected to "hold" the contested terrain, as Marines moved into a less visible role. Collaborators with diverse backgrounds were going to be key in achieving anything, and in many instances they knew this. We had money to spend, and they needed money. Quid. Pro. Quo. Then repeat.

Fawzi had the routine down. He would lift each hand a parallel six inches or so above a folding table while leaning back in his plastic chair, black loafers scraping the dirty gym floor that doubled as our main meeting room.

"This, how much," he would say, estimating the height of $50,000, separated in two stacks.

"In 50s and 20s only?" I would guess.

Rather quickly we turned into the city's primary banker. Cash diplomacy you could say, or as a follow-on manual issued by the U.S. Army's Finance Corps would make explicit within the ranks: "Money and contracting in a COIN [counterinsurgency] environment are vital elements of combat power." Junior Marines would arrive early, usually on the morning convoy from Camp Fallujah, and stand next to Marine Civil Affairs officers and me to distribute U.S. Mint–fresh dollars. Fawzi got to know these Marines better than just about anyone.

I acted as one of his biggest advocates. We needed locals like him to help, even if that proved expensive, as our disbursers with their bulging backpacks of cash counted out the funds.

"Okay, first the 50s, fifty, one hundred, one-fifty, two, two-fifty . . .

"And the 100s, one hundred, 2, 3, 4, 5 . . .

"Sign this, and we'll see you next week."

In all of Fallujah, Fawzi stood out as the cleverest businessman. His role as a city Rotarian of sorts meant he had a say in many rebuilding projects: the new sewer line, the promised Iraqi government fund to rebuild houses, repair of power lines, even some city beautification plans. Fallujans liked green space too, and their kids hoped for a playground or two, ones that were safe enough for them to play in.

A doer, he was not above bargaining with us over these piles of cash for projects. Fawzi kept his business empire local—not tempted by the bigger markets of Baghdad—and employed Fallujans. That mattered. Neighbors remembered. He had not maneuvered himself into a central ministry job, for instance, like ambitious others had, but rather stayed close to his Anbar roots, a Sunni homebody and proud of it.

In his forties, Fawzi had a magnetism measured in wry smiles and easy laughs. He never appeared to be in a rush, whereas we always tended to give that impression, even if we were not in a hurry. Counterinsurgency could not be fast-forwarded, though we tried every way possible. When not counting U.S. currency, he used his hands to emphasize in broken English where Americans were going wrong, placing both palms on my shoulders. Some things could not afford to be lost in translation. His grip put into bold his words, including his memorable warnings.

"America watch set too fast, voting can't be rushed in Iraq."

"Sunnis still very angry about your invasion."

"Many here do not believe Marines will leave."

"Iran has hidden hands in Baghdad."

In such comments, I realized he was as much a local politician as anything else. That made him even more valuable as we tried to navigate Fallujah's complex political terrain. Fawzi had never run afoul of Saddam's henchmen; he was too smart for that. But for such a tough operator, Fawzi resembled a teddy bear. With groomed hair and clipped dark beard, his paunch signified a tradition of long lunches with platters full of rice with raisins, saffron, bread, and kebabs, even during Iraq's sanctions era. He often smelled of this plentiful buffet.

Already plugged in as a former Baathist, Fawzi managed the sprawling cement plant just outside the city during Saddam's rule and situated not far from the Potato Factory. At one point it employed hundreds. He continued in the job after Saddam went into hiding. His employee payroll dropped to the single digits about the time the Americans in the Coalition Provisional Authority, my onetime colleagues, showed up preaching free market economics and heralding privatization plans—while also firing the whole Iraqi Army.

High walls throughout Fallujah made for uneasy, untrusting neighbors, and the beginning of drone surveillance only made things worse. They were foreign and unidentified (among Iraqis at least) flying objects, unseen to this extent in war before. Fallujans said they sometimes could hear something high above them, hovering atop mosque minarets, but did not know what it was. Iraqi women, even with covered faces and bodies, feared hanging clothes outside. They felt like they were always being watched. Growing anti-American paranoia had a real basis and the mounting points of friction not imagined. Fawzi warned us these tactics would result in more resistance.

In one meeting he reemphasized this point, while reclining in another flimsy plastic chair that somehow managed to support his weight.

"You see, it is all about the women, mothers, our daughters in Fallujah.

"They fear what they cannot see, but think you can see them. In homes, through windows, inside compounds. When they send their children to school."

"Fawzi," I replied, "we do have some valid concerns about who might try to come back into the city. I mean, Al Qaeda did find support here. Zarqawi himself used to live here," referring to Abu Musab al-Zarqawi, the Jordanian-born leader of Al Qaeda in Iraq.

"Mr. Kael, let me explain. The only way Fallujah becomes safer is when we see and tell Marines who does not belong here. You can spend millions on drones and send in more Marines, but they are blind to what Iraqis have here," as he pointed to his head.

"Terrorisms begins in heads, not in streets."

He was right. But we did not listen.

We remained in more of an armored cocoon than we wanted to admit, particularly all the troops not based at the CMOC downtown or in combat outposts. They were Fobbits before they knew what the word meant. In other words, they were service members who rarely, if ever, left increasingly cushy military bases, aka FOBs or large Forward-ing Operating Bases. Grunts and Fobbits, needless to say, tended not to get along. The former were at war. The latter were not so much, even in Iraq. Grunts saw buddies killed next to them. Fobbits read reports about the KIA in office cubicles, air-conditioned in summer and heated in winter. More than a few had enough downtime during their deploy-ments to draft a debut novel, compose a short story or two, perhaps craft stanzas of poetic verse, or apply to MFA programs. And many read, a lot.

In contrast, some of the Marine and Army infantry guys I knew in both war zones kept personal journals filled with unadorned and unstudied and uncrafted prose written for their own eyes only. These were the eyewitness-to-war accounts. Words recorded during the war that perhaps came from a different place, a more pained place.

Both species within the U.S. military, grunt and Fobbit, got combat pay.

Just down the road from Fawzi's cement plant, for example, Marines had moved into the Baath Party resort compound nicknamed "Dreamland." They renamed it "Camp Baharia," a word that meant "oasis" in Arabic. There, corporals and captains occupied lakeside villas and jogged along palm-tree-lined paths and bridges. It served as a satellite base not far from Camp Fallujah and became the rotation location for incoming and outgoing Marine battalions.

Indians and Bangladeshis were hired to sweep the roads with extra-large brooms—despite all of us living in one of the most sandstorm-prone parts of Iraq. Some of these workers, whom we imported to scoop, cook, scrub, and wash our laundry, took their own lives, hanging themselves in their cramped bunk-filled trailers. I wondered if we made sure their bodies made it back to their native lands. Perhaps another clause in another cost-plus contract. There were no memorials for the help. We never knew them well enough for that.

Ugandans guarded our bases. Some hummed soothing African tunes while checking identification badges and echoing "Jambo" (Swahili for hello).

Dreamland, despite the lake, villas, and palm trees, always felt cursed to me. The CMOC setting did not make me feel like I was part of an American military empire, but this place, Camp Baharia, sure did. And the vast bases in Baghdad, populated by thousands of stationary U.S. troops, and in the rest of the country even more so. They became truly gilded and grossly extravagant.

Across these new massive encampments, Kellogg Brown & Root (KBR), the Texas-based corporate behemoth (with ties to Vice President Cheney), had money to spend, piles of it. Supplemental funding bills in Washington meant automatic approval outside normal Congressional budgeting procedures. We never asked how much anything cost. More expensive dining facilities replaced tents for chow halls, as troop levels escalated along with supply lines and meal options. In the last years of the war, lobster and steak became Sunday night staples, with five-gallon cartons of Baskin-Robbins ice cream. Vanilla. Strawberry. Chocolate.

Larry Nicholson refused to eat the ice cream.

This piqued my interest. Particularly because I never said no to any flavor of ice cream as a matter of war zone policy. My logic being "tomorrow we could die" and that was not an overstatement, so "tonight we should partake of ice cream" . . . at least when we could get it. Not often in Anbar. Never in downtown Fallujah.

The colonel disagreed.

"It's excessive and unnecessary. Most Marines and sailors are living in hardscrabble and spartan conditions in remote outposts. Having ice cream available in the big chow halls is over the top and ridiculous," he said.

I dropped the subject.

This "war is a racket" largesse that went well beyond ice cream also reminded me how Larry and I used to joke that our linguists, both very good ones, each made in pay more than double what we did with our Pentagon and State Department salaries. It also meant the corporations providing language support to U.S. military forces charged double or triple linguists' net salaries to corresponding Pentagon accounts. In other words, amounts much higher than the take-home pay of the commander in chief.

By this time, Larry and I had grown close. After his return to Iraq from Walter Reed, we met regularly in Ramadi and Fallujah. He liked to talk about State Department anthropology as much as I liked to talk about Marine Corps anthropology. In prior tours and well before the wars, he had been an officer based in Brussels at NATO, as well as in Italy. We both had a Euro-side. Larry's stemmed from his time stationed there, while I gained mine as a graduate student in the U.K. and the Netherlands, a time when each of us listened to more "Euro-trash" music than we cared to admit publicly (and before Larry switched to Katy Perry albums and I went back to a lot of Ennio Morricone). We also agreed having more allies, from Europe and beyond, in a war made a difference, which was not the prevailing view during the George W. Bush administration.

One morning, Fawzi unexpectedly invited me to see more of Fallujah, beyond the razor wire and Marine guard towers surrounding the CMOC. I feared he might be raising the topic of bodies in the city, including more questions about Marine procedures in the Potato Factory. I did not want to revisit that place, that topic, in any way.

"Close. Not dangerous," he said.

"Okay, but let's not do the full Fallujah tour. I'm still the U.S. government rep here, and the city has seen better days." Marines had warned me to stay close, as talk in town had already spread, making me a key Al Qaeda target. Who better to target than the unarmed civilian in Fallujah whose job was to talk Iraqi politics and find more collaborators?

"Promise, close."

We walked a few hundred meters to a neighborhood of large brown stucco-like homes surrounded by high walls and iron front gates. Chunks of metal lay all around. A burned-out vehicle sat in front of a mosque, much smaller than the Hadrah mosque—earlier identified by Marines as "key terrain" to be taken. Turning a corner, Fawzi motioned me to stop. In front of us, I saw only remnants of a two-story house. Others in the Askari neighborhood had been damaged from U.S. missiles, rockets, and mortars, but this one had taken several direct hits, now nearly flattened. A giant palm tree, still intact, had been blasted, horizontally, into the front yard. What once looked to be a rooftop of concrete had collapsed, tent-like, with a massive metal frame jutting out, skyward.

By the way he looked, I could tell this had been his family home. Fawzi did not need to say it. I knew it. I felt it.

We ducked through a hole, tunnel-like, into the front hall of an adjacent house and a few meters later entered into what resembled a "secret garden" courtyard. Its greens stood out from the browns, with fallen electrical lines mixing with tree branches. From a tangled bunch, leaning heavily toward the ground, he grabbed an orange and handed it to me. Then he reached for one for himself.

And so Fawzi and I sat, silent, sharing oranges, in winter, amid the rubble, amid the rubble that had been his home, that had been his garden.

In those weeks, while dogs remained a target, Marines did not shoot the cats under Fallujah's skyline of broken minarets. The felines were too nimble, too sneaky, having found better places to hide. They made new friends as well, quickly and smartly. I saw a few curled up next to welcoming grunts. Some of our toughest Marines (just ask them) became the first to adopt war zone pets, kittens and some puppies, though dogs were harder to keep close, especially given their orders. Still, they defended the need for their new friends as essential morale-building mascots.

What was left unsaid but clear to most of us: these adopted pets were a reminder of home and of one's humanity in one of Iraq's most inhumane environments.

The senior officers sometimes looked away, permissively, sometimes not. Unlike many Marine leaders, I was rooting for the hidden dogs to stay hidden—as mascots and as Marine animal therapists all in one.

A first sergeant and Louisiana-Georgia native assigned to fight in the eastern quadrant of Fallujah described the setting best, after explaining to me his infantry company suffered thirteen KIA and forty-eight wounded.

"The dogs were on the dead Iraqis, while the cats were licking Marines. No one can relate if they weren't there. Not a day goes by that I don't think of it."

Late November 2004, a small group of us ventured into the industrial section of town, with clearing operations still happening in various other sectors.

Most of the human bodies had already been picked up and taken to the Potato Factory for processing. But the smell of death remained, hanging heavily over the city, the stench like a cloud that would not move or dissipate. Under Fallujah's main water tower—the one with a U.S. military tank round hole through the middle of it—our Humvees sank half a foot in swampy water. A grunt said he thought the water had not only fallen from above, "like a giant taking a piss" until the tank was empty, but also had seeped up from below, from shattered sewer lines.

Feces mixed in with decomposing human remains. A concoction served up from Hades.

Our driver found a bit of higher ground and stopped. That is when I heard the growl, from behind a compound wall. A massive dog bounded out from a gap in the front gate. He was different. The dogs back then usually kept a wary distance, like the Fallujans we initially encountered. This big Anbar hound reminded me of a German shepherd on steroids. Exhibiting no fear he charged and tried to bite the back of our iron Humvee. Several times.

A Marine pointed his rifle downward; he had orders to shoot after all. I told him not to, mainly because the aggressive dog had already started to retreat, but not before trying to take another bite out of a rear wheel well. With a swish of his tail, he went back into the empty compound that once housed a family, almost certainly his owners.

The whole episode lasted only a minute, but I sensed that dog possessed a clear knowledge that his new neighbors, the Americans, were the enemy, strangers killing Arabs. His people. He would guard that compound until a bullet finally killed him. As a dog owner, I respected that. He was remaining loyal to his people. He knew an invader or two, or a few thousand, when he saw and smelled them. Saw and smelled us.

A few stops later, I peered into a rubbled building that looked like it had once been a pharmacy. On the shelves were bottles, most of which remained right side up, unbroken. It had a broken satellite dish above. And, below, a single calico cat—it stared at me as much as I stared at it. While not at all scenic, the setting seemed calm, too calm. The cat had found a good place to hide in the shattered city. We had not. We were exposed. A dilemma of our own making that would only grow as insurgents also found their own perfect places to hide all around us.

In those darkest days, Stephen King would have been the ideal war reporter assigned the Fallujah beat. Alongside, perhaps, H. P. Lovecraft, whom King himself has lauded, a long-dead writer of surreal worlds. Edgar Allan Poe too, who had enlisted as a private in the U.S. Army in 1827 and later was a West Point dropout, would have been at home in Fallujah. All three could have easily found the best horror story lines amid war's insanity without having to invent characters or scenes. The city's red streets under gray skies almost demanded macabre verse. No ravens but plenty of drones, though a later hand-launched model with an almost five-foot wingspan would, in fact, be named the RQ-11 Raven.

Inside half-destroyed compounds and next to mud-caked Humvees, I noticed some Marines writing in their journals. A new William

Styron or E. B. Sledge (both Marines) among them, I bet, or a prolific Hemingway, I hoped. But unlike the famous writer who liked Cuba, bulls, his cigars, and his daiquiris, these troops' scars were deeper, redder. Authentic ones. They were recording the war at its worst, as they were living it. I sensed their pages would not be adventure stories, replete with neat, heroic, and happy endings. "Truer" stories. Stories probably most easily, if not readily, shared among other Marine combat veterans and not at family reunions or in literary seminars.

All of which comprised "the real war" that would never get in the books. But more of the other kind, hero-less, full of foreboding ambiguities, as the mercurial Papa himself had written: "I was always embarrassed by the words sacred, glorious, and sacrifice and the expression in vain. We had heard them, sometimes standing in the rain."

I took a quick trip from the CMOC back to Camp Fallujah for some meetings about tribal outreach and engagement, which was being spearheaded by the intrepid chief of staff, Colonel John Coleman. Fawzi had assured me he would help get word out that Marines were serious about reengaging these traditional power brokers in Anbar. This was exactly why our collaborators were so important. Bremer and his political team had unwisely alienated them during the CPA era. Now we had a chance to reengage. I passed the good news on to Coleman, and told him that knowing Fawzi the sheikhs would probably be asking for projects, i.e., well-funded cost-plus projects, D.C. Beltway-style, paid in cash. But it would be worth it.

Afterward, he pulled me aside.

"We're getting a big VIP here soon. You should try to be here for it."

I guessed that a four-star general was inbound.

"Wrong," Coleman replied.

"I don't know. Another senator who wants to be commander in chief?"

"Wrong again. It's Secretary Rumsfeld."

"Got it. I'll definitely make it."

Before then, I spent days with the Marine Civil Affairs team monitoring the progress of the early "build" phase in Fallujah. The multimillion-dollar sewer line project was a popular topic among returning residents. We knew why. They were tired of their own feces running in the streets. But the biggest part of our focus remained on housing compensation. With half the city proper more or less leveled, we spent hours matching claims with estimated costs. Fawzi and his local reconstruction team colleagues employed engineers to estimate damage costs, all recorded by hand. These reports were then sent to ministry officials in Baghdad. We even were monitoring a twenty-first-century solar light project in the city. It began to stall, however, when workers received flyers with death threats.

And of course, there were the soccer fields and parks some Fallujans still wanted our help in building. One site's location? Not far from the railroad tracks. Not far from the mass grave. Not far from all those buried secrets.

The same day Secretary Rumsfeld received his Fallujah "accomplished" update memo, November 12, 2004, eleven U.S. service members were killed in Iraq—most in Fallujah:

Spc Raymond L. White (22, of Elwood, Indiana, pop. 8,514); Cpl Jarrod L. Maher (21, of Imogene, Iowa, pop. 69); Sgt Morgan W. Strader (23, of Crossville, Tennessee, pop. 11,246); LCpl David M. Branning (21, of Cockeysville, Maryland, pop. 20,776); LCpl Brian A. Medina (20, of Woodbridge, Virginia, pop. 4,055); Cpl Nathan R. Anderson (22, of Howard, Ohio, pop. 242); Cpl Brian P. Prening (24, of Sheboygan, Wisconsin, pop. 49,288); 1st Lt Edward D. Iwan (28, of Albion, Nebraska, pop. 1,611); Sgt Jonathan B. Shields (25, of Atlanta, Georgia, pop. 447,841); LCpl Nicholas H. Anderson (19, of Las Vegas, Nevada, pop. 603,488); and Sgt James C. Matteson (23, of Celeron, New York, pop. 1,091).

The same day Secretary Rumsfeld's autopen would be readied to sign, mechanically, the KIA condolence letters for the families of these eleven service members, now dead.

It is valuable for any top policy official to visit the theater of operations. One can never be reminded often enough that national security policy is ultimately about human beings.

DOUGLAS J. FEITH

Helo Down

By December 2004, twenty-one months after the initial U.S. invasion that began in March 2003, the Iraq War was not going well, to say the least.

No weapons of mass destruction found. "Dead-enders"—as official Washington at the time had referred to those Iraqis trying to kill us—turned professional insurgents. Bodies processed amid bags of potatoes and buried in trenches. Dogs shot by the dozen. Week after week. Month after month. Public opinion about Iraq at home was well on its way to new lows. Voters had begun to question the wisdom of the decision to invade. This was a contrast to the early days. When there had been a conflation about Bush administration war policy and, in the public's mind for a long while—too long, about Saddam's alleged ties to Al Qaeda and the 9/11 attacks.

In truth, there were no ties. Never had been.

I could tell Marines were feeling it. I was as well. In smoke pits and at chow halls, where the smell of sausage mixed with the smell of sweat and nicotine, the faces were long and the stress levels high. More and more of my friends in uniform said that family members back home were wondering where all this was headed. The politics of the Iraq War in D.C. was likewise heating up, within both Republican and Democratic parties, as KIA and WIA numbers reached a new high following the assault into Fallujah. Iraq's vast stretches of western desert had long since turned cold, clouds grayer than usual, full of more rainfall than normal.

So when Secretary of Defense Rumsfeld arrived with his Pentagon retinue, led by his talkative press spokesman, I could not help but notice his constant glare. He did not seem to be in a good mood. But then Fallujah never tended to lift the spirit of anyone. Those of us there would know. We lived Iraq full-time, without refuge.

The squinty-eyed Illinois native and former Princeton wrestler renowned for his quick fireman's carry takedowns stood before me in a muddy corner of Camp Fallujah under heavy and low skies. I had read that the former congressman had introduced legislation during my dad's and uncles' war in Vietnam to end the draft—a position he still maintained, arguing an all-volunteer force to be the much better option . . . And thereby probably easier to start wars, I reckoned, because there would be less pain to be shared by fewer families, a more apathetic public in a time of war. I still had my own Selective Service card printed on yellow paper, number 72-0033084-8, mailed to me by the federal government the same year the Gulf War started.

Rumsfeld's visit to Iraq happened on short notice, an implied though unacknowledged *mea culpa* of sorts. He brought a lot of reporters with him. The media had just revealed the defense chief's KIA condolence letters were autopenned. His office countered with a statement to the U.S. military paper, *Stars & Stripes*, a week earlier, on December 17, 2004, where Rumsfeld responded to critics: "I wrote and approved the now more than 1,000 letters sent to family members and next of kin of each of the servicemen and women killed in military action. While I have not individually signed each one, in the interest of ensuring expeditious contact with grieving family members, I have directed that in the future I sign each letter."

Larry Nicholson wrote his letters in longhand, signed and personalized every one, and did not need to "direct" his command staff or himself to do so and expeditiously. He would instead take careful mental notes about each Marine, based on comments from their buddies and information gathered by the regiment's sergeant major—sense of humor, type of music they liked, favorite sports team, and so on. "I always write them late at night," Larry would tell me. "Everything is quiet. I'm alone."

After returning to Anbar as commanding officer of 5th Marines, he composed them in the same office in which the rocket had exploded two years earlier almost killing him. As Larry sealed envelopes, the gouge marks from that rocket's shrapnel still scarred the ceiling above. It looked as if a giant bear claw had been raked across the plaster. I can only imagine how that setting made his words that much more heartfelt and authentic. He was writing condolence letters as a Marine who, if not for a few inches and a few seconds, would have been the subject of one autopenned to his wife, Debbie, and his sons from the "Office of the Secretary of Defense."

No shrapnel marks there, in that Pentagon office suite.

Given the autopen controversy, Rumsfeld wanted to be seen with the troops, and what better constituency and backdrop than United States Marines at war. Grunts from a base in Hawaii—part of the 1st Battalion of the 3rd Marine Regiment, nicknamed "The Lava Dogs"— gathered to meet Rumsfeld in a crowded, makeshift cafeteria on Christmas Eve. The facility and nearby infantry headquarters were decorated with gaudy plastic poinsettias, Saint Nicks cut out of green and red construction paper, and dangling candy canes. Some Marines across the base, though hardly Fobbits stationed behind desks perusing Tolstoy, even sipped bad knockoffs of eggnog and read after-action reports under the soft light (no kidding) of cinnamon-scented candles.

Rifles used to kill Sunni insurgents only days before lined the walls outside.

When Rumsfeld entered, he made his way to a reserved seat with a colorful placard that read SECRETARY OF DEFENSE.

But not before passing a wood board listing the unit's KIA, such as LCpl Richard P. Slocum (19, of Saugus, California, pop. 41,743); Sgt Kelley L. Courtney (28, of Macon, Georgia, pop. 89,981); Cpl Christopher J. Lapka (22, of Peoria, Arizona, pop. 162,592); LCpl Travis A. Fox (25, of Cowpens, South Carolina, pop. 2,217); LCpl Jeremy D. Bow (20, of Lemoore, California, pop. 24,973); Cpl Michael R. Cohen (23, of Jacobus, Pennsylvania, pop. 1,841)—and SSgt Theodore Holder III

(27, of Littleton, Colorado, pop. 44,275), LCpl Kyle W. Burns (20, of Laramie, Wyoming, pop. 31,814), and LCpl Blake A. Magaoay (20, of Pearl City, Hawaii, pop. 47,698). The last three were the names I had seen etched on a wall in the middle of Fallujah, near the fire station, during the height of the battle.

Dozens of other names were on the wall as well, most with photographs of the mostly young and now dead Marines. On either side of the secretary's designated chair sat two enlisted Marines, names and rank placard-less, needless to say—one was Corporal Wise, how appropriate, I thought. On the table in front of them stood Tabasco sauce bottles and mixed nuts and a lot of Mountain Dew. Above them hung the American flag and the Marine Corps flag with a message in big block lettering:

BATTALION LANDING TEAM 1/3, UNITED STATES MARINE CORPS, TERRORISM STOPS HERE.

Behind a podium covered in green camouflage with a Christmas wreath on it, the secretary of defense gave a short speech, laced with altogether too many "isms." He referenced the Iraq War in the same context as America's role beating back Nazism and communism (!)—both very much Missions: Accomplished—then walked outside for pictures with Marines. Once he was freed up, I approached him, partly because Colonel Coleman, the chief of staff, had dared me to, thinking I would back out. I did not. I had a long list of concerns. We were stretched thin in Anbar province. We needed more MRAPs (Mine Resistant Ambush Protected vehicles), for example, and, most important, the right political deals between Iraqi leaders in Baghdad—ones that would last.

I stepped forward.

"Who are you?" Rumsfeld grumbled.

"The State Department representative working with Marines here."

No reaction.

"Marines are stretched."

"We are at the highest level since the war began," he uttered. Indignant.

I was tempted to challenge him on the whole "preemptive" invasion concept that became U.S. policy but kept my composure. I figured he did not need me to remind him that this war was not being "won." And definitely not as fast as he had heralded—the war had, so far, gone on for one year and nine months, four times his five-month-max prediction.

"We're stretched big-time," I replied.

Again, no reaction beyond the single statement he had made. I noticed members of his staff motioning for him to pose for more photos with the assembled Marines. Case closed, at least in his mind. He walked away to be choreographed by the official photographers, standing as close as he could to as many Marines as he could.

I took a picture of Donald Rumsfeld that gray day. He is surrounded by enlisted Marines, who weeks earlier had cleared the city. Ninety-five would be killed, and more than 500 more wounded according to the final red tally. In the foreground, the battalion sergeant major towers over all, including the shrunken-looking Rumsfeld. Within the frame, I noticed something only later on, an image inadvertently captured in the lower left side—a set of crutches lying on the ground.

A wounded Marine honored, I am sure, to be standing next to the distinguished visitor. Next to a man whose challenge coin would only be outranked and outdone at a bar by the commander in chief's own, which trumped all. I wondered how many "SecDef" coins he handed out, and what he said to the Marines when he did, if he did.

I doubted very much he acknowledged to any troops how wrong he had been about how hard and how long the Iraq War was proving to be. How many of their buddies were being sent home dead and how no one was welcomed back in big parades. The kind of celebration Americans in American cities and towns alike held once one of those isms, Nazism, was defeated.

Not long after the secretary of defense's brief stop in Iraq, I visited a Marine platoon and Civil Affairs team based in Jolan Park, scene of some the most intense fighting across the prior month. It had morphed into election central.

Fallujah's families lined up for Humanitarian Assistance (HA) supplies next to the dilapidated Ferris wheel. Some asked questions about polling sites. The quadrant, which had once been home to a thriving Jewish community and academy in ancient times, resembled a blitzkrieg setting, virtually every house damaged or destroyed. A few dogs barked in the distance. A heavy, smoky smell hung in the air. We could almost taste it through our nostrils, the sort of olfactory veil so strong it is almost visible. Fires lit by returning residents to stay warm in a shattered city caused a surreal glow at morning, lasting into evening and throughout frigid nights.

And yet, the people kept coming home, leaving tracks in muddied streets as the unusually wet and persistent cold fronts continued to sweep through the city that winter. The women's black clothing matched the shared mindset.

Behind a winding zigzag of razor wire, a Marine motioned to me. I did not recognize him at first. Then he took off his helmet and I knew he was a corporal from Northern California who had been stationed near the cloverleaf and ECP-1. We used to talk about the Golden State, where he and I both had family. I had given him a State Department challenge coin for good luck before the big battle. He pulled it from the front of his flak jacket, declaring it had kept him safe during the battle. Then he described the death of his platoon commander, Lieutenant J. P. Blecksmith (24, of San Marino, California, pop. 13,327), on November 11, the day after the Marine Corps birthday, shot by a sniper the day after I first stepped foot into the city.

"I tried to revive him. I did mouth-to-mouth, but then he just went white."

Blecksmith had died right in front of him.

The Marine wanted to know if the election in Fallujah meant Marines could go home sooner.

A question I wished I could pass on to Rumsfeld directly, or anyone in Washington for that matter.

Nearby, two Marine Civil Affairs officers showed me all the preparations for the election, which was now two weeks away. Sergeant Todd Bowers and Captain Alex Henegar had shifted seamlessly from removing bodies out of the city to moving ballots into it. Many Marines asked me whether the State Department could save some blank ballots for them as mementos. I asked Henegar to keep a boxful. He did, but only after recording my request on official USMC letterhead and emailing me a scanned copy of it. With nothing to hide, I confessed to the embassy what I had done and forwarded the letter. Radio silence ensued.

During his next visit to Camp Fallujah, Ambassador James Jeffrey, Negroponte's gruff deputy and a former U.S. Army infantry officer himself in Vietnam, told General Sattler, "Weston is one step away from insubordination." What would Iraqi and international media think if they knew an American official had sequestered blank ballots before Election Day? Conspiracy theories already abounded, and Sunnis definitely did not trust us. After we had invaded their country because we could, then occupied it badly and ineffectively, they had a point—so did Ambassador Jeffrey.

But I kept the ballots.

I knew more than a few Marines wanted to believe Fallujah's ballots would mean fewer dead bodies—ours and Iraqis'—as did I. I had also been told some KIA parents wanted ballots to hang on their walls at home. Fighting cynicism comprised another daily battle in Iraq, while our capital, Washington, remained full of it. And maybe the family of a fallen Marine would take comfort in thinking, believing, an Iraqi ballot, and what it represented ("democracy"), somehow made the death of their son, daughter, brother, sister, mom, or dad a bit easier to accept.

Election time was upon us by January 2005. An impressive CIA case officer (circumspect, serious, and deadly, I was sure, if need be) who spent time with us downtown at the CMOC said his station chief in Baghdad had decided to ground all agency operatives that day—too dangerous. I told him the ambassador wanted his State Department political officers based in the provinces, like me, out talking to the people near polling sites.

"I wish I could go with you," he said. "I have a pistol. You don't."

"True, but I've made a few friends in Fallujah. I trust them. Most of them mostly anyway." Still, I could have used a well-armed and well-trained civilian counterpart at city polling sites and almost encouraged him to defy CIA orders and join me.

In advance of the voting, top Marine commanders and I had to determine the level of support U.S. Marines would provide to Iraq's electoral commission. Over 7,000 candidates were running for office associated with 111 party lists. The battle in Fallujah had been fought to rid the city of terrorists and insurgents, but also so Fallujans could vote. Washington wanted to shift public focus to ballots instead of bullets. Fallujah had become synonymous with violence—and symbolic to a growing number of people, to voters in the U.S., of a failing war. The overriding policy question before us: should we focus our assistance to the principal population centers, Fallujah and Ramadi, or rather "go wide" and order troops into remote parts of the province to secure additional, if a lot smaller—and more exposed—polling sites?

For Sunni politicians, and the Bush administration for that matter, the more "purple finger" Iraqi voters observed by the media the better. As a minority group, Sunnis had perhaps the most at stake in a country now dominated by Shia politics and parties. For Marines and me the calculation centered on different dynamics, as insurgents continued to plot and pick us off whenever they could. Enabling extra polling sites to be established (via USMC muscle, manpower, and lift capacity—in the form of an armada of planes and helos) might mean more votes, but it surely meant greater risks for our frontline grunts.

At Camp Fallujah, decision time had arrived. PowerPoint slides briefed; logistics options compared and timelines established. All detailed planning, even to the extent of how best to gather, stage, and then strap into cargo hold seats Iraqi election workers alongside pallets of ballots they were charged with overseeing.

Sitting at my right, Brigadier General Denny Hejlik, the deputy commander of the 1st Marine Expeditionary Force, turned to me. Growing up on a farm in Garner, Iowa, a small town of a few thousand, he was one of my favorite Marine leaders—a Marine without airs or manufactured alpha male attitude, albeit an occasional curmudgeon. I like curmudgeons. And wars tend to produce them at all ranks, all ages.

He understood what the embassy's priorities were: more Iraqi voters given the opportunity to vote, no matter the U.S. military logistical effort required to make it happen.

Another well-regarded general based in Ramadi, however, had dispatched a small group of Marine staff officers—colonels, lieutenant colonels, and majors—to argue the opposing case. The expected Sunni boycott of the election backed up their position, plus the questionable wisdom of putting more demands on limited USMC resources and personnel. Even the Marine Corps had its limits, though Marines were not likely to admit as much. A Marine friend and proud native of Buffalo,

New York, once reminded me: "There is no mission Marines believe they cannot accomplish." I said I liked that attitude even if reality sometimes might get in the way. The Ramadi contingent sat across the table, outnumbering me five to one.

Their leader, their general, who all predicted would wear four stars one day, had made his position clear. Weeks earlier, he had educated me bluntly and yet diplomatically—and gratefully—on how best to deal with top Marine brass. I tended to be as blunt as they were at times, although unlike most Marines I tried, usually successfully, to avoid using "fuck" and "fucking" as transitions in my vocabulary.

This already legendary Marine's name was Joseph Dunford, a Bostonian by birth and the son of a cop who fought in the Korean War as an enlisted Marine. The Praetorian Guard strategists he had sent on the 1st Marine Division's behalf did not look pleased. The Marines knew what was coming. I was about to pull civilian rank. As Hejlik had said, the issue before us, after all, constituted a State Department–led matter.

With the floor now mine in the small plywood conference room, I made my points, but not before draining the coffee cup in front of me, probably my third by then.

"If we don't provide election support across Anbar, it will be like de facto gerrymandering. The day after the election, Sunni politicians will want to know why their tribes and people did not get to vote. The only polling sites that open will be the ones we make happen."

I went on to explain that Sunni politicians were raising the issue in Baghdad with the ambassador, asking whether their people and tribes would be able to cast ballots. It was clear Shia areas would have high turnout—one-man, one-vote meant they would control a majority of seats in the new parliament.

For good measure, I added the ultimate kicker.

"Insurgents will also think we are caving if we limit our support, and Marines don't cave, right?"

Then came Brigadier General Hejlik's concluding statement.

"It's your call, Kael, this is a State Department political issue. We'll do this election your way."

"Okay, I'll let the embassy and ambassador know, and pass on that more Marines will be going to a lot more places than just Fallujah and Ramadi to get ready for the election," I replied.

The meeting soon ended. I had won the debate, though it was really a nondebate. Dunford and I worked well together, and I greatly respected his judgment given the gap in years between us, almost two decades, and experience and wisdom in him that went along with it. And yet, I still opted to go the other way.

General Hejlik heard my position, my decision, and saw, I am sure, the 1st Marine Division staff officers looking agitated. With a nod to me, no cinematic fist landing on a table, he ordered them to begin preparing for a support mission across the vast area of operation, home to over 30,000 coalition troops, under our command. This would start the mobilization of thousands of Marines and the movement of tons of Marine equipment so more Anbaris, well beyond Fallujah and Ramadi, could cast ballots. Our helos. Our forklifts. Our convoys. Our troops. Our sweat. Marine lives. The mighty Marine military machine would be shifted in this way in support of the Iraqi political process. Without which nothing would have happened across Anbar to reinforce U.S. political objectives. The government of Iraq simply did not have the resources to hold elections in the huge and volatile province.

Whether Iraqis chose to vote or not was another matter. Almost all I met with said Anbar's Sunni community would boycott the election. They said they opposed our attempts to democratize Iraq on our schedule, which would place Iraq's future in Shia hands, including overtly sectarian ones guided by Tehran. Waleed, Fawzi, among others; they all echoed one another. Fallujans did not believe in the political process we were forcing on them. Plus, the province remained a combat zone. Showing up at a polling site might mean death, with insurgents openly vowing to target voters.

Four days before the election in the early hours of January 26, 2005, two CH-53E Super Stallion helicopters full of Marines, many of whom had volunteered for the special mission to help secure polling sites, headed west, flying low toward Ak Ashat, a Sunni town of about 5,000 midway between Baghdad and the Jordanian border. It was as remote as a place could be, Mojave Desert–like.

The second helicopter, call sign Sampson 22, crashed en route. Its metal hull and massive blades slammed into the desert—a steel bird crumpled in an instant. All onboard died, a total of thirty-one U.S.

service members—thirty Marines and one U.S. Navy Corpsman. It remains the single largest casualty incident from the Iraq and Afghanistan wars. Only days away from redeploying home to Marine Corps Base Hawaii, the service members met a sudden and violent end: the young now the dead, torn bodies recovered by fellow Marines amid jagged metal on hot sand. They were part of Battalion Landing Team 1/3, the same unit Secretary Rumsfeld met a month earlier at Camp Fallujah. It was to be their last mission before redeploying—and it became just that, but not in the way any of us expected or could ever have imagined.

I remember hearing someone declare that long night: "Helo Down"—and then later, after receiving confirmation: "Thirty-one Angels."

We all knew the translation. What it meant. What it meant for families back home.

My decision, by not agreeing with General Dunford, had led to this mission—to their deaths. I was devastated. As Marines began to gather more information, I stepped outside, looked up at the Anbar sky before dawn, and saw no constellation of stars I recognized. Everything was a blur, inside my head and all around me. In my brain, at the time I believed I had done the right thing. In my gut, I now felt, I knew, the opposite. That day I was the U.S. government's messenger—not to Iraqis but to the United States Marine Corps—and I stayed on message: Iraq's elections would be supported by the USMC . . . at tremendous cost in lives.

Usually, under any night sky virtually anywhere, I could eventually locate Orion, the Hunter. As a kid, I had learned three stars marked his belt below Betelgeuse, Orion's right shoulder. I would later learn astronomers classify the massive celestial object as a red supergiant and estimate it to be at least 300 times the sun's diameter. The star Rigel forms part of a knee and is a very hot blue supergiant. And the sword? The Orion Nebula, a giant, fluorescent cloud of gas and superstellar dust 1,500 light-years from earth—a place where new stars are born.

I could not locate it that night when I most needed it. But even looking for Orion reminded me of my youth, camping under dark Utah, Colorado, Wyoming, and other American West skies, a time well before the wars, when I read Ray Bradbury's *Martian Chronicles* and not Defense Department counterinsurgency manuals. When my dad, a zoologist and hawk expert and amateur astronomer, would describe the vastness of the universe along with our small but not inconsequential place in it.

If the Weston family had an enduring religion, it was located somewhere in the night sky. He explained the physics and science behind the relativity of space and time. How a child on earth would age differently than a child of the same age traveling at the speed of light. This expanding universe of ours, its possible beginning, a Big Bang—and its possible end, a more depressing Big Crunch. Dad even spoke of the possibility of life-sustaining planets in galaxies far away, reminding us kids that by looking up we were looking back in time—the light reaching our eyes billions of years old.

Standing in the middle of Camp Fallujah, I wondered if any of the thirty-one had looked up at the night sky as well, and felt the same, when they were younger. I missed that era, that innocence, a time well before I knew anything about war. Anything about violence and death and about how easily humans could kill, or be killed—and did kill.

Anything about places named Fallujah. Or Anbar. Or Ar Rutbah. Or Ak Ashat. Or even Baghdad.

"Always remember," my dad would tell my brothers, older sister, and me, "to look up."

"Humans walked on that moon. I was in Vietnam when they did."

That night I felt as if I matched the Iraqi sky. A black hole above me. A black hole within me.

I remember thinking if only we could have avoided the war altogether by not invading Iraq in the first place.

So much less loss, pain, and deceit.

So much less death.

A war to what end?

A war without end?

The war all of us were stuck in.

Soon after hearing the tragic news, I went to my shared, cramped room, grabbed my running shoes and started to run around the base perimeter. And I kept running. And I kept running. I ran well beyond sunrise with nowhere to go but in circles, loop after loop. Knowing full well there was nowhere I could escape to. Knowing full well that two and a half dozen doors plus one more would be knocked on, many in Hawaii, in just a few hours. The official "next of kin" notifications they would hear changing lives forever. Families made son-less. Brother-less. Father-less. Grandson-less. Husband-less. Fiancé-less. I could not go back to that conference room and instead say: "General Hejlik, let's only do election support in Fallujah and Ramadi. Dunford and the Division are right."

Throughout the first meeting that day following news of the crash I avoided eye contact with a lot of Marines, particularly those who knew how the "election support" decision had been reached—and who spe-cifically had made that decision, not a Marine general officer, but a civilian no less. What was General Dunford thinking in Ramadi? He never said. I never asked. I knew.

Within days after the helo crash, we learned the January 30, 2005, election had resulted in huge majorities for Shia politicians, led by the United Iraqi Alliance. Across Anbar province, an overwhelmingly Sunni electorate, only a small number turned out to vote, a few thou-sand at most. Anbaris had said they would boycott, and they did.

Still, inside Fallujah, there were some voters. I spent Election Day at the Jolan Park poll site, which Marines had helped set up in the aban-doned and half-destroyed amusement park. I stopped under the broken Ferris wheel, standing next to a rusty child-sized space capsule with Mickey Mouse on it holding an American flag. Hundreds of Fallujans lined up between winding layers of razor wire, with gutted homes and destroyed buildings in the background. I noticed Marines positioned on rooftops, providing overwatch to protect the purple-fingered voters.

These Iraqis voted, but most also looked shell-shocked.

In Ak Ashat, where Marines were headed before the helo crash, I doubted more than thirty-one locals voted—or in the bigger, nearby town of Ar Rutbah for that matter. I preferred not to know the final count in either location.

There had been no de facto gerrymandering. Marines had not caved, providing security and other support at polling sites for the two-point-something percent of Anbaris who eventually voted. These Marines ordered to assist the election process in the province outnum-bered those purple-fingered Iraqis by at least tenfold.

"Just following State Department orders, just trying to make the election work in the middle of a war" could be my excuse, I thought while on my next, very long, nighttime run.

It would not be my excuse.

Those thirty Marines and Navy Corpsman should never have been close to Ak Ashat and Ar Rutbah, Iraq. My call. My regret. Though regret is not the right word. My reckonings. A decision I could never take back.

Thirty-one families stateside left devastated.

Thirty-one hometowns across America left to mourn.

Thirty-one gravesites I promised myself, there, that day, I would visit.

Thirty-one dead.

Thirty-one Angels I would not forget.

The Arab respected force a little: he respected craft
more, and often had it in enviable degree: but most of all
he respected blunt sincerity of utterance.

Collaboration

How did we get to the point of Marine helicopter after helicopter being
dispatched across Anbar's deserts full of Iraqi ballots and poll workers? So much had happened that none of us could have predicted post-
invasion, or been taught at Quantico or the State Department's own
training institute, since the return of Fallujans to their homes. Warfare
in Fallujah had entered new phases all at once. New skill sets would be
required among grunts, having less to do with the size of their weapons
and more to do with the degree of their endurance—and finding Iraqi
partners while spending large sums of U.S. reconstruction funds. Even
though the Iraqi government officially asked Fallujans to return to the
city across the winter and early spring of 2005, it remained in ruins.
Broken sewer lines spilled sewage. Holes had punctured compound
walls and front gates, some the size of tank rounds. The main industrial
section was leveled. The Jolan Park neighborhood still smoked.

An estimated 200,000 residents left before the battle. The first waves of the displaced reentered just before Christmas Eve, the exact same day Larry Nicholson arrived back in Anbar after being wounded just over three months earlier. The first time I saw him, I was tempted to get a general to order him back to Bethesda to recover fully. "Larry, we need you in fighting shape, not bleeding from your shoulder," I said. "I'm fine, I'm fine," was his standard reply. He mostly was, but I knew it was always very hard, if not near impossible, to redirect a Marine, especially a USMC infantry officer away from a front line, any front line.

As Fallujans returned across those weeks, we saw women covered in black holding their children in bright orange and pink clothing, small peacocks of energy surrounded by somber mothers. Seeing sons and brothers proved not as common. Many of them stayed away, out of anger and in fear. And rage. The city smelled of kerosene and dead bodies, except for the few hours after intermittent rainstorms. Back at Camp Fallujah candy canes and imported shiny Christmas tree ornaments were still strung next to racks of rifles, flak jackets, and Kevlar helmets. Our intentionally extended holiday season had coincided with a season of woe for Fallujans.

Residents initially approached by foot, single-file, before being processed. The place and our procedures seemed to mimic earlier wars in Europe, the ones I had seen chronicled in military history documentaries such as British television's iconic 1973-74 *World at War* series. In those scenes, no one looked victorious, just devastated—stooped but most not from old age, eyes cast down, pale—fitting the post-battle cityscape backdrop.

This did not feel victorious either.

The poor weather continued to match the setting, casting many more cold winter days in more gray and in succession. Even Anbar's usually intense sun did not reappear. Scarred people on both sides, new neighbors, in a scarred city, left shivering. In those earliest days, we worked hard to "welcome" Fallujans back despite the rubble and temperatures and conflicting allegiances. Many wore sandals, while Marines wore combat boots. Day in, day out, sunrise to nightfall, our worlds continued to collide.

Each morning, Marines and I lined up to begin another commute around the city in our Humvees, often within sight of the Blackwater Bridge, now decorated with Marine graffiti:

THIS IS FOR THE AMERICANS OF BLACKWATER
THAT WERE MURDERED HERE IN 2004. SEMPER
FIDELIS. 3/5. FUCK YOU.

3/5 was the tag for 3rd Battalion, 5th Marines, one of the Marine
Corps' most storied regiments of the Camp Pendleton–based 1st
Marine Division (Guadalcanal, Inchon, Chosin, Da Nang, and now
fuck you Fallujah).

Beyond the notorious bridge, numerous large tan tents with
card tables sprung up just inside city checkpoints, a barrier intended
to keep terrorists out and Iraqi civilians protected. I entered some to
observe the reentry process and ask Marines how their work was going.
Between coiled razor wire, Fallujans lined up in winding lines, waiting to be given the signal it was time to have their irises scanned via
high-tech gadgetry—Biometric Automated Toolsets (BATs)—and fingerprints recorded as well. American teens in uniform standing face-to-
face with Iraqi teens wearing dishdashas. Thousands of Fallujans waited
for hours in these lines, separated by razor wire—from each other and
from us—hundreds of meters long. Biodata first. Complaints later.

I asked a sergeant what he thought about all this technology in
Iraq's City of Mosques, where the sewer lines were still not functioning
nor wires for electricity or pipes for water.

"Sir, it makes companies back in the U.S. a lot of money and keeps
the generals happy."

I pressed.

"But is this database we have in Fallujah actually accurate? Have
we found a lot of insurgents because of all this processing we are
doing?"

"You want my personal opinion?"

I indicated I did.

"No, but it keeps us busy."

This BATs system would remain in place for years.

On one side stood the black-clad women, on the other crouched
men. I saw a row of young Marines, almost as if they had been trained
to trade shifts at a war zone help desk. Each was suited in full body
armor and with Kevlar helmets on.

I asked one corporal if he had heard any, or maybe many, complaints or problems.

"No one throwing a fit, sir. But most don't look very happy."

"Do we tell them what this is all about, or just scan their eyes and say 'Next'?"

"We just do it."

"Got it, but I'm not sure how I'd feel if our government was doing this to us, even in the middle of a war," I replied.

"I stay in my lane, but this is right out of a sci-fi movie," the Marine said.

"I'm thinking a George Orwell book."

"Who's that?"

I opted not to tell him, clearly not an author on junior Marines' recommended reading list but probably should have been.

Just past the scanners, we positioned Marines with backpacks full of crisp bills recently transported to Camp Fallujah by helicopter. Into our database Iraqi lives would go, then payment—and only then—would follow. De facto bribes as incentive to cooperate; they needed the money, and we needed to show that Fallujah could be rebuilt. Many appeared incredulous, humiliated, unblinking. E-interrogated, E-archived. Hundreds of thousands of American dollars paid out in hours.

Marines handed one old woman two $100 bills. She looked at them strangely, holding each at the edges like a dirty rag, walked to a nearby market, got a few vegetables for her Ben Franklins, and then went on her way. The seller, clearly a keen capitalist, did not give back any change—even if he had enough in the new, colorful Iraqi dinar notes, printed in shades of sand with palm trees, monuments, and historical sites on them, to make the swap. A few Marines, like Larry, raised questions about why we were paying in U.S. dollars, our currency, and not Iraqi currency. After all, Fallujans often asked, weren't we trying to build confidence in the "new Iraq" versus the old one? (Saddam's face and mustache dominated the most used pre-invasion note, the 250 dinar bill.) Our American currency stacked and handed over, most of which featured the faces of our American presidents, our former commanders in chief. Not a helpful visual for us.

Larry pressed the issue informally with me.

"Kael, we can't keep paying Iraqis in U.S. dollars. We need to show them that we are serious about using their currency."

"Larry, I agree, but you know how much harder it is to get and transport dinars compared to dollars, that's what MEF planners keep telling me. They say we have stacks and stacks of the dinars in Conex containers on base."

"Well, then . . ."

"Okay, I'll talk to General Sattler about it and see what we can do."

Soon, more and more Marines had colorful dinars in their hands, not greenbacks. Thanks to Larry's initiative, a practice he would continue once back in Fallujah, as the commanding officer of his own regiment.

Fallujah by then had already become the most exclusive gated city in the Middle East—whether Iraqis liked it or not. Marine guards on watch 24/7. In addition to eyes, they also scanned the metal and the iron and the rubber and the plastic and the glass of Iraqi vehicles via backscatter technology (using X-ray machines designed for military checkpoint use)—or opted to randomly search them by hand. During those days, insurgents wisely and dangerously melted back into the population. Patience always favored them. They had time to regroup and wait for the right moment to strike the right people. Fallujah was full of targets, especially anyone who openly collaborated with us.

The muezzins fell silent for long periods, no calls to prayer. Mosques instead filled with worshippers' whispers. Our unarmed drones buzzed overhead, unable to penetrate Iraqi minds below, just as Fawzi had said, while tracking Iraqi footsteps. Quiet plots among anti-American imams and sheikhs proliferated as our jets flew just above stockade-like minarets—a flyover tactic intended to demonstrate "dominance" by self-described U.S. military "battle space owners." But in doing so, we guaranteed the opposite outcome.

During one early meeting inside the city, a senior cleric robed in gray and bearded almost to his waist, sat still as mortars landed a hundred or so meters away from us. I flinched. He did not. A brief exchange followed.

"We're used to these sounds," he said.

I tried my best to sound assured. "Marines will be only a temporary presence in Fallujah. Imams like you will be here forever."

The Americans would go home one day, I repeated. We would leave. I was unsure he believed me. I was unsure I believed myself. Ambrose Bierce wrote that diplomacy was "the patriotic art of lying for one's country." I suppose, but not always wittingly or convincingly.

Washington did not give me talking points—they did not know what to say, anyway—and I likely would not have echoed them, anyway. The further we Americans kept ourselves from the Iraqi people, the more enemies we made. I could tell early on very few of us would get to know the people we had invaded. Very, very few of us.

What is more, our lives were deemed more valuable than theirs. That is the perception we gave. Our casualty counts detailed and recorded and mourned, but not theirs. We did not speak their language, understand their customs, or really know their stories.

All the while, the Green Zone parties in Baghdad continued: Middle Eastern Dance Night; Baghdad Karaoke; Flag Football 8 on 8; Viva la Salsa; 2nd Annual Baghdad Regatta; Country Night: One Howdy-Doody Good Time . . .

. . . as Iraq's City of Mosques, my adopted Iraqi home, was falling apart.

There were many ways to die in Fallujah. And those most at risk of dying were our Iraqi collaborators, not us. As we began the rebuilding phase, it would be our collaborators, the locals, and the ordinary Iraqis who would be most crucial to our effort and making any sustainable progress. They had a target on their backs almost 24/7. But we needed collaborators. Fast. And to get them we would need to connect to the real people of Iraq.

The imam who had sat next to me as mortars exploded outside asked me for money to repair his damaged mosque and to buy fuel for a generator. I said yes, and doubled the amount. The incoming insurgent barrage continued month after month. Those who launched the rounds called themselves the "noble resistance." We called them the enemy. Iraq's resistance had a rationale. I hated to admit it to myself and especially to the Marines.

What was this insurgent logic?

They were resisting us. The Americans. Period. And said they would never accept occupation. Fallujah was a neighborhood full of former Baathist generals and senior party officials, those now out of power after our invasion. They believed they had lost everything in the war, and since the army leadership and soldiers had been fired from their jobs, the embers of the insurgency would never truly go out. No matter our cause or the case we made, with American words or dollars or weapons. And Al Qaeda, absent in Iraq before our invasion, took full advantage of that reality. That truth. They co-opted the most extreme Sunnis into the terrorist fold. And killed the others.

The checkpoints, while helping secure the city, blocked commerce. Hundreds of vehicles in lines would back up each day, as young Marines and a growing local police force checked drivers for identification—and randomly examined cars and trucks for bombs. These were among the highest-stress jobs imaginable, conducted by eighteen-, nineteen-, twenty-year-olds, many of whom had never before left Omaha, Oakland, Sioux City, or Columbus, let alone the United States.

To be mayor or a city council member in Fallujah during the Americans-are-here era usually meant a death sentence. And yet Iraqis kept standing up to take over after predecessors were shot dead in front of their homes, in front of their mosques, in front of their families. The teenaged sons of city leaders, not yet old enough to grow the Arab world's ubiquitous beard, served as impromptu bodyguards. They had to seek Marine approval for weapons permits, our go-ahead for their own self-defense.

I wondered how many U.S. politicians would seek public office knowing their odds of survival were 50-50—at best.

By early 2005, I became the chief American collaborator, persuading as many local leaders as I could to join the cause. My State Department case to them:

> Come work with us. It's in your interest. We have millions to spend to rebuild. Schools. Soccer fields. Parks. Shops. Sewer lines. Let's focus on Fallujah's future, not its past. There are more elections coming up and you don't want to be left out. Issue the fatwas, religious edicts, in support of voting. I'm here not because I've been ordered to be in Iraq, but because I choose to be. Don't question my motives. Marines make no better friends, but also no worse enemies, like you Fallujans. Put down the weapons. Vote. Help us leave sooner. We are not here for the oil. Again, vote. Did we hand Iraq to Iran on a "golden platter" as you claim? Well, let's focus on other things.

Sheikh Dhari, the collaborating mayor I knew most, rarely donned traditional white tribal garb. When he did, his expensive fabric never had a smudge. Typically Dhari wore brown and charcoal silk suits, imported leather wingtips from Amman, and had a way with words that both annoyed and entranced fellow Iraqis during weekly city council meetings. A Marine lieutenant used to time the mayor's Tuesday morning arrivals—always sartorial entrances, he was usually the last to arrive—by singing under his breath a bad rendition of Right Said Fred's "I'm too sexy . . ." lyrics.

Everyone knew Dhari came from a famous Sunni family centered just outside a Baghdad suburb called Abu Ghraib.

After one city council meeting, the mayor asked to have a private conversation. I agreed, figuring he probably wanted to press me on helping secure more reconstruction funds from the central government. Much of Fallujah had been leveled and the prime minister's office promised a $100 million transfer to cover the costs. The money only started to flow when then New York senator Hillary Clinton raised the matter in Baghdad following her visit to Fallujah. Even the most pro-Republican Marines took note. General Sattler had told her it was our top priority, and I was about to tell Ambassador Negroponte the U.S. government would need to consider footing the bill if the Iraqi funds did not come soon.

But the mayor and I did not talk about money. Dhari proved to be a succinct interrogator. He wanted to discuss something much bigger than millions of dollars. He wanted an answer about the U.S.'s preemptive invasion of his country.

His was a one-line question, a one-line indictment.

"What did Iraq have to do with September 11?"

I knew this question was coming, but it still pained me to hear it. Pat Carroll, a talented polyglot Marine officer, sat next to me, transcribing my conversation with the mayor. He leaned a bit closer, pen in hand. Our reports went straight to the National Security Council at the White House and State Department headquarters in Washington. They requested we forward verbatim notes on our conversations with our collaborators. The city's political gyrations exemplified the Sunni mind-set in Iraq's most rebellious city, commentary colored in bloody reds as U.S. and Iraqi casualties mounted.

I knew this meeting would get top-level attention, probably in both the Oval Office and Vice President Cheney's conference room.

"Sheikh, I personally believe Iraq had nothing to do with 9/11."

And I believed it, knowing full well such an admission would not sit well with many in the Bush administration, that is, many of my highest-level bosses.

"You Americans turned Iraq into your stadium to fight the terrorists. They came only after you arrived," he replied.

Check and mate. And even if I were to push back—and I had no desire to because I agreed with him—his question said everything. We were in the middle of a war of choice and occupation, the wrong war. The terrorists appeared when we did. Not before.

Saddam had many deadly traits, but he did not welcome extremism that would later buttress Al Qaeda in Iraq and germinate the roots of the Islamic State. City leaders said Saddam only visited Fallujah once. After having a dream that Anbar tribes would "ambush and kill him" on the road between Fallujah and Ramadi, he stayed away, they said. They further claimed Saddam mistrusted Anbar sheikhs more than Shia imams. One cleric said he remembered how Iraqi state television used to run popular programs on Fridays, during prayer time, to try and move devout Iraqis away from religious messages in the mosques.

Saddam the Secular, in other words, not Saddam the Sectarian.

Once again, Pat Carroll, the Foreign Area officer, son of a Massachusetts surgeon, and linchpin of the CMOC team, recorded my exchange with Dhari in detail. He had the harder end of our partnership; I talked a lot, he wrote a lot. The report went to Washington unedited. The Bush administration at the time still pushed an Iraq-9/11 conflation and Vice President Cheney declared the insurgency in its "last throes."

Some Marines used Sharpie pens to inscribe "Never Forget September 11th" on their helmets. Black ink layered over a sandy camouflage pattern. Some even had a linguist translate the words into Arabic, reminding me of that unforgettable image in the coalition palace in Baghdad. In the main dining hall there, Ambassador Bremer's staff hired an Iraqi artist to paint Manhattan's Twin Towers on a wall bordered by gray marble Saddam had imported under ceilings etched in gold leaf. I wondered what other Ground Zero artifacts might have been placed inside the palace walls in those days, while none should have. No part of lower Manhattan belonged in Baghdad.

Saddam's palace of mirrors had become ours throughout the country. Like him, we saw what we wanted to see. Manufactured images, our own Potemkin Iraq.

Mayor Dhari eventually proved his mettle to Marines. Many considered him to be only a political poser and not brave at all—but chasing a would-be assassin off his property with his pistol in hand demonstrated another side. After the mayor fired a few rounds, the wounded attacker fled. Dhari showed up the next day in the council meeting, telling us about his close call in animated and exaggerated fashion. He too had learned how to tell a good war story.

Mayor Dhari's near-death experience aside, the odds always worked against the Iraqi leaders. We had our walls, armored Humvees, and a PSD, personal security detail—a dozen Marine grunts with M-16 carbines—to protect us. Leaders like Dhari had two or three bodyguards at most, unarmored vehicles, and a constituency increasingly uneasy with or outright opposed to the American presence, no matter our money and our promises.

He also quizzed me on local history, knowing that I had been a political science and history double major in college. As I was the only full-time U.S. official in Fallujah and all of Anbar province for most of the period between 2004 and 2007, Dhari asked whether I knew anything about the "unfortunate" British diplomatic representative who preceded me eighty years earlier. I said I knew how badly our U.K. friends tended to draw maps in the region, but the specifics of their experience mostly remained a blank.

"His name was Colonel Leachman."

Dhari's subtle message: study him.

And so I did. In 1919, Gerard Leachman was shot in the back near Fallujah after visiting another sheikh named Dhari, a blood relative of the one I knew so well. The once untouchable U.K. political officer and envoy met his end with bullets during what was likely a furnace of an August day in the Iraqi desert. He was buried in the Baghdad Military Cemetery.

The mayor of Fallujah and I never had a follow-up conversation about Leachman. His message, his warning, reverberated. I did not need or seek another reminder of what happened when distant empires reached too far, across the Tigris and Euphrates Rivers and into modern Babylon.

Marine colonels and generals had their own well-rehearsed floor speeches in meetings with our growing list of Iraqi collaborators. While I talked politics, they talked security. Larry proved especially adept at these tough topics. Checkpoints. Weapons permits. Detention operations. Rules of Engagement, ROE. Solatia payments for Iraqi dead and wounded. Night raids. Search procedures.

And especially the badges, who got which kind, and which levels of access, and for what reasons.

Iraqi contractors had their badges.

City council members too.

Tribal sheikhs got theirs.

Baghdad-based ministry representatives got a version as well—different stripes, different colors, all worn around the neck. Even a local turkey, which Marines had adopted, got his own badge . . . before being killed and eaten for Thanksgiving.

Of course these badges, associated with prerogatives and security in our eyes, could serve as nooses for our Iraqi friends. Any tie to us—and a U.S.-issued badge was the surest indicator of "collaboration"—meant automatic death if found out by the wrong militia member or Al Qaeda terrorist.

After one of the first Fallujah city council meetings, which Marines and I attended weekly at the CMOC, a council member approached me with two things to say. I was surprised none of his points had to do with badges because that was often the first, or sometimes only, request.

He had a warning and advice: "There are people in the city who want to kill you. But more of them are beginning to believe you want to help the city rebuild.

"You have to keep telling us in the council meetings that your troops will leave one day. The people need to hear that, over and over."

I appreciated his honesty, but did not like the feeling of still being a principal target in a city that had been the scene of the most intense fighting of the war. I began to think I was earning my State Department danger pay (35 percent of my base salary) and then some. Every corner in Fallujah rated as "outside the wire" and our casualty rates reflected as much. Before long, Marines began to call the city Sniperville.

The collaborators, those who stepped forward, became my friends. Many were assassinated. Their names and roles did not mean much to most Americans who passed through the city.

But they did to me.

One local leader put it this way: "I used to know my hometown, but not any longer."

The war had turned his hometown upside down. He meant the political ecosystem as much as the economic one. New power plays were under way. Local bosses were no match for Al Qaeda terrorists who were beginning to reinfiltrate and identify America's closest partners.

In addition to Mayor Dhari, we relied on other collaborators too.

Sheikh Kamal had a round belly, thick fingers, and preferred political talk to preaching in his mosque. He had been assigned to be the clerics' lead voice. Selected as chairman of the Fallujah city council, he lasted less than a year. Many Marines were annoyed with his speechifying and wanted him gone—not killed, but sidelined. And others thought I myself had been co-opted by Fallujans. I had not, but then these same Camp Fallujah–based Marines never heard how bluntly I challenged Fallujans about the problems in their city, the many problems. And most were Fobbits, and they had no intention of giving up that title and its associated comforts.

In one instance, I overruled a Marine regimental commander's reluctance when Kamal's sons asked for weapons permits to protect their dad. It was the right thing to do in a city where local politicians were being killed regularly, week after week. The colonel, a good leader who was quiet and introverted by Marine standards, reconsidered. Kamal's sons got the approval and necessary paperwork. Each night, one of them stood guard in their home, rotating duty. Eventually, on his way to meet us for the first time in weeks, Kamal was shot, six times, while driving alone to make our appointment. He bled to death. Kamal and other city leaders had been boycotting meetings because Marine rifle companies had been occupying dozens of homes in counter-sniper operations. The tactic was not working. The snipers remained, and we were alienating droves of Fallujans in the process. Kids and moms corralled in corners, with corporals atop their house rooftops, did not equal a good dynamic. I ended it.

Within a day of Kamal's assassination, his brother brought me the badge we had issued him as council chairman. It had a bullet hole through it, the cracked plastic identification coated in dried blood. The message did not need to be translated. I turned it over to a Marine intelligence officer, my fingerprints now on the badge alongside Kamal's.

In my diplomatic cables to Washington, I described Sheikh Kamal's death, like so many others, in formal and flat language. His was titled:

FALLUJAH CITY COUNCIL CHAIRMAN ASSASSINATED

It had neutered subheadings too, "Assassination Blow to Local Governance" and "Lasting Impact?" My job in the State Department meant putting feelings aside in order to analyze. And analyze some more, robotlike:

How would Kamal's death, on top of all the others, affect U.S. interests?

With him gone, what do we lose?

Who is next in line to take over?

Forget the friendship, only recount for the ambassador, Main State HQ, Pentagon, and White House, the whole interagency, why they should notice another death of another anonymous Iraqi.

And even then, they tended not to take note for long.

The least we could do for Kamal and for all the other "martyrs" was put their names and a small part of their life story into the U.S. diplomatic archive, right? I believed that the records of the superpower that invaded their country because it could, not because it had to, should contain these foreign names. The Occupied. Not the Liberated. I like to think my cables became their obituaries of sorts, or at least an epitaph—e-archived, before and after WikiLeaks, for a very long time.

I wished I could have attached Kamal's bloodied badge to my cable, the one with the bullet hole in the middle of it. Not a picture on a scanned document but rather the badge itself. The texture and color of it, shattered, and the human absence it signified. His brother would have approved. Washington of course would not have.

Kamal had a family. Kamal had children. Kamal, in other words, had a story all his own. His oldest son used to ask me questions that had nothing to do with what I would expect from the son of a Sunni preacher of Islam. He liked to know about America. It humanized his dad in a way that only a son might, a son who had to protect his dad with a pistol at night in their compound.

One conversation stood out more than the rest because of all the good questions he asked me in a dank, dusty, small room in the downtown CMOC. I never told Kamal about it.

"Do you think my father will be safe enough?"

"Do you think he can protect himself when I'm not around?"

"He doesn't sleep at night. None of us do."

"What happens when Marines leave Fallujah?"

My answers went along the standard lines I was by then practiced at: Your father is a brave man. He is standing up for Fallujah. We work with him and the council because the city needs leaders right now. I respect his decision. The weapons permits are the least and best we can do. I cannot imagine how hard it is at home for your family. We will do our best to keep Fallujah safe.

And so on and so on. Kamal's son did not look reassured.

My war words became anodyne as well in my wartime cables. I was well trained in State Department–speak and wordage. Here is how policy makers in Washington read about Kamal-the-collaborator's death. A note on the cable's content: CF = coalition forces. PolOff = me. KHALILZAD = the ambassador at the time. (While political officers write cables, all of our reports are transmitted under the ambassador's name and final approval authority to State Department headquarters, relevant U.S. embassies in the region, and other national security–related agencies.)

I summarized Kamal's death in this way:

> Sheikh Kamal's assassination will set back our local governance efforts in Fallujah, at least in the short term. The number of leaders willing to continue in or assume top leadership jobs in the face of renewed threats remains unclear; the Fallujah bench, however, is not deep. Unconfirmed reports of imams fleeing the city do not bode well. As a group, they have generally been cooperative or, at a minimum, preached messages of stability. Other intimidation efforts in spring and summer 2005 effectively silenced senior tribal leaders. Following Sheikh Kamal's assassination, all other groups, including the area tribal sheikhs

council, mukhtars (neighborhood watch-type individuals and resident advocates), and junior imams in Fallujah who had regularly interacted with CF and PolOff, decided to suspend any further meetings. A prolonged city leadership and civic engagement vacuum would heighten citizen unease. A new Marine regiment assumes control of security operations in the city within two weeks. This transition comes at an especially sensitive time and will need to be carefully orchestrated.

My detached tone belies the vibrancy of the admittedly controversial man, as some Marines had a hard time accepting him in his leadership role, not to mention his occasional, politician-like theatrics. The report exemplifies how distant our Iraqi partners remained from U.S. officialdom, even from me at a certain level, and I knew them best.

And, of course, I received an email from a well-meaning Marine regimental staff officer who rarely left the wire, unlike all of us who lived basically full-time downtown. He had one question: "Isn't there an opportunity for us in Kamal's death?"

Valid enough point in a we-are-at-war-shit-happens kind of way, but not the kind of email or question I wanted to get just then. I did not answer it.

A Fallujan present when Mayor Dhari visited Kamal's family to offer condolences said one of his sons angrily challenged him.

"Why didn't you do more to protect my father?"

And why hadn't we?

Lawyer Najm came next. He volunteered to take the city council chairman job after Kamal's assassination. I wanted to tell him, yell at him: "No, don't do it!" Of course I did not. It was not my job to push Iraqi collaborators away in order to help save their lives. In hindsight, I should have made that my job.

A legal man, Najm had a narrow mustache, always well clipped. In meetings, he smiled more than he debated. His main issue with us centered on ensuring proper condolence payments for Fallujah's dead and wounded. It was a long list. Najm advocated for the poorest in the city. His son was gregarious and seemed proud his father held a top governance job working with the Americans. A new local political dynasty, he imagined, perhaps. He got his weapons permit, for a pistol but not for a bigger weapon. Another son-turned-bodyguard. Occasionally, I could see it bulging in his suit coat pocket or at his waist. Both Najm, in his mid-fifties, and his son, mid-twenties, were killed in their vehicle. Shot multiple times through the windows and doors.

Sami, a proud Arab nationalist, used to stand up and openly challenge Al Qaeda in city council meetings, some of whom undoubtedly sat in the room while pretending to be cooperative citizens. He was bald, had blue eyes, and chain-smoked. Prayer beads always in hand, he did not come across as a devout Muslim. Like Jack Mormons I knew, he seemed to be a Jack Muslim. He talked more about Egypt's Nasser (second president of the country and an anti-monarchist who nationalized the Suez Canal) than the Quran. Sami was Colonel Nicholson's favorite leader. Two tough men who spoke in blunt language. They bonded immediately. Then we got the call early on a Sunday morning.

"Kael, bad news. Ops just said Sami's been hit."

"Let's go," I said.

Thirty minutes later we stood in front of Sami's brown compound with its front gate partly opened. His oldest son, still shaken, greeted us. It was sunny and cold. No rain that day.

"They shot Father here, less than an hour ago. They had a vehicle. It pulled up, bullets all around.

"At first he wasn't shot, but then he went back toward them, running with his pistol. But behind him, others he didn't see shot him in the back."

Larry spoke first.

"He was one of the bravest men in this city. I am not the only Marine who saw that courage in what he said and what he did for Fallujah. Please accept our condolences."

"I am so sorry," I added. "Your father never hid his voice in the city council meetings. He told everyone the truth, tough messages, including to us Americans."

Toward the house, there was some motion behind window curtains. Probably his daughter and wife looking out at us, but remaining hidden. I wondered what they thought of Larry and me. On that day, it must have been anger. Deep anger. Our association with their father and husband had put a terrorist target squarely on him. Our friendship with their father, her husband, got him killed.

Sami's body would be buried before sundown, keeping with Muslim tradition. His eldest son said he did not want to move the family out of Fallujah, but would. The whole time he stood next to us, his eyes darted around. He was nervous. Larry and I knew the longer we stayed there, the more likely our presence put more of his family in danger, even by expressing our condolences in a conversation that lasted a few minutes at most.

Sami's killers were never identified. (And Larry, over a decade later and now a three-star general, still keeps the prayer beads Sami had given him as a gift in friendship. "Colonel Nicholson is a Marine leader," Sami often told me, "who cares enough to really get to know the people of Fallujah.")

Even with these tragic deaths, our collaboration was working. The city began to be rebuilt, if slowly and mostly with American money— not the promised and projected Iraqi government funds. The Fallujah reconstruction committee met weekly. A typical session focused us on the usual projects. We talked sewers. We talked electricity. We talked water. We talked roads. We talked schools. We talked soccer fields even, that enduring topic favored by the leaders with children back in their broken homes.

And it all felt better for a while. Marines, while highly trained in killing, are also schooled in civil affairs. Some of the best among them could easily have been diplomats or USAID workers. Iraqis used to tell me that what made U.S. Marines so fearsome in fighting, more than any other U.S. military branch in their view, also made them so effective in rebuilding. By 2005 the city council members were able to tell Fallujans that life was getting better, and they were right—even if the scars still ran deep and reconstruction tab remained big.

Despite the long-term dispiriting odds, the Marines and I tried to keep our collaborators alive.

But we were never able to come close.

The bullet hole through the center of Kamal's bloodstained badge marked "FCC Chairman" was proof of that. His brother had handed it to me for a reason. His dead brother's chief American collaborator had been John Kael Weston, U.S. State Department representative in Fallujah, not a Marine general or colonel or captain or corporal.

Kamal's brother was seeking accountability in me—and assigning blame too. If our roles had been reversed, I would have done the same thing, or probably more.

The murder of a man is still a murder, even in wartime.

MANFRED VON RICHTHOFEN
"THE RED BARON"

KIA in Mayberry

According to the Quran, the angel of death, Malak Am-Maut, returns the souls of the dead to Allah. My dead Iraqi friends were believers. This Islamic teaching must have reassured their families. But before that journey's end, Muslims believe other angels, Munkar and Nakeer, question the soul about past good deeds and bad, a final measure of character and actions. Judgment Day.

Islamic doctrine says there are no fallen angels, but Iraq's battlefields were filled with them. Both sides. Death did not discriminate. That equal opportunity reaper stayed busy every day with no guardian angels intervening between us. Marines died. Fallujah's leaders were killed. Sniped. Blown up. Bled out. Definitions of the mode of death did not matter to us. Dead is dead. Technically, it was only Iraqi politicians who were counted in our records and my diplomatic cables as "assassinated." While on our side, we used the shorthand of KIA for killed in action.

Among Marines, Lance Corporal Ryan McCurdy's death hurt

most. He was one of a small group of us who lived full-time downtown at the CMOC. Ryan, nicknamed "Dirty" McCurdy, wore blue Crocs. His feet clopped and shuffled.

Late one night after brushing my teeth, I ran into Corporals Joerndt and Clifton Trotter. Both were good friends with Ryan. Like me, they tended to be night owls. But this time they had bathroom-cleaning duty (restrooms are called "heads" by Marines).

"Lucky you," I said.

"Beats other kinds of duty around here," Joerndt replied.

"Yeah. It is getting even more dangerous around Fallujah. Fallujans coming in to meet with me are saying some of the Al Qaeda guys are returning."

"Yup. That's why we are getting into a lot of firefights down here about every day."

Trotter spoke up. "Are all these meetings you are having with the mayor and those sheikhs doing any good?"

"Some days I think so, some days I am not sure."

They said they had better finish cleaning because they had to get up early. I noticed on the wall near the sink a "duty roster" for the unpleasant job. Each CMOC Marine had been given a day.

"I don't see the Department of State guy on the roster. Maybe you can pencil me in, say, two years from now."

Joerndt got the joke and laughed. "Well, I sure don't plan to be here then."

"The way things are going, I might be," I confessed. "Besides, keep this top secret but one of my first jobs was cleaning shitters in public park restrooms, and I have retained that special skill, I think."

Trotter pulled out a pen and wrote my name down, next to the year 2015, which was ten years later.

"If any of us are still in Iraq by then, things will definitely not be good," I said before making my way through a dark CMOC corridor to the room I shared with several Marines, already asleep. Though shuteye never lasted long in downtown Fallujah, I got on my cot and tried to think of anything but war. And tried to sleep.

Within eight hours, Ryan McCurdy would be dead and Trotter almost. Of course, in war one never knows when that last night, day, or hour might be. Everything seemed "normal" until it happened, until the sniper team struck.

I had gotten up early, off my sunken cot, and begun competing for bad black instant coffee with Marines. Starbucks SOS shipments did not always reach our little outpost. I had a meeting with a member of the Fallujah city council to prepare for, plus an update for the embassy to finish. I usually also sent notes to the generals on base, keeping them informed about Fallujah's ever-gyrating political dynamic downtown.

The radios suddenly erupted, "Marines down! Marines down!"

Outside, shots rang out. The Iraqis, in line for their meetings, scattered. Each of our corporals was under direct fire. Corporal Trotter was the first down. He had just been shot in the neck by a sniper. Corporal Joerndt, also on gate duty, began to try to pull him behind a HESCO barrier. Corporal McCurdy was helping as well, when suddenly a second round penetrated his chest from the side and he too fell to the ground.

"Marines down! Marines down!" the radio continued to ring out.

As the chaos grew, Ryan lay dying, with Trotter near death, his neck bleeding profusely, and Joerndt kneeling close by.

At first we thought something had happened at the Marine rifle company headquarters located a few hundred meters away. We shared the same radio frequencies. But then familiar voices sounded. Our team. My CMOC Marines.

I hurried back to the dusty reception area where Fallujans, by the dozens, had already gathered that morning, and I saw Sergeant Green walk in.

A laconic NCO from Ohio, he never seemed to lose his cool. Week after week, he had helped move Fallujans in and out of our building through layers of security, rarely complaining. I always felt reassured with Green around. Not just because he was a rifleman but also because he had composure reflecting his age—he was several years older than the typical infantry grunt.

He changed that day, and I could understand why.

Green threw his helmet on the floor with a loud clunk and yelled at the Fallujans: "You know who did this! Goddamnit, you know who did this!"

Every Iraqi stared at the floor, while I stared at Green. I was thinking to myself about all the foreign faces in the room: *Show us your spine. Turn in the bastard who did this.* Fallujans had been coming in daily to the CMOC to get badges, discuss projects, submit claims for property damage, and probably to spy on us. Their routine. Our routine.

Tribal sheikhs had just informed me that security in the city was deteriorating. The regiment, meanwhile, was debating whether to shut down our operations in the city—a position I opposed, but that many Marines shared. Marine CMOC duty was among the most dangerous in the city. I held my ground, however, and the CMOC stayed open for business. The leaders we met in that building helped keep Fallujah safer for the hundreds of other Marines rotating in and out, year to year. Tribal sheikhs. Imams. The mayor. City council.

As Green moved into another room, fuming, I noticed an old man in the room start to shake. A young boy in a dark shirt with "NY" on it fidgeted in his seat. Several children stopped playing with a plastic ball that Marines kept in the lobby along with other toys. And all the mothers began to gather near the door, ready to leave en masse. They looked fearful for themselves and more so for their children. We soon asked all of them to vacate, and they did, in a jumbled rush.

Doc Reed, our Navy Corpsman from Maryland, followed Green and walked to our makeshift gym, shaking as well, and sat close to me on the bent bench press. His uniform had a lot of blood on it, streaks of crimson atop its camouflage pattern. Doc unloaded in stream-of-consciousness fashion. A sniper's bullet had come out of nowhere and hit Ryan in the chest while pulling guard duty that morning directly in front of CMOC. Doc said he tried to save him, doing all he could, but it was not enough. He described treating Corporal Trotter too, who was heaving after being shot, his neck tissue severed a fraction of an inch away from his carotid artery. Doc was not sure he would make it. Trotter was being transported back to the main base. We all knew his wife was pregnant.

I do not remember what I said to Doc, just what he said to me.

Joerndt arrived back in the CMOC and kept repeating to us throughout the day the same thing: "I didn't go back out, I didn't go back out."

In his mind, he had panicked. He had failed. With two Marines down, first Trotter then McCurdy, he eventually remained behind a HESCO barrier, but only after exposing himself to the sniper as he aided Trotter. This was the right call, the toughest kind in combat. We would have had three Marines down if Joerndt had gone out again.

I grabbed him, saying, "Remember, you did everything right today. Remember that, for the rest of your life."

My words came out sounding like an order. They were. I repeated to all of them, not just Joerndt, how important it was to keep the CMOC open, the house-office-fort all in one we shared and practically under siege daily.

It was a speech I had to give, but it felt like half lies. Some of our collaborators had ties to the insurgency and worse. Of all Americans in Fallujah, I knew that. And I had a sick feeling Sergeant Green was right. Some Fallujans in our very lobby probably supported snipers killing us. You could never tell, but you could sure surmise, more than just suspect.

That night, we held an impromptu memorial for Ryan. Each Marine offered words. I told them that without their work at the CMOC and Marines throughout Fallujah, there would have been no elections, no chance for this war to end. I gave Corporal Joerndt some ballots.

"These are the cleanest symbol of what we are trying to do over here," I said, trying to sound convincing—to him and to myself.

He said he wanted to take some to Ryan's family in Louisiana when he got home.

If the ballots helped them, that is all that mattered, if those ballots helped Marines still fighting in Fallujah, that is all that mattered. But in my own mind, the doubts about U.S. policy and our ability to stabilize the situation in Iraq had only grown.

I kept such thoughts to myself. They comprised a list of painful secrets, in a sense, because I knew too much about what was not working in Baghdad, or in Washington. Few Marines, even the generals, knew as much as I did—because I was the only one with a direct line into the policy making side of government. Including by then a back door to the National Security Council, with one senior staff person, Brett McGurk, reaching out to me directly and regularly, which I appreciated.

"We brief President Bush on the bad news too, rest assured," he would email me. A talented lawyer who had clerked for Chief Justice Rehnquist on the Supreme Court, Brett seemed committed to Iraq, while perhaps too close to Iraq's Shia power brokers. But then, the same could be said about the Sunnis and me, and was said, I am sure—a Weston-Is-Too-Close-to-the-Sunnis indictment of sorts—in various State Department circles in Baghdad and Washington.

But I was not reassured. I was angry. Marines were dying around me, and I had no good answers for their very good questions about "what's next" in Fallujah . . . and Anbar . . . and Iraq.

That night I did something that surprised me, and perhaps I should not have. I handed over some mini-bottles someone had given me, unopened, not being much of a drinker myself and definitely not in a place like Fallujah. Numbness came in a host of other ways.

"I'm overriding General Order Number One, a State Department right, I think, in special circumstances. There's not enough alcohol here to do anyone any harm, or any good, anyway."

With that, each Marine took a swig. Green drank last. And I began to prepare for my full day of meetings the next day in the CMOC: at 10 a.m., the mayor; noon, the reconstruction committee; and at 2 p.m., the police chief, who was bringing in Iraqi police officers so I could thank them for their work securing the city—and protecting us in the CMOC.

I also opted to go ahead with a meeting of tribal sheikhs. I refused to cancel it, which would be the wrong signal to Fallujans and to Marines. I walked out beyond the Marine-manned checkpoint to where Ryan had been killed, figuring the sniper or snipers would not shoot in the same place twice. All the Marines on post watched me traverse the forty meters to the outermost perimeter. It did not take long, and I did not feel brave. I was sad. But it had to be done.

Sheikh Abdul Wahed al-Janabi greeted me. He had an Obe-Wan Kenobi way about him. Probably close to seventy-five years old, quiet but strong-willed, and robed in white. I looked down as he leaned in to greet me with a customary kiss on the cheek. It had been another cold winter morning, but not a lot of rain. Near his feet, I saw a puddle of blood where Ryan had died the day before.

Don't step there. Anywhere else, just not there, I thought.

His right foot missed the pool of blood by inches—a grimy part of Fallujah that would forever be America. I wanted the Iraqi skies to open up and pour down on that very spot, for an eternity. But the stain of what happened there I knew could never be washed away.

My other meetings went ahead too, and the senior-most Marine officers based at the CMOC and I made sure the regiment upgraded the netting and protective barriers at the gate. The improvements came too late, and I had no good reason to tell the Marines why the deadly delay.

Within a few days, a video of the snipers who killed Ryan had already been uploaded to the Internet. It was accompanied by chanting in Arabic, with the refrain "Fallujah." They filmed Trotter being shot first, falling to the ground. Then Ryan, hit in the side, as he tried to drag Trotter to safety. It looked like the sniper had been positioned across the street because we could see cars passing before the attack.

A week or so later, I sat in the commanding general's conference room at Camp Fallujah. Two Marines straight off a recruiting poster stood near the head of a long wood table, demonstrating the arrival of new side-SAPI (Small Arms Protective Insert) ceramic plates. They were designed to protect the stomach and chest from bullets entering below the shoulders. Our technology always seemed to arrive a bit too late, even though Marines pushed hardest to get it. Meanwhile, some Pentagon chiefs in Washington seemed more focused on equipment than others—Robert Gates trumping Rumsfeld by a blood-red mile.

As a tribute to Ryan, we named our dilapidated recreation room in the CMOC in his honor: "McCurdy's Blue Shoes Lounge."

We placed his blue Crocs on the wall next to his name and "RIP."

Not long after, Sergeant Green told the rest of us that Ryan, a Baton Rouge, Louisiana, native and Christian Life Academy graduate, was buried back home. In East Baton Rouge Parish's Resthaven Gardens of Memory and Mausoleum, his tombstone reads "son," "purple heart," and "Operation Iraqi Freedom."

He was twenty years old.

PFC Joshua P. Klinger, twenty-one, of Easton, Pennsylvania, was another of our KIA. I attended his memorial in the northern part of the city—sometimes I attended three in a day, most often with Larry—just below where we had buried the Iraqi dead in trenches. Close to the old railroad tracks. Some of the new Marines did not know that part of Fallujah's history, and I did not tell them. Secrets, again, best left buried.

Klinger died after stepping on a bomb while on patrol. As I stood for the playing of Taps, the muezzins' calls to prayer began as well—in sync. The stereo-like effect bothered me. Our Taps and the Muslim siren call to their faithful, echoing from dozens of mosques, only reminded me how foreign we were.

American strangers in a strange land, killing Arabs, and Arabs killing us, strangers in their homeland.

We had other casualties too.

Marine leaders and I used to visit the "boneyard." Where troops would haul all the military vehicles blown up by roadside bombs. A military junkyard but not full of old and run-down trucks and cars with rusted chrome, just all those split open by insurgent explosives getting more deadly by the week. Earlier, a car bomber had driven into one of the few MRAPs (larger, more armored transport vehicles with a V-shape hull) we had. Marines inside were banged up, but not killed. The bomber's scalp landed on the top of the vehicle. We heard the explosion before the team pulled their damaged truck into our compound.

We heard another Marine had been killed by a massive IED, so we stopped at the boneyard. A Marine on the colonel's staff wanted us to see how big the bombs were getting. The left passenger seat of a Humvee had been sheared off, almost as if by a giant sword. That was the KIA seat, we were told. Sand had been placed in the vehicle to soak up blood. The two-inch-thick front windshield had been blasted out. The front seat, however, where the driver sat, looked perfect. Undamaged.

The driver survived. His buddy seated a half foot behind died instantly.

Whether them or us, life or death came to a matter of inches and seconds.

And then there were the "Lionesses" on June 23, 2005. Some of these female Marines and Navy personnel worked with me at the CMOC. They were in the city to search Iraqi females across checkpoints, a sensitive job in a branch dominated by alpha males and wannabe alpha males. Each day, the Lioness group commuted between base and downtown in a convoy. Sometimes, I sat next to them. Another car bomber clearly knew our route. The women were seated side by side in the open-back seven-ton when the bomber rammed their truck broadside. Two died instantly. Incinerated. A third would die a few hours later.

On base, I remember the electricity had gone out that day. The general and his team and I discussed the tragedy. The single largest casualty incident for women in the Iraq War had just happened in our city. Someone brought in candles and flashlights. The dark room hid everyone's eyes.

And each of us knew the families of the dead women, LCpl Holly A. Charette (21, of Cranston, Rhode Island, pop. 80,566), Navy P01 Regina R. Clark (43, of Centralia, Washington, pop. 16,660), and Cpl Ramona M. Valdez (20, of the Bronx, New York, pop. 1,419,000), had yet to receive their knocks on the door back home.

Our convoys continued on the same road throughout that summer and beyond. And for weeks, we passed the spot of the attack, now blackened where the asphalt had melted due to the heat of the blast.

I tried to look away, but could not.

Then there were their deaths, the Iraqis'. And they were no easier.

I once had to play mortician myself. A "MAM" (military-aged male) had been detained, taken to Camp Fallujah to be questioned. At some point during his interrogation, a lone Marine in the room shot the Iraqi dead with a round to the chest. The Marine said the detainee charged him.

A he-said, he-said situation—except one was dead.

I had no reason not to believe "our" side of the story. But my job required I consider both sides. I would be the person who had to explain what happened to Fallujans—my own credibility, which amounted to U.S. credibility, once again, on the line.

Soon after, I met a senior tribal leader in central Fallujah on another windy, dusty day, as so many were. We had to hand the body over, and I had the closest ties with Sheikh Thamer, this noble-looking Sunni with a trusted track record with me—and me with him. After coordinating with regimental staff, I asked Marines to bring the body downtown. They showed up in a truck with the body in a plywood coffinlike box, body fluids leaking out of the bottom of the simple container. Not blood, something else. It reminded me of the Potato Factory, the smell too. I had hoped to put that period, the bodies, all those bodies in various states of decomposition, behind me.

A Marine handed over the paperwork that went along with the dead Iraqi but suggested we consider keeping it. I looked at the form, which contained the outline of a man's body on it (again, just like the records I had seen Mortuary Affairs Marines use during the body retrieval process), with a coroner-like statement inscribed in English: "Cause of death: single gunshot wound (GSW) to the chest."

Sheikh Thamer said he already had told the tribe and family members the young man had "died of food poisoning" while in Marine custody.

Had I misheard him?

Food poisoning?

I knew he wanted to help reduce tension but that explanation sounded impossible to explain. With the body moved to the back of Thamer's sedan, I began to hand him the death certificate. This kind of paper trail, even in English, could cause more violence, but Thamer and the tribe were entitled to it, our official record of the cause of death.

He waved it off. He would not take it.

"Better this way," he said.

There were so many others—a little girl, probably age eight or so, got too close to a Marine checkpoint.

Troops fired warning shots into the pavement. Fragments of the bullet penetrated the vehicle through the floor and badly wounded her lower leg. We treated her on base because we had better medical facilities. After about a week, it was time for her to go home. I went to the hospital to help begin the transfer. We had been receiving intermittent mortar rounds, and the Navy doctors told me she felt the blast waves the prior night and had a hard time sleeping.

"It is time to take you back to your family."

Clad in a bright pink and light blue outfit, she said through an interpreter, "I don't want to go."

"They miss you, I'm sure."

"I feel safer here."

We eventually brought her back to her family in Fallujah. She looked scared. Not afraid of us, or the Marines whose bullets had wounded her, but fearful of what her own hometown had morphed into since the Americans arrived.

I heard shots being fired all the time. Firefights were almost a daily, even hourly, occurrence around our central location. Often it was a group of insurgents, but this time it was not a group, just one person, a kid really, with a hell of a lot of bad luck and no gun.

A slow and mentally challenged Iraqi had approached our main gate. Marines yelled and motioned for him to stop. He could have been a suicide bomber, they explained later. So when he did not stop, they shot him. A round blew off the lower part of his face, severely wounding him. Teeth, tongue, chin, and bone. I understood why the Marines did what they did, but how do you explain that to family members?

I was always the messenger to them in such situations.

The next day, the wounded Iraqi's older brother requested a meeting with me. One on one. On such occasions, Fallujans avoided every Marine they could. He began to unravel in front of me, crying out, saying his brother had just been trying to find his car, to get it back. Marines, he said, had confiscated it. I promised him I would look into the matter.

The next day I saw a couple of junior Marines doing donuts along dirt roads on base, in a Toyota sedan with Iraqi plates on it. I asked Larry what the Holy Hell was going on with Iraqi vehicles at Camp Fallujah. He stopped some Marines, instantly putting the fear of a regimental commander in them, and soon found out we had a corral full of Iraqi cars.

He ordered they be returned to city leaders. I met with several of them in a big sandy lot where the sedans and trucks were assembled. They said thank you, "Shukran," but most of the vehicles were badly beaten up.

All their eyes reflected the same message: *This is not how you win friends in Iraq. This is how you guarantee enemies. This is what gets you Americans killed. This is what gets us Iraqis killed.*

War is impossible to forget.

And of course those of us who experienced it firsthand should not strive to forget just because some, or many, memories are bad or hard or often unwanted. But even (especially?) in Fallujah, we tried, if only for a night, to mute the war outside, to mute the war that had moved inside each of us, deep, as well. During the hardest days, Al "Top" Blankenship, a six-foot-four master sergeant, a native Southerner, used to invite—rather require—all of us to watch *The Andy Griffith Show*. Top would have been a perfect member of the cast: big, friendly, with a slow-moving saunter and neighborly in every way, including with Fallujans. He set up the projector in the CMOC at least once a week, usually Monday nights.

And so in Iraq's most dangerous city, we immersed ourselves in Mayberry, North Carolina—Andy, Opie, Barney, Aunt Bee, Goober, and Gomer Pyle and all the rest. Where the television series scripts included comedic story lines, for example about pickles, moonshine, a lost wallet, cow thefts, counterfeiting, banjo playing, the local barber-shop quartet, and mismatched love interests in town, among dozens of other unwarlike vignettes. All fit the show's buoyant opening music theme ("The Fishin' Hole") and oh-so-carefree whistling.

And yet there was never a true escape for any of us, or very many laughs. Constant mortars, small arms fire, even an occasional RPG impacted our building or compound, forcing Marines to stop, leave the world of Barney Fife, and, once again, help man our fort, the biggest target in the city. Needless to say, the nearby meandering Euphrates River did not serve as a bucolic fishing spot for any of us either.

In all my years in Iraq, I never heard an Iraqi whistle, Mayberry-style.

An Andy Griffith quote echoed with me during that time: "You know when you're young you think you will always be. As you become more fragile, you reflect and you realize how much comfort can come from the past." It was fitting that Don Knotts, the actor who played Deputy Sheriff Barney Fife, had enlisted in the Army. He spent his war entertaining troops—very well, I am sure—in the Pacific theater of World War II as a member of a GI variety show . . . just as he had for us, as well, in Fallujah, sixty-plus years later.

I realized each Marine had his or her own Mayberry, as did I, a place to escape to mentally, no matter in which state of the fifty or the size of our hometowns. In those days, I witnessed how war made everyone fragile—and forced us all to reflect. Fallujah had now become part of that past, part of our new past, and an expanding part of the American past.

Ryan McCurdy's Mayberry?

East Baton Rouge.

Not long after Ryan's death, I visited the infantry company head-quarters next to the CMOC. On the wall, I noticed some Marine graf-fiti: "I was very weary of bartering the lives of young men for worthless real estate. (Then) Lt Dan Marshall speaking of Iwo Jima." Another Marine had added his own postscript to this quote in thicker and darker ink with an arrow pointing down, writing in all caps: WHAT WE SAY NOW IN FALLUJAH.

. . .

Trotter and Doc Reed would still be mourning, unsurprisingly, and remembering that day, posting online tributes in honor of Ryan many years later. The kind of memories in the kind of words about the kind of experiences in war, and the kind of reflections after war, that would never make their way onto etched marble along the National Mall in Washington, D.C.:

> This is SGT Trotter Clifton R. Ryan gave his his life to save mine, out of a act of kindness, careing mabe a bond between Marines no it was pure sacrafice of love for another human-being. As he lay on top of me dieing i remember telling him i loved him and he was going to be alright. when the doc got there i kept trying to tell them to take care of Ryan and leave me be. but no one could hear me because i was shot in the throat so only a whisper came out . Ryan I LOVE YOU SO MUCH!!!!!!!! I think about u every day &every min. I know when i get to heaven ill see u again guarding the gates of that beautiful city they call Heaven" SGT Clifton R Trotter of LUverne AL USA

> My name is HM1Reed i was the corsman assigned to that division he was a good marine and a better friend he passed in my arms after I performed cpr. HE has been on my mind for a while and I am so sorry that it took me so long to write. I did all I could to save him not a day goes by that I think that I could have done more.so please contact me and I will tell you more COrey Reed of waldorf, md

For the veterans of Iraq and Afghanistan, their community, and scars, and pain, and tears, have moved online—a different kind of VFW gathering hall, a digital one. If one looks, if one looks hard enough to find them, they are there. The very personal and the very private made very public, where it is possible to hear the rest of the stories, the rest of their stories.

GENERAL JACK D. RIPPER: Mandrake, do you recall what Clemenceau once said about war?

GROUP CAPTAIN LIONEL MANDRAKE: No, I don't think I do, sir, no.

GENERAL JACK D. RIPPER: He said war was too important to be left to the generals. When he said that, fifty years ago, he might have been right. But today, war is too important to be left to politicians. They have neither the time, the training, nor the inclination for strategic thought.

Dr. Strangelove (1964)

When Senators and Generals Talk

I never imagined a certain subject would ever, could ever, come up in a war zone, let alone in Fallujah of all places, until it did. Death pervaded many more days in Anbar than laughs. Our Iraqi collaborators and their families knew that, just as Marines and their families knew, better than anyone else.

And yet one day a question came up that I could not possibly have predicted. None of us could have—then we heard it.

"General, what about the high cost of dental care?"

On this particular day in August 2006, Indiana congressman Steve Buyer seemed to have rotten teeth on his mind. A Marine friend and I guessed there might have been a House bill he sponsored on the topic. We later would learn our hunch proved right (the representative's brother was a dentist) . . . but still. All in the room were taken aback that he wanted to shift the conversation to flossing habits and the price of root canals. Military leaders and I had just finished briefing him on the violent realities in Anbar, which at that time—in the middle of the Iraq War—was leading to the almost daily death and maiming of numerous people on both sides.

The response from the head of the table came immediately, pitch-perfect in a way that only a Marine general can utter in a combat zone.

"Well, Congressman, I'll make sure all of my Marines get their teeth checked tomorrow."

Every one of us in the crowded conference room chuckled at the Marine general's remark—except the congressman and another VIP who had joined him at Camp Fallujah: the Bush administration's veterans affairs secretary, Jim Nicholson, a Vietnam War veteran, U.S. Military Academy graduate, lawyer, and Colorado real estate developer.

The general had other topics on his mind: like keeping his troops alive.

As did I: keeping Marines alive and keeping our Iraqi collaborators alive as well, or as many as possible.

Unlike our Washington guests, we attended memorial services for grunts blown apart by roadside bombs. Marines, like Ryan McCurdy, had been fatally shot by rounds to the head, neck, chest, and heart by well-trained Al Qaeda snipers wielding Russian-made Dragunov rifles, which had a longer range than the ones used by our own Marine snipers. We had listened to grunts break down during impromptu remarks about their best friends, dead in their teens. I recall one hardened infantry guy in particular. He publicly recounted how a friend, now KIA, had comforted him with bear hugs during the worst days of Fallujah's house-to-house assault. He described a kind of warrior bonding, even a kind of love, rooted in warfare.

Another Marine, who had made the cover of *Time* magazine, told me how a friend had been killed in the kitchen area at the back of a Fallujah house—and how other Marines in his unit believed he had been a coward for not going back into the room. He sounded as if he had already rendered a verdict about himself to himself. Guilty as charged.

All of us in Anbar had other matters than dentistry on our minds—particularly that blunt general (a rugby player in college), who rightly preferred not to talk about teeth. I had joined him on visits to entry control points across the province, listening to him explain to junior Marines how avoiding more EOFs—escalation of force incidents in which Iraqi civilians were shot, sometimes killed or injured, as they drove vehicles toward Marine checkpoints—meant taking on more risk for grunts, for us. They listened. More Marines inevitably got hurt so more Iraqi families would not.

I was relieved the Marines across the rest of the province had missed out on this latest galling episode of "D.C. Does Iraq"—deployments of a different kind, the most surreal kind of interaction I had experienced to date. The Marine general would later attest by email from his follow-on tour that I had remembered our brush-teeth-and-floss meeting correctly, describing it as the most "bizarre" visit by a congressman he could recall.

I had not imagined it after all. I wished I had.

In both Iraq and Afghanistan, members of Congress traveled thousands of miles to see "the troops." Yet, they arrived at Camp Fallujah with stylish Tumi bags, usually carried by staff, only to stay for a few hours before transiting back to plush accommodations in Kuwait or Amman or Dubai. Their questions often surprised us, sometimes unsettled us, and rarely reassured us. We always hoped otherwise. One congressman requested time to watch college football (Oklahoma vs. Texas) rather than meet with Iraqi leaders. A former senator insisted on seeing "the real" Fallujah, much too dangerous at the time, so Marines took him on a "battlefield circulation" tour of "Fallujah's outskirts"—which was an uninhabitable desert area between bases. He never knew the difference. He did not need to know. He was a lot safer that way. So were his Marine escorts.

There were many other memorable visits in both Iraq and Afghanistan.

Far from Fallujah and years later in Afghanistan's Helmand province, for example, one congresswoman, wearing heels, wanted to visit an Afghan market . . . to shop, for what we were not sure, but she proved to be a star among the Afghans. She sat on the floor, ate with the tribal elders—everything offered, including stringy, undercooked goat meat. Three male congressmen traveling with her, nearly half her age, all wimped out. The Afghans noticed the difference in grit and spunk and level of respect toward them.

A senator visiting Helmand's Garmsir District wondered whether he needed to wear body armor as he strolled along shops and among Afghans. A Marine general, acting as a host, replied, "I'll leave that up to you, sir—guess it depends on your level of insurance." It was Senator Mitch McConnell.

Despite some of their inexplicable behavior, at least these elected officials had made the effort to come all the way over. They deserved credit for that, even if none of them warranted an automatic pass on what they did and said once on the ground.

Theirs was the Middle East as viewed mostly from the Amman Four Seasons—and then there was the Middle East as viewed from the middle of Anbar province, our daily deadly grind. State Department officials abbreviate these visits as CODELs, for Congressional Delegations. European stopovers usually found a way into many, if not most, trips abroad. Paris and London and Rome undoubtedly helped platoons of U.S. politicians gear up for their war zone treks and readjust postwar with some R&R. European capitals meant for these nondiplomats better food, lots of alcohol, and plenty of protocol. Baghdad and Kabul meant rice, tea, and a lot lost in translation in palace parlor rooms.

A friend recounted a post-9/11 CODEL to Paris that has since entered State Department lore. A group of House representatives and "spouses" stayed at the Hotel Intercontinental (635 euros, or over $1,000 at the time, per night). Before arriving in France, the politicos sent a forty-four-page fax detailing what every member wanted in their minibar. "Not Smirnoff Vodka, but Grey Goose. Not Seagram's gin, but Tanqueray. Not Johnnie Walker Black, but Johnnie Walker Blue. Red Bull, fresh-squeezed pomegranate juice, and Pop Tarts, as well as a premium selection of French wine and cheese upon arrival." Once in France, the CODEL received a private tour of the Louvre, "pushing people out of the way in front of the *Mona Lisa* and then jumping a very long elevator queue to go up the Eiffel Tower."

When departing France via C-130 military aircraft, a congressman showed up with two full-sized bronze stags and two 10-foot-by-15-foot paintings. The amount of champagne the group had bought (at discount at the U.S. embassy shop) and later loaded onto the plane's pallets was so great that there was not enough room for the statues or paintings.

My friend concluded by saying, "So the paintings were shipped, not knowing if we could tack on the shipping bill to the CODEL's travel account."

This diplomat recalled top Baghdad moments as well while I was in Anbar. A senator falling asleep in a meeting with Iraqi prime minister

Ibrahim al-Jaafari, "who liked to show off his knowledge of U.S. history, such as Ibrahim Lincoln cutting down the cherry tree." Another prominent senator and onetime Republican presidential candidate insisted on a sidebar discussion with Prime Minister Nouri al-Maliki and had "a tantrum in Maliki's lobby." He refused to leave until he saw the Iraqi leader.

And when he did, the senator's question?

"So, how's it going?"

We all knew the two-word answer to that kind of question.

Not. Well.

(Years later, the same senior senator would lecture a top Marine general at the end of a Senate confirmation hearing, going so far as to publicly question whether the combat-tested nominee understood the scale and toll of U.S. casualties in Iraq. Unlike the scowling and sanctimonious-sounding senator, a key supporter of the Iraq invasion, the general had attended many KIA memorials in Anbar where Taps echoed across remote desert outposts. And, unbeknownst to the dismissive politician, the Marine leader under cross-examination still kept with him a list of the names of all the service members who died during his twelve-month deployment—including those from the senator's home state of Arizona.)

Before CODELs landed in Iraq or Afghanistan, U.S. military units would poll troops on which state they called home, by birth or by upbringing. After finding a match, corporals, lieutenants, and sergeants would be asked to sit amiably at a table in a chow hall and interact with their elected representatives over cafeteria food. I noticed how many of the pols mostly pecked at the bland culinary options in their trays while draining Diet Cokes. Jet lag got the better of most, no matter one's exalted title. Military photographers would capture each CODEL within carefully aligned digital camera frames. Before long, pictures of smiling politicians alongside captive but excited, often bashful, grunts would be posted online. These "troop morale" visits amounted to good politicking back home, even as the wars became increasingly unpopular—and forgotten.

Who would not want to see Representative "Smith" who had gone to Washington shaking the hand of the local high school graduate who had gone off to war?

What was left out of these Kodak moments in the post-Kodak age happened behind closed doors. When the generals and I met the politicians; when the generals and I heard the politicians. Such occasions usually left me more disillusioned than when I first entered the room. I would like to characterize what the generals thought as well, but probably should not. Let's just say our forced smiles most often mirrored the politicians' forced smiles.

I remember one junior congressman, a former service member no less, who walked into a Marine commanding general's office wearing a backpack and with his shirt untucked.

The first words out of his mouth?

"General, you're not reading terrorists their Miranda rights, are you?" he said flippantly, as if we were treating dangerous detainees as U.S. citizens with constitutional protections against self-incrimination.

His lecture went on for several minutes. The general and I opted not to lecture him back about the more important issues in our bomb-filled province.

Most VIPs looked nervous boarding and exiting Black Hawks—and for good reason. Statistically, the most likely way of dying at war is in an "air mishap." Senators John Kerry, Chuck Hagel, and Joe Biden once experienced an emergency landing in a mountainous part of Afghanistan. Their Black Hawk helicopter pilot had wisely opted not to continue flying in a snowstorm. The cold senators waited for a few hours until they were picked up by a ground convoy from Bagram Air Base. We all were relieved they were safe; too many of their colleagues in the Senate never visited either war zone.

Beyond the surreal/bizarre exchange about Marine teeth, there were other notable instances. As memorable, but not in the way any of us preferred to recall even years later, when Washington came to the front lines. Then quickly left, while we stayed, month after month, year after year, into the decade-plus category.

Take for example one CODEL to Camp Ramadi. By December 2006, like much of Anbar, the base had suffered the brunt of the Sunni-led insurgency. It had the feel of a massive bunker. Flights there risked small arms fire, including our early morning helicopter ride from Camp Fallujah. Before taking my seat, I asked a top Marine a question in the form of a statement really.

"We know what he wants. More troops here. The Surge. We don't need any more, at least in Anbar, right?"

"We will always take what we can get."

True, the military always could use more to do more, but to what end? More lives lost. More legs lost. More psyches damaged. And, yes, more medals won.

The brief conversation under rotating helicopter blades did not sit well with me. Not because of what the Marine had said but rather the situation we found ourselves in. Washington seemed intent on saying to general after general: go, fight, win, and see you back here when the war is over. And so this particular meeting with this particular politician would be especially important. For it included a veteran-turned-politician and a man we all knew wanted to be commander in chief one day. And might be.

His name: John McCain.

As the Marine high command based in Fallujah and I walked into the cramped, un-fancy conference room, I noted this CODEL included not only Senator McCain but also his Senate colleagues, the "independent Democrat" Joe Lieberman, Air Force Reservist Colonel Lindsey Graham (the other two who comprised the "Three Amigos"), and Maine's Susan Collins. There might have been others there too, but it is these four I remember.

A few minutes into the brief, McCain raised his voice my way after I offered a differing perspective on Iraq's future. I had intended to remain silent, but the Arizona senator posed a question about Fallujah. Since I had spent more time there than any American, Marine Major General Richard Zilmer turned his head slightly, asking me to reply . . . which led me to decide to extend my commentary into the real issue as I saw it: to surge or not to surge tens of thousands of U.S. troops into Iraq.

This was the biggest debate driving political discussions in Washington, the overall strategic question centered on troop levels, not Fallujah's internal dynamics.

McCain believed a troop surge would stabilize Iraq, a position he had made clear weeks earlier as the bipartisan Iraq Study Group finalized its recommendations—which would advocate against a surge.

"Senator, if I could raise another subject, even with a troop surge there doesn't seem to be the political will among Iraq's leaders to—"

He interjected right away.

"You tell me, when has there been political progress in any insurgency without security first?"

That is when his fist hit the table. Not a slam per se but an audible enough smack.

I kept my mouth shut and the conversation moved on. McCain added minutes later a clarification, rather unexpectedly. "I did not intend to denigrate anyone's comments earlier."

Denigrate. It was the first and only time I had heard that word used in a meeting at any point in my State Department career. Some words stick. "Denigrate" did.

To McCain's credit, it came across like a half apology, even if his prior commentary and tone sure sounded denigrating to me, probably to others as well who called Anbar home. His peace offering accepted, the discussion continued, but I wondered whether I had said too much. McCain was a leading senator and self-described "maverick"—a word I liked; Washington needed more. Maybe I was out of line. I respected his story, as my own father and two uncles had served in Vietnam, one uncle almost dying there.

Like my dad, McCain had been part of a "surge" in that other unnecessary war a commander in chief—with a lot of support in Washington—had escalated.

But I stayed quiet, out of respect. (I remembered his first visit to Camp Fallujah, in late 2004. The biggest battle of the Iraq War had just ended, or mostly. Almost a hundred Marines had been killed. McCain stood up in the briefing room, in front of rows of troops, wanting to thank them. Overcome with emotion, he could not finish his remarks. All of us were moved by the former Vietnam POW that day.)

During the same December 2006 CODEL, a Ramadi-based Army brigade commander detailed the "Sunni Awakening" in Anbar. It was all U.S. Army, without any reference to the long-standing role of Marines serving in the province, including the sizable contingent based in the provincial capital. This prompted a Marine leader to remark to me under his breath, "Sure was a lot of 'Marine' in that brief to the senators, huh."

"Yeah, I noticed that as well," I said.

The Sunni Awakening Myth in Anbar had been born.

While the U.S. Army would seek and get a majority of the credit—there was plenty to go around—it was U.S. Marines who had most effectively and most persistently engaged Anbar tribes throughout the war in Iraq's Sunni west. Everyone knew the United States Marine Corps comprised the strongest tribe—especially Iraqis, not just other U.S. military branches. The USMC's olive-branch outreach and strategic shift toward Anbar tribes had started in 2004, when U.S. civilian leaders in Baghdad and Washington showed little to no interest. I had been around since then, so I knew the details well beyond the Power-Point slides. Not enough others did.

Senator Collins came up to me after the meeting ended. The senator said she shared my concerns about whether a large troop surge would equal lasting political agreements in Baghdad, beyond any short-term security gains.

"I hope we're wrong," we both said almost at the same time.

Half a year earlier, in summer 2006, a top Fallujah leader, the city council secretary, told me Sunnis had begun to "awaken" (his word, and expressed in English) in Anbar province. I would have told the senators this story perhaps if, well, the tone had been better and more conducive to frank dialogue in the room that day. I reported this unexpected good news to the embassy—the first time I had heard an Iraqi use, in English no less, the words "awaken" and "awakening." Outreach efforts by Marines and me to tribal leaders, including those that had been attempted early on in Amman, were finally paying off. Reconciliation between former enemies continued, if quietly.

This earliest part of the story is what McCain, and the Army brigade commander for that matter, did not hear. Marines in the room that day were too uncharacteristically humble (and/or too annoyed) to elaborate. The dynamics were complex and any U.S. military leader, in whichever branch, would have been wiser to give more credit to Iraqis sooner versus claiming ownership of any "awakened" part of Iraq. Such a gesture would have been both accurate and generous.

We Americans were always quickest to cite our "successes" (and implied heroics) while being slow to acknowledge Iraqi efforts and sacrifice (very real and very extensive).

One insurgent, who fled Baghdad when violent sectarianism had reached its high point, put the remarkable shift this way: "We are only 20 percent against you, 80 percent against the Shia militias."

That 20 percent enemy remained deadly, expert at attacking and killing us.

I wished Senator McCain had been able to interrogate such an Iraqi in a nondenigrating way, get an unfiltered take on their motivations—and persistent concerns about a Baghdad government more directed toward Tehran than rapprochement with moderate Sunnis.

Senator John Warner became a regular visitor to Iraq and my favorite political VIP. It seemed to me the more the war went badly, the more the conscience of this Senate giant got to him. The onetime husband of movie star Elizabeth Taylor (her sixth) helped lead the floor debate in support of resolutions related to the Iraq War authorization. A stately Virginian—gray hair, high cheekbones, a cadence and Southern demeanor that reminded me of Gregory Peck's Atticus Finch—he came to Anbar to listen more than to talk. In one visit, two of us from Camp Fallujah convoyed with Marine Major General Steve Johnson to brief Warner, Senator John Kerry, and Senator Ted Stevens of Alaska.

Beyond Warner's gentlemanly ways, I remember a few other things about that briefing. How John Kerry wolfed down an Otis Spunkmeyer muffin in record time. (Who could blame him? He seemed to be starving. I myself had wolfed down plenty of the chocolate variety in prior months.) Ted Stevens asked us repeatedly about possible WMD that U.S. troops had yet to find "buried"—but would, he assured us, with new technology—under Iraq's sandy western desert. Some variation of "No, Senator, no WMD here in Iraq" from all of us did not seem to persuade him.

But it is what happened after the briefing that has stayed with me most. Per standard practice, the three senators met their uniformed "constituents" on base. The Marines, about a dozen, stood attentively as each senator made his way down the line—Warner with Virginians, Kerry with Massachusettsans, Stevens with Alaskans.

Toward the end of the visit, I thanked Senator Warner for being one of the few "leaders" who made it all the way from Washington to one of the most remote and dangerous places in Iraq.

His reply was as simple as it was devastatingly reflective of his mindset. "I am not feeling very much like a leader right now."

I did not ask him why. His expression seemed to reinforce my impression: the chairman of the Senate Armed Services Committee had mounting doubts about the Iraq War. He had helped ensure the invasion had congressional support, and yet I sensed a genuine acknowledgment that he would not continue to support the war if he believed it no longer worth the human cost. He was the type of politician, a statesman, I could never imagine talking about troops' teeth in a war zone.

We had just reminded the Senate CODEL he led about the number of KIA and WIA in Anbar, which continued to top the list of U.S. casualties. He looked pained the entire time.

Once back in Washington, Warner—a World War II veteran—quoted a Marine who had told him the situation in Iraq was moving "sideways." He agreed with the candid assessment. This both surprised and unnerved the Bush White House. If they were losing Chairman Warner, a Republican legend and congressional power broker, they would be without their standard-bearer who wielded great influence over dozens of other senators—and those senators' war-related votes. Reading his comments in the papers, I was reminded of a quote by that most supreme of war-tested politicos, Winston Churchill: "When the eagles are silent, the parrots begin to jabber."

On the same visit a friendly female helicopter pilot shook hands with Senator Kerry as I stood a few feet away from them. Months later, while piloting a CH-46 Sea Knight, an insurgent rocket brought her helicopter down near Fallujah, killing all seven on board. Captain Jennifer Harris died at age twenty-eight, a native of Swampscott, Massachusetts (pop. 14,412). A Marine friend later told me that she had volunteered last minute for the flight, only days before her scheduled redeployment home. She wanted her last flight to be with the medevac crew known as "The Purple Foxes."

Every time a group of senators visited, I wanted to ask them if they had read the 2003 National Intelligence Estimate (NIE) report on Iraq's alleged WMD. Had they made the time to review in detail this ninety-two-page classified version—versus the five-page unclassified one—before deciding whether to support the invasion of Iraq?

Only a handful ever read it, the long version that went into a lot more detail about State Department and Energy Department doubts about the alleged Iraqi WMD program.

Indeed *The Washington Post* reported just six senators in fact had, page after page—they had to sign logs to enter a classified reading room, so there is a record. But I never had the guts to ask elected representatives when they visited us in Iraq this straightforward question and a follow-up one.

If they had not read the NIE before voting for the Iraq War authorization, well, why not?

Why. The. Hell. Not.

I had images in my mind of many fancy dinners in D.C., while senatorial "homework" of the gravest kind went ignored and many lobbyist checks were deposited into (D) and (R) reelection accounts.

Senator Sam Brownback of Kansas and his staffers must have wished they had stayed home by the end of their own CODEL visit. In February 2005, they ventured all the way into Fallujah, downtown, beyond the usual confines of Camp Fallujah. South Carolina senator Jim DeMint, Ohio congressman Rob Portman, and South Carolina congressman Bob Inglis joined them in Iraq. I had helped persuade Lieutenant General Sattler, the commanding general at the time, that senators had become somewhat bored with Green Zone visits (embassy colleagues had related as much), so perhaps they should see the "real" Iraq. Why not help them do that in Anbar, provided we not get any of them killed or hurt?

"If they say they went to Baghdad, that's one thing. But if they say they were in Fallujah, that is going to help us get support we need to help rebuild the city for a long time."

"Okay, we'll try it with the next group," Sattler replied.

I pictured what bragging rights a "CODEL to Fallujah" must have entailed in Senate cloakrooms and coffee sessions.

Brownback and his colleagues would be our first group to be escorted into meetings with Fallujah's leaders. The mayor, the police chief, the top tribal and religious leaders—all of whom trusted me when I asked them to show up for a meeting, even when I could not share with them exactly the why behind my request or with whom. Such situations only increased the danger for Iraqis, making each Fallujan appear even more as the Americans' suspicious collaborators gathering in secret.

And yet they showed up—again and again and again.

Marine Captain Dave Meadows, fluent in Arabic and one of the most popular Americans with Fallujans, and I arrived early. We wanted to be sure Fallujah's leaders were briefed minutes before the special visitors arrived. Senators tended to prefer formalities and reinforcement of their special status in the U.S. political hierarchy.

Marines passed on to us that the CODEL convoy had left the gates at Camp Fallujah. We could expect them to arrive in fifteen or twenty minutes. After they had just passed the midway point, we heard mortars exploding in the general vicinity. They did not fall on top of us, or on Senator Brownback's Humvee, but close enough that the blast waves were heard and felt by all. That included the no longer cocooned senator and his entourage. Marines ordered the convoy to continue to the CMOC, the site of the meeting, passing the long line of Iraqi vehicles waiting at one of the multiple city checkpoints to enter the city. Marines stood guard at each location, randomly checking vehicles for car bombs. Hundreds.

That was *their* nine-to-five job. A bit stressful, you could say, and a lot more stressful than senatorial duty in Washington, one might argue. Perhaps the senator and his colleagues noticed the difference in job descriptions.

When the CMOC doors opened and Brownback entered with a few staffers, they looked scared, pale, and on edge. Dave and I glanced at each other, enjoying the moment. We were relieved the mortars had not landed too close, but we knew our D.C. guests had heard what war really sounded like. Felt like. No escape from it in Anbar.

As they sat around the table to listen to Fallujah's leaders, the VIPs from Washington tried to stay composed, but it was clear they wanted out of Anbar's Dodge—and fast.

After they departed, I told Dave that the next time a senator visited, we should call our quasi-insurgent Iraqi friends (those Fallujans in survival mode who worked with us and sometimes against us in parallel) to make sure the mortars fell a bit closer but not close enough to do anyone any harm. Such was Fallujah humor. But we were only half kidding.

That same afternoon, our Iraqi collaborators left on their own, on foot, unarmed. Theirs was always the biggest target on any back in the City of Mosques. Our side wore body armor, boots, and carried rifles. They wore dishdashas, sandals, and carried prayer beads.

. . .

Across seven years in both wars, I witnessed only one senator bring anything to give to frontline troops. In Fallujah, Senator Jack Reed, a former Army officer and paratrooper, asked Marine leaders and me to make sure troops got the Dunkin' Donuts coffee bags he had brought over with him. He and a top aide placed a stack on the general's conference room table. We delivered them.

Senator Reed (another eagle) left a lasting impression, like Senator Warner had, in all the complimentary ways we hoped to see in so many more of our elected leaders—but largely did not. Not only had he brought coffee, but the Rhode Island senator asked good questions. As did John Warner, who showed he had a conscience. The Virginian helped start an unwise war, then he took a stand to try to end it.

Both senators came across as un-D.C. They cared about what happened after a congressional vote for, or against, war. Too many Washington politicians (jabbering parrots) seemed to have come to see us in Iraq and Afghanistan for different reasons, perhaps mostly self-interested ones. Hard and personal reflections about the wars, John Warner–like, required effort and honesty. It required character—"A man's character is his fate," as Greek philosopher Heraclitus famously said.

There is one congressman on a CODEL I never met, but wished I had. Walter Jones represents a North Carolina district that includes Marine Corps base Camp Lejeune. A former supporter of the Iraq War, he later believed the invasion to be an unconscionable failing. He has written to all family members of American service members killed in Iraq and Afghanistan.

The Republican politician told a Young Americans for Liberty group (a self-described "pro-liberty organization" with chapters on hundreds of college campuses in the United States) that "Congress will not hold anyone to blame. Lyndon Johnson's probably rotting in hell right now because of the Vietnam War, and he probably needs to move over for Dick Cheney."

Oh, you're marvellous! All those ribbons. You gotta tell
me what they all mean. But not now.

Sara al-Jumaili and
the Last Grand Mufti

CODELs never seemed to arrive when we had the best case studies
to show them what could, and too often did, go wrong in war. Senators believed in U.S. military heroics, and there were plenty of well-
publicized examples of that. But it seemed they had a harder time
understanding when things fell apart. Good intentions badly implemented with deadly consequences. SEALs and Delta Force teams
behaving badly and irresponsibly, at times, irked Marine infantry captains, corporals, and generals. No case study showed that more clearly
in Fallujah, and at much personal risk to our Iraqi partners, than what
happened to a young Iraqi named Sara al-Jumaili.

Her story shattered much of the equilibrium that Marines and I had
worked so hard to achieve. It did not need to be so.

Members of an Army Delta Force team detained her twice about
midway through my time in Fallujah. They held Sara, a young woman
from Fallujah and member of a prominent local Sunni tribe, against her
will—enraging the local population to near revolt.

We had a problem suddenly. A big one.

We needed the help of the imams, needed the help of Fallujah's grand mufti.

The junior imams showed up first, as they always had. Those with the real power waited a few days before meeting with us on the most sensitive subjects. For a long time now, Al Qaeda in Iraq had intimidated Muslim leaders, forcing the imams out of their mosques to the outskirts of the city in an attempt to co-opt them. Failing that, they had begun to kill them—Kamal's fate. Even Sheikh Hamza had at one point been run out of town, to a satellite community called Ameriyah. A mufti scared by Al Qaeda, though not controlled by them.

But now he had since returned and, as always, the grand mufti looked as humble as he was sincere in words and actions. I understood why terrorists and associated hard-line ex-Baathists feared him and his personal following. They numbered in the tens of thousands, an army of the faithful that formed the most important power bloc of residents, not just believers, in Iraq's City of Mosques. Fallujah's imams led by Hamza—which means "steadfast" in Arabic—approached us warily, slowly. Gray-bearded in white robes, hunched over, their palms rested atop Qurans.

When Sheikh Hamza and his inner circle finally returned to the center of the city, a sense of possibility came with them. Not only had he deescalated rising tensions about the Potato Factory, he also encouraged Fallujans to participate in the referendum on the new constitution. Sheikh Hamza and another imam made their case to me in private conversations, which I dutifully reported to Baghdad and Washington. The biggest step forward was Hamza's decision to issue a fatwa. In his words: "The city is completely ready for the referendum, but the more important question is whether appropriate changes will be made to the constitution. If there is not, we will reject it. We would like to vote for it, but not in its present form."

I had just heard news that would make Robert Ford and Ambassador Negroponte very pleased. The Sunnis seemed to be giving democracy, however circumscribed in a war zone, a chance. Along with Hamza, another senior imam, Sheikh Ahmed al-Janabi, said he had delivered five Friday sermons urging participation in the political process, although Fallujah's council of imams had not yet agreed to a joint position. Then came his warning: "I will vote no because of dangers in certain paragraphs [of the constitution], many of which could lead to a splitting of the country . . . you will have many different parties with no centralized control."

I conveyed these mixed signals to Baghdad, but politics rarely drove most conversations in Fallujah. U.S. military operations did.

Case in point: when the Delta Force squad detained Sara al-Jumaili, the city's attention morphed from ballot boxes to fury.

It happened as these things always did. (Still do?) Without any warning to us, Black Hawk helicopters descended over Fallujah on a cool October night in 2005. The team located Sara, put a blindfold over her eyes and bound her hands, and flew away with her to a base well outside the Marines' area of operation, declaring they needed to question her about Zarqawi, Al Qaeda in Iraq's self-proclaimed leader and one-time Fallujah resident.

An infantry grunt said his platoon had heard rumors that the housing compound they were asked to help secure was home "to Zarqawi's girlfriend. A lot of us got a kick out of that, even if we didn't know if it was true or not."

The corporal added, "We ransacked her house, but the only thing we found was a lot of anti-American propaganda type shit buried in the yard."

If any city would have a lot of that kind of material, it was Fallujah. Not a crime in Iraq—or in the U.S. of A. itself for that matter.

All of our hard work began to disintegrate right away, based on a decision the Marines and I had no input on whatsoever. We were Fallujah's full-time residents and most knowledgeable about the various sticky webs of egos, deceit, and vendettas layered and intertwined within the city.

Male Fallujans fixated on the worst conspiracy scenario imaginable: a young woman taken from their hometown in darkness by helicopter-borne American "brutes"—their image of bearded, muscled, Oakley'd, and very aggressive and very well armed operators. Minds became inflamed. The detention risked becoming the ideal flashpoint extremists needed to turn Fallujans against us, and for good.

Sheikh Hamza refused to join others and rile up the people. The courageous grand mufti would not be intimidated, but he was still afraid of Al Qaeda and associated insurgents. While sitting one-on-one in the sandbagged CMOC compound surrounded by razor wire, he offered brief but pointed comments. The mufti's message was clear. "You Americans are putting me personally at risk. The terrorists want me to support public demonstrations, but I will not do it."

I knew he spoke the truth. His decision put him in a precarious and exposed position. Long considered untouchable because of his status and popularity, he had now openly defied Al Qaeda. He had defied Zarqawi himself.

"Sheikh Hamza, I will do everything I can, but Marines do not have Sara."

The grand mufti did not add anything more and departed into the street, without looking back and without bodyguards.

It was the last time I saw him.

The Marine two-star commanding general, who shared my concerns, said the matter was out of his hands. Delta and SEAL teams had a separate chain of command—all the way back to Joint Special Operations Command at MacDill Air Force Base in Tampa, Florida, under Lieutenant General Stanley McChrystal. Technically, not even the top four-star general in Baghdad could order Sara's release.

Iraqis, including the top leaders we dealt with most frequently, did not understand how our conventional forces were separate from our Special Operations Forces (SOF), including high-velocity Delta Force and SEAL teams. Our internal organization charts did not matter to them; they wanted Sara back. Marine operations officers, in charge of de-conflicting airspace and battlefield priorities, often complained to me in private about the special prerogatives the elite teams had. Sometimes both sides played well, infantry and SOF, other times not so much. Besides, Marines and soldiers were fighting the biggest parts of the war, not our most elite units. The narrowly focused nighttime missions conducted by SEALs and Delta Force units usually lasted a few hours at most, not the week upon week upon week of effort that had come to define our counterinsurgency strategy.

I had few options but decided to act outside my usual State Department channels and directly contacted General George Casey, the senior U.S. general in Iraq. We had established an informal back channel via email by then. I found some comfort in telling myself with pre-act-of-insubordination logic, "What is Washington going to do, send me to Fallujah as punishment?" I also needed to reinforce with him that the top U.S. government focus in Fallujah remained the Iraqi political process—we had just had an Iraqi vote on their constitution. That is, trying to get Sunnis to participate and not shun their role in the "new" Iraq. He knew this, but perhaps despite his top rank also was constrained by special operators with special prerogatives and separate chain of command.

So I sent General Casey, the only four-star in the country, an email—"Sara's face will launch a thousand IEDs in Fallujah." When Friday prayers commenced the following day and if she still remained in our custody, I predicted uncontrollable violence. Radical clerics were on the verge of ordering a citywide revolt. Even Iraqi friends began to boycott meetings and warn of a return to bloodshed. I followed up with another warning from my keyboard in downtown Fallujah: "It is 1651 [4:51 p.m.] on Thursday. If Sara al-Jumaili is not released before Friday prayers, Marines and civilians will die. I am going on the record now."

This message amounted to what Marines called a "red star cluster"—a full-on SOS in military slang. If and when used, there had better be a good reason why. I had one. In several earlier instances, U.S. troops and Fallujah civilians had been killed when demonstrations erupted into violence. Insurgents and terrorists knew how to get us to react—and overreact. In spring 2003, just after the invasion, for example, U.S. soldiers fired hundreds of rounds at a combustible crowd near a school, leaving several dead, including children. An Army soldier and friend, who was there at the time, described hearing the "wailing of Fallujah mothers all night long, and the next morning, little kids' shoes filled with blood." All it took was one insurgent shooting his weapon in the air during a protest march for a Marine to engage. The crossfire would guarantee casualties on both sides.

General Casey listened and ensured a speedy release, cc'ing me on his message to the three-star McChrystal in Florida. Casey, wisely, was showing the JSOC commander what could go wrong—and was, quickly, going wrong in the iconic city of Fallujah, with the political and security risks outweighing any potential Delta Force mission gains.

I also sent a similar message to a close State Department contact in Tampa, who was serving as the political adviser to the four-star CENT-COM (the U.S. military's regional command responsible for all troops deployed to the Middle East) commander. I asked whether any top civilians in the U.S. government were closely overseeing these operators, or at least informed about the details of the missions. He said he would look into the matter.

Luckily, the Delta team brought Sara al-Jumaili back later that evening, back to Camp Fallujah. She arrived by helicopter blindfolded. Marines then transferred her to the CMOC, where I oversaw Sara's release back to Fallujah's mayor, Sheikh Dhari, who met us close to midnight for the handoff.

It was then I saw Sara for the first time after being escorted, eyes covered, into the CMOC's main meeting hall by a female Marine, with others lining the walls. She had dark straight hair, a slight build, and a shyness and quiet composure about her that did not yell "terrorist"— the short-lived, explosive claim as to why she needed to be detained in the first place. Sara said nothing, but as she reached for a cup of water placed before her, I saw her recoil. This was not a good sign. We were not trying to poison her, but given what she had just gone through, the thought might have crossed her mind. Mayor Dhari hurried forward and grabbed both of my hands in thanks before escorting her into a waiting vehicle.

Could Sara have had ties to Zarqawi? Perhaps. But the case was never made to the Marines or to me. We had built a relationship with Fallujans, hard earned, and had the most to lose. The rage of the streets would have equaled more roadside bombs. It was a question of their collective sense of honor. Sunni men would never trust a woman to be in Americans' hands, no matter our explanation.

After Sara's release, a senior tribal leader—Sheikh Thamer again, who had come up with the unforgettable "food poisoning" explanation earlier—told me the tribes had decided to kill her. I asked him to repeat what he had just said.

"We have decided to kill her."

He said Fallujah could not risk having Sara taken for a third round of questioning. He was not kidding. They had done the math: one life or many? I immediately requested they not take such a step "officially on behalf of the U.S. government but also speaking as a friend of Fallujah." Thamer tipped his head forward, but only slightly, appearing as if he was still considering what to do.

The war had changed me, but I held on to an earlier version of myself. Barely, I had to admit, a disconcerting acknowledgment. An old, before-war, and a new, at-war, self merged together. While I believed they should not kill Sara, there was a hard logic at work among the tribes. A third Delta Force operation, a third detention of her, would have meant scores dead, Iraqi and American, as Fallujah's minaret skyline filled with bullets flying above and blood running below. This kind of career dynamic would never be incorporated into any of my annual State Department employee evaluations, which lacked boxes to check for "pre-war" and "post-war" qualities and lessons. I wanted to scrawl on the forms:

"FALLUJAH"

In bold and in all caps and maybe even with an exclamation point or two. One word, one place, sometimes can explain everything.

With Sara's return, the city quieted, and top Sunnis in Baghdad conveyed relief to our embassy leadership. Ambassador Ford would later tell me that a senior Sunni politician, Tariq al-Hashimi, had alerted him about the firestorm the detention had caused. We barely avoided a rampage, one that neither Marines nor I could have contained despite our solid and hard-won relationships on the ground.

Five days after Marines and I celebrated Thanksgiving, a month after Sara's release, terrorists gunned down Sheikh Hamza outside his unpretentious and unprotected mosque. The grand mufti's white robe turned crimson as steel-cased slugs pierced his chest. The leader who had long been deemed untouchable—un-killable—died. Another Fallujah tragedy—the list of dead was already long and would only get longer.

Fallujans by the thousands gathered at their mufti's grave. I viewed images captured from a surveillance drone directly above his burial. We were voyeurs, even though Hamza was my friend. I imagined SEALs and Delta Force watched too, but not realizing the connection between their operation and this funeral. All those Fallujans, the greatest gathering I had ever seen in the city, moved slowly, with many staying hours at Hamza's gravesite. They had lost their beloved leader, their revered spiritual leader, Fallujah's most moral one even in the face of Al Qaeda death threats. I could not help but think that Hamza's death was akin to an Iraqi version of Henry Purcell's "Dido's Lament," a story full of war, but instead of her suicide and an aria, his was an assassination and a chorus quieted. An entire community of the faithful left to lament him, left to remember him. ("When I am laid, am laid in earth . . . Remember me, remember me, but ah! forget my fate. Remember me, but ah! forget my fate.")

Iraq's City of Mosques, the first time in a long while, fell silent. The sounds of war and the sounds of the muezzins silenced by shared sorrow. But I wanted to yell. I wanted to yell so loud that Baghdad and Washington and especially Joint Special Operations Command in Tampa could hear my voice. Anger so deep, if conveyed in an email or call to the embassy or D.C., might finally get me kicked out of the State Department.

Looking back, it might have been worth it. Irrevocable insubordination—but with cause.

With so much on my mind, and so much soul-deep sadness mixed with quiet anger in me, I came close to requesting a Marine convoy. One that would take me to the middle of the cemetery, the risks be damned, so that I could pay my respects. Confess. That would have been stupid and suicidal even, but also the honorable thing to do. The right thing to do—what a real friend should do, by instinct and without hesitation, at the end of another friend's life.

And yet I would be putting young Marines' lives at risk, and I could not do that. Hamza's death was enough. Far too many Marines, young and old, had already been killed in Iraq.

So instead, I stared into a computer screen. To my left and right sat committed and efficient lance corporals and sergeants and captains and a lieutenant colonel or two managing Fallujah's persistent needs: still the repair of those electricity lines, still an unfinished and multimillion-dollar sewer, still the soccer fields, still the road repairs, still mosque "refurbishment" projects.

It is likely Fallujans had heard the drone hovering above. To us it always sounded like a flying lawn mower. To them, it must have sounded like something else, whatever the metaphor or metaphors. But the message remained: *The Americans are watching us closely, during the funeral of our grand mufti, in our most sorrowful moment, in an ancient city built under mosques, not drones.*

I never felt as far away from Fallujah, or from America and the government I represented, as I did that day. I wanted to swat every drone right out of the sky, everything detached and clinical and mechanical and cold that our drones represented. The exact wrong face and misdirected gaze of America and not nearly as omniscient an overwatch asset of Iraqis and Iraq as we imagined our dear and increasingly expensive drones to be. On such a day, Fallujans deserved a bit of privacy—a lot of privacy. They were not in a mood to revolt. They were in a mood to mourn.

After Sheikh Hamza's assassination, moderate clerics fled en masse to Syria, to a place known as "Little Fallujah" because of the number of Fallujans who had relocated there. A half year later, the terrorist leader Abu Musab al-Zarqawi—the Delta Force unit's target—lay dead, killed by an F-16 laser-guided bomb strike in Baqubah, hundreds of miles away from Fallujah. More Marines and Iraqi civilians would die in the city as anti-American imams gained influence. When I later inquired about Sara al-Jumaili, an Iraqi friend told me, "We took care of that problem." I could only assume they killed her. While I had made the case to spare her, the tribal leaders seemed hesitant. Then another Fallujan, a town lawyer, added they had forced her to marry and move to a remote part of the province. He sounded mostly convincing, but I will never know for sure.

Sara might have become a casualty of the Delta Force raid, after all.

I emailed Larry Nicholson, who was back at Camp Pendleton. "You'll never believe what a Delta Team just did, twice."

"I can imagine," he replied.

"It is worse. What happened got Sheikh Hamza killed."

Years later I raised the matter with General McChrystal. The top coalition commander in Afghanistan and I were waiting for Ambassador Richard Holbrooke to arrive from Pakistan, transferring from a C-130 transport plane to a helicopter (called a "tail swap"), as America's top diplomat for the region continued his journey farther into Afghanistan.

Given the 115-degree temperature, I had a water bottle in hand. McChrystal did not. He reminded me of a reptile, in his element, weathered by sun and sand, not needing much to survive in the harsh environment. A perfect fit for the war zones. I liked him.

"Mind if we talk about Fallujah?"

"Sure, let's talk about Fallujah."

Although it was four years later and we were thousands of miles away, the general listened to what happened after the consecutive Delta Force night raids. McChrystal knew I had challenged the wisdom and necessity of the SOF operation.

He said right away, "Sara . . ."

I quickly followed.

"Sara al-Jumaili."

McChrystal heard from me the rest of Sara's story. I sensed the general had never been told what happened in Fallujah after his forces detained the Iraqi woman and then returned her. He nodded, looking regretful. Perhaps he was thinking, *My guys were wrong to take her both times*, but he did not say it. Admit it.

One of his SEAL aides in Kabul did, however, commenting to me rather remarkably: "Oh yeah, after that Sara incident happened we took all the other females off of our targeting list." I did not want to imagine how many other women had been on their top secret "let's grab and talk to this woman next" document.

In both wars we should have traded our "compartmented" secrets, those in the State Department and those in JSOC, in real time but did not. "Same team" should have meant shared—and much better coordinated—political-military fights. I had as high a U.S. government security clearance (Top Secret/SCI) as they did. And certainly a "need to know" in a war where local politics drove everything else. This kind of coordination did not happen often enough in either war, particularly in the early years, even at the ambassador and four-star general level.

That disconnect cost Iraqi lives.

That disconnect cost Afghan lives.

That disconnect cost American lives.

Holbrooke's plane landed and McChrystal joined him. Across the tarmac a few hours earlier Marines and I had stood at a ramp ceremony in honor of more KIA. Far from Fallujah. Far from America. I wished Holbrooke could have been there for that. I knew McChrystal went to many of these ceremonies. I wished even more that the commander in chief and his White House team could have stood in the long line of Marines, three deep, as another coffin was placed in the belly of another cargo plane for another long flight home.

Such ceremonies remained, however, absent from the official diplomatic records. We called them among ourselves "dignified transfers."

. . .

Sara's detention ranks as one of the most challenging, and raw, experiences in my decade-plus-long State Department career. Its repercussions in Fallujah and beyond would echo for the rest of the war. Heroic SEAL and Delta Force teams do not always only get the bad guys in the zero-dark hours after midnight. This time, they went on a mission after an Iraqi woman, got her, and caused us to lose our most important local ally in the process.

Grand Mufti Hamza.

I was complicit as well in the outcome.

In the wars, the tempting blame game only made sense if our fingers could point all the way back to Washington, to where policy or, rather, nonpolicy was deliberated. Decided by the deciders. But we were too busy for that, trying our best to end the mismanaged wars in our little but still deadly parts of them. Generals and grunts, SEAL teams, Delta Force units, and, yes, State Department commissar-grunts had more in common than differences.

We fought on a shared front line. They used bullets. I used words.

Both could kill. Both did kill.

The death of Fallujah's last grand mufti, my friend, proved as much.

When the embassy asked me who killed Sheikh Hamza, I had an answer prepared.

"We did."

The only way you get Americans to notice anything is to tax them or draft them or kill them.

JOHN IRVING, *A Prayer for Owen Meany*

A Farewell to Fallujah

About midway through my final year in Fallujah and not long after Grand Mufti Hamza's assassination, a city council member's comment surprised me in a crowded public meeting.

"Mr. Kael, you can't leave until Fallujah is happy again."

Larry Nicholson gave me a hard time declaring that the local leader's statement meant I could never leave.

"You've been cursed now," he added.

"True enough, but we all wear a Scarlet A for Anbar on us, Larry, including you and every Marine or soldier who has ever fought here."

Fallujah certainly was not happy. And by early 2007, the time had come for me to leave. I had to go. There would be no grand farewell speech, either. We had entered Fallujah loudly and violently. I preferred to leave Fallujah quietly. Peacefully had become impossible by then. Ninety-three American service members had been killed in the last twelve months, many hundreds more wounded, all our dead dying inside a relatively small circle on a map around one violent city.

That focused our pain even more. Some were friends. Until the day he redeployed and I left, Larry and I still were attending almost every memorial, as many as two or three some days. I was physically tired. I was mentally tired. I was exhausted. Fallujans, of course, even more so. Unlike them we always had the chance to go home one day. War, however, had settled into their hometown.

Larry and the regiment he commanded, 5th Marines, were set to leave about a month before I was. He pulled me aside outside the CMOC one day. "Kael, you have to stay until the new regiment has settled in a bit. You know how left-seat, right-seat transitions go."

"Yeah, I do. Like the time a new battalion did not get the map from the old battalion that showed where the mayor of Fallujah lives. A classic moment in counterinsurgency in this dear city of ours. Sheikh Dhari is still pissed about it."

"We all screw up once in a while. But will you stick around?" he pressed again.

"We do, including me. Yes, I will."

"Good. Plus the city council won't let you leave."

Around the same time Larry persuaded me to stay in Fallujah a bit longer, one of my closest Iraqi friends and most reliable collaborators, Abbas Ali Hussein, also had a relevant and revealing question for me. His dark eyebrows arched, the round English teacher asked: "What does fiasco mean?"

If only I could put that question before the senators and CODELs, I thought—and with the whole Fallujah city council, imams, and Anbar tribal sheikhs gathered in the room to hear their answers. And then inform the VIPs, American public servants—charged with voting for or against war—whether their replies were sufficient given the state of the American invasion and occupation of Iraq.

Abbas, who would have loved such an opportunity to interrogate U.S. politicians, waddled when he walked, books under arm and sheets of paper in hand—a happily disheveled image that made me grin. Of all of our collaborators—Hamza, Najm, Kamal, Sami, Dhari, and many more—I felt a special bond with him. He spoke English fluently, his language skills highlighting our lack of them, in particular my own glaring deficiency. Often in city council meetings, Abbas would do the translation, usually during the most heated moments. He prided himself on his ability to ensure little would be misunderstood. For decades Abbas taught English grammar to children in Fallujah, sharing with the older ones the American literature he safeguarded in his small library.

If the U.S. invasion of Iraq ever had a chance to end not so badly, it would be through the efforts of Iraqis like Abbas. He was Shia, no less, in the middle of perhaps the most Sunni city in Iraq—a difference that did not equal an automatic divide, at least in the early days after our unrequested and sudden arrival in their country. Abbas did not quit his job, even though other council members had been assassinated while holding supposedly safer positions. As city council secretary, his ties to our side could not be explained away.

He knew that. We knew that.

Glances and whispers in open-to-all weekly city council sessions recorded his every move, his every word. Hidden to our foreign eyes, Al Qaeda operatives had a seat, as did former Baathists and the full range of insurgents moving in and out of the city. We were blind to almost all of these machinations and double-cross and triple-cross agendas. Plots. Secret asides. Coded threats. Enmity.

Abbas was not. Some who wanted him dead most likely were his former students, those who knew him best, his daily routines.

And where he lived.

For much of the war, rage and revenge defined Iraq. Adrenaline followed by grieving on all sides—actions, reactions, and then more vengeance. Abbas represented a chance at better relations. He wanted to help, and did, over and over.

For instance Abbas aided a father and son. The duo's entire Sunni family had been killed in their home in a mixed Baghdad neighborhood. They had been drinking tea at a Shia neighbor's compound when the Jaysh al-Mahdi militia entered their house. No one else survived. Within a day father and son sought refuge in Fallujah. The kid never looked up, as if peering into the abyss below that had swallowed his mother and sisters and brothers.

He already had seen too much . . . by age eight or nine. His eyes still pierce me.

In such moments—coming face-to-face with the faces of war—I could not recall whether Muslims believed in heaven and hell in their religion and, if so, how Allah judged who went where. Wars do not lend themselves to forgiveness or forgetting. This child of Iraq and his father could not forgive or forget, I was certain, and so Iraq's cycle of violence would continue. In Shia slums, other kids would lose family members to car bombs.

The same story, the same faces, the same abyss. Civil war was coming. Our invasion marked the beginning of the unraveling.

I asked the embassy whether Baghdad was still the largest Sunni city in Iraq. They got my point. Sunnis from all over were fleeing to Fallujah, the most gated Sunni Arab community in the country. I even heard Iraqis say they were relocating because their grandfathers had been born there, though they themselves had never been to Fallujah.

If not for collaborators like Abbas, the very bad would have been very much worse.

It was in this dark period I made my decision to leave Fallujah, despite the Fallujah leader's request I remain until Fallujans were smiling, more or less, again. I had simply seen too much of the human costs of the Iraq War to stay any longer. This was hard to admit to myself, particularly since I did not want to think about how long it might take another State Department "commissar" or senior diplomat assigned to the Marine command to get smart on the city, in addition to the province.

Such was the dynamic in late January 2007 as I sat around a table near the outskirts of Fallujah—and such was my burned-out mindset. Weeks had passed since I had talked with the father and son who had fled Baghdad. Only days before my scheduled departure I sat with Abbas, my impromptu interpreter to my right, and three teenagers who surrounded me. Their fathers—council chairman Kamal, deputy police chief Khudairi, and Grand Mufti Hamza—had been assassinated. I was there to offer condolences and make amends of a sort, via U.S. dollars. Hard looks, language, and the invasion separated us. A Marine corporal counted out $50 and $100 bills with thick fingers trained to pull a trigger, not shuffle money like a Vegas teller. Then he left.

Blood money. Each Iraqi boy got 2,500 bucks, about five times what we paid for damaged vehicles or homes. Math that never made sense, and I never wanted to have to explain why. It just was—a reflection of our impenetrable accounting of Iraqi lives and property. The same sort of arithmetic would hold true in Afghanistan as well.

It was not as if we could be sued for more money. Defense Department rules authorized $1,500 for "permanent disability or significant disfigurement." Part of the deal meant that we never formally admitted responsibility, offering only "our condolences" instead through a translator. We became practiced at sounding sincere in our language, not theirs, without any formal acknowledgment of guilt. Some of us, but not enough, were sincere. Nothing written. No legalities, all marked down as "collateral damage." As official documents read: "Payment is not an admission of legal liability or fault."

American lives had been priced out as well.

Before Iraq, American KIA, our boys, were valued at an incremental automatic death gratuity that grew over time. The maximum payouts were $10,000 in 1965, $50,000 by 1986, and $250,000 in 2001. As casualties went up and the politics of the 9/11 wars made the front pages of even the hometown papers, the guarantee increased—an insurance program with roots after World War I and revised in the Vietnam era. If troops checked a nonmandatory insurance box before deploying, which virtually all did as the wars dragged on and buddies got blown up, families or surviving spouses could get up to $400,000, tax-free. (The same amount given for suicides or training accidents, or motorcycle crashes, and so on.) For immediate burial and funeral costs, $12,500 was provided. Uncle Sam and the associated insurance company priced American lives in Iraq and Afghanistan at almost 200 times the amount we typically paid out to Iraqi families.

The Law of Armed Conflict, or LOAC, sounded reassuring in principle but proved hard to adhere to in practice. Disbursements for the war dead did not figure into the rules devised and agreed to among long since deceased foreign ministers who met in striped three-piece suits within the ornate salons of Geneva, Switzerland. Words agreed to over leisurely meals, between cigars, and facilitated by liquor— diplomacy famously described as "a life of protocol, alcohol, and cholesterol." They had concerned themselves with the conduct of warfare between nations ("conventions") and their mechanized armies and air forces, not tribal allegiances, murky insurgencies, or civil wars within them.

The treaty to "end" World War I was, appropriately enough, signed in Versailles's Hall of Mirrors outside Paris. World War II had its beginnings in that very room. British artist William Orpen captured the diplomatic facade—old bearded men, most black-suited and a few uniformed, all aligned in a row after millions of young men left dead on both sides of the trenches in another unnecessary war. His remarkable 1919 painting of the postwar/prewar gathering: *The Signing of Peace in the Hall of Mirrors*. Orpen's *To the Unknown British Soldier in France*—featuring a Union Jack–draped casket—is also a moving preview of all the bloodletting across Europe to follow. Of all the future wars to come, including the American wars in Iraq—row upon row of Old Glory covered coffins in the back of U.S. military transport planes arriving at Dover Air Force Base in Delaware.

I used to tell Marine generals I would rather have been a political commissar working with them on Okinawa or during the Inchon landing, not along the western front of Iraq. Big and "right" wars that somehow seemed cleaner in their basis and logic, if war could ever be described as such. Numerous atrocities happened in these wars (firebombing cities, gory rapes galore, enemy bodies mutilated) but their basis, and stakes, were much clearer on behalf of a mobilized American home front. Abbas himself read enough U.S. history to know America had "won" wars—and then stuck around to help rebuild defeated countries, on a scale much more vast than the war-torn city and country we shared.

But history would not serve as a prelude for what was happening in Iraq. We were losing the war. Iraqis felt it—and so did we. Expressions of "our condolences" followed by a passing of U.S. bills across tables marked the slide.

My meeting with the city leaders' sons did not last long. Neither they nor I wanted it to be prolonged. For two of the three, it was our first time meeting. It happened in the same room that Ambassador Neumann, General Sattler, and I had sat in with Fallujah's last-chance delegation before the battle, Phantom Fury renamed New Dawn or Al Fajr.

Full circle.

Our green currency could not bring back their dead fathers. Just as our government's money distributed to the families of fallen American KIA could not bring them back. I could tell the sons did not want to take the American cash, but they needed it. Now father-less, avoiding poverty trumped pride. The sons, all under twenty years old, had suddenly become responsible for their mothers and siblings.

Kamal's son's comments stood out: "We only wish our government would do this, remember and show respect for our fathers."

I did not know how to reply and said nothing. What I wanted to say is that their government did not care, and probably would not anytime soon, either. And the government I represented only cared in the form of money.

All told, $7,500 in "martyr payments" passed over the table, my side to theirs. I also asked Marines to authorize a separate disbursement for an Iraqi girl likely hurt by our bombs years earlier, found by troops in the initial days of Operation New Dawn. Her still body, with a gash to the head and sliced nose, lay amid clumps of dirt and puddles. Twenty-six months later, the little girl dressed in Santa red sat at the table too, arriving just after the three sons had departed. Probably age four or so by now, in the lap of her grandmother wearing all black, her eyes under curly dark hair darted unfocused in all directions below a dented, scarred forehead. The little girl had permanent brain damage. Marines told me they thought both parents were killed during the battle . . . killed, accidentally, by us.

I remembered the rest of her story. I was the one at a city checkpoint who had seen this same woman waving the same girl's photo. That's when Marines and I began to follow the trail, one that now included this postscript years later.

Before the group departed, with U.S. cash triple-wrapped in plastic bags, Abbas said one day we would pay his family, predicting his own death.

"Don't say that, Abbas," I said. "Fallujans have already suffered enough. So have Marines."

But I knew he was probably right.

Few words baffled Abbas. Fiasco was one and is why he asked me about it. It was the only definition he seemed confused by. I had previously handed over a book by Tom Ricks with that title, one of several tomes the English teacher wanted to translate into Arabic. Abbas believed Iraqis deserved to read American books by Americans about our "shock and awe" war. I told him Americans needed to read Iraqi books by

Iraqis about our inept occupation. But I knew that would not happen soon enough.

The blood money meeting was the final time I saw Abbas. He had in his hands the last set of books I saved for him and his translation project: John Irving's *A Prayer for Owen Meany*, the 9/11 Commission report, Tom Clancy's *The Sum of All Fears*, Michael Gordon and Bernard Trainor's *Cobra II*, and Paul Bremer's *My Year in Iraq*. Abbas said he believed translated accounts authored and read by "different" peoples, but not so different really, might reduce misunderstandings and help prevent conflict. And result in more empathy. That is why he had undertaken his monumental English-to-Arabic literary project. The humble library of this one individual in Fallujah had both Iraqi and American stories in it.

I wish I had left him other literature, including nonwar subjects— and refused to hand over the Bremer memoir. Abbas had the picture-book of the Western U.S. national parks I had given him, so he could better understand the nonwar me. The before-war me. And, perhaps, the after-war me as well. I had planned to give him more John Irving, who had written in his tale of Owen Meany, "my life is a reading list."

Abbas would have liked that quote.

In turn, he unexpectedly handed me two books in Arabic.

"Mr. Kael, these are for you. Now you must learn our language. You have been here long enough and should know more by now."

He, yet again, was right. I could have made a better first impression by being at least conversational in Arabic, but perhaps had made up for it in other ways.

I opened the books. The larger one, with a blue and gold cover and the outlines of eleven mosque minarets on it, contained an inscription:

A gift to my best friend among Americans in Falluja. I know him as a great politician and humanitarian. Thank you. Abbas. 2007.1.30

I felt like neither. And only one had a positive connotation in my mind.

Then we parted. Abbas waddled out of the room, and I made my way to a Humvee.

When I got back to Camp Fallujah, outgoing Marines said Brigadier General John Allen, the incoming deputy commanding general, wanted to meet with me. He had heard I knew more about Fallujah than anyone else. True enough, but still more a curse than a compliment. In my unclassified in-box was a PowerPoint presentation to review and to provide input.

One of the last slides read: "Redeployment and TRICARE Information." Neither of which applied to me, though I wished they did. The U.S. military's basically socialist health care plan (TRICARE) beat the State Department's plan, and I knew my post-Fallujah assignment would not be a redeployment to safe Washington. I was leaving one war, Iraq, for the other, Afghanistan.

I did not go see General Allen. The new Marine generals needed a new U.S. embassy representative. Someone else to debate with them, agree with them—or disagree with the generals privately. Or, when need be, express differences publicly in front of HQ staff, on good days, and particularly on the bad days.

I had seen too much, heard too much, smelled too much, survived too much, since arriving in Fallujah almost three years earlier. I sure felt like a "veteran" but knew that label, back home, would never apply to me. I was a "civilian"—a category ("State Department type") often derided as lesser in Marine and soldier circles. No VFW membership. No VA benefits. No veterans discounts for me, whether at Amtrak, Cabela's, Jiffy Lube, or at the drive-thru of my first employer, Dairy Queen. No free U.S. National Park Annual Pass labeled "military" either. (I have gladly paid the full-price, eighty-dollar R&R investment every summer.)

And certainly no "did you kill anyone over there?" questions—though, truth be told, my policy decisions led to the deaths of many Iraqis and many Americans. Many U.S. Marines. Dozens made dead, including good friends on both sides.

The wrong words, I learned, could be more dangerous to human life than rounds fired from rifles. So many deaths had taught me that lesson, that truth.

And so it goes in war.

And so it would go once I was back home, after war. A question about killing I should be asked. A question both Republican and Democratic war cabinets, all the policy makers, in the White House should be asked.

And perhaps asked more than once or a few times, but repeatedly: "Did you kill anyone over there?"

I went to my room at Camp Fallujah to pack a couple of giant black footlockers before shipping them back to the U.S. Soon, I came across many items that would forever mark the Iraq War for me and represented all the mixed emotions. All the things I carried deep inside—and would for a long time.

There was an American flag, properly folded in a triangle inside a box. A *Time* magazine cover, dated December 29, 2003, with a picture of U.S. soldiers in uniform under the heading, "Person of the Year: The American Soldier." And two *New York Post* "late city final" papers printed on January 24 and February 14, 2003, which I had kept from my time at the U.S. Mission to the U.N. One with a headline that read, "Axis of Weasel: Germany and France Wimp Out on Iraq," and the second: "UN Meets: Weasels to Hear New Iraq Evidence"—with weasel heads superimposed on the French and German foreign ministers seated around the circular table in the Security Council chamber. An information card that began, "Leishmaniasis is caused by a parasite that gets into people when infected sand flies . . . there is no vaccine or preventive drug." Two Iraqi oil paintings I had bought in Baghdad. One had Arabs seated under a tent during a sandstorm. The other, a much larger canvas in bright yellows, contained a mass jumble of black, snaking power lines. The young artist told me at the time that we Americans were still promising to bring more electricity to Baghdad—but had not. He said that is what his modernist-type painting represented.

There were several Iraqi election ballots scripted in Arabic. A coffee mug emblazoned: "Happiness is CPA Iraq in my rear view mirror!" A spoof Kenny (of *South Park* fame) uniform patch, which read: "You sent me to Iraq! You Bastards!" Another Marine-related item: a signed mini-USMC flag with its Eagle, Globe, and Anchor, a gift from a group of Infantry and Civil Affairs Marines, one of whom wrote, "DOS u Ok"—as in Department of State; and lots of "stay safe"—an often heard message with the sincerest of meaning for all of us in a place like Fallujah. I had even kept with me in Fallujah a folded and frayed confirmation letter from "EduServ" verifying repayment of my college student loans. Year after year in the Iraq War had at least allowed me to get out from under that 24K of undergraduate and graduate school debt.

I held a stack of Marine KIA Memorial pamphlets as well, paper-clipped together, with a picture of each Marine centered on the covers: *In Memory of* . . . Cpl Jason Jarrard Corbett (23, of Casper, Wyoming, pop. 59,628); LCpl Jeremy S. Shock (22, of Green Springs, Ohio, pop. 1,368); Cpl Joshua D. Pickard (20, of Los Banos, California, pop. 36,822); Cpl Christopher E. Esckelson (22, of Vasser, Michigan, pop. 2,639); LCpl Nicholas A. Miller (20, of Clifford, Michigan, pop. 324); LCpl William D. Spencer (20, of Paris, Tennessee, pop. 10,166).

And one that honored Major Megan Malia McClung of Orange County, California, a popular public affairs officer across base and ranks. The picture on the front cover showed her, a devoted runner, in full stride; and a wide-smiled close-up of her on the back cover. A Naval Academy graduate, she was born in Honolulu the same year I had, in 1972, and died December 6, 2006, in Ramadi—the final month of her deployment. Megan was the first female Marine officer to be killed in Iraq, and the first female graduate of the Naval Academy, founded in 1845, to be killed in action. Her mantra: "Be bold, be brief, be gone."

All of us missed Megan.

My well-used Kevlar helmet, covered in Marine Corps Desert Tan Digital Camouflage Fabric, coated in Anbar sand, was there too.

And perhaps among the most memorable things I prepared to pack away from my years in Iraq? A plastic bag full of dried-out cigars and Muslim prayer beads. One symbolized Marines. The other symbolized Iraqis.

No better friends. No worse enemies. Both.

Surprisingly, there was a Quran, with an elaborate cover shaded in blues, reds, and gold, still wrapped in protective plastic. I wanted to think Sheikh Hamza, the last grand mufti of Fallujah, had given it to me. But I could not remember, and that made me feel both embarrassed and sad. Perhaps I had already repressed, but not really forgotten, more of Fallujah than I thought. Than I thought possible.

I even found a 3x5 Fujifilm color photo of me with Bassam and his teamsters and diesel mechanics in a Baghdad truck repair shop. Had they survived the Sunni-on-Shia-on-Sunni-on-Shia cycle of violence, i.e., civil war, as they moved food across Iraq?

And another picture—Larry and a battalion commander kneeling over, rubber mallets in hand, a game that a platoon kept at one of their combat outposts: Whac-A-Mole.

A final item stuffed into the back of one of my files was a transcript of a Pentagon press briefing from mid-November 2004, during the big battle. A reporter had asked a very good, if loaded, question—one that got to the fundamentals of everything that had gone on in Fallujah.

I reread it, wondering how would I, called "Kael al-Falluji" by Fallujans, answer that question now?

Q: Colonel, Jamie McIntyre from CNN. Some critics back here have invoked the old Vietnam-era phrase, "We had to destroy the city to save it." I assume that you reject that comparison. But can I just get your thought about somebody who thinks that that's what's going on in Fallujah?

A: . . . So I would say to you, I am responsible to the commander on precision targeting. Is this like Vietnam? Absolutely not. Vietnam had Hue City, and that was leveled and there wasn't precision targeting, and they didn't secure it in the amount of time that we've secured. . . . But again, yes, there will be and there has been buildings damaged. And it now becomes our responsibility to help the country of Iraq clear up this with the reconstruction efforts, which have already gotten under way, really, a couple of days ago. I'd mentioned Mortuary Affairs. Yesterday and today we started working on the meals program. We've worked electricity yesterday. We've put guys in to see where and when they can turn on the electricity. We've got many, many forces in line just to go into that city and set up a CMOC, a civil/military operations center, in the government building right next to the incoming provincial mayor of the city. He's pleased with it. In fact, tomorrow he and I will participate in a brief to General Casey to explain some of the phase four, which is reconstruction of this city and how we're aligned to start doing that in the near—not too distant future.

After thinking about it for a while, I believed I would have to answer the question differently in 2007 regarding my adopted Iraqi hometown.

We might not have destroyed all of Fallujah in the battles and ongoing firefights since—more like half—but we certainly had not saved the city in the process either. And while Iraq was now post–Saddam the Tyrant, Al Qaeda had followed us into the country, as Mayor Dhari often reminded me. The country had become more violent with our arrival, not less. Thousands of U.S. troops dead and injured. Hundreds of thousands of Iraqis dead and injured and even more, millions, made homeless.

I recalled Marines patrolling Fallujah with rifles in one hand. Using their other hand, they would show thumbs-up signs to Fallujah kids gathered close by saying "Mista, Mista." Their interactions reminded me of a helicopter gunner crouched in front of me during a flight above springtime fields, irrigated by the wide and meandering Euphrates River. He kept his left hand on the trigger of a machine gun, and his right hand on a bag of rainbow-colored hard candy. He had tied a red ribbon to the bag's top—to make it easier for the Iraqi children below to find it.

In the end Abbas, my friend, my very good friend, had been right. He was dead three days after we parted, small bullets filling his big body. The English teacher of Fallujah was gone. The afternoon I left Fallujah by helicopter, Jason Brezler, a reservist civil affairs officer and New York City fireman, forwarded me an email from another Fallujan, an engineer on the city reconstruction committee. I read it when I landed. He described Abbas's family as being in "very hysteria" after seeing his crumpled body lying in front of their home.

> My friends
> I am so sorry to tell that our teacher Abbas Dabas, the nobleman was killed before 30 Minutes agao, I was sent some mail with my one team to his houes and he saw him on the land killed and his family in very hysteria.
>
> Khaled

From the military airport in Baghdad, I contacted the Marine commanding general, Richard Zilmer, at Camp Fallujah, one of the Marine Corps' best leaders, who innately understood and empathized with Iraqis, the last of a long list of impressive Marine general officers. All based in Anbar and who—along with plenty of USMC corporals and captains and colonels—taught me a lot about the Corps and about war and about service in a time of war. Generals Conway, Mattis, Sattler, Hejlik (as well as Generals Natonski, Johnson, Patton, Zilmer, Neller, Reist, Williams)—and especially General Dunford, who had called Ramadi home, well before earning his second, third, and fourth star and becoming the United States military's top officer and principal adviser to two commanders in chief on America's longest wars.

Zilmer replied he had already approved a $5,000 payment, emailing me, "Already done . . . like you, I am very angry and sad. Both Mr. Abbas and Mr. Najm were two of the most genuine and committed people to advancing our joint objectives. . . . Have passed along the info to Col Nicholson, who I know will be devastated when he hears this news . . . V/R Z"

We Americans had priced out another Iraqi life, doubling the usual amount. It did not make me feel any better. Their lives, Abbas's now too, tendered yet again with our money.

Fiasco.

I never was able to provide Abbas with an answer to his question that felt good enough or right. Tom Ricks had picked a spot-on and devastating title for his bestselling war book, *Fiasco*: everything Iraq had become, and Washington, D.C., represented, captured in a single word. All of us in Iraq lived the Iraq fiasco. The American military's bloody misadventure, the United States of America's bloody and tragic and avoidable misadventure, amid millions of Iraqis who suffered most. And would for a long time to come.

Abbas's exit coincided with mine, but his was final. Some words used by nonnative English speakers convey the most. No qualifying. No nuance. No thinking too much about proper usage. No editor or editing. No writerly craft. No imagination necessary.

The last two words in the email did that.

"Very hysteria." That's how it described Abbas's family on the day he was killed.

The day I said farewell to Fallujah.

The day I escaped Iraq.

The day I left the quagmire we started.

The day I said farewell, from afar, to a good friend, a good man, now dead.

And then the long night that followed after I boarded a C-130 to Jordan. The military craft's flight path taking us high above Fallujah and Abbas's small home library, across the wide western deserts of Anbar, including over Ak Ashat near Ar Rutbah—the site of thirty-one KIA.

Where, in an instant, 31 Angels fell from the sky.

When people speak to you about a preventive war, you tell them to go and fight it. After my experience, I have come to hate war.

DWIGHT D. EISENHOWER

The 93

I arrived at the military airport in Amman for a quick one-day layover. Dating back to Roman times, Jordan's capital was a welcoming and relaxing hilltop city, nineteen hills in total, where a cool breeze always seemed to blow in contrast to Iraq's hot winds. A line of taxis waited outside the small terminal, drivers hoping to score fares paid in U.S. dollars. Decades before, it would have been British pounds from British imperialists. Many of the taxi drivers, Palestinian by birth with Marlboros in hand (produced by Philip Morris in Jordan), gathered in clumps. One got to me first and I jumped into his parakeet-yellow car. He guided our way to my nonmarquee hotel where economy-minded Jordanians stayed.

Most American expats, not to mention congressional delegations from Washington, preferred Amman's Four Seasons on Al Kindi Street. Just as the many rich ex-Baathists did and some even richer Anbar sheikhs, who now inhabited the city after our invasion. The spacious, white and tan marble hotel ("coffee, tea, and muffins in the foyer" and "twice daily housekeeping") had a terrace-top pool too, but not as large as the one at the Coalition Provisional Authority HQ palace, once Saddam's very own. A five-star hotel vs. street-level disconnect amid so many others. Rome could be burning, as Baghdad was, and one might never know while sleeping in under high-thread-count duvets in such grand accommodations just beyond the war zone.

A friend from my time at the U.S. Mission to the U.N. in New York, a Jordanian diplomat, wanted to meet. His older brother worked for the king of Jordan. We gathered at a local restaurant not far from the U.S. embassy. A good Muslim, he did not drink, and I was in a tee-totaling mood. He had, however, picked up another kind of vice in the U.S.—Starbucks frappuccinos by the gallon (the extreme sugar intake rationalized in his mind, he used to say, after eating sushi and sashimi by the pound across Manhattan). I kept mostly quiet, still thinking about Abbas's death, about how I had just left Anbar with the province worse off than when I had arrived years earlier.

Iraq had indeed slipped into a civil war by 2007, with drill bits the preferred torture weapon of Shia militias and car bombs the deadly tactic among Sunni terrorists with ties to Al Qaeda. This was bloodletting on an industrial scale with no signs of ending anytime soon.

My friend tried to steer the conversation away from the sectarian meltdown under way next door in Iraq.

"Kael, remember that Iraqi ballot you sent me from the first Fallujah election?"

"Yeah, I remember."

"Okay, well, I was on eBay the other day looking around and guess what? Someone in Florida is selling a sample ballot like the one you gave me for one hundred dollars!"

"I am pretty sure now that all those elections we forced on Iraqis only divided Iraq," I replied.

I did not tell him that the father of a Marine killed outside Baghdad in 2004 had sent me a letter from Wisconsin all the way to Camp Fallujah just before Thanksgiving 2006. His son, Lance Corporal Daniel Wyatt, had proposed to his girlfriend twelve hours before being called by his command informing him that he would be deploying to Iraq. He was killed a few weeks after arriving in country. The Marine's dad, Dave Wyatt, wrote:

Dear Mr. Weston,

The Iraqi ballots have arrived and there is no way that I can even come close to expressing my gratitude. . . . I will never forget January 30, 2005. I was in almost constant e-mail contact with Daniel's battalion commander and was glued to the Fox News coverage. That ballot is the essence of what it is all about. All of those purple fingers meant that my son, and all the other fallen, did not die in vain. Two of the January 30th ballots are, as I write this, at a frame shop being professionally matted and framed. One will hang in a place of honor in our home and the other will be presented to Fox Company to be placed on a special wall that they have reserved to honor the five Marines who did not return from Iraq. . . . Once again, I cannot even come close to expressing my gratitude.

In October 2006, I had sent the Wisconsin family three sets of ballots (2005's January 30 election, the October 15 constitutional referendum, and the December 15 parliamentary election) after hearing from a Marine friend that the family wanted to honor their son's memory in this way. I used to tell Marines in Anbar that 2005 was the U.S. government's experiment in "three intense democratic experiences for Iraqis in one year." A very bloody experiment too. My letter to these parents, which I wrote in Fallujah, concluded: "Your son's sacrifice to help the Iraqi people achieve a better future is the purest example of what this fight still represents. His service to our country, and on behalf of Iraq's families, will always be deserving of two nations' everlasting gratitude."

My Jordanian friend continued to mention past conversations. "When we were in New York at the U.N., I warned you, so did a lot of other diplomats from around here."

"I remember what you said about our invasion, what it would mean for a 'small country' like yours. You guys caught up in the geopolitics between the U.S., Iraq, Iran, Israel, and the Saudis."

"Jordan is very small. We live in a very dangerous neighborhood, even more dangerous now," he replied pointedly.

I confessed in my own way.

"Yeah, thanks to us, I know. After Fallujah, I would do anything to go back to 2003, when we spent all that time drinking coffee in the North Delegates Lounge, when Secretary Powell made his damn WMD speech in the Security Council. We both watched him that day."

"You really think he could have prevented the war?"

"I don't know. But Colin Powell was probably the only one who could have made a difference, make the American people pause, maybe make Bush think twice and not side with Cheney, Rumsfeld, and all the rest. I wonder if he would take it all back if he could."

My friend offered to drive me to the airport the next morning to Queen Alia International Airport. I said I would be fine and take another cab. It was late. We parted ways, planning to stay in touch by email.

During my brief stopover in Amman, I was reminded of a conversation I had several years earlier in the fall of 2003, about six months after the U.S. invasion of Iraq, when I was part of CPA's imperial staff. A number of Jordanian trucking business owners had invited a group of us for a series of meetings. They considered the Bassams of Iraq across the border as potential teamster partners—or, more likely, cut-price competition. Trade between Iraq and Jordan totaled billions, with the trucking routes particularly lucrative given the dangerous Anbar transit points between the two countries' capitals.

Over that weekend, a few State Department colleagues and I stopped by the closed Iraqi embassy. After the invasion, we Americans had become the new government in Iraq. Saddam's diplomats had disappeared. Only one person remained—the night watchman. Slow-moving and with a clipped mustache, he walked up to me. I introduced myself, saying I was part of the American contingent based in Baghdad and on a short visit to Jordan.

"*Shukran, shukran, shukran,*" he repeated. Thank you, thank you, thank you. Before shifting to very good English.

"Iraqi people have nothing to worry about now that you Americans are in our country. We are like a fifty-first state."

I did not know what to say, but knew my trucker friends hauling food across Iraq were not nearly as hopeful. Or naive. He motioned us inside the building after unlocking a side door. The watchman pointed to a pile of papers that lay scattered about a desk in a dark, wood-paneled office. One looked like a contract with a Russian company for some kind of weapons system, with a printed drawing on the cover of what appeared to be an antiaircraft mobile rocket platform. Perhaps he had planted the document. Whatever the case, it reminded me that for many years U.S. jets had patrolled the skies over Iraq in a no-fly zone. Seeing the image, I recalled how in early 2001, Rumsfeld's Pentagon had shifted to a more aggressive military posture in the region. Ramped up F-18 flights as if to trigger an explosive "incident" . . . half a year before the attacks on September 11, 2001, gave Rumsfeld and his higher-ups the very pretext they sought.

What had been a mostly cold war of sorts between Washington and Baghdad after the Gulf War had by 2007 become a new war post-invasion that was very hot and very out of control.

Iraq as America's fifty-first state . . . the night watchman's comment echoed for a long time inside my head. I wondered if some Afghans might be thinking the same thing, years later and in the other war. I would soon find out.

Within two weeks after departing Jordan, I was standing in Southern California at Camp Pendleton, the massive oceanside Marine base that is home to almost 40,000 Marines under the command of the 1st Marine Expeditionary Force. Some 70,000 more USMC retirees live within a few miles of it. While Twentynine Palms is remote and in the middle of a high California desert, Pendleton is urban, not far from San Diego, and home to prime beaches with wave conditions ideal for surfing—a hobby more than a few Marines take up in between their warfare training. At 4:59 p.m., in other words, many begin to trade rifles for boards.

Larry Nicholson had invited me to attend the regimental memorial service for the 93 KIA we had suffered. All dead in the space of a year in and around Fallujah under the command of the 5th Marine Regimental Combat Team, the most decorated unit of its size in the Corps—and described by one top Marine, a Fallujah alum no less, as "the sledge-hammer of war." (This same Marine leader, known for his aggressive battle tactics even by infantry standards, would also ask me privately, "After Fallujah, how do you sleep? I am having a hard time myself.") For the memorial, I had put on a suit, the first time in years. The sun was out, blue skies above the base's palm trees, predictably beautiful California weather and a scenic setting for this very sad occasion.

Gold Star parents and families (those who had lost family members in America's wars) from across the country had been sent invitations, and a dozen or so gathered, having made the trip to Pendleton on their own dollars and dimes. As the ceremony got started, I stood back. Not wanting to meet any of them just yet, unsure what I would say if a mom, dad, sister, brother, or grandparent asked me what my job had been in the Iraq War.

"State Department guy" was the easy answer, and leave it at that.

A more honest and expansive one would have been: The civilian government guy, who worked with the generals and colonels and captains and sergeants and corporals, and Iraqis too, lots of Iraqis, to try to unscrew all that was going wrong. And despite our efforts to succeed in that mission, the KIA figures proved otherwise.

A more honest admission would have been: Some of what we did got them killed. Some of what we did not do got them killed. And sometimes no matter what we did or did not, they died.

No parent or family member asked. So I did not need to consider whether I should lie to them—I imagined I could not have, I imagined I would not have—as the U.S. government had been doing for so long regarding the Iraq War. Lying about the war's premise. Lying about the war's conduct. Lying about the war's costs.

About the war's outcome.

If any of the visiting Gold Star family members had said they wanted an Iraqi ballot to frame and put on their wall, I would have sent it to them—or many if that was what they requested—to any of the fifty states and to any hometown. But I also would have kept quiet about what I thought an Iraqi ballot now represented, versus what others in Washington still said it did. And what I myself once believed the Iraqi elections symbolized as well.

Sometimes it is the mirage that gets people or oneself through the desert. Through the wilderness. Through night.

Larry Nicholson, who had departed Fallujah a few weeks before me, walked over. He looked a lot more rested. As he should have. One month before leaving Fallujah, he and I had visited every combat outpost in and around Fallujah on Christmas Day 2006. Across those twelve hours we had been shot at, RPG'd (I instinctively ducked in the backseat of a Humvee as a second RPG exploded on the corner of a nearby building), and had a big IED detonate in the front part of our convoy. And at no point did the good colonel declare over Marine headsets a TIC (troops in contact), which is the equivalent of a 911 call. That had been his "farewell tour" of the city, Marine-style.

"Got your speech ready?" he asked.

"I don't do speeches. Only did that in Fallujah, all those city council meetings we went to, week after week. That's your job, Larry."

"I think today is going to provide some closure for families," he said. "And maybe even a little bit for me."

"I hope so," I said. "There are going to be a lot more devastated families based on how things looked when I left Iraq a couple of weeks ago."

"We do what we can. We did what we could," Larry added.

He motioned for his wife, Debbie, to come over. Dark-headed, South Carolina–born, a Jeep aficionado, and known for being perhaps the best cook on base, Debbie looked relieved to have Larry back. It had been his second tour to Anbar, the first one almost killing him when the rocket landed in his office and she spent many days with him at Bethesda.

I had only one request.

"Debbie, make sure Larry gets lots of ice cream now that he's back," I said. "He never had any in Iraq when we had the chance."

"Look at his waist. Larry's doing okay, can't you tell?"

Of course he had not gotten too soft around the middle, but I trusted Larry was back to at least a scoop or two of ice cream after dinner. He deserved a lot more from the Marine Corps and his nation than thirty-one flavors of ice cream in his fridge.

Iraq had taken a toll on me too. I saw it in the mirror. A few gray hairs, a lot more wrinkles (having earned every new one while over there, I suppose), and often a heavy head full of heavy thoughts that caffeine or aspirin could only temporarily alleviate. But I also felt resilient in a newfound and unexpected way. Larry and I and so many Marines and even more Iraqis had been tested to a degree that makes war the ultimate four-letter word. A forging of something deep inside, a soul, a spirit, made larger, in a way, amid all the broken parts.

Standing in the California sun to honor young Americans now dead, I knew I would take some of the Iraq experience back if I could, but not all of it. The war had made us weaker. The war had made us stronger. We had persevered. And that, I believed, counted for a lot.

Perhaps that is what mattered most in Fallujah and what mattered most of all after Fallujah.

Even if the deaths, on both sides for me, would haunt, would hurt, for a lifetime.

The ceremony soon started. It took almost half an hour to read the names of all of the Marine KIA. Each name was called out, then the chiming of a bell.

Larry kept his comments brief, describing the losses as numbing.

"It is like losing a son," he said, with those present not realizing one of his own sons had served under him as a lieutenant at a small combat outpost on the outskirts of Fallujah, in a place called Saqlawiyah. Dodging bullets and bombs, just like his dad.

A local journalist attended the ceremony and quoted Paul Buerstetta, the father of Lance Corporal Richard Buerstetta, from Franklin, Tennessee (pop. 68,886), in an article. The dad described the disconnect among the American public and the war front, saying, "I see people laughing and having a good time, and I don't think they understand there's people dying for them."

His son was one of the ninety-three across one regiment killed in one year in Iraq.

As the sun moved a bit farther west, the ceremony reached its end. Long shadows from well-watered palm trees stretched across the well-watered parade ground lawn. California's drought had not yet prompted the sprawling military base to shut off its sprinklers, turning lush greens into desiccated browns in ensuing years—perhaps a more fitting Mother Earth frame for a memorial for the dead. The last KIA Marine's name was read. The last bell sounded. And following the playing of Taps, I quickly left and went back to my motel room as seagull after seagull, squawking loudly, darted above the blue ocean filled with swimmers, snorkelers, and surfers near I-5, the always busy thoroughfare that bisected the sprawling base all the way to Hollywood.

I preferred to be alone, as I am sure more than a few families did by then.

Hearing Taps at memorial after memorial in Anbar, and back at home in the U.S., killed a part of me every time. Historians say the singularly mournful tribute started as a reminder of "lights out" for troops during the Civil War, an early version of which reportedly was Napoleon's favorite composition.

Now the brass bugle's notes bid last farewell among the living for America's military dead. For Iraqi dead, like Abbas, the only sound was the wailing of family members. All those who were buried in Iraq would always and vastly outnumber our own.

At Camp Pendleton that day, Taps served as a reminder of ninety-three lives lost across a twelve-month Marine-led deployment. Among hundreds of others in the years before and all those, hundreds and hundreds and hundreds more, that would follow amid hundreds of thousands of Iraqis. Not to mention the dead in the Afghanistan War.

In San Clemente, a picturesque seaside community whose slogan is "Spanish Village by the Sea," town leaders dedicated land on an oceanfront knoll to build Park Semper Fi instead of another luxury condo development. A statue of a Marine in his dress blue uniform (modeled after a sergeant who deployed to Iraq and now lives in Oklahoma) stands watch, facing westward to the ocean.

At nearby Dana Point, another high-rent part of the California coastline halfway between San Diego and L.A., Marines and community patrons unveiled a gray granite memorial. Built with local donations, it is in the shape of a Texas-sized T-wall—fortress-like concrete barriers ubiquitous in Iraq that kept most Americans in and most Iraqis out.

During the December 2007 ceremony to mark this second memorial's unveiling, Larry, speaking as the outgoing commanding officer of the 5th Marine Regiment, offered a personal assessment. Standing in front of family members who had gathered from across the country, he said, "This is more than just a roster of names carved into stone. It takes your breath away."

It did mine.

Engraved with the ninety-three names of troops killed in and around Fallujah across one year (part of a total of 221 representing all of the regiment's casualties in Iraq up to that time) and a promise, the memorial reads:

FALLEN AND NEVER FORGOTTEN: OPERATION IRAQI FREEDOM

Their deaths, America's war dead buried coast to coast, leaving all those who loved them more alone:

The PFC Sean T. Cardelli Family
of Downers Grove, Illinois, pop. 49,670
age 20

The PFC Javier Chavez, Jr. Family
of Cutler, California, pop. 5,000
age 19

The Cpl Ross A. Smith Family
of Wyoming, Michigan, pop. 74,100
age 21

The LCpl Benito A. Ramirez Family
of Edinburg, Texas, pop. 80,836
age 21

The SSgt Raymond J. Plouhar Family
of Lake Orion, Michigan, pop. 3,062
age 30

The Cpl Jason W. Morrow Family
of Riverside, California, pop. 316,619
age 27

The LCpl Rex A. Page Family
of Kirksville, Missouri, pop. 17,577
age 21

The LCpl Geofrey R. Cayer Family
of Fitchburg, Massachusetts, pop. 40,383
age 20

The Cpl Johnathan L. Benson Family
of North Branch, Minnesota, pop. 10,087
age 21

The Cpl Dustin J. Libby Family
of Presque Isle, Maine, pop. 9,402
age 22

The Cpl Richard P. Waller Family
of Fort Worth, Texas, pop. 792,727
age 22

The LCpl Philip J. Martini Family
of Lansing, Illinois, pop. 28,508
age 24

The LCpl Marcus S. Glimpse Family
of Huntington Beach, California, pop. 197,575
age 22

The LCpl Stephen J. Perez Family
of San Antonio, Texas, pop. 1,409,000
age 22

The PFC Steven W. Freund Family
of Pittsburgh, Pennsylvania, pop. 305,841
age 20

The LCpl Robert G. Posivio III Family
of Sherburn, Minnesota, pop. 1,128
age 22

The Cpl Ryan J. Cummings Family
of Streamwood, Illinois, pop. 40,351
age 22

The LCpl Brandon J. Webb Family
of Swartz Creek, Michigan, pop. 5,636
age 20

The PFC Christopher N. White Family
of Southport, North Carolina, pop. 3,137
age 23

The SSgt Benjamin D. Williams Family
of Orange, Texas, pop. 18,922
age 30

The LCpl James W. Higgins, Jr. Family
of Frederick, Maryland, pop. 66,893
age 22

The LCpl Robert L. Moscillo Family
of Salem, New Hampshire, pop. 28,776
age 21

The Sgt Elisha R. Parker Family
of Taberg, New York, pop. 3,063
age 21

The Cpl Jose A. Galvan Family
of San Antonio, Texas, pop. 1,409,000
age 22

The Cpl Kyle W. Powell Family
of Colorado Springs, Colorado, pop. 439,886
age 21

The LCpl Derrick J. Cothran Family
of Avondale, Louisiana, pop. 4,954
age 21

The Cpl Pablo V. Mayorga Family
of Margate, Florida, pop. 55,456
age 33

The PFC Ryan G. Winslow Family
of Hoover, Alabama, pop. 84,126
age 19

The Cpl Joshua C. Watkins Family
of Jacksonville, Florida, pop. 842,583
age 25

The LCpl Jesse D. Tillery Family
of Vesper, Wisconsin, pop. 573
age 19

The LCpl Luke C. Yepsen Family
of Hillsboro, New Jersey, pop. 38,303
age 20

The Cpl Joshua D. Pickard Family
of Merced, California, pop. 81,102
age 20

The SPC Dustin R. Donica Family
of Spring, Texas, pop. 54,298
age 22

The Sgt George M. Ulloa, Jr. Family
of Austin, Texas, pop. 885,400
age 23

The LCpl Jason K. Burnett Family
of St. Cloud, Florida, pop. 40,918
age 20

The LCpl David J. Grames-Sanchez Family
of Fort Wayne, Indiana, pop. 256,496
age 22

The 2ndLt Michael L. LiCalzi Family
of Garden City, New York, pop. 22,552
age 24

The Cpl Steve Vahaviolos Family
of Airmont, New York, pop. 8,824
age 21

The Sgt Brock A. Babb Family
of Evansville, Indiana, pop. 120,310
age 40

The LCpl Joshua M. Hines Family
of Olney, Illinois, pop. 9,108
age 26

The LCpl Richard A. Buerstetta Family
of Franklin, Tennessee, pop. 68,886
age 20

The LCpl Tyler R. Overstreet Family
of Gallatin, Tennessee, pop. 32,307
age 22

The Sgt Thomas M. Gilbert Family
of Downers Grove, Illinois, pop. 49,670
age 24

The LCpl Jonathan B. Thornsberry Family
of McDowell, Kentucky, pop. 3,415
age 22

The LCpl Troy D. Nealey Family
of Eaton Rapids, Michigan, pop. 5,211
age 24

The LCpl Minhee "Andy" Kim Family
of Ann Arbor, Michigan, pop. 117,025
age 20

The Sgt Bryan K. Burgess Family
of Garden City, Michigan, pop. 27,153
age 35

The LCpl Jeremy S. Shock Family
of Tiffin, Ohio, pop. 17,832
age 22

The LCpl Brent E. Beeler Family
of Jackson, Michigan, pop. 33,423
age 22

The Cpl Christopher E. Esckelson Family
of Vassar, Michigan, pop. 2,639
age 22

The LCpl Nicholas A. Miller Family
of Silverwood, Michigan, pop. 1,274
age 20

The PFC William D. Spencer Family
of Paris, Tennessee, pop. 10,166
age 20

The Sgt Jonathan J. Simpson Family
of Rockport, Texas, pop. 10,036
age 25

The 1stLt Nathan M. Krissoff Family
of Reno, Nevada, pop. 233,294
age 25

The Cpl Stephen R. Bixler Family
of Suffield, Connecticut, pop. 15,735
age 20

The Cpl Cory L. Palmer Family
of Seaford, Delaware, pop. 7,325
age 21

The Sgt Alessandro Carbonaro Family
of Bethesda, Maryland, pop. 63,374
age 28

The HM3 Lee H. Deal Family
of West Monroe, Louisiana, pop. 13,094
age 22

The Cpl William B. Fulks Family
of Culloden, West Virginia, pop. 3,061
age 23

The Sgt Mark T. Smykowski Family
of Mentor, Ohio, pop. 46,979
age 23

The SSgt Christopher M. Zimmerman Family
of Stephenville, Texas, pop. 18,561
age 28

The LCpl James D. "JD" Hirlston Family
of Murfreesboro, Tennessee, pop. 117,044
age 21

The LCpl Howard S. March Family
of Buffalo, New York, pop. 258,959
age 20

The Cpl John E. Hale Family
of Shreveport, Louisiana, pop. 200,327
age 20

The Cpl Bradford H. Payne Family
of Montgomery, Alabama, pop. 200,332
age 24

The LCpl Stephen F. Johnson Family
of Marietta, Georgia, pop. 59,089
age 20

The Cpl Nicholas P. Rapavi Family
of Springfield, Virginia, pop. 30,484
age 22

The LCpl Nicklas J. Palmer Family
of Leadville, Colorado, pop. 2,580
age 19

The Capt Brian S. Letendre Family
of Woodbridge, Virginia, pop. 4,055
age 27

The Sgt Matthew J. Fenton Family
of Little Ferry, New Jersey, pop. 10,806
age 24

The Cpl Paul N. King Family
of Tyngsborough, Massachusetts, pop. 11,292
age 23

The LCpl Kurt E. Dechen Family
of Springfield, Vermont, pop. 9,373
age 24

The LCpl Michael D. Glover Family
of Brooklyn, New York, pop. 2,592,000
age 28

The Capt John J. McKenna IV Family
of Brooklyn, New York, pop. 2,592,000
age 30

The Cpl Jordan C. Pierson Family
of Milford, Connecticut, pop. 53,137
age 21

The Cpl Jared M. Shoemaker Family
of Tulsa, Oklahoma, pop. 398,121
age 29

The LCpl Eric P. Valdepenas Family
of Seekonk, Massachusetts, pop. 13,722
age 21

The HM2 Christopher G. Walsh Family
of St. Louis, Missouri, pop. 318,416
age 30

The LCpl Christopher B. Cosgrove III Family
of Cedar Knolls, New Jersey, pop. 3,163
age 23

The SSgt Gordon G. Solomon Family
of Fairborn, Ohio, pop. 33,213
age 35

The Cpl David G. Weimortz Family
of Irmo, South Carolina, pop. 11,742
age 28

The LCpl Donald E. Champlin Family
of Nachitoches, Louisiana, pop. 18,323
age 28

The PFC Colin J. Wolfe Family
of Manassas, Virginia, pop. 41,705
age 18

The LCpl Cliff K. Golla Family
of Charlotte, North Carolina, pop. 792,862
age 21

The LCpl Philip A. Johnson Family
of Hartford, Connecticut, pop. 125,017
age 19

The PVT Ryan E. Miller Family
of Gahanna, Ohio, pop. 34,051
age 21

The LCpl Rene Martinez Family
of Miami, Florida, pop. 417,650
age 20

The Cpl Eric W. Herzberg Family
of Severna Park, Maryland, pop. 37,634
age 20

The Sgt Luke J. Zimmerman Family
of Luxemburg, Wisconsin, pop. 2,515
age 24

The LCpl James E. Brown Family
of Owensville, Indiana, pop. 1,273
age 20

The Cpl Michael C. Ledsome Family
of Austin, Texas, pop. 885,400
age 24

The Cpl Joshua M. Schmitz Family
of Spencer, Wisconsin, pop. 1,925
age 21

The LCpl William C. Koprince, Jr. Family
of Lenoir City, Tennessee, pop. 8,981
age 24

Many, many more families and many, many more hometowns left to mourn.

If there is such a thing as being conditioned by climate and geography, and I think there is, it is the West that has conditioned me.

WALLACE STEGNER

To Monument Valley

After leaving California, I had about a month until I was due in Washington. From there I would be heading to Afghanistan, my new State Department assignment. Ambassador Neumann, who had engaged Fallujah's nonpeace delegation just before the November 2004 battle, was now the U.S. ambassador in Kabul. He wanted me on his team working with Afghans directly in a frontline province called Khost.

I agreed to go, hoping to put Iraq a bit behind me by shifting to the other war, the only one that had a direct connection to the September 11, 2001, Al Qaeda attacks. A place and a war where no Afghan mayor would ever ask me: "What did Afghanistan have to do with September 11?" as Fallujah's mayor, Sheikh Dhari, had done regarding his own country, Iraq, after the U.S. invasion. I could only hope high school and college history books one day would declare in bold print and without any asterisks:

Afghanistan had something to do with 9/11 and was the right war.

Iraq had nothing to do with 9/11 and was the wrong war.

The American people, the Iraqi people, and the Afghan people were owed this truth. And given the Iraq War's many effects on many other countries, big and small, allies or not, I believed the U.S. owed this kind of reckoning with the wider international community as well. After all, when the world's sole superpower with its half-trillion-dollar-plus defense budget decided to invade Iraq, numerous nations began to bear the tremendous human costs of this decision. And they would continue to do so for a long time.

But before heading to Kabul, I needed some mountain and desert time first—the only kind of R&R that seemed to sink in fast and last. I needed to reconnect with the American West. I always felt best in the Rockies and the red rock, where my pioneer roots were strongest and the landscape big enough, wide enough, and deep enough to escape Washington's dysfunction and schadenfreude. The Great American West . . . where, as a Dutch friend from college once reminded me, remote highways ran a hundred miles long and in a straight line. And, unlike crowded Holland, travelers could traverse big valleys, horizon to horizon, with ridge tops edged by Ponderosa and spruce, not crowded canal houses along the Amstel River.

John Wayne country, John Ford country, Clint Eastwood country, Wallace Stegner country, Maynard Dixon country, Mormon country, Navajo country, and Weston country, generation after generation.

A scarred land of insurgents and insurgencies, generation after generation.

And so, after three and a half years in Iraq, I went on an overdue road trip, a long one, which would begin in Utah and end along the Arizona border of the Colorado Plateau. The trails my pioneering ancestors took by horse, wagon, and handcart, I would do via asphalt and in a 4x4. I decided my final stop would be Monument Valley, but before then I would trek to Milford, a small Utah town, and, if I had time, the nearby Topaz Mountain area, both places with family resonance and wartime resonance. In one, I had heard stories about nuclear radiation courtesy of the U.S. government, and in the other, stories about American citizens ordered to internment camps courtesy of the U.S. government. These were mostly unknown American stories in settings far from Iraq and in a different era—when the American impulse to do right went awry, and in a big way. Lives devastated and the American mirror left cracked.

As I began my early springtime trek, the news from Iraq continued to be bad and getting worse by the week as U.S. troops surged into the country's most violent areas, including Anbar and particularly into the worst pockets of Baghdad's Sunni-Shia sectarian inferno. I tried literally to tune it out, listening to a recycled audio blend of NPR's Click and Clack *Car Talk* and FM country stations that dominated the airwaves, as well as an entertaining and quirky local call-in show called *Tradio*—a platform for trade-me-this-for-that deal making.

Within my family, warfare had long become its own American story line. My maternal grandfather Warren, my father, Brad, uncles Chad and Ron, and my brother-in-law, Mike—all veterans—World War II, Vietnam, the Gulf War. Only after I left Anbar, however, did I learn about a great-uncle, Harold. The grandson of poor Danish and English immigrant farmers, he survived the Battle of the Bulge, Hitler's last armored charge. Only to die, alone—according to the coroner's esti- mate, over three hours—in a single vehicle car crash, probably a suicide (his death certificate read: "a crushed chest"), near a bridge after coming home with a drinking problem—"not the same"—from the bombed- out frozen forests called the Ardennes in Belgium full of frozen bodies. An estimated 19,000 Americans fell dead there in one month among thousands more German casualties and 3,000 civilians.

Harold, like so many other veterans of his day, and today, would not be buried at Arlington National Cemetery but rather a graveyard that measured only about 100 meters by 100 meters in Pinto, Utah (pop.: fewer than a dozen or so now in the unincorporated ultra-rural area that once served as a rest stop for pioneers and U.S. cavalry, a horse watering hole along the Old Spanish Trail, as well as a transit point for traders of animal pelts—and Indian slaves). A place only reach- able by bumpy, washboard dirt roads, where rattlesnakes and ants find cover and shade in the sagebrush-filled and very unmanicured grounds, surrounded by a chain-link fence and rusted barbed wire. And where some tombstones, simple lichen-covered rough-hewn slabs of rock, tilt at 45-degree angles under scarecrow-like juniper trees as ravens circle above.

My family's larger experience with war also happened, insidiously, under Great Basin skies, in Milford, Utah, not far from Pinto. Where in the 1950s warfare's ultimate weapon—atomic energy—introduced itself into my ancestral DNA with summer breezes, over and under backyard fences and through redbrick walls. It took four decades, but the U.S. government (landlord over two-thirds of the state) eventually classified my family, the Weston clan, as "downwinders."

As I drove into this town of irradiated ancestors, where I used to search the white-yellow sand for arrowheads as a kid and shoot a .22 rifle before I was a teen, the stench from football-field-sized corporate pig farms filled my nostrils. Only a bit of piñon pine buffered the smell. This was a land crisscrossed first by pioneer trails, stagecoach, Pony Express, and rail, then later civilized to a degree by gravel and pavement below the community's solitary high point, a gray water tower.

A place now home to that most modern of symbols: a massive wind farm outside town that helps power Los Angeles.

The area's abandoned silver mines attract only jackrabbits and opportunistic birds of prey. A few valleys over, Robert LeRoy Parker, aka Butch Cassidy, grew up on a cattle ranch in Circleville before becoming an expert in banditry and bank robbing in Utah, Colorado, and Wyoming. A great-great-uncle, a Gillies, a rebel we like to brag about on our genealogical tree, rode and hid along with his friend Butch. Outlaws. Even after surviving Fallujah, at times barely, I liked to think my own family of Western renegades and outcasts could have held their own in Anbar against Sunni outlaws.

Probably, but my family was no match when pitted against the U.S. government.

As I stopped to fill up my gas tank and grab a Coke (but not sprinkled with salted peanuts this time, a redneck recipe my quasi-redneck family long favored), I remembered these other "war stories" from my paternal grandpa, Jack Weston. He himself began work as a teenager in Milford shoveling coal into the fireboxes that powered the steam engines of Union Pacific locomotives, traversing before age twenty the largest rail network in the U.S. He would retire half a century later after sitting at the front of trains, an engineer, powering across the West—a yellow and black blur of railroad steel.

As a younger man on predawn depot duty, he would wake up my dad and his younger sister around 4 or 5 a.m. before a scheduled nuclear test. Under receding starlight, they would sit on the front porch stairs and look to the west, near the Nevada state line, for a sharp flash in the sky. About thirty minutes later, the sound of the above-ground atomics would rumble through the "UP" railroad town of 1,500, a small burg of alfalfa farmers, miners, and railroaders in a wide valley bordered by the Mineral Mountains on one side and Wahwah Valley and Frisco Peak on the other. No mountain range, however, and no matter how high, afforded protection from these nuclear blasts.

After seeing the horizon brighten a hundredfold in a single second—a form of instantaneous man-made radioactive lightning—my dad said the family would have a sit-down breakfast before he would head off to elementary school. A handful of teachers taught eighty or so students across all six grades. The next public announcement about the next A-bomb test would follow on the radio and be printed in *The Milford News*. Alarm clocks once again would be reset. He recalled that the early morning single-strobe blasts of unimaginable wattage and subsequent shockwaves, which ever so slightly lifted parted bangs, were always "an event" for kids.

The nuclear age had begun.

In America.

After Hiroshima. After Nagasaki. After the U.S. government introduced its new weapon to the warring world—at 0815 local time, above Hiroshima's Shima Hospital.

With these other atomic detonations now stateside, the American Southwest desert sky filled with free entertainment, compliments of Uncle Sam ... the same federal government that would be my own employer decades later, first in the Netherlands, then New York, then Iraq, and finally, in Afghanistan.

Between 1951 and mid-1962, the Nevada Test Site conducted eighty-six nuclear tests at or above ground. They were timed to detonate when wind patterns were blowing toward the Beehive State of Utah and away from the Golden State of California. Another fourteen were tested underground.

My great-uncle Heber operated a large ranch in those unhealthiest of days, with thousands of sheep milling about the West Desert. During the atomic testing, he found hundreds sick, lethargic, dying. Sheepherder and sheep irradiated alike. An estimated eighteen to twenty thousand in various flocks in the Nevada-Utah area were exposed in 1953 alone, with burns to the animals' faces and lips after grazing on isotope-laden fields and pastures. Ewes miscarried and wool came off in unnatural chunks well before shearing season. Some ranchers lost as much as a third of their herds. These animals succumbed faster than the herders on horseback around them. Sheepdogs were quieted across those years, and Heber himself died of cancer carried by Western winds monitored by the Feds when they blew over certain parts of America but not others.

Only much later would downwinders, including my relatives, be informed that government scientists already understood how destructive the nuclear early morning matinees were to the human genome. At the cellular level, the human body could be made—in an instant—as weak and vulnerable by science as it had evolved over millennia to be strong and resilient. These other kinds of bullets had now been invented, microscopic, and just as deadly in the end as those Marine grunts dodged in Iraq, even if death took years, not seconds.

The New England Journal of Medicine concluded in a 1979 study: "A significant excess of leukemia deaths occurred in children up to 14 years of age living in Utah between 1959 and 1967. This excess was concentrated in the cohort of children born between 1951 and 1958, and was most pronounced in those residing in counties receiving high fallout." In 1990, Congress passed the Radiation Exposure Compensation Act (RECA). All who could prove unusual family deaths from the approved list of health conditions due to nuclear fallout were paid $50,000 by the federal government. The law allowed uranium miners to apply for $100,000 payments, and $75,000 for those closest to the atomic test sites. Tax-free.

More lives priced out in U.S. cash, a different kind of blood money. This time, Americans, my own relatives and parents' neighbors, whereas in my role in Iraq, I had been paymaster for Iraqi families and their neighbors. Killed by made-in-the-USA radiation. Killed by made-in-the-USA bullets. Same difference, although the dollar amounts were significantly greater for the Utah, Nevada, and Arizona downwind dead. As a federal government employee myself, I was appalled when I read how a U.S. Department of Energy official at the time remarked, "Those people in Utah don't give a shit about radiation."

Well they did then, and we still do.

Give a shit.

Every time I thought of these mini–mushroom clouds, I was reminded how in Iraq I had heard some troops offer dismissive comments about "Hajis" or "fucking Muslims"—who, early in the Fallujah battle, were burned by curtains of white phosphorous (aka "Willy

Pete") used to conceal Marine movement and protect American lives, while melting Iraqi skin.

These wartime reflections and reckonings filled my mind for the initial three hours of my journey, until I got to my first stop. After parking, I walked for a bit along Milford's dilapidated Main Street. It had a lot of potholes. Once straight picket fences lay twisted in front of unkempt front yards. Some gutters were filled with soil and trash. Fallujah almost looked better in a few places, at least after the multimillion-dollar "build" phase began to take hold in the city. Milford's economy had bottomed out, making it appear semi-abandoned. I walked past 1,500-square-foot houses in my parents' old neighborhoods, wondering which families had lost relatives to the radiation. The odds were stark: my mother lost five aunts to cancer, mostly leukemia. As my dad put it, "We watched the bomb explosions, then years later our friends began to die of cancer. Mitch, Mel, Elaine, Carroll, Dale, and Jerry and more."

After an hour or so of wandering through town, past the closed Chinese restaurant, former Spanish-style railroad depot, a yellow Union Pacific caboose set on a square lawn, and the boarded-up tan brick Hotel Milford, I knew it was time to get back on the road. I needed to get to Monument Valley before a forecasted storm moved through and passable dirt roads became impassable mud roads.

But prior to leaving, I made my way back to Main Street to stand below a curvy retro blue and yellow sign that read "Norge Appliances." This marked a key part of the Milford map for me. My mother's side, the Johnsons, had kept a small furniture store open here despite the Great Depression and across three twentieth-century wars. The plain brick storefront once welcomed "Sam's Furniture and Appliance" customers to shop for linoleum and sofas ... not far from a 1940s-era Japanese-American internment camp. It was called Topaz, encircled by barbed wire and guard towers—and U.S. Supreme Court–approved (*Korematsu v. United States*, a 6-to-3 ruling in 1944).

The store's large glass windows had been updated and now read, "Derailed Bar & Grill, Totally Off Track! Get Your Caboose In Here!"— but with an orange and black "For Sale by Owner" sign taped below. Three other electronic signs advertised three brands of Budweiser beer. After looking at my grandparents' furniture store turned dive bar gone bust, I had seen enough of Milford. Full of Edward Hopper–like scenes, the stark uncompromising variety where shadows reveal just as much, if not more, than light. A rough town where tough people somehow survived—the kind of hard-luck place that could, and did, produce soldiers and Marines for all of America's wars. Like my father. My uncles. My grandfather. My brother-in-law. My great-uncle Harold.

The kind who enlist. The kind who got drafted.

The kind of kids who got killed. The kind of kids who still get killed. And probably the kind of kids who always will get killed in America's future wars, far from their hometowns across the USA.

Within a few minutes I was back on the road, on state route 257-N, headed to Topaz for my next road trip stop outside another small town called Delta. Along the way, top-of-the-hour radio newscasts had a few Iraq updates but not many.

I preferred other audio. A bunch of bands—Tears for Fears ("It's a very, very Mad world"), The The ("The world is on its elbows and knees / It's forgotten the message and worships the creeds"), Echo & the Bunnymen ("Oh how the times have changed us . . . Men not devils have claimed us"), the Byrds ("a time to kill, a time to heal"), singer Stan Ridgway ("Things are never quite the way they seem"), some Joaquín Rodrigo (Concierto de Aranjuez), a bit of David Guetta (before Memories), a lot more Johnny Cash ("Everyone I know goes away / In the end"), including "The Ballad of Ira Hayes," and especially an Ennio Morricone collection, which fit the American West setting—all made for good company.

The Good, the Bad and the Ugly movie soundtrack particularly reverberated with a new kind of meaning after Fallujah: "Smoke hides the valleys and fire paints the plains / Loud roar the cannons till ruin remains . . . All hope seems gone, so, soldier, march on to die . . . How ends the story, whose is the glory / Ask if we dare, our comrades out there who sleep . . . This devastation once was a nation / So fall the dice, how high is the price we pay."

The wars were still very far from most Americans, I could tell, with the only "old news" being more bombs or more dead or more wounded—often all three. Bad headlines easily tuned out since few knew anyone serving in Anbar or Mosul or Baghdad. Or in Afghanistan.

I would not have a long time to explore this other place, this other tragic American war story. But as a history major in college, I was intent on making sure I walked the place. See it firsthand. I imagined it would have the kind of ghosts that tend to hang around certain notorious places in a democratic republic that likes to pride itself on doing what is right, not what is wrong, even (especially?) in wartime.

Driving along flat fields, I almost missed the turnoff, but then I saw a green sign with a big white arrow: "Topaz Relocation Site."

The word "relocation" struck me as a bit Orwellian, a bureaucratically neutered term. The Japanese-American citizens who "relocated" to Utah had no choice. They were forced to leave their families and homes in Northern California, with Topaz being just one of several camps overseen by the War Relocation Authority. I remembered how Fallujans were forced to abandon their homes just before Operation Phantom Fury, which we renamed New Dawn.

The hurried timeline was straightforward enough.

After Pearl Harbor the mechanics of government moved quickly, spurred by the momentum of prejudice and a presidential executive order. Such that by springtime 1942, in the Presidio near San Francisco, large posters went up with big print:

NOTICE
Headquarters Western Defense Command and Fourth Army
Civilian Exclusion Order No. 61
Wartime Civil Control Administration
Instructions to All Persons of JAPANESE Ancestry . . .

The official notification listed all the local hometown areas from where individuals "both alien and non-alien" would be required to be "evacuated" and limited to the following possessions: "bedding and linens (no mattress) for each family member," "toilet articles," "extra clothing," and a final restriction that must have devastated many families and children: "no pets of any kind will be permitted."

The end of the order stated the two, and only two, specific days those of the wrong ancestry had to show up, between the hours of 8 a.m. and 5 p.m., "for processing." Again, I thought of Fallujah: we had badged the people, processed them in our tents, and handed out two $100 bills after scanning their irises and fingerprints.

That was how the journey from California to Topaz began. Once in the remote western Utah desert, the unlucky thousands were moved into crowded military-barracks-like huts behind barbed wire and armed guards. A total of 11,212 people would pass through the Topaz front gate across three years. They were part of more than 120,000 sent to nine other "War Relocation Centers" and related "Department of Justice"–run facilities located primarily in the West, with one camp in Wyoming named Heart Mountain.

In front of me, not much of the Utah camp was left and a planned museum still unbuilt. Not much to reinforce the hard history and hard stories of the site. I could see some twisted metal, shards of glass and tile, mounds of soil, a stone fence, and cracked concrete. While stepping between anthills, however, I came across something unexpected. A placard that read: "The marker signs throughout the site are an Eagle Scout project. Please help us preserve them."

Now that, I thought, was a worthwhile scouting project.

As I left my footprints amid the sagebrush plain, I could only think how war, whether in Iraq, or in World War II, could bring out, and inevitably did, the worst human instincts—and the worst government policies. Not just overseas along distant front lines but back home too, when fear itself, contrary to FDR's admonition to the American people, became a contagion. All around me was proof of that, as were the featured stories within publications of the time.

An October 1942 *Coronet* magazine, for example, showed wartime propaganda at its very worst, but probably very effective as well at the time. Inside, an article was titled "Concentration Camp, USA Style" with an italicized preface: *American style internment camps—where brutality is unheard of and democracy is the rule—are both a protection against our enemies and an investment in the future . . .*

Incidentally, some of the magazine's other stories in the same issue ("Cover Girl, North Carolina–born Ava Gardner") included:

"Your Role as a Guerilla Fighter"—The preface: *A Veteran of the World War, a fighting man who did post-graduate work in Mexico, Palestine and Spain, tells how to stop the enemy in your own back yard . . .* ("It could happen here. . . . We could be invaded. And if that should happen— then you might be a guerilla").

"Plain Talk About Sterilization"—The preface: *Sterilize the mentally defective? A California research foundation has surveyed the results of sterilization in that state. Here are the findings . . .* (citing a Supreme Court majority opinion in 1927: "Three generations of imbeciles are enough").

"Psychosurgery Cured Me"—The preface: *A tonic of the headline blues: this inspiring story of a nervous wreck, miraculously restored to normal life and happiness by a surgeon's knife* . . . (a first-person—and indeed favorable—account of a lobotomy).

And, "Should Roosevelt Be Elected to a Fourth Term?" (. . . *do not change the helmsman in the middle of a storm* . . .).

My how times change—or mostly?—and gratefully.

Iraqis, post-invasion, sure could relate to the how-to-be-a-guerrilla article, I thought. Abbas would have liked to add this magazine to his personal library, though I would have encouraged him not to share it with his English students in Fallujah.

I would not have told Abbas either that my grandpa, a very good man, who had served in World War II and owned the small furniture store not far from the camp, a town leader, a member of the local VFW and American Legion, called the Japanese "Japs" until the day he died of a heart attack at age seventy-four. In the early 1940s, official U.S. Army posters declared: "JAP . . . You're Next! We'll Finish the Job!" and featured a fearsome-looking Uncle Sam, with both shirtsleeves rolled up, wielding a big tire wrench.

I knew plenty of Americans had even more dismissive names for Iraqis, for Muslims.

Abbas knew it as well. He had heard the derogatory names, read the derogatory names.

After walking through a small part of the vacant but still scarred fields—the Topaz site encompasses more than 600 acres—I noticed there had been another visitor in the desolate area, though I had seen no one else all afternoon. I had missed the item at first, which was delicately balanced on the scouting project sign. Someone at some point had left a pair of glasses, and not by accident it seemed. I got closer and saw they looked to be a very old pair, maybe even a pair worn more than half a century earlier. Perhaps a student at the Topaz Art School, finally back to reflect and remember? Start a new drawing maybe. I wanted to think so anyway, eyes that had seen Topaz firsthand.

A witness.

I recalled how the celebrated progressive, and ever-bespectacled, Earl Warren was once asked, long after retiring from the U.S. Supreme Court, what he thought about this particular American chapter in a time of war. As state attorney general and governor of California in the 1940s, he had approved of the internment camps "USA-style." According to one account, upon hearing the question, the former chief justice broke down and cried.

In a place that had experienced plenty of tears but rarely saw rain in a Western state with the second lowest annual average rainfall, storm clouds began to gather. Time to leave.

As I departed, making my way toward I-70, another part of local war history came to mind, when war front and home front mixed. I recalled how my hometown's fruit orchards grew in the same place where World War II POWs worked in agricultural labor camps until 1945, when Nazi Germany and the rest of the Axis Powers surrendered to Allied forces. The foreign laborers included Germans, officers from the North African campaign who had served under "Desert Fox" Erwin Rommel. Area farmers said several of the POWs spoke English and acted like "gentlemen."

So many young American men had gone off to war in the 1940s there was a rural labor shortage. Families needed help with the agricultural work: picking peaches, pears, strawberries, and cherries. While their sons and brothers fought other German sons and brothers, these POWs sent to the Rocky Mountains gathered fruit in the same fields that small-town soldiers and Marines had harvested while growing up.

In 1970, camp buildings were dismantled to make way for Orchard Elementary School, located not far from my own grade school with its nuclear attack warning siren painted cherry red, towering forty feet above the playground and a concrete bunker dug out twenty feet beneath a cafeteria managed by a stern crew of "lunch ladies," who had been born just after World War I.

A mostly unknown fact from this period as hundreds of thousands of POWs worked in agricultural camps across the United States seemed particularly ironic after I had placed my own feet atop the crumbled concrete and between the rusted barbed wire that day at Topaz: some German POWs were able to walk around under an "honor system," and all were afforded protections under the Geneva Conventions (e.g., paid for their labor, living conditions similar to those provided to U.S. troops: forty square feet for enlisted, 120 square feet for officers, top-ranking ones even getting garden space).

Many German soldiers as POWs, in other words, enjoyed more

rights and better wartime treatment than many interned Japanese-American citizens—and their children.

My road trip was half done. Leaving Topaz, I remembered how I felt while visiting Abu Ghraib Prison in Iraq, not once but twice. The first time to secure the release of Iraqi detainees mistakenly rounded up in Baghdad in fall 2003. I had never seen two more relieved Iraqis as they huddled, shaking, in the backseat of our SUV, both silent the entire drive back to the Iraqi capital. They got out of the prison a few months before news of the abuse scandal broke in the U.S. The second time, three years later in 2006, I went with Larry Nicholson to the mostly deserted Abu Ghraib, full of wind and dust and a very bad aura. On behalf of the coalition, we handed responsibility for the prison back to the Iraqi government. An Iraqi Army soldier said to me at the time: "No one likes what this place represents in the mind."

I put his comment verbatim in my cable to Washington, later WikiLeaked.

Plenty of Americans, I suspected, had heard about Abu Ghraib and what had gone on there. But not enough knew about Topaz and the other places like it—all the camps located much closer to home.

Field trip distance.

After turning onto I-70 and heading toward Colorado, I crossed the jagged San Rafael Swell—an arid maze-like region of stone canyons, including Robbers Roost, where Butch Cassidy and my great-great-uncle hid from lawmen—and onward into the former uranium boom-town of Moab. Where the fuel for America's nuclear arsenal once was mined and at great profit, based on prices guaranteed by the federal government wanting to out-stockpile and out-war the Soviets.

By this time, my interstate traveling speeds matched my '80s music flashback playlist: The Church ("Under the Milky Way"); Duran Duran ("Don't say a prayer for me now"); The Cult ("I'm sure in her you'll find / The sanctuary"); and Paul Hardcastle ("All those who remember the war / They won't forget what they've seen / Destruction of men in their prime . . . All we want to do is come home.")

As the red mesas and rust-colored lower layers of sediment called "Chinle" and "Moenkoep" came into view, I stopped at another important historical marker. One that echoed the internment camp I had just

left. On a dirt road easy to miss, just west of Arches National Park—
Edward Abbey land ("You can't study the darkness by flooding it with
light")—a small sign describes what happened there, at a scenic place
with a soothing name: "Dalton Wells." Unlike at Topaz, the script
provides an unflinching summary of "the facts" under the heading:
Japanese-American World War II Concentration Camp, 1943 and reads:

> On January 11, 1943, a train pulled into the Thompson Station
> north of here with armed Military Police guarding sixteen male
> American citizens of Japanese ancestry. While the locals of the
> town waited to cross the tracks, the entourage was loaded and
> transferred to the old abandoned "CCC" [Civilian Conserva-
> tion Corps] camp located here at Dalton Wells.
>
> Their crime? They were classified as "troublemakers" in
> the Manzanar, California Relocation Center where they and
> their families had been forcibly located at the start of World
> War II. Removed from their homes and lands in California
> under a Presidential Executive Order, they were subject to the
> whim and mercy of poorly-trained bureaucrats and military
> personnel in the center. This Executive Presidential Order was
> the result of wartime hysteria, racial bigotry, and greed.

The already bad-enough story got worse. "Trigger-happy soldiers"
killed two of the "inmates" during a protest at the site. All of the men
had U.S. citizenship —and, as the historical marker notes, "some were
veterans of World War I."

A few hours more, beyond the mountain biking and Colorado
River rafting recreational magnet that Moab had since become, I finally
arrived at my road trip destination, Monument Valley, which straddles
the Utah-Arizona border. The winding drive beyond Topaz had taken
six hours.

As the late afternoon sun began to set after gray cloudbanks lifted,
reflecting off the massive red sandstone buttes, I began to wonder . . .
*How would America memorialize the Iraq War? And the other war I was
soon going to, in Afghanistan? Would the wars' pain and scars be acknowledged or ignored in noble rhetoric somewhere on a new monument along the
National Mall?*

Were these conflicts ever even winnable?

Iraq did not feel that way. The kind of staged "surrender" ceremonies for public consumption in wars past no longer seemed possible in an age of more insurgencies, more troop surges, and more transnational terrorism.

More drones. More deployments. More war.

With some slow hiking ahead, I had time to give these questions some deliberate thought. In front of me towered the iconic geology. Sheer walls under big sky located in the middle of an Indian reservation, a "sovereign nation" that measured over 27,000 square miles—but a lot smaller than the tribe's original vast lands.

Like so many Native Americans, including the Lakota who lived near the Little Bighorn River in Montana, the Navajo had fought their own battles, waged their own wars, against a bellicose government in Washington that commanded a bigger army.

I wondered how they, the Navajo, memorialized what others called "The Navajo Wars."

How they chose to remember their war dead and their wartime sacrifices—in those unwinnable wars.

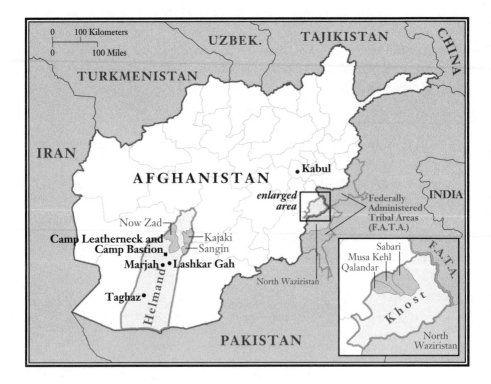

PART II

The Right War

The war was a mirror; it reflected man's every virtue and every vice, and if you looked closely, like an artist at his drawings, it showed up both with unusual clarity.

GEORGE GROSZ
ARTIST OF *Eclipse of the Sun, Fit for Active Service,*
The Pillars of Society, Shut Your Mouth and Keep on Serving,
Bow to the Authorities, Peace, II

Diplomats and military men remember with nostalgia the first alien lands in which they served, and I suppose this is inevitable; but in my case I look back upon Afghanistan with special affection because it was, in those days, the wildest, weirdest land on earth and to be a young man in Kabul was the essence of adventure. . . . I thought again of the violent land and the even more violent contradictions that surrounded me.

JAMES MICHENER, *Caravans*

Deeper into the Muslim World

It was a scenic flight.

The ground below me unfolded in a blanket of reds and oranges bordered by towering passes and sunken, hardpan deserts. Sun-cooked and cracked, this in-between land resembled worn, crumpled sandpaper, dotted with isolated mud compounds connected by few visible roads. Caravans of horses, donkeys, and camels carried nomads called the Kuchi across the ancient setting, as they always had. Faint remnants of archaic encampments could be discerned, not yet having succumbed to wind and time. I saw what looked like piled stones in places, circular and buttressed by high ground primed for combat. This was territory that Mongols and Alexander the Great had invaded, defended, and then abandoned. The only signs of water, and life, were intermittent green crags fed by hidden springs.

The commercial airplane navigated Iranian airspace and was scheduled to touch down in Afghanistan within the hour. We easily cleared Iranian territory, a land of Mahmoud Ahmadinejad, ayatollahs, American embassy hostages, crude oil, and nuclear reactors. From my window seat, I felt uneasy, contemplating the obvious. It was spring 2007. Some in Washington still harbored remake–the–Middle East designs. The same individuals inside and outside the George W. Bush administration who claimed the Iraq War had been "a last resort."

A Safi Airways ("The International Airline of Afghanistan") flight attendant dressed in soft shades of blue with a delicate matching scarf, and who reminded me of the young Sophia Loren, all angles around those eyes, offered me a plastic cup. She filled it with lukewarm water, no ice, as is custom.

Five and a half years after 9/11, two wars were sapping the superpower I represented. The United States was on the verge of a mortgage meltdown and "too big to fail" billion-dollar bank bailouts loomed.

During my short stint stateside on leave, I heard grumblings about our nation-building needs at home, not in western Iraq or eastern Afghanistan. Our infrastructure, not theirs "over there." In August of that year, a sudden bridge collapse outside Minneapolis—thirteen people killed and another 145 injured—graphically reinforced this theme across U.S. newscasts. The fallen structure, emblematic of a broader state-by-state level of disrepair, had been completed four decades earlier in 1967. Experts estimated 8,000 outdated "fracture-critical" structures across all fifty states needed urgent repair, including New York State's Tappan Zee and San Diego's Coronado bridges.

Looking down from the plane, I noticed Afghanistan's springtime poppy fields and shiny mineral deposits, some of which were laid bare, amid treeless hills, glinting in the mid-afternoon sunlight. The country's untapped copper resources equaled multiple kings' and queens' ransoms in market value. By November 2007, the Chinese convinced the Afghan government their investor pockets were deepest and surest, and finalized a $3 billion joint mining agreement to exploit an estimated $88 billion copper bonanza. The math was simple. Communist Chinese trade delegations offered the best deal to the Afghans, reportedly influenced by fistfuls of bribes.

The view of Afghanistan from 25,000 feet exceeded everything I had read or could have imagined. Only the peaked topography of the American West—minty sagebrush instead of the purple-pink poppy fields—approached the mesmerizing effects of this country. Half an hour from my hometown, one of the world's largest open-pit copper mines, Kennecott, still produced tons of metal ore annually. In World War II, it supplied Allied nations with 30 percent of their war mobilization copper needs. Like China's Great Wall, the vast mine could be observed from space, both testaments of manpower and national will.

Ready and yet wary, I neared entering this new war zone, a region that remained largely unchanged, its lifespan counted in eons. Here, the Hindu Kush took their own time, geologic time, to rise up and touch the sky in sudden jolts of relief, just like the Rockies I knew so well. The stockade-like 14,000-foot range still corralled expansionist armies led by proud generals, as it had for centuries. Such views might help heal the Iraq occupiers' psyche, my own and those of my friends in uniform. Marines who already had served in "The Forgotten War" echoed my optimistic sense of this neglected front.

I was going from one war right into the other because I wanted to justify my country's actions, to remind Afghans and myself what America represented. I wanted to show what we could accomplish. I was not just seeking collaboration or commiseration in my new State Department assignment. I was looking for more. I wanted to regain a sense of place and purpose and to connect with the Afghan people.

Most of all, I wanted to convince them what the United States of America still stood for—not what we risked becoming because of Iraq. We were not just an incompetent occupier and naive nation builder, human rights abuser, and even self-justified torturer—waterboarding "enemy combatants" and facilitating the "extraordinary rendition" of suspected terrorists to and from secret CIA "black sites" where jailers were known to interrogate without moral or legal constraints.

It seemed there was a new post-9/11 vocabulary confusing America's conscience. Torture tapes destroyed. More fear. More surveillance. More drones. More young kids left dead on both sides.

Afghanistan did not yet feel like my country's Mission: Impossible. America, the historic standard-bearer of democratic ideals and conduct on the international stage, could do big, good things in a desperately poor, war-torn country half a globe from home.

Couldn't it?

Surely, U.S. actions in Iraq had not damaged irreparably our American core—America's spirit—and traditions. Our better angels enshrined in laws and ethics, I believed, had to win out. But at the same time I could envision the alternative: our national mirror so cracked, its reflection so warped. One we might collectively choose to look away from, not wanting to acknowledge the image that stared back—a scarred and new kind of wartime countenance now increasingly unrecognizable.

What next, another war amid Muslims, somewhere else, fought by the same few?

While landing in Kabul, the sprawling brown city of millions spread out before me. The pockmarked capital from decades of continuous warfare, located within the most heavily landmined area in the world, showcased ramshackle earthen huts. All built on terraces layered upward, like a giant mud cake, enveloped in a hazy mist of stagnant carbon-dioxidized air.

I embraced this uncertainty and challenge. This country. After my long detour in Iraq, I was finally about to set foot into 9/11 territory, the training ground of Al Qaeda terrorists, including Osama bin Laden and Mohammad Atta. From the very beginning, my nation should have sent me, all of us, to Afghanistan—diplomats, aid workers, Marines, and soldiers alike.

To the necessary war. To the good war.

To the right war.

After exiting the plane at Kabul International Airport, first constructed by Soviet engineers in the early 1960s and remodeled decades later with Japanese funds, a young man approached me. Bearing a steady gaze from green-gray eyes set above a black beard, the proud-looking Pashtun extended his large hand and said, in practiced but still broken English, "Wehl-cuhm to Off-gun-eh-stun."

His greeting sang with an accent I immediately liked. I already felt at home. For the first time in a long while, I did not feel like an occupier. I could sense the weight of Iraq begin to lift. Walking to the convoy of armored vehicles waiting to take me to the U.S. embassy compound, built like a fort, I noticed several other Afghans nearby, kneeling on small multicolored prayer rugs and facing Mecca.

After about a week of in-processing at the embassy in Kabul, I was on my way back to another frontline job, in Khost province, one of

Afghanistan's most violent regions, bordering North Waziristan in Pakistan and about 140 miles east of the congested capital. Overwhelmingly Pashtun (close to 100 percent), tribal law had long dominated the rebellious region, particularly in remote villages and valleys. Khost measures approximately 1,600 square miles, with a population of around 600,000. Over 90 percent live in rural areas, with a sizable Kuchi (or nomad) population of around 100,000. They move with the seasons and treat countries' borders as resting stops, not where passports are required and checked for onward travel.

The year I arrived, the Afghan government estimated that 40 percent of males were literate, but less than 10 percent of women, even partially. In Khost, agriculture dominates the local economy, with a low amount of poppy production compared to southern Afghanistan, particularly Helmand, which had long topped the list. In 2010, only 4 percent of Khost's population had access to electricity, while two thirds of the province had mobile phone service. Pakistan's close proximity influences all facets of life in Khost. From goods being sold in its markets to the currency most commonly used (widespread use of the Pakistani rupee)—and shared instability, reflective in the number of CIA drones overhead and black operations conducted by SEAL and Delta Force teams. Sometimes conducted jointly with Afghan forces, but sometimes not.

The notorious Haqqani Network, led by former mujahideen commander Jalaluddin Haqqani and his son Sirajuddin, retained close ties with the Taliban's Quetta Shura. In the 1980s, the CIA funded this powerful tribal network to fight against the Soviets. The Haqqanis have long been both a favored and feared family anchored in Khost. They have deep pockets and long tentacles that reach into the remotest mountain ranges and valleys, winning friends out of largesse, fanaticism, and fear.

In the center of Khost there is a large mosque, built and funded by the Haqqanis. The province, due to its temperate wintertime climate, was also a favorite get-away spot for Osama bin Laden, who had established a terrorist training base in one of Khost's districts. The United States bombed it with cruise missiles in August 1998, but missed bin Laden. The strikes were in retaliation for the terrorist attacks on the U.S. embassies in Tanzania and Kenya earlier that month. After returning from a summer vacation in Martha's Vineyard, President Bill Clinton said, "There will be no sanctuary for terrorists." Taliban leader Mullah Omar said the U.S. attacks showed American "enmity" toward the Afghan people.

After arriving in Khost, I realized my long road trip to Monument Valley had helped put things into perspective, allowed me enough time and distance, measured by U.S. highways and remote byways far from Fallujah, to recover a bit. In Iraq I had seen the worst of warfare and conflict. Afghanistan held more promise, and better days perhaps, even with its violent history. I wanted to think so anyway, even in a place like Khost and with all of its challenges—and danger.

I had no real marching orders, other than to try to get along with the military in a province that was home to U.S. Army brigades rotating under the command of the 82nd and 101st Airborne Divisions.

In the first days there, I received an email from Larry Nicholson, asking how the new assignment was going and how I liked working with the Army compared to Marines. I emailed back that many of the soldiers seemed solid, while others had some challenges because they had never deployed before or had been in billets that meant they were tied to various Fobbitvilles. It was also unfair for me to compare an Anbar vet with soldiers who had deployed to much safer parts of Iraq. I did offer one observation though: "For a long time there were too many generals in Iraq, especially in the Green Zone. But there sure are not enough over here." Larry got my point, I think: the right general in the right place can help unstick things. And a lot in Afghanistan needed to be unstuck, and quick. Colonels sometimes, even brigade commanders, just did not have the heft to do it, either in theater or back in Washington.

"Well keep me updated," Larry wrote back.

"I will. You know how I still think this war needs more Marines in it, and Iraq needs a lot fewer in Anbar. Let's hope General Conway gets what he wants." (Conway, the Marine commandant at the time, was pressing to refocus the Marine Corps toward Afghanistan, away from Iraq. He had met some resistance at the highest levels, given the Bush administration's focus on Iraq—and its legacy in that war.)

In Khost, I would also be working with the Provincial Reconstruction Team (PRT). Our primary mission was to ensure U.S. funds—millions of dollars—were spent on the right projects: schools, district government centers, roads, water wells, bridges, and so on. Despite our significant resources, this would not be easy. The Taliban had long been embedded in Khost, even if they had been put on the defensive by this point in the war. They had a plan and strategy of their own. Iraq had taught me never to underestimate your enemy, and never to overestimate your side in any war.

U.S. government bosses also expected me to get to know the political dynamics among the local tribes as quickly as possible. My work in Anbar had shown me how complex that could be. I had also been given some background information on Khost's governor, Arsala Jamal, who had been born in a neighboring province and whose family resided in Canada. A former NGO employee, he would be my partner in all things political. Embassy Political Section officers said they welcomed any inside assessment I might have about him because he was close to President Hamid Karzai and, they said, perhaps "a bit corrupt." I did not intend to take on an FBI-like role, I told them. They meant well but I also saw in my embassy meetings just how far removed most Americans remained from most Afghans. Just as most Americans in Baghdad had been from Iraqis.

The PRT and I had our simple office and simpler housing on Forward Operating Base Chapman. The base, a former Soviet airstrip, had the best jogging route in the province, year-round. Between two-mile loops, I was always awed by the transfixing, layered imagery: Afghan army soldiers praying daily on top of the rusted wings of Soviet airplanes, bracketed by a mountain range border that had long been the transit point for armies, traders, Taliban, terrorists and the occasional imperial envoy. In my afternoon runs, I was reminded of what this country and region had always represented—and always would: a combustible mix of history, religion, and geography. The place seemed to be whispering: *All foreigners beware.*

After arriving at FOB Chapman, I met Arif, my Afghan linguist. I had heard good things about him from some of the soldiers and the diplomat who preceded me. Much of the American effort depended on Afghans who spoke our language because few of us spoke theirs. Arif became both my voice and bridge into the intricacies of Afghan society. He was about five years younger than I was, but like many Afghans, he said his exact birth date was unknown. Arif kept his black-going-gray full beard trimmed and had studied engineering. His family was part of the influential and largely pro-U.S. Mangal tribe.

"Mr. Kael, welcome," he said as he offered me his hand.

"Do you like these mountains we have in Khost?" he asked. The diplomat before me must have briefed him on me.

I looked into the distance. "I can't wait to get up in them."

"Good, because one of our first missions will be that way and all the way up there," he pointed.

Atop a hazy layer of clouds I could see a ridgeline east of where we stood.

"That's Qalandar District. That's where we will go."

"I like any mountain."

Arif paused a bit before adding, "The Taliban like mountains too."

The next day, as we climbed the terraced valleys and ridgelines in our Humvee caravan, I noticed that the trees looked to be dying, reminding me the way beetles had infested and killed swaths of forests in Utah, Wyoming, and Colorado. Patches of leaves had gone brown, appearing rustlike, due to a spreading infestation of something deadly and small and insidious. *Damn bugs are here too*, I thought. Still, the farther we went, the greener the terrain became. Compared to Iraq's Anbar, Khost was lush, especially in the deep crags that were fed by deep springs or spring runoff. If there were any people in the world who could manage limited water supply, I could see it was Afghans. Over many decades, even centuries, they had shaped the earth to capture rainfall, channel, and store it—and mostly without twenty-first-century, or even twentieth-century, tools and technology.

While far from an expert in forestry, let alone in Afghan foliage, I thought the doomed tree stands resembled spruce and ponderosa pine, a resilient species that had thick, toughened bark, practically fireproof and smelling vanilla-like. The mountainsides also appeared scarred, as if old horizontal mine shafts had long since caved in. I counted half a dozen.

When we stopped, more than a dozen Pashtun tribal elders sat gathered. Behind them congregated their twentysomething-year-old sons, and a third line of teens, all in a row, watching but not speaking. Their penetrating gaze focused in my direction.

They had traveled from isolated villages to mark the opening of a new district center. Funded by hundreds of thousands of U.S. dollars, it would be the provincial government's outpost in Qalandar District, populated by approximately 9,000 sturdy Afghans whose compounds (Afghan homes are compounds, often rather large) spread across pointed outcroppings. Our Humvees had maneuvered around 1,000-pound boulders to get to the remote site, departing Forward Operating Base Chapman well before sunrise. The setting was so high that hawks circled below us.

It was to be a quick visit, so I kept my speech short. I spoke a bit about the district center, our hopes for it, and in closing, I asked them about the trees.

The senior elder spoke first.

"You are the only American who has ever asked us about our trees."

"I'm from mountains in America. I care about trees, wherever they are."

We could get along, I thought, a mountain guy among mountain people.

Within minutes, a young boy was summoned. He walked forward, hands cupped. In his palms, several dark beetles rested with only the slightest of movement. I put a few in a plastic bag and said I would have our Department of Agriculture representative look into it. I guessed Afghan snowpacks and temperatures were affected by global warming like those in the Rockies. Again, *damned beetles*, I thought.

The engines of our Humvees hummed nearby, signaling time to go. Diesel exhaust fumes always preceded the Americans' arrival and our departure. Afghans could probably smell us before they could see us. Governor Arsala Jamal and the Provincial Reconstruction Team commander, Dave Adams, had already left by Black Hawk. I had decided to stay and ride back with the soldiers.

A five-hour commute was ahead, boulder-to-boulder, our tailbones and heads receiving an equal measure of thuds along the way. Thirty minutes into it, however, we became stranded. The driver's-side axle of the lead Humvee had crashed into the corner of a hippopotamus-sized rock in a narrow ravine. Metal crunched like a 7Up can. All of us knew our one-day trip would at least be an overnighter, if not longer. And these hills undoubtedly had eyes.

I volunteered to take three Afghan guards with me to seek help from elders who lived up the wadi, part of the same group I had met earlier. U.S. soldiers in uniform would complicate things. Qalandar remained a mostly "red" district, often frequented by Taliban fighters and in open support of the rebellious Zadran tribe, which in the past had reportedly maintained links with Osama bin Laden and Al Qaeda.

About twenty minutes later and hundreds of meters up the valley that was more like a ravine, we exited our Hilux. All the Humvees remained far behind. Arif joined me to interpret. The Afghan guards carried AK-47s. We had firepower, but not a lot, and I never carried a weapon. I had taken off my body armor and Kevlar helmet and left them in the truck. The equipment made me feel like a bad version of RoboCop and did not convey a "trust me, because I trust you" message. If we were ambushed, which was very possible, we would not last long.

A huddled gathering of Afghans eyed us as we walked toward the "intersection" of the small village. Instead of dirt roads, streams formed an "X." The smell of fresh naan-like "foot bread" filled the air. Pakistani imports, including crackers, rubber sandals, and small teapots, crowded shelves in dilapidated shops. Wheat fields spread out in all directions, up and along well-tended plots of land.

"Mista, mista, here. Good things."

A young man motioned toward a small wood table, containing nothing I was in the least tempted to buy or haggle over. Security, not shopping, was on my mind.

"No thanks, next time." The young entrepreneur looked irritated. Below him I saw the bottom half of an AK, the Gun of the Ages—the AK-47, perhaps the former Soviet Union's most enduring export. Bury the AK in sand, pick it up, point, and it will still fire off rounds—and chunks of soil undoubtedly, forget any grease. The sight of a gun, not unexpected but the sort of observation that makes one wonder just how many other Russian-made weapons there might be in more hidden places.

It was time to move on, and we did, walking through calf-high green undergrowth.

Earlier that day, some of our soldiers swore they had seen marijuana plants. I could not resist at the time and replied, "I'm surprised the U.S. Army and National Guard have deployed so many pot experts."

A few grinned but admitted nothing. By no means was I an expert.

Arif and I walked through the plants with our local Afghan guards. We had to figure out just what kind of neighborhood this was, friendly, not-so-much, or the opposite: enemy territory. I was not sure yet.

As we entered the village, I recognized two of the Afghans from our morning meeting. This was a good sign. They invited us into one of the nearby shed-like structures. I took a seat on the dirt floor.

"We know you are stranded. Our sons saw your Humvees stopped in the wadi," the senior elder said in slow words that had to be translated from Pashto to English.

"You are safe tonight. We will have our arbakai watch over you."

Arbakai, a welcome word, a centuries-old traditional term that roughly translates into Afghanistan's definition of a "posse" comprised of young Pashtun warriors. Those beardless youth, who had sat silently in the meeting that morning, could, like nimble mountain goats, traverse hidden trails faster than any ultra-marathoner or Boulder, Colorado–based climber.

"But beyond the turn in the road, we have enemies. We are fighting with that tribe," he added.

Time to get out of Deadwood, I thought.

Before I could excuse myself, they invited me to stay for tea.

"No rush. We protect. We keep our word."

He sounded sincere at least.

The tea was milky, brown, and full of pungent goat milk. I never mixed milk with tea, but knew when best to just smile and drink, almost as if I was back on the Tigris with Bassam, enjoying his gruff company and grilled carp. The conversation became particularly interesting around the time my fermenting stomach started to rebel. The main elder reminded me about how I had noticed the condition of their forest, implying it mattered a great deal to them.

Initially, these Afghans in Qalandar had held back, opening up not because of what I did, or the powerful nation I represented, but because I cared enough to see their trees—their dying trees.

The lead elder unexpectedly went on to answer my other question from earlier in the morning, about the gouges in the mountainside.

"That is where the Russians dropped their bombs. They killed some of us, but we dug tunnels into the hillsides."

This district, like the rest of Khost province, had been mujahideen central. It was the first place where the Soviets lost a key part of the map to insurgents, eventually beaten back all the way out of the country. The Soviet pullout marked the beginning of the end of their empire, and none of us yet knew just how long the U.S. would be fighting in Afghanistan as well, at the time only six years in and not yet America's longest war.

These elders had helped lead the fight against the Russians when they were young, with our made-in-America Stinger missiles. This valley had been a front line, indeed, among the most important and vicious front lines, in Charlie Wilson's war. (Mr. Wilson being a rambunctious Texas congressman, who had played a key role in securing U.S. funding for Afghans fighting the Soviets in the 1980s.)

And then I noticed something else that drew my attention.

On the wall behind the elders, to the left of the door, I saw what looked like an odd-shaped axe. It did not appear to be a tool used to clear wheat or poppy fields, or even to chop wood. It was then they gave me the warning in the form of a story.

With clear intent, one of the elders looked toward me. "We still tell our children about the last Russian killed in Qalandar."

Afghans are the best storytellers. They never lost their oral tradition, with tales usually shared before and after unhurried meals.

I had to hear the rest of the story, even though I sensed their message was not meant to entertain, but to convey something much different. Power in their mountain range—who had it and always would, and who did not and never would. We, in other words, would not be talking about the trees anymore. The oldest tribal leader motioned to the axe, which suddenly looked to me what it was: a weapon, one that could do a lot of damage and fast.

My guards began to look anxious. None were from that district, which meant even they would be unsure in just which kind of company we now sat, cross-legged. If this were a trap, they had set us up well, and I had been dangerously naive. But I listened. To excuse myself too soon would be the riskier step, perceived as a sign of fear and disrespect and weakness—a bad, possibly fatal, combination among the Pashtun.

"We used explosives to trap the Russians, in front of them and behind their convoys. Then at night, we would finish them. The last Russian was killed with that kind of weapon. It split his head in two."

He motioned, tomahawk-style, with his large, calloused fingers bunched together.

I thanked them and said we needed to make our way back to the stranded convoy. I tried to sound self-assured. I estimated our odds of survival to be a decent 60-40, maybe even 70-30.

Before leaving, I asked one question.

"When was the last time a representative from the central government visited Qalandar?"

I wanted to include a calendar date in my diplomatic report to the embassy and Washington. That is, if we were allowed to go unharmed. I had my doubts there had been any recent or successful outreach by the government in Kabul. The old men glanced at each other with smiles.

Another tribal elder spoke up.

"A long time ago, King Zahir Shah sent his tax collector. He came once. We never saw him again."

As my Afghan guards and I began to leave, with all three clasping their AKs closer than when we had arrived, the senior elder added one more comment, prompting me to ask one more question.

"You Americans have nothing to worry about, as long as you respect us and our religion."

Above him I saw the dying trees and the still visible holes from Soviet bombs.

"What do you think when you see us?"

"From up here, your military convoys look like snakes. It is best to leave snakes alone. But sometimes snakes must be killed."

The small group of U.S. soldiers and I spent the next two nights in the wadi, protected by the arbakai. The elders kept their word. But unfortunately, they were unable to keep sheets of rain from pelting us. I had decided to sleep outside, under the stars, per my longtime habit since being a kid. I did not locate Orion, my go-to constellation, or Ursa Major or Minor or really anything because the clouds were so thick most of the time.

And by then my adrenaline had kicked in. We might not be in enemy territory, but we were far from home. Regardless of the weather, I did not sleep much.

When I woke up, I walked a hundred or so meters up a side canyon. I had to relieve myself—a biological process always speeded up in a war zone. Without notice two Afghans appeared out of a clump of trees. I did not speak Pashto. They did not speak English. One placed his arm across his chest—a good sign. And I did the same.

"Problem?" I asked, though I was certain they did not understand by their blank looks alongside their silence.

I figured they had been spying on me the whole night. As I certainly would have spied on a stranded convoy of Afghans if they had been stuck, say, near Sheep Ridge in the Mosquito Range of the Colorado Rockies.

I did not envy the job of the arbakai. They were caught between sides. And while we had more military hardware and money on our side, the Taliban were dug in, the newest brand of fighters in a country that had been fighting for decades. Even on this early trip, I was beginning to see how Afghanistan's youth were pulled in opposite directions. Ties to tribe and family on one side, and the attraction of the Taliban and insurgents on the other. Which way their friends went would likely determine which direction they would go—and arguably the country as a whole, a generational struggle as much as anything else.

By the third day of our predicament, I had plenty of time to think about bigger issues beyond our damaged Humvee. The setting, verdant and wild, prompted overriding questions about U.S. wartime strategy and what might be ahead. I remained convinced, despite being stranded and unnerved a bit by the axe story, that I should be in this war, having left Fallujah exhausted. The scenery itself provided a welcome change. Not just because it reminded me of Utah and Colorado, but also because I believed there remained a chance for success still in this war and for things to turn out okay and not deteriorate like Iraq had into an open sectarian battle. After having met just a few Afghans, I sensed they would be easier for me to befriend, to collaborate with, and that degree of human potential felt promising. Perhaps most of my collaborators here would survive, unlike so many who had been killed in Fallujah.

Fortunately, an Afghan "jingle" truck driver stopped, leaning his head and arm out of a large vehicle decorated in gaudy fashion with dangling items that caused the jingling. After a few hours of volunteer mechanic duty, he somehow managed to repair our Humvee enough so that we could tow it back to the base. His forearms were as thick as the axle he worked on. His massive hands coated in grease. If not for this mechanic-from-God/Allah, we would have been ordered to destroy the Humvee, leaving another rusted remnant of another foreign army's ill-fated attempt to maneuver the jagged terrain, inhabited by a proud and self-sufficient people.

As we slowly made our way down the mountain, I understood why the king's tax collector had only visited Qalandar once. But knowing the American instinct to try to do all things and in record time, we might not be so wise.

After a several-hour journey between more boulders and at a much slower pace going down the mountainsides than what it took our convoy going up, we arrived back at base in the late afternoon. I asked Arif to make sure he reached out to the truck driver who had repaired our Humvee. We agreed that a few hundred bucks seemed fair. As usual, our money made things seem easier, at least for a while. We could indeed buy our way out of some dilemmas in the middle of the war.

My attention soon shifted to other matters, including one that I had not anticipated. A subject that no amount of U.S. dollars, piled however high, could fix.

Or forgive.

Beware how you take away hope from another human being.

OLIVER WENDELL HOLMES, JR.

Dilawar of Yakubi

Over tea and coffee, Arif began to open up a bit more about his family. I knew enough about Pashtuns to avoid asking too many personal questions, which amounted to a lot that Americans took for granted: kids, spouse, and religion were particularly sensitive subjects. And yet it was Arif who opened up a taboo topic first.

"I am worried about my sons' education."

"Aren't the schools we are building helping? I know we are hoping to get dozens more funded and done this year," I replied.

We were sitting at a table, just outside the main Provincial Reconstruction Team building. Birds chirped overhead in trees that must have been planted by the Russians when they controlled the airstrip, now operated by a CIA contingent. We never really interacted that much with these rotating groups of U.S. spies, which was very intentional on their part.

"I'm still concerned," Arif said.

Occasionally, a soldier would walk by while we were talking and ask for a smoke. Arif had quit and I had no cigs to offer. Nearby, Afghans who worked on base were making flatbread. The smell made me hungry. The hum of our imported A/C units reminded me of the universality of Americans at war in hot climates: we would send in the Marines to such places, for sure, but the A/C units and generators often were delivered first for all of us who followed USMC grunts—the Army, the Air Force, the Navy, and the State Department. War had its own kind of pampered pecking order. Marines were the least demanding and least cosseted, without question. The Air Force I found to be the most, next to some of my State Department and USAID civilian colleagues, that is.

"Yes, but where will the teachers come from? There aren't enough and many don't want to leave Kabul for Khost. It's a lot more dangerous here along the Pakistan border."

"Maybe we can see if there could be some kind of bonus pay."

"Well, you should try it. I also have daughters."

This unexpected and unusual admission almost prompted me to semi-interrogate Arif on girls education in the province, but he moved on to another topic, as if planting a marker that we would return to at some point when he was ready, but not then.

"Have you heard of Dilawar?"

"No, why?"

"He and his family come from Yakubi, a hilly area that is part of Sabari District. You will get asked about him." He looked me in the eye as he said this. It clearly was a serious issue.

And with that, he said it was time to leave for the day. His sons would be waiting. I bet his daughters were just as excited.

In the weeks that followed, I realized Arif was right. Afghans asked if I had heard of Dilawar.

But when I pressed locals for more details, the replies were couched in general terms: Dilawar was a poor taxi driver; Dilawar came from a big family; Dilawar was "not a terrorist." This last comment often came with a raised voice. That struck me most, along with the glancing eye contact reflecting obvious unease. I confessed I did not know his background, which visibly let them down.

How could I not know Dilawar's story? I was the newly arrived U.S.

government's representative in the frontline province, a place that mattered in the war. Hadn't I done my homework?

It all happened before I arrived, I said to myself in an attempt to justify not knowing Dilawar's story. The demands of the present filled my days. We had an insurgency to counter, and I was in the middle of it. The Pakistani government had already struck some deals with Taliban fighters just over the border from Khost. The embassy wanted me to figure out if they would last.

I also had internal Army dynamics to address, and fast. The maneuver units had a tendency to direct soldiers assigned to the PRT to do their bidding, when I believed the missions should remain as distinct as possible. For instance, if a PRT project opening ceremony were scheduled in one district, but a combat mission in an adjacent one, the resources allocation would not be equal. The U.S. military, which I had a lot of respect for in both wars, remained primarily a blunt instrument of hard power. That worked when fighting the Taliban, but not so much when trying to win over local leaders and average Afghans. The two faces of America: We will kill you if we must. We will help you if we can.

In Iraq, I would have had the final say in PRT priorities, where State Department officials were in charge. But in Afghanistan, the PRTs remained military-led.

All that said, I took Arif's warning seriously, so I started to research what happened.

We had tortured to death Dilawar of Yakubi.

Dilawar's story begins just after September 11, 2001.

When the Mullah Omar–led Taliban government in Kabul refused to hand over Osama bin Laden, a U.S.-led massive air campaign followed. Small, cash-rich teams of CIA and U.S. Special Operations Forces moved across the rugged terrain of eastern Afghanistan. They had lots of money to hire "allies" via stacks of American currency. The Tora Bora range bordering Pakistan, where bin Laden had taken refuge, became a pounded zone of man-made mini-earthquakes.

The "bad guys" on the run, as we "good guys" chased them. It became the easy narrative and, for a while, more truth than fiction.

In places like Khost, U.S. forces detained a number of Afghans. Just

before the Muslim holiday of Eid al-Fitr, Dilawar was questioned outside the main military base in Khost, called Camp Salerno. Dilawar had
picked up three men in his taxi. Local Afghan guards, who had established ties to U.S. military units (often based on sharing intelligence),
reportedly found items in his vehicle they said looked suspicious. Since
there had been a rocket attack on the base earlier that morning, all four
men were detained and transferred to U.S. custody. The three passengers were eventually returned home (after fifteen months in Guantánamo), but Dilawar had it much worse.

While Iraq had Abu Ghraib, Afghanistan had another American-
run detention facility, known as Bagram, located in the sprawling airport outside the Afghan capital. Bad things happened there as well.

At the time, the U.S. found itself fighting two war fronts, one in
Afghanistan and one in Iraq. Bush administration lawyers had ruled
each theater to constitute different threats. Trained in America's top
law schools, and now ensconced inside the government, they issued
memoranda that did not give Afghans like Dilawar the same legal status as Iraqis. In other words, the fight against Al Qaeda did not meet
the definition of an "international armed conflict," so protections for
certain captives, these lawyers argued, did not apply. This led to the
creation—and conundrum—of Guantánamo.

Unlike Iraqi prisoners, Afghan detainees were not deemed to be
prisoners of war under the Geneva Conventions. As such, U.S. forces
could handle them outside treaty-mandated standards of humane
treatment (not that they were honored always in Iraq). This is why
Afghans comprised the most sizable population of detainees in U.S.
custody. Some would later be released back to their communities. Once
detained, however, there was no judicial process. No evidence would be
required for continued confinement. They had a special, intentionally
obtuse, designation: "unlawful enemy combatants." This new category
amounted to a legal black hole—by design.

Interrogators basically had free rein. There were few rules and little
oversight, particularly early on in the war. And some members of the
U.S. military at the Bagram Theater Internment Facility committed
violent and inhumane acts to people who may or may not have been
guilty of anything. By then, top policy makers and their top legal advisers in Washington had approved the operative mind-set: waterboard

first in secret, ask questions later in secret. And, by the way, P.S.: no crimes have been committed should anyone ask—for example, bothersome questions coming from some members of Congress with wartime consciences, such as, eventually, from California senator Dianne Feinstein.

Two Ivy League–educated lawyers named Jay Bybee and John Yoo, in particular, issued legal memoranda with subject lines like "unlawful enemy combatants" followed by their determinations of what was permissible or not, that is, legal in their view, or not.

The George W. Bush administration lawyers' memo from the esteemed Office of Legal Counsel began with this introduction:

MEMORANDUM FOR ALBERTO R. GONZALES
COUNSEL TO THE PRESIDENT

Re. Standards of Conduct for Interrogation under 18 U.S.C. §§ 2340-2340A

You have asked for our Office's views regarding the standards of conduct under the Convention Against Torture and Other Cruel, Inhuman and Degrading Treatment or Punishment as implemented by Sections 2340-2340A of title 18 of the United States Code. As we understand it, this question has arisen in the context of the conduct of interrogations outside of the United States. We conclude below that Section 2340A proscribes acts inflicting, and that are specifically intended to inflict, severe pain or suffering, whether mental or physical. Those acts must be of an extreme nature to rise to the level of torture within the meaning of Section 2340A and the Convention. We further conclude that certain acts may be cruel, inhuman, or degrading, but still not produce pain and suffering of the requisite intensity to fall within Section 2340A's proscription against torture. We conclude by examining possible defenses that would negate any claim that certain interrogation methods violate the statute.

Approximately forty-seven pages later, they concluded their legal rationale.

CONCLUSION

For the foregoing reasons, we conclude that torture as defined in and proscribed by Sections 2340-2340A, covers only extreme acts. Severe pain is generally of the kind difficult for the victim to endure. Where the pain is physical, it must be of an intensity akin to that which accompanies serious physical injury such as death or organ failure. Severe mental pain requires suffering not just at the moment of infliction but it also requires lasting psychological harm, such as seen in mental disorders like post-traumatic stress disorder. Additionally, such severe mental pain can arise only from the predicate acts listed in Section 2340. Because the acts inflicting torture are extreme, there is significant range of acts that though they might constitute cruel, inhuman, or degrading treatment or punishment fail to rise to the level of torture.

Further, we conclude that under the circumstances of the current war against al Qaeda and its allies, application of Section 2340A to interrogations undertaken pursuant to the President's Commander-in-Chief powers may be unconstitutional. Finally, even if an interrogation method might violate Section 2340A, necessity or self-defense could provide justifications that would eliminate any criminal liability.

Please let us know if we can be of further assistance.

Jay S. Bybee
Assistant Attorney General

This so-called torture memo—full of the worst kind of legalese and keep-the-bosses-happy logic, as in keep the president and vice president of the United States of America happy—was signed in August 2002, four months before Dilawar's death. It includes a macabre Appendix listing "Cases in which U.S. courts have concluded the defendant tortured the plaintiff." They did not mention, even in a footnote, that it had been President Ronald Reagan who urged the Senate during his presidency to support the U.N. anti-torture treaty, which senators eventually did ratify, thereby making it U.S. law. (Reagan had written in May 1988: "Ratification of the Convention by the United States will clearly express United States opposition to torture, an abhorrent practice unfortunately still prevalent in the world today.")

To make matters worse, Afghans would sometimes use and manipulate our own military forces to settle decades-old tribal rivalries. So that while the torture illegalities were being reinterpreted as legal in Washington, or simply ignored, revenge between tribes drove much of the warped dynamic on the ground in Afghanistan.

I once asked a brooding SOF team leader based at Camp Salerno if his units had given large sums of American cash as rewards to Afghans for rounding up suspected insurgents.

"Sir, I'm not going to answer that question."

His non-denial said everything.

Our money could do good things, like build schools and roads, but also cause desperate or plain greedy people to report someone else for attacks on coalition troops they did not commit, or by using the most common refrain that got our attention, "X, Y, or Z has ties to the insurgency."

I was surprised that Governor Jamal never mentioned Dilawar to me. After a few weeks working with him, I had gotten a sense of the top Afghan official in the province. He did not seem corrupt. He wore small glasses on the bridge of his nose that gave him a bit of a scholarly air. His fluent English made all conversations easy, even though he would occasionally ask me what a certain American idiom meant. In discussions with Afghans, I sensed right away that he was as smooth an operator as any Iraqi I had worked with in Anbar. I could see why President Karzai considered him a confidant and had sent him to Khost. Jamal knew how to work deals with tribal leaders and mullahs. And he knew how to work deals with us Americans offering wise advice:

"Remember, our people here have a saying that all you Americans should take seriously. 'The harder you beat an Afghan, the stronger he becomes.' We have been fighting for decades. The Taliban know these mountains and valleys because they were born in them and never left."

He and I also had something in common. We both believed too many U.S. troops were undercutting the partnership we needed in the country. Our occasional brute force tactics were backfiring. We were creating terrorists. Not eradicating enough of them. Of course, we both knew Afghanistan had plenty of insurgents, but it was how we differentiated them from innocents that had grabbed his and increasingly my own attention. We both saw a system failing and alienating the people caught between the Taliban and us. Over time, more were turning against us. Governor Jamal and I needed to go to Bagram and see how the detainees were being treated. He had his suspicions, and I had mine, about what was going on behind the walls.

Jamal said he wanted to be able to explain to Afghans the "details" about our in-country detention facilities. I wanted to better understand the place where Dilawar died.

It was not easy to get clearance for the trip, but Governor Jamal, a crafty politician, made it official. He requested in his role as the top Afghan leader in Khost a visit to the Bagram detention facility. His argument? Afghan constituents demanded more detailed information on conditions there, not bland reassurances, which he detailed in a letter to the U.S. ambassador, my boss. I said I would pass it on, and did. After some further exchanges, I persuaded the embassy to support Jamal's request, backed up first by an understanding Army leader, Major General Dave "Rod" Rodriguez, who saw the benefit in being flexible with a star governor, whom he had previously met and liked.

With the visit approved, Jamal and I departed Khost for Kabul. After arriving, Governor Jamal and I shared a cramped room at the base, cots with frayed bedding, flat pillows, and a bad smell emanating from adjacent urinals. He did not complain. The evening before we were scheduled to visit the Bagram facility, he asked for some advice, pulling out a notebook in one hand, prayer beads in the other.

As he rubbed the small ruby-colored stringed plastic pieces together, I sensed some unease. While Jamal had always been blunt with us, he still knew that the power equation was unequal. We Americans had the money and, if crossed, had been known to ask Karzai to relieve certain governors from their positions. I objected to this kind of heavy-handedness, but he also had been around Americans long enough to know that some felt it their job to review Karzai's personnel decisions. It was in this context that he asked me for advice, making sure that our visit did not get him, or me, in trouble. The ambassador was watching me. Karzai was watching him.

With his prayer beads draped from his hands he asked, "What

should I ask the detainees? Will your government be angry if I challenge the conditions here?"

I tried to reassure him. "That's up to you, Governor. You have the right to question our detention procedures, how we operate behind closed doors. I am here to find out as well."

The next morning we arrived early. Governor Jamal continued to look and act nervous. All around us were uniformed American soldiers and a few from NATO allies, walking leisurely to and from bounteous chow halls. More than a few had acquired the bellies of a Fobbit. The nonchalance of a Fobbit at war. None looked our way. None knew who Jamal was. Bagram itself was a hive of activity before sunrise, even in this secret quadrant. Our rooms had been close enough to the prison facility to walk over, thereby avoiding the congested roadways that crisscrossed the base. Overhead, jets continued to fly and a few helicopters hovered farther down the main tarmac.

I leaned toward the governor. "Are you ready for today? You are the first governor to visit. I think they'll try to impress us, especially you."

"President Karzai is looking forward to my report. What if I see things that will upset him?" Governor Jamal asked.

"Tell him the truth. We are partners and need to be for as long as we are here." While stating as much to the governor, I knew relationships between top levels of my government and the Afghan government had already begun to deteriorate. And if this visit went badly, that dynamic would only worsen. We Americans were about to provide access to one of our most sensitive and secretive sites.

A lot could go wrong.

After passing through metal gates topped with razor wire, an Army officer escorted the governor and me into a holding room. For a minute, I thought they were going to hand search Jamal and perhaps me as well. Several plastic chairs had been placed behind a rectangular white card table, where we sat. The room was dark except for a few bright lights in the center. It felt like an interrogation room, right out of a movie, with a hint of diesel fumes in the air.

I asked the U.S. soldier how long he had been working at Bagram.

"I've done other tours here."

"Anything change since then?" I asked.

"Yeah, it's a lot better."

The stocky and graying guard understood the implication in my question. The governor and I had just been given an overview of all the humanitarian improvements at the site—larger rooms, outdoor exercise options, better food, health checkups, and so on.

Had he been there when Dilawar was transferred from Salerno?

Part of me wanted to ask, but another part of me refused to. Better not to play interrogator myself. I imagined how addictive that role might easily become in a war zone. Instead, the governor and I listened as he noted that "about 650" detainees were being held in the Bagram facility, adding, "all designated as unlawful enemy combatants" (hence no POW status, hence no process or procedures required under binding treaty law). He said the International Red Cross had access to all parts of the facility, "except where classified documents were stored."

Our conversation was cut short when other soldiers brought in three detainees originally from Khost. They had hand restraints and wore orange jumpsuits. The last time I had seen that incarceration uniform was a five-minute video of Nicholas Berg, an American beheaded in Iraq in spring 2004 reportedly by Abu Musab al-Zarqawi in Fallujah. Al Qaeda terrorists had forced him to wear the blaze-colored jumpsuit as they filmed his graphic execution.

Two older men sat down in folding chairs before us, maybe age fifty or sixty—but then almost all faces in Afghanistan belonged to far younger men than they appeared to be, usually by a decade or two. The other one looked about thirty-five or forty. We listened to their stories. Governor Jamal interpreted for me as I took notes in my green notebook.

"I would have come in to be questioned if they had asked. We are victims of bad feelings between tribes."

"I have been interrogated eighty-seven times. Just tell me I am a Taliban commander. No evidence shown to me."

"One soldier asked if I was a mullah? I am. I said I was, asking him, 'Is that a crime?' The soldier got angry and left the room."

"Can I be transferred to Cage 9 because it is closer to the showers? Walking distance."

"I'm number 3415. The Americans don't call me by my name."

"Cage 9." I underlined that description.

I asked the guard whether any of them had been told what an

"unlawful enemy combatant" meant according to our government's definition. He said there was a general reference to the label during their in-processing, nothing more, then added, "but do not mention the Geneva Conventions to them because they might think they have rights."

U.S. military jets continued to roar overhead as our brief introduction came to a close. One of the detainees made a final request when a young soldier wearing blue latex gloves appeared, standing by to take all of them back to their cells.

"Can he put the blindfold on me after we leave the room?"

The soldier readied a set of goggles and earplugs for detainee number 3415 but honored his request. The blindfold would wait. I think he could tell I would have ordered him to do just that—wait—if he had decided otherwise.

After returning to Khost, I dug deeper into the story of Dilawar's final days. The circumstances of his death were even worse than I imagined. A Military Police soldier, Sergeant Thomas Curtis, drew a sketch for investigators of how Dilawar had been chained to the ceiling of his cell, spread-eagle. Arms stretched above his head, V-shaped, with his legs also chained below. He dated the drawing 5 December 2002, 1930 (using military time for 7:30 p.m.). *The New York Times* chronicled how another MP claimed Dilawar spat at them. Specialist Corey Jones said he "retaliated" by giving him a number of "peroneal knee strikes." Jones recalled Dilawar crying out, "Allah! Allah! Allah!" He estimated over a twenty-four-hour period Dilawar's lower body suffered "over 100" blows.

Interrogators said they considered the young detainee to be "non-compliant."

An interpreter, Ahmad Ahmadzei, who was present at the time, saw the situation differently. He later testified that a female MP named Selena Salcedo "berated [Dilawar] for being weak and questioned him about being a man, which was very insulting because of his heritage." He said she and another interrogator repeatedly slammed him against a wall. Ahmadzei went on, "About the first ten minutes, I think, they were actually questioning him, after that it was pushing, shoving, kicking and shouting at him. There was no interrogation going on."

These "interrogators" kept Dilawar in shackles, chained to the ceiling overnight.

The next morning, a guard recalled Dilawar pleading with him that he would die if he remained in the same position for another hour. "He said that he didn't feel good. He said that his legs were hurting." Another guard checked Dilawar's circulation by pressing down on his fingernails, declaring, "He's okay, he's just trying to get out of his restraints."

He was not okay. The (ridiculous) fingernail pulse check—after a 100-count series of body blows—failed.

On December 10, 2002, Dilawar was found dead in his cell, five days after being detained. An autopsy conducted by an unnamed coroner reported the tissue in his legs "had basically been pulpified." Major Elizabeth Rouse, an Army pathologist, ruled Dilawar's death to be a homicide and further added: "I've seen similar injuries in an individual run over by a bus."

The coroner's autopsy would later note that even had Dilawar survived the beatings, his legs would have required amputation given how badly they had been damaged.

Only after the *Times* front-page reporting did the U.S. Army launch a formal internal investigation. Lead interrogator Specialist Glendale C. Walls pled guilty, and was sentenced to two months in a military prison. Two other soldiers found to be complicit also received sentences but would not serve any time. Sergeant Salcedo admitted to some offenses, had other charges dropped, and was reduced in rank to corporal. She was issued a letter of reprimand and docked $250 a month in pay for a total of four months.

Governor Jamal and I returned to Khost with a better understanding of treatment at the "new" Bagram. But the ghosts of the old Bagram haunted the minds of Afghans. And Dilawar's ghost haunted my own. Jamal met privately with provincial religious and tribal leaders to inform them about our visit. He reassured them that past U.S. abuses were not continuing. Most, he said, trusted him and did not want to believe the American government tortured people.

I reported to the embassy the joint trip had been a "success" but it did not feel that way. The governor saw us make an effort, and he was

proud to be the first high-level Afghan politician to visit Bagram. A
small victory, perhaps, but it felt hollow. I kept thinking about Dilawar
and the one detainee asking that he not be blindfolded again until after
he was away from the governor's eyes and mine. That shackled old man
had more dignity, I thought, than some within the highest levels of my
government. I did not need to read his "guilty" file to see that. I never
learned his name, just his number. Our jail had broken his body, but
not his spirit.

I realized then that a key part of my job in Khost would be to try
and undo some of the damage of America and Americans at our worst,
regardless of the schools we were building and millions of dollars of
projects under way.

In this right war, in this necessary war, how could we have begun in
such a wrong way?

What I did not know at this time, however, was that in Washington, just before Dilawar was beaten to death in our custody, Donald
Rumsfeld wrote a relevant memo to Deputy Secretary of Defense Paul
Wolfowitz. He later put the document on his website under the heading "The Rumsfeld Papers":

> Call Condi Rice. She said to me that we have got to get the
> detainee mess sorted out, that nobody is able to get answers.
> I think she is getting this from the UK. Call her and find out
> what she is talking about. She always comes in with these cryp-
> tic messages as thought [sic] the Pentagon is messed up, and I
> don't have any idea what she is talking about.
>
> I told her that everyone who has wanted to see their detain-
> ees has been able to and it is baloney. But you should check it
> out and get back to her.

The Pentagon chief gave his deputy two days to respond.

In a second memo, also made public, Rumsfeld approved the expansion
of interrogation techniques by U.S. military personnel. It concluded:
"Our Armed Forces are trained to a standard of interrogation that
reflects a tradition of restraint."

Rumsfeld, known to suffer from chronic back pain, had a standing desk installed in his large office suite, not far from an oil painting of George Washington and a poster of Uncle Sam that read in red lettering, "We're at War, Are You Doing All You Can?"

At the bottom of the memo, with a line drawn to white space from the SECDEF "approved" box—now checked—the Pentagon chief handwrote with regard to limiting the amount of time a detainee could be forced to stand:

"However, I stand for 8–10 hours a day. Why is standing limited to 4 hours?"

D.R.

Thirteen days later U.S. military guards stood before Dilawar's tortured corpse.

And within three months of his death, in March 2003, the U.S. Senate confirmed lawyer Jay Bybee as a federal judge on the United States Court of Appeals for the Ninth Circuit. In the roll call tally, seventy-four senators voted yea and nineteen voted nay. Seven members of the "world's greatest deliberative body" declined to vote.

Since 1993, John Yoo, the *summa cum laude* graduate of Harvard University in American history with a Yale *Juris Doctor* degree, has been a professor of law at the University of California, Berkeley. In 2003, he also became a "scholar" at the American Enterprise Institute in Washington, listing his specialties to be "international law" and "constitutional law."

I could not help but wonder whether Donald Henry Rumsfeld of Taos, New Mexico, and "Mt. Misery" in St. Michaels, Maryland (the former plantation where Frederick Douglass was enslaved). Or Condoleezza "Condi" Rice of Palo Alto, California. Or Jay Scott Bybee of Las Vegas, Nevada. Or John Choon Yoo of Berkeley, California. If any of them knew the story of Dilawar. The story of Dilawar of Yakubi. And if so, whether they remembered him. His name. Where he was from. And how he died.

The same goes for Vice President Richard Bruce "Dick" Cheney, of Jackson, Wyoming, and St. Michaels, Maryland, and President George Walker Bush, of Dallas and Crawford, Texas, formerly of 1600 Pennsylvania Avenue.

The White House.

Our White House.

War is what happens when language fails.

MARGARET ATWOOD

Khost U.

After my Bagram visit with the governor, and with Dilawar still on my mind, I opted to shift focus a bit. I began to think that perhaps the younger generation of Afghans might be a receptive audience to our positive efforts. I also imagined they might, via the Internet, be familiar with the best traditions of America, ones that had nothing to do with detentions and detention policy, whether as devised in Washington or implemented in one of our CIA-run black sites or in a U.S. military–run facility and by U.S. military personnel. Abu Ghraib had cost us enough; Bagram was still mostly a secret, at least to Americans and the world, but not to Afghans.

And so on a mid-June day in 2007, our Humvees pulled up to Khost University unannounced. Its location struck me as ironic and appropriate, situated near the city's biggest mosque, the one Taliban mastermind Jalaluddin Haqqani had funded. The religious structure had a massive sky-blue dome, just like Fallujah's most imposing mosque. The greater portion of Khost University students must have spent at least as much time inside the mosque as in the university, a reminder that the United States was attempting to partner with the Islamic Republic of Afghanistan, where freedom of religion amounted to one faith.

In the distance above leafy trees seemingly always covered in a layer of dust sat an old fortress with two-foot-thick walls of stone, almost medieval-like in appearance. The Soviets had once occupied this high ground. We ever-confident Americans chose to establish an outpost there as well. We called it "Matun Hill." Though predictable, it was not a low-profile or wise location for us. It just sent the wrong message. Black Hawk helicopters buzzed back and forth above the mosque. The thump-thump of rotors accompanying a foreign military presence could aggravate locals just as much as the visual reminders, metal armadas airborne and hulking convoys below snaking between forward operating bases.

Khost University's chancellor, an energetic man who appeared to be in his sixties, greeted us. The Afghan academic wore glasses and a Western-style suit jacket outlining a bulging waistline. He quickly demonstrated his fluency in our language. He also looked surprised and a bit nervous. When the Americans visited, everyone noticed. And he surely would be asked after we left just what had been discussed and why.

The Taliban, who were still very present and influential in the area, had a way of silencing words with bullets. "Night letters" were slips of paper with variations of "you and your family will soon be dead if" warnings left near doors or compound gates. Arif had told me he had received them himself. Just like our collaborators in Iraq, those brave enough to work alongside us here were always in jeopardy.

The university chancellor escorted us to his cramped office. It was a throwback to an earlier Afghanistan, the one of the 1960s and 1970s. When students, both men and women, attended college classes and libraries were stocked with books in multiple languages. A time when there was no need to have guards posted in front of a campus.

I wanted to meet with some students. The chancellor thought that the political science and law students would be the best group to engage, but he also warned me that some of them held virulent views about U.S. efforts in Afghanistan. "We have fundamentalists and radicals here," he said.

"They could be the future leaders of Afghanistan, right?" I replied.

He nodded.

Good, I thought. Afghan government officials tended to tell us what they thought we wanted to hear, not what we needed to hear. These students will get extra special attention, I figured—a worthy challenge. I was about to enter a room full of, well, future Afghan lawyers. While they were honing their use of words, I knew in their country each student had first been trained in how to use an AK-47, possibly an axe or two as well. And in a place like Khost, several must have had friends or cousins, even brothers, somehow linked to the Taliban.

Nonetheless, I felt ready. I had almost four years of counterinsurgency behind me. How hard could it be to talk to students? Confident verging on overconfidence, which is not a good place to be in a war zone.

The chancellor escorted me through the door of a second-floor classroom. It had shiny floors that reminded me of my elementary school. Surfaces that required sweeping followed by polishing, hard surfaces that accumulated dust and echoed conversations. As I stepped forward and met the surprised gaze of two dozen students, I hesitated—a moment when being the newcomer in a distant land grabs hold and unsettles you. Not panic, just an immediate and unavoidable at-war reckoning.

What am I doing here?

What had my country sent me here to do?

Behind me, I noticed looping Pashto script several inches wide scrawled in chalk on a blackboard. And on one side stood a man with dyed orange-ish hair who must have been the professor.

"Welcome to Khost University," he said.

The students' looks communicated the opposite. Penetrating glares from black eyes set atop unsmiling faces.

Through Arif I said I was from the Provincial Reconstruction Team. I went on to outline some of our projects—the Khost–Gardez road (important to students because it was the main route to and from Kabul), bridge repairs (a common need given the prevalence of flash flooding), and even shoes and clothes for the Kuchi families (donated by American humanitarian aid groups). I told them that the U.S. embassy had sent me to Khost for at least a year, and I wanted to meet students.

I think I even mentioned that my mom had been an elementary school teacher, the fifth grade, in a long redbrick building, in a district named Alpine, reflecting the nearby mountain setting not so unlike Khost.

More silence, as more leaned back in their chairs, not forward.

I looked to the professor for help, and he motioned toward the chalkboard, noting they had just started a new subject. As I turned around, he went on to decipher what was written on it: AMERICAN FOREIGN POLICY. I grinned. Who better to be on the spot than me? A few smiled back. I encouraged them to have at it. Q&A time.

One student, who said his name was Sohaib, asked an unexpected question right away. (I would later learn that the Arabic name Sohaib roughly translated to "fiery head" and "hot temper.")

"Why did it take you so long to come here?"

I replied that I had been in Iraq for the prior three years, but I was there now. It was a weak answer. He knew it. I felt it.

"You Americans could have walked down the streets of Khost with no security. It was that safe for a long time after your troops arrived."

The student spoke the truth. By the time I had arrived in the province in spring 2007, the Taliban had been conducting escalating attacks throughout the eastern part of the country. The most dangerous places for coalition troops could be counted quickly based on KIA and WIA rates: eastern Afghanistan, including Khost, and southern Afghanistan always ranked highest. While Washington and I were focused on Iraq, the insurgency expanded and the Taliban got a second chance to reinfiltrate into numerous hard-to-reach places, as well as into the minds of Afghans. This is what the indictment in the student's comments amounted to—and he was not exaggerating.

I admitted to the class I wished my government had sent me only to Afghanistan, not Iraq. When I mentioned Fallujah, several of the students said they had heard of the city, but none seemed interested in hearing more about it. Like many Americans, Muslims across the Arab world associated the Iraqi city with death and destruction.

Over the next hour, I answered dozens of questions nonstop. Iraq. 9/11. Israel. Pakistan. And more. As each question escalated, I could see the students lean forward in their chairs. A few became agitated, while most seemed inclined to listen.

Sohaib was their ringleader. A native of Kunar province, he had challenged me to convince them the U.S. invasion of Iraq did not mean the American military planned to occupy the whole Muslim world. This important topic, I assured him, would require more time. I congratulated Sohaib along with the other students in "making it" to Khost University, noting how challenging getting even a basic education remained in their country. I meant it. Most did not have anyone else in their families in the educated category, let alone anything advanced or specialized. Most kids worked in the fields.

The barrage of questions continued:

"What about a war with Iran?"

"Are you willing to help Afghanistan in the battle for our hearts?"

"Is there a worldwide definition of terrorism?"

"The coalition arrests one person an hour with no evidence. Many are innocent. This leads to casualties. Why won't you stop this?"

"Do you admit the CIA is involved in terrorism?"

"What's the difference between terrorism and the Taliban?"

"Do you think Afghanistan can be built with projects only? It can only be built with security."

At this point I introduced to them, out of necessity given their interrogation of me (though a welcome one), the American concept of a time-out. I made a "T" with both hands and explained that we would pause when necessary to explore topics in more detail. No BS from either side. Honest differences, but no propaganda to be left unanalyzed, whether emanating from our side or theirs. Sohaib elaborated on his earlier claim, setting off excited reactions among other students: "I still believe your government is responsible for the attacks in New York."

A few motioned with their hands in "T-for-time-out" fashion and laughed. They said they liked the concept.

Progress.

Khost U., I realized, would be more important to the future of what happened in the strategic province than any debate I had been part of or witnessed in the U.N. Security Council.

It seemed we, the Americans, had arrived in time.

One student replied, when I asked this question: "Is it too late?"

"No."

Before leaving, I suggested we might work with the chancellor and their professor to organize a weekly seminar on political issues. About a third of the future lawyers seemed to think that would be a good idea.

A majority stared back, unconvinced. Still, I knew I would be back. This was where a real counterinsurgency could begin.

Local guards had positioned themselves outside Khost U. as we departed, with rusted-but-ever-functional AK-47s arrayed around us. We paid our black-bearded Afghan protectors well, in dollars. U.S. soldiers formed an inner ring. They were never paid enough. We had arrived to start a new relationship—to listen more than we talked—but were unsure what our reception would be. It went better than expected. Team America's entrance did not amount to a good first impression. It rarely did. Armed and armored. Hard power—hardly the "soft power" we hoped to demonstrate through projects and patience and a message of "help us help you."

This "we don't trust you" theme pervaded both wars. All of us had been told, trained really, to take off our sunglasses when we talked to Afghans or Iraqis. But we also had been ordered to keep on our body armor and Kevlar helmets. Suicide bombers. Snipers. Roadside bombs. Omnipresent threats. Did American lives matter more? Some Iraqis and Afghans said the bombs and bullets followed us—to them and their communities.

They had a point. And their government did not issue them body armor.

I regularly violated the order in meetings. Just as I had that day in the classroom, leaving my gear on the floor, like some of the more experienced or contrarian counterinsurgents in our military. We pulled off our ceramic plates. We took off our helmets. I had more flexibility than most troops, and did so not because I was brave. My bosses simply were not within shouting distance, sitting in Kabul about 140 miles away, and beyond, in Washington.

The old university campus had been scheduled to close soon. Students and faculty, who numbered around 2,000, were moving to a sprawling new one funded by the oil-rich United Arab Emirates on the outskirts of town (renamed for the UAE's ultra-rich ruler, Sheikh Zayed University). Khost province was home to hundreds of laborers who helped build and staff Dubai alongside many Indians, Pakistanis, and Bangladeshis. The current downtown college location had several madrassas close to it. Hundreds of girls attended a school along the same road. They walked to class in groups. Education central. If not for the overwhelming threat of violence, it could have almost felt a bit cosmopolitan.

I began to hold weekly seminars with the Khost U. law students. I got to know dozens of them very well. Sohaib never gave up on some of his conspiracy theories (shared by some Americans too). But he acknowledged that an indefinite, large-scale U.S. military presence in Afghanistan would not be feasible or welcome by Americans or Afghans. The native of Kunar province implied he had family members in the Taliban. His forested village had long been a transit point for fighters, not far from the infamous Korengal Valley. Slowly, I deputized him. We became partners in choosing which topics to cover each week, as varied as U.N. negotiations, Guantánamo, the invasion of Iraq, U.S. policy toward Israel and Palestine, Pakistan, and how Americans elect a president.

One of the other students, from Tani District, with unworldly jade- and amber-colored eyes, said he remembered when American cruise missiles exploded in Khost. "They flew over our compound, when I was a child." The year was 1998. President Clinton had launched an attack against Al Qaeda training camps. Several Arab fighters died, but not Osama bin Laden, who was at the location. The same student, now studying law at Khost U., said the Arab fighters infrequently left their high-walled compounds, but when they did the kids stayed away.

"Parents warned us about them."

I had to ask in response: "Are Khost parents warning children here about us and our drones?"

"Some are. Some children are now afraid of the sky."

Given this momentum at Khost U., I asked the governor to support an education-related project. The PRT and I wanted to connect students from the most remote districts to the university. After much back-and-forth with Bagram-based military personnel, I finally got approval for $5,000 in funding to help cover the cost of travel for students. I had to say something along the lines of: "I'm the U.S. government representative in the province where Osama bin Laden once lived. Fund it." They did.

So we hired Hilux trucks as taxis to bring about 100 of the province's best young students to Khost University. Getting paperwork approved to build infrastructure projects always proved easier than building people. A new water truck, for instance, costing around $20,000 had been funded in a few days, few questions asked. Human infrastructure mattered more, but for years we had yet to make it a funding priority.

Before leaving the university campus, the young students received specially designed certificates marking the day and their participation in the field trip. On it, we had imprinted a shaded photo with the striking outline of Khost University. At no point did any of them interact with any of us. By design, the day was Afghan-to-Afghan.

After surviving Fallujah, I knew the map that mattered most in either war zone had nothing to do with the GPS grid coordinates for our battalions or the red circles we placed over Taliban locations. The lasting battles occurred inside Muslim minds. If university students doubted or, worse, opposed our efforts, then sustaining any progress would be that much harder. Besides, college students were at an age when their questions would, and should, comprise a key reality check for us.

The Khost U. group kept me honest. We Americans needed to be kept honest, and challenged. Whether when we were seated in suit and tie around the negotiating tables at the U.N. in New York or sitting with crossed legs on a red carpet in easternmost Afghanistan.

In one session, Sohaib, never one to miss an opportunity, led a small group of students in asking me the first question. Topics in prior seminars had focused on U.S. foreign policy, but as faithful Muslims they raised another matter that day. They were ready. I was not.

"Mr. Kael, our teacher, we would like to offer you our religion. The Quran can teach you more than other books. We invite you to join Islam."

I looked in front of me. Over twenty Afghans were waiting for their chance to welcome me into their religion, as Sohaib smiled.

I thought, *well played*.

In the Islamic Republic of Afghanistan, the religious alternatives were . . . none. Few of the students—even the most open to challenging their own preconceived notions—understood what "freedom of religion" meant in the American context.

My mind flashed back to the last time I had been invited into Islam.

It happened in Fallujah when the City of Mosques' top cleric, Grand Mufti Hamza, voiced the same words. He too wanted me to become a Muslim, despite my obvious occupier status among Sunni Arabs there.

Seconds passed in our outdoor meeting room. I stood still. Then my reply came out in the same way it did more or less in our other war in the middle of the Muslim world.

"The grand mufti of Fallujah also asked me to join your religion, and I was honored, like I am now. But I represent a country of many faiths. Hindus, Jews, Christians, Muslims, and others. . . . It would be unfair for me to choose one over the other. Our Constitution protects all religions and the freedom to join any one or none of them."

My reply seemed to work. Sohaib and the others did not press me. Just then, one of the soldiers I had brought along with me for this session, who was deployed with the Arizona National Guard and a friend of mine as well, Mark Bradford, decided to elaborate on my point.

As if it were nothing, he said, "My wife used to be Muslim, but I convinced her to convert to Christianity."

Arif, with an anxious glance my way, said he preferred not to translate that statement, but I could already tell several of the students had understood. A few laughed. More grimaced. Sohaib helped me change subjects, gratefully. I owed him, and he knew it.

Mark, who now realized he had almost started a Muslim vs. non-Muslim uproar, apologized to me. I told him not to worry, but added, "Just don't try to convert anyone else over here and tell your wife back in Arizona hello from me."

We had avoided one potential flashpoint as strangers in a strange land. But more verbal and cultural landmines in this land of Pashtun Muslims lay ahead, among even tougher Afghan skeptics toward America and toward us.

Perhaps Allah will make friendship between you and
those whom you hold as enemies.
And Allah has power over all things, and Allah is Oft-
Forgiving, Most Merciful.

QURAN, VERSE 60:8
SECTION 2, CHAPTER 60
Friendly Relations with Non-Muslims

A Handshake, or Two

Academic schooling, like that offered at Khost U., was not the only
kind available for school-aged Afghans. Some teenagers (and often
those younger) entered madrassas, the more traditional kind of education throughout the Pashtun tribal belt. Where the college-level
law and politics students sought out textbooks—and the Internet—
madrassa students seemingly were focused only on one: the word of
Allah. Divine. Undebatable Truths. They studied the Quran, daily and
in earnest, memorizing it verse after verse, lesson after lesson.

I decided this was the next group I needed to focus on, even if they
probably would be less welcoming and more close-minded to my role
in the province. No one in Kabul had suggested I do this, and I knew
there was no constituency inside the U.S. government for this kind of
outreach. Too politically sensitive back home, particularly with certain
members of Congress, I had been told, especially with one senator from
the state of Georgia. But I believed this kind of outreach to be impor-

tant, if risky. When I told my plans to Arif, he simply said: "Be ready. It might not go well."

I asked Governor Jamal to help arrange most of my initial meetings. He said he would, but when I mentioned ranking madrassa students and mullahs at the top of my list, he questioned their willingness. The governor warned me that talking to them would likely be considered antagonistic.

"If I can handle Fallujah's imams and students in Iraq focused on Islam, I should be able to handle them here."

"Okay, but I am not sure how this will go," he said, echoing Arif's concerns.

Jamal and I then spent some time discussing how the U.S. was still perceived to be anti-Islam. Night raids in madrassas had made both the students and mullahs feel like enemies. He said many of his meetings dealt with their concerns.

The governor would arrange the meeting as soon as possible. I was more nervous, and underprepared, than I let on. Jamal predicted the sessions would end badly. My own doubts grew. Maybe I was pushing too hard.

Jamal excused himself to go pray. I never saw him skip a prayer for a meeting, whether with a military commander or with me. I respected that. I sensed he had been a good student in his youth, in regular school and college—and in a madrassa before that.

Not schooled in Islam myself, I knew my first contact with madrassa students in their home turf—high in the peaks—would be tricky, if not potentially explosive, even deadly. Iraq had taught me that the wrong words at the wrong time, even at the right time, could get people killed. Bullets had a physical velocity, whereas words—most of them translated, which only added to the complexity of wartime "dialogue"— carried an emotional velocity. Neither, once used, could be taken back. Among Muslims, I had learned any affront to their faith was deemed an affront to all of the faithful. And, they believed, to Allah Himself.

It was late afternoon when we arrived in Musa Kehl District, located adjacent to Qalandar, but not as rocky and with more green than brown yet just as many low-swooping hawks. The slanted sun stayed hot. The air blew peak to peak, dry. No thunderstorms had been predicted before our convoy departed early that morning, well before sunrise. But I knew they could come fast, rolling down from mountaintops far away. Those layered and too distant to see, almost mirage-like. They appeared spiked, a curvy spine of rock like the back of a giant stone Stegosaurus, asleep. The day seemed primed for lightning strikes. And not the man-made variety unleashed in the air via drones, now armed (in Fallujah, they had been just for surveillance).

We slowly approached the school. I could hear dozens of young men inside reciting the Quran, their madrassa surrounded by flowering bushes and what looked to be orange marigolds. Through opaque windows I saw the outlines of bodies, rocking back and forth in unison. As in Fallujah, with the muezzins' calls to prayer below dozens of minarets, I found this chorus to be beautiful and eerie, familiar and foreign. Arif was with me, of course, but I had asked Mark and other U.S. soldiers to remain behind. I knew any sign of weapons would only complicate the discussion. And, even then, this kind of interaction, or what might be a confrontation, could go badly.

Village elders had warned me that the mullah in charge of their religious school ruled viciously, violently. They said he had found his wife in the compound of another man, and shot them both dead. I believed the story. In this culture, neither a real nor a perceived adulterer had a chance at survival.

Arif gathered a dozen or so students. They formed a wall of white clothes, as if they intentionally encircled me for added effect. The strength of their numbers made evident. I was probably the first American they had met, or seen up close. Big risk. Big opportunity. I had the first chance among Americans to make a decent first impression.

With all that on my mind, I did what came naturally when meeting someone. I extended my hand. A minute passed. Or maybe two. It felt longer. Then one of the students, a tall teenager, who had the presence of a leader, held out his own. Most of his arm remained covered in his light-colored shalwar kameez. He had bunched the loose material along the sleeve to enclose all five fingers, clenched, almost fistlike within a makeshift glove.

We shook hands.

But our hands did not touch.

He made sure of that because of the clumped cloth covering his own fingers. I would only understand exactly why later on.

Unseen eyes peered at us, far more enemies than friends. This visit had to be short. I did not want to appear rushed, but the commute back to Khost was four hours. Traveling by night was tricky, and I did not want to repeat the situation we had in Qalandar.

The tall madrassa student, who did not tell me his name that day, the one with his hand covered, had a question—and request—that came in the form of a single word.

"Radio?"

"Yes, I can get radios, but first let's talk."

Now uncovered, I saw each of his fingertips had been colored deep red-orange, natural ink from the henna plant. Some hands you never forget, but I also sensed it was not the coloring that had caused him to hold back. No, it was because of who he believed me to be, not what I might say or bring with me as a gift.

With the madrassa students now sitting before me, I fully introduced myself. The usual: "I'm the U.S. government's representative in Khost." "I'm here to help." "I'm here to listen." "No one ordered me to Afghanistan. I volunteered." "There has been enough violence. Time to cooperate." And so on.

Over the next hour, they talked, and I listened. The three closest to me wanted to attend regular schools and the madrassa. The most charismatic was named Akbar, which translated to "great." He was inseparable from his quieter friend, Rahmatullah, or "mercy of Allah." They understood why Americans had come to their country. They were hopeful the U.S. could build a better future. The middle three or so said little, but turned their heads back and forth, as the first and last sets of students spoke. Arguing, but in quiet yet forceful and confident voices. Those who were seated farthest away from me wanted the Americans gone.

They made their case.

"The Taliban were right to destroy the Buddha statues."

"You are here to disrespect Islam."

"The terrorist attacks in your country had a reason behind them."

"You say you want to help, but you send soldiers to shoot and planes to bomb."

And a refrain that echoed the Khost U. students almost verbatim: total occupation of the Muslim world by the U.S. military.

Iraq. Afghanistan. Where next, Pakistan? Iran? They were convinced of this escalation.

And the unanswerable question: "Why did America invade Iraq?"

Rather than debate then and there, I promised we would continue to meet. I wanted us to tell each other stories and show each other our cultures.

Then one of them admitted a darker personal tale.

"I am still ashamed to tell my father what happened in Pakistan," he said.

He went on to explain that the eldest sons in most Pashtun families were sent to the best madrassas for the best Islamic education. The premier places—with electricity, water, and better-educated mullahs—were not in Afghanistan but in northwest Pakistan. In the extreme madrassas, he said, "they take advantage of the weak-minded. They call it 'special training.'"

Translation: they made suicide bombers, with precision.

These madrassas comprised a small minority, he said. He had been recruited but did not "complete" the indoctrination. He never explained why. But I remember how his legs bobbed up and down, nervously, as if he feared a mullah's spies might be near.

None of the other students spoke up.

"Please don't tell our mullah what I told you. He believes going to Pakistan is good."

"I will not tell him. I respect your honesty. The government here is trying hard to support you."

I added a question. "Will you ever go back to Pakistan, to North Waziristan?"

"No. Never."

I knew in that first meeting only one ratio mattered—two to one. If the group seated next to me could convince those in the middle, the anti-American contingent would become a shrinking minority.

More than language separated us in these encounters. Suspicion, like a thickening fog, did too. Suspicion that refracts words in unintended ways, no matter the skill of the negotiator or interpreter—and Arif was one of the best.

But I was determined, and they were willing to meet again.

I arranged funding for computer and English classes for them, which grew to support over 200 in central Khost. When they asked about Muslims in America, I repeated a sincere mantra: if the U.S. were at war with the Muslim world, the U.S. government would be at war with part of its own population.

"We have millions of Muslims in America," I repeated again and again.

I said mosques could be found throughout America and if they walked down New York City streets dressed as they were, no New Yorker would consider them to be non-American or odd. I added, however, they might not as easily blend in if visiting or living in other parts of the country. Freedom of religion meant freedom for Muslims to pray to Allah. Freedom to be clothed in white dishdashas, to wear prayer caps, and to hold prayer beads. The same held true for Christians, Jews, Hindus, and nonbelievers.

Eyes widened. I could only hope they believed me. There was no modern-day American crusade. None, fortunately, mentioned President George W. Bush's comment to that effect right after 9/11: "This crusade, this war on terrorism, is going to take a while." It sure was taking a while.

And then one of the madrassa students asked me an unexpected but logical question.

"Do you think Americans would ever elect a Muslim president?"

I paused and said, "I don't know the answer to your question."

The student looked disappointed, as if my inability to say "yes" meant "no." I wished I had told him at the time, told all of them, that one of America's first and greatest presidents, Thomas Jefferson, not only had read the Quran but also kept his own copy in his personal library.

I sent Washington my formal policy recommendations, essentially arguing for more resources for madrassa students through the Afghan government. But only after I had listened to hundreds of them—the only American official in either Afghanistan or Pakistan who had to this extent. Their words, I believed, needed to be heard.

Before long, the embassy in Kabul agreed to my request, shared by the PRT commander, to help facilitate a visit by Afghanistan's minister of education, Hanif Atmar, to Khost. I joined him on the flight from Kabul in a Russian-made helicopter that looked destined for a sudden, final descent into the Hindu Kush. Upon boarding, the words "flying jalopy" came to mind.

I briefed Atmar on the situation in Khost. More central government outreach was needed, alongside the construction of more "Centers of Excellence"—which would merge religious instruction with nonreligious topics, such as math and science. He welcomed the initiative in support of his policy, suggesting Khost might become a model if done right and carefully. The plan was straightforward: show the madrassa students that the Afghan government was as invested in their future as secular students'. Better facilities with registered mullahs and madrassas. A message of "you're welcome here" and thereby stemming the flow into the ungovernable parts of northwest Pakistan.

After landing, I escorted Atmar to a large gathering of students in Khost. Along the way we talked U.S. politics too, and I could tell he was up on the backstory of a certain "young senator from Illinois" who, Atmar said, was saying positive things about the long-term U.S. commitment to Afghanistan. I sat in the very back, said nothing, and watched. Before him sat rows of boys, as well as girls. They looked both excited and intimidated. Their teachers hung back as Atmar answered every question. After a full hour, as the sun began to sink over the western peaks, he excused himself. He nodded my way before huddling with the provincial education director.

Atmar promised to return and departed later in the day back to Kabul, on the same Russian-made helicopter that somehow, given its condition, remained aloft. But before then, I pitched to him one more time the importance of better integrating madrassa students.

"That is a priority for me, but it is also a controversial policy among some members of the government in Kabul."

"It is controversial in my government too," I replied.

I had found an ideal co-conspirator.

In one of my last visits to the mountainside madrassa in Musa Kehl District, I noticed the setting had changed. We had heard reports of more Taliban infiltrating the area, though the new district center had not yet been directly attacked. The under-construction high school, made of stone and cement, still stood. The dirt road remained passable. And so we loaded up another Humvee convoy and went. We would hold a medical clinic for Afghan girls, as our engineers checked the status of the various projects under way, such as diversion dams. Do-good Americans at work, yes, doing good things in a genuine sense.

Toward the end of the day I ventured up the hill again.

"Arif, let's go say hi to those madrassa students we met a while ago."

As we walked farther along a narrow path, debating the relative danger in the area, I remembered how earlier in the year I had played volleyball—more like jungle ball—with locally recruited police. While learning Afghan rules (few, really, beyond a court lined with rocks), I realized these Afghan teens could spike as well as any UCLA or SoCal beach pickup team, and some were even tall enough to dunk basketballs, though that sport was as foreign to them as cricket was to Americans.

During one game, where I demonstrated less-than-perfect skills compared to them, my digital camera went missing. Stolen. When I asked about it, two players looked at each other, determined. One ran across the wadi. Within the hour, he had returned it. There were a few new images on it . . . a family, unfamiliar with the high-tech gadget, had taken it inside their compound. I saw, for the first and only time, images of Afghan life behind the mud brick walls. Dirt floor. A fire. Women. Children. A man with a mustache, who wore a traditional woolen Pakol hat. Their inner sanctum, which made me feel like a voyeur, but a justified one. After all, they had "borrowed" my camera.

"That was a good game, even if I almost got my camera stolen."

Arif replied, "I still can't believe they brought it back to you. Either it scared them or they actually felt guilty about it."

"Probably both," I said.

We were now just in front of the madrassa. The neat rows of the same orange marigolds blew gently in the wind, next to a red bush that looked as exotic as the setting. I could tell they were regularly clipped and watered. In my backpack, I had brought a final gift. Radios. Making good on the first request I had received upon arriving. It turned out the madrassa students liked to listen to the BBC World Service. They did not say it outright, but I sensed they found comfort in hearing about distant places, more peaceful places. Curious too about what lies beyond their mountains. While Afghans largely detested the British, they could not get enough of their global service's broadcast waves in their own tongue, as part of the BBC's World Service programming included Pashto. But the students would only ask for the radios when the mullah was gone. I could not imagine how painful the punishment would be if he caught them, or me, but they seemed undeterred.

Their arms motioned me forward, an invitation. I entered the madrassa compound. Most of the faces looked familiar.

I reached for the radios and handed several out—the better-quality version of the two varieties we had in stock at the PRT; Afghans knew the difference. The convoy was waiting for me. Again, rushed. I turned around, looking for one madrassa student in particular. I found him. He still had a leadership aura about him. The same kid, the same charisma. I wished Minister Atmar had been there with me, one generation of Afghans encouraging the next.

I reached out to shake his hand. Temporarily, and for just a few seconds, I covered my hand with my shirt, before pulling my sleeve back.

He smiled. A few friends around him laughed. He then extended his own hand, uncovered. We shook, palm to palm.

Afghan to American.

Infidel to Muslim.

Friend to friend? And then the question: "Will you come back?"

"I am not sure," I admitted. "I would like to."

Arif and I got into the convoy. I turned around and noticed all of the madrassa students were looking our way. They looked sad. I felt sad myself. Perhaps they realized shaking the hand of an American was not such a bad thing, regardless of what their mullah had taught them.

Not all infidels were the same. Not all Afghans were the same.

Individuals deciding for themselves what to believe and what not to believe.

We had our propaganda about them. They had their propaganda about us.

Even so, it seemed the barriers between us had begun to come down. Perhaps just a bit but more than either side imagined possible that first day, high up in the mountains of Khost, when we met.

When one handshake could easily have been the only handshake, first and last.

A smart enemy is better than a stupid friend.

PASHTUN PROVERB

Reformed Taliban

He was a senior mullah.

What Sheikh Hamza had conveyed in his quiet and restrained way in Fallujah, always dressed in white, Mullah Sardar got across in a more direct and somewhat unnerving manner. A man who had a dark past and who kept dark secrets, I could tell. Rumor had it he had maintained close ties to the most extreme elements of the insurgency, including other mullahs who dominated some of the Pakistani "hate" madrassas that I had heard about from the madrassa students as well as some of the Khost U. students. A smaller group of them had themselves attended the religious schools in their youth, and most often not by choice even as devoted and believing Muslims.

This disquieting quality piqued my interest. Unlike so many other important and self-important types in any land, Mullah Sardar arrived alone, an entrance of a different kind that was noticed by all. This also intrigued me. No posse necessary with this man. He was an entourage of one. The message: he could protect himself and, by extension, as a religious leader, Allah would too. Willowy in frame, black-bearded, six-foot-one or so tall, just under my height, and probably in his mid-forties, I noticed how he moved the first time I met him. It seemed like he floated. Ever observant, he happened to have been one of the Taliban's senior-most leaders in the area—but only in his "past" life, he reassured me.

He provided a quick overview of his own story that first day we met in summer 2007. Though he spoke some English, we communicated mostly via Arif, who had again warned me beforehand. And as he was my closest adviser, I always listened.

"These senior Taliban leaders are very clever."

He went on. "I don't know about Iraq where you lived for so long, but I know my own people. A leader like Sardar only got in that position in the tribal areas because he was feared."

Arif's implication: Sardar had killed people, most likely Americans among them.

True words, I guessed, an important warning too, but just the kind of Afghan the embassy had sent me to deal with, at least until I could hand him off to them at a higher level. Khost, unlike much of Afghanistan, had a reputation of fierce tribal loyalties that reminded me of Anbar, but at an even deeper level. The fiercest Taliban elements split their time between Afghanistan and Pakistan, an insurgent highway of sorts. U.S. drones had already begun frequent bombing runs in the skies overhead, with many bombs exploding in Miran Shah, a forty-minute drive over the border into North Waziristan and long considered Taliban HQ.

"I appreciate your warning. You'll be close when we talk to Mullah Sardar, so let me know if I start to cross any line, because I know I have in the past."

Arif paused before responding. "I'm worried about my family. They have received more night letters and threats lately. If this meeting and the rest we are having with the Taliban go badly, they will pay the price. My wife and children can't move into FOB Chapman."

I did not know what to say because while all of us on the American side had armor and guards and HESCO barriers to protect us, our local partners like Arif did not. He commuted between home and FOB Chapman in a private vehicle, and I could see the strain growing every day. His wrinkles. His graying hair. His voice.

"I understand," I said. But that was a lie. We both knew it. I had no way of knowing how difficult his home life was getting now that he and I were focusing on ex-Taliban outreach.

Sardar opened our initial meeting by describing his reentry into Afghanistan after years in Pakistan.

"President Karzai sent an entire convoy, a dozen vehicles, to meet me at the Pakistan border when I decided to come back to Khost. I left hundreds of fighters behind the border," he added, as if it was no big deal.

"I have given up my support for the Taliban. I want peace." He did not avert his eyes from me, as so many Afghans tended to do. He was in no way intimidated by the hundreds of U.S. Army soldiers who called central Khost home, or me. We were in his neighborhood.

I asked him if Karzai's government made this kind of reconciliation easy. It seemed he could have expected handcuffs at the border, not open arms. Afghans could be unforgiving and brutal in their vengeance. And the Afghan government in Kabul had not gained a reputation for either efficiency in their outreach programs or competence.

"I understand my own people. I understand Karzai. He must reach out to senior mullahs like me or Afghanistan will be at war forever. The president of Afghanistan needs people like me more than I need him."

A bold statement boldly delivered.

Yet I believed he was right. There were enough Taliban in Khost to make the province unstable for a very long time unless more Sardars left the tribal areas of Pakistan to cooperate with Kabul. And if Khost stayed unstable, the entire eastern part of the country would be a battle zone given its central role in the region.

I was about to offer him tea, which would have led to multiple Q&A rounds, but Sardar ended the conversation. We would meet on his terms, and he would let me know when he was ready for round two. I promised him I would continue to meet whenever he wanted and see how the U.S. embassy could facilitate more reconciliation between high-level Taliban leaders, that is, Sardar's onetime peers, and the Afghan government. I reiterated U.S. policy: "You are not reconciling with us, you are with your own government." He said he would rather deal with us than with Kabul.

Before we parted that first day, I had to ask him a final question. "Have you ever talked to an American before?"

Arif translated right away.

"No. You're the first."

Not the answer I hoped to hear, but expected. We had been at war in his country for six years by that time.

There were other reformed Taliban. Like Sardar, they comprised a sensitive and complex part of my job. I needed to find a way to get more of them to support the government, while not having a mutiny among the American soldiers who worked and lived alongside me. I was essentially bringing former enemies into our home base. It was an unpredictable gambit. The American soldiers did not like it.

To ease the dynamic a bit, I always held my outreach gatherings in the same place, neutral territory far enough away from American military bases to blunt the wrong sort of first impression. The Pashtun themselves had by reputation perfected hospitality—and revenge. Arif reminded me that one of their proverbs held true over the centuries— "the sword's fellowship is sweet." It stuck with me. This strict code of conduct, called "Pashtunwali," had led Mullah Omar to protect Al Qaeda and Osama bin Laden.

Our meeting compound was situated in the middle of Khost, not far from the governor's barricaded residence. It symbolized a half-century history of the troubled land. The Taliban had built an open-air gathering spot, without walls, just a ceiling to drain rain, and several columns painted light green, rosebushes and other blooming plants aligned neatly on all sides. Its Mediterranean feel contrasted with tough talks about violence, corruption, assassinations, and Al Qaeda influence. Bees pollinated. Birds chirped. Occasionally, gunfire could be heard in other parts of town. It was a stark contrast.

Nearby, within the same walled square, the Soviets had constructed a brick building, imposing and left unfinished. It had the thickest walls and smallest windows. The main building had been erected during King Zahir Shah's time, in the 1950s, a multi-roomed, spacious two stories, now dilapidated. And then there was our contribution, recent and sandwiched in the corner: a quickly assembled functional structure that cost a lot, too much, tens of thousands of dollars. This amalgam of buildings, crowded within a 100-meter-square compound, chronicled Afghanistan's past.

None of the structures had the appearance of permanence.

The location did not stop things from getting heated at times between the soldiers and me. Tom Roth, a New Jersey native and U.S. Army lieutenant, directly questioned the value in reaching out to the Taliban. He was a good soldier, active duty, who wanted to make a career of it, even though his girlfriend back home had other ideas. When Tom was not in the gym, he was asking me sharp questions about the rationale behind various U.S. government policies—not that I could often answer him in a way that demonstrated much of a rationale.

"We can't trust any of them," Tom said.

I understood why he was distrustful, but told him we had to do it.

"They've killed our guys," he continued.

"Some have, I'm sure. The truth is, Tom, we'll never know who they are unless they confess in front of us. And I don't think they are going to do that anytime soon."

"Bullshit. We should just detain them again. Besides, you're risking a lot by bringing them into meetings like this. All the guys talk about it."

I paused before responding. I considered Tom to be a friend.

"That's bullshit too. If we don't try to get them on our side, you and all of our other troops here are going to be stuck here in Afghanistan for even more years than we've already been."

I continued. "You think this war will end with us fighting it out in these mountains and along a border that is anything but a border? We need the good Afghans fighting the Taliban from the inside."

Tom nodded, but grudgingly. He said he would have the Taliban ready for me when I finished my first meeting I had scheduled with a group of mullahs from several districts.

Before the session began, I made sure my notebook contained plenty of blank pages. I had a feeling this exchange would require a lot of note taking. Few Americans, other than CIA case officers, had sat in a room with former frontline Taliban fighters—wisely so. Arif and I also made sure the room's chairs were assembled along the walls. We had a better line of sight that way, just in case one of them, or a few, opted to cause some trouble.

These former Taliban were much more junior than Sardar, but they had a lot more testosterone and I could see why Tom and the U.S. soldiers were nervous. It was like two gangs eyeing each other, waiting for one side to make the first move. But instead of a knife fight, both were armed with a lot of guns. I kept reminding myself that they were no longer Taliban. The group had joined the local police force after "reintegrating" back into Afghan society. Or so they had promised. That was our mantra. That was our policy. They had AK-47s with them, but were not wearing their new police uniforms, which was a bit of cause for concern.

Tom approached me again.

"Let me take their weapons. It's too risky."

"Tom, no. We can't," I said. "Otherwise, they'll be pissed even before I open my mouth and they open theirs. But you can escort them to the second floor."

"Okay, but I'm telling you, if something happens . . ."

"I'll be ready when my meeting with the mullahs is over," I replied.

"Roger, but I'm telling you, this could get ugly," and with a slight nod he conceded.

In truth, I was not looking forward to this meeting. I could not tell Tom, or the other soldiers who were my friends as well, that I estimated 50 percent were probably self-identified Taliban still, trying to play both sides. Those were not good odds. And while I was certain some had killed Americans, I was also certain we must have killed some of their family members. Whether by design, because they were shooting at us or by mistake, or due to bad intelligence shared between sides, or plain counterinsurgency sloppiness.

I did not want the meeting to last longer than necessary, nor did the soldiers standing guard duty twenty meters away.

Leaving the open-air veranda, I made my way to the second floor into a cramped space in the main building, where I had asked Tom to bring my guests. I entered with Arif to see two open seats opposite us. On either side sat the Taliban-turned-cops, AK-47s leaning between their legs and dishdashas including some Pakistani carbines I had never seen before. All of a sudden, I thought Tom's instinct had been right. Arif glanced my way with a look of "what were you thinking?"

Good question. I was an American official, unarmed, surrounded by former enemies—and Arif my number one collaborator. Most of them, I am sure, believed the U.S. topped, along with the British, the hierarchy of NATO coalition infidels. We droned villages in Pakistan's tribal region from above, high-tech and invisible thunderbolts. This would be a challenging session.

I had arranged the meeting in order to understand how well the Afghan government's reintegration program for former Taliban fighters was working. The provincial director told me it had already failed. I wanted more opinions.

Only a few looked me in the eye, a now familiar pattern I was not getting used to among Afghans. They must have been the leaders, the Taliban's equivalent of our infantry company commanders, my target group. The ambassador and generals could deal with high-level enemies. The rest shuffled their feet and said nothing. One, about my age, almost looked Swedish, sharp features, but colored in browns and blacks. He introduced himself as Habib, short for Habibullah.

His name meant "beloved of God."

I listened to his story for the next ten minutes as Arif translated.

I learned how Habib was like many midlevel Taliban commanders. His words did not surprise me but reinforced how much work remained to win more like him over from the border, drop their weapons, and stay. He was brief: "I brought over forty of my men from Miranshah back to Afghanistan. One day, we were around the fire in the morning and decided to leave Pakistan and the Taliban. By evening we were back home here in Khost."

Habib held up both hands.

"I got these scars after attacking the border checkpoints. We knew your helicopters would arrive in sixteen minutes. That is how much time we had.

"The Taliban paid us, had air-conditioning, and provided DVDs from the Pakistani markets. We saw the orange jumpsuits of your prisoners in Iraq. The dogs and women."

I confessed. It happened. There was no escaping the shadows of Abu Ghraib. The place had stained my country, I admitted. No excuses. I told Habib that I had been to the Iraqi prison, twice. It did not impress him.

"You make the Taliban job easy.

"One of my friends brought his men back. But no one welcomed him home. He returned to Miranshah. The Taliban beheaded him."

My response?

"We won't do that. You all at least have that going for you. The government program is broken. I'll do what I can to help but there are many poor people in Afghanistan. You have reintegrated but that does not mean you should be rich. I will make sure our military has your names on their 'reintegration' lists." (They didn't.)

"My friend Zahirullah and I will come back to talk with you some more," Habib replied before walking away at a measured pace.

Tom, the good lieutenant, asked with a semi-smirk how the meeting with "the enemy" went. I said fine. It looked bad to be sitting with former Taliban fighters who had killed Americans or tried their best but failed. The interaction did not make me feel any better, but it was the right thing to do.

On the short trip back to Chapman I looked out my Humvee window. On the two-inch-thick Plexiglas, one of the soldiers had written a message traced in dust, directed toward Afghans along our return commute. He did not realize that I would sit in that Humvee seat.

"Fuck you, I want to go home."

True to their words, Habib and Zahirullah, the two midlevel commanders who had led dozens of Taliban foot soldiers back to Khost from the Northwest Frontier province of Pakistan, worked with me to get more fighters reintegrated. Together we hatched a plan.

Habib, who had young children, wanted them in school. Zahirullah said the sons of former Taliban needed to be in classes as well, for only then would the current and violent stalemate begin to end.

Ours was not an elaborate or complex counterinsurgency initiative that would require hundreds of thousands of dollars, the movement of U.S. soldiers, or high-level intervention.

We focused on two simple things—wheelbarrows and blue school uniforms.

If big wars often begin with bombs and jets strafing strategic targets, I had learned long wars could only possibly end via the smallest of steps taken, cumulatively. Among the people who never would meet a U.S. ambassador or become a rich contractor building another U.S.-funded project. The Average Omars and Alis in Iraq. The Average Juma Guls in Afghanistan. All the people the future of Afghanistan depended on.

Our wheelbarrow-and-uniform plan, however, would not happen easily. Distrust remained, particularly when any soldier learned of my weekly meetings with former Taliban fighters. And yet the battalion staff and soldiers had a point. Bygones were never bygones when it came to a place like Khost, on both sides. We had to make deals, but not at any price. The U.S. government sent me to the province to facilitate such deals—between the insurgents and the Afghans, not between the bad guys and me or us. It represented a delicate balance to get right—and a fairly dangerous business to be in.

But in order to move ahead with the plan, I first had to make the case to Washington. The questions came fast: *What exactly was I proposing?* and *How did such an initiative not amount to reverse collaboration?*—that is, getting too close to the U.S.'s onetime enemy. Those, in other words, who could not really be trusted, even in a transactional way.

For help I turned to a man who knew how to get things done, and asked Governor Jamal to be in the lead. He began to contact other governors in the east, but more important, relevant ministry officials in Kabul. Soon, word got out to the ambassador and his staff that we were coordinating efforts in Khost. With Jamal's cover, things moved a lot more quickly. We Americans long liked to tell ourselves that "anything with an Afghan face on it" could be sold to Washington as "progress" or, rather, "good enough progress."

In two other separate events, we distributed school uniforms to the onetime fighters' children (mostly sons but some daughters too). The local education director reassured the groups that "all children" of former Taliban fighters would be welcome at Khost schools. They just needed uniforms. It was as simple as that.

You could sense the excitement that day—from both the students, but also among many of the dads. And if you looked closely enough, the girls appeared excited too. More than a few former Taliban fighters had brought daughters, not just their sons. Who would have thought that former Taliban fighters believed in education for their daughters as well?

Khost's provincial education director voiced a clear message: whatever your fathers might have done in the past, the government would not hold that against you. In other words, the "sins of the fathers" should not, would not, mean any school door in Khost would be shut to their families. I could not have scripted his speech better myself.

He then handed out dozens of blue school uniforms purchased for about $7,000 of U.S. funds I had approved and coordinated with

USAID. America could do good things, lasting things, a storyline increasingly lost amid headlines focused on attacks and violence. A typical Predator drone costs millions of dollars. Here we made a difference with a tiny fraction of that amount.

The wheelbarrows followed a similar logic. In a province where we spent millions of dollars on roads and bridges and buildings, it seemed former Taliban foot soldiers' needs remained much simpler: they had been lacking the means to join the local day labor market. With a wheelbarrow and a pick, they could get hired.

Without, it would more likely be the Taliban who rehired them. Or killed them as traitors.

So we bought dozens and dozens of wheelbarrows, and we called them the Khost Wheelbarrow Brigade. Habib particularly got a kick out of that label, reminding me he had dreamed in his former life of leading that many, a brigade's worth of Taliban fighters, into Khost.

"I could have been a great Taliban commander," he said.

I too knew he could have been, and would have been . . .

"But I'm glad you're not, my friend," I replied. "Besides, Mullah Sardar chose a better future as well."

"Isn't it better to be on his side in any fight?"

American leadership is indispensable. But leadership means cooperation with allies and pressure on adversaries. Neither rule was followed in Iraq, with disastrous consequences.

RICHARD HOLBROOKE

The Ego Has Landed

I had come to know many key parts of Afghan society and communities by this point. Whether it was Khost U. students, madrassa students, or former Taliban fighters. PRT colleagues and I were beginning to see that there was a degree of hope in the province, a counterinsurgency strategy beginning to show results. The people had faith not only in their religion, but more than a few in their war-torn but still resilient country. It was time to introduce some of them to one of America's most prominent ambassadors, indeed that most rare of breeds in Washington, a true American statesman. His name: Richard Holbrooke.

It was not just for their benefit, but for his too. This legendary diplomat should meet, I thought, the "little people" in this longest of American wars. He was on a multi-day trip to the region facilitated by the United Nations. I knew enough of the itinerary to see his engagements before Khost, and after—sessions with those who inhabit the upper echelons, such as prime ministers, ministers, and top generals.

I wanted Holbrooke instead to experience Afghanistan at the street level, not more meetings in more fancy parlors and five-star hotel reception rooms. Besides, he had a reputation for being up for a good challenge. (One of his favorite quotes from *Moby-Dick*: "I love to sail forbidden seas, and land on barbarous coasts.") Of course, I probably should have told him of my plans first, but I also figured he could handle being surprised. He knew I would gather an unusual group but did not yet know the details of who exactly would be facing him in the room.

"Welcome to Khost," I said upon greeting Holbrooke. "I think we have several good meetings arranged for you."

"That's good. When we last met in New York at my office, I asked you why Afghanistan mattered. Do you remember what you said?"

"Yes, you had just shown me a picture of you walking along a street in Vietnam."

"Right. And?"

"I said in Vietnam we could walk away. The domino theory did not hold, but along the Af-Pak border there sure could be. Plus, I remember telling you that Pakistan's nukes changed the picture completely."

His questions showed he was still testing me.

Holbrooke was one of America's greatest U.N. ambassadors. Under President Clinton, he had managed to get the anti-U.N., archconservative senator from North Carolina, Jesse Helms, to agree to fund hundreds of millions of dollars in U.S. arrears (legally required payments to the U.N.'s budget). And for the first time, he had convinced the world's top diplomats in New York to treat HIV/AIDS as a threat to international security. Holbrooke also brought global attention to the African continent, whose endemic challenges had long been pushed aside as third-order concerns by the world's wealthiest nations.

He had attained undisputed legendary status, despite being abrasive and headstrong. Holbrooke had basically brought an end to the Bosnian war. In peace talks at an airfield in Dayton, Ohio, he had stared down Yugoslavia's president Slobodan Milosevic, as America led Europe in ultimately saving hundreds of thousands of Muslim lives. If anyone represented Teddy Roosevelt's advice that it was necessary to "carry a big stick," it was Dick Holbrooke, though he hardly spoke softly while doing so. All appreciated his enormous intellect, one matched by a proportionate sense of self.

And that is why I gravitated toward him—even while others openly (and, arguably, justifiably) could not stand him. An attraction, he was, for a few, but repellent to many more. Too many hurt feelings, too many opinions eviscerated among the bureaucratically minded, Holbrooke couldn't care less; his was a long track record of abrasiveness and theatrics that yielded success. Holbrooke got things done. He was a doer in a system of book-smart talkers, deliberators, committee member types, and platoons of staffers, all nuanced in the politics of politics, where following "the rules" often got in the way of results but ensured promotions.

As one of the few remaining great American statesmen of a bygone era, Holbrooke had come to Khost to explore the contours of the most complex chessboard in play. He knew the next U.S. president would be trying to end not just one long war, but two.

Holbrooke complained to me upon arriving. "No one in Washington knows anything about Afghanistan."

"Don't tell me that," I said.

"And what they do know is mostly wrong," he added.

Everyone inside the U.S. foreign policy establishment saw Richard C. Holbrooke as a likely—indeed inevitable—secretary of state, so long as a Democrat he campaigned for sat in the Oval Office. In past elections, before Hillary Clinton's campaign, he had worked to elect Al Gore and John Kerry. In the 2008 presidential primary among Democratic candidates, however, Holbrooke had alienated Senator Barack Obama's key foreign policy advisers—one of whom, Susan Rice, once flipped Holbrooke off in a meeting years earlier. Many governments dependent on good relations with the world's superpower had made the same calculation and treated Holbrooke accordingly, almost royally. This shared expectation led most U.S. diplomats to show him, a maker or breaker of careers, a respectful wariness. He had long followed the Machiavellian maxim: better to be feared than to be loved. When his travels took him abroad, American embassies were known to mark his arrival by declaring, "The ego has landed."

The gathered political science and law students from Khost U. had been closely following the U.S. Democratic Party's presidential primary. When I had first met with the students, the surging junior senator from Illinois had not yet beaten Holbrooke's candidate, Senator Hillary Clinton. By now tension between the sparring campaigns had crescendoed, with Clinton mounting a comeback of sorts in Midwest Rust Belt states. Mostly, though, the political outcome seemed certain: an eventual Hillary Clinton loss. Everyone knew it—Holbrooke too. The delegate math was just not adding up for the once unbeatable senator from New York. The grassroots upstart Obama machine of "hope and change" had masterfully built a commanding lead.

To begin the meeting with a bit of suspense, I asked a leading question: did the students favor one candidate over another?

After a brief pause, they replied in unison and with a resoundingly loud echo: "Obama!"

Holbrooke's broad shoulders visibly shifted as he rocked back in his chair. I smiled. I had set him up. But the Afghan students had been genuine in their proxy vote. Even the would-be secretary of state (if Hillary Clinton became president, that is) could not deny that the wave of enthusiasm for Obama had reached the easternmost edge of Afghanistan.

Momentarily taken aback, Holbrooke recovered, declaring in his trademark authoritative tone and New York City accent: "Hillary Clinton will help this country get the attention and resources that it has long needed, but not received. Afghanistan will no longer be America's forgotten war."

Ambassador Holbrooke spent the rest of the day doing what he did best. He met more of the Average Juma Guls in Khost than he ever could have imagined, the same segments of Khost that I had interacted with. The statesman parried clever yet substantial statements with all of them—ranging from Khost's street-smart tribal elders (from safe and unsafe districts alike); the Islamic madrassa students, who came dressed in their signature white; and former Taliban commanders, sharp-eyed and self-assured in his presence. The university students were particularly impressed that Holbrooke would join them for a long lunch and no-holds-barred Q&A session over goat meat, crusty wheat flour bread, almonds, raisins, and tea, several cups of which the distinguished visitor himself poured.

Holbrooke had just left Pakistan after meetings with Islamabad's top political and military government officials. I sensed he felt this was just as important, maybe even more enjoyable, because these Afghans comprised a more unpredictable group without the usual agendas or talking points.

At the end of his day-long marathon meetings, Holbrooke insisted on walking down the steep hill that surrounded the fort atop Matun Hill to the adjacent governor's compound, declining body armor in favor of his sky-blue sweater and khakis: an easy target should a sniper be in the vicinity. Holbrooke indicated he needed to stretch his legs, but I knew he was itching to experience the province up close—not through a Humvee's Plexiglas window. The Army battalion commander (a descendant of George Armstrong Custer who shared the same surname) was responsible for Holbrooke's safety and looked at me, tense. He urged me to intercede, to talk some sense into our headstrong visitor. I defended the headstrong statesman instead.

"It's Ambassador Holbrooke. He does what he wants. Besides, I've also always wanted to take this walk down to Governor Jamal's house."

I joined Holbrooke on his deliberate stroll.

"Kael, you have quite a view here."

"Yeah, it reminds me of the Rockies a bit. But a lot more dangerous and not many hiking options."

"Telluride is better." (He owned a home in that pricey Colorado ski town.)

As he moved down the hill, with Army soldiers arrayed around him, Holbrooke asked me about the politics in the province.

"You think the government here is welcomed by the people, or most of them anyway?"

"I should probably defer on that question. Let's just say we keep hearing concerns about corruption."

"Not surprising. What about our forces here?"

"Afghans hate the raids, even when SEALs get the guys we're after. I think they are even more sensitive about it all than Iraqis were in Anbar," I said.

"Civilian casualties?" Holbrooke asked.

I replied, "More than there should be. Get Governor Jamal's opinion. He has to deal with all the fallout more than we do."

"Okay, after talking with the governor maybe I'll give Bob Gates a call." (Defense Secretary Gates would visit Khost as well—and hold meetings in the exact same room atop Matun Hill.)

Holbrooke, some of his traveling staff, and I continued our downhill trek together. The only time I was allowed to make it. The views were unmatched, a broad valley spanning miles surrounded by high peaks marking the Pakistan border and ungoverned tribal areas. This was dangerous territory and exactly where one of America's foremost states-men should be spending time.

Scheduled to meet Afghan leaders later in the week, he decided to spend the night in the Provincial Reconstruction Team's modest head-quarters. We hosted Holbrooke in the best room available. It had a cheap red rug at least, plywood walls for privacy, a satellite television connection, working A/C window unit, and a cot with an extra-thick foam mattress. He seemed fine with the primitive VIP guest suite, as it did have a television that received U.S. cable channels via the Penta-gon's Armed Forces Network. He could thus watch and loudly critique pundits who were chronicling the latest political developments in the race for the White House. This provided him ample entertainment.

When South Carolina senator Lindsey Graham appeared on-screen, Holbrooke rolled his eyes and remarked, "It sure would help if our senators got over here and stayed awhile."

"Well, they do manage a day or two, which is better than noth-ing." Graham, in truth, was one of the most regular visitors to Iraq and Afghanistan and a reservist colonel in the Air Force.

"Washington is full of war tourists, you know that," Holbrooke said.

"True. Marines and I sat through one delegation in Fallujah when a congressman wanted to talk about teeth. And in Ramadi, Senator McCain once basically yelled at me."

"Well, I hope you told him something worth getting yelled at."

Holbrooke then grabbed the remote control, a bottle of water, and switched the station. I sensed he wanted to avoid any news update con-firming that Hillary Clinton's loss to Barack Obama in the Democratic primary was now a matter of when she would concede, not if. That outcome would doom his chances to become secretary of state.

. . .

Late in the evening, Holbrooke invited me to talk one-on-one. No set agenda or topic as we had already covered Afghanistan in detail. I had stressed that Afghans sought an enduring partnership with us and that the challenges remained marathon in length, generational in nature. We had long confused rising troop levels with signals of commitment. I argued we needed to keep up a fast pace in transitioning as much control as we could to Afghans, without abandoning them.

Holbrooke listened before opening up specific topics of his own. He had done his homework.

"What about the tribal elders in Khost? What are their concerns?" he asked.

"They keep telling me the same thing. The welcome mat would be out as long as Western troops respected Afghan customs and, most important, their Muslim faith. Too many U.S. military boot prints on that red carpet would wear out our welcome in a country of proud warriors."

"How close do you think we are to that point?"

"Closer than we like to admit to ourselves," I replied.

Perhaps it was my informal proximity to Holbrooke, with his shoeless feet propped up on a wobbly coffee table, that prompted me to raise another subject. He had been a supporter of the Iraq War—what many, including myself, still considered to be the greatest strategic disaster in American foreign policy in a long time, maybe ever. So I asked another leading question.

"Ambassador, when are you going to visit our other war, Iraq?"

Holbrooke's expressive, bright eyes narrowed and glared just a bit, but he did not take the bait. Instead, after a brief awkward pause, he replied simply: "I see no need to go to Iraq."

And he left it at that.

Holbrooke proceeded to give me some very good career advice. Even if that meant, he cautioned, I would have to spend more time in Washington among Washingtonians. A place the native New Yorker said he himself did not like very much. The statesman also offered for free a related jab of his own. He commented on what title I should have achieved by then in the State Department, given that he had been an assistant secretary by his thirty-sixth birthday, the same age I was at the time.

"State Department war zone grunt" did not cut it in his mind.

I replied by saying that my career would have taken off if only I had joined the U.S. Forest Service and stayed in the West. The happiest and healthiest-looking people I had ever seen in D.C. were not locals. I recalled how on the Washington Metro one summer day I sat next to a dozen National Park Service rangers who had gathered in the capital for a conference. All had their uniforms and distinctive hats on. None of them got off at the "Pentagon City," "Pentagon," or "Foggy Bottom" stops. I was jealous, in a good way.

Holbrooke said I could retire to Colorado or Utah, even to Yellowstone, but having a Washington zip code "and dumb government badge that everyone wears around their necks" remained a necessary bureaucratic requirement. U.S. foreign policy, he informed me, did not get done in national park campsites.

But perhaps it did get done while paddling under the Tetons, I thought, as I recalled how George H. W. Bush's top diplomat, James Baker, invited his Russian counterpart to visit Wyoming. I did not argue with this could-be secretary of state and NYC devotee on that point. The Great American West, in my mind at least, should be the preferred place to cut the toughest deals with America's friends and enemies and frenemies. Baker, a Texan, got it. In September 1989, he and Eduard Shevardnadze, the Russian foreign minister, talked trout while fly-fishing in Wyoming waters. This kind of informal interaction between two key people must have lessened U.S.-U.S.S.R. tensions. In follow-on formal talks about nukes at Jackson Lake Lodge, they reached a deal, with Baker declaring at the time, "We have moved from confrontation to dialogue and now to cooperation."

I wondered whether Iranian diplomats had ever been invited west of the Mississippi to meet, ideally near a national park. Diplomacy that might require Teddy Roosevelt–style tactics—but also in the part of the country Teddy Roosevelt, also a New Yorker, loved most.

The next morning, as I grabbed another cup of black coffee, I bumped into Ambassador Holbrooke in the cramped, dusty corridor outside his room. We both were up early, before most everyone else. He had bed-head and wore pajamas—appearing to me as attire from the racks at JC Penney rather than a high-priced Manhattan store outside his Central Park West apartment in the Beresford, a famed building with neigh-bors that included Diana Ross, Jerry Seinfeld, Glenn Close, and John McEnroe. Perhaps the "real" Holbrooke was a more modest man, in private. Others, much closer to him, had told me as much.

After exchanging "good mornings," he asked if I had any aspirin. I went back to my room, retrieved some Advil (all I had) and found him by then in front of the television, surfing for the latest MSNBC political update. As I handed over the little, reddish tablets, Holbrooke stopped me.

"Thanks, but I need aspirin, for here."

He motioned to his heart. In that moment, and just for a split sec-ond, I saw for the first time a degree of frailty in the larger-than-life diplomatic legend.

I got him the aspirin.

The world, that understandable and lawful world, was slipping away.

WILLIAM GOLDING, Lord of the Flies

Life After Guantánamo

Larry Nicholson's email did not come as a surprise. He continued to regularly check in on me in Khost. He had been following the news and knew that things were heating up in eastern Afghanistan. I had also told him about all the Afghans I was meeting, beyond the usual types. That included my planned interaction with former Guantánamo detainees. I suspected this session would be particularly interesting for Larry. He and I had long discussed, and occasionally debated, detention policy, including how we handled insurgents or might-be insurgents in Fallujah and Anbar. His message was straightforward and welcome: "Good luck with the Gitmo guys."

And my reply?

"Thanks, I'll need it. Too bad you can't send me a rifle company or two just in case the meeting does not go so well."

And I meant it.

.   .   .

The Afghan who had formerly been held at Guantánamo—the final stop for many beyond Bagram—said he did not want to tell me his name. He opened our conversation with a cutting comment. Given where he had spent the last four years, it should not have surprised me. But it did.

"Sometimes you Americans have ears and no eyes, or eyes and no ears. You do not want to see or hear certain things."

If only Holbrooke were here, I thought. He needed to hear such comments directly, not in an email from me at some point down the line. After leaving Khost, Holbrooke had called me from India to get input on a *Washington Post* column he was writing. Given who sat in this room, I knew which topic I would suggest he tackle in a future piece, perhaps under the title "Guantánamo Damage Control." Or "Gitmo Fallout on the Front Lines." Or, even more urgently, "Gitmo Gets American Troops Killed."

Instead, I answered some follow-up questions he had about the PRTs, and my related work in Khost—all "human capital" groups we were engaging, in addition to all the U.S. dollars we were spending. After hanging up, I wished I had asked him a question of my own, along the lines of the one I had put to him about Iraq: "Mr. Ambassador, when are you going to go visit that prison in Cuba?" If anyone could figure out a way to close the facility sooner, it would be he, known inside the U.S. government by his initials: R.C.H.

Holbrooke titled his March 2008 *Washington Post* column "The Longest War."

Short, wiry, and skinny below a gaunt face, with long fingers topped by long fingernails, the Afghan who would not share his name sat across a small table in front of me. Already seeking control of the room, he looked as if he had much to say. And being fluent in English, he made sure nothing would be lost in translation during our meeting. His verbal fury dominated a session that lasted for two hours but felt like a hundred . . . to the point, I believed, he might opt to use his fists as well.

If he had lunged my way, I would not have blamed him.

I wished Mullah Sardar could have been seated at my side if only to run interference, perhaps even vouch for me, as if to declare: "Give my friendly American infidel here a chance." Or Habib and Zahirullah would have been good protection as well—at least they could speak to the wheelbarrows and school uniforms. Small steps but concrete ones versus more talk.

By way of introduction, this agitated and aggressive Afghan said he had survived almost fifty straight months at the Guantánamo Bay prison, approximately 1,500 days in total.

"I was held from September 22, 2002, to October 16, 2006."

His anger still burned within, even after receiving his "get out of jail" notification from prison officials in Cuba. I sat before him not only as the face of the official U.S. government representative in Khost province. In me, he also saw the face of his former American jailers. And to him, it would forever be an ugly one masking unforgivable treatment. In a small way in this small room on the easternmost edge of Afghanistan, I was hoping the gap between jailer and jailed might close, even if just a bit. Guantánamo had damaged numerous lives and represented a major crack in the U.S. mirror, what the United States believed it represented to the world versus what the nation I represented meant in the eyes of non-Americans.

He was not the only one here. There were others. All equally as broken. Today would be their day to tell their stories to me, and I would be their messenger to Washington. I did not expect the prison in Cuba to close based on a single cable from me, but perhaps a few high officials in Washington would start to reexamine their own consciences on the matter.

Our meeting had been delayed almost two weeks. A fan blew hot air across the room and disrupted the flight patterns of a few nonaerodynamic flies trying to land on a sugar spoon. Over hot cups of tea on that hot day, I played host and tried to be a good one.

Before seating themselves, the four Afghans entered as a group, three looking down, only one at me directly. Two were from the same family, gray-bearded and with the most wrinkles. One appeared not even twenty years old. He limped as he took a seat farthest away from me. The last one, who spoke first and the most, got closest. He would challenge my personal space from beginning to end because he could. I sensed he knew how to be an interrogator, not just be interrogated. Closing the physical distance had his desired effect. There would be no escape for me, and a more intense dynamic than what Governor Jamal and I had experienced at Bagram months before with those detainees.

Tom, the ever-vigilant soldier verging on paranoid—not a bad quality in a war zone—asked me to let him stand guard in the room, "just in case—they are Gitmo guys after all." I said that would not be a good idea, even though he made a great one-man Praetorian Guard. I did not feel brave but knew any soldier in the room with a weapon, however well intentioned, would undercut my goal: listen to what they had to say, then report back to Washington, verbatim, as much as I could. Plus, they could rush us and acquire an American soldier's loaded rifle in the process.

So I sat alone, except for Arif, who translated when necessary. We held the meeting at the mayor's complex in central Khost. Tom and all the U.S. soldiers gathered outside the building, near our Humvees. Far enough away not to unnerve the Afghans—or for the Afghans to unnerve the soldiers, but close enough to yell for help, if need be. I knew enough about Gitmo to understand that not all of the individuals there had been mistakenly imprisoned. Some had ties to Al Qaeda.

The former detainees did not hold back, starting off with a litany of complaints and accusations based on U.S. conduct from the time they were first detained. One described telling American soldiers, "We are not afraid of handcuffs. You can take our names." He said he got the handcuffs but "you Americans waited a long time before asking my name." After being moved to a facility, he described his new conditions: "I got sick, fungus on my head. They did give me medicine but it did not work. They gave us one blanket, but it was freezing anyway. The room was like ice. We were fed bread and cauliflower. We had a choice to either eat or pray."

The youngest of the former detainees interjected in a soft voice, "They said we will release you if you help us find terrorists. I told them I was sixteen years old and a shopkeeper. My family thought I was dead."

His tone was not as angry as I expected at this point in our conversation. He sounded more resigned than anything. The oldest-looking man in the room described his own circumstances, citing a large civilian casualty count.

"Your military dropped bombs on my home, killed twelve elders, women, and children. It happened in Nadir Shah Kot."

He went on to complain that his uncle was still in Cuba, despite not being Taliban or Al Qaeda. His own release date, he said, had been recorded on documents that listed a month and a day eighteen months prior. He wanted to know why there had been such a long delay.

Acting as a spokesman of sorts for them by now, he said that upon release he had been blindfolded and "locked to a metal chair" as he was transported from Cuba to Kabul, at which point he was given 1,500 afghani (about $30). He eventually made his way back to Khost.

I asked what he had been told about the reasons for his detention, which led to an immediate eruption. He claimed the "knock" came at four in the morning when men in U.S. uniforms scaled his compound wall and broke the front gate. He said local tribes "used coalition forces to settle internal feuds" and added, "Americans make the best tool, like a trained dog for this purpose." Elaborating on his own profession, he added, bitingly, "An Afghan intelligence officer can find out if someone is guilty or not in one week. Why did it take you four years to do the same?"

I looked toward Arif after he translated this latest outburst. I could see in his eyes that he was not sure this meeting, like many others I had arranged, had been a good idea. I was beginning to doubt it myself. And yet, ground-level counterinsurgency was all about these kinds of sessions. Face-to-face dialogue forced a certain degree of honesty not possible in the far more detached environment of a fortified compound or U.S. embassy conference room.

He raised his voice further.

"What you do is terrorism. Helicopters above our houses, they make our children afraid. You fire your weapons from Camp Clark. So now I don't know who the terrorists are! My kids are still afraid by what happened. What would your kids do or think if they saw handcuffs and hitting of their father's head? What kind of impression?"

He claimed that at Chapman, the next stop, he was not allowed to sleep for two days, stood in the sun for two more days while loud music played and dogs were allowed to bite his legs. Then he was transferred to Kandahar, which he said was "more normal" than Chapman. Then onward to Bagram for twenty days, where he said he was hung from a ceiling with blindfolds and a bag placed over his head in a very cold room. Detainees were allowed fifteen minutes to eat, but could not sit. His story reminded me of Dilawar's—but unlike Dilawar, he had survived.

When he finally reached Guantánamo, he said he was put in isolation. After two years, the food improved. There were different kinds of punishments, he explained further—for example, no toilet paper. No soap for the shower. No toothpaste. No blanket or mattress.

But it was alleged U.S. mistreatment of the Quran that got him most enraged, as he lifted himself out of his chair toward Arif and me and continued in very good English:

> Sometimes we got the Quran. During General Miller's [Army Major General Geoffrey D. Miller] time, three incidents happened. A Quran was placed in a toilet, another dropped from shelves, and Americans always searched them. . . . It is forbidden to touch the holy book. During one interrogation, they placed a foot on the Quran. They interrupted our prayers and would tell us to go to interrogation.

After another incident, the details about which he left vague, he said he was put in a cold "isolation cabin" for four months. Based on his aggressiveness, I imagined this former detainee was probably one of the most resistant and vocal in Cuba.

"We were not expecting this from Americans. We thought you wanted peace. A military judge said 'I'm sorry.' I told him I did not want his sorry."

His face grew red, as one hand hit the table next to Arif.

"Your court said I'm innocent, right? Your government owes me! I need compensation for my losses! Those who gave you wrong information should be prosecuted now!

"My belongings need to be returned! No more, 'I'm sorry, I'm sorry, I'm sorry'!"

Arif went to get more hot tea. For the first time in either war, I felt that my words would only make the dynamic worse. Escalate the anger. While I listened and spoke very little, his combined physical reactions became volcanic.

He leaned over the table. Eyes wide. Almost yelling.

"Your government had me for years, then released me. Does that mean I'm innocent? Does that mean I'm innocent after you kept me for four years? I have no business anymore! What about my family? You could have kept me in the prison forever, but you didn't. Am I innocent then?"

When Arif returned, he could tell there was a problem. The session, about two hours in, needed to end.

Or maybe not.

This is where I should be, and I knew their stories mattered more than the hate directed my way by one, while three others watched.

And then I saw it was time for them to leave—not me. They, too, had had enough. The older ones, who had said so little, left first, followed by the furious one and, lastly, the youngest, who limped.

As I trailed him, not knowing if or when I would see any again—not that I wanted to actually—he turned and asked one question in broken English: "Name?"

"Kael. You, your name?"

"Mohammad."

He reached out first, to shake my hand. "When first . . . Guantánamo, so young, no beard" using motions toward his face.

His black beard was now thick. He hobbled down the stairs from our second-floor meeting room. I never saw him again. I never saw any of them again. Dozens of former detainees now called Khost home. They would be an important group, depending on how they decided to reintegrate—or not—into their communities. Washington's focus unfortunately remained on what went on in Cuba, not life after Cuba.

I could only imagine what the much larger contingent in Khost of "Gitmo alums" must be thinking given their treatment in Cuba before release. During Holbrooke's visit, I had briefly mentioned the subject to him. I said I was concerned that Washington's dismissive attitude was making Khost more dangerous. The family members of former detainees regularly approached Governor Jamal looking for explanations. Some, he said, asked for compensation "but most just want answers."

Getting some answers is what had prompted me to push for the session.

And the embassy had to be persuaded to allow the first meeting and any others that might follow.

"Will you support me? Governor Jamal believes it is an important session I try to do. Plus the provincial council chairman's own brother had been detained by us."

Several days passed before the embassy in Kabul got back to me with a phone call.

"The ambassador says meeting with the Guantánamo detainees is okay. Go ahead. A lot of other people here thought it was a bad idea, some still do."

"Please tell him thanks, and I'll be sure I write it all up and send a formal report back to you. I have a feeling these ex-detainees are going to have a lot to say."

We had struck a deal, and that is what I did. It also helped that the Khost provincial council chairman's brother had once been held at both Bagram and Guantánamo, another "justification" for the unusual and sensitive meeting. What I did not tell the embassy, however, was that the tribe both brothers came from remained among the most suspect we had in the province. The Zadran tribe.

Still, on such occasions, the State Department's best traditions came to the fore: truth telling amid bureaucratic pressure to do the opposite by political operatives within Washington officialdom, whose loaded agendas usually centered on protecting the boss at all costs and making him or her look good. Protecting the long-standing traditions of the United States did not always factor in first—or at all. I never got the chance to thank the ambassador in person for sticking up for me, but his support made the difference. Instances of moral courage always jumped out.

The meeting constituted the first and only one of its kind officially reported via diplomatic cable as far as I knew. If any Afghans were going to call the American bluff about our detention process and abuses, it would be these men.

Deep down I knew there would be no way to explain how 9/11 seemed to have warped all sense of law or rules, particularly for anyone not holding U.S. citizenship and came under "Global War on Terror" scrutiny. In total almost 800 detainees would be held in the prison, cases adjudicated outside any normal legal process. In 2004 the U.S. Supreme Court ruled in *Hamdi v. Rumsfeld* that detainees had the right to appeal their detention before an "impartial" tribunal. The Supreme Court later ruled that detainees had the same protections as those afforded under the Constitution (describing military tribunals as "inadequate" substitutes).

But these steps came too late for the Afghans I met that day. I had gone into that meeting with the Gitmo guys confident we should hear what they had to say, unedited, and not hide it. But would anyone really care to hear what these once condemned men had to say?

That became the premise of what followed. My cable: "Life After Guantánamo."

Why push the system this way?

Simple: I made the case inside the State Department that what happened to detainees after they left the prison was crucial. How these men transitioned back home, particularly in a place like Khost, could inflame local dynamics—and increase the chance all of us might dodge more roadside bombs and bullets. Or their return could be a net neutral, perhaps the most realistic outcome.

I reminded the embassy about other governments and the programs they had initiated for post-Guantánamo detainees. The Saudis, for example, provided platinum "welcome back" treatment that included a generous reintegration package, such as accommodation and funds to live comfortably; some even provided assistance in finding a wife. The Saudi government argued this kind of formal program would increase the likelihood of a smoother readjustment into society. No repeat offenders, in other words.

Could we help the Afghan government do more, even if they lacked anything close to Saudi resources? It was at least a model. I knew NATO allies had a far more skeptical view about many aspects of the Cuba facility, including the need for it to be established in the first place, its internal detention procedures, its legality, and the potential to inflame hatred toward the U.S. and its allies. Perhaps by more closely examining the transition of this population, European governments would see a better angel of the United States.

There was also the moral dimension. I could not be as blunt about that part of my rationale—I represented the U.S. government after all—but it mattered in my mind just as much. I had a bad feeling that after spending four, five, or six years in Guantánamo, their release did not amount to the long-standing American notion of rule of law and human rights, whatever the Department of Justice lawyers were submitting to political bosses via various memos. I wanted to be proven wrong.

Several Khost University law students, as well Khost governor Jamal himself, told me privately that while they knew there were plenty of insurgents and terrorists in Afghanistan, what continued to be critical was how the U.S. went about dealing with them.

Jamal added: "Guantánamo is what the Taliban and Al Qaeda want." He mentioned that many Afghans in Khost had discussed a case where a "ninety-six-year-old grandfather" had been detained, enraging the entire district. (The governor later explained this very old man—whose purported age, he agreed, seemed to be a rather large exaggeration— had been released, although the friction over his detention had not dissipated.)

When my cable landed in Kabul, it got some attention: the ambassador and embassy classified it "NODIS," which meant "no distribution" and thus it would be severely restricted. Only a select few would read it inside the U.S. government, and no sharing even with our closest NATO allies. (Too embarrassing in many ways, I figured.) As such, it also was not made accessible to Defense Department computer networks, thereby staying out of the WikiLeaks trove.

If one cable deserves to be widely and publicly read, however, among the hundreds I wrote across seven years in both wars, I believe it is this one—"Life After Guantánamo." But it remains shelved in some e-archive and will probably stay there as a government secret for a very long time. Perhaps longer even than—the eventual closure of?—the American prison in Cuba, still open for business at a total cost of over $5 billion as of 2015.

Before the day's meeting ended, I asked the former detainees what documents any U.S. official or military officer had given them upon release from Guantánamo. Each had spent between three and five years in the prison. They mentioned a piece of paper as the only one handed over upon being flown from Cuba to Kabul. I asked if I could get a copy.

A few days later Arif received the release document from one of the Afghans.

"Mr. Kael, here is what he gave me. Just this."

My eyes quickly scanned it.

"Just this? You have got to be kidding. Are you sure he didn't say there were more documents, anything else?

"Nothing. He looked nervous and wanted to leave."

"I can't blame him. We had him in Cuba for years and I'm sure he has flashbacks every time he sees an American, even one who is there to listen to his side of the story."

I held in my hands the only documentation issued by the U.S. government or any military officer following a former detainee's transfer back to Afghanistan:

UNCLASSIFIED

NOTIFICATION OF THE DECISION OF AN
ADMINISTRATIVE REVIEW BOARD

ICO ISN XXX TO DEPART GUANTANAMO BAY

An Administrative Review Board has reviewed the information about you that was talked about at the meeting on 02 December 2005 and the deciding official in the United States has made a decision about what will happen to you. You will be sent to the country of Afghanistan. Your departure will occur as soon as possible.

UNCLASSIFIED

Nothing else. No other explanation. Just seventy words. And poor Pentagon prose at that . . .

This single piece of paper would mean more American troop deaths. More Taliban recruits. Not only was I convinced of this point, so was Governor Jamal. He had already warned me.

And more suicide bombers plotting away—and heading our way.

Remember the rights of the savage, as we call him. Remember that the happiness of his humble home, remember that the sanctity of life in the hill villages of Afghanistan, among the winter snows, is as inviolable in the eye of Almighty God, as can be your own.

WILLIAM E. GLADSTONE, 1879

The Dead of Sabari District

With the troubling accounts of Guantánamo still on my mind, I glanced over Arif's shoulder, noticing the hazard lights flashing yellow on a Toyota Hilux. They reflected off a nearby mud wall, and the branches of a line of trees overhead. The vehicle had stopped after the L-shaped turn a few hundred meters from FOB Chapman, our "safe" destination in an unsafe province.

I heard the lead gunner in our Humvee convoy call out the vehicle on our "comms" (radio headsets)—"Toyota Hilux, right side"—and for an instant my mind wondered why the SUV had parked in that spot. They almost always pulled over when Humvees came near.

Earlier that day, we had finished an opening ceremony for a diversion dam in a hilly district along the Pakistan border, about an hour away from the Khost center. The governor gave a speech, as he always did, while the Afghans knew it was American money that funded the project. For a while, the facade worked for all sides. The sun was setting, and we needed to get Jamal back before dark, when things always got more dangerous.

The Hilux remained at the corner. Waiting. It should not have been.

The main convoy gunner up front called out a second time.

"Suspicious Toyota. Watch it."

And then . . . kaboom. The bomb, I could tell, I could feel, I could certainly hear, had been big, with my ears ringing still, and the beginnings of what felt like a bad headache coming on. An "IED migraine" is what Marines called them in Iraq. This was the biggest I had ever experienced, even compared to those in Fallujah and Ramadi.

Our convoy stopped along the paved road we had funded, the blast wave throwing us forward. My head almost hit the driver's seat as our Humvee rocked with a jolt. It had been a bomb meant for us, and a close one. Contrary to training and embassy rules, I got out of the vehicle and stepped "into the X"—the area in which a usual defensive perimeter would be established in case of follow-on small arms fire or other secondary attacks.

Meters away lay twisted metal, scattered. Human remains clung to tree branches, bunched above, which also dotted the road farther down. A soldier told me later on that they found the bomber's severed hand, but not much else. I am glad I missed that visual, no need to repeat another Potato Factory–like experience in Khost. Still, the images before me stuck—a blur.

Dusk. Hilux. Lights blinking. Blast. Metal parts. Body pieces.

Flashes of war imprinted in memory.

Several of the governor's guards were badly wounded, and the provincial council chairman, Mujahid from Musa Kehl District and a friend, died—but not from the blast. He collapsed of a heart attack, not yet forty years old, fingers still clamping the steering wheel of a Corolla, one of two in our convoy.

Suicide bombers picked their targets carefully. We depended on luck. And somebody always got unlucky. But not the governor this time, as he had called a wise audible prior to joining our convoy and switched vehicles. Instead of traveling in the dark blue armored Toyota Land Cruiser we provided him (one of several), he moved back into the other old white Corolla. The model ranked among the most common vehicles in Afghanistan, like seeing a rusting but ever-reliable Honda Accord along I-70.

Jamal had already been targeted several times by 2008, including by a teen would-be bomber who believed flowers would spread into the air after exploding his suicide belt. That is what he, like impressionable other youths, had been told by the extreme mullahs in Pakistan. Afghan police detained him before he could get close to the governor. Karzai pardoned the fourteen-year-old, named Rafiqullah, and gave him $2,000 to return to his family across the border. Jamal told Afghan reporters at the time, "He is a child. I don't believe it was his idea. He was brainwashed. Actually it was my decision to free him. I told the president he should be free."

Given this past and his value as a top target for the Taliban, the rusty sedan hid Jamal's VIP profile. The bomber must have thought the governor would not trade imported comfort, steel-plated and inch-thick, blast-resistant glass provided by the Americans for an ordinary Corolla. Jamal had few of his nine lives left to spare, and by this point he had gained the respect of the most hardened U.S. soldier. Most, like me, had been in Afghanistan long enough by then to understand the most dangerous jobs were not our own—but rather those held by Afghans. And the top of the target list? Afghan politicians, like Jamal, who lived in the provinces, not in Kabul.

Near the bombing site, Texas native Dave Adams, the commander of the Provincial Reconstruction Team and a Navy nuclear submariner-turned-able-counterinsurgent (he knew how to get a lot of Pentagon money approved and how to spend it fast), asked me to get back into the Humvee. He was agitated and then some.

"You should have stayed in the Humvee."

"You're right," I replied. "I know the rules, but I also needed to see who was hurt."

Mark stood next to me, agitated as well. He raised his rifle in a sweeping motion in case an RPG or small arms fire followed the blast. I hoped he would not tell his wife back in Phoenix about what happened, just as I did not intend to tell my own family.

I paused before turning around. Instinct atop numbness from Iraq got in the way of better judgment in Afghanistan, but Adams was right. My presence complicated the situation. The State Department did not pay me to assess battle damage, metal amid tissue. Good political analysis and good counterinsurgency strategy was supposed to reduce the odds of these scenarios. No diplomatic cable or employee evaluation, needless to say, could capture the texture of being in a suicide car bomb attack while on the job.

In contrast to us Americans, Afghan leaders took such attacks mostly in stride. Such day-to-day risks were assumed, but never easy to deal with personally or obviously for their families.

Governor Jamal received a call on his phone just minutes after the explosion and told a Reuters reporter what happened. "The attack was against my convoy. I am fine, but I see some people in flames in cars ahead of me."

Hanging up, he broke down into tears, turning my way.

"I am not sure I can continue in this job. My family will hear this news. What do I tell them? Another bomb?"

After taking him into Chapman, we walked outside for half an hour and said little. I could see moonlight glinting off the old Soviet planes rusting on the compacted dirt tarmac the Soviets had built during their invasion. Looking up I thought I saw a shooting star, but it moved too slowly.

Probably one of our spy satellites. I knew such technology could not get into the minds of suicide bombers. That required person-to-person homework and ground-level insights. That required working closely with brave and undeterred Afghan collaborators like Governor Jamal.

When the Hilux truck bomb (SVBIED in military terminology—Suicide Vehicle-Borne Improvised Explosive Device) went off, Arif and I were talking about eastern Afghanistan tribes. Some wanted our help and money. The Mangal, his own people, fell in that category. What better spokesperson than my trusted albeit biased interpreter to advocate his district's needs? But some Afghans did not—those in Sabari, for example. To them, American money was dirty money.

American money was blood money.

And no other district in Khost had more of a reputation for violence than Sabari. Of course this meant Arif and I needed to go there and talk to the people. We did not expect to find many friends.

With us on this mission came two of our most trusted Afghan guards: Qadir and Fassal. Hired by the military to be the day-to-day protection force for us, I had already grown close to them. Along with a dozen other guards, they helped us maneuver through the province. Qadir served as the lead guard of a dozen. Bearded and always laughing, he had regaled PRT soldiers and me with stories about his past work in Khost during the Soviet era.

"I laugh now, but didn't then. Russians were killed in Khost while peeing in the streams."

Fassal, by contrast, was one of the youngest guards. Curly haired and jumpy, he used basic English to crack jokes—we rarely understood what the jokes were, but the way he told them made us laugh as well.

"I am tough guard.

"I am toughest guard.

"I never run."

Despite his skinny appearance and nonmilitary bearing, I believed him. Afghans, like Marines, run toward gunfire.

Qadir carried his AK in a precise way. Fassal, who had a lot less experience with weapons, treated it almost like a toy. I was glad both would be joining us on the mission.

Before departing, Qadir asked me how long he thought we would be in Sabari. He had a large family to take care of and hoped to be back within a week.

"Don't worry, we'll get you home by then. I don't plan to spend more time there than we need to."

He thanked me and asked me to join him and the other guards for lunch. Fassal, he said, needed a new uniform. He wanted to look professional.

"We'll take care of that when we get back to Chapman."

"Qadir, do you know anyone in Sabari?"

"No. I try to avoid that place."

Qadir's warning about Sabari tracked with what many Afghans had told me, so much so that by the time our convoy stopped to make camp for the night, the sight of a group of Afghan soldiers only partly reassured me. They were on our side, I knew, but I wondered about their views on having been ordered to Khost's most dangerous district. The sun began to move quickly over the peaks, with their high-altitude winter chill flowing directly upon us, forcing one Afghan National Army soldier to be a full-time fire keeper else the flames would die out and we might just all come close to suffering from near-instant hypothermia.

"Where were you before coming here to Sabari?" I asked.

"Telman," he pronounced slowly, dragging out the sound of an "e" instead of an "i" for a few seconds. That is, the base named for Pat Tillman. A former NFL player, he had enlisted in the U.S. military (leaving a multi-million-dollar-per-year football career), deploying to Afghanistan, where he was killed in a friendly-fire incident—a fact that only came out after his family pressed the Pentagon to release more information. A partnered local militia soldier was also killed.

Next to U.S. Marines, I always felt safest around Afghan National Army soldiers. The ANA did not look the part, exhibiting no Marine spit-and-polish or regimented standard operating procedures. Their uniforms were never pressed or creased, often fraying and covered in dirt and mud. I felt we could relate, at least in the choice of war zone fashion. I preferred jeans to khakis.

Unlike so many Marine friends of mine—with their precise haircuts, bench-pressed chests, strutting habits and attitudes to match—the bony Afghans kept their facial hair unshaved and the greasy locks on the top of their heads swept back behind their ears. Few if any spent time in a weight room, but they had been well trained in mountain warfare from a young age. And they made good scouts, whom we needed on a mission like the one we were on given the difficult and dangerous terrain.

Where our Humvees could maneuver on this Sabari mission, we left tire tracks—all easily identifiable wide lines in gray streambeds full of dust and rocks and often mud, ideal places to bury roadside bombs. If insurgents needed a roadmap directly to us, these would be it, almost as if "Here There Be Americans" were stamped across the soil. Put another way, no matter how hard we tried, we stood out. Each convoy did its best to plot newer, more clever paths in order to avoid the IEDs, while also not hitting a boulder or landing in soupy muck that would get us stuck. That kind of mechanical predicament could become the other kind of Khost predicament. Small arms fire or mortars launched by the Taliban, who always seemed to know where we were going before we did; before we got there, before we got anywhere, really.

Even so, the same people took point over and over and over in unarmored vehicles, Hiluxes or smaller trucks: our Afghan security guards, with Qadir and Fassal in that role on this trip. They had the eyes, ears, and noses that only a born Pashtun could use to figure out which turn would be the wrong one that got us killed.

During this particular multiday winter trek in Sabari, I spent the windy night talking to this same small group of Afghan soldiers. Temperatures had continued to drop to the 30s, and we were not going to be back at the base for a few more days. The area represented the most difficult in Khost to conduct counterinsurgency operations. Sabari not only had close ties to the Haqqani Network, but also geography that made it impassable in many areas, especially in winter. Insurgents could not have picked a better home base.

We set up a makeshift camp in the foothills near a local cemetery. Multicolored flags flapped in the air. The sun had already set, leaving the sky dark after shades of orange and blues. Across the valley, smoke billowed up from mud compounds as families persevered through another Afghan winter. Still cold despite my North Face jacket, layers of fleece, and long underwear, I wandered over with Arif to the fire to strike up a conversation and warm myself. The closer I got to the flames, the friendlier everyone seemed. The Afghan soldiers had only basic winter gear and shivered a lot less. My focus? How did they view our troops, particularly their training mission?

"Do you think we are doing a good job?"

Several nodded.

I tried again.

"Do you feel like our troops trust you?" Arif moved his hands together to keep them warm, all the while eyeing the perimeter. By now, I had come to appreciate how his instincts in any environment counted for just as much as the words he translated. If there was going to be a problem with any of the Afghan army soldiers tonight—a time largely before "green on blue" insider attacks (when Afghan army soldiers or police turned their weapons on American trainers)—he would know first. While Khost had not had any confirmed cases since my arrival, Arif and I had discussed the possibility. It only took one disgruntled soldier to decide which American would be the easiest target, and as the only one on most missions without a weapon, I easily could be that American.

The Afghan army sergeant, who spoke for the rest, said Afghans welcomed U.S. support, but I was hoping for more details.

"You know the differences between our troops. Is there a part that you prefer to train with?"

A few looked at each other after Arif translated my follow-up question. Then paused, as if unsure they should declare any preferred part of the U.S. military.

"Yes. Marines. They are like this with us."

The Afghan sergeant, who had wide shoulders, a beard starting to go gray, and massive hands, stretched out his arms in a wide-sweeping and circular motion before bringing them together, like a bear hug.

Governor Jamal was always looking to expand the government's reach into the wildest areas, while also educating me on "Pashtunistan" dynamics. He wanted his American co-conspirator to gain a visceral feel for his native land. Jamal's commitment to Afghanistan ran deep, like the steep mountain passes we often traveled together along with the PRT in order to check on the status of various U.S.-funded projects. It was for this reason we had ventured into Sabari, but also to gain firsthand insights into why the district remained "red." Had locals given up on the Afghan government? Had they given up on even American dollars and our projects?

On those key questions, I would soon meet another American civilian who had arrived to help. He was, of all things, an anthropologist by training. That boded well. As a student living near Seattle my first year of college, I had taken an anthro class. The homework about other cultures proved to be a highlight from all of my coursework that year. In Khost I still remembered Polish anthropologist Bronislaw Malinowski's Trobriand islanders as a famous case study of the "other" and the importance of fieldwork. If anything, successful counterinsurgency required an anthropologist's instinctive openness toward that which is different and foreign.

"I'm Michael, nice to meet you."

The bearded thirtysomething-year-old had the studious look

of a pre-tenure professor. Michael Bhatia was his full name. Brown University–educated and a Californian by birth, his academic focus fit nicely with his new environment: the mujahideen, who had long populated Khost, whether arming themselves to fight the Soviets or now us. He tilted his ears toward the Afghan side of the table, pen and notebook in hand. A good sign we all noticed. In earlier meetings with Governor Jamal and other provincial leaders, Bhatia had explained to me that his job was to help the U.S. military better understand Afghan culture and society.

"I am here to help improve that dynamic."

He had a big job ahead of him, particularly given how many civilian casualty incidents Khost had experienced in the past and probably would well into the future. In turn, I was blunt.

"Good luck. I'm in that business too, but am glad as a civilian I'll have reinforcements for as long as you're here."

"When you have time, you'll have to tell me more about the State Department. What you like about it. What you don't. And what this kind of assignment will mean for your career."

"All good questions. These wars have forced State to do things we have never been trained to do, but that's mostly a good thing. I wish there were more anthropologists like you back in D.C."

"Yeah, there might be fewer wars," he replied.

We agreed to meet the next time I was at Camp Salerno, where he was based. Before Bhatia left the room, I said what I told all Americans who had arrived in Khost, whether for a short stay or a longer assignment.

"Be safe. This place is a lot more dangerous than Kabul."

He nodded and left. Bhatia would have joined us on our mission to Sabari, but we did not have room in our Humvees, so instead of waiting for another time, we went ahead with the mission. I wish we had not.

After the fires died down on the hillside, and I excused myself from the group of ANA soldiers, I crawled into the back of a Humvee, put my legs up over the front seat, and fell asleep. In the morning, over instant coffee from MRE packets, I reminded our PRT soldiers why we were there, what the mission was all about: try to win friends in one of the worst districts. Some tribal leaders said they wanted to help us, even if most were either neutral or working against the government and coalition. They listened but only half seemed convinced. I made the case nonetheless. We sure could have used Bhatia on this mission, I thought. I could tell he got Afghans, and sometimes I wished I was not the only civilian embedded in a pack of U.S. soldiers, some of whom simply did not like Afghans.

We needed allies in Sabari, even if the stares had the icy look of some of the worst I had seen in the worst days of Fallujah. I would tell the governor as much. The soldiers said they got my points. I added, however, we also needed to admit the limits of U.S. power in such places. Limitations mechanical (our Humvees could only go so far) and verbal (my translated words could only close cultural gaps so far) became apparent soon enough.

A conversation surprised me during one of our final stops before returning to Chapman. It reflected both of these limits. I sat next to several elders who had their grandsons gathered close. But as in so many other instances, the testosterone-filled teenagers stayed away. The grandfathers remembered the era of U.S. Stinger missiles, and the grandsons sat fascinated by us foreigners—U.S. soldier uniforms, the occasional volleyball we gave out, a radio if they were lucky, even my light-colored hair. All of us wondered what the missing teens might be up to atop rooftops or behind the compound walls. Our Afghan guards kept close watch.

Arif, who had just told me that he remained concerned for his family's safety, translated a list of projects the village leaders said they needed beyond wants. I took notes and repeated the line I often used: "I keep the promises I make, which is why I don't make very many." But I qualified that declaration by adding I would discuss a few of the more realistic possibilities back at the PRT, such as a diversion dam, a few wells and schools.

And then came the surprise.

Arif translated the words of the group, not just from a single tribal leader, but from many.

"Bring back Captain Barr."

"Bring back Barr."

"Barr."

"Where is Barr?"

"Barr different."

I thought I had misheard them. Captain Barr? The U.S. force lay-down did not reach into their area, but they clearly meant an American.

"Who?"

"Captain Barr."

Arif leaned toward me, as he often did when a particularly impor-tant subject required my full attention. As he got closer, I noticed more gray hairs than when I had first met him. Captain Barr, he said, was a Marine company commander who had been based in the province years earlier. Like the elders, Arif attested to his true Superman status. Afghans loved him. He was one of them. He made the province, even a place like Sabari, safer.

I wrote down his name and promised myself I would email General Dunford and encourage him to track down this Barr hero and put in papers to promote him right away. Hell, I would even give him his own battalion if I were a Marine general.

Maybe we Americans had a chance, I thought. Even in a place like Sabari.

Qadir nodded. "I remember Barr. All Khostis remember Barr."

"Should we try to get him back here? I can ask some Marine leaders to find him."

"If you had more Barrs standing next to us Pashtun, you would have already won this war," he added.

"Sounds like we need to find him, then clone him."

Arif tried to translate what that meant exactly, but had a hard time.

As our meeting ended, Fassal and Qadir assembled with the rest of the guards in order to take a truckload of humanitarian assistance supplies back to Chapman. They asked to leave about ten minutes early. We said okay. They hopped in a dark blue Toyota and started out.

I said goodbye to the elders and eventually moved into the right rear backseat in the lead Humvee. We estimated it would take about two to three hours to get back, and we were ready. The weather had cleared but the temperatures remained frigid.

Our convoy began to creep along the wadi, moving like a slow, steel python. Minutes later, an IED exploded in front of us. A boom rever-berated through our Humvee, rocking us in our seats. Another IED migraine that none of us needed. After rounding a small bend, I saw the dark blue Toyota split in two and a narrow column of dirt drifting away. The front end of the vehicle had lodged bumper-first into the ground, the back end the same. The unarmored car's metal spine had been broken, inverted, forming a perfect upside-down V shape.

Within minutes, our surviving guards were picking up body pieces, scattered in several directions. It was Fassal. Qadir had been blown meters away. His back lay flattened amid gray stones in the dusty riverbed, unblinking eyes directed upward.

We radioed for assistance and soon a Black Hawk hovered overhead. But it would not land. Because no American was KIA or WIA, they would not take the risk. It was policy. We eventually moved to the nearest U.S. Army fort-like base still in Sabari. The major stationed there openly hated Afghans. In an earlier meeting in central Khost, he had glared at me when I suggested we share some lunch at an event with Afghan guards. That reaction stuck with me. I asked him to let the helicopter take our Afghan guards' remains to Chapman, so the bodies could be buried before sundown, in line with the Muslim custom. He refused.

"I'm not gonna land our helicopters. Too dangerous for my men. Besides, you told me there are no Americans wounded, so as I see it, no need for casevac" (casualty evacuation in military lingo).

I wanted to boot him out of the country on the spot but kept my mouth shut and turned around, exiting his command post, which, I now realize, lacked even the most basic sense of Afghans. The most basic sense of what could lead to green-on-blue attacks.

And so we left. I decided not to raise the matter with the battalion or brigade commander, but I should have. Khost remained too important a place for a key U.S. Army officer to serve and lead, someone who hated Afghans and seemed intent on making every effort to show it. The Qalandar elders' basic message echoed in my ears: *You Americans have nothing to worry about, as long as you respect our religion and us.* With the remains of Fassal and Qadir now wrapped in a blue plastic tarp, the rest of our Afghan guards got ready to depart, but not before one declared the truth.

"If they were American, your helicopters would be taking them back to the base right now."

I had nothing to say. To say something other than "you are right" would have been a lie.

Of course he was right. I was furious. The helicopter had left the immediate vicinity but we could hear it in the distance heading in the opposite direction, rotors thumping, empty except for the crew. I could see a second helicopter farther out but also flying opposite our direction.

We sped as fast as we could back to Chapman and gathered in an informal memorial, next to the former Soviet airstrip. Fassal and Qadir were buried before sunset back in their villages, transported by our remaining guards and relatives who had raced to Chapman upon hearing the news.

As I walked into the PRT's main building, Commander Adams came up to me, declaring, "I heard you got out of the Humvee after the IED attack." I had. Just as I had gotten out of the vehicle when the suicide bomber targeted the governor's convoy.

But I worked for the U.S. State Department, not the U.S. Army or a general or a Navy nuclear submarine commander. My words came easily. They ended the exchange.

"Yes, I did. We had to pull the body bags for Fassal and Qadir from behind my seat."

Sabari District only grew more violent after that mission. I never saw the elders again, and since I had not made them any promises, I believe they received funds for a few diversion dams but not much else. Had they known in advance about the IED? I did not want to know. All the while, I kept thinking of those ANA soldiers I had met over a fire, and the "bear hug" they had received from some Marines.

Michael Bhatia, the anthropologist assigned to work with the Army, died in a massive roadside bomb in Sabari District on May 7, 2008, along with two U.S. soldiers: Specialist Jeremy R. Gullett (22, of Greenup, Kentucky, pop. 36,519) and Staff Sergeant Kevin C. Roberts (25, of Farmington, New Mexico, pop. 45,426). The explosion left another two service members critically injured.

Michael had been traveling in the convoy's lead Humvee. His was not an assigned seat in the front vehicle, always the most dangerous one to be in when convoying through IEDvilles, but a voluntary one.

Let us pick up our books and pens. They are our most powerful weapons.

MALALA YOUSAFZAI

The Commander and
the Top Student

It just so happened the best U.S. strategy on women's issues had nothing to do with money or memoranda from Washington. No, it came through the role of one person, the new Provincial Reconstruction Team commander in Khost: Erika Sauer.

Standing almost five-foot-ten, Erika had spent a lot of time at sea, far from landlocked Afghanistan. But I welcomed this new dynamic mainly because it would test both the Afghans we worked with, including the governor and his top advisers and provincial officials, but also test the U.S. Army and its command team based in Khost.

Sauer, who grew up just outside Erie, Pennsylvania, had been a basketball star in high school, member of the National Honor Society, and class valedictorian. She later played basketball at Rutgers and graduated with a BA in microbiology. After enlisting in the Navy in 1984 as a meteorologist, she served in the Joint Typhoon Warning Center in Guam before going to Officer Candidate School in Rhode Island. She would later serve on the USS *Belleau Wood*, named after an iconic

World War I battle, and the aircraft carrier USS *John F. Kennedy*, named after a president not known for particularly strong views on women's rights, even when considering "it was a different era back then" logic.

Before Commander Erika Sauer's arrival in Afghanistan the U.S. Army brigade commander, outgoing PRT commander Adams, the battalion commander, and I debated views on whether we thought she could succeed in the province. They voiced their indictment.

"Afghans won't accept her."

"You know how they are with women."

"She is going to be run out of this job."

I listened, but eventually made my position clear.

We Americans needed to respect Afghan sensitivities. But in a province where we were spending millions of dollars, including on girls education, they needed to get to know us as well. We had women in positions of leadership, powerful women. Period. Plus, in my mind, I knew that all girls we would visit at various girls schools would see me, the usual male American, but also the new PRT commander, a woman. The battalion commander said he could see her role working, with a lot of effort on both sides, but the others remained skeptical.

All of us knew a related battle—one of perceptions—would happen inside the traditionally male-dominated U.S. military, who only slowly were getting used to women in greater positions of authority. In Iraq I had witnessed U.S. Marines—the most self-described macho of branches and the definition of maledom (less than 10 percent female; the U.S. Air Force has the highest number, roughly 20 percent)—increasingly debating how women might transition into frontline combat roles.

And if Khost province was anything, it was a laboratory for many things. Now to include just how much Afghan elders would, or would not, be willing to work with the Americans' newest reconstruction team leader. A woman put in charge and in uniform, not another man in camouflage.

One of the first places Erika and I visited in Khost was a school that had been built for $50,000 max, I estimated. One drone overhead, or one helicopter hovering, or one Humvee for that matter, cost a lot more by many, many multiples.

I paid most attention to the patient Afghan teacher who met our group outside. It was his big day. The young, serious-looking man, who was probably only a few years older than his oldest students—teens—wanted to showcase his class. Before the walking tour of his school, he offered the Pashtun staple diet for meetings: tea, dried yellow raisins, and homegrown walnuts, half shelled, in small, carved wooden dishes. We made our way down the line as he gave a brief overview of the school. The students looked bashful, shuffling their sandals in the dirt, swinging arms at their sides. Many, yet again, avoided direct eye contact, as I would have done if some Afghan foreigner—one that did not even speak the same language—had visited my school at their age.

Just before reaching the end of the first row, a willowy girl with long black bangs looked straight at me. I could tell the teacher wanted to stop and say a bit more about her.

"She's my best student, my top student."

As if rehearsed, she piped up without pausing, in a bit of English but most of her words requiring translation from her native Pashto.

"I am also the class president." Arif focused on that comment.

I congratulated her, confessing I too had held that position while a junior in high school. Hers of course was a lot more difficult, and dangerous, role to have in a place like Khost. I wondered whether she had been elected by other students or selected by the teacher but did not ask. I sensed she could win any election at any age at any level.

"And what do you think about us Americans here? Do you want us to stay?" I asked.

"You can leave. But only after I graduate from university."

I could tell she meant what she said and had to give her credit. She knew how to deliver a demarche—State Department lingo for official messages between national capitals. To me, and through me to the U.S. government, her words had been offered on behalf of herself but also her generation and gender.

I figured her age to be fifteen, sixteen tops. A quick calculation based on her request meant she believed that U.S. troops in Afghanistan should remain for at least six more years. That is, if she managed to secure a spot at Khost University, let alone in Kabul.

Despite innumerable cross-cultural barriers, there was something special and resilient about her, which made me think she could do it.

She could be the star student who went to college despite the overwhelming odds. And then? A leader, in whichever field she chose . . . or was allowed to choose.

As I turned around to answer questions from other students, I noticed Erika had stayed back. She had even more students gathered around her, including all the girls. I realized then the incalculable value of a PRT commander who stood out, for all the right reasons, in Pashtun culture, and from the male-dominated U.S. military culture for that matter. The girls encircled this patient American, questions from all directions, making it hard for Erika's interpreter to keep up.

"What's your name?"

"Where do you come from?"

"Are you married?"

"Do you speak Pashto?"

"When will you leave?"

"What do you think of Khost?"

"You in charge of soldiers?"

And so on.

I am certain that more girls that day began to think about attending university, not because of anything I had said. But rather because they had seen the Americans arrive with a confident and caring woman, one who also happened to be in charge of the soldiers around her.

Arif had daughters, but he still had not spoken about them. After several months, he told me that teaching girls would never be easy in a place like Khost, even in the most moderate areas. But what happened behind the mud compound walls would surprise us Americans.

"Mothers in charge. My wife in charge."

I asked him to explain, knowing full well the common understanding of this part of the world: men dominated in all matters. Money. Business. Politics. And fighting. Another linguist jumped in at this point and said that once the Americans had arrived and broadcast intentions to educate not only boys but also girls, the reaction proved mixed. Proud Pashtun fathers and brothers simply did not trust U.S. intentions, even if more than a few believed their daughters did not belong in a lesser category.

"The teaching stayed behind our gates and walls. Many did not want girls taught in your schools but that did not mean education for them did not continue away from your eyes."

I was skeptical, but then Arif opened up more about his personal experience, even while he never conveyed the names of his daughters.

"My wife and I want them educated too. But they are not safe at schools where there are no women teachers and little security."

"Can't they attend classes with your sons? We have been to schools where on one side it is girls, on the other side, boys."

"No, that is not allowed. Until there are more girl teachers, our culture will not be comfortable with teaching this way."

That top student must have benefited from this kind of parental support. I wondered how many sisters had been left waiting for their own time to leave the compounds and begin more formal instruction. A magnet school in central Khost would be the one place—indeed if any place could make such an educated future possible for more than just a small number of girls. The Afghan government and foreign NGOs had celebrated this model location.

After a meeting with Governor Jamal earlier that same week, Commander Sauer, PRT members, and I walked about a hundred meters down the road to this largest girls school. It had a small gate, but one that did not hide the activities within: the education of girls. It seemed the teachers and families who were sending their daughters believed the site to be safe and protected because of its proximity to government offices and a police station. In many ways, they assumed right. Plus, we Americans knew too many visits by us would only increase the risks for the girls and their teachers.

With donated book bags (but without books in them) in hand, we entered and soon found ourselves surrounded by dozens of girls wanting to know what the American PRT had brought this time. Compared to the remote regions in the province, everything about this school appeared to be working. The government had provided not only teachers but also sufficient school supplies. According to the provincial education director, the curriculum remained the most advanced.

Before leaving, I asked one of the teachers—a woman who had spent time working with several international NGOs—what made this school so successful, when so many other attempts had failed. Her once black hair had long since gone white, and, like her students, she wore sandals.

"You would be surprised how much the women here in Khost whisper under their burkas."

And with that, she turned her back to me, effectively declaring, though without words: *Thank you for what you do, but we are already doing much on our own.*

As I made my way to the waiting Humvees, I looked across the street. On one side, young men lined up by the dozens in front of a mosque. Their education would continue to be Islamic first, foremost, and last. On the other side of the street stood a butcher in front of his shop. He had laid out his meat for sale in the warm morning air as flies buzzed around and on top of the fresh pink and white flanks of goat. Behind him, a woman knelt in a blue burka, alone. I could not help but think none of her whispers involved education or women's rights. She was clearly trying just to survive.

Of all the Americans who called Khost home for a while, Commander Sauer's impact ranks among the most long lasting—while, in many ways, remaining the most invisible. Hundreds of girls will remember the American commander who was different, and different for all the right reasons in their eyes. The important American in an important job looked and sounded like they did.

Arif confirmed as much later, in a detailed email update.

Girls' education in Khost is growing, trend is up, especially in downtown and the districts nearby.

In contrast to older years, nowadays more parents are becoming supportive. In previous times, parents would only allow their younger girls to go to primary school or a mosque-conducted village class.

Parents used to remove them from class before the age of ten, but that concept is vanishing. Many parents hope to see their daughters in doctor uniform, lawyer and qualified teachers.

But aside from remote districts where insurgents still pose threats to girls' education, those in close-by districts, including downtown Khost, the ratio between girls and boys is close to 50/50.

He added a final number that surprised me.

About 1,300 adult girls are seeking higher education at Khost University and other private universities in town.

Plus the girls' schools we used to visit have been expanded. One has been moved to another more decent building, next to the grand mosque that used to be Haqqani's madrassa during his period of rule. A good size girls' dormitory has been built at Khost University as well.

He ended his message on a very personal note:

My wife as you know didn't go to school, but she is very pro girls' education. She always encourages our daughters to go to school so they can become doctors and teachers. One day I overheard her saying, "it is over for me to go to school but it is a golden chance for you to become a somebody, a person."

By this time in Khost, I was on my fifth year straight in a war zone. I had started in the Green Zone in Baghdad and now found myself in its exact opposite: an un-plush and gritty outpost almost within walking distance of the Pakistani border. And yet, I preferred this place to Baghdad, and I preferred this place to Anbar, and I preferred this place to Fallujah.

In some ways, I even preferred this place to the U.S. Life more dangerous, but life more simplified too. Life tended to get streamlined in the wars. My routine at Chapman by then was not at all that bad. Sure, there was the violence, reinforced by regular warnings about incoming mortars, but the job itself was rewarding in a way that I did not imagine possible in the middle of a war.

I saw the U.S. government and the U.S. military getting things done. Building things. Making friends. Developing ties. That "better face" that contrasted so much with the stereotypical "ugly American" image. And the PRT was full of good soldiers and leaders, some with multiple tours.

Plus I had made good Afghan friends. I used to spend a lot of time with our local guards. Usually, we would sit in their separate chow hall, sharing beans, bread, and tea, while a small television monitor flashed melodramatic soap operas from India.

It was during these quiet times that I developed a deeper appreciation for the Pashtun, long derided as the ethnic group responsible for all the woe in the country. Even Holbrooke had gotten himself into trouble when he had made public comments implying that the Taliban and terrorist problems in Afghanistan were first and foremost a Pashtun problem. Hour after hour my Afghan friends showed me how tough a people they were. Some guards had lost their parents at age forty-five; others had lost children at childbirth or at age three. And yet, these personal stories were not conveyed as complaints, but rather "this is our life."

My own family by now had begun to question how long I had been at war. My dad's Vietnam tour had been thirteen months, and my grandpa's in World War II about two years. And yet when they saw the photos from Khost, they understood. The landscape was dramatic, and the people appeared deserving of American investments and my own. My mom, a former schoolteacher, often asked me about the schools and the students. I told her I had adopted a village in Qalandar, paying teachers out of my own pocket—two hundred bucks a month for two teachers seemed like a bargain. She agreed and sent some money.

My twin brother, an anthropology major in college, also "got" the work in Khost. In certain districts, I could have imagined Clifford Geertz, the famous anthropologist, sitting among the Afghans, notebook in hand, observing and participating, and documenting the "thickly described" experiences one can accumulate whether as a well-behaved guest or inquisitive visitor among "others." Khost was that kind of place, mesmerizing really, even amid its violent past and the violent tendencies of some of its residents.

The progress felt real. The progress made me think: we can do this. America just might be able to succeed in this war. That is, as long as our Afghan partners stayed close and trusted that we would endure along with them the many challenges still ahead.

It had been a long time since I had last seen us show our worst side, our worst actions, our worst way of fighting a war. These better days in Khost were about to end.

In the name of "force protection," the military often rolls up windows, builds walls, and points rifles at the outside world. The best force protection, however, is to be surrounded by friends and allies.

ERIC GREITENS, U.S. NAVY SEAL

Jackpots and Dryholes

By mid-2008 I was nearing the year-and-a-half mark in the province. Ambassador Robert Ford, who had been my boss in Baghdad while I was in Fallujah, had asked me to return to Iraq. I reluctantly said yes, because, as he had put it, "Iraq is still the national priority." And, under the Bush administration at the time, that was true. Democratic presidential candidate Barack Obama was promising in his campaign to refocus U.S. attention and resources on Afghanistan, but he had not been elected yet.

Robert told me I would be the embassy political officer responsible for covering the political dynamic in Baghdad, with some trips to Anbar. Lucky me. Unlucky me. I knew even from Khost which part of Baghdad mattered most: Sadr City. And how much Anbar remained far from being "won"—in whichever way that concept of winning was being defined in Washington.

Until then, I had more work to do in Afghanistan. The school visits were going well. As were the various projects the PRT had funded throughout Khost. Approximately $50 million had been directed from Pentagon coffers for these efforts—serious levels of U.S. cash. So the call I received that day came as a surprise—of the very bad variety. I picked up the phone to hear Governor Jamal nearly screaming. "Check your email!" It was as upset as I had ever heard him.

I logged on to my computer right away, noticing there was an attachment to his email message: a photo of a young Afghan boy with a bullet hole in the middle of his forehead. He had been shot at close range, not from a distance, in his mud-brick home during an American raid.

Incidents like this could destroy the trust between the people in Khost and American forces that the PRT and I had been working so hard to build.

"The province will explode.

"I am trying to keep people calm. Tribal elders will be visiting me tomorrow.

"I emailed you more pictures.

"This can't happen again."

Then he hung up.

The situation was as bad as any Governor Jamal and I had faced. In these rare instances, he treated me, rightly, as the U.S. government official in Khost, not the friend I had become, and thus offered no softened words. I respected that quality about him. Jamal similarly told visiting U.S. senators, a defense secretary, and other VIPs what they needed to hear but often did not want to hear.

Jamal and I both had tough messages to deliver to each other when need be, even as we worked together against the efforts of insurgents who targeted us with bullets, mortars, and bombs.

I alerted the embassy and talked with the brigade commander at Salerno, the province's main coalition base, asking one question.

"When we raided the compound, did they, did the SOF team, have Afghans with them? That's U.S. policy."

"I don't know."

He said he would find out, but I had my answer.

The local Special Operations Forces team, including elite SEALs and Delta Force, shared Khost province with us, but on a part-time basis.

With dedicated helicopters and fixed wing aircraft, their units dropped in and out at will. For this mission, which left some innocent civilians killed, they believed they had scored "jackpot"—terminology that meant terrorists and/or insurgents left dead or detained. Their targeting cell had, it seemed, identified a compound of insurgents. The special operators, America's most highly trained killers, had a recurring, if debatable, mission in my border province.

How SOF went about their essential job sometimes caused conventional troops and me some concern—at times, a lot of concern. Even more so, we questioned how necessary the high-speed operations were, particularly in the later years of the wars. There were also the long-lasting repercussions when "mistakes were made" and SEALs departed for another super-secret operation in another part of Afghanistan. This kind of conduct, unfortunately, became a pattern that Marines and I had first experienced in Fallujah, with Sara al-Jumaili's detention perhaps the most glaring example. The grand mufti of Fallujah, Sheikh Hamza, shot dead as a consequence.

The dilemma remained: Who would be left to deal with the consequences as full-time American residents of the province once SEALs went elsewhere? And the resulting Afghan fury after civilians lay dead, leading to more roadside bombs?

Us. Not them.

I remained anything but naive about the dangers in Khost—the same with Governor Jamal—just as I had been realistic about the dangers in Fallujah. As much as anyone, I believed certain terrorists needed to be captured or killed. Those who lived in Khost represented the most vicious and well-trained variety in Afghanistan. An Afghan diplomat, part of the Karzai clan, once told me, "Haqqani and his men are different. In Kandahar they talk politics, but in Khost, it is like this." He then motioned toward a nearby fireplace, with orange flames low but hot.

"No, in Khost, they would just grab these embers by the handful and not even blink."

The imagery and his warning, as a Kandahar native no less, stayed with me.

And yet a mother and two children had been shot dead, three of a total of six Afghans killed in one operation. The photos Jamal had sent me showed the bloody result, one after another. The governor wanted

me to join him in a subsequent meeting with local elders. Soraya Sarhaddi Nelson, the Kabul-based reporter for NPR, happened to be visiting the province and asked to sit in.

She brought her recorder.

Alongside Jamal, we would meet with the family, make a condolence payment, and try to help calm down the province.

After the governor's emergency post-midnight call, it took some
time to arrange the meeting. Meanwhile, the governor continued to
press me in private on these U.S. "mistakes" in blunt language. He visited the PRT in advance of our session with tribal elders and conveyed
more frustration.

"Sending humanitarian aid to families is a slap in the face: 'we just
killed your sons, but here are some beans.'

"Minister Popal [a close Karzai aide and popular with American
officials in Kabul] told me not to show the photos to President Karzai,
who has requested them. They are too brutal for him to see.

"You must rely on our system, not just on your relationship with
me. In almost every case, Afghans can detain the targets you want.

"You take weapons from compounds. I even keep an AK in my
room!"

And a pointed statement, more like an accurate indictment, which
hit hardest: "Your Special Forces are trained for Fallujah, not here!"

I passed on the governor's comments informally to Kabul and
Washington under the heading: "Losing Khost, one SOF operation at a
time." Embassy staff told me they did not believe a "tipping point" had
been reached yet in Khost, whereas I was beginning to sense otherwise.
We would only know such a marker had been reached . . . afterward,
when it would be too late.

Days later, with the meeting with the family's elders set, I exited a
Humvee and walked silently into the governor's corner office. By the
time our group got there, about a twenty-minute convoy ride from
Chapman, the elders still had not yet arrived. When they did, we stood
as they passed by, one by one, and sat down. We were on the right side
of the room. They remained on the left. I noticed a young man among
them. *He must be one of the sons whose family members we shot and killed,*
I thought, *probably the oldest.* The governor had told us that one would
now have to take care of the rest in the large family.

The men surrounding the governor sat hunched and wore gray and black turbans. In 2008, Taliban had yet to hide bombs in the traditional Pashtun head garb, so these local leaders would only have been searched on their bodies. Meeting with the governor of Khost translated into one kind of shakedown; when we Americans arrived, the process proved even more thorough—and, in their view, more disrespectful. More hands searching in more places.

All of us were seated in semicircular fashion. More tea, more walnuts, and some plastic-wrapped Twinkie-like snacks made in Pakistan covered the tabletop, though no one reached for the food, even for the tea. It was that kind of meeting. Jamal conferred privately behind his desk with the senior elders, words not translated, and that was a good thing. One elder looked furious. But he was not yelling. His low tone conveyed as much pain and hurt as anger. As Jamal clasped him on the shoulder, the Afghan kept his back to us, almost as if he would have preferred never to look our way.

I wondered how this conversation would go, but first indications were bad. I was glad Soraya Sarhaddi Nelson had joined us in the room because she knew Afghanistan and Afghans well. She was also one of NPR's most experienced reporters in a war zone. Everything would be on the record. I hoped the exchange could at least show us trying to bridge, however temporarily, an impossible gap. I would be one of the American faces and voices in the room. Commander Sauer would be another. We had brought the cash with us, which we gave to Jamal, so he could take care of the actual handoff of currency. Unlike in Iraq, we had carried with us local currency, not U.S. dollars. I felt better about that.

At the outset, the Afghan delegation from hilly Nadar Shahkot District let one speak for the group. I looked at his large wrinkled hands, thinking he, like so many Afghans, had worked the fields since a young age. With a commanding voice, he said he wanted those responsible for the deaths "brought to justice" and the villager who had made the claim of ties to the Taliban identified and questioned. It was false information, he said. "Each village has friends and enemies." The Afghans detained that night also should be released; otherwise any American apology would be "meaningless."

The points he made were similar to those the former Guantánamo detainees had put to me: you Americans get bad information from unvetted sources, often pay for it, then detain and raid compounds at nighttime, rather than question us in an open meeting. The underlying dynamic, they claimed, was feuding between tribes, not the activity of terrorists.

The elder concluded, "If we were at fault, I would say that. All we want to do is just live. We want no connections on either side, yours or the Taliban. We are in the middle."

Commander Sauer spoke first, understandably hesitantly. Nothing in her Navy background had prepared her for such an encounter. I was glad that room had a woman's voice in it, the only voice that would sound like a mother's voice.

"This is a very great loss, but we are here to try and help you get through this situation."

I followed, with Arif pausing between his translation of my "apology."

"Our goal today is not to try and explain away what happened, but as Commander Sauer said, to help you get through your loss, but to also try and make sure it does not happen again."

We received blank stares.

Governor Jamal then handed over the Afghan currency, orange-colored and with few creases in the bills. New money for an old tradition, we were hoping to buy forgiveness and had put a price tag on it.

Two thousand dollars times six dead equaled $12,000.

Huddled before the governor and me were the surviving family members, including the youngest adolescent, who introduced himself as Ghader Gol. In a barely audible voice, even after his family's tragedy, he said something remarkable: "That the Americans build schools and roads does mean something. But this shouldn't have happened."

His comments hit me very hard. I had been sent to Khost to do just that: "build" not only projects but, more important, people. This next generation, in other words, who populated eastern Afghanistan—those Ghader Gol's age. In one night much of that progress was now at risk, and we had put Governor Jamal in another very difficult position.

Would we ever learn?

I imagined Jamal had similar thoughts. His day job just got a lot more dangerous, as more enemies had a new reason to target the governor, who was already considered too close to the Americans—and to our money.

The frustration between Marines and SOF in Anbar had been significant. Sara's detention represented a strategic-level case study—one that merited to be studied in detail at JSOC HQ in Tampa but most likely was not and never would be. In Khost, it seemed the Army preferred to look the other way. It was not an equal power equation, but one that, ideally, should have been reversed: SOF deferring to commanding generals at a minimum, and regimental or brigade colonels under certain conditions. I knew Washington policy makers had little sense of these frontline dynamics because it was much easier to think we always got the terrorists and "collateral damage" could be written off. Children's lives and mothers' lives are never written off in places like Nadar Shahkot and Khost, no matter how much money we handed over.

As the group began to signal their departure, I asked to speak to the oldest son, Ghader Gol, privately. Arif thought it would be a good idea, but we should be prepared if he said no.

Surprisingly, the young Afghan agreed. We walked into a glass-enclosed side room, behind the governor's ornate desk area. Arif translated for us.

I had one question.

"What happened that night?"

Before answering he repeated to me that he believed he needed to attend our school, try to get a better education, or his family would not have a chance. This willingness to see the positive side of our efforts in Khost, despite the recent deaths in his family at our hands, amazed me. He then described how his dogs started to bark outside their compound around midnight. American soldiers "jumped over the walls" as his father, unarmed, went out to see what was going on.

Ghader Gol said he had to kneel down as bullets "sprayed through the windows," injuring his mother right away. He said he did not know if it was intentional, but she was shot again. The SOF team "after killing my family" told villagers not to come out of their compounds and shot one of the family dogs. Ghader Gol said he was roughed up and everyone put in one room after being zip-tied.

Then they left.

I asked what happened to his younger brother.

"We all heard the shots, they started shooting at the door. Then they released their dogs. When my mother was shot, a dog bit her in the arm. She was shot in the leg first. She tried to pull me and my brother in and that is when she was shot again."

He said the operation took fifty minutes.

I asked what our SOF unit did when they realized his mother and younger brother had been killed, what did they say. He said "nothing."

"We would have come to Salerno for questions if you had asked!"

I had heard enough. "You said you would still go to the school we are building in Nadar Shahkot. I do not think I would be strong enough to do that, if my family members had been killed like yours, no matter the reason or mistakes."

In this boy of thirteen or fourteen, I saw a kid forced to grow up in an instant. I told him I would try to visit the school and see how else we might help them. Would he meet us there?

He did not reply.

The brigade commander, whom I liked and respected, told NPR that while our SOF units tried to do joint operations with Afghans when raiding compounds at night, which reduced the chances of deadly mistakes, "sometimes they need to act independently." He added that in this instance, those targeted were insurgents and "linked to hundreds of Afghan deaths."

The colonel explained further.

"And so we go in there to try and constantly refine the procedures and techniques we're using to reduce the chances that any casualty—let alone civilian casualties—are going to be incurred."

I asked the brigade to get from the SOF unit details on the operation. I held the highest-level U.S. security clearance (TS/SCI), but they declined. No colonel or general or State Department official, even an ambassador, could force them to provide it (though an ambassador probably would trump and get what he or she wanted in the end).

Once back at Chapman, I put on my running shoes and did more circles around the former Soviet-built airstrip than I ever had before. I probably clocked a two-hour run and fifteen miles. I could not get the image of the dead kid or my conversation with his older brother or with Jamal out of my mind. The meeting had left me more mentally exhausted than the 26.2-mile marathons of my youth had ever physically exhausted me. The brain, like quads and calf muscles, I realized, could get bruised and worn out too. There would never be aspirin or any number of colored pills, even if I wanted those kinds and I did not, which could heal the wounds of the soul and conscience.

How did Afghans (or Iraqis) deal with even more pain?

Soon after, while at Salerno, I saw two SEAL types walk by. Muscled. Bearded. Shades. Sauntering. *Had they been the ones on the mission that night?* I moved a few steps closer with the intent to ask them what really happened. They or their comrades must have known.

But I turned around. I left. I did not want to know their side of the story. I did not want to know more about our side of the story, as the brigade colonel had already qualified the events that night.

Why not?

Because I would not believe them—believe what we told ourselves, let alone the family of the dead, who now had twelve thousand of our dollars counted out in Afghan currency as proof of something. We did not have to pay the blood money, but we did.

Was Ghader Gol's side of the story accurate? I don't know, but I believed him. The operation's outcome proved nondebatable: his family members were dead. And I knew this kind of operation gone very wrong, with mothers and children killed, is how we fed the insurgency, how we guaranteed hidden if not outright support among the local population for the Taliban—not for weeks but for years.

And how more Americans became targets, alongside our Afghan partners, like Jamal.

Weeks later, I tried to meet Ghader Gol at the school we were building in his village, the one he said he knew he must attend in order to get a better job maybe and provide for the rest of his family. But when our convoy arrived, Ghader did not appear. I suppose I would not have either. While still a young teen with both parents buried, in addition to his younger brother, he now had become responsible for eight brothers and sisters. He had other, more important responsibilities than meeting me—and unresolvable anger, I could only imagine.

I was reminded of a quote I once saw: "One man's collateral damage is another man's son."

Or one boy's father, one boy's mother, one boy's younger brother. Ghader Gol did not need Arif and me to translate the expression "collateral damage." He had witnessed it firsthand, right in front of him.

When SEAL and Delta Force units don't get a "jackpot," they report the mission as a "dryhole"—dryholes that can orphan an entire family.

And in Ghader Gol's case, we Americans did just that.

I wish I could have scripted a different ending for him, his family, and for us that night in Khost. Imagined something better. I could not have imagined something worse.

Governor Jamal said he never sent the photos of Ghader Gol's dead mother and younger brother to President Karzai because they were too unsettling. I wished I had not seen them. He recounted a meeting in Kabul with the Afghan leader regarding civilian casualties.

"We feel you Americans are not taking us seriously. The president spent the last three weeks on this case and others like it. And then the next one happens."

Jamal concluded, "President Karzai appeared helpless."

What had begun as a good year was ending not so well. The civilian casualty incident in Nadar Shahkot would be repeated in other places. More unilateral SEAL operations in more parts of Afghanistan would also generate more distrust and fury among Afghans, amid some of the SEALs' important successes in targeting terrorists.

Arif knew my frustration better than anyone. But he also knew the limitations of the State Department function in military matters. Unlike in Vietnam, when military officers had actually been put under the formal command of civilians (John Paul Vann being the most famous case study), Joint Special Operations Command HQ in Tampa still had the last word. And absent strong U.S. ambassadors, the political-military vacuum could be even greater. I kept reminding myself that "political" came first, followed by "military." This was a key distinction that should have made more of a difference. Marines, to their credit, usually got this equation more right than wrong.

During one of the PRT's final visits to a madrassa and nearby girls school hundreds of meters from the Pakistan border, a mullah I had met previously but did not know well approached me unexpectedly.

"I have a gift for you, Mr. Kael."

Arif looked at me with a shrug. We had delivered solar panels earlier in the month, which helped provide light at night, a rare thing still in most parts of the province. The panels, I imagined, were also used to power up radios, but I did not mention that in any conversations with any mullahs. Best to keep that a secret.

The religious leader, who had a dozen students in tow, asked one to pull the blanket off what he was carrying.

Inside was a puppy.

I was surprised.

"Thank you very much. I grew up with dogs, and always wanted one here."

I kept to myself, however, that I would be leaving the province before long. And the State Department, let alone the U.S. military, had made war zone dog adoptions nearly impossible. Our troops were more used to killing canines.

"Do you have a name to suggest?" I asked.

"No, that's up to you." Several of the students probably would have answered differently, but they were not given a speaking role that day.

When we got back to Chapman, Arif and I sat in our usual spot, on the long table near the Afghan chow hall. The same soap operas, dubbed from India, seemingly morphed into even more melodramatic episodes of spurned lovers in colorful garb, flashed on the small TV screen.

"Arif, I hope you'll take care of the puppy. You could use another guard dog when he gets bigger."

"We could. My family is still getting night letters. I hide them from my wife but sometimes she finds them before I do," he said.

"It makes me so angry that we cannot do something about them. You are safe here at Chapman but not at home. But if we get close to your compound, that will create even more trouble for you.

"I do have a name for the dog, I think," I said. "My sister used to have a great and stubborn Siberian husky named Mojo. Do you mind if we call him that, even after I'm gone?"

"Mojo . . . what does it mean?"

"Well, it's hard to explain, but it is a good word. It means good things."

"Okay, Mojo. I'll introduce him to my kids with that name. How do you spell it?"

. . .

In the remaining weeks I had in Khost, I said farewell to Commander Sauer and to Governor Jamal. These were not easy exchanges. Both had become close partners, and I knew the governor's family remained worried about his safety. In one of my last meetings with him, he said he kept not one but two AK-47s in his room, near his bed.

"Just in case."

Commander Sauer meanwhile continued to face some bias behind her back among Afghans and inside the U.S. military because she was a woman in charge of men and in the company of mostly men in a war zone. But things had improved. More and more Afghans were beginning to request that she be at more and more events. Other military commanders took notice of that.

I told the battalion and brigade commanders that one day there would be a female commander in chief, from either party, so they should get used to it. I had expressed the same thing to Marines in Iraq. And when that day arrived, I said I planned to fly to Camp Pendleton in California to see a madame president's grand welcome in front of her most martial, and most manly of course, troops.

Larry Nicholson always said he could easily and happily work for a woman seated behind the desk in the Oval Office, "no problem with that whatsoever." The more I thought of it, the more I realized any commander in chief, male or female, Republican or Democrat, would be very lucky to have a Marine leader like him, or General Dunford, close. Too many policy makers had been too far removed for too many years from the wars, whereas U.S. troops had spent deployment after deployment in the most dangerous locations in each war.

Iraq and Afghanistan had made them war-wise, more than war-wary or war-weary. And Commander Sauer had now joined their ranks.

I am no hero. I just acted as an Iraqi who witnessed the pain and bloodshed of too many innocents.

MUNTADHAR AL-ZAIDI

Motor City

Another flight, another war zone, I thought, as I sat in the gunmetal gray C-130 flying from an aesthetic Amman to a battered Baghdad. I had brought in my backpack just one book, recently published—*The Forever War* by Dexter Filkins. It was a title that matched the U.S. predicament, the Iraqi predicament, and my own, written by a *New York Times* reporter renowned for his in-depth, viscerally described dispatches. Next to me was Ambassador Robert Ford, my old wartime boss and once again new wartime boss. Our pilots were maneuvering through airspace along the same route in the same type of aircraft I had flown after leaving Fallujah a year and a half earlier. The black hole of Iraq remained, sucking thousands of U.S. troops, as well as Robert and me, back. While boarding this uncrowded military flight from Amman's military airport under darkness, I did not even try—a habit since childhood—to locate any familiar stars in the sky above. Given my mind-set, all of the planets would have been colored red.

Swaying in our canvas seats along one side of the plane, I turned

to Robert, who had been directly asked by Secretary of State Condoleezza Rice and Deputy Secretary John Negroponte to return to the
U.S. embassy in Baghdad—he was that valuable to the American effort.

Without a filter, I said: "Well, back to Iraq already. I have you to
thank for this, Robert."

I could not retract what I had just said, an undiplomatic comment
I should have kept to myself, even if offered in the dark-humored way
that Iraq tended to bring out in many of us. And yet, I was beginning to
wonder if the Iraq War would ever end. It felt in many ways as if I had
never left. War had taught me, all sixty-three months by then and five
Thanksgivings in a row spent in the Iraq and Afghanistan conflicts, that
its centripetal nature endured, while not much else did—a violent vor-
tex that trumped man and machine and American money. Everything
that could go wrong in a war usually did, eventually.

Robert, still the most well-respected U.S. diplomat in Iraq among
Iraqis—and they were no easy constituency to win over—shifted his
head toward me and said he thought I would like my new assignment,
the one he had asked me to consider while I was in Khost. I had in effect
saluted, telling Robert at the time that I considered him to be like a top
Marine general. If he said I needed to be somewhere, I would be there.

"You'll be able to get back to Anbar, talk to the Sunni Arabs given
all your time in Fallujah and Ramadi, but I also think you'll like covering Baghdad and the Shia political dynamics."

"You're about the only boss I'd do this for," I replied. "Khost was
pretty nice and a lot more scenic than Iraq. And most of the people
wanted us there. I got out a lot among all kinds of Afghans."

"Iraq is still the national priority," he repeated as he had before, and
alluding, I knew, to the fact that George W. Bush remained president
for a few more months. The stubborn/resolute Texan and 43rd commander in chief was still adamant that he would not leave office with
the Iraq War—Bush's voluntary war—"lost," at least in his mind.

Upon landing, we transferred from the C-130 to a helicopter. A
haze hung over the Iraqi capital. I saw the Dora Power Plant with its
towering four stacks amid some mosque domes and minarets, but not
nearly in the concentration that Fallujah had. Below us, somewhere
amid the blinking lights that cast an orange glow over everything, not
far from the banks of the Tigris River, was Sadr City.

If Fallujah had a mirror opposite, this sprawling part of Baghdad was it. I had gone native with Marines. I had gone native with Fallujans. Perhaps I would go native with the Shia in Sadr City too. I had been cursed once with "al-Falluji" behind my name; I did not seek another nickname like it, which would be "al-Sadri." Though to be a U.S. government official with both monikers would do a lot for my street credibility among all Iraqis, regardless of the version of the Muslim faith they practiced—or sectarian agenda they pursued behind closed doors.

On both the C-130 and Black Hawk, Robert and I wore body armor and a Kevlar helmet, as did all the American soldiers seated near us. The U.S., the country we represented, was fully five years into the war after the initial invasion.

I already missed Afghanistan. I had not missed Iraq. Soon enough, I would be back in Iraq's violent mix.

The young soldier did not stand a chance against the explosive projectile. Shia militia members in Sadr City's bustling Jamilla Market, using deadly technology imported from Iran, had angled the device for a trajectory that would decapitate the armored vehicle's turret gunner. It did just that. The molten metal traveled several times the speed of sound, penetrating the thickest steel plating like magma buckshot patented in hell. A rudimentary version of the weapon was first developed in World War II and used in the Battle of the Bulge, Great-uncle Harold's war front that he had somehow survived but then was unable to, postwar, on the home front.

By the time I walked the same Iraqi street days later in late 2008, a foot-wide dislodged chunk of asphalt from the trash-littered curb and gutter marked the only evidence of the bomb that had killed the young American. The memorial service had already been held. Iraqi teenagers played soccer in a nearby dirt field. Soldiers patrolling on foot around me pointed rifles outward as they guided our movement at a quick pace. Sweat drenched our body armor despite the cool early mid-winter temperature. None of us chased down a stray soccer ball that passed by us, bouncing along, in order to helpfully kick it back into the neighborhood sports field.

I had been back in Iraq for several months. And this place, Sadr City, was my new part-time home, just as Robert Ford had suggested it be. I was getting to know the Shia and passing my observations on to the ambassadors and Washington, particularly how this part of Iraq's population, the vast majority, lived day to day on the Iraqi streets. How they saw their own government as well as ours. And, crucially, how they viewed the U.S. troop drawdown and possible complete withdrawal.

I had tried to locate Bassam and some of the truckers, but they had disappeared. I hoped they were still alive after all the sectarian bloodshed, but not all probably would be given their odds.

The battalion commander, my escort, paused during the patrol. I asked what mission the soldier's unit had been assigned when he was killed. I had already guessed what his answer might be.

"They were checking the status of a new sewer line," he replied.

The young soldier, in other words, lost his life over a metal pipe project to transport human waste.

Lost his life over infrastructure, that is, for shit. I had imagined maybe a road-related project, or to deliver a big generator perhaps. That knowledge stung.

Our day and the foot patrol (no Humvees or MRAPs) had started at Joint Security Station Sadr City, the U.S. Army outpost established within the vast Shia slum that comprised almost half of the Iraqi capital. The walled compound, lined with sand-colored MRAPs, served as my satellite office when away from the claustrophobic confines of the embassy. The largest in the world, it had cost almost one billion dollars and was staffed by thousands. American imperialism architecturally defined, leaving no room to doubt which country had invaded which—but still remained cut off and in a crouched position behind tons of concrete and steel, and plenty of armed guards.

I slept on the floor at the site, ate MSG-filled MREs and soupy, grayish tray rations with the soldiers, developing an iron stomach but enjoying better company than the largely cynical discussions among colleagues within the Green Zone. In some ways, it felt like I was back at the Civil Military Operations Center in Fallujah. Such Joint Security Stations, very isolated outposts in most cases, were deemed crucial for improved security when American troops surged into Baghdad in early 2007, with General David Petraeus in the lead. America had found its four-star hero, one who thought he knew how the Iraq War should end after famously wondering aloud to a reporter in Mosul, "Tell me how this ends." The general had also declared, "Money as a weapon system would win hearts and minds."

A new Pentagon doctrine codified and one I was intent to explore in detail. My time in Anbar and Khost had given me antennae for money well spent—or not so much. I started to ask around the JSS about the various projects under way. A captain told me they included a performing arts center, swimming pool, a modern art sculpture for a park, and trash collection.

A modern art sculpture?

I had heard right.

By then in Sadr City—a place dominated by the politics of the anti-American Shia leader Moqtada al-Sadr—third- or fourth-tour U.S. troops had morphed into supreme nation builders, city builders, really, and at the micro-level. I joked all of us knew more about the infrastructure of our adopted Iraqi towns than hometowns in America, whether Dubuque, Denver, or Dayton. But we did not laugh much or for long because the line was not really a joke. Most of us remembered service members, our friends, killed or injured while on similar nation-building missions across the new Iraq.

The soldier who had been killed by the molten IED while on sewer patrol represented only the most recent instance.

It was better that his parents and family, I thought, like so many others back home, rarely learned about the mission details before the death of their son or daughter or brother or sister or father or mother was recorded as another KIA. ABC News' Sunday political talk show *This Week* would list his name on-screen along with others recently killed in the wars. Just before ending its weekly segment, the network host would lead in with the following: "And now we honor our fellow Americans who serve and sacrifice. This week the Pentagon released the names of *x* service members killed in Iraq and Afghanistan."

The names of the dead would be shown. Depending on how many KIA there had been, the tribute took a second or a few, at most: name, military branch, age, and hometown.

A comedy excerpt from one of the night shows or Comedy Central usually preceded ABC's weekly KIA segment—a jarring sequence later discontinued. Sometimes I recognized the names because they had been my friends. The Sunday ritual never felt broadcast in earnest, or earnest enough. Let alone proportionate to family pain, but at least

ABC tried to connect the war front to the home front for a few seconds every Sunday morning. The day of the week such a notice seemed most appropriate—however brief the KIA mentions were and however restless that Seventh Day remained for some.

Such thoughts stayed on my mind as we marched on. Our V-shaped patrol in Sadr City lasted most of the wintry day as we made our way through the winding Jamilla Market streets. The area doubled as the capital's wholesale product breadbasket. Five-meter-high piles of potato chips in wire stalls and soda bottles in stacked crates dominated the congested urban landscape. Intersecting this Shia section of Baghdad, home to more than three million Iraqis, snaked a massive concrete wall. Erected by U.S. troops in spring 2008, during a fierce street-to-street battle, it walled off a third of the district, a mission named "Operation Gold Wall." To keep "them" out or "us" in? I wondered. In total, U.S. soldiers emplaced around 3,000 twelve-foot-high T-walls, weighing nine tons each, forming an almost five-kilometer-long barrier. (Years later I would meet a soldier named Baylen Orr, who had been stationed in the area during the violent time. He helped put up the Great Wall of Baghdad and would tell me what really happened in those days, based on blunt entries in a detailed journal he had kept.)

U.S. military commanders cited security gains post-wall. Sadr City residents complained about disrupted commerce post-wall. Again, war as a kaleidoscope of interpretations, it all depended on which side you were on at any given point in the fight.

Just before sundown, we stopped to talk Iraqi politics—my job description with the State Department. In such exchanges, I continued to work hard to bring Washington-based policy makers the views of ordinary Iraqis, the "average Omars and Alis" who mattered most. Given the danger of Iraq's internal political machinations since the invasion, it usually took me a short amount of time to gauge how far a conversation might or should go. Or should not go, and therefore would not go.

Silence equaled safety. Political talk both indicted and divided Iraqis based on sect, Sunni versus Shia. After a few minutes, I could assess the degree of anger toward Americans, which most often resembled embers in a fire pit. Cooled on the surface but still hot at the core—and with sectarian winds never far. The legacy of the American invasion most American leaders back home did not want to admit, but I felt viscerally and often daily from many Iraqis.

The U.S. exit from Iraq had begun by then, even as we surged troops into the capital. Washington ordered the influx so that if (when?) the country reverted to a civil war after a period of semi-stability, we could blame the Iraqis after claiming victory. What was that indictment we were waiting to issue toward Iraqis?

"Not fighting hard enough."

"Not working hard enough."

"Not compromising hard enough."

We were good at that, pointing fingers toward them in a war they had not asked for but then got after we sent in the Marines and soldiers, around 150,000 U.S. troops in total alongside almost 50,000 British forces, a couple of thousand Australians—and scattered contingents numbered in the dozens from a few other countries. Not entirely a unilateral invasion, but mostly.

While walking in the middle of Sadr City with this bunch of U.S. Army soldiers, I recalled a recent headline-grabbing event. I also knew it would probably come up in discussions I would be having that day. Two weeks prior, in mid-December 2008, during a press conference in Baghdad with President Bush and Prime Minister Maliki, a young Iraqi reporter and native son of Sadr City named Muntadhar al-Zaidi threw two shoes at the visiting U.S. president. He narrowly missed hitting the commander in chief. The Iraqi PM tried to deflect one of the size-10 projectiles.

"This is a gift from the Iraqis; this is the farewell kiss, you dog!" Muntadhar al-Zaidi yelled. "This is for the widows and orphans and those killed in Iraq!"

Bush was fortunately unhurt. He survived the shoe attack. Millions soon viewed the raw video footage on YouTube.

The shoe-throwing incident dominated worldwide newscasts. Wealthy Arabs sought to bid on them as trophies. One Saudi reportedly offered as much as $10 million, but the pair was destroyed, symbols that might inflame a mob. The television images recycled across Iraq for some time.

The topic resonated locally in Sadr City as well, but did not always come up right away. Toward the end of our wintertime patrol, a local electrical shop owner and self-described fan of American movies invited us into his cluttered shop. Other, more polite subjects came up first. He said he liked Arnold Schwarzenegger and "Opera." Verdi or Wagner? I was no expert in opera and at a loss for words. Soon I realized he meant Oprah, the same thing Iraqi army soldiers had told me years earlier in Ramadi and Fallujah.

"Iraqis love Oppperrrraaah!" he said loudly.

I told him so did millions of Americans.

The shop owner's floor space smelled of diesel fuel, used for a humming generator. The billions we had invested since the invasion in Iraq's power grid had not reached him. Next to a space heater, he offered me a plastic chair to sit in to warm my frozen hands, almost assuredly an item imported from Iran. U.S. Army soldiers stood guard outside. The Iraqis looked nervous. I removed my body armor, the ceramic plates, and Kevlar helmet.

The shopkeeper very quickly raised the shoe-throwing incident. I sensed it was time for me to just listen, not say much.

"He should have just asked President Bush tough questions to embarrass him, such as why U.S. investments had not led to more job creation, only more corruption."

He went on to state how moved he was while watching the recent U.S. presidential election results. When Senator Obama beat Senator McCain, Arab media showed images of "so many crying, but happy and excited crying" in America. I had watched the results in Baghdad and called Mark in Arizona, the soldier from my time in Khost and an African American, to discuss the results. I kept that to myself.

A half dozen other Sadr City residents gathered close by and listened in, snooping with permission but remaining quiet.

"What do you think about Obama?" the shopkeeper asked.

"Complicated topic, but he talked a lot more about Afghanistan than Iraq during the election."

"Yes, we Iraqis have noticed."

I thanked him for his time, not wanting to get into a sticky political exchange about America's newest commander in chief. Much, I was sure, would be lost in translation. I put my body armor back on and left the shop as we traced our way back to the Sadr City fort we called home.

This time, on our return trip, we took a different route—just in case. The streets were empty. Locals feared Iraqi nights as well, not just we Americans.

A few months later, I made a final return trip to Sadr City. Larry Nicholson, now a one-star commanding general, had requested that I return to Afghanistan and serve as the 2nd Marine Expeditionary Brigade's political adviser. Robert Ford agreed to the shift, and to the credit of the State Department, they approved my redirection to Afghanistan.

I never felt entirely comfortable in Sadr City. The district chairman's office had been bombed the summer prior to my arrival. The explosion killed two American civilians, two soldiers, and injured the chairman, Hassan Shama, who had since become a key contact of mine. Before my first meeting with Sadr City's chief politician in his well-tailored, shiny, silken suit that reminded me of Sheikh Dhari in Fallujah, U.S. soldiers pulled me aside. In whispers, they said they believed Shama had been complicit in the attack despite being wounded.

One summarized the plot.

"Mr. Weston, you need to know we think he knew the bomb was in his office before it went off. Yeah, he was injured, but his furniture had been moved at least three feet. How many people wouldn't notice that, moved furniture, in their own office? Be careful in there with him."

"Got it."

And I thought Anbar had been an interesting challenge.

For the next hour, my mind focused on the chairman's new furniture, not his words. Then it was time to talk to the Iraqi politician's "constituents" beyond the locked gate of his compound.

Outside the district governor's own fort, not far from ours, crowds of Iraqis gathered, as they did about every day. Most voiced loud complaints: no electricity; bribes required for identification papers; abusive police; failing food distribution networks. Akin to an open-air town hall, the chaotic pulse at the heart of the slum energized me—flashbacks of Fallujah, but in a good way. Retail-level interaction. Retail politics. Unpredictable and authentic voices mixed together. These were the once oppressed people, no longer in Saddam's deadly grip, even with now protected Shia extremists and death squads in their midst who wielded electric drills as torture weapons.

When I looked out on their dozens of faces, bunched together, I could not tell which was which, who was who, friends and foes. But I reported their words without bias in my cables to Washington. Whoever lost the Iraqi street would lose Iraq. And I increasingly sensed that we had—but were not yet ready to admit it to ourselves.

Standing close to me, an old woman extended a clawlike hand, likely curled inward due to decades of labor and arthritis. She held a small badge and waved it toward me. In it the visage of a teenage youth with large brown eyes peered out. She looked eighty, but was probably closer to fifty. Everyone looked older in Iraq, as they did in Afghanistan, and that included us by our second tours. After a brief exchange outside the front gate, I learned she wanted help receiving promised Iraqi government "martyr payments" for her dead son. They had not paid her, a common complaint. When I asked what happened, she said he had been killed while serving in the fledgling Iraqi Security Forces.

Then she revealed where. "He died in Fallujah."

I took down her name but promised nothing, repeating the same line I still echoed throughout both wars. "I always keep my promises, which is why I don't make very many." Once translated, most Iraqis laughed, at least a bit, with me. As had Afghans.

In the middle of the throng, a U.S. soldier asked if he could respond to the accusations of one vocal Iraqi teen in particular, who spoke enough English to heckle us in our native language. The youth kept repeating "Jobs, jobs, jobs!" and said Iraqis blamed the U.S. for failing to improve living conditions. He waved his right hand over his head, back and forth, in a motion an American would liken to a Tom Brady football pass. But to an Iraqi, the gesture had only one meaning at the time: shoes held aloft and thrown at the U.S. president.

Several of his friends stood together, laughing, and pressed us in an enveloping circle, inches away. The American soldier, who had always been among the calmest in the unit, a Midwest stoic, rarely spoke. This day proved different.

"Mr. Weston, sir, can I respond? Can I?"

"Of course, say whatever you want." I was curious what choice words he would utter.

In a low, forceful voice—a single sentence—he made his POV very clear.

"Listen, I am from the Motor City, Detroit, and my own dad has been out of work for years."

Nothing more.

It was then I knew nation building in Iraq, far away from America's own economically gutted and over-mortgaged cities, all our hometowns, had never been sustainable. I included the Iraqi teen's and soldier's comments, he himself only a few years older, verbatim in my cable to Washington. To my surprise, Robert did not edit them out. Diplomatic reporting could often turn formulaic and dull via multiple rounds of internal embassy editing, but my cable's extra "texture" as Robert called it stayed in. (Holbrooke himself, a prolific writer and author of the book *To End a War*, often criticized the limp prose of official State-speak.)

The Motor City native's words conveyed far more than any analysis of my own. This Detroit soldier stood as the most honest American ambassador that day. I wished he could have repeated his line to the Iraqi prime minister and our own outgoing president, George W. Bush, in the Oval Office. And that the Associated Press, Al Jazeera, NPR, Fox News, *The Washington Post*, *The New York Times*, as well as the blogs had been there to report it—and especially the *Detroit Free Press*, founded in 1831.

The blunt soldier, whose dad would have been proud of him, had called the situation for what it was. While policy makers continued to trade official memos based on a mythology: preemptive invasion and then the surge equals war won and worth the costs.

Or not.

The soldiers and I walked back into the district center that day without saying anything more. Sadr City's council chairman greeted us with a smile and led me to a large, green-cushioned chair with gaudy gold trim in his spacious office. He seemed proud of his furniture collection and its careful placement in the room.

I titled my first cable, "Sadr City's Son and His Shoes: Muted reactions, so far, in the street; questions remain regarding planned U.S. drawdown and Iranian influence." I reported how a group of eight new Iraqi policemen expressed concerns about the planned U.S. troop drawdown, with the senior police officer telling me, "We need U.S. support here because Iran is already living beside us in the city."

Soon after, I drafted another cable. Its title: "Kissing the Koran: Electioneering in Sadr City." It focused on . . . another Iraqi election . . . more ballots . . . Iraqi "democracy" after the American invasion. I wrote how one Sadr City politician who sat on the district council declared to me, "[Political] parties are destroying us," adding that key ministry jobs were being awarded based on sectarian agendas. This local Iraqi leader reminded me how truckloads of fake ballots had been intercepted in the January 2005 election along the Iran-Iraq border. He implied more of that was ahead.

In September 2009, the Iraqi government released Muntadhar al-Zaidi (the shoe-thrower) for "good behavior" from an Iraqi jail after serving nine months of a three-year sentence, enabling him to move to London and lead a humanitarian organization focused on Iraqi civilians.

In 2010, he came out with a book titled *The Last Salute to President Bush*. In the Arab world, he is considered a hero among many, including in places the U.S. government classifies as allies.

I never learned whether the sewer line project in Sadr City was completed.

Not that it mattered. In truth, I did not want to know. And I surely did not want that soldier's family ever to know about that mission's objective the day he died.

City building in Sadr City, before the soldier's death by EFP— explosively formed penetrator, molten metal slugs—had included the following projects, which I reported to Washington in an unsuccessful effort to get money, hundreds of millions of dollars, for such well-meaning initiatives restricted at the four-star and ambassador-levels, and thereby save American lives.

I wrote: "An estimated $43.2 million has been spent in various sectors, including almost $11,000 per day for trash collection . . . [and] 17 sewer, 30 school, 27 electric, 18 trash, seven health and eight economic development projects."

Inevitably, more U.S. troops conducted more "sewer line patrols"— with more KIA and more WIA the result. The U.S. money flow did not stop. In some places, it even increased. And I was certain few recalled that in his run for the White House in 2000, before 9/11, before Afghanistan, before Iraq, candidate George W. Bush said (promised?): "Are we going to have some kind of nation-building corps from America? Absolutely not."

During my last week in Baghdad before joining Larry Nicholson and 10,672 Marines in Afghanistan, I said farewell to embassy colleagues. I also said thanks to Ambassador Ford, one of the most effective U.S. diplomats in the Foreign Service and still proving as much in how he navigated the political minefield that was Baghdad, among Iraqi leaders and among fellow American diplomats as well, for that matter.

"Iraq was the national priority, Robert. Now it is Afghanistan, right? New president, new priorities."

"Yes, Kael. President Obama has made that clear. Afghanistan is a top focus now. Safe travels to Helmand, and don't let Marines get you into too many crazy and dangerous places that I know they like to charge into."

The 30,000 additional troops that I am announcing tonight will deploy in the first part of 2010—the fastest possible pace—so that they can target the insurgency and secure key population centers. . . . Taken together, these additional American and international troops will allow us to accelerate handing over responsibility to Afghan forces, and allow us to begin the transfer of our forces out of Afghanistan in July of 2011. Just as we have done in Iraq, we will execute this transition responsibly, taking into account conditions on the ground.

PRESIDENT BARACK OBAMA
DECEMBER 1, 2009, WEST POINT

Escalation

After landing in Helmand province in June 2009 and throwing my one bag to the ground, Larry Nicholson, now a brigadier general and in a command billet, walked up to me with a familiar expression. The one I had gotten used to in Fallujah. Half smile, half grimace, it signaled both "good to see you" and "let's get to work." After having somehow survived Anbar during the most intense fighting of the Iraq War, I wondered what our survival odds would be in southern Afghanistan.

Extending his hand, Larry said, "It's about time you got back to Afghanistan. We have a real fight on our hands here in Helmand."

"I've been reading all the reports," I replied. "I thought Khost was tough."

"Helmand will be harder. I've got everything ready. You'll have an office right next to mine, and I'm giving you my part of the tent, fit for an ambassador."

"What?"

"Come on, I'll walk you over to your fancy room."

While I did not expect anything five-star or even 2.5-star, I had not realized all Marines were living in tents, with the nearest shower trailers and port-a-johns almost a hundred meters away. That same stink, from the early days in Anbar, hung in the air. And the setting seemed as hot, dusty, and dry, if not even more arid. I recalled how Marine corporals used to joke in Fallujah that if the U.S. was going to invade anywhere else after Iraq, it should be a series of tropical islands, not landlocked countries full of insurgents and big-fanged camel spiders that pack a very big bite. And yet, Marines, I knew, ran to these kinds of edge-of-empire places on maps full of new and strange names because that is where the toughest fights were.

A five-minute walk from the all-plywood command building nicknamed "the Ark," we entered a twenty-foot-by-twenty-foot large canvas tent. It was one of dozens and dozens, all aligned in neat rows encompassing a football-field-sized USMC at-war community. The whole place looked like an encampment of soldiers dispatched from Holy Rome, and not in a Hollywood set kind of way.

Larry remarked, while pointing left and right, "You're lucky. You'll only have four roommates. The deputy commander, chief of staff, sergeant major, and command master chief.

"There, see the back of the tent? That's all yours, and the A/C works."

"Thanks, Larry. This makes me miss the CMOC in Fallujah."

"Welcome to Camp Leatherneck."

In U.S. military-speak, Helmand ranked as the "main effort" in what, by then, was fast becoming the longest war in U.S. history. Larry and the 2nd Marine Expeditionary Brigade were expected to pacify the vast province. It measured almost 23,000 square miles, home to a thousand villages, most in remote areas, spread across thirteen districts. Within its oblong borders, hectares and hectares of poppies were farmed (an estimated three quarters of all opium production in the world)—amid a lot of Taliban, many of whom worked as part-time day laborers during the poppy harvest. The province's population of over 1.4 million is majority Pashtun, and the Helmand River, which stretches 700 miles north to south, feeds a verdant agricultural area along its banks, including famous melons. Notably, in the 1950s, Helmand benefited from large, multimillion-dollar USAID investments and infrastructure improvements (canals, bridges, roads, schools).

The Marine Area of Operation (or AO) stretched from northern Helmand (Now Zad, Sangin, Kajaki) all the way to the Pakistani border in the south to Khan Neshin and its ancient "castle" (built more like a mud castle than anything out of Sir Lancelot) and adjacent Taghaz. Fallujah had been a focused effort in terms of battlefield geography—one city and its surrounding area. Helmand, in contrast, would be an expansive one, measured in helo airtime not Humvee time. The province had experienced some of the most intense fighting before U.S. Marines arrived in force. British troops had suffered the greatest toll.

The base Marines had built, basically from nothing, sat in the middle of a gray-yellow desert by day, turning orange by dusk and again by dawn, in between cloudless daytime skies. The place looked like Mars, I imagined, but instead of Martians, I saw only hundreds of Marines whose MARPAT uniforms blended into the landscape. A State Department friend asked what I thought upon arriving. I said to her it was like I had landed on "Planet of the Marines."

The British had arrived in Helmand first, building a far more accommodating base called Camp Bastion (with much better food, ironically, such as great pasta and beef, not beans-on-toast fare), which served as the primary NATO base in the region. It would eventually rank as the largest U.K. base constructed since World War II. Former prime minister Tony Blair, in a blue shirt and a blue blazer, told traveling British press during one visit in late 2006 (reported in *The Guardian* newspaper) that the stakes could not be higher, his rhetoric virtually Churchillian:

> You are here for a reason. This was the training grounds for al-Qaida and terrorism, so when you defeated the Taliban, your defeat is not just on behalf of the people of Afghanistan, but the people of Britain and the wider world. If this goes wrong in Afghanistan, the whole region feels the consequences. Here in this extraordinary piece of desert is where the fate of world security in the early 21st century is going to be decided.

The U.S. view about the province would be different, not nearly as sweeping, which became clear just after I arrived. Larry explained we had a VIP delegation arriving from Washington. President Obama was sending his national security adviser, Jim Jones, who also happened to be a former Marine commandant and Supreme Allied Commander Europe (SACEUR), to meet with us. Leatherneck, in other words, would be the setting for a war council of sorts. And I was getting a prime seat in the room.

A few days later, NSA Jones and his staff landed at Leatherneck. Larry's aide-de-camp, George Saenz (a Texan and A&M alum fanatic, who also maintained the best imported candy and snack collection in Helmand), helped get the group situated. But they were expecting something different, better. What the VIPs got was some of our tent space. That was it. The famous *Washington Post* journalist and author Bob Woodward was traveling with them. He had been focused on "Obama's War" as a theme, digging around D.C. for high-level insights and, as ever, a bit of spicy cabinet-level gossip. I always found his books on Iraq to be worthwhile reads, but also depressing. Washington backstabbing had become an art form, it seemed, and not just sport or pastime— particularly over the wars and failing policies that were anything but bipartisan.

George said I would have a new roommate for one night: Woodward. So I met the acclaimed *Post* reporter outside my shared tent, taking him back to the "suite" that would be his. When he looked at the green cot, dusty floor, and stacked footlockers that were probably hiding a few spiders and scorpions somewhere, I sensed he was, well, a bit anxious but nevertheless put a Braveheartish face forward.

"Do you have a phone I could use? Need to call my wife, Elsa, let her know I arrived okay."

"Sure."

I handed my State Department–issued cell phone to him, which usually worked—and surely would be tapped by the National Security Agency (NSA), given that its signal emanated from the middle of a war zone. Perhaps Woodward remembered that whistle-blowers, employees of the spy agency, had claimed only months earlier that Green Zone calls in Baghdad, from soldiers and aid workers to girlfriends and boyfriends back home, had been intercepted over several years. And some of their raciest comments, revealing very personal things, had been shared "best of"–style at NSA HQ, in violation of agency policy and U.S. law. (Edward Snowden had not yet initiated, via his leaks years later, a national debate on secrecy, citizen rights, and national security.)

As Woodward got settled in my un-lux canvas abode, tent flaps flapping in the wind, he asked me a few questions about the war. I explained I knew a lot more about the east than the south, having just arrived back from Baghdad, but said I believed Afghanistan would test American endurance, not firepower. On the question of a troop surge, I cautioned that Marines were not built for marathons. "They are sprinters, great at the hundred-meter dash. And there is no bridge too far in their mind." That usually worked to our country's advantage in a war zone filled with more enemies than friends, I added, but the clock mattered and the context.

I moved my sleeping bag to the top bunk in another part of the tent. Woodward said he was jet-lagged and was calling it a night, adding that he was looking forward to the Marine brief to General Jones.

"So am I. I have a feeling there will be some surprises tomorrow."

Early the next morning, as the sun was heating up the desert air to 90 degrees already by coffee time, one of the Marines assigned to guard Larry during any travel off base approached me.

"Hey, sir, who was that visitor, that older guy, who was staying in your tent last night?"

"His name is Bob Woodward. He got famous by writing about Watergate, Nixon resigning."

"Umm, okay. I'm asking because some of the guys and I saw him leave the tent in the middle of the night. We had our NVGs on [night vision goggles]. He walked around a bit, then stopped next to a T-wall and took a piss on it."

"Well, I guess he couldn't hold it. But let's not tell the general," I replied. (Larry remained a stickler for proper war zone etiquette. Taking a leak on a concrete barrier would not go over well with him, no matter who the "leaker" was.)

At about that time, the Marine and I saw a wet-headed Mr. Woodward walking between two rows of tents with only a towel wrapped around his waist and bathroom sandals. Noticing him on his way back to the State Department tent non-suite to get ready for the meeting, we were glad he had found the showers.

. . .

General Jim Jones looked every bit a four-star-general-turned-statesman. His demeanor reminded me of Virginia senator John Warner, both men almost of a different era. I could have pictured either representing the U.S. at Versailles (like I could have imagined Holbrooke, though he probably would have threatened to break some glass in the Hall of Mirrors). Where treaties and international relations were the focus, not the grit and grime and grind of tactical warfare fought at the edge of empires.

General Jones sat next to Larry, who provided an incisive half-hour brief of the Helmand fight ahead, the overall terrain, and a bit on a place called Marjah—which, as Taliban Central, eventually would need to be addressed, he said, but it was too soon just yet. Plus there was the most immediate question of additional U.S. troops: to surge or not to surge.

After winning the presidency, Obama had agreed to an initial influx of U.S. forces into Afghanistan (about 20,000 additional troops), a decision left to him as George W. Bush vacated the Oval Office. But if there were any question whether a second iron and human wave was going to be approved by the White House, Jones made clear that Situation Room deliberations were basically over.

His was not a mixed or "let's see first" kind of statement. No, he told the Marines that Commander in Chief Obama would not respond very well to any request for more forces, saying the new president would have a "Whiskey Tango Foxtrot" (WTF/What The Fuck) reaction. In the plain plywood conference room sat many Anbar alums—indeed, several of us had spent years in Iraq. NSA Jones further made clear this effort would be different: "We are not going to build that empire here that we did in Iraq." And yet, as Woodward later reported (he took good and detailed notes, as I compared them to my own), Larry had remarked, "We are a little light on troops," extending the argument that in order to properly do the upcoming Central Helmand River Valley operations, more Marines could be useful. But the main takeaway from the gathering had been what Larry said in closing and with a lot more emphasis: "We don't need more U.S. forces. We need more Afghan forces."

I could not have said it better myself. It was a topic Larry and I had previously discussed in private. Without more Afghans, Americans would continue to be fighting for, not fighting alongside. Side by side, shoulder to shoulder, needed to be the frame, not Marines in the fore and charging ahead into new valleys and across the remotest ridgelines. The war had already gone on too long for that, we both agreed.

The Washington Post ran a story on its front page that summarized the meeting. Larry and his top officers did not like that Woodward described them in a specific way when NSA Jones made his WTF comment. The journalist wrote: "Nicholson and his colonels—all or nearly all veterans of Iraq—seemed to blanch at the unambiguous message."

More than a few Marine officers came up to me for days afterward, with the same message: "We are Marines. Marines do not blanch." The word "blanch" became my favorite to use around Marines for many weeks to follow.

Within six months, President Obama would order the Pentagon to surge 30,000 more troops into Afghanistan, the exact opposite approach NSA Jones had put forward as having been already decided. Larry, his aide, George, and I were sitting with an Afghan general named Mohay-aden drinking more tea and eating more raw almonds and more yellow raisins when we heard the news about the second troop surge.

George received a call with an update. "General, we have another WIA report. Ops just called."

"Any details yet?" Larry asked.

"It doesn't look good—they are saying 'lost legs and currently with a tourniquet still on him.' They are sending the WIA to Bastion right now."

The Afghan general shook his head, acknowledging the wounded Marine. He also noted that Afghan army soldiers had been taking high casualties as well. All of us understood that their ability to medevac their wounded nowhere matched our own. For every Marine wounded or killed, Afghans took ten times as many losses. Or more.

Toward the end of the tea and almond session, the Afghan military leader asked us how much one of our HIMARS missiles cost. This High Mobility Artillery Rocket System was launched from a truck, a platform that weighed 24,000 pounds, and had a range of almost 300 miles, with the missiles traveling at about 50 miles per hour. Larry estimated the cost to be a few million dollars.

General Mohayaden raised both eyebrows and both hands, noting that kind of money could "make many jobs and schools." And he spoke as an Afghan general who had experienced a lot of fighting in some of Afghanistan's most dangerous terrain.

Larry, George, and I said we agreed. I knew, though, that with President Obama's decision, announced earlier that same day at West Point, Helmand would be seeing a lot more HIMARS in the months ahead, a lot more Marines (a doubling of our current force level, which would rise to almost 20,000), and our own pace would pick up proportionately. Sprint after sprint after sprint, despite the marathon distance that this war still represented.

And so the real American war in Helmand got under way.

The escalation.

Larry, the 1st Marine Expeditionary Brigade's CG (commanding general), was known among his troops to stir a sixth- or seventh-round cup of Starbucks instant VIA coffee after midnight. There are generals and then there are commanding generals (aka the alphas in any war, even if others might wear more stars on collars but hold billets as "staff" generals and lack "commanding" in their title—a big difference). Larry was the latter, and everyone knew it. His command was arguably the most demanding and highest-priority in the whole country. Putting him in charge showed how much the Marine Corps trusted his judgment, and I knew how much Afghans would benefit, as Iraqis had. There was no artifice in his counterinsurgency mind-set. Collaborators could also become friends, and around him they did.

Larry never finished work before 2 a.m. and was awake by 6 a.m. to prepare for our daily 7 a.m. staff briefing. Only on Sundays did our days start a few hours later. Even then we were often on helicopters to visit our spread-out Marine combat units, as war, we all learned, tends to keep a 24/7 schedule, and thus Marines had to as well. The one-star general and I, his aide, and sergeant major were shot at numerous times—by small arms fire, a Taliban machine gun, even an RPG overhead. But our closest calls, all adrenaline stories without any heroics, came while flying above a 200-square-kilometer area of operation flat in the middle and bordered by steep peaks to the north.

Some flight patterns took us to the Iranian border, which, the British embassy had warned the U.S. embassy, "lit up the Iranian grid." This only made Marines, and me, more gung ho to get closer. Our daily gamble in the air proved threefold. Dual tilt rotor Ospreys fly high and fast but are vulnerable to bullets; buslike CH-53s tend to "brown out" under their massive rotors and obscure everyone's vision in sandy landing zones, a dangerous predicament for all; and even the ever-reliable workhorse C-130 can surprise the most experienced of pilots when a strong Afghan desert wind blows across a moonlit tarmac, forcing a plane off course by a few crucial meters.

Late one night our plane from Kandahar to Helmand came within a few feet of clipping a building upon approach at Camp Bastion, which led me to offer a black-humor comment after landing, grateful to be alive and not scraped to death with everyone else along the landing strip.

"Well, a crash tonight would have either been very bad or very good for the strategic effort."

Only Larry got the joke. The Marine pilot, one of the best, never flew again during his tour. If not for an "oh-shit, override" button on the new model of the C-130—immediate flaps up and engine thrust—the plane would have disintegrated into fiery pieces along the tarmac. It appeared he lost his nerve, as we all tended to do sometimes in the wars.

Each of us seemed to have been given nine lives. I remember a dozen times we thought we would die by bullet, rocket, or crash. Five, in just one week, met the requirements for a Combat Action Ribbon. I never told the State Department, or my family. Larry never told his military bosses, or his family.

We were not brave. We got lucky. We knew Marines who were brave and got unlucky. They died.

We were entering what was said to be the last phase of the war and the number of killed and wounded was spiking in Helmand.

More than courage, the fight in Afghanistan's southernmost reaches demanded inhuman amounts of endurance. Along with Kandahar, it had the most concentrated Taliban numbers. No caffeinated concoction or marked redeployment calendar could alleviate the compounding effect of USMC-style battle practiced by the infantry and supporting units:

intense and unrelenting. I learned overseas there were no true breaks, physical or mental, once in the kind of combat zones to which U.S. Marines were sent. But we enjoyed plenty of esprit de corps, which made up for a lot.

And we had strong allies on the ground with us: the Brits, as well as Danes, Estonians, Georgians, and a contingent of Bahrainis. I also, by then, had found my strongest ally: Farid, who was my interpreter, as Arif had been in Khost. Part Pashtun, part Tajik, he had family in Kabul and Herat. And like Arif, he was wise to the ways of Afghanistan in ways that a *ferangi* (foreigner) like me never could be. Besides, before arriving in Helmand, he had also spent time in Afghanistan's east, near FOB Tillman. If Afghans had been awarded Combat Action Ribbons, Farid would probably have earned more than any other.

He also understood how Afghans really felt about the British, even a century-plus after their very bloody withdrawal from Kabul.

If I should die, think only this of me:
That there's some corner of a foreign field
That is for ever England.

RUPERT BROOKE, "THE SOLDIER"

Our British Friends

With tens of thousands of U.S. Marines now ordered to battle by Washington across two presidencies, a new and complex dynamic was under way. We Americans had sent in the Marines—infantry battalion upon infantry battalion—during the Bush administration and now under Obama's.

Some called it a surge. Others, including me, kept calling it an escalation. Echoes of Iraq. Echoes of Vietnam? Time would tell, and then the war historians would tell all, I figured. But the present, the urgent here and now of war, was what occupied Larry, our allies, and me.

With this U.S. troop influx the so-called special relationship between the United States and the United Kingdom took on new meaning and meant unforeseen challenges in Afghanistan. Despite the avalanche of Marines in their Eagle, Globe, and Anchor uniforms, British forces continued to suffer in that initial period more killed in action than we did. U.K. troops were being blown up in open-air vehicles called "Jackals"—not built to deflect increasingly sophisticated roadside bombs. Lacking V-shaped hulls and thick metal armor, they were more mobile but also much more vulnerable. Inadequate transport equipment resulted in numerous lost lives and limbs unnecessarily in my view. The U.K. soldiers' odds of survival were lower than they should have been and lower than ours.

The British casualty count affected me a lot. While jogging around Camp Leatherneck and Camp Bastion (the British side of our sprawling base in the middle of Helmand's Nevada-like desert), I listened to British Forces Radio. I liked the news updates and their Euro-music playlist. The announcers, many with precise Queen's English accents, described the latest arrival of U.K. KIA at Wootton Bassett, a small village where British remains were repatriated. The radio reports conveyed the way the United Kingdom mourned the dead: caskets covered in the Union Jack; a church bell sounding above St. Bartholomew's; and townspeople lined up several rows deep as black hearses passed by. Unlike in the U.S. under the Bush administration, U.K. media were never barred from recording these images.

The American public still supported the Afghanistan War, though by a shrinking margin. The British public did not. They wanted their boys home.

A few weeks after arriving in Helmand, I walked into Larry's office to raise a subject that had been on my mind for a while.

"Can't we transfer to the British some of our extra MRAPs? They don't stand a chance in their vehicles when they get hit."

"I'd like to, but you know it would never be approved. They couldn't take them even if we offered."

I dropped the matter about a possible MRAP transfer to the Brits and went back to my office. It had a small fridge, stacks of bottled water, a coffeemaker, and a pile of instant oatmeal I had brought with me. On a wall near my desk, a sheet of paper I had taped there showed "the longest wars in American history." By 2009, Afghanistan was near the top of the list. I shared the plywood wall behind me with Larry's adjacent office-bunkroom combination.

Larry was right. We both knew in no way would our government or Her Majesty's Government accept the transfer of U.S. equipment to British forces. The London-based press would pounce. So would ours. Leading American news organizations like *The New York Times*, NPR, *The Wall Street Journal*, and *The Washington Post* kept their reporters

out in the field and close to our troops, thereby in the know. So did
the London-based broadsheets. Such a shift in combat zone resources,
or even open talk of it, would be hard to record in logistics and supply
records let alone explain to the public: British soldiers dying due to
inadequate equipment, and U.S. Marines arriving in Helmand in order
to "rescue" the overwhelmed and undersupplied Brits.

"Here, take a few of our Made-in-America MRAPs . . ."

It would have made for an indicting and politically inexplicable
headline, atop an important story. And it would have put even more
pressure on the increasingly defensive No. 10 Downing Street and
White House about the stalled war front.

We kept our extra MRAPs, and more British soldiers died.

At Camp Leatherneck, I needed civilian reinforcements.

The expanding Marine base had a *Starship Troopers* feel to it, our
imperial grunts ordered to the empire's farthest reaches. Our spartan
side, opposite the British, had sprung up from the desert in weeks. Tents
formed canyons of canvas with diesel generators attached in order to
pump into them a steady flow of un-desert-like cool air. As in Iraq,
we had perfected climate-controlled warfare. The nineteenth-century
British had brought fans with them; we had General Electric with us.
I did not mind my cot that year, but I did mind when the generators
stopped.

Into this spare environment (we were still eating tray rations and
slept between tent flaps), the U.K. embassy sent a political adviser to
share my office space and gain a seat at our command deck conference
room table.

Caroline of Helmandshire ventured into Marinestan in order to
help ensure the U.K. government's strategy helped guide Marine tactics. That comprised a big challenge, especially for a non-American. I
performed the same task for Washington. Unlike me, however, Caroline Mulcahy had never worked with the U.S. military, let alone proud
and tribal jarheads. Plus, she was a female in an environment where
men outnumbered women 100 to 1.

Despite these challenges, Caroline soon became everyone's favorite
political adviser. I could hardly compete. Not yet thirty, she had short
blond hair, angular features, and a clipped way with words that went

beyond the precise English accent and vocabulary, which in combination always impressed us less eloquent Yanks. While she served in Helmand, her boyfriend remained in London and her parents continued their sailing trip across most of the world's seven seas.

Caroline was the type of person who could have easily avoided war. She instead chose to go where the Afghanistan War was at its most intense. Marines noticed. She was their kind of expeditionary diplomat. I had found an ideal counterinsurgency partner to help rein in the twitch-muscle instincts of U.S. Marines. Like me, she viewed Afghanistan as a marathon.

When Larry Nicholson urged me to visit Now Zad, a former lush pomegranate paradise now dotted with IEDs, Caroline said she wanted to join me. It would have been oh-so-convenient and justifiable for her to avoid the dangerous place and instead spend more time in meetings in Lashkar Gah, the much more posh headquarters location her Foreign and Commonwealth Office (FCO) colleagues called home. Infamously, British and American diplomats once hosted a party there advertised as "Lash Vegas Pimps and Hos." When I heard news of their jubilant gathering, I almost asked, indeed ordered, Marines to lay siege to our occasionally Nero-like colleagues in the provincial capital.

Now Zad, in contrast, represented everything Lash was not: the real war front. Our helicopter landed under moonlight, a timeframe in the twenty-four-hour flight cycle when we had the advantage over the dozens of insurgents in the area. We got out and walked a few hundred meters, escorted by Marines, into FOB Caferetta. The whole place had an Alamo feel to it. HESCO barriers. Sand berms. Razor wire. Towers. The British had formerly occupied the contested terrain. The adjacent market reminded me of Fallujah's warren of streets—mainly because they were abandoned and had been obliterated over consecutive battles.

And we had Marines here in northern Helmand for what reason? I thought. The main effort in counterinsurgency had long been: go where the people are, spend the money where the people are, and not least, "send in the Marines" where the people are.

Early the next morning, with temperatures still in the 80s, I bumped into a lanky junior Marine. I nodded. The lance corporal nodded back. It seemed we were the earliest risers that day, just beating the sun over craggy, gray peaks to the east. His nametag read Bernard. It had been a while since I was this ensconced in Marine culture, and it reminded me how Marines used to insist that their uniforms not list any last name, just "U.S. Marine." Marine first. Marine foremost.

Unlike other U.S. military branch uniforms, adorned with all sorts of He-Man badges denoting past service locations, Marines kept theirs simple, badge-less. Almost Borg-like, the collective identity outweighed that of the individual. And I understood why. Small-unit combat depends on camaraderie, not distinctions. More bragging rights did not need to mean more uniform patches. Some Marine friends called their Army and Air Force counterparts "war peacocks."

The only other civilian I noticed on base at the time was a staff photographer, Julie Jacobson, for the Associated Press. As Marines hunted for the least lukewarm bottle of water (the ones stacked in front of the half-functioning A/C wall unit were most prized), the photographer and I compared our how-we-got-to-a-place-like-Now-Zad stories. Quiet in demeanor, she mentioned how she too preferred the Western U.S. to the East Coast, recalling a river rafting expedition down the Colorado River. We talked about Moab, Utah's red rock deserts, and Colorado's mountains for a while and then parted.

I respected her as a media embed—embedded in Now Zad of all places. This photographer, like several others in Afghanistan, had opted to chronicle the most difficult parts of the war. She mentioned she would be joining our platoons a few weeks later in operations to clear Dahaneh Pass. I had looked at the infantry company commander's maps and knew how challenging that area would be to patrol. Hours later, I experienced what kind of "welcome" the local Afghans—more poppy farmers than wheat farmers—preferred to give us. Near Dahaneh, Taliban fighters on an adjacent ridge began to fire a Russian-made Dishka, cannon-sized, in our direction. The rounds landed wide, but we did not want to give them time to readjust their sights.

After moving back toward the FOB at max speed, I decided to join a foot patrol along the market. I had seen some Afghans gathered and wanted to hear their take on us, as well as give them the opportunity to ask me about our take on them.

A Now Zad elder spoke first.

"Will you stay?"

"Marines will stay for a while," I replied. "I'm only here for a few days, but my government hopes to help build up your own army and police force so our troops can go home to their families."

"The Taliban have not left this district. They are only waiting. They will return when you leave."

He placed one hand under his chin and began to scratch his long gray beard, as if contemplating whether to keep up the conversation or go quiet.

"I know the Taliban are here. But will you and the people here prevent them from coming back, even after we leave?"

"Some will, but I think not enough."

Then he turned around and began to walk away, wearing sandals and carrying an empty plastic bag.

I began to follow him down the street when another Afghan elder approached me, asking me to make way for an open-bed truck that was slowly moving in our direction.

"We need to bury our dead. A family had gone to Kabul to buy things for a wedding. On their way back, their van hit a bomb.

"They are dead, except one girl," he added.

"I am so sorry. I'll make sure we stay out of your way."

Before long, the truck passed with a large piece of canvas in the back. It covered most of the bodies, but not all. An old woman's arm dangled to one side as children gathered close. One boy lifted it up, with a blank stare toward the jumble of bodies.

Other little kids gathered to peer under the tarp at more bodies.

Within an hour, Marines and I watched as young boys and old men shoveled dirt over the remains in hurried graves. Both sides knew the roadside bombs were there because we were there.

After they were done, I asked one what happened to the girl, the lone survivor.

"We sent the girl to Kandahar. Those are the only relatives she has left."

After two scorching days in Now Zad, Caroline and I returned to Camp Leatherneck. She had joined me, despite reservations and stricter U.K. security requirements, because the Marine presence remained a controversial topic among British diplomats and military officers. Caroline, to her credit, had wanted to do some due diligence of her own before reporting back to Lashkar Gah and Kabul, as well as to London.

Larry asked us what we thought.

We echoed each other: It is remote. It is full of Taliban. It is a ghost town.

I would turn my visit into a cable titled "Helmand's Now Zad Challenge: What's Next?" In it, I questioned the need to keep troops there. The situation looked like a stalemate to me: a Marine infantry company versus a Taliban company, operating in places our troops had nicknamed "Pakistan Alley" and "Sherwood Forest."

I recounted conversations I had while seated cross-legged with wary Afghans (about a dozen elders and one mullah—and a kid who reached for a Marine interpreter's pistol). Their most pointed comments included one from an old man who said, "We are like rocks here; you kick us, the Taliban kick us, no one listens to us; no one will give us our freedom." Another elder's critical view of Kabul: "Where is the government? There is no government." And a comment that stayed with me longest: "I remember as a child when Americans visited to eat our pomegranates."

Later that summer, a contingent of U.K. diplomats from the provincial capital joined Marines and me in Now Zad. We brought Helmand's governor, Gulab Mangal, an animated and active leader who enjoyed watching *Meet the Press* reruns. He came, via Marine helicopter, to mark the formal commitment of the central government to the isolated region's future. Under clear skies and a slight breeze, Mangal began to raise the Afghan flag, colored red, black, and green. Local media had brought their cameras. Just as the flag ascended past the midway point, mortars began to explode between our location and the forward operating base. After three or so rounds, we all opted to take cover. The ceremony ended abruptly.

I could not forget the dichotomy of the image, the sounds. As the Afghan flag went up, Taliban mortars rained down. The message was clear: we were not winning this part of the war.

Days later the Marine operation to clear Dahaneh Pass got under way. During one patrol, in the middle of an abandoned market, a Taliban RPG tore into the legs of the lead Marine, Lance Corporal Joshua Bernard. The same Marine I had previously met. As he fell, Julie Jacobson, the AP photographer still embedded with the unit, took a series of photos. In one, reddened stumps can be seen, as other Marines attempt to aid the crumpling young man, twenty-one years old from rural Maine, who liked to read literature. Though the photo is blurred in grayish green hues, Bernard's pain, his look of shock, is evident. He would eventually die on the operating room table.

Jacobson recounted what happened in an article co-written with AP's on-site reporter that day, Alfred de Montesquiou, citing her own journal entries. She described seeing the wounded Marine only ten yards away, and how "for the second time in my life, I watched a Marine lose his." The RPG had blown off one of his legs and mangled the other. Bernard, she said, lay on the ground. Two Marines stood over him trying to stop the bleeding. The first tourniquet "broke," forcing the medic to apply another. Jacobson recounted how she could hear Bernard's voice: "I can't breathe. I can't breathe."

She watched as other Marines dragged him to the MRAP, saying "Bernard, you're doing fine, you're doing fine. You're gonna make it. Stay with me, Bernard!" A Marine held Bernard's head in his hands when he seemed to go limp, trying to keep him awake. Jacobson also recorded in her journal how two Marines ran in with a stretcher.

And then the scandal erupted. Bernard's family and Defense Secretary Robert Gates did not want the photograph released. The Associated Press, in the end, opted not to censor it, leaving editors at individual papers across the U.S. to decide whether to publish it or not. Many did.

I questioned why Marines like Bernard were stationed in Now Zad, though I understood Larry's side of the policy argument: the need for Marines to press the Taliban, in addition to being close to Musa Qala, an area where U.K. troops were sparsely deployed. The general argued Now Zad represented "everything wrong with the war" to that point and had to be fixed. I had only briefly met Bernard but believed Bernard's photo, the photo of this one Marine's death, should be seen. Filtering war made more deaths more likely, not less. To edit out war would be to edit out truth. The way he died—graphically, painfully— did not need to be imagined. It happened. It was.

Jacobson's photo of the dying Lance Corporal Joshua Bernard won a World Press Photo award.

. . .

In late 2009, the outgoing British foreign secretary, David Miliband, asked Larry and me to support the expedited departure of British forces from Helmand. We had flown from Leatherneck to Lashkar Gah. Seated at a table in a dark room, the lively, energetic British politician—reportedly Hillary Clinton's favorite counterpart—said he saw "more light than heat" in the way the general and I traded views on troop priorities in Helmand. I confessed I had been a "nerd" in high school, watching the PBS programs *Prime Minister's Questions* and *I, Claudius*, based on books by Robert Graves. I kept to myself, however, that I also had watched *Benny Hill* reruns just as much.

Toward the end of our meeting, a U.K. military officer passed a note across the table to Foreign Secretary Miliband. The message informed him that two U.K. soldiers had just been killed by an IED in Sangin District.

In order to assist the British, more Americans would die.

Miliband had just asked us to urge Washington to move U.S. troops to that location. He said it was time for the overdue shift between allies. The Brits wanted out. Larry and I understood the new math.

On the flight back to Camp Leatherneck piloted by a female officer, on my favorite helicopter model—the newest Huey (UH-1), which floated in the air like a feather—I kept thinking about the request, about the note. About how many more Lance Corporal Bernards there would be as we took over British areas of operation. The numbers would shift: a lot more Old Glory–covered caskets arriving at Dover AFB and fewer Union Jack–covered caskets arriving at Wootton Bassett.

That same year, 2009, incoming UK Prime Minister David Cameron sat next to us with the same sort of message. Dressed in black corduroy pants and a brown V-neck sweater, he appeared lackadaisical. Perhaps due to jetlag, or perhaps it reflected uncertainty. I had met few top politicians who seemed fit for a war zone. The British brigadier general, James Cowan, seated across from his PM-to-be, opened the meeting by stating there remained "a question about dedicating so many troops to an empty city"—clearly implying an unwise Marine deployment to Now Zad. Larry replied by pointing out how U.S. Marines were aggressively patrolling Helmand, in line with our larger combat footprint.

The aristocratic Cowan, who maintained an air of I-still-go-foxhunting-on-the-weekend about him, went on to describe the high—

but unequal in his view—cost to coalition troops in Helmand. This led to the most remarkable and unfortunate exchange I ever witnessed between allies at war. The British brigadier compared amounts of spilled blood on the battlefield.

"I went to Bastion hospital. I checked and was told 80 percent of blood transfusions were going to British and Danish troops, 20 percent to Americans.

"We are patrolling, Larry, and at high cost."

He had his future prime minister in the room. Maybe that led to the cutting comment. I liked Cowan, despite his well-known fussy and officious behavior (a few years later he would write a memo about how British troops should eat sandwiches properly—with knife and fork, like at least one of our own West Point generals surely did, after I had seen in Larry's office this top U.S. Army officer cut melon into bite-sized bits with the precision of a surgeon). But on this day I could not believe what I had just heard. None of us Americans in the room could.

An awkward silence hung in the air. I kept waiting for PM-to-be Cameron to intervene and remind Cowan that all U.K., U.S., and other nations' losses reflected how difficult the allies' combined war front remained. He said nothing. I was hoping for a moment of statesmanship—we all were—and yet no words came from the youthful Conservative Party leader.

I fumbled to find my own.

"Sir, there's a dynamic with Afghans that you need to know. I spend a lot of time talking to the average guy on the street. They have different expectations about us, with our deeper pockets and more troops, than they do of your troops. You also have your colonial history in this country, which makes your job much more difficult."

And then I offered an inadequate rejoinder about our casualties.

"There has been plenty of blood shed here by all sides."

Brigadier Cowan said he "did not disagree" with my assessment. Cameron explained it was important for the British, but also the Afghan, public to see Afghans doing more. True enough, but was that it? No grand speech?

What I thought of saying—but a minute too late—was a reference to World War I poet Rupert Brooke. I wish I'd had the wit to conclude differently, pointedly.

Mr. Cameron, plain and simple, there are far too many parts in Helmand that will be forever England, forever Denmark, and forever America.

There was no such poetic moment.

After the meeting, I wrote a formal recommendation to Washington, arguing that our two countries, the U.S. and U.K., had reached a "crossroads." We needed to help get the British out of Helmand. Ambassador Karl Eikenberry agreed, but because of the sensitivity of the subject he opted to turn my cable into a memorandum for Secretary Clinton in advance of her upcoming meetings in London. Though I had supporters in Washington, including Richard Holbrooke, who was now the Obama administration's special representative for Afghanistan and Pakistan, I failed to convince a shift in U.S. strategy. Both nations would instead "surge" troops into the province—and with a stated public deadline for their redeployment. (Different country, different year, but same John McCain position: the surge in Iraq, he believed, "worked," so a surge in Afghanistan, he argued, would "work" too. Left unsaid in Helmand, however, was another view: the surge in Iraq had *not* worked in any strategic sense—the political deals between Iraqi politicians were never reached—and I, more than the general and Marines present, believed it would not work in Afghanistan either.)

McCain's position represented just what our Afghan partners did not advise or want. Even Helmand governor Mangal, closely associated with us in the eyes of Helmandis because he was, remarked sarcastically to me in private: "Of course 40,000 more troops will solve terrorism in Afghanistan!"

I put that memorable quote in an official report to Washington but to no avail, even if I had been told Holbrooke privately agreed with my position.

We failed to listen. Yet again, political masters in Washington and London believed they knew better.

. . . knew better than we on the ground.

. . . knew better than our Afghan partners.

You don't have to be straight to be in the military. You just have to be able to shoot straight.

BARRY GOLDWATER

Ask and Tell

Much of the talk in Helmand by early 2010 was that "Marjah was the new Fallujah." It was the main effort in southern Afghanistan. And a big chunk of the additional troops President Obama had decided to deploy in the poppy-filled area were now ready for battle—against not just insurgents but also more than a few insurgent-farmers. Marjah itself had approximately 100,000 Afghans living and farming in its borders. It had benefited from massive USAID project investments begun in the 1950s, so much so that the imprint of America on its geography ran deep despite the intervening decades. But the canals that still carried irrigation water were now planted on either side with poppy crops and increasingly deadly IEDs. The British called it a "crust"—a crust to be avoided unless or until paths had been cleared. Not enough had been by the time the battle was about to begin, once President Karzai finally gave his approval after much convincing from General McChrystal in Kabul.

Ironically, there was one parallel with Fallujah that I agreed with (the others not at all): Marines, with no experience in Fallujah, used to show a slide with a map of Marjah on it during internal briefs. On one visit by General Hejlik (now a three-star whom I had not seen since our time in Fallujah), he and I both looked at each other at the same time with the same comment: that map sure reminds me of Fallujah, square in shape and shaded in a way that was similar to the neighborhoods that had cost us so many Marine lives. A bad omen.

But it was the arrival of another general, James Terry Conway, that marked the real denouement. He was as legendary a general as they get within Marine ranks. As with Hejlik, I had not seen him in a long while, not since our time in Anbar years earlier. This top general would be deploying with an entourage, as only four-stars can in the middle of a war zone.

Half helicopter, half plane, two futuristic Ospreys with dual, metallic-gray tilt rotors that defied gravity arrived on schedule. They always did when this particular passenger landed in Afghanistan's battlefields.

Hundreds of Marines had gathered in early February 2010 in Helmand province to hear Conway, the Marine commandant, deliver a rousing speech on the eve of the war's largest battle to date. He had not changed since Fallujah. The Walnut Ridge, Arkansas, native had achieved mythic status in line with his matinee-script fit (tall stature, booming voice, imposing bearing) as the top Marine boss and one of the most vocal members of the Joint Chiefs of Staff. So impressive were his leadership qualities, had he ordered an infantry charge on the spot upon landing in Helmand, I would have been first to follow him into the breach then and there—with thousands of Marines right behind, I am sure.

If the Marine Corps had ever produced a Caesar, Conway fit the mighty mold. Seeing me, and referring to my time still in the wars since Fallujah going on year six-and-a-half by then, the commandant said, "I thought you'd be dead by now."

So did I.

Only days away, the big fight in Marjah between Marines and the Taliban filled everyone's minds. A kind of final countdown had begun that early part of February 2010. President Obama had ordered America's storied Devil Dogs into Helmand in order to reverse insurgent momentum—and they were ready to do just that. I almost expected the lean (but green) lance corporals, Iraq-hardened NCOs, and gung-ho company commanders to pull out sword and shield in thumping, Roman legion–like unison as their leader spoke.

Adrenaline, anticipation, and a palpable degree of fear hung heavily in the unusually damp Afghan winter air.

General Conway spoke eloquently in a martial cadence:

> Marjah will be where the war begins to end. We are about to write another page in our history. As the days get closer, each of you is going to have to deal with this thing we call fear. Look to your left and to your right and take care of your buddies because they will help you get through this. Fear can be a good thing—can make you grow quicker, maybe make your shots better. You all will be in the main attack. This will be the biggest thing we Marines do, and you will show the enemy, and our nation, that we remain the strongest tribe.

Then, rather unexpectedly, he raised another topic.

As thick rain clouds mixed ominously overhead, muddied boots remained firmly planted alongside rows of rifles. Out in front, the towering four-star general asked the assembled grunts about possible rumors regarding repeal of the military's so-called Don't Ask, Don't Tell (DADT) policy. He got to the point quickly, referencing the ongoing debate among politicians and general officers' obligations to convey accurately Marine views. He asked whether service by "openly homosexual" Marines would affect unit morale. Some Marines raised hands in the affirmative; others kept their hands down, seemingly unconcerned with the issue. Many appeared not to have heard the question. The visit occurred within one month of President Obama's State of the Union address, in which the commander in chief had declared that he would work with Congress to bring DADT to an end.

At the time, I was just over halfway through my twelve-month assignment, along with Larry.

We had an enormous political-military task before us: jointly formulating and implementing a frontline strategy for just under 20,000 U.S. Marines in Afghanistan's most dangerous province.

DADT was the last issue on my mind, or his.

The killing fields of Helmand had become very deadly by the time of the commandant's visit to the outskirts of Marjah, with double amputations from IEDs already the signature wound. The poppy-filled part of Helmand remained a den for Taliban, narcotraffickers, and disgruntled farmers and tribes. Per square meter, it arguably produced more opium than anywhere else in Afghanistan—drugs that made their way to European streets and cash into the pockets of the Taliban and their affiliated networks. Some of the Marines assembled that day would be maimed or die. All of us knew as much, as did Commandant Conway. Old Anbar province alums, those invaluable staff sergeants, first sergeants, and senior NCOs, had by then schooled the youngest grunts (some not yet eighteen) on what battle really meant, only hours away.

The hardest part remained not knowing who exactly—of the hundreds standing or kneeling on one knee before us, face-to-face—would ultimately be added to the Marjah killed-in-action list. *It is old men who die—or should die, not our nation's young,* I kept thinking. But war had long since reversed that natural evolution.

Following General Conway's compelling eve-of-battle speech and unexpected impromptu DADT poll, a sandy-haired lance corporal quickly approached General Nicholson and me. He was equally as blunt as his commandant had been.

"Why is General Conway asking us about gays in the military? It's not a big deal. We are about to be in the biggest fight of the whole war. We don't care about that issue."

A few of his buddies stood close, but a couple of steps back, seemingly for moral support. Marine corporals rarely, if ever, approach a Marine general directly, let alone when several general officers are gathered: in total, one four-star, two three-stars, and a one-star commanding general. I had long witnessed Marines, including bull colonels, become starstruck and suddenly silent in the company of just one general officer.

What the junior Marine did took guts.

"I take your point, admire your honesty."

Looking back, I should have introduced him to General Conway, then and there.

No filter. No partisan Washington BS. No rank barriers.

Old Marine Corps meet new Marine Corps.

Instead, the junior Marine turned around and walked away, but not before saying in a flat voice, "Thanks."

I first knew DADT repeal was mostly becoming a nonissue—on the front lines at least—when various Marines, junior to senior, began to discuss the subject with me increasingly frequently if informally. We all sensed the shift.

As the brigade's State Department commissar in Helmand, I was referred to by Marines as both "The Inquisitor" and "The Confessor"—my dual, designated call signs. No subject was off limits. I asked few but pointed questions in briefings, and also served as their buffer and sounding board before taking an issue to the commanding general, who happened to be a close friend as well. Many Marines did not seem to be overly concerned with openly gay service members. To those who did, my message remained consistent.

"Get over it, because our country already has."

I remember a Marine sergeant who pushed back against an anti-gay remark voiced by another Marine grunt. He said that at his last high school reunion in small-town Tennessee his best friend had come out of the closet, then added in his forceful NCO "outside" voice: "And he's still my best friend." American public opinion had changed dramatically since DADT's implementation under President Clinton. And Marine views seemed increasingly—though not uniformly—in sync, indicative of former Joint Chiefs chairman General Colin Powell's own evolution on the matter. Open service, several predicted, would probably be uncontroversial. We discussed how our military needed to welcome into its ranks all qualified Americans. Lying to serve in the USMC— the effective outcome under current policy—seemed to be entirely un– Marine Corps, if not fundamentally un-American.

DADT contradicted the qualities of honor, integrity, and character instilled within the proud and long USMC tradition. This had been former Joint Chiefs chairman Admiral Michael Mullen's own argument in advocating repeal, forcefully conveyed in congressional testimony. I believed the policy also contrasted with America's own persistent march toward greater equality for its diverse array of citizens, not least its citizen-soldiers ordered to serve, repeatedly, in two wars.

Largely status quo silence among gay and lesbian Marines may have ensured their military careers, but at a personal and often cor-rosive cost. One Marine said he knew of cases where closeted Marines got out, when they should have stayed in the service, because of the cumulative toll.

"We have lost some great Marines because of this."

The issue being debated in Washington politico circles really was not a hot-button one for us in the combat zones. We were busy fighting the real wars, not an outdated and overly politicized one.

One top general (not Larry Nicholson) put it this way to me in Helmand: "Marines are first and foremost Marines. That is who we are. Whether gay or not, it doesn't matter in the end. We will still respect and take care of each other, on the battlefield and off."

DADT repeal was not simply an intra-Corps generational matter, pitting younger, next-gen Marines against older, stereotypical recalci-trant ones who "don't get it." I found views across ranks to be more nuanced than that. As a four-star Marine general and self-described "AARP G.O." reminded me, the Pentagon DADT study highlighted that state of origin and religious beliefs tended to shape views at least as much as age group. He added in an email, "As an 'old guy' . . . I actually try to be objective and adaptive on occasion!"

A company commander based at Camp Leatherneck perhaps summed it up best: "Americans are ready for this change and want it done, and we are America's Corps."

Among those assembled on the dank Helmand plain on the eve of the Marjah battle were several Afghan army units, all who would fight alongside Marines. General Conway's question became lost in transla-tion to them—by design. Farid, my linguist, and I both knew that "gays in the military" constituted a fact of life among Afghans. Pashtuns espe-cially were known for the close ties that developed between them. Farid noted that traditional Pashtun poems sometimes celebrated this bond. It is what it is and has been so across centuries, he basically told me.

I asked him to sprint to the Afghan National Army contingent, which had gathered opposite General Conway, adjacent to a row of hulking Marine troop transport vehicles.

"Farid, run and go tell the 'terps not to translate what Conway is saying," I said just above a whisper, not wanting any of the assembled generals to hear.

"I'll try, but it might be too late."

"Well, we gotta try."

I suspected that Afghan and American troops had other and more pressing matters on their minds just before the battle, in line with what the lance corporal had just conveyed.

I watched Farid sprint and interact, face-to-face, with half a dozen linguists, most of whom nodded, as if understanding that their job that day would be to remain silent and not translate the commandant's DADT poll.

But many of the Afghan soldiers looked puzzled, as Marine arms went up or down on either side of them. Only a few feet separated the American grunts from the Afghan grunts. A nearby Afghan general, who spoke English well, later told me confidentially that this topic would cause confusion among his men and likely bad feelings.

"Not good. Not good for training and friendship."

A few days after the commandant's visit to Helmand, hundreds of Marines serving alongside their Afghan army counterparts stormed Marjah. Dozens died in service to their countries. Young bodies fell, gay and straight, amid poppy fields that would soon be covered in vibrant purples and pinks—the deadly battlefield transformed into a stunning kaleidoscope of colors.

Following the official repeal of the DADT policy in September 2011, the Marine Corps became the first branch to send recruiters to interact with interested gay and lesbian candidates at a location in heartland America, in the middle of Oklahoma. And in 2012, the photo of a Marine's return home from Helmand's battlefields circulated across the Internet. In the picture, a Marine sergeant is shown jumping up, embracing his boyfriend—backpack nearby and a large U.S. flag draped in the background of the Marine base in Hawaii.

A Marine friend in California who had served multiple deployments in Iraq and Afghanistan emailed me about the photo. "I don't give a damn either way. I hate public displays of affection whether it is same sex or opposite."

. . .

This much publicized "Battle for Marjah" or Operation Moshtarak (the Dari word for "together") that had commenced mid-February 2010 would last many more months. Dozens of Marines and British troops would be killed or wounded, as would Afghan civilians. By the time General McChrystal and President Karzai visited a "pacified" Marjah, many of the locals had already told Larry and me, "We are Taliban." Some of their greatest fears, they said, were the return of abusive local police, not the Taliban "insurgents" that many considered to be cousins—and literally were cousins, or brothers or fathers or sons.

Kabul's designs to bring into the area a quick-results "government in a box" did not work out so well. The new district governor, Haji Zahir (who had spent many years in Germany), would later be assassinated. And General McChrystal was quoted as calling Marjah "a bleeding ulcer." And yet Marines and British troops had succeeded in pressing large segments of the Taliban out of the area, if only for a while. Poppy production did go down, but not in any sustained way. "Sustainable"—what was and more often what was not—continued to be the watchword throughout the Afghanistan War, a standard of progress that left more than a few Americans and NATO allies disappointed by the end of their tours.

Marjah did have its adrenaline moments, of the kind I had hoped to put well behind me in Fallujah. During one visit into the middle of the district, a young Marine approached me to say, "We see General Nicholson everywhere, even out here with us." That same week Larry and I, the sergeant major, and George, the general's Job-like aide, narrowly avoided small arms fire (AK rounds) directed at us, as well as an RPG and even a Taliban machine gunner who put a series of rounds a few feet to our left.

By early spring, Helmand's governor Mangal, perhaps the Marine Corps' biggest fan in all of Afghanistan, invited Larry and me to join his convoy from the provincial capital in Lashkar Gah to the new district center in Marjah.

Larry, ever a to-the-front-I-will-go type of leader and genuine friend to Afghans (as he had been with Iraqis), said of course. And so with no Marines near us whatsoever—not one—only an armada of drones watching us overhead, we joined the Afghan convoy. To show that, well, American lives were no more valuable than Afghan lives, whether a general officer's or State Department official's. Marines back at Camp Leatherneck were basically freaking out. Not because of my exposure, but rather because of their commanding general's across areas that, while "cleared," were far from safe.

Larry sat next to the governor. I sat next to Helmand's top mullah.

After an hour or so, we arrived via SUVs in Marjah. Once in a central market, I managed to acquire a memento that I had always wanted: a poppy scraper, the small wood and metal tool used to scar poppy bulbs. When the bleeding sap, milky white in color, has dried out, it is collected and becomes the basis for opium.

The made-in-Helmand item would remind me what an escalation of U.S. Marines into a war zone could accomplish. But also what such a policy decision made in remote Washington could not achieve on the ground, as Marines—gay or straight, all well armed, all well trained—maneuvered in a windblown sea of poppies.

Most of them avoided the buried bombs and Taliban bullets, staying alive and keeping their limbs, but not all.

But if the cause be not good, the King himself hath a heavy reckoning to make, when all those legs and arms and heads chopped off in a battle shall join together at the latter day, and cry all, "We died at such a place"— some swearing, some crying for a surgeon, some upon their wives left poor behind them, some upon the debts they owe, some upon their children rawly left. I am afeard there are few die well that die in a battle, for how can they charitably dispose of anything, when blood is their argument? Now, if these men do not die well, it will be a black matter for the King that led them to it— who to disobey were against all proportion of subjection.

WILLIAM SHAKESPEARE, *Henry V*

A Dignified Transfer and The 91

Well beyond Marjah, our Osprey aircraft landed in a placed called Taghaz amid hard and unfriendly stares directed our way from shopkeepers, as if we were aliens descending from the sky, armed, armored— and unwelcome.

Our group noticed a black nanny goat giving birth as we walked along the dirt road to where the "Combat Outpost-in-a-box" was being built. Once we got there, I saw one of the Marines quickly shaving, cutting his chin, because "the general" was near. No scruff allowed. Close by, a little Afghan girl caught my attention, dressed in bright colors, as Afghan kids always seemed to be, amid the surrounding landscape's brown palette. She wriggled her way through razor wire to grab a piece of candy one of the Marines must have thrown her way just before we arrived. An old man, still farming, looked at us with squinting eyes.

Larry and I asked the Marines, all standing at attention, what they did "back home."

Most of the reservists came from Maryland. Their non-Marine jobs included: "mechanic," "community college student," "supervisor of a hospital guard force," and "welder." We shook hands. Before long, it was time to go and continue our visit to a newly built outpost. I walked with a young Marine at the front of the patrol for forty or so minutes as we made our way through salty, wet soil to this new base. The lance corporal joked "the officers are getting tired" as we kept up a much faster pace.

His name was Rick. I saw "Centanni" on his nametag. On the short side, with brown hair and blue eyes, he had an understated way about him. I had nieces living in Southern California at the time, close to where he was from, Yorba Linda in Orange County. Richard Milhous Nixon, a future Navy lieutenant stationed for fourteen months in the Pacific in World War II (South Pacific Combat Air Transport Command), had been born there in a small bungalow in 1913, on his father's modest lemon farm. Rick talked about how he wanted to follow in his dad's footsteps and become a cop. We got to the next base well ahead of the rest of the group and agreed that after the war, it would be time to stay home, in the West, for good—nice people, better weather, a laid-back life—even if the war was still going on. Our way of saying we were homesick without really admitting it. We both pretended we were tougher than that.

The next day, back at Camp Leatherneck, I received an urgent message from a colonel based in Kandahar. "An Afghan man had walked into the market and . . . right where you and the CG just were . . ."

Soon, we heard the rest of the story. The Afghan had walked up to a group of grunts in Taghaz and blew himself up, taking them with him. The suicide attack occurred eighteen or so hours after Larry and I had returned to Leatherneck by Osprey Air, while the Marines stayed back in one of the most dangerous parts of Afghanistan.

I sensed the general and I had been the magnet for the bombing.

The worst news like this always arrived in the same way with the same words, an all too common email headline in Helmand.

RIVER CITY IS NOW IN EFFECT

The subject line seemed pastoral, not funereal. The email went to everyone on the distribution list declaring one thing: death had visited again.

A "River City" alert signaled a communications blackout until family members back home were notified about their dead, only a matter of hours until they faced their new reality. Life without their Marine, killed most often by bombs, sometimes by a sniper's bullet, or in a helicopter crash. No one could predict how long it would take. Marine Casualty Assistance Calls Officers (CACO), spread across all fifty states, had one job ahead.

"Notification of next of kin."

Only when they had completed their knocking at a front door— "On behalf of the Secretary of the Navy, I regret to inform you . . ."— did we receive the other message, that email and phone restrictions had been lifted. CACO teams visit no later than midnight and no earlier than 5 a.m. and do so in pairs, wearing their green-and-khaki-colored service uniforms, the USMC's version of a suit. The protocol is precise. I imagined, however, the reactions to them were anything but.

My knowledge went a lot deeper than the initial e-blackout notice regarding more U.S. troop casualties. Given my role at Camp Leatherneck, I knew right away how our Marines died, and I saw the survivors before they were transported to Landstuhl in Germany. If they made it past the medical machines there, Bethesda Naval Hospital in Maryland awaited them. Larry and I always went together. We talked to the best friends of the dead. We heard how the dead died. We heard how the survivors survived.

All our KIA received a "dignified transfer." This meant Marines and I lined up several rows deep, often at night, sometimes in the middle of the day on a desert-summer-hot or desert-winter-cold tarmac, as bodies were transferred to a C-130 for the flight home. As we stood still, Mortuary Affairs duty Marines (whose job specialty had since been formally renamed as "Personnel Retrieval and Processing") always pulled up last in a jeep-like vehicle. It looked several decades old, World War II era even, with a wide and high back camper-like area, big enough for multiple bodies. A chaplain read their names as each was carried thirty or so meters to the waiting cargo plane. On these trips the only cargo was the flag-draped coffins.

In Helmand that year, summer 2009 to summer 2010, we had ninety-one KIA, ninety-one dignified transfers.

The first goodbyes for our dead happened at the platoon level, in unscripted and authentic words, before the formal transfer of our KIA home for good. These were the most personal of memorials, the most raw. Words I wished could be put in stone along the National Mall in Washington, verbatim, or at least broadcast, in real time, to the offices of senators and executive branch bosses. Old men forced to hear dead young men's war stories from those who knew them best.

A Navy Corpsman described how his friend "fought to get back on the deployment list" and, before leaving for Afghanistan, wrote on one of his personal checks the following:

"To the United States of America: Paid in Full."

Then he signed it. The "just in case" happened.

"I wish I could have done more to save him. He loved *Star Trek*."

The Corpsman said both of them had attended another KIA memorial earlier in their tour. Afterward, his friend said he did not want his own tribute to be similarly sad and made him swear "to make it funny" if he died.

He kept his promise. I heard Marines laughing, if awkwardly, during the memorial. In addition to the *Star Trek* line, the buddy recounted jokes the dead Marine had played on other platoon members.

Another grunt remembered his friend this way: "I came in the Corps screwed up. I tried to break him, and he ended up changing me."

After the dead Marine's buddy delivered his tribute, he walked back to his other buddies who had been luckier, staying alive for one more day, one more week, one more month. The odds were with them so far, but as in poker, someone always draws losing cards.

This particular memorial at Forward Operating Base Fiddler's Green marked more Marines gone—one of whom, I had been told, had been decapitated by a buried bomb.

That night at our daily 5:30 brief—which recounted all the day's events and, often, firefights throughout our 200-square-kilometer area of operation—Larry, ever the stoic commander, said it had been a "tough day, but there would be more."

. . .

After the meeting, we made our way to Bastion hospital, as was our unfortunate routine. As we entered, the first wounded Marine on a gurney moaned in the operating room. The Navy doctor on duty briefed us right away.

"He was very lucky. Shrapnel just missed his aorta."

There was so much antiseptic splashed on the junior Marine, I thought it was blood at first, but by then I knew the fluid's orangish red color was not quite the crimson shade of what pumped through human veins and hearts. I had seen too much of the real thing in both wars. He would likely survive, we were told.

The next WIA was the welder from our Taghaz visit. The doc said he was still in shock, but wanted to talk to us. The Marine described what happened.

"We were just off duty, heard an explosion . . ."

He went on, "I turned and saw my buddy dead. I knew he didn't make it. There was so much blood on the ground and some of it on me."

His eyes drifted downward as his words trailed off. The firsthand suicide bomber sitrep (situation report) ended. I could tell he was replaying the image of the attack, grinding a middle fingernail into another finger, trying to continue to tell the story. The general was there, after all.

"I haven't told my wife yet."

I asked if he needed anything—not that I had anything to give. His friends had just been blown up next to him, a few feet away.

"I'm fine, sir."

As we left, he tried to stand up next to his bed at attention. The general ordered him to lie back down on the mattress.

That night we attended the dignified transfer ceremony for all the KIA that day. I counted four boxes for three bodies. Sometimes, remains could not be matched with the bodies—or the remains were found later. I hated seeing when the numbers did not match up, because I knew someone had the job of recovering body parts, including times when they landed in deep green canal water or were scattered along a weed-filled path near canals the U.S. had funded and built half a century earlier.

We had been briefed on how two Marines stood guard all night near the location of a bomb that had killed a fellow Marine. As the sun rose, they stepped left, right, forward, in some direction—probably just a few inches but enough movement to trigger another IED, killing them both.

There would be many more visits to Bastion's operating and recovery rooms, as well as to the flight line as our KIA were loaded into the bellies of more C-130s to begin their final journey home. Only the luckiest of the most severely wounded made it within the "golden hour" to medical personnel. The rest died in *Hell*-mand, as the Marines called their new desert home.

The British ran Bastion hospital. Some of our Navy doctors helped staff it alongside the Brits. But most memorably for countless Marines, a contingent of Danish nurses did as well. One in particular was very good at her job and made sure every rule was followed, even for us know-it-all and entitled Americans. This no-nonsense Dane was the boss, outranking the general and me in her mind and in ours, once we entered her hospital.

Larry and I visited the wounded there almost nightly, the double, triple, quadruple amputees. Corporals, captains. One named Corporal Nicely—a name that stuck—had survived quadruple amputation. He had a tube in the side of his rib cage, what was left of him under a green blanket with some blood on it—and "Fi" from a "Semper Fi" tattoo inked above, on his pale chest. A medical technician, working on a vein in his arm, said the doctors "usually start to cut just below the knee, if they can." We were told he had been the lead Marine on the patrol when he stepped on the IED, and was only the second U.S. service member to survive quadruple amputations.

Looking down, I wanted to look away but did not. I wondered how someone could still be alive after so much damage, so little of him on the bed. He had been twice as tall only hours earlier. Machines buzzed. Tubes pulsed. Digital displays blinked. Transfusion bags dangled. I smelled rubbing-alcohol-like antiseptic. Corporal Nicely's eyes stayed closed.

Larry teared up, along with the rest of us. The sergeant major kissed the corporal on the forehead. In my notebook that night I wrote, "So sick of this, about this. Don't want to go to hospital again."

But we did, again and again and again.

In the tent on my cot, I kept thinking about the other person doctors had saved that day. In a bed across the room from Corporal Nicely, an armed Marine stood guard, which drew our attention right away. The wounded man, who looked only a few years older than Nicely, sat up, surrounded by similarly high-priced and top-line medical equipment. He was Afghan. He was in much better shape.

A nurse saw us looking.

"He's Taliban."

In a separate hospital visit, Senator John McCain would ask staff about the same man. "Who's that guy?" The doctor replied, "An insurgent. We treat the bad guys here too." McCain did not look pleased.

Some patients made it through until morning, but not all. One shredded Marine died while we stood at his bedside. So young, he went so fast, barely half of him left on the slickened operating room table, white-then-red surgical gloves and shiny, sharp trauma room instruments—a frantic but failing blur of motion under unforgiving bright lights.

Week after week, more wounded Marines shared their stories of survival with us, when life and death could be measured in inches or minutes or armor. A banged-up corporal had a tube sewn to his lip so that it would not move. From the neck up, massive facial lacerations made him appear like a young Frankenstein, his body built like a linebacker. The stitches zigzagged across both cheeks, under his chin, and above his eyebrows. He said the IED had been hidden in an unusual place.

"We didn't check up on the wall, then it went off on me."

Another Marine, from Wisconsin, also had bad cuts on his face and below both eyes. He confessed to the general he had been "stupid" for not wearing his eye protection (goggles) because he said it fogged up his "nerdy" glasses. I told him I had a twin brother with a scar under one eye, which women liked.

His blue eyes widened. "Well, I guess I'll be able to find me that one special brown-eyed girl then."

A Marine in the bed next to him said he had called his mom.

"She did not react that bad, but my ex-girlfriend started to bawl."

When the IED exploded, he said he remembered seeing smoke, then hitting the ground in a lot of pain. He asked the general for permission to return to his unit.

"Denied," said the commanding general of almost 20,000 U.S. Marines.

"I concur," I said.

Nearby, another grunt, with a black eye right out of *The Little Rascals*, told us a sniper had missed him by "half an inch. I popped my head up one last time and he got me. I'm the luckiest guy in the world." The bullet ricocheted off his helmet. I did not ask how he got the bruise because it did not matter. He was alive.

A Marine from Detroit, our final stop among what seemed to be an endless list of wounded, showed off his "Motor City" tattoos, reminding me of the Army soldier from Detroit I had met in Sadr City. But it was his other tattoo that grabbed our attention right away. An image of scissors and "Cut here if captured" inked just below his neck. Tough guy, we could tell. When Larry asked him about his "MOS" (Military Occupational Specialty), i.e., job, he broke down.

"I can't stop thinking about who is going to take over the squad."

He explained another Marine had just lost his sister in a car crash, and the next in line to take charge had a pregnant wife.

"I keep thinking how I don't want to put them in that position."

As we left, I noticed a container on a table bedside with small metal fragments from IED shrapnel—a different kind of war booty for war's survivors.

On another long night at the hospital, when the head Danish nurse was in a good mood, we walked in just as medics carried in a British soldier. Half of his scalp was gone and chunks from his right side. He cried out but appeared blind, motioning with one hand toward his head. He looked and sounded like he was dying, a voice of panic and pain in equal measure amid dwindling volume. A trail of blood marked the twelve feet or so they moved him to the trauma ward. Larry and I sat outside as the front door swung shut, in two empty wheelchairs, the only seats around.

We were girding ourselves for another round in the hospital.

Once inside, the Navy doc briefed us per the usual protocol. Again, more than I wanted to know. Needed to know. The first Marine we met had a "decent" prognosis according to the expert with an MD and who gave us a precise rundown of the injuries: "Lower leg wound, testicle damage, left hand, he's breathing hard. He doesn't know yet, but the other two Marines with him are KIA."

He doesn't know yet . . . that part would hurt him most, I thought, when he does know. *And that news might be what kills him in the end—survivor's guilt.*

We walked down the corridor, which reminded me of the shiny tile floor of my elementary school and some of the schools we funded in Afghanistan. The kind of surface that is continuously polished, but in this case not for playground dust but mopped for battlefield blood.

The general looked my way. "I don't see how anyone can work here. Glad someone can."

"I hate hospitals," I said.

Larry and I entered the rooms of our battlefield wounded for a reason. To witness. To listen. To remember. To tell. This time we found ourselves among Afghans.

In one corner, I saw a young boy, probably no older than seven or eight. He had a big smile on his face and played with the stump of a leg, an amputee just below the knee. Next to him sat his father, head held low, between legs, sitting, pretzel-like, the way only Afghans or world-class gymnasts can. The son looked at us; the father did not, as if he was trying to disappear into his chair. Odds were it had been one of our bombs that had landed in their compound. The kid had survived, luckily, and was treating his shortened leg as a new toy, courtesy of Uncle Sam's best ordnance.

In a hospital bed near the Afghan boy, a Marine wore a head brace, "fractures to his upper spine," the doc said. What I initially thought were freckles were dirt and rock fragments, small bloody ones, across his cheeks and forehead. He had been sandblasted by the IED. A Danish nurse continued the narration for us.

"No hearing from the blast, he's another one who doesn't know about his friend yet."

Larry talked to the Marine, but we knew he could not hear us. The whole time he cried, tears streaming out of both eyes, and said nothing. The general and I could only imagine what kind of images were replaying in his mind. He was watching a horror reel, but a real one. His buddy had lost both legs, above the knee, before dying. He must have seen enough to know. Even if hospital staff had not yet told him that his friend did not make it after they placed him on a helicopter for urgent evacuation.

His friend being another American KIA in Afghanistan, in America's longest war, after the war was escalated—twice in one year by two commanders in chief.

And then there was the English patient.

A British photographer had been in an MRAP in Nawa District when a huge IED, estimated to be 200 pounds of HME—homemade explosives—detonated. Marines told me it hit the "sweet spot," lifting the entire multi-ton, V-shaped hull ten feet in an instant. His lower shin disintegrated from the shock wave, requiring his lower leg to be removed.

The blast killed Marine Lance Corporal Mark D. Juarez (23, of San Antonio, Texas, pop. 1,409,000), along with a British reporter, Rupert Hamer (39, of the East Anglia region of the United Kingdom, pop. 5,847,000), while the MRAP's driver was lifted out of the wreckage, paralyzed from the chest down. I was told both were the first KIA in a Marine MRAP.

Since no British government representative was available, I volunteered to pass on any message the wounded photographer had to British diplomats in Lashkar Gah and Kabul. For that night, I became his official messenger.

He only had one request: "Just make sure someone is there to hold her. Will someone put their arm around her?"

He repeated. "Will someone put their arm around her? My partner, she's four months pregnant."

I said I would. I could tell he loved her in a way I could never convey in words. It was in the way he asked, the way he looked, the way he wanted her to be taken care of.

He made no requests for himself.

Before General Nicholson and I left for the night, a Marine who had lost a testicle when a piece of metal passed through his scrotum offered a self-diagnosis.

"Well, now I guess I'm like Lance Armstrong."

This comment made us all laugh, including himself.

Recognizing Larry, he went on to explain some shared war biography.

"I remember you, sir, from Fallujah," explaining he had pulled security at the regimental command after the rocket that almost killed Larry had exploded in September 2004, five years earlier. Of all things, we three were having a Fallujah reunion in a combat hospital in Helmand. He added he was also one of the Marines blasted into the wall when another rocket hit the front gate outside the regimental head-quarters at Camp Fallujah. I told him I recalled both days as well. Mortars tended to be exclamation points in the brain's wiring.

All of us agreed we had been in the wars too long.

"I work for the State Department, which means I get to say thank you on behalf of our country, even if our country is disconnected from what is going on over here. You are serving at a very important time."

I do not know if my words helped. They did not come out how I wanted. I sounded anesthetized myself.

Two of the hardest conversations came toward the end of my year in Helmand. A young Marine had survived a medium-sized blast. Doctors stopped Larry, his aide, George, and me before we reached him.

"He doesn't know it yet, but when he gets to Germany, they are going to have to take one leg."

For the next fifteen minutes, we had to keep that secret from him. He was in a good mood. He and his buddies had survived, he said. A close call, but someone was looking out for them, he went on. At least for a few more hours, he could continue to believe he would keep both of his legs, both covered by a blanket crumpled just above his waist.

I thought about when doctors would tell him the news at Landstuhl—before or after the operation?

Doctors had temporarily stabilized a badly wounded Marine we met earlier in the evening. He was plugged to a machine, unconscious, and looked really bad. A different doctor, with a British accent, walked over to the general and me as we were leaving after midnight to go back to the Ark, our plywood office.

"We had to take both legs off at mid-section. He is going to lose his fight. We found parts of his boots blasted into his stomach.

"The metal parts that hold shoelaces in."

Less than two months after we met in southernmost Helmand, Rick Centanni died at age nineteen. He was the driver of a Light Armored

Vehicle (LAV) destroyed by a massive IED, which also killed Sergeant Major Robert Cottle, a twenty-year member of the LAPD and its SWAT team and married father of a nine-month-old daughter.

It took Marines over a day to recover their remains. Parts of the LAV had melted.

At Lance Corporal Centanni's and Sergeant Major Cottle's dignified transfers and memorials, many men, many boys, cried.

River City restrictions, the mandated communications blackout between the warzone and the U.S., were eventually lifted after a pair of front doors had been opened at two homes in Southern California.

The ninety-one KIA during the 2nd Marine Expeditionary Brigade's deployment to Afghanistan in 2009–2010:

LCpl Joshua R. Whittle
of Downey, California, pop. 113,242
age 20

CWO2 Ricky L. Richardson
of Franklin, Missouri, pop. 97
age 33

LCpl Charles S. Sharp
of Adairsville, Georgia, pop. 4,716
age 20

MSgt John E. Hayes
of Middleburg, Florida, pop. 13,008
age 36

LCpl Roger G. Hager
of Gibsonville, North Carolina, pop. 6,640
age 20

Cpl Matthew R. Lembke
of Tualatin, Oregon, pop. 26,879
age 22

MSgt Jerome D. Hatfield
of Axton, Virginia, pop. 6,645
age 36

LCpl Pedro A. Barboza Flores
of Glendale, California, pop. 196,021
age 27

GySgt David S. Spicer
of Zanesfield, Ohio, pop. 25,435
age 33

Sgt Michael W. Heede, Jr.
of Delta, Pennsylvania, pop. 728
age 22

Sgt Ryan H. Lane
of Pittsburgh, Pennsylvania, pop. 305,841
age 25

LCpl Jeremy S. Lasher
of Oneida, New York, pop. 11,262
age 27

Cpl Nicholas G. Xiarhos
of Yarmouth, Massachusetts, pop. 23,793
age 21

PFC Donald W. Vincent
of Gainesville, Florida, pop. 127,488
age 26

LCpl Gregory A. Posey
of Knoxville, Tennessee, pop. 183,270
age 22

LCpl Jonathan F. Stroud
of Cashion, Oklahoma, pop. 832
age 20

PO3 Anthony C. Garcia
of Tyndall, Florida, pop. 2,994
age 21

Cpl Christian A. Guzman Rivera
of Homestead, Florida, pop. 64,079
age 21

LCpl Travis T. Babine
of San Antonio, Texas, pop. 1,409,000
age 20

LCpl James D. Argentine
of Farmingdale, New York, pop. 8,239
age 22

Sgt Jay M. Hoskins
of Paris, Texas, pop. 24,912
age 24

LCpl Dennis J. Burrow
of Naples, Florida, pop. 20,537
age 23

LCpl Javier Olvera
of Palmdale, California, pop. 157,161
age 20

LCpl Patrick W. Schimmel
of Winfield, Missouri, pop. 1,418
age 21

LCpl Bruce E. Ferrell
of Perdido, Alabama, pop. 1,218
age 21

Sgt William (Bill) J. Cahir
of Washington, D.C., pop. 658,893
age 40

LCpl Joshua M. Bernard
of New Portland, Maine, pop. 718
age 21

LCpl Leopold F. Damas
of Floral Park, New York, pop. 15,907
age 26

GySgt Adam F. Benjamin
of Garfield Heights, Ohio, pop. 28,378
age 34

LCpl Donald J. Hogan
of San Clemente, California, pop. 65,040
age 20

LCpl David R. Hall
of Elyria, Ohio, pop. 53,956
age 31

LCpl Christopher S. Baltazar, Jr.
of San Antonio, Texas, pop. 1,409,000
age 19

PO3 Benjamin "Doc Stiggy" P. Castiglione
of Howell, Michigan, pop. 9,557
age 21

LCpl Christopher S. Fowlkes
of Gaffney, South Carolina, pop. 12,657
age 20

LCpl John J. Malone
of Yonkers, New York, pop. 199,766
age 24

LCpl Jordan L. Chrobot
of Frederick, Maryland, pop. 66,893
age 24

SPC Kevin O. Hill
of Brooklyn, New York, pop. 2,592,000
age 23

SSgt Aaron J. Taylor
of Bovey, Minnesota, pop. 816
age 27

LCpl Alfonso Ochoa, Jr.
of Armona, California, pop. 4,156
age 20

LCpl David R. Baker
of Painesville, Ohio, pop. 19,933
age 22

Capt Kyle R. Van De Giesen
of North Attleborough, Massachusetts, pop. 27,143
age 29

Cpl Gregory M. Fleury
of Anchorage, Alaska, pop. 300,950
age 23

Capt Eric A. Jones
of Westchester, New York, pop. 968,802
age 29

Capt David S. Mitchell
of Loveland, Ohio, pop. 12,326
age 30

LCpl Cody R. Stanley
of Rosanky, Texas, pop. 679
age 21

Sgt Cesar B. Ruiz
of San Antonio, Texas, pop. 1,409,000
age 26

LCpl Justin J. Swanson
of Anaheim, California, pop. 345,012
age 21

LCpl Shawn P. Hefner
of Hico, Texas, pop. 1,347
age 22

LCpl Nicholas J. Hand
of Kansas City, Missouri, pop. 467,007
age 20

LCpl Jonathan A. Taylor
of Jacksonville, Florida, pop. 842,583
age 22

Cpl Xhacob Latorre
of Waterbury, Connecticut, pop. 109,676
age 21

LCpl Omar G. Roebuck
of Moreno Valley, California, pop. 201,175
age 23

LCpl Mark D. Juarez
of San Antonio, Texas, pop. 1,409,000
age 23

LCpl Jacob A. Meinert
of Fort Atkinson, Wisconsin, pop. 12,482
age 20

Cpl Nicholas K. Uzenski
of Bozeman, Montana, pop. 39,860
age 21

Cpl Jamie R. Lowe
of Johnsonville, Illinois, pop. 77
age 21

SSgt Matthew N. Ingham
of Altoona, Pennsylvania, pop. 45,796
age 24

Sgt Christopher R. Hrbek
of Westwood, New Jersey, pop. 11,075
age 25

LCpl Jeremy M. Kane
of Towson, Maryland, pop. 55,197
age 22

PO2 Xin Qi
of Cordova, Tennessee, pop. 34,728
age 25

LCpl Timothy J. Poole, Jr.
of Bowling Green, Kentucky, pop. 61,488
age 22

Sgt Daniel M. Angus
of Thonotosassa, Florida, pop. 13,014
age 28

LCpl Zachary D. Smith
of Hornell, New York, pop. 8,473
age 19

Sgt David J. Smith
of Frederick, Maryland, pop. 66,893
age 25

LCpl Michael L. Freeman, Jr.
of Fayetteville, Pennsylvania, pop. 3,128
age 21

Cpl Jacob H. Turbett
of Canton, Michigan, pop. 90,173
age 21

PFC Jason H. Estopinal
of Dallas, Georgia, pop. 12,415
age 21

LCpl Noah M. Pier
of Charlotte, North Carolina, pop. 792,862
age 25

LCpl Alejandro J. Yazzie
of Rock Point, Arizona, pop. 642
age 23

PFC Eric D. Currier
of Londonderry, New Hampshire, pop. 24,129
age 21

LCpl Larry M. Johnson
of Scranton, Pennsylvania, pop. 75,806
age 19

Sgt Jeremy R. McQueary
of Columbus, Indiana, pop. 45,775
age 27

LCpl Kielen T. Dunn
of Virginia Beach, Virginia, pop. 448,479
age 19

PFC Kyle J. Coutu
of Providence, Rhode Island, pop. 177,994
age 20

LCpl Joshua H. Birchfield
of Westville, Indiana, pop. 5,956
age 24

Cpl Gregory S. Stultz
of Brazil, Indiana, pop. 8,171
age 22

SSgt Christopher W. Eckard
of Hickory, North Carolina, pop. 40,361
age 30

LCpl Matthias N. Hanson
of Buffalo, Kentucky, pop. 498
age 20

LCpl Adam D. Peak
of Florence, Kentucky, pop. 31,423
age 25

LCpl Eric L. Ward
of Redmond, Washington, pop. 57,530
age 19

LCpl Carlos A. Aragon
of Orem, Utah, pop. 91,648
age 19

LCpl Nigel K. Olsen
of Salem, Utah, pop. 6,928
age 21

LCpl Garrett W. Gamble
of Sugar Land, Texas, pop. 83,860
age 20

Cpl Jonathan D. Porto
of Largo, Florida, pop. 78,409
age 26

LCpl Justin J. Wilson
of Palm City, Florida, pop. 23,120
age 24

SgtMaj Robert J. Cottle
of Whittier, California, pop. 86,635
age 45

LCpl Rick J. Centanni
of Yorba Linda, California, pop. 67,032
age 19

LCpl Jacob A. Ross
of Gillette, Wyoming, pop. 31,797
age 19

Sgt Frank J. World
of Buffalo, New York, pop. 258,959
age 25

LCpl Tyler O. Griffin
of Voluntown, Connecticut, pop. 2,603
age 19

LCpl Curtis M. Swenson
of Rochester, Minnesota, pop. 106,769
age 20

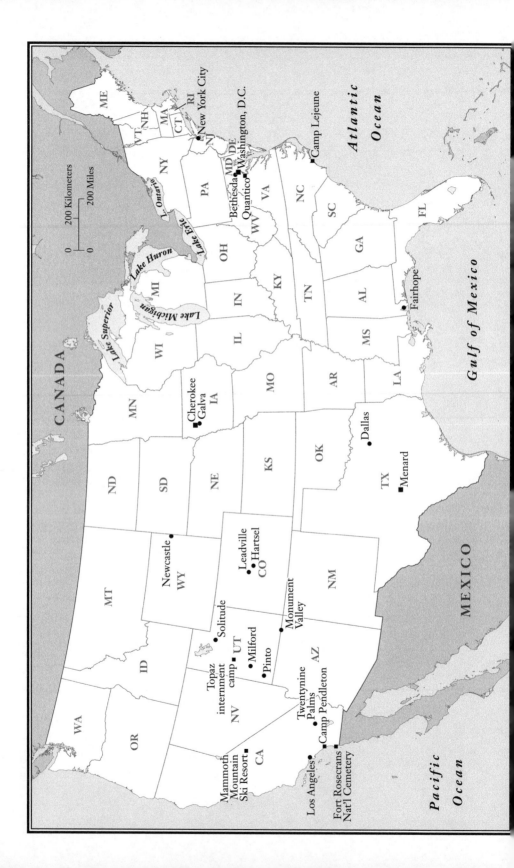

PART III

Home

The mirror follows us, but it's not a friend.

CHARLES DE LEUSSE

You just can't believe the joy I did receive
When I finally got my leave and I was going home
Oh, I flew through the sky my convictions could not lie
For my country I would die and I will see it soon

"LOVE VIGILANTES," NEW ORDER

To Cherokee, Iowa

I had finally left the wars, even if the wars had not left me, any of us. My dad and uncles could relate. They still had Vietnam in them. One with shrapnel embedded inside him. Another battled the health effects of Herbicide Orange (aka Agent Orange) decades after his job had ended, part of Operation Ranch Hand clearing jungle roads and destroying crops with the poisonous defoliant. The Vietnamese people we sickened with our 2,3,7,8-tetrachlorodibenzodioxin compound, TCDD for short—an estimated 20 million gallons dumped and sprayed—suffered on a much greater scale. Millions.

For me, Helmand had taken its toll. We had ninety-one KIA, almost matching the number in Fallujah across 2006, ninety-three KIA, and ten times as many wounded in both places. Good friends were killed in southern Afghanistan: in October 2008, Trevor Yurista from a Taliban IED, detonating below his Humvee, the blast breaking his neck; and in August 2009, Bill Cahir from a Taliban bullet in the chest. Two junior Marines, Nigel Olsen and Carlos Aragon, had also been killed a few days apart in southernmost Helmand. Both graduated from my high school years after I had. Lance Corporal Aragon was born in Chihuahua, Mexico, a month after I got my diploma, Olsen the year before, reinforcing just how young they were when they died, fighting on behalf of the nation, a nation of immigrants.

As I had for Bill, I attended their memorial service held in a windy, dusty Marine combat outpost. A Marine who spoke that day said he would miss sharing early morning breakfast, a quiet ritual they enjoyed in a loud war.

Weeks later, one of the KIA Marines' mothers told my mother she wanted to talk with me about the Afghanistan War.

What might she ask? What would I say?

The mother never asked. So I never had to say.

Many more troops had been wounded while patrolling between U.S.-built canals and purple poppy fields—all those WIA Larry and I had visited so often in the Bastion field hospital. And then there were the Afghans, hundreds and hundreds dead, most by insurgents but some by our errant bombs or after U.S. military night raids had gone wrong or were conducted without enough discipline. I knew I would be thinking of Ghader Gol and his family in Khost for a long time, Dilawar and his—and so many Marine families.

The Helmand Experience, on top of the Fallujah Experience, made me reconsider my profession, my career in the U.S. government. A job that, by tradition at least, was all about preventing warfare, not dealing in real time with not only one but two wars, both fast becoming America's longest. A job that had entailed a painful red spectrum:

The Potato Factory, in Iraq, where we processed Iraqi dead.

Dignified transfers, in Afghanistan, where we said farewell to our own.

There had been some good days in Khost too, but not enough. Four years in a wrong war, three years in a right war, and now home.

What next? What next. What does one do, or not do, after coming back from seven consecutive years in two wars? Surviving, somehow, seven consecutive years in two wars.

·   ·   ·

I recalled how when I took the State Department's Foreign Service Exam over a decade earlier, it contained standard questions about English grammar and usage, the U.S. Constitution, and the history of American wars: World War I, World War II, even a couple on Vietnam—an American war lost.

There was also a nonwar topic that had always stood out in my mind in the years since. One of the test's multiple-choice answers listed Jelly Roll Morton, a jazz musician. American diplomats were expected to be "well-rounded." Know your twentieth-century wars. Know your twentieth-century jazz. I knew my wars. I am not sure I got the music question right. And yet in both wars, I met Iraqis and Afghans who could name numerous jazz and pop and rap and rock "Born in the USA"–type musicians. Soft power exemplified and underappreciated in Washington, I think, in a time of these two very hard and very long American conflicts, in a time of expanding drone warfare and torture-as-policy.

Another problem-solving question, randomly assigned on exam day, dealt with cross-border infant adoptions. I was given this hypothetical case study about diplomatic friction between the U.S. and Russian governments. I did my best to try to help solve, via my imagination, this bilateral dilemma. A separate role-play team scenario had us test takers, seated around a table as a group, prioritize a mock U.S. embassy budget. I had a weak project to pitch and acknowledged as much, speaking last and finishing early, well before my allotted time was up.

With some luck, I passed the exam's two parts. Of course nothing in the written test or the oral interview that followed related to Iraq and Afghanistan, America's twenty-first-century wars. Or Daesh—aka ISIS or ISIL or the Islamic State. All of us back then had been quizzed and vetted in more peaceful times. After being told I had made the cut-off score for new political officers (one year before September 2001), State Department overseers asked me to confirm that I understood the profession's cardinal premise and nonnegotiable condition for employment: "worldwide availability."

"Yes," came my one-word reply.

I was almost tempted to raise my right hand for emphasis, having no idea that soon a U.S. invasion would be under way in Iraq and, seventeen months before that, a massive bombing campaign along the easternmost part of Afghanistan. The latter justified, the former not at all. Along with U.S. troops, U.S. diplomats would be at war.

My name was put on a rank-ordered "eligible hires" list, and I went about filling out paperwork required for a medical clearance and a Top Secret security clearance. The most memorable question in that process being, "Have you ever done anything that would embarrass the U.S. government?" I did not hesitate and I did not plead the Fifth and I got my Top Secret clearance. In the years and State Department work that ensued, I realized that starting but not being able to end an unnecessary war, à la the Iraq invasion, amounted to a much bigger indictment, and tragedy, than any youthful indiscretion.

A question of my own came to mind for American leaders and politicians: "Has the U.S. government done anything, of late particularly, that would endanger international peace and security?" "If yes, please elaborate." Now that would be a conversation worth having, an American mirror to gaze into for a long time and not look away.

Today, in an updated version of the exam, Foreign Service candidates are asked to provide a "personal narrative." Examiners want to verify a candidate's "leadership," "interpersonal skills," "communication skills," "management skills," "intellectual skills," and "substantive knowledge" through real-life examples.

Fallujah, Khost, Sadr City, and Helmand had taught me a lot about all of that, and perhaps a bit more. Still, I had to wonder what kind of hire-me essay I would write after my nonstop State Department wartime deployments. How much of a war narrative it would be, and not by choice either. I wanted to think I would begin with a focus on Iraqis (Hamza maybe, or Abbas), or Afghans (Sardar probably, along with Arif), or Marines (Larry, of course, and General Dunford and several infantry NCOs, Civil Affairs officers, and rifle company commanders)—all those who also had persevered through both wars. It would be a long essay with many firsthand examples.

Before leaving the country, some Afghans had given me farewell gifts, like Iraqis had in my last days in Fallujah. When I left Helmand, I had no desire to reminisce. A contradiction soon became apparent after my return home: War nostalgia, both imagined and manufactured, across the United States among those who had never experienced war firsthand—or knew anyone deployed to either war.

My black footlockers eventually arrived stateside. I had triple-taped and shipped them from Camp Leatherneck. They had "SFO" labels, marking the West Coast airport transit point on their way to the 11,000-foot Wasatch Mountains. Where I had begun to decompress a bit at Utah's scenic Solitude Mountain Resort, aptly named, a place surrounded by aspen and spruce, mountain bike trails and ski lifts. And where two blue jays dependably showed up, I was told (and sometimes saw myself while on leave), each spring on the deck and left, together, each fall.

It was, at long last, time to unpack in every way. As I emptied the dented, dirty, and once mini-padlocked containers with FPO AE stickers still on them (the U.S. postal designation for military bases), it all came back. Khost and Helmand came back as I sifted through items in my hands.

Surprisingly, strangely, gratefully, and, yes, finally, I felt ready to go through what was inside them . . . inside me.

One of the first items I held was a plaque from a friend, who had helped coordinate de-mining efforts in Now Zad District. It read:

> Pressure-plate for an improvised landmine constructed by the Taliban out of a humanitarian cooking oil can donated by the American people.

The can's silver metal plating shows the blue USAID symbol, below which, mostly rusted away, is the agency's signature handshake. A lot of these bombs had taken the legs of a lot of Marines. There were Pashtun music CDs inside, which madrassa students in Khost had given me, reminding me how much many of them liked radios and thereby rebelled against the more strict mullahs. Several black and gray turbans lay at the bottom of one footlocker. Afghan tribal elders had presented them, arms extended, after a final chai-filled negotiation about deteriorating security in their districts. And a gray Pakol hat, made of wool, which a Khost U. student from a rural area wanted me to have, and even a sequined Khandari cap, like those madrassa students wore, reminding me that two or more handshakes are always better than one in a country far from home and where war had made its home for three decades and counting.

I dug up a bright, shiny basket, covered in reflective gold-colored foil wrapping (looking like an Easter egg basket). Former Taliban fighters offered it as a farewell gift. Inside was a bottle of jasmine perfume spray . . . also a gift from the former Taliban cadre. There was an alabaster carving, with my name on it, next to "Presented by Governor Mangal" of Helmand; I had accidentally dropped at the Dubai airport near passport control the other alabaster carving he had given me, shattering it in a dozen pieces. *Just jinxed myself,* I thought at the time. Three small teakettles clanked together, colored light blue and yellow, oxidized on both the inside and out. I had bought them in Musa Kehl District, not far from a district center we had funded but that remained half built. They were just like the ones Qalandar elders used to serve milky tea to guests (at least well-behaved ones who noticed the ill-condition of their forests).

I saw a rough red brick, made locally in Khost, the kind used to build schools for boys and girls. I pulled out dozens of Marine-issued lime green notebooks as well, which served as a journal of sorts in both wars. These were where I had recorded the details, almost transcript-like, of Dilawar's death, the concerns and hopes of Khost U. students, as well as the voices of the former Guantánamo detainees, and so many more true war stories.

I had also stowed dark green sheets with white trim that I first bought at a Camp Fallujah PX on base in summer 2004 and used to cover my cot through both wars. They still had a bit of Helmand sand in them. Wrapped in one set were a few books: *The Poetry of Rahman Baba, Poet of the Pukhtuns* by Robert Sampson and Momin Khan, a 2006 printing of a *Pashto Dictionary and Phrasebook*, an old edition of *The City of the Saints and Across the Rocky Mountains to California*, by explorer-writer Richard F. Burton. A book I would later place on a shelf next to another favorite character and story with a Western theme: *Silas Soule: A Short, Eventful Life of Moral Courage* by Tom Bensing. (Maine-born Silas S. stood up against the slaughter of Cheyenne and Arapahoe tribes in Colorado, later known as the Sand Creek Massacre. He refused to shoot his rifle, and had a tragic end himself because of it, dead at the age of twenty-six only one month after getting married.)

Ken Burns's compact-disc series *The Civil War* and his production of *The West* were in a shoebox. The former had storylines that reminded me of Larry and Marines and how common people and common soldiers lose biggest in war (the journal of Private Samuel Rush Watkins, for instance, of the First Tennessee Infantry Regiment, Com-

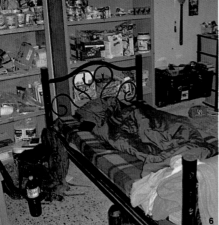

FACILITY RULES
قوانين الموقع

RULE 1: You will obey all written and verbal orders from all American military personnel.

قاعدة رقم ١: سوف تطيع جميع القوانين سواء الشفهية منها او المكتوبة التي تصدر من جميع العسكريين الامريكان

RULE 2: You will immediately sit down and place your hands on your head with fingers interlocked whenever you hear three whistles or horn blasts or the word "Halt". The Marine guards are authorized to use force, up to deadly force, if you do not obey this rule.

قاعدة رقم ٢: سوف تجلس على الارض حالا واضعا يديك متشابكة على رأسك كلما تسمع ثلاثة صافرات أو صوت البوق او كلمة "قف". حراس المارينز مخولين باستخدام القوة المميتة اذا لم تطع الاوامر

RULE 3: You will not interfere with, threaten, or harm any American military personnel.

قاعدة رقم ٣: يجب ان لا تقوم بتهديد او الحاق الاذى بالاشخاص الامريكان

RULE 4: You must have your capture tag and wristband or badge in your possession at all times.

قاعدة رقم ٤: يجب ان تحمل طوال الوقت قيد الاعتقال او بطاقة التعريف

RULE 5: You will keep your body and your living areas clean. You will only urinate or defecate in designated areas.

قاعدة رقم ٥: يجب ان تحافظ على نظافتك الشخصية والمنطقة التي تعيش فيها وسوف تتبول وتتغوط في الاماكن المخصصة لذلك

RULE 6: You will not attempt to escape. The guards are authorized to use deadly force if you attempt to escape.

قاعدة رقم ٦: لا تحاول الهرب الحرس مخولين باستخدام القوة المميتة اذا حاولت الهرب

RULE 7: You will not leave your fenced-in living area, or move past designated boundaries, without an escort.

قاعدة رقم ٧: سوف لن تغادر المنطقة المسيجة التي تعيش فيها او تتحرك متعمدا خارج الحدود المسموح بها بدون مرافقة من الحرس

RULE 8: You will not fight with, or physically harm, any other detainees. If at any time you fear your life is in danger or that you may suffer physical injury at the hands of other detainees, you are to report this immediately to a guard.

قاعدة رقم ٨: سوف لاتقوم بمقاتلة بقية المحتجزين او الصراع الجسدي معهم او ايذائهم و اذا خشيت على حياتك او امكانية ايذائك جسديا من قبل باقي المحتجزين عليك باخبار الحرس فورا

RULE 9: You will not steal or take food, medicine, clothing, blankets, or any personnel items from any other detainee.

قاعدة رقم ٩: سوف لا تقوم بسرقة الطعام او قذه او اخذ الادوية او الملابس او البطانيات او أي شيء يعود لباقي المحتجزين

1. Waleed, Iraqi highway patrolman, and Colin McNease, Marine Civil Affairs officer
2. Regional Detention Facility Rules, Fallujah
3. Marine combat outpost, Anbar
4. Lieutenant General John Sattler, Ambassador Ronald Neumann, and the Fallujah delegation led by Sheikh Khaled al-Jumaili at final meeting just before Operation Al Fajr (New Dawn)
5. Marine message on the "Blackwater Bridge" over the Euphrates River, Fallujah
6. Civil Military Operations Center (CMOC), downtown Fallujah

7. Marine helicopter gunner dropping bags of candy over Anbar
8. Entry Control Point One (ECP-1), Fallujah
9. Combat outpost, central Fallujah, Christmas Day, 2006
10. Fallujah city center during Operation Al Fajr (New Dawn)
11. Navy Corpsman treating an Iraqi girl injured in an escalation-of-force incident, CMOC
12. Fawzi Mohammad, standing in front of his destroyed home, Fallujah

13. Mortuary Affairs (MA) Marines burying human remains in trenches north of Fallujah

14. Potato bags, Potato Factory

15. Body bags, Potato Factory

16. MA team, Potato Factory

17. MA team using a grappling hook to ensure dead bodies are not booby-trapped, Fallujah

18. MA Marines assessing human remains, Potato Factory

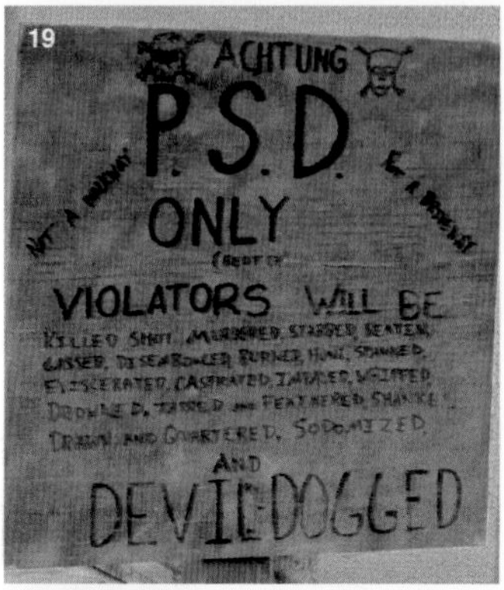

19

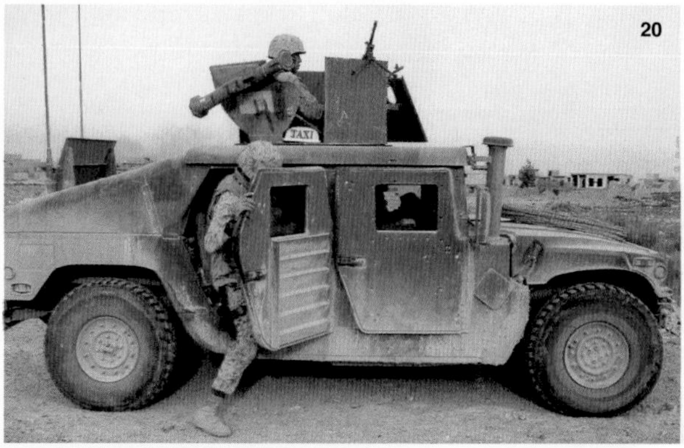

20

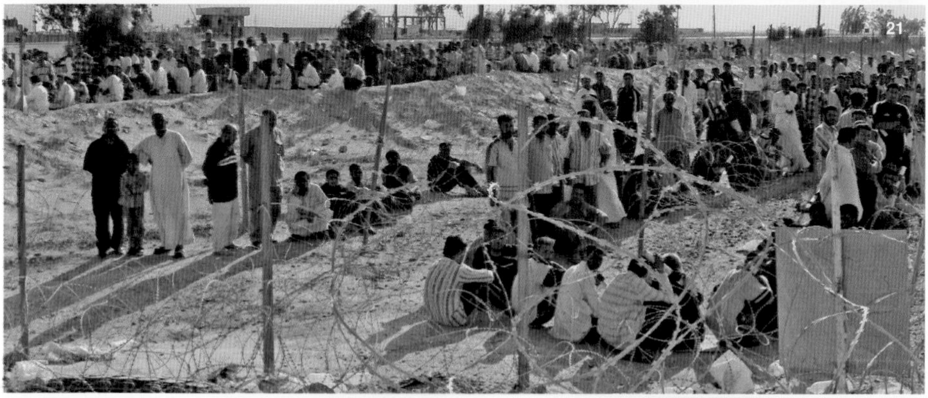

21

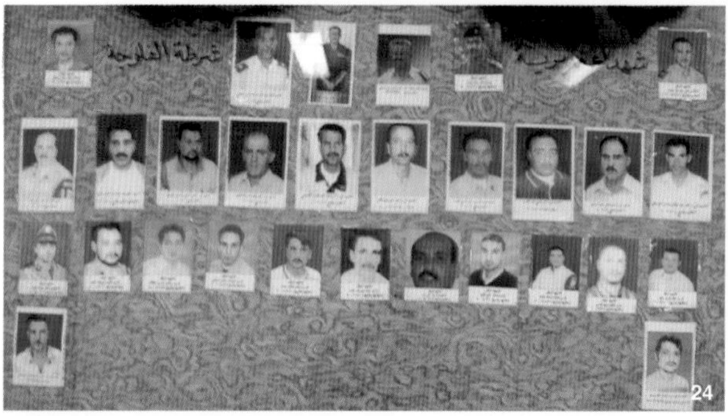

24

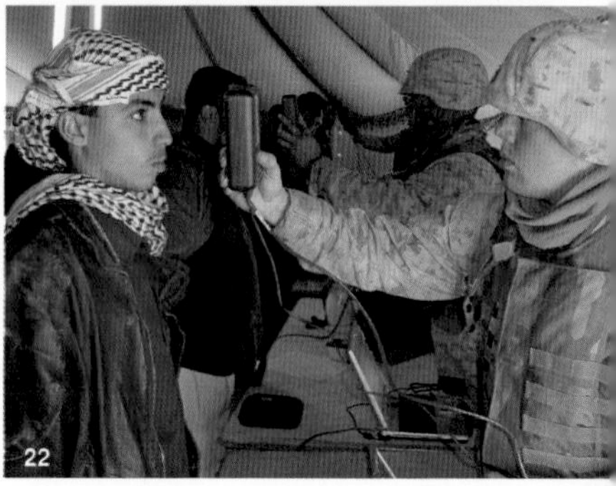

22

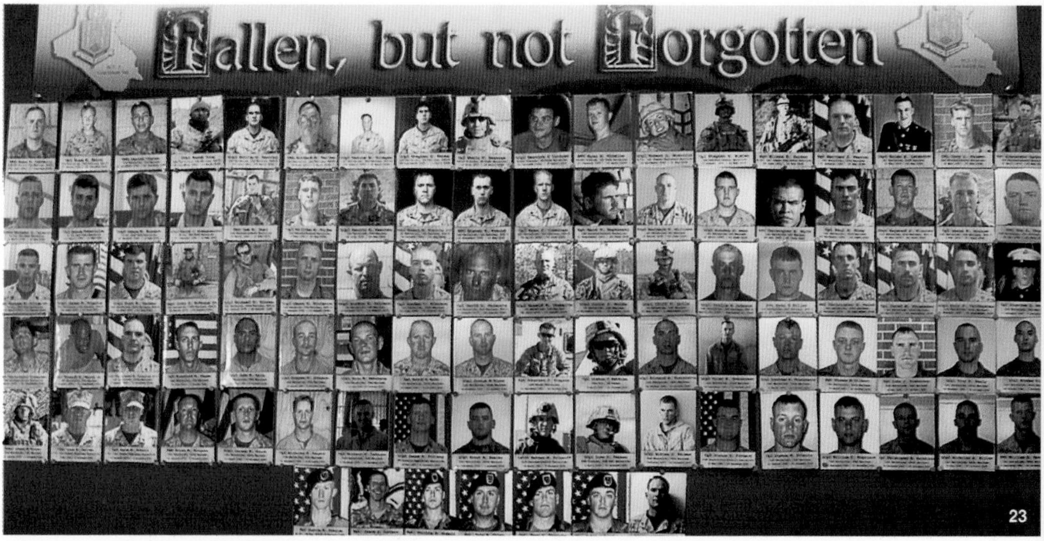

23

19. Marine personal security detail "warning" sign outside barracks, Camp Fallujah
20. Marine Civil Affairs team, Fallujah
21. Displaced Sunnis from Baghdad to Basra waiting for badges to be issued before entering Fallujah
22. Marines scanning the irises of Fallujans returning to the city after Operation Al Fajr (New Dawn)
23. U.S. KIA, Fallujah, 2006–2007
24. Iraqi KIA
25. CMOC Marines standing under the blue Crocs of Ryan McCurdy, KIA
26. Fallujah families waiting to receive humanitarian aid after Operation Al Fajr (New Dawn)
27. Senator Hillary Clinton (NY) on a visit to Camp Fallujah
28. Senators John Warner (VA), John Kerry (MA), and Ted Stevens (AK) visiting troops in Anbar
29. Colonel John Coleman, chief of staff, and Lieutenant General John Sattler, commanding general, 1st Marine Expeditionary Force, Fallujah
30. Sheikh Kamal, Mayor Dhari, Fallujah
31. Raid on a family compound outside Fallujah

32. Fallujans lined up to vote during the January 30, 2005, election in the Jolan Park neighborhood
33. Iraqi "MAMs" (military-aged males) bound during a raid outside Fallujah
34. Secretary of Defense Donald Rumsfeld on a visit to Camp Fallujah
35. Iraqi Army graduates, Habbaniyah, Anbar
36. Anbar governor Ma'moun and Major General Richard Zilmer reviewing Iraqi Security Forces during a graduation ceremony
37. Memorial for 31 Angels, Anbar, February 2, 2005
38. Sandstorm, central Fallujah

9. The English teacher Abbas, Fallujah
0. CNN crew interviewing a Provincial Reconstruction Team (PRT) service member, Khost
1. Marines paying displaced civilians $200 as they return to Fallujah
2. PRT project, near Pakistan border, Khost
3. Iraqi dinar used to pay "solatia" (compensation payments, aka "blood money") to Fallujans for deaths, injuries, and property damage
4. Left to right: The sons of General Khudairi (deputy police chief), Sheikh Hamza (grand mufti), and Sheikh Kamal (city council chairman). Each of their fathers was assassinated.

45. Dilawar of Yakubi
46. Hands of a madrassa student stained with the henna plant, Musa Kehl District, Khost
47. Girl at PRT-sponsored health clinic, Musa Kehl District, Khost
48. Governor Arsala Jamal with two mechanics, Khost
49. Qalandar District students in their outdoor classroom and with PRT-donated radios
50. Khost University students and graduates

51. PRT guard Fassal
52. Governor Arsala Jamal holding a meeting, Khost
53. Khost tribal elders
54. Kuchi (nomad) children along the Afghanistan-Pakistan border
55. Wheelbarrow project for former Taliban fighters, Khost
56. Daughters and sons of former Taliban fighters, Khost

57

57. Richard Holbrooke meeting with madrassa students, Khost
58. IED built with USAID-donated cooking oil can, Now Zad District, Helmand
59. Boy at camp for displaced families, Khost
60. Girl and women in burkas during meeing on education, central Khost
61. Marines asleep with a military workindog named Blue after a foot patrol
62. Larry Nicholson, Now Zad District, Helmand
63. PRT soldiers, Khost
64. Helicopter flight over northern Helmand (aka Mordor)
65. FOB Caferreta, Now Zad District, Helmand

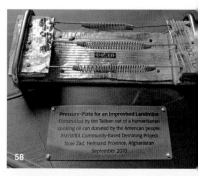

58

60

59

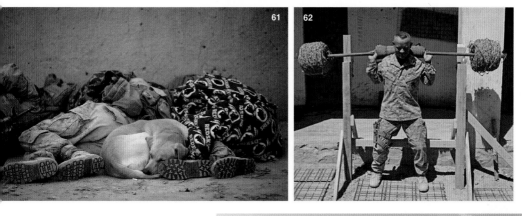

66

IRAQ STAR INC.
FREE Reconstructive Surgery for Battle-scarred Warriors of the Iraq and Afghanistan Wars
Shrapnel Removal • Scar Revision • Laser for Facial Sandblast
Includes Active Military & Veterans
Nationwide   www.IraqStar.org   310.245.6775

67

NEWCASTLE
POP   3532
ELEV 4334

70

68

HISTORIC SITE
—Topaz—
Internment Camp
Visitors Welcome
PLEASE Do Not
Remove Artifacts.
NO ATV'S Or
Motorcycles.

69

71

72

73

75

74

66. Road sign advertising postwar procedures for wounded Marines (Shrapnel Removal/Scar Revision /Laser for Facial Sandblast) in Twentynine Palms, California

67. Newcastle, Wyoming, road sign

68. Japanese-American internment camp, Topaz, Utah

69. Monument Valley, Utah/Arizona

70. Marine recruit graduation, Marine Corps Recruiting Depot, San Diego, California

71. Pinto Cemetery, Pinto, Utah

72. Near Main Street, Menard, Texas

73. Corporal Nicholson, WIA, and General Nicholson, WIA, not related, Bethesda, Maryland

74. Gravesite, Nathan A. Schubert, KIA, Cherokee, Iowa, buried at Galva Veterans Memorial, Iowa

75. Gravesite, P. Christopher Alaniz, KIA, Menard, Texas

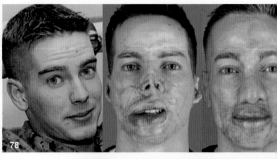

76. Matt and Rocky
77. Wounded Warrior ski event, Mammoth Mountain Ski Area, California
78. Aaron Mankin, WIA, Operation Mend's first patient
79. Memorial honoring Nick Palmer, KIA, Leadville, Colorado
80. Brad and Rochelle Palmer, Larry and Debbie Nicholson, Leadville, Colorado
81. Gravesite, Brian D. Bland, KIA, Newcastle, Wyoming

82. "Iraq is sovereign" note, George W. Bush Presidential Library and Museum, Dallas, Texas

83. KIA/MIA bracelets and Barney dog bowl, George W. Bush Presidential Library and Museum, Dallas, Texas

84. One World Trade Center, New York City

85. 9/11 "memories" computer terminal, George W. Bush Presidential Library and Museum, Dallas, Texas

86. 9/11 display, George W. Bush Presidential Library and Museum, Dallas, Texas

87. Wheelchairs at the entrance of the National Museum of the Marine Corps

88. Palmer home, Leadville, Colorado

89. James Cathcart's tattoo honoring Mourad Ragimov, KIA

90. World War II Memorial, National Mall, Washington, D.C.

91. Jason Brezler, Marine and New York City fireman, National September 11 Memorial and Museum, New York City

92. World Trade Center building steel column remnants, National September 11 Memorial and Museum, New York City

93. U.S. KIA memorials from Iraq and Afghanistan wars left at the Vietnam Veterans Memorial, National Mall, Washington, D.C.

94. PFC Dan Bullock, USMC, KIA, age fifteen, the youngest American to die in the Vietnam War, Vietnam Veterans Memorial

95. James Cathcart visiting Mourad Ragimov's gravesite, Fort Rosecrans National Cemetery, San Diego, California

pany H, proved as much). The other CDs' images and storylines reinforced how much I missed the American West. Only the 1973 British television documentary series, *The World at War*, had stayed with me more than Burns's groundbreaking work. Particularly episode 18, titled "Occupation: Holland (1940–1944)," which is narrated by Laurence Olivier and includes the story of a sister and her younger brother . . . a story of Resistance, a story of Resilience. I even found a prized bootleg copy of the movie *Blade Runner*, with its unforgettable final scene that had a new kind of wartime resonance: "I've seen things you people wouldn't believe. Attack ships on fire off the shoulder of Orion. I watched C-beams glitter in the dark near the Tannhäuser Gate. All those moments will be lost in time like tears . . . in . . . rain."

Geert Mak's *Amsterdam* was also there, the paperback book crammed into a corner, a reminder of my more relaxed Euro-life at Euro-pace before the wars. I also missed those days. I missed the carefreeness, the *zorgeloos*, indeed the whole *gezelligheid* of the sunken mountain-less country. And I missed my decades-old yet sturdy Dutch bike that had served me well traversing many canal bridges and pedaling around Vondelpark.

Life before the wars.

After unpacking the last footlocker, I imagined how many more were stored in basements, garages, or attics across America. Approximately 2.5 million service members have deployed to Iraq and Afghanistan, plus tens of thousands of civilians. I mentioned to a Marine friend how it felt to get through my own war archive.

"Yeah, my footlockers are downstairs, haven't gotten to them yet. Not sure I want to really," he said. "But my wife wants me to."

"You should," I replied. "I actually felt better digging through them."

Following my arrival back in the U.S. from Helmand, a maintenance crew showed up at the mountain condo to fix a window. While we worked on the problem for about an hour, one of the younger guys mentioned his friend had served as an Army sniper in Iraq. I did not say much but admitted I had spent some time there.

"He's lost."

He went on to explain his friend's postwar homecoming.

"We were deer hunting. We got a buck and started to clean it. When we went over to the truck, he was crying. The blood reminded him of his buddy who had been killed. He did his tours and is thinking of going back to school."

As the crew left, they wrapped their ladder and equipment in the back of a small Toyota pickup, in a blue tarp. It resembled the kind we had covered Fassal's and Qadir's bodies with after they had been killed by the big IED in Sabari. They had guarded us, while we could never protect them. I remembered how I sat with soldiers in the lead Humvee behind our guards' SUV that day. If not for the order of some minutes passed and some meters covered by them first, it could very well have been us dead.

I kept that war story to myself. And realized it had been over two decades since I had been on a deer hunt with my dad and brothers, well before the wars. I doubted I would ever go again. I had seen enough blood too. Iraqi, Afghan, and American. I did not want to see one more living thing die too soon.

A few weeks later, I read a local newspaper story about a former soldier who had taken a gun into his friend's garage, away from his wife and family, and shot himself in the head. I do not know if he was the same veteran I had heard about while fixing the window. But he came from the same town, a very small one on the other side of the mountain pass. My gut told me it had to be.

The obituary said the "avid outdoorsman" had received a Bronze Star and two Purple Hearts after two tours of duty in Iraq, and was the dad to a young daughter, a daughter named Autumn.

Those long summers in 2010 and 2011, after I returned from the wars, for good, I began to keep the promise made to myself that one starless black night into early morning at Camp Fallujah, January 26, 2005. It took me a while before I was ready—ready to end my hibernation at Solitude Mountain. After visiting Newcastle, Wyoming, and feeling better because of it, I began an even longer drive to Cherokee, Iowa. I had another Marine's hometown to visit and to remember. The highways of America helped me reframe the wars, while seeing new states and small communities between big cities, places touched by the wars and not covered in the headlines.

Following I-80 east, opposite the usual direction I drove, the landscape flattened. Utah's, Colorado's, and Wyoming's still white-topped peaks, the same ones that had stalled my pioneering and warring ancestors a century and a half earlier, gave way to wide grasslands. I could tell the families scattered about in these parts had been anchored for decades. One house here, another there, surrounded by vast tracts of alfalfa, corn, wheat. Every once in a while, I would see a Union Pacific locomotive chasing the wind, or fighting headwinds, depending. The railroad my grandfather, on my dad's side, had devoted his life to for half a century—from working at the back of the trains to guiding the steam-powered engines at the front, always moving the cargo and passengers east to west.

Crossing into Iowa, it was all cornfields, a green carpet dotted with red barns, white clapboard houses, under a slate sky. Each town had its name proudly painted on the highest point for miles around: on water towers. Massive grain silos sat next to rail lines, some still in use but not all. John Deere equipment surrounded ranch-style homes, as if a garage sale for farm vehicles. But they were not for sale. Just parked on the front lawn until dawn when the next workday in the fields would begin.

After about twelve hours, passing by Rock Springs, Laramie, Cheyenne, North Platte, and Omaha, the last big city on my route, I hung a right on U.S. Route 30, aka Lincoln Highway, then U.S. 59. Cherokee, Iowa, was less than an hour away. After seeing a sign that read "Worms" as a pheasant flew over my truck, I turned the radio dial just in time to hear the regular commodity report with a baritone announcer summarizing prices for corn, soybean, meal, wheat (Chicago and St. Louis market), livestock, and heating oil.

Pulling onto Cherokee's Main Street and some adjacent ones, I noticed most of the stores were housed in brick buildings dating from the nineteenth century. I saw signs for Sequins Bridal Boutique, Carey's Furniture, Darren's Clothing Co., Liquor on the Corner, and FireIce Firearms. Of course Cherokee had its own Dairy Queen as well in a state full of dairy farms.

On the radio, a country music song played, Alan Jackson's "Where I Come From" ("I said where I come from it's cornbread and chicken, Where I come from a lotta front porch sittin' / Where I come from tryin' to make a livin', And workin' hard to get to heaven / Where I come from . . .."). And where I was now is where Marines come from, reminding me of Milford, where my own family had come from, a town in Utah like this one in Iowa that, year after year, decade after decade, produced more soldiers and more Marines. A cycle. A kind of citizen-nation contract, an enduring compact in times of war—whether in right or in wrong American wars—I suppose.

The weather had started to shift toward rain, with an unusual degree of humidity already making clothing stick to skin. All around me rolling early-growth cornfields were as verdant as anything I had ever seen, such lush land compared to Anbar's arid deserts on either side of the mighty Euphrates River. Fertile and farmed in all directions, I realized the Hawkeye State was the bread (and corn) basket of the country, and I could see why Gene Roddenberry made Iowa the home of Captain Kirk. Americana, idealized. The state is even home to Winnebago County, reflective of perhaps the best way, a slow and meandering way, to see America along its highways and byways between RV parks. Iowa, I learned, was also the longtime headquarters for the "lonely" Maytag repairman of television ad fame, the washing machine company founded there in 1893.

Maybe, I began to think, this small state warrants its disproportionately big political voice, whether in wartime or not. Residents caucusing amid the cacophony of presidential candidate voices, and determining who is worthy to be commander in chief of millions of troops and leader of a global superpower. Ninety-nine counties whose votes set the stage for the outcome across forty-nine other states that follow every four years—grassroots vetting between cornfields and silos. The up-close-and-personal degree of debate and first and last impressions of striving Rs and striving Ds had to count for something.

But a tourist stroll through Cherokee or Iowa caucus sites was not my intent. I was there to visit the local military cemetery, situated just outside town. Before heading that way, I decided to jog. My legs needed the exercise after hundreds of miles of driving, plus I wanted to explore the town via my ASICs, not just my 2003 Tacoma, which needed a break itself. I had passed a high school on my way in, before checking into a bargain-priced motel. I knew that is where the Marine who died in Anbar, one of the 31 Angels, must have gone to school: George Washington High School. And he did, graduating in spring 2001, just a few months before 9/11.

As I jogged past, I noticed the school mascot was a Brave—reflecting the Native American history in the area. A sign on the school's chain-link fence read: "Braves Honor Parking: We honor those who temper their bravery with knowledge and dedication." During construction in the early 1970s of Cherokee's municipal sewer, archaeologists uncovered a site where some of the earliest Indians butchered bison.

The town itself (pop. 5,253) doubles as the seat of Cherokee County and is named for the tribe—now, like the Navajo, its own Cherokee Nation. Its people having plenty of their own war stories—forced relocation via a 1,000-mile march, internment camps, and repeated broken treaties with Washington. There were also the Indian raids, with hard-to-break revenge cycles. A local one was the Spirit Lake Massacre of 1857, reported as "red men" butchering "white men." I could not help but think that in tribal warfare no one wins, even if the "victors," not the learned historians, write the quick history. And declare that they have won whichever war in the meantime—sometimes then holding victory parades in an attempt to prove it.

Turning left, I opted to finish my jogging route in town, crossing Railroad Creek, which helps water the Little Sioux River Valley. I navigated leafy streets as the sun rose. Only the early delivery trucks were on the roads, as I passed the stately American Theater, which was playing *Battleship*, *Men in Black 3*, and *The Avengers*. A sign above Gustafson Realty read, "Farm for sale, Cedar twp, 154 acres, farm this year." Sweating quarts now, I knew I had to get on my way. After my predictable morning routine, instant coffee to go with my instant oatmeal, I located on my iPhone map my destination: Galva Veterans Memorial. This is where the Marine I had traveled to remember was buried, about twenty miles outside Cherokee near the town of Holstein and not far from Storm Lake.

I pulled up at the memorial half an hour or so later, making a couple of wrong turns amid endless Iowa fields. No one else was there—at first. The gray sky had become grayer. Mist blanketed the deep greens that bordered the cemetery on all sides. Below an American flag, a large granite monument read: "All gave some, some gave all" and "In tribute to the men and women of Galva Area who served this country." In the background above was a white water tower with "Galva" painted on it. I walked the neatly trimmed and pristine lawn until I found the grave marker I was looking for. On one side of the shiny black stone surface was a picture of the Marine and below his name inscribed:

NATHAN ALAN SCHUBERT

Cpl US Marine Corps
Jan 27 1982   Jan 26 2005

Operation Iraqi Freedom
Honor
Courage
Commitment
Semper Fidelis

On the other side, an engraved picture of pheasants in flight, with a forest of pine trees etched in the background. A cement block below, with a bronze Eagle, Globe, and Anchor medallion embedded in it, read: "If love could have saved you, you would have lived forever." Next to Corporal Schubert's headstone was another, that of his father, Drew Alan Schubert, April 27, 1952–June 19, 2004. This meant two deaths in one family within seven months.

I said what I needed to say, and left what I needed to leave.

I then began to make my way back to my truck, at which point a woman pulled up in the gravel lot. She looked to be in her mid-fifties. I feared she might be Corporal Schubert's mother. I froze. Again, what would I say if she said hi, asked who I was and which gravesite I was visiting? She walked closer but passed, and instead stopped before another tombstone, which read: NASLUND, EARL LEROY NASLUND, Cpl US Marine Corps, Korea, Mar 16, 1930, Feb 9, 2005. Only one other person showed up that morning while I was there, a white-haired man in a silver sedan. With a back bent from age, he exited his car with some items in his hands, slowly making his way to honor another veteran or veterans from another war. I thought probably, given his tilted posture, World War II or Korea.

I sat on a nearby cement bench for half an hour before loading up to leave the cemetery and town. I did not mind the light rain, which had replaced the mist. I heard a train whistle in the distance. And thought: *Nathan died just before his birthday.* I had not realized that until my visit. He was killed the day before he would have turned twenty-three. It also pained me to think that "Operation Iraqi Freedom" had not made very many Iraqis feel free, certainly not free from terror and terrorists. How did the Schubert family handle that knowledge? How did so many other KIA families think about the stated rationale for, and outcome of, the war that had killed a member of their family?

Corporal Schubert was scheduled to redeploy from Iraq back to his battalion's home base in Hawaii on February 4, 2005, nine days after he died.

As the lush fields became a blur of more green ribbon, I saw farther down the two-lane state road a sign that read "Republican Women's Club of Harrison County." I could not imagine a place more different from Anbar than Iowa. And I could not imagine another nation that for so long had sent its young men and women in uniform so far away to fight, whether in a "right" fight or not. That, I believed, was remarkable amid the immense cost in lives.

A tremendous cost counted out in so many futures, like Corporal Schubert's, prematurely ended in youth in a foreign country, and not of old age back at home.

As a student of history, a reader of history, I knew very few countries had military cemeteries with acreage dedicated overseas, thousands of miles away, ocean-distance away, memorializing their own dead sons and daughters.

The United States was one.

Over so many decades and so many wars, we had buried most of our war dead on American soil, but not all.

I was born an American, I live as an American, I shall die
an American. And I intend to perform the duties incum-
bent upon me in that character to the end of my career.
I mean to do this with absolute disregard to the personal
consequences.

DANIEL WEBSTER

To Menard, Texas

If the military cemetery in Galva, outside Cherokee, Iowa, had an
exact opposite, it would be the graveyard I visited in Menard, Texas.
This road trip would require a plane ticket first. As my Delta flight
descended over the Texas Hill Country, the partly cloudy skies allowed
for my first sense of just how big the Lone Star State truly is. After
crossing into what looked to be the start of Texan (sovereign?) airspace,
the flight went on and on and on until finally we were asked to prepare
for landing.

While not a Western state as I understood the distinctive mountain-
into-desert category to be (i.e., Wallace Stegner's *Angle of Repose* and
The Big Rock Candy Mountain country), Texas did reflect the American
West's sense of scale and Big First Impression at 30,000 feet. And, I
reckoned, the sense of privation. (Stegner in his own words: "The lessons of life amount not to wisdom, but to scar tissue and callus.") I had
transited the state's airports during layovers, but this visit to deep in the

heart of Texas would be the first that extended beyond the confines of a passenger terminal.

My plane landed a bit ahead of schedule in San Antonio. I had not checked any bags, so quickly made my way toward the rental car counter. On the ground floor, a huge white banner with red and blue lettering read, "Welcome Home Troops, Thank You! City of San Antonio Veterans Affairs Commission." A bit farther on, another permanent sign: → To Terminal B → Military/USO. These were good indications, I thought. This sprawling metropolis had a feeling for the ongoing wars perhaps that endured. Granted, San Antonio was home to one of the nation's largest military burn centers and bases, where Aaron Mankin had been treated for his injuries and scarring. The same city where, I recalled, Richard Avedon had been visiting to photograph the Iraq War wounded when he died in 2004 at a local motel of a brain hemorrhage.

But a city neighborhood or suburb would not be my destination. Menard, Texas, was that—still another two-hour drive away. After getting the keys for my small hatchback, I pulled out of the airport and headed northwest. I missed my truck but not its gas bill. A blanket of cooler air had descended, with a cold front forecast to move through but not until after my scheduled departure late the following day. This would be a short trip, reflecting my limited personal travel budget. The days of U.S. government per diem rates and expense accounts were behind me.

Beyond the relative greenery of the San Antonio metro area, Interstate 10 transitions into brush-filled plains that reminded me of hilly Nevada in places. A persistent drought had decimated larger plant life, with only the hardiest species persevering amid the ever-hardy oak. My late midday flight put me on a tight schedule. The skies had cleared and I hoped to make it to Menard before sunset, wanting to get a sense of the place as soon as possible. A sense of where this Marine, Captain Paul Christopher Alaniz, a copilot of the CH-53 Super Stallion that crashed outside Ar Rutbah in Anbar, called home. I needed to see where his remains were buried, far from Arlington, just as Corporal Schubert's had been in rural Iowa.

Across the years in Iraq, I certainly had a sense of that country. It only seemed right, an after-war requirement in my mind, that I would try to gain some sense of where these Marines had come from before Iraq—and returned to after dying in Iraq.

About an hour and a half into my drive, this time opting for an oldies station over more country music, I decided to stop, gas up, and eat in Junction, Texas. Another Dairy Queen had been the draw, a fast food joint proving to be a staple in my road trip diet, on top of a personal reminder of where I made my first hourly wage as a sixteen-year-old semi-trained "fry guy" and "Blizzard blender." I pulled into the parking lot and noticed a beat-up truck with Mississippi plates, with several military-themed messages affixed above the rear bumper. They included, all aligned in a row: Indiana Soldiers' and Sailors' Children's Home, Knightstown, Indiana; Veteran Vietnam War; US Navy; and a final one in bold red with silver writing, VFW, Post 6731, LIFE MEMBER.

I had put a few Marine stickers on my own white Tacoma, which Larry had given me. I suppose I had the right. Besides, grunts told me the chance of being issued speeding tickets goes down proportionate to the amount of Marine propaganda you have affixed to your rear bumper. (A theory that I found proved to be true in the following months and years as I traversed at a good clip more highways and byways throughout the West. I began to think state highway patrols had more than a few members of the Marine mafia in their radar gun ranks, thankfully.)

I walked into the DQ, ordered two wraps and a Snickers Blizzard, and finished the Blizzard first. A woman behind the counter said, in a friendly Texas accent, that Menard was up the road, "close, 'bout half 'n hour 'way." I said thanks, gave her a giant tip, not explaining why, and headed out. Across the street, a shop advertised "Welcome Hunters: ice, beef jerky, fried pies, deer corn." I was glad I had opted for the DQ menu instead, though I imagined the jerky was good quality. But deer corn? I did not want to know. After the wars, I preferred that Bambis remain alive despite having been an expert and towheaded deer hunter's assistant across many fall hunting seasons back in the day.

The sun was hanging low on the western horizon as I neared town, spying finally a small roadway sign I had been looking for—"Menard City Limit, Pop. 1471." From Junction onward, I counted only three vehicles that passed me in either direction. This was remote country. Several closed iron gates on either side of the road signaled ranches beyond. They looked like big spreads, hundreds of acres. Perhaps modern-day J.R.s, Sue Ellens, and Jock and Ellie Ewings had opted to get out of Dallas for good. I passed another sign that read "Eden," which made me grin a bit given the non-Eden-like context before at last entering the town's boundaries.

I had made a reservation at Motel 83, in large part because it advertised (of the three in town) that it doubled as the home to "Shifty's Bar." ("We are the only Motel in Menard with a bar featuring Music, Pool, Ice Cold Beer, and Set-ups.") With promises like that, I had to check it out. Of course, when I got there Shifty's was closed, looking to have been that way for months. I checked into the semi-abandoned establishment. An older woman said a few words with a shrug, handed me an old-style key, and pointed toward the back. The place felt a bit like the Bates Motel, honestly, but it would do. It would have to do. I saw one other car in the lot, hoping there would be a lot more. Just in case "Shifty" had other connotations at the run-down establishment as well.

Instead of jogging through town at sundown, I decided to walk it, at least for a mile or two. Managing a decent pace, I passed the Menard Church of Christ sided with yellow aluminum, Menard Elementary School, constructed with a tan stone facade resembling the colors of some schools in Khost we had funded, and an old brick building with "The Menard News" above it. The place looked closed, for good. I also saw a park dotted with benches painted red. It housed a light gray granite memorial for the town's youth of yesteryear who had gone off to war over the last century. World War I. World War II. Korea. But I did not see "Vietnam" listed. Its message etched in the stone:

IN MEMORY OF THOSE WHO DIED

> They held in their keeping the safety of the Republic. They kept alight the lamp of liberty. Their record of service to God and Country helped to preserve the American way of life. They lived and died so that the eternal values by which men live shall not perish from this earth.

I noticed no names yet listed from either Iraq or Afghanistan, and I wondered how applicable these grand and moving and heroic words would be for either war. I supposed that like the United States itself, small towns had yet to have that discussion. Have that debate. Have that reckoning. Iraq as a place that "kept alight the lamp of liberty"? "Helped to preserve the American way of life"? "Died so that the eternal values by which men live shall not perish from this earth"?

What instead would be those words, what instead *should* be those words?

The clear skies had started to darken. A few cars passed. Some dogs barked, but the stillness of the place is what struck me most. Not only did Menard feel and look dead-tired, it felt and looked like a dying town. It had lost its sheen a long time ago. And yet, it retained its character. Underneath the dust, cracks, weeds—and an unemployment rate that must have been triple the national average—I sensed an enduring toughness. I liked that. A much smaller Motor City on the plains of Texas.

On the largely vacant commercial street, I saw a sign for the Boys and Girls Club of Menard . . . "Great Futures Start Here." An adjacent brick building had the date "1928" atop it, and a solitary American flag leaning toward a weathered sign in wood spelling out "Woody's"— not that different from the look of my own grandparents' shuttered furniture-store-turned-failed-bar in another part of small-town, forgotten America.

I myself was tired and ready for bed, but before heading back to the Bates Motel, I made one last round in the park, a mini-oasis of sorts. I realized I had missed two key parts of the local history and was glad I had gone back.

One large historical marker was headlined: "Great Western Trail." Below which began the rest of the story: "Some seven million head of cattle & horses went up the Great Western Trail from 1874 to 1886. This trail lasted more years, carried more cattle, and was longer than any other cattle trail originating in Texas. The trail brought economic recovery to the post–Civil War economy in Texas and helped establish the ranching and livestock industry as it moved north." Menard had been one stop in that migration of horned animals below ten-gallon-hatted men. I sure wish I could have experienced Menard back then, as well. Experienced the town, the state of Texas, and the (Re)united States of America . . . after the Civil War.

And then I saw the other local claim to fame, which surprised me most. A bronze plaque affixed to more gray granite noting that legendary Marine General Oliver Prince Smith had been born in Menard in 1893. The town rightly remained proud to call O. P. Smith one of its own (before he moved farther west, to California). It read: "He is most noted for commanding the 1st Marine Division in Korea during the Inchon invasion and the Battle of the Chosin Reservoir where his Division was completely surrounded by 8 to 10 Chinese Divisions, outnumbering the Marines 10 to 1. He led the 'Breakout' which saved the Division . . ."

Historians termed this feat a "strategic retreat."

This was the same historic Marine division that Larry Nicholson would soon himself be leading. The tradition would continue and the legendary 1stMarDiv (aka the Blue Diamond—its flag insignia) thereby remain in very good and very war-tested hands.

Before arriving back at the motel, I also took a photo of Menard's fort-solid Art Deco courthouse designed by Elmer G. Withers (what a name) of Fort Worth and finished in 1932, at the height of the Great Depression with its "Mayan influences" in the design. I also stopped at a small store to buy some food and try some local fare I had seen in the aisles: "Hot Pork Cracklins" (described on packaging as "Fried Out Pork Fat With Attached Skin" / "Especial Para Cocinar También Como Botana") and Goodart's peanut patties—"Now!!! 69 cents." Partaking of both once would be okay, I figured, and not result in any permanent damage to my innards. Hopefully. I fell asleep on a full if unsettled stomach not much later. The next day would be long, and be focused on the cemetery.

The following morning, after more instant coffee and more instant oatmeal (not unlike my usual breakfast in Fallujah and Helmand), I drove to where Captain Alaniz was buried. Two narrow pine trees rose twenty-five feet on either side of a simple archway at the cemetery's entrance. A "Garden of Memories" sign hung below a cross. This Marine, my age when he died, had reportedly been at the controls of the helicopter. "Sandstorm" had been the immediate explanation for the crash. A brown dirt road without any gravel divided the simple grounds in two. I entered on foot the 75-meter-by-75-meter or so enclosure a bit uncomfortable. Next to hospitals, and before the wars, cemeteries had ranked pretty low on my list of places to spend free time. They just did not feel like peaceful places. On one side along a roadway into town, semis rang out as they barreled past. On the opposite side there was scraggly brush beyond a barbed-wire fence with old wood posts. I even heard a few coyotes, as if on cue.

The names on the tombstones were overwhelmingly Latino, with many tributes etched in Spanish. They included other veterans, such as: RAYMOND S. ORTEGON, PFC US Army, World War II, Oct 31 1924 Nov 11 2009. He had lived a long life, to age eighty-five. JULIO MORALES JR., US Army, World War II, Dec 10 1914 Jun 16 1995. He too pushed through many years, all the way to eighty. JESUS MARTINEZ, PVT, US Army, Jul 28 1916 Apr 12 2004. Eighty-seven years old. I began to think maybe, just maybe, there was something in the water here that equaled longevity.

Or maybe these soldiers, these veterans, had been born in Mexico, just across the border, less than 150 miles away, or beyond, fought hard for their adopted country—which I wanted to believe had welcomed them before they put on the uniform—and then fought as hard as they could to enjoy, for as many years as they could with family, the United States of America after coming home. That made the most sense to me. That would be just as much an American story as any, including my own immigrant family story that began in nineteenth-century Denmark and England.

And then I came to Captain Alaniz's burial site, black marble above a big cement block. It was surrounded by more Latino names.

Beloved Son, Brother, Husband, & Father

CHRISTOPHER ALANIZ

Dec 7 1972   Jan 26 2005

Gentleman, Scholar, & Inspiration to All Who Knew Him
"Siempre serás lo más grande en este mundo para mí. Jamás te olvidaré."
("You will always be the biggest in this world for me.
I will never forget you.")

A second slab of granite had a color photo of Alaniz, standing in a white-collared shirt, tan vest and slacks and with a big smile in the middle of a field of yellow flowers. Two bottles of beer had been put in front, one with a Modelo Especial label.

Perhaps most moving, however, were the six handmade colored tiles affixed to the cement. I could tell right away some had been done by the hands of a child under the watchful and artistic eyes of a mother. One, most certainly from Alaniz's wife, Thelma, showed a skeletal wedding couple, standing side by side, a bouquet in her hands and a sky-blue background. American Gothic reinterpreted in a time of war, giving new meaning to "till death do us part." Another featured a bluebird. A third one, a light yellow tile, had the words "Daddy Always in My Heart . . . Love Lourdes." A fourth decorated with a blue and red tie, dated 2012: "A classy tie for a classy guy. Papa, Happy Father's Day, All Our Love, Mama & Lil Mama." A montage spread across one placed nearby in pink, red, orange, and blue with a red heart in the middle, with the initials LB and HB next to each other.

There was even a tile that had, of all things, a handpainted solar system, with the planets etched in a circle surrounding a yellow-blue sun. Though small, Mars, the red planet, stood out most to me. As it, I suppose, always would.

After only a minute, I realized this Marine, who was a son, brother, husband, and father, had someone else buried next to him, as close as one can be, four years later. Her name:

MARIA CYNTHIA QUIROZ

July 17, 1950   July 31, 2009

His mother. In Iowa it had been a dad. Here, a mom.

I said what I needed to say, again to two this time, and left what I needed to leave, for one.

Turning around I noticed, across from mother and son, the simplest graves I had ever seen. Mounds of piled dirt. Small rocks outlined each. Bricks and small pebbles placed on one. No granite. No sculptures. Handmade simple crosses. And behind them all a sign on the barbed-wire fence that warned, "No Dumping."

It was a long, slow walk back to my rental car. A few semis continued to barrel down the road toward the town center. I heard no more coyotes. This cemetery was the antithesis of the one in Iowa. It was also the most opposite setting I could imagine from pristine Arlington National Cemetery.

And it moved me the most.

As I drove out of Menard, just before noon, I passed a couple of businesses I had not seen while arriving the day before. One sign read "Deer Processing" in front of "Devine Outdoors Taxidermy Wild Game Processing" and not far away, another, "R.B. Bagley & Sons, Inc. Pecans, wholesale, retail, buy, sell, custom cracking, shelling." Captain Alaniz—Christopher that is, who like me was called by his middle name—perhaps spent time as a kid at one or both. I would have.

During the first hour on the road back to San Antonio my mind circled back to what my Jordanian friend in Amman and I had wondered about after I left Fallujah, about a setting and event years earlier when we both worked at our country's missions to the United Nations in New York.

Could Colin Powell, considered by many to be one of America's most trusted leaders at the time, have prevented the Iraq War? Could lives like Christopher Alaniz's and Nathan Schubert's and so many others, American and Iraqi, have been saved if America's chief diplomat and former top military officer had chosen a different course, the harder one?

I was there, in the room, an eyewitness, when he made the case for war.

What I had seen still troubled me a decade later. My mind on replay, and full of "what ifs" and "only ifs" . . . I recalled it all like a tragic but historic scene in hindsight in a tragic movie featuring a historic man. A statesman. A statesman who chose not to make the case against a voluntary war. A secretary of state, former four-star general, and Vietnam veteran who might have resigned in protest, but did not.

In February 2003, I observed Colin Powell present "evidence" on Saddam Hussein's alleged weapons of mass destruction program. I heard his words offered in a grave tone at a grave time, a time of real but also manufactured fear. It was quite the diplomatic rollout. Not since October 1962 had so much global attention been focused on one circular table in midtown Manhattan, fifteen seats reserved for the world's top ambassadors. Both gatherings, separated by four decades, were right out of a Barbara Tuchman book.

The Cuban missile crisis neared its climax in 1962. In the august formal chamber of the United Nations Security Council, a dramatic display of high-stakes diplomatic poker was under way. With actual photos of missile sites in hand, U.S. ambassador Adlai Stevenson challenged the Soviet representative directly in the crowded room:

> Well, let me say something to you, Mr. Ambassador—we do have the evidence. We have it, and it is clear and it is incontrovertible. And let me say something else—those weapons must be taken out of Cuba . . . let me ask you one simple question: Do you, Ambassador Zorin, deny that the U.S.S.R. has placed and is placing medium- and intermediate-range missiles and sites in Cuba? Yes or no—don't wait for the translation—yes or no? [The Soviet ambassador would not respond.] You can answer yes or no. You have denied they exist. I want to know if I understood you correctly. I am prepared to wait for my answer until hell freezes over, if that's your decision. And I am also prepared to present the evidence in this room.

President Kennedy had already sent former Secretary of State Dean Acheson to Paris to make the same case to French leader Charles de Gaulle. But de Gaulle replied that Acheson had no need to have done so.

"A great country such as yours does not act without evidence. You may tell your president that France will support him."

It was just over forty years from the Stevenson-Zorin showdown in the same U.N. chamber when I watched the other American "case" to the world. Behind Powell sat the gruff, Queens-born CIA director, George Tenet, and my boss, the prototypical foreign policy mandarin, U.S. ambassador to the United Nations John Negroponte. He and Richard Holbrooke began their storied diplomatic careers in Vietnam's river deltas. Powell, the former chairman of the Joint Chiefs of Staff and leading cabinet member—whose popularity and gravitas were unequaled in the George W. Bush administration—held up a small vial and uttered "anthrax" to illustrate, rather dramatically, his argument. It was his presentation's exclamation point in the case for war.

My colleagues, every statement I make today is backed up by sources, solid sources. These are not assertions. What we're giving you are facts and conclusions based on solid intelligence. . . . We know that Saddam Hussein is determined to keep his weapons of mass destruction; he's determined to make more. . . . Leaving Saddam Hussein in possession of weapons of mass destruction for a few more months or years is not an option, not in a post-September 11th world.

When might the world community nod and say: "Okay, we will, because you're the Americans"? That is, when we asked them to . . . "just trust us" again?

All this "history" in a time when so many said there was no point in "litigating" the Iraq War. Well, on that stretch of freeway between Menard and San Antonio I was doing exactly that. Litigating. Relitigating. Remembering the facts. What had happened back then compared to everything that followed, measured in violence and casualties and so much family pain. Two gravesites in Iowa and Texas forced a reckoning of this kind in me, even if there was no way to hit rewind and script a different set of public comments from Secretary Powell, a different decision by President Bush.

A wrong war avoided.

The storm had missed the city, so I-10 was dry. I was glad the rain skipped that part of Texas, despite the drought. Once I was back on the freeway, a big, black Dodge Ram 1500 passed me, among the dozens of other vehicles. But it stood out. I noticed the truck had "Handicapped" plates on it, with a Purple Heart symbol, driven by a young man who looked to be no more than twenty-one based on the glimpse I got of him.

I wondered where this soldier or Marine, or Navy or Air Force guy, had served, where he had been wounded. *Operation Iraqi Freedom* in Iraq? *Operation Enduring Freedom* in Afghanistan? Both maybe? Where he was from, where he was headed, how many friends he had lost "over there."

And I also wondered whether President Bush, a Texan by choice, had ever visited Menard, either as governor or president. And if not,

Texas is a very big state after all, whether he had been to a cemetery like the one where Christopher—a Texan at birth, as well as after, a Texan in death—and his mother, Maria, were buried.

I know the forty-third president and son of the forty-first president had often gone to the always picture-perfect Arlington, a short motorcade trip across the Potomac River, like so many other commanders in chief had done and still do each Memorial Day Weekend. I could only hope an American leader, one day, would venture to a cemetery in a forgotten yet still resilient part of the U.S. like Menard. It might do a president, and the nation, some good to see that kind of visit on their television screens—far from Washington, a lot closer to the hearts of America.

A long list of American commanders in chief also had awarded medals to American troops once back home to mark their service in America's wars.

Sometimes they even did it in person.

No more Hope, no more Glory, no more parades for you and me any more.

FORD MADOX FORD

The Parade

Parade Day had arrived. Marines congregated in pressed uniforms because they had been awarded a medal—a very important one among U.S. service members—called the Presidential Unit Citation. Using acronyms, troops have nicknamed it a PUC (pronounced "puck").

General Larry Nicholson had flown in from Kabul and hundreds more Marines and family members gathered in front of the most prominent redbrick building at Camp Lejeune, North Carolina, the 2nd Marine Expeditionary Force headquarters. He and I had stayed in regular contact since I had returned to the U.S. and he was given a new assignment in Afghanistan. When he saw me without jeans but in a suit, he had his quip ready.

"You are finally dressing the part. Congratulations."

"That's my former life, Larry. I've graduated from foreign policy to being a professional in hiking and biking out West. A good postwar career move, no?"

"Yeah, for a while but not forever. A lot of people keep asking me when you'll get back into the fight."

"One day, maybe. The views in the Rockies beat those in D.C., for sure."

And North Carolina, for that matter, I thought. But kept that bias as a native Westerner to myself, and knowing that Larry's wife, Debbie, was a native of Charleston, South Carolina, the architectural and atmospheric belle of the South. (I also kept to myself the feeling that writing a blunt book about Iraq and Afghanistan would be a more valuable public service than taking on a high-level job in the Pentagon or State Department. Had I said as much, Larry probably would have agreed.)

Despite the heavy blanket of humidity, honor guards and brass bands rotated through practice sessions before the featured speech by Secretary of the Navy Ray Mabus, a former governor of Mississippi. The commandant of the Marine Corps, General James Amos, and General Nicholson did not speak. President Obama chose not to attend, and the White House did not send a representative in his place. No politicians holding office graced the honorees with their presence—"not even the mayor of Jacksonville, who lives right outside Lejeune's front gate"—as one Marine pointed out to me pointedly. The only civilians present apart from me were family members and a few reporters, including one from the *Marine Corps Times*.

From my view in the back of the reviewing stand, I noted the American flag had been lowered to half-staff. Two days earlier, on September 12, 2012, the American ambassador to Libya, Christopher Stevens, had been killed in Benghazi along with three other U.S. citizens. All of us knew Marines were on their way back to reinforce the American embassy. (They first marched to the "shores of Tripoli" across 600 miles of Libyan desert in 1805 to rescue the kidnapped crew of a U.S. ship, dispatched by commander in chief Thomas Jefferson.) After Benghazi, the Pentagon ordered other teams of Marines to reinforce security at the U.S. embassy in Yemen and similar Middle Eastern hot spots.

You could feel unease in the air. All gathered here had fought "over there" and many knew they would be heading back, despite talk in Washington that all U.S. combat forces would redeploy home before President Obama left office. Afghan friends were emailing me that they were not as optimistic. Several Khost University graduates described the growing influence of the Taliban in Kunar, Khost, and Paktika—the students' home provinces. Of course they never had a seat at our policy making tables, or those in Kabul.

This day's gathering of military men and women stood at attention, but not amid a "welcome home" Norman Rockwell setting. It did not feel like a celebration. The troops recognized they had been forgotten a long time ago by the nation that had sent them off to war. Some to known places like Kabul and Khost, but others to unknown front lines like Taghaz, Golestan, Bakwa, Nawa, Garmser, and so many more. Places where friends had died and many more had been wounded. Many had also served in Iraq.

Their wars never had an Iwo Jima moment. Their wars would never have a Victory Day parade.

But they did get their medals.

Since the war in Afghanistan commenced with a massive bombing campaign along the Hindu Kush mountain range near Tora Bora in late 2001, the president of the United States up to that point had awarded very few PUCs, the nation's highest group commendation for efforts during Operation Enduring Freedom.

Navy SEAL Team Six earned the distinction for killing Osama bin Laden on May 2, 2011, in Abbottabad, Pakistan. Shortly after, President Obama traveled to Fort Campbell, Kentucky, to meet the men who ended bin Laden's life. In a public ceremony, he told over 2,000 assembled troops recently returned from Afghanistan: "We are ultimately going to defeat al Qaeda. We have cut off their head. Our strategy is working and there is no greater evidence of that than justice finally being delivered to Osama bin Laden."

He concluded, "We're still the America that does the hard things, that does the great things."

While the death of bin Laden represented an important marker in America's longest wars, terrorist ideology had already become viral. (This became apparent before long as the Islamic State pursued their own strategy, on Syrian and Iraqi territory and on social media, to include videotaped beheadings, ransacked museums full of antiquities, and the burning to death of a Jordanian pilot.)

After meeting with the now famous SEAL team, who later gained

more attention through movies, controversial book deals (prolific coau-
thors), and consulting for shoot-'em-up video games as well as an "I
shot Osama bin Laden" television special, Obama told the traveling
press, "They practiced tirelessly for this mission, and when I gave the
order they were ready. They're America's quiet professionals."

The commander in chief also requested to meet, and then thanked,
the canine that had been assigned to SEAL Team Six for the top secret
mission: a Belgian Malinois military working dog named Cairo.

This day, the almost 20,000-strong 2nd Marine Expeditionary
Brigade, led by Larry Nicholson, was receiving the Presidential Unit
Citation for their fight in Helmand province. When President Obama
decided to escalate and surge (the second time, after NSA Jim Jones
emphasized otherwise) more than 30,000 troops into Afghanistan in
2010, the initial wave arrived in the southern reaches of the country
in the form of U.S. Marine companies and platoons. By "sending in
the Marines" in the war's eighth year, the White House signaled the
fight would go on but only for a few more years, and with West Wing
clocks synced to the voting public's expressed uninterest in and discon-
nection from the war. The commander in chief put a 2014 deadline on
the troop increase, a professed-to-be-certain timeline on which troops
would return home. Across the brigade's deployment, ninety-one U.S.
military service members were killed in Helmand, with several hundred
more badly wounded.

President Obama's calendar date for withdrawal, however, continued to slide as more troops deployed during and after the surge were
killed and wounded. The wounded included dozens of double, triple,
and quadruple amputees. And now they were home.

When the Pentagon first released news about the award in 2012,
Marines of all ranks, officers and enlisted, sent me messages of excitement and anticipation. The PUC remains one of the most coveted ribbons to be worn on Marine and Navy dress and service uniforms; no
other unit award rates higher. The ribbon reserves a special place within
rows of color perfectly aligned on proud chests, all tales of service or
combat. The day of its awarding was one to memorialize the sacrifices
of the entire Corps on behalf of a grateful nation.

Expectations grew that President Obama would make a personal
appearance, as he had with the SEALs. If a one-day operation with
spectacular results warranted the presence of the commander in chief,

didn't their 365-day frontline tour as well? But the Marines' optimism proved to be misplaced.

To my left and right Marines of all ranks gathered in clumps. The band was assembling, their shiny instruments reflecting the morning sun. Some of the youngest Marines, who had not deployed, hung around to hear "gray wolf" Marines recall how tough the Helmand fight had been: IEDs hidden in walls, along canals, at times daily firefights. Ambushes—planned more by the crafty Taliban than by very-well-trained-in-the-art-of-war Marines. And so on.

Overhearing these war stories being passed from older to younger grunts made the day that much harder. Because I knew the politics of the war virtually guaranteed a no-show outcome by President Obama. Given the presidential election year in which the economy was still dormant and thereby the dominant issue, neither President Obama nor his challenger, Governor Mitt Romney, wanted to talk about Afghanistan. It was as if the nation's longest war needed to be made the nation's quietest war. Votes would not be won by reminding anyone of how difficult the challenge (way) "over there" remained.

While I believed the odds remained long, I thought the president's team might advise him to visit North Carolina, a swing state, and reprise his role as the commander in chief welcoming home his troops. Or, better yet, I thought he might overrule any aides who might have urged Obama not to attend. I was wrong.

As a few hundred of us stood in front of him, Secretary Mabus delivered his parade-day remarks. Gentlemanly in demeanor, silver-haired and slight, he looked the part of a distinguished former Southern governor with close ties to Bill Clinton, who had nominated him decades earlier to be the ambassador to Saudi Arabia. Marines and their families respectfully listened, but his words fell flat. A "Presidential" Unit Citation is hard to award if you are not the president, even if it is viewed as the tradition among Navy secretaries. The gravitas is impossible to substitute, regardless of the speechwriter's skill.

I watched as rows and rows of Marines remained at attention. Families stood close. Kids wandered, but not too far. People began to use their programs to fan themselves. Across the grounds, the North Carolina coastal waterway had a few boats on it slowly crossing the flat horizon. Afghanistan seemed a million miles away, at least geographically. I knew most of us still had it very much on our minds, that day, and most days.

When the parade itself commenced, it was a picture-perfect version, made for a Hallmark Sunday night feature, but lacking any sense of nation.

The whole day was as manufactured as the setting was manicured. By Marines. For Marines. They had been ordered to war, sacrificed deeply, and returned home. Yet here they were, welcomed only by their own and not by fellow citizens or their commander in chief—or, for that matter, the local mayor.

I left the event proud of our Marines and disappointed with everything else. The Marines were too. But they were more disciplined than I was in expressing their level of disappointment, apart from quiet conversations under parade ground trees as a Marine color guard, flags aloft, marched neatly in step. Later that evening, well past midnight at a local bar filled with flags, medals, recruiting posters, mugs, and Marine Corps memorabilia emblazoned with their mantra "Semper Fi"—Always Faithful—several voiced their discouragement over beers without it sounding like a complaint.

"He didn't come."

"He's a busy man."

One of them, a lance corporal, ordered half a dozen beers—all for himself. It seemed to be his way of drowning out not only Helmand memories but also his frustration with the day's perfunctory nature. The middle-aged bartender kept the glass moving across the counter for us all, her arms a well-oiled machine. I paid for the first round. By round five, I noticed the youngest Marines were the drunkest. They were old enough, I thought, to vote for a commander in chief, go off to war, see friends die, but not old enough to grow much of a beard— which Marine standards forbid anyway.

Meanwhile, up the coast at Andrews Air Force Base in Maryland, President Obama and Secretary of State Hillary Clinton welcomed home the remains of Ambassador Stevens and the three other Americans killed in Benghazi.

A Marine honor guard, clothed in their finest dress blue uniforms, carried the caskets.

This "welcome home" from war could have been different, proportionate to the troops' sacrifice, but was not. Inside the main gates, Camp Lejeune is, after all, a great place to hold a parade. It is a place one would think politicians facing reelection would want to be seen, want to participate, give a speech, shake many hands, and ensure campaign photographers were near.

Smile. Click. Post online. Attract more votes.

Unlike the lunar setting of its West Coast counterpart Twentynine Palms, military engineers constructed Marine Corps Base Camp Lejeune in the middle of a marsh in Onslow County, North Carolina, not far from the now named Ronald Reagan Freeway. Marines at "Camp Swampy," as they refer to the base, pronounce it properly, with a Southern "luh-jern" emphasis. West Coast–based Marines, mostly endearingly, refer to their rural brothers as the "redneck side" of the family, citing extended cabs with rifle racks; an obnoxious addiction to dip, cigarettes, and chewing tobacco; varmint hunting; and "mudding" in their gigantic trucks on weekends. In turn, Swampy-based infantrymen sarcastically call their San Diego–area brothers stationed at Camp Pendleton "Hollywood Marines."

Lejeune's sprawling 156,000 acres—encompassing eighty live fire ranges, forty-eight tactical landing zones, thirty-two gun positions, and eleven miles of beach—ensure its uniformed residents do not enjoy too long a break from the wars when redeployed or on leave. Aircraft and helicopters, including a fleet of new tilt-rotor Ospreys, fly and hover overhead on their way between Marine Corps Air Stations Cherry Point and New River.

The road into Jacksonville, the adjacent town, is lined with competing advertisements for military-style barbers: Pro-kutz, First Choice, Head Styles. Park 'N Pawn, Fantasy Tattoos, and a store advertising "3 rooms of furniture, $69/month" entice the primary customer pool who transit a main route named "KIA, WIA, and POW Freeway." As does the airport roadway shop named Gruntz with a sign that reads "dvds, lingerie and mags."

On the base, sweeping green lawns and redbrick buildings accented by white trim provide a sort of 1950s-era backdrop. New dads and moms on short leaves home from war push strollers along leafy paths, and temporarily single moms, and a smaller number of temporarily single fathers, form jogging clubs to pace away the days until their spouses return. Each house, proportionately sized according to rank, has a small sign with nameplate in front. Lieutenants in a row. Captains in another row. Majors in another. And so on. Only the general officers' public housing cul-de-sac could qualify as a bit ritzy by normal standards.

It is a jarringly idyllic place for trained professionals who have perfected the ugly business of warfare and killing. As one Marine friend put it, "Lejeune is where Marines routinely bring their own firearms to work for show and tell."

The Beirut Memorial, which reads "They Came in Peace" and lists the names of the dead, dominates the place and sets it apart from other Marine installations. One ornamental pear tree is planted on Lejeune Drive for every Marine, soldier, and sailor killed on October 23, 1983, when terrorists detonated two truck bombs beneath a multistory barracks in Beirut, Lebanon. Among the 241 killed, 220 were Marines. Marines serving in 1983 remember where they were, like Americans in the 1980s did upon hearing news of the assassination attempt on President Reagan or the Challenger shuttle explosion. The bombing represented the highest single-day death toll for Marines since Iwo Jima in World War II, and for the U.S. military since the first day of the Tet Offensive in the Vietnam War.

Larry told me, "The Beirut bombing meant the end of our innocence. It snapped us out of our post-Vietnam malaise like cold water. Who had ever heard of a suicide bombing as a military tactic? The attack marked the beginning of what others would later call 'the Global War on Terror.'" (President Reagan ordered the remaining troops back to the U.S. after the attack.)

A few hours after the parade ended, my iPhone began vibrating with a barrage of text messages. Insurgents had launched an attack in Helmand province on the British airfield located next to Camp Leatherneck. A British diplomat, the U.K. ambassador's chief of staff, emailed news that a group of Taliban had attacked the British side, Camp Bastion, killing two Marines and destroying several jets. The suicide mission had been intricately planned. Later we learned that Marine aircraft squadron commander Lieutenant Colonel Christopher Raible rallied his mechanics—"every Marine a rifle man"—to beat back the attackers. He was killed in the process along with Sergeant Bradley Atwell.

I noticed another email, from the Obama campaign finance team in Chicago. I did not want to open it because they had sent so many mass fundraising appeals asking for the same thing: "urgent" campaign donations.

In the subject line, a cyberspace Beyoncé Knowles proclaimed, "I usually don't email you."

No kidding.

Her "friend-to-friend" message on behalf of the Obama campaign read, in part: "I have an amazing invitation I have to share. Jay and I will be meeting up with President Obama for an evening in NYC sometime soon. And we want you to be there!" Followed with a bold and underlined additional tag: "Until midnight tonight, if you pitch in $75 or whatever you can, you'll be automatically entered to be flown out to join us."

E-Beyoncé's concluding words?

"The countdown is on—this opportunity ends at midnight" and a sign-off that read, "Can't wait to meet you! Love, B."

Below in very small print, the fundraising appeal noted, "Odds of winning depend on number of entries received," with a final declaration, "Paid for by Obama for America."

Though I like Beyoncé, I opted not to donate.

Post-parade it was time to leave North Carolina. I arrived early for my flight. I had no checked baggage, and soon found myself surrounded by Marines in jeans and T-shirts, coming to or from leave. It always seemed strange to see them not in uniform, but rather in civvies. After so many years in both wars surrounded by MARPAT digitals—a popular design later copied by other U.S. service branches, which both made Marines I knew proud and a bit annoyed—even I was struck when seeing that they dressed pretty much like I did. The enlisted, that is—officers still wore in my view way too much belted khaki below tucked-in polo shirts . . . non-assimilation simply not an option once "an LT."

The gate attendant announced the flight to Atlanta. It reminded me of another time I had departed Lejeune. It had been for the memorial held in April 2010 in honor of the ninety-one killed in action in Helmand during my year in the province working with Larry and the 2nd MEB.

A few feet away, two mothers were also waiting to board the plane.

One said, "My son lost both of his legs. I heard his death was quick and he didn't suffer."

The other mother, whose back was to me, said something in response and reached to put her arm around the other one, who mentioned she was from Wisconsin.

After boarding that flight a few minutes later, I sat down in seat 2B. Next to me in 2A was the mother whose son had died after stepping on a bomb. She settled into the window seat. I noticed on her wrist a bracelet that read, "LCpl Jake Meinert, KIA, 10 Jan 10." I had attended his memorial in Helmand with Larry. He and I went to them, almost all of the KIA memorials. I began to open my mouth to tell this mother that, but I did not. I feared she might ask me, "So, Mr. State Department, what was our plan in Helmand anyway? And what is it now?" She had every right to ask. My answers would be the problem.

Shortly before the door closed, a Marine seated in 1A, who must have been no older than twenty, received a phone call. I overheard him say only one thing, "It was rough." Then he hung up.

When our commuter plane landed in Atlanta, I stood up to let Jake Meinert's mom pass me into the aisle. I had not said a word to her the entire flight.

There would be only a few big-city or small-town parades in America marking U.S. efforts in Iraq and Afghanistan, even as the Marine bands played on at their military bases. These wars did not end well. Or even "end." Confetti and brass are for winning, and ending, the right kind of wars. Missions that could be, and were, accomplished.

Republican presidential nominee Mitt Romney did not mention Afghanistan or the troops in his 2012 convention speech. President Obama's own Democratic Party convention that year, coincidentally held in North Carolina, shortly followed the Republican gathering in Florida. It featured a prime-time lineup of veterans onstage and a video montage saluting their service in both 9/11 wars.

As Election Day neared, the Democratic and Republican presidential campaigns went to war over who supported the troops most. Both Obama and Romney claimed the mantle of worthiest commander in chief. Well-staged appearances proliferated with Marines, sailors, soldiers, and airmen.

In the 2012 election, each presidential candidate raised over one billion dollars. President Obama and the Democratic National Committee: $1.123 billion. Mitt Romney and the Republican National Committee: $1.019 billion.

Both men, who sought the top public servant job in the country—hired, rehired, or fired every four years by voters—now ranked as record-breaking fundraisers in chief.

Reading about these astronomical (unimaginable, unconscionable?) dollar amounts, I was reminded how a Marine infantry corporal from North Dakota told me he had barely survived a seven-month deployment in Ramadi. He said he was excited to spend the $9,000 or so saved during his combat tour as a down payment on a new pickup truck. I also recalled Sergeant Todd Bowers, the friend I first met in the middle of Fallujah. He had bought with his own money an upgraded specialized scope for his rifle. The purchase saved his life after a sniper bullet was stopped inside the metal and glass casing, inches before entering his skull through the left eye socket.

Political analysts have predicted the 2016 presidential election cycle will result in over $2 billion of campaign cash being raised and spent—by each side. More fundraisers, more you-owe-me-now checks written by donors to politicians, with America's troops still at war and the nation voting for, indeed hiring, their next commander in chief.

If I have any beliefs about immortality, it is that certain dogs I have known will go to heaven, and very, very few persons.

JAMES THURBER

Semper Fido and the Sierras

There are other kinds of reunions that involved Marines after they return from war.

In 2012, I received an email from a Marine's mom, Jody O'Hara. I did not expect the SOS message. It was about her injured son, Matt, and his dog, Sergeant Rocky. The two had been separated during the war in Afghanistan. She was asking for help to get them reunited. She also described Matt's challenges returning home, writing: "Unfortunately (or fortunately), my son's injuries are not visible"—explaining he had suffered a traumatic brain injury and depression. She thought getting his dog back would help. Like her son Matt, the black Lab had been wounded in Helmand, hit by shrapnel from an RPG, leaving a scar on the left side of the dog's neck. Both man and dog served on a Marine counter-IED squad together, and their joint duty was among the most dangerous in Afghanistan. Sometimes the bombs, once sniffed, once sat upon, went off. Sometimes the dogs died. Sometimes the dogs and the Marines died together.

Jody O'Hara had reached out to me after I had begun to help reunite another Marine, Sean Belliston, with his dog, Sergeant Freeze. Her son and Sean were friends and had traded notes on how best to try to get their dogs back. I had met Sean at a restaurant fundraiser ("Medieval Madness") in Alexandria, Virginia, for the Semper Fi Fund. Over dinner, Sean, from Ohio, and a humble and hesitant narrator of his own story, told me about his work as a dog handler, stationed at a small outpost in Kajaki. The area remained most famous for a massive dam project that the U.S. had helped fund fifty years earlier—and was still funding (hundreds of millions of dollars) half a century later.

I used to tell Larry that Kajaki Dam had become Afghanistan's "biggest, bloodiest white elephant."

My logic stemmed from devastating casualty numbers in the area. Essentially, after U.K. forces moved out of northern Helmand, U.S. Marines took over. Sangin, Musa Qala, Kajaki: a crowded KIA and WIA list for British forces while they were there that only got more crowded as our troops moved in. And a lot more Taps played. The deployments to these districts happened after I left the war, but I kept a close eye on what was happening across all three places. These parts of the map had been imprinted on my conscience.

And it was not good news I was hearing and reading about. Our Marines were patrolling the remotest areas (their "no bridge too far" mind-set ensured as much), attempting to clear Taliban strongholds with little, if any, local support. If COIN (counterinsurgency) had a case study of limits, these areas represented it. Marines even brought in tanks after Larry Nicholson and the rest of the 2nd Marine Expeditionary Brigade and I had departed.

I emailed a four-star general, whom I had known since 2004 in Anbar, and asked what had prompted us to send in the tanks. If Afghans asked for tanks, that would be one thing—but I knew they had not. To move tanks into the war zone in year nine of the war signaled in my view everything that was going wrong, had gone wrong. To send in the Marines was one thing; to send in the Marines in and atop their tanks something else entirely.

Rusted Soviet models still dotted the country. Had we forgotten?

In response to my message "Let's talk tanks in DC," the general wrote back, "Look forward to it."

I asked Sean what the Afghans' reactions were to Americans in the area.

"They mostly didn't want us there." He told me the details of when he got injured, as if a further case study of the resistance in the area.

One evening, as he sat on the roof of a mud compound with another Marine, the Taliban launched an RPG from the tree line, about fifty meters away.

"It exploded between us."

One of Sean's hands was badly damaged, bits of metal tearing into him. He was knocked out. Freeze was not injured but forced to stay behind as Marines evacuated Sean.

It was a full two years after I left Helmand when Sean asked if I could help him get his dog back. Of course, I said. I raised this new and welcome mission with Larry, and we both said we would do everything we could.

I asked why it was Sergeant Freeze, canine stripes and all, and not just Freeze.

"The dogs always get one rank higher than our own during training. Shows them respect."

"And who is really in charge," I replied.

Sean's reunion with Freeze happened relatively fast. Freeze had been medically retired, so Larry and I managed to locate him quickly. And with an impatient civilian and patient general working together (his stars made the biggest difference), we got it done.

Sean sent me a final note of thanks. In it he opened up about how Freeze had saved his life.

I shed a tear or two just because it made me really thankful how lucky I was to have a dog and thinking about how many lives he saved, including my own. Quick story: we were at a tree line one time about to cross basically looking for a place to cross, and I leaned in to look in between the brush. Freeze jumped in the brush and was going crazy, kept looking down and then at me etc. There wasn't any place for him to do his usual way of notifying me. Then I stepped forward and he literally pushed me backwards. Sure enough I looked down and saw all kinds of wires that were hidden by dirt and brush. Taking a step further

I looked at my feet. I was an inch or two away from stepping on the pressure plate. So I can attest to that dog saving my life on more than one occasion. He used to lay down in front of me when we were getting shot at, his way of protecting me.

Matt O'Hara and Sergeant Rocky were a different matter. Their reunion proved not so easy.

Rocky, a laid-back and agreeable and altogether un-alpha dog, had not been retired, but rather promoted and in a big way. Not just promoted, he had been assigned duty with Marine Helicopter Squadron One or HMX-1—the pilots and crew assigned to fly the commander in chief, President Obama, around the world. Whether departing from the White House's West Lawn or skipping between European or Asian or South American capitals overseas. Rocky, in other words, had assumed first-among-equals dog duty.

I emailed the colonel in charge of the presidential fleet, John K. "Jed" Faircloth, about Rocky, a POTUS dog. I also learned he was the Marine One pilots' and crew's top dog. Faircloth wrote: "Yes, Rocky is attached to our unit. He is doing a great job, having been retrained as an airfield dog, specializing in chasing birds. He has reduced our number of near misses and actual bird strikes between our helos and Canadian geese. What can we do for you?"

Simple: *Give Rocky back to Matt . . .*

A few days passed and the HMX-1 Team did the right thing. I knew they would. Though their deliberations about their favorite dog must have been hard to bring to an end so quickly, following such an unexpected request.

I talked to Matt, for the first time, to pass on the news. Until then I had only had conversations on email and over the phone with his mother. When he picked up the phone, Matt said he was cleaning his gun.

"I think we're going to get Rocky back."

He was as excited as his mother.

Matt knew this mission was as good for me as it was for him. Triple therapy it would be: Matt, Rocky, and me—and probably for General Nicholson and his wife, Debbie, for that matter, who had lost their own pet while Larry was deployed, a bulldog named Chestnut (the female version of Chesty, as in Chesty Puller, one of the most decorated and revered Marines in the USMC pantheon).

After the big reunion, I met Matt and the whole family outside Richmond, Virginia—and of course Rocky. Jody had earlier sent a message with photos attached that made my day, week, month, and year. "My house is so full of joy. No one more than me. Okay maybe Matt and Rocky. Have a good night."

And so on a humid afternoon behind a stately redbrick home, I played fetch and more fetch and more fetch, then all over again, with this special dog and croquet with the O'Hara family. They said Rocky never got tired of playing. Neither did I that day.

In the kitchen, before dinner, Matt showed me a fancy plaque that had come from the HMX-1 crew. It featured a prominent color photo of Marine One landing at an aerodynamic angle in front of the White House. I thought how considerate it was of them to give Matt such a cool and unique memento. These troops flew the most powerful person in the world, after all.

I soon realized, however, the gift was not for Matt . . . it was for Rocky, with handwritten messages spread all around the framed photo.

"Dear Rocky, it was our privilege to serve with you." "Rocky, you are a true patriot and Great American!" "You deserve the good life." "Great playing with you, be a good dawg." "Arrg, Arrg, Woof, Woof. Arff, Arff." "To the most amazing K-9 I've had the privilege of meeting." "Enjoy retirement, the life of cookies is well deserved." "Rocky, thanks for always putting a smile on my face." "Thanks for keeping morale high. You did a great job keeping the birds away. You will be missed." "Sorry for giving you peanut butter your first day and making you puke in the O-lounge." "May your dog bed be soft, your dog bones plentiful, and cats to chase numerous, little best pup."

After reading all the tributes, I almost felt bad about forcing the issue—until I saw Rocky and his new life.

Matt said Rocky quickly adjusted to life in rural Virginia. At first, though, his dad had used fertilizer on the lawn, the smell of which caused the spunky black Lab to experience "former life" flashbacks. IED dogs, not surprisingly after redeploying, get their own kind of post-traumatic stress. And for a few weeks, he would traverse the back lawn in sweeping fashion, as he had been trained to do in Helmand, when looking for buried bombs. It took Sergeant Rocky a while to trust there were no IEDs and no Taliban bomb makers in the greater Richmond, Virginia, metropolitan area.

I received one last email from the colonel in charge of the Marine One fleet. They had replaced Rocky with another bird dog.

Sir,
It was our honor to assist in this event. Glad they are back together. We all miss Rocky, but Taz, another black lab is on the job. Not quite as outgoing, but we will spoil him too.
   Again, it was our honor.

S/F

Jed
JK Faircloth
CO, HMX-1

Soon after I met the O'Haras and played fetch with Rocky, Matt sent me another update. He said he graduated from the fire academy and had started EMT training, still had his girlfriend, and was feeling a lot better. So was Rocky. He had attached the dog's post-Helmand retirement photo. It showed Rocky lounging on a hot Virginia summer day in a tub of ice surrounded by beer bottles, both black Lab and drinks clearly well chilled.

Rocky had, finally, redeployed for good.

The next war dogs I would meet would be near ski runs in the high country of California, not trained to sniff out IEDs but rather to assist wounded veterans, many wheelchair-bound, at a ski and snowboard week held in the jagged Sierra Nevadas near the California and Nevada border, about a two-hour drive from Donner Pass.

Marine Staff Sergeant Dean Sanchez, in charge of USMC Wounded Warriors in the Rocky Mountain region, traveled with me from Denver. We covered hundreds of miles in half a day, reaching

California's highest peaks after passing near Las Vegas, Area 51, and a number of "bunny ranches" along the desolate route. The grayish yellow desert terrain reminded us of districts in northern Helmand province, but without the Taliban, purple poppy fields, and roadside bombs.

The roughly fifty people we joined for the week did not comprise the usual outdoor recreation enthusiasts at Mammoth Mountain Ski Area. Instead, Marines on skis and snowboards congregated, several with leashed canine companions at their sides. This late-January group, a majority out of Marine Corps Base Camp Pendleton, had served in both Iraq and Afghanistan, and almost all were wounded. Doctors categorized their Purple Heart status in clinical terms: L leg limb salvage; TBI [traumatic brain injury] balance issues; L leg gunshot wound; paralysis of left shoulder; shrapnel wounds; PTS/anxiety; cerebral inflammatory disorder; bullet in lung; C1 fracture.

Mammoth locals did not wait to be asked by a president or a Veterans Affairs Administration official to act. Rather, they knew they could do something and then did.

It seems the farther one gets from Washington, D.C., not only do the geographic vistas improve, a lot, but so too does the can-do attitude among citizens.

California native Corporal Jorge Elizio Salazar lost both legs in Kajaki, Afghanistan, in August 2012, when a buried bomb detonated beneath him. Yet soon he would be skiing the Sierras. "I remember everything," said the father of two. "I've never been on snow before. This is the best kind of therapy, not like a vacation." A member of the Marine Corps' Wounded Warrior Olympics Team, he swims the 50-meter free, 100-meter free, and 50-meter back. He plays on the volleyball and basketball teams, and just started surfing.

What amazed Jorge most about the ski week in Mammoth? "How quickly the organizers turned the idea into action and all the planning behind it. The town and resort are amazing." He said he learned from his mother, "who herself has been through a lot," how to stay positive despite any unexpected challenges.

Sergeant Leroy Johnston, a Houston native, served five deployments, three in Iraq and two in Afghanistan. A sniper shot him in the upper left arm, at sunrise, just outside Fallujah. His service dog named Apache, an Australian cattle dog, always stays close and "loves the snow." What makes the Mammoth event so special, he said, is "how they invite our families too." Wives and partners need such activities as well, Leroy added. "Getting on the mountain like this helps us and helps our home life." For both Texas natives, the week marked the first time skiing for him and his wife.

Leroy said people should know that for many wounded veterans after war, "No matter the limits we can live a full life."

Kathy Copeland, an energetic Vermont native, arrived in Mammoth in the early 1970s and never left. A whirl of activity on and off the slopes, Kathy heads the local chapter of Disabled Sports, Eastern Sierra region. With several colleagues and a town full of volunteers, they have built the Wounded Warrior skiing event into an annual celebration of alpine therapy—and fun. Orange parka–clad instructors escorted Marines up and down the mountainside. One New Zealand–born senior mountain guide remarked during a conversation with me on a ski lift, "I've helped train Olympian Tommy Moe. What I see with these veterans is the same kind of determination. It's in their eyes and attitude."

At a luncheon with Vietnam and Korean War veterans and others from the community, the CEO of Mammoth Resort, Rusty Gregory, noted how the scrappy ski town defined boom-and-bust resiliency. As he spoke, a blizzard—the first time since early December—funneled big flakes outside massive lodge windows. The Great Snow Gods, finally, rewarding us all. He reminded everyone of the only-in-America bootstraps-to-ski-straps story of Mammoth's founder, Dave McCoy. McCoy celebrated his 100th birthday in August 2015 and still lives with his ninety-five-year-old wife, Roma, in a scenic big valley not far away. All the week's participants, Gregory added, could ski free for the rest of their lives.

Earlier that morning, resort employees "saluted" the veterans with their ski poles held aloft, forming a thirty-meter-long inverted V archway—reminiscent of crossed Marine swords—for them and their service dogs.

Mammoth's "Operation Mountain Freedom" marked its tenth year in 2016, and is set to grow even bigger. Kathy Copeland and the town have launched a fundraising effort to build a National Wounded Warrior Center for veterans and their families adjacent to Cerro Coso Community College. Once completed, it will be open year-round and a much-needed home base for further educational opportunities and more tailored programs.

Author Dean Koontz and the family of *Peanuts* creator Charles M. Schulz have done their part. They help fund a program called "Canine Companions for Independence." It provides free of charge specially trained dogs. An ever-serene black Lab named Augie, for example, demonstrated his skills in picking up a dropped iPhone for his wheelchair-bound companion, Lance.

Leaving Mammoth and the town of Lone Pine, Dean and I drove to San Diego, my Tacoma carefully weaving along State Route 395 as semis and clumps of bikers reclined on their Harleys traded pole position. There we met with a Marine drill instructor stationed at the Marine Corps Recruiting Depot (MCRD), i.e., boot camp for all would-be Marines west of the Mississippi. The almost century-old facility and grounds have been designated a national historic site. Recruits train amid the Spanish Colonial Revival structures colored golden in America's Golden State.

It was graduation day for Company F when we arrived on an unusually gray and wet afternoon, reminding me of Fallujah in February and Khost in November. Hundreds of friends and family members had gathered at the ceremony to cheer on the newest members of "the Few, the Proud." Near an internal road named Iwo Jima, dozens of bags with a camouflage pattern crowded the pavement, all perfectly aligned, end to end, as if part of a G.I. Joe LEGO set. Marines made their way to the ones marked with their names. With bags slung across shoulders, they departed to enjoy a short leave period before reporting back to duty.

These enlisted grunts mostly would be deployed at sea on ships, or assigned guard duty at U.S. embassies. They would not have to fight in Anbar again or maneuver across bomb-laden poppy fields in Afghanistan.

Or so I thought.

Despite the political rhetoric in Washington, however, both wars have yet to end. And Marines are returning to Iraq, back to Anbar, while others continue to be deployed to Afghanistan.

Many of them were in kindergarten, or preschool, on September 11, 2001.

I woke up in the ICU, and there was a mirror in my room that I willingly ignored for weeks. When I finally got the courage, I cried for the longest time. It's such a disconnect looking at yourself and you expect to see someone that resembles you, and it was a stranger staring back at me, and it was a lot to deal with. . . . Beauty is who you are. It's not the way you look.

AARON MANKIN

Operation Mend

News from Iraq and Afghanistan remained bad and growing worse. I knew more veterans would come home wounded—and that the longest wars in American history were only getting longer. That meant more KIA. More WIA. In another part of California, down the coast, I met another group of Americans who were doing things to help veterans on the home front. Their story all started with an elbow nudge.

Ron Katz said he and his wife, Madelyn (Maddie), were watching Lou Dobbs's show on CNN in bed one night. They saw an interview with Marine Aaron Mankin about his service in Anbar province and the IED attack that left him almost dead.

"You have to do something."

His wife elbowed him and said again, "You have to do something."

Katz, a wealthy Los Angeles–based inventor and businessman, decided it was time to see what private donors could do to help Aaron and others like him. His father, Mickey Katz, had been a famous vaudeville performer and musician. Katz holds dozens of patents (automated calls, ATM processes) and owns a company that actively licenses associated technology.

Before long, the seventy-nine-year-old inventor and a team of specialists based at Ronald Reagan Medical Center—the primary teaching hospital at UCLA's David Geffen School of Medicine—created what he told me over dinner was "a cocoon of care" to help heal a face, a person, disfigured by war.

They called it Operation Mend.

We met at a white modern-style home in Pacific Palisades—the kind with a pool, a view of the palm-tree-lined foothills above the Pacific Ocean and leafy yards throughout the neighborhood that seemed perpetually in bloom. As I pulled up in my economy-class rental car, I noticed all the other vehicles were a lot newer and a lot more expensive. Not quite Beverly Hills, but shades of it. I was surprised and glad to see one car parked nearby, not a 4 x 4 either, that had a "Leadville, Colorado" sticker on it.

As Katz, balding and casually dressed, walked in, I introduced myself.

"Thank you for taking the time to tell me about your organization. I'm looking forward to hearing what private citizens are doing."

Katz exuded calm confidence, a vibe that went beyond his obviously sizable bank account and multiple entrepreneurial projects. I sensed that when he started something, he finished it.

"Well, we had to figure out a way to do it, and we have. I like a good challenge."

Over pasta, chicken, and a cheese plate, he explained this multistep process requires dozens of operations and can amount to half a million dollars or more per patient—complex procedures with financial costs not always covered by the U.S. government, which sent its young men and women, whole, to the war. Battered psyches and souls, moral injuries—to the mind, to the spirit—may even be harder to repair.

From elbow nudge to reality, Operation Mend has grown into a privately funded program based at Ronald Reagan UCLA Medical Center.

Katz explained the early days, when there was doubt about the level of support and sustainability of the idea. He said medical professionals in the Department of Veterans Affairs medical system "understandably" were wary of having patients receive care outside the usual procedures.

"There was some initial resistance to what we were proposing. But we can do what sometimes the VA system cannot do."

Partnering with VA staff and advocacy from family members and the success of the first patient, Aaron Mankin in 2007, enabled Operation Mend to grow. Quickly.

After Mankin's first surgery, Katz said the sight "caused Aaron's father's knees to buckle" in a hospital corridor. Many surgeries later, Aaron serves as a main spokesperson for Operation Mend and veterans overall, home from war—changed, scarred, but also resilient.

Diana Mankin Phelps, Aaron's mother and proud daughter of a coal miner and oil roughneck, has written a book, *A Mother's Side of War*. In it she describes her own process of coming to terms with her son's injuries. "I became a Marine mom with the signing of a paper, but it would take a phone call, late one night, for me to fully absorb the impact this new title would have on my life." She goes on, "I saw the world changed in an instant. My eyes were opened to a need in this country that was just beginning to be recognized. The floodgates were opened, and our battle-injured warriors filled our military hospitals." Aaron's mother (he is the youngest of her three children) also maintains a blog: "Writing to Heal."

Katz noted some patients can be served in other medical settings, but for those who cannot, "no one is turned away. We find the money."

What began with facial reconstruction expanded to include specialists in mental health, orthopedics, urology and reproductive issues, repair of airways, and design of new prosthetic ears. Family members, hurt in their own often hidden ways, receive support as well.

Throughout the L.A. area, "buddy families" work with Katz and his team. They volunteer to host wounded veterans for the days and weeks, sometimes months, required to complete the surgeries and follow-on care. One couple I met, part of the buddy family group and employed by a leading commercial real estate company, told me it helped their children understand the wars, their costs, as well as veterans overall.

"We are in L.A., Pacific Palisades. We don't bump into many veterans here. We get families from rural Minnesota, for example, from places where they have never been to the ocean. We take them there."

The next day I met Dana Katz, the daughter-in-law of Ron Katz and linchpin of the charity, at a restaurant just across the street from Operation Mend's UCLA medical center office.

The place was buzzing, with a Hollywood sheen to it. Diners' eyes focused on who's seated where, more than what's on the menu. Dana walked in, sat down, and provided an in-depth overview. She described how one patient, after receiving initial surgeries, felt comfortable enough to ask about the possibility "of one more procedure."

In Dana's words: "She was hesitant. Shy. Then finally asked if our doctors might be able to help heal her hands, saying, 'I'd like to be able to wear my wedding ring again.'"

Operation Mend surgeons made it possible. She now wears her wedding band on her ring finger.

Dana also described how another patient made only a single request. It took the form of a question.

"Do you think you can help me smile again?"

They did. He got his smile back.

In early March 2009, Ron Katz's wife of fifty-two years, Maddie, a Sioux City, Iowa, native, died from pancreatic cancer. Days before she passed away, three Operation Mend patients visited her bedside. One was Aaron Mankin, who, by coincidence, had named his own daughter Madelyn well before he deployed to Iraq and met Ron and Madelyn.

Katz said the physicians and hospital staff remain a special and motivated bunch. He described how one of the nation's leading hand surgeons, based at UCLA, had three patients scheduled around the same time on the same day: a very wealthy and a very famous member of the Hollywood establishment, Katz himself, and an Operation Mend patient.

"When I arrived, the doctor leaned over and said, 'I hope you don't mind, but I'm going to see our Operation Mend patient first.'"

Katz said of course. He and the Hollywood A-list Somebody waited.

As of June 2015, 127 service members have participated in the program, from all four military branches, 116 men and 11 women, with 69 from the Army, 47 Marines, 6 Navy, 4 Air Force, and 1 from the Army National Guard.

Operation Mend describes its focus this way: "Our mission is to partner with the United States Military to jointly heal the wounds of war by delivering leading-edge patient care, research, and education and using the best medicine and technology available."

Patients' stories and pictures (before and after procedures) are provided on the organization's website.

MARINE CORPORAL OYOANA ALLENDE: She is married, studying occupational therapy, and living in New York City for the summer. She was injured on June 23, 2005, when a suicide bomber rammed his car, wired with explosives, into her Marine convoy truck. Fourteen female Marines were riding in the bed of the truck at the time, being dropped off at various military checkpoints where they helped search Iraqi women for weapons and explosives. Three female Marines were killed in the incident, plus the driver of her vehicle, the gunner, and a rescuer. She sustained extensive burns to her face, hands, and knees.

ARMY CAPTAIN JAMES BARCLAY: He is married, father of three children. On August 19, 2006, while serving as an infantry platoon leader for 10th Mountain Division, CPT Barclay was wounded in Afghanistan by a roadside bomb. Three soldiers died that day; CPT Barclay and his driver were the only soldiers who survived. 47 percent of his body was burned, 35 percent third-degree burns. The enormous amount of scarring limited his ability to fully open his mouth and disfigured his face and hands. The surgeries he has undergone at UCLA have restored much of his mobility and function and reduced the scarring tremendously on both his face and his hands.

SPECIALIST FRANCESCA DUKE is currently living in San Antonio, Texas, with her family. Her job as a military police officer was to train and maintain an Iraqi police station in Ramadi, Iraq. On August 21, 2006, the IP station she was assigned to was blown up by a VBIED carrying propane tanks and explosives. She was burned on her legs, arms, back, trunk, and face. She will be having her first surgery at UCLA at the end of this year [2014] and is home celebrating the new birth of her beautiful daughter.

ARMY SERGEANT DARRON MIKEWORTH is active duty living in North Carolina and is stationed at Fort Bragg with his wife

Dea and two young boys. In April of 2005, as a Humvee gunner on the way to Balad Air Base in Iraq, he saw a suicide bomber approach his convoy. The attack nearly killed Sgt. Mikeworth and left him terribly disfigured. It broke every bone in his face. He lost his nose, left eye, and almost lost his right arm. He is in the process of a series of operations with Christopher A. Crisera, M.D., that include constructing a lower eyelid in which a prosthetic eye can be placed, reconstructing his nose and reforming his lips.

ARMY SPECIALIST JOSEPH (JOEY) PAULK is now retired and living back in his hometown of Oceanside, California, with his girlfriend and two dogs. On July 5, 2007, he was injured in Afghanistan when his tactical vehicle hit three anti-tank mines, flipping it over and igniting the fuel tank. Tragically, his team leader lost his life during the attack, and Joey was left with significant injuries. He suffered 40 percent burns to his body and face, smoke inhalation, paralysis of his vocal cords, and complete amputation of all ten fingers. He has had to re-learn how to walk, talk, swallow, and cope without the use of his hands.

MARINE STAFF SERGEANT OCTAVIO SANCHEZ is a married father of four and is currently retired and living in California. He was the victim of a makeshift roadside bomb in Ramadi and suffered third-degree burns over 70 percent of his face and body in June 2005. Before arriving at the V.A.–Greater Los Angeles, he was told there was nothing more that could be done for him. Operation Mend doctors were able to construct a nose, using skin from SSgt Sanchez's forehead. Once the blood supply was in place, one of his ribs was implanted to provide structure to the nose. Nostrils were fashioned out of remaining ear cartilage and his lips and cheeks were rebuilt. He has undergone several surgeries on his face and hand and now enjoys a more natural and normal appearance.

ARMY SERGEANT RICHARD (RICK) YAROSH currently lives in Binghamton, New York. He was deployed to Iraq in December

2005 (then a PFC) as a driver of a Bradley fighting vehicle and then moved to the gunner position. On September 1, 2006, Sgt. Yarosh and his fellow soldiers were on patrol in the Abu Ghraib region of Iraq when their Bradley vehicle was hit by a roadside bomb. The explosion ruptured the vehicle's fuel cell and engulfed the entire crew and vehicle in flames. Sgt. Yarosh's face and body were on fire when he jumped from the top of the Bradley's turret. His jump broke his right leg, severing an artery, which resulted in an amputation (below the knee). He suffered burns over 60 percent of his body, lost partial digits and full use in both hands, and lost both of his ears and part of his nose.

Upon her death, the Maddie Katz Fund for Operation Mend was established.

My springtime visit to L.A. and meeting with Ron and Dana Katz reminded me of the last time I had been in a hospital with medical professionals dedicated to helping wounded veterans from the Iraq and Afghanistan wars. In late June 2010, Larry Nicholson and I went to Walter Reed National Military Medical Center in Bethesda, Maryland, to see wounded Marines. We walked down the fourth-floor corridor (the Marine wing), when Larry leaned over to me.

"That's the room I was in, after the rocket attack."

We walked in, greeting a wounded Marine and his family.

"This used to be my room," Larry said.

This opening introduction brought a smile to the badly wounded Marine and his family. They knew then this two-star general could relate. He would understand. He too had a Purple Heart.

"Sir, not many generals come in here who have Purple Hearts."

"All of us can get unlucky, and Fallujah had plenty of those days," Larry replied. "Seems like they are taking good care of you here."

"Yeah, food's not bad either and they keep us busy with physical therapy."

We visited a number of other Marines that day. Corporal Nicely, who had survived the quadruple amputations, was there. We had not seen him since Bastion hospital in Helmand months earlier. Tubes and medical equipment lights reflected off of his pale skin. A nearby television set showing music videos was on mute.

He was asleep, so I asked an on-duty Marine to give him a State Department challenge coin when he woke up.

Larry and I walked into another room.

"General, thanks for visiting," said a double amputee.

His parents standing nearby remarked, "We know you commanded Marines in Afghanistan. It means a lot to see you after our son came home."

"It was a hard job over there for everyone."

"Where's home?" I asked.

"Kaysville, Utah."

"Ahh, great skiing near there. I used to spend a lot of time in the Wasatch Mountains."

"Me too. I'm hoping to get back on the slopes," said the Marine, adding, "It might take me a while, but I'm working hard to do it, on my snowboard."

"I bet you will. Maybe I'll see you at Solitude or Snowbird."

"I hope so."

What I did not tell him is how the howitzers the ski patrol used for avalanche control along the Wasatch Range reminded me of those Marines had used to shell Fallujah. Sounds of war blasted between snowbanks tens of thousands of miles away and many winters since leaving the Iraqi city. Perhaps he, too, shared these echoes.

Just over four years later, I would read that this Marine, Staff Sergeant David Lyon, age thirty-two, an Explosive Ordnance Disposal technician, died in a San Diego hospital from "heart complications and stroke" tied to his initial IED wounds. His father had served in the Navy, other brothers in the Marines, Air Force, and Utah National Guard. A local news article said Lyon felt proud about his service in Afghanistan among Afghans, his dad recalling his son saying, " 'They have freedoms that they never would have had before.' He was very proud of that and said, 'I would do it again in a heartbeat.' " David Benjamin Lyon had one son, Ethan Jayce Lyon, and was buried with full military honors in Kaysville, Utah (pop. 28,876).

As we left the room and walked out of earshot of the Utah family, a nurse told Larry and me about another wounded Marine who had a "bad fungal infection, but he's making it." She added, however, a comment about other patients not as fortunate. "Sometimes we get human IEDs. The remains of the suicide bombers blown inside our patients."

On a lower floor, Larry and I met a wounded pilot from Iowa. He was comatose, but had both eyes open, glassy and unblinking. His dad said, "Over there in Afghanistan, he was fighting. Now he's fighting for his life." The pilot's family said he did not have much time left. The doctors could do no more.

"General, will you sign this?" the pilot's father asked, holding his son's blanket in both hands.

"Sure, I'd be honored."

In the background, a respirator rose and fell. The tube down the pilot's throat protruded, one of his hands held by his mother, the other by his fiancée.

Larry and I left the emergency room area, allowing the family to spend their last few hours alone and in privacy.

A young twentysomething-year-old woman approached us unexpectedly. "You have someone here?"

"No," I said, "but he and I spent a lot of time in some tough places over there."

In her hand, I noticed a Big Gulp cup.

The Navy nurse motioned us down the hall, while explaining the condition of this young woman's husband.

"He's in very bad shape. We don't think he'll make it. That's his wife. She's been bringing in a full Big Gulp every day—and we know it's not full of Pepsi."

Larry and I began to make our way back to the fourth floor. As we stepped into the elevator, I saw more family members visiting their wounded sons and brothers. They stared at the floor, some zombie-like. I knew many had been there for days, weeks, even months.

As we reentered the Marine floor, I glanced at Larry. "I knew this would be rough, but the look in those families' eyes says it all."

"Bastion hospital was hard. This might be even harder because of all the parents, sisters, brothers. We see them all bedside," Larry added.

"For me, it sure is," I replied. "Some of these spouses and kids are so young."

Back on the fourth floor, we had been told that a junior Marine had heard a general was visiting. A nurse said this particular Marine usually did not want to see "any generals." But when he heard it was General Nicholson, "he asked us to bring you in."

"Sir, I still remember what you called us. 'Marjah Marines' and 'Phase Line SGLI.' That got us motivated." (SGLI is the acronym for Servicemembers Group Life Insurance—automatically enrolled, automatic maximum coverage in case of injury or death.)

I noticed both sets of eyes were watering—the corporal's and the general's. The last Marine amputee we met was another corporal who shared Larry's last name: Nicholson.

I also noticed an inexcusable absence at Walter Reed on that day—and I was not the only one. Arnold Fisher, a New York–based philanthropist, stood before an audience to mark the opening of a one-of-a-kind new facility to treat traumatic brain injuries and various psychological conditions for veterans. His family's foundation has funded numerous Fisher House buildings across the U.S. for families to stay in at no cost during ongoing treatment for wounded service members.

Looking around, the Korean War veteran (a onetime corporal himself) saw no politician or cabinet member present. No elected official on stage or in the audience.

Not one.

Fisher offered pointed remarks: "Here we are in the nation's capital, the seat of our government, the very people who decide your fate, the people who send you to protect our freedoms. And yet, where are they? And while we appreciate that much of our military leadership is present, our government should be behind this effort. I know these are difficult times. I read newspapers. I see the news. And still, where are they? They call you out. You are injured. We are all here.

"Where are they?" he repeated.

Indeed, where were they?

And where are they now?

My dream is of a place and a time where America will once again be seen as the last best hope of Earth.

ABRAHAM LINCOLN

The Spirit of America

"I was shaving."

Jim Hake was about to take his seven-year-old son, Sam, to school at Palisades Elementary. A friend and native New Yorker called and told his wife to turn on the television. A second L.A.-bound jetliner had crashed into the South Tower at 6:03 a.m. Pacific Standard Time. In recounting, he told me: "From California we watched the Twin Towers smoking, smoldering. It was after both towers had been hit but before the first one collapsed. I remember just standing there in disbelief, towel around my waist, half naked, half my face covered with shaving cream."

Hake, a former Silicon Valley entrepreneur, decided on 9/11 he would do something, as Ron Katz did by founding Operation Mend. "I took some comfort in knowing there would be people across the country who would do the same."

Before long, he learned that a friend from college, Richard "Woody" Woodwell, a Wall Street trader, had been killed in the second tower. They had studied together in Mexico on a Dartmouth foreign study program, surviving an army of Oaxaca cockroaches while learning the history of Latin America.

A Pennsylvania native, Hake had moved west to the Bay Area decades earlier to be part of a similarly minded community inventing new technology. He maintains his Pennsylvania accent while adopting a California-induced laid-back demeanor marked by polo shirts and colorful Nikes. His energy—solar-powered, one could argue—fits a man constantly in motion and bouncing ideas off all who join him for a long lunch or dinner as he hunts for America's best Bolognese Italian dish.

In high school, a teacher argued that "America the Beautiful" should be the national anthem because it was not about war and conflict. But a young Jim disagreed.

"I'd rather be free and brave than beautiful. To me freedom and opportunity—who you want to be—is important beyond my ability to describe it. I'm an entrepreneur. I really like creating things. America provides the freedom to create, to express oneself with a set of ideas, ideals, and principles. Yes, life, liberty, and the pursuit of happiness."

When the attacks in lower Manhattan, Washington, and over a field in his native Pennsylvania occurred, Jim had been winding down a company called BigButtons. "A great idea, but it had failed," he said, an unsuccessful predecessor to today's iPhone and tablet apps. The idea? To make getting information as easy as pushing a button: "I had founded the company. It was a huge disappointment, a really tough thing to go through." Based on his own experience in technology start-ups, Hake became convinced he could play a role in helping the United States respond in creative and citizen-initiated ways to the September 11 attacks.

"I had done enough various ventures to have some idea about the difference between what is good versus what sounds good. I wanted to do something useful, not just satisfy an urge to do good."

Hake's lightbulb moment came, as he called it, a year and a half after 9/11. Disappointed with what he saw as a weak public diplomacy effort by the U.S., he was convinced more could be done. "Our government was not doing a great job of demonstrating who the American people really are." In February 2003, he saw a *National Geographic* program showing Special Forces soldiers playing baseball with Afghan kids, boys and girls. One of the soldiers, Jay Smith, had taken his baseball glove to use during his free time. Soon, village kids were using it, so the soldier called his wife and asked her to send bats, balls, and mitts for the village kids to play a real game. With donations from friends and family, she sent him enough equipment so that the entire village could learn how to play America's favorite sport.

Hake tracked down Jay through the producer of the show, flew to Fort Bragg, North Carolina, and met with him and his team. Jay and his guys "were just about jumping out of their chairs" and kept saying that this idea would save lives. Jim thought Jay might be overly enthusiastic, but then Jay conveyed how in Afghanistan Al Qaeda had been crossing the Pakistan border at night and firing rockets on the team's camp. Because of the strong relationship Jay and his team had built with the villagers, the Afghans formed a night watch patrol to protect the American soldiers. The rocket attacks stopped.

Jim called his new organization Spirit of America, to reflect the initiative, generosity, and optimism demonstrated in Jay Smith's work, qualities Hake thought might help prevent another 9/11. The first projects were funded on a small budget with Hake working out of a spare bedroom. The highest-ranked military personnel he had talked to was Sergeant First Class Jay Smith, not a general officer, let alone a colonel or a captain.

"I figured if it made sense to him and it made sense to me, we could figure out everything else in between."

Over the next three months Hake translated ideas into action, leveraging the Internet to connect frontline troops with Americans willing to help fill their needs. Jim began to match donors from his California home base to soldiers and Marines. Before long, dozens of small projects were under way: soccer jerseys, dental supplies, musical instruments for Iraqi children, and carpentry tools, among others.

Within a decade, the Los Angeles–based Spirit of America start-up would transform into a multimillion-dollar initiative helping thousands in Iraq and Afghanistan.

And beyond, in less well-known places, places not yet as ravaged by war.

In June 2013, I arrived outside Spirit of America's office just as L.A. police were closing palm-tree-lined Wilshire Boulevard. I had to see for myself Hake's small brain trust, a team that included innovative former U.S. Army and Marine veterans. One cop announced to a group of us standing outside our cars, "Just so you know, the president is coming." Impatient Angelinos stuck nearby, as traffic backed up, were not pleased. A woman on the corner, close to the Literati coffee shop, said President Obama was doing a fundraiser in the area.

"It's Santa Monica. Lots of money here."

Local media reported the lunch at Hollywood producer Peter Chernin's house cost $10,000, $16,200, or $32,400 per person. The $10K ticket covered food but did not include the "photo reception." The White House press pool described the event: "Tables and chairs were set up in the grass, with cheery yellow roses and bowls of lemons adorning each table. A large, beige curtain cordoned off the yard. There were 11 tables with 10 guests each."

The median annual household income for Americans in 2014 was just under $54,000. And the starting basic pay for a Marine private first class in 2015 equaled $1,645 per month.

Minutes later, sure enough, the presidential motorcade passed by. Through tinted windows, the president remained hidden. I did not see many Californians looking too excited in the City of Angels filled with limos and countless VIPs. I took a few pictures with my iPhone. It had been some time since I had last seen President Obama in person. Over six years earlier in Springfield, Illinois, to be exact, on the formal announcement day, February 10, 2007, of his presidential candidacy. He had come a long way since then. So had I, geographically at least—two wars across eighty-four consecutive months since 2003. Hundreds of thousands of veterans from Iraq and Afghanistan had done their repeat tours as well.

After leaving Fallujah and just before joining Larry at the memorial at Camp Pendleton for our ninety-three KIA, I had decided to fly to Illinois to try to get a sense of the junior senator and presidential candidate. Iraqi deaths, including Abbas's the same day I left, and numerous Marine deaths, including friends, had made me feel hopeless about the Iraq War. I wondered whether Obama could be a different kind of leader in a time of seemingly endless war. Once his campaign team heard I had flown in from Iraq, they walked me to the basement of the old statehouse to meet Senator Obama. An assistant said as she guided me toward him and his wife, "You'll like Barack, and you'll really like Michelle."

She was right. And about a year later the campaign asked me to introduce Michelle Obama at an election rally, which I did. It was an honor.

As the armored vehicles zoomed by, sirens blaring under green palm fronds and a gray sky, I imagined the president, or at least a key national security staffer, stopping. Visiting Spirit of America and Operation Mend at UCLA, located on the other side of Wilshire Boulevard, a mere thirty-minute drive. I knew such thinking, such hoping, such a change in protocol was a mirage.

Jim Hake runs Spirit of America (S of A) from a small office with maps and clocks on the walls. They cover the regions of the world where the organization supports ongoing projects in Honduras, Peru, Guyana, Mauritania, Niger, Djibouti, Afghanistan, and the Philippines. On dry-erase boards I saw a list of "top 10 projects" that included wheelchairs, eyeglasses, boots and shovels, and sewing machines. U.S. military command acronyms scribbled on the board also reflected the extent to which S of A coordinates with them, including Joint Special Operations Command.

As Jim told me, "We have picked a side: the U.S., the American side."

As if to underscore this principle of nonneutrality, a giant poster covered part of a wall. In it a red-white-and-blue Uncle Sam points, and "I want you to take a side" is printed below in large lettering.

But my favorite quote on the S of A headquarters dry-erase board comes from Larry Nicholson.

While in Afghanistan, a *Washington Post* reporter asked the Marine general about the USMC partnership with their Afghan army counterparts.

Larry said bluntly: "You can't surge trust."

S of A had adopted the mantra—while officialdom in D.C. still seemed deaf and dumb to the notion.

During my visit, Hake's team provided an overview of priority projects. Two jumped out, both in the preventive category.

The organization's staff members, for example, have worked with the State Department Bureau of Conflict and Stabilization Operations in Syria to support radio stations. S of A provided information to help strengthen moderate groups in key communities. Hake said they had also begun to supply hand-crank, solar-powered radios for the stations to expand their reach. The initiative sounded a lot better to me than what Washington policy makers had previously considered: launching a few hundred cruise missiles into Damascus, which Islamic State terrorists would have approved of and in even greater numbers. I also recalled how effective and popular radios had been with the madrassa students in Khost.

In Niger the S of A team is supporting a civil-military initiative that U.S. military officers describe as an effort to "help prevent a war" like the one in neighboring Mali. They are assisting key tribes and traditional leaders with priority projects focused on livestock health and youth employment. Some locals are being trained in engine repair, while others have been given dirt bikes so veterinarians can reach remote areas. Again, an initiative small in scope, but one that would affect average people, even while the U.S. ambassador continued to meet high-level officials in Niamey, Niger's capital city.

Jim also said the nonprofit is providing books in Vietnam and the Maldives. In Afghanistan, we used to call small, open-access State Department–funded reading libraries "Lincoln Centers"—after the self-taught and very well read sixteenth president of the United States.

As I walked out, I noticed a banner, which encapsulated the entire effort:

S of A Model: *Decentralized. Private + public. Not neutral.*

Hake also showed me an email about a proposed donation:

Dear Sir/Madame,

I am not a wealthy person and feel that I can't donate money in large amounts. However, I do have a very little used harmonica that is in excellent condition and is capable of putting out excellent music in capable hands. Can you use it? I would sanitize it with a wipe of alcohol. I'm the only person that has ever used it and it has been well taken care of. I am a perfectly healthy 69-year-old former Marine officer (Cuban missile crisis era).

Hake and Spirit of America welcomed the donation and soon received the Marine's harmonica in the mail.

I left L.A. feeling optimistic that this small organization could continue to contribute in new and innovative ways, as it had via projects in Iraq and Afghanistan, but also in many other important locations. Hondurans, Mauritanians, and Filipinos, among others, were experiencing American greatness through American goodness. Private citizens performing a public good.

And the newest group to benefit from America's generosity through Hake's organization? Iraqis and Syrians in migrant camps in northern Iraq, displaced by the Islamic State—displaced by the Iraq War the U.S. started but could not end. These families include many from Fallujah, among them the Iraqis who had collaborated with Marines and me. Our friends. America's friends.

Fairhope, Alabama, ain't New York City or Los Angeles—in several complimentary ways. The author Winston Groom, who wrote *Forrest Gump* and is a Vietnam War veteran (the topic of his first books), lives in the area. As did Fannie Flagg, whose book *Fried Green Tomatoes at the Whistle Stop Cafe* celebrates Alabama's "sweet home" setting, downhome cuisine, and spicy heroines. The bucolic town sits across the bay from Mobile and has survived numerous natural disasters, which come in the form of hurricanes. Residents trade that omnipresent Mother Nature threat for the breeze that blows across Mobile Bay and top-quality seafood served fresh, any time of day or night.

As I drove into town from Pensacola, Florida's airport and crossed the Alabama state line, I noticed one stretch named "Vietnam Memorial Highway." I doubted any current freeway signage in the entire U.S. interstate system read "Iraq Memorial Highway"—or would, perhaps, ever. A bit farther along, I saw an even bigger sign: "Who is Jesus?" I knew my country had many versions of that sign along its winding highways.

I went to the coast of Alabama to meet a couple in their fifties who also decided to do something after 9/11. They chose Spirit of America as the nonprofit to support. Chris Toney, a gregarious Southerner, grew up in Texas and later moved to California. And a more introverted Marcella Franssen, who was born and raised in the Netherlands before working in San Francisco—where the two met. They got married and moved to Alabama, where both jointly operate their own computer systems consulting business.

I spent a weekend with them in Fairhope to understand why they had decided to become involved with S of A.

"We liked how it was small but doing big things," said Marcella.

Chris added, "It also gives us a choice in how we can help, and their projects address problems before they get bigger."

In a forested backyard, full of colorful jays, manic squirrels, and baritone toads, they explained their donations have enabled them to help with girls education projects in Afghanistan, a priority. Marcella also spoke of her European upbringing, noting that the world began to see the U.S. differently after 9/11. What began as positive perceptions turned negative, particularly when images of America locked in perpetual war took center stage.

"The wars in Afghanistan and Iraq have not helped tell the right story about America. The one I grew up hearing about," she explained. "Some Europeans wonder whether Americans only want more war."

By chance one evening on our way to pick up Domino's pizza in town, I happened to see a house just a few hundred meters down the street from Chris and Marcella's. The ranch-style home had a gold star hanging in the window of what looked like one of the bedrooms. I knew what the symbol meant—a house where a family lived whose son or daughter, brother or sister, had been killed in one of the wars.

I got on the computer and found the only name that seemed to match: Lance Corporal Bradley Faircloth, native of Mobile but whose mother lived in Fairhope.

He was killed in Fallujah, November 25, 2004. Thanksgiving Day. I read that the twenty-year-old Faircloth had received a Purple Heart for injuries on November 16, followed by a second one a week later after being wounded in the leg, two days before he died. I too called Fallujah home at the time—and would for almost three more years.

Ten months after Lance Corporal Faircloth's death, eight Marines from his company visited his mother to help repair her house from damage caused by Hurricane Katrina.

On my way to the airport, after Chris and Marcella introduced me to Southern-style, French-originated beignets (think donuts but better), I left Fairhope by way of the same stretch of highway memorializing the Vietnam War. Once in my cramped seat on a crowded plane, I noticed the headline of a *USA Today* the passenger seated next to me held in his hands. "U.S. Evacuates embassy in Iraq, Blasts Kill at Least

15 in Baghdad; Another City Falls." I asked him if I could keep the paper once he was done with it.

"Sure, you know anyone over there?"

A final Spirit of America–related trip meant I had to be in New York for a dinner, the American city where the 9/11 scars still feel deepest to me as a onetime New Yorker myself.

There was one caveat, however, the gathering was off the record.

The guest of honor, a military man, seated at the center of the long table, wore a gray suit. But in his day job, in pressed uniform with four stars on each collar, he was responsible for a geographic area home to hundreds of thousands of U.S. troops and massive amounts of Pentagon-funded hardware. His assigned part of the globe encompassed some twenty countries, including the world's most violent and unstable regions. To foreigners, the general personified American "hard power."

The dinner took place in the low-lit dining room of a posh Park Avenue apartment with multiple doormen, an oval marble foyer, and designer furniture. Thick walls and double-paned windows blocked out the 24/7 sounds of Gotham. The hosts owned one of New York's most eclectic, edgy, and expensive art collections—Picasso etchings, Chagall, but also Helmut Newton nudes. Several billionaires sat around the table. One had bought a major-league sports team—players that would later win the Super Bowl. Others helped manage some of America's largest hedge and investment funds. To my immediate right sat the president of Fox News Channel and chairman of the Fox Television Stations Group.

For the first time, I was among the .0001 percent. I felt out of place. In a massive way, you could say. My first jobs were at Dairy Queen ($3 an hour), delivering gooey Godfather's pizza, mowing weedy lawns, fixing drippy sprinklers, and cleaning runny toilets and rusty urinals after Little League baseball games in a public park. I imagined some of the others might have pulled fast food or maintenance duty as well in their youth. I wanted to think so, anyway, perhaps from hourly laborer with a timesheet to corporate titan ... the American story. Andrew Carnegie had done it: son of a Scottish hand-loom weaver turned U.S. steel magnate; author of a book called *Triumphant Democracy*; participant in the American Anti-Imperialist League (he once volunteered to give the Filipino people millions of dollars to buy their independence . . . from the United States—Mark Twain was also a member of the group); and, not least, America's greatest public library benefactor.

Across several courses while the rest of us ate, the top officer described current geopolitical dynamics, as well as the effects of a decade-plus of constant warfare involving battalions and more battalions of U.S. service members in two war-ravaged Muslim countries. The Spirit of America organization could not have asked for a better spokesperson. As he talked, I could tell this general traveled the world as a first-rate listener, not as an ego-driven lecturer, the more common and grating "voice of America" I had heard in the wars. Where many self-important-sounding U.S. politicians often treated their visits to Fallujah, Khost, and Helmand as part of a prerogative-filled lecture circuit. Marines called this unique military leader the "warrior monk."

After finishing our sculpted desserts, conversation shifted in more frank and informal directions. Perhaps it was the wine, poured by the platoon of attentive wait staff. Their silent culinary glide paths between guests demonstrated amazing training and talent, of the luxe Manhattan variety.

When it was my turn, I asked an open set of questions to everyone at the dinner party. It had two parts.

"Which word or adjective do you most associate with our country, the U.S.?

"And which word or adjective do you think non-Americans associate with us these days, after 9/11 and in light of our wars in Iraq and Afghanistan?"

While noting some of their answers, which included references to democracy and the much and rightly lauded American traditions of "freedom" and "opportunity," I told them that I had heard a lot in both wars about drones, Abu Ghraib, Guantánamo, and unconstrained U.S. military power. A mirror on America that did not reflect the values we wanted Iraqis and Afghans to see in us, as well as the rest of the world.

The dinner discussion continued in animated fashion.

I may have disagreed with some of their politics, but I respected these guests. They embodied a major, if at times legitimately controversial, part of the entrepreneurial American tradition. A broken system that many Americans believed had been, for some time, stacked against the common person, the common interest. To their credit, however, this elite group had assembled not just to write a check. They wanted to share ideas about how to make America better and do something about it.

The general did make one comment that requires, I think, a slight exception to the off-the-record understanding we had that night. In a subdued voice, he reminded us all of the reckoning under way. The reality.

"I am like the Roman general Aurelian, Lucius Domitus Aurelianus Augustus. Also known as 'Restitutor Orbis,' who reigned from 270 to 275. No one has ever heard of him. He's not in the big history books. Why not? His job was like mine is today. To help pull the empire back, closer to home, back to Rome."

Had our own country (overstretched empire?) reached its limits for good? Or perhaps would the "Spirit of America" endure and rebound despite two long and costly wars gone wrong? Two big wars both ongoing and both unwon.

None of us at the Park Avenue apartment that night left with easy answers, just a shared sense that all of us, along with other Americans— no matter the differences in net worth—could and should do more.

Months later, in the same towering city of concrete, steel, and glass, John Phelan, a Florida native in his early fifties, was telling me about how September 11, 2001, changed everything for him.

"I was right here. We saw the first plane. Our office windows actually rumbled and vibrated. It was a beautiful day, just like today.

"We were on the phones with Cantor Fitzgerald. Believe it or not the phones stayed connected. Then they said they had to get off." The trading firm's headquarters were located between the 101st and 105th floors of One World Trade Center.

Friendly and charismatic, the onetime Goldman Sachs employee has helped invest and grow computer mogul Michael Dell's money, along with his own sizable portfolio. I was tempted to tell Phelan how very reliable my (very heavy) Dell Inspiron E1405 laptop had been in Fallujah and Khost, impervious to the dust and dirt and to being dropped a dozen times. The two were classmates at Southern Methodist University in Dallas. At one point during the U.S. economic meltdown, Phelan and allied investors had considered a bid for Fannie Mae, the country's huge mortgage clearinghouse. The U.S. government said thanks, but no thanks.

I had inquired to see whether he was willing to discuss his involvement with S of A. He agreed and invited me to visit at the end of a Thursday workday. On the top floor of a sleek office building, his investment company—lean by NYC standards, numbering fewer than a hundred—hummed. It felt like a place where the speed of computers and their connections had premium priority as millions of dollars zoomed back and forth in deals few knew about and fewer, like me, understood.

While walking over, he began to explain what went on that day in September, thirteen years earlier. His desk was bordered, fan-like, by several large computer screens and commissioned artwork displayed all around. The setting reminded me of a pricey coffee table art book— but with the museum-quality items hanging on the walls, not printed on pages.

"I walked home from the office, like everyone in the city did. I was mad. I was angry. It was upsetting. We lost a lot of personal friends. Who can ever forget those jumpers from the top of the towers? Even days later, you could smell death in the city."

Like Chris Toney and Marcella Franssen, Phelan decided to do something to help U.S. troops, who, he said, "everyone knew would be at war" soon. He began by focusing on Special Operations Forces, particularly the SEAL community. After helping them fund a building on a military base for family members, he heard about Spirit of America. Though small, he said its efficiency attracted him ("I use Charity Navigator to check organizations out"), in addition to the "character references" of the low-profile nonprofit, including those from Marine General Jim Mattis.

"Part of it is the narrative. We Americans need to tell our story better. And Spirit of America helps do that."

He and his wife, a former Dallas Cowboys cheerleader, are well-known and respected art collectors. Phelan, who serves as co-president of the Aspen Art Museum in Colorado and on the Whitney Museum's Executive Council, began to help organize fundraising events, tapping into donor networks in New York and elsewhere.

Phelan described the influence of his father, a military doctor.

When his father died, he decided it was time to help in bigger and more concrete ways. He first started looking into medical areas, which later grew into military issues as service members deployed to Iraq and Afghanistan.

Across the years, he has helped a number of SEALs find employment after they have left active service and remains close with many, for example, joining a few on a getaway trip to Las Vegas.

As I looked out of his office window down a glittering Fifth Avenue below, soundless, I could see the new Freedom Tower at the far end of the motorized rivers of red and yellow lights. I figured it was my turn to tell Phelan a story of my own.

I spoke about how I met Jamshid, a medical student, in Khost years earlier. He sent an email to me in August 2012, all the way from eastern Afghanistan, after learning about the death of Neil Armstrong:

> So sad about the death of nail armstrong he was the real poineer who had shown his heroism & persuade human to seek & try more and has made clear that nothing is impassable.

Jamshid's was the only note or message I received about the great astronaut's, the great hero's, death. And wondered how many American youth today, or young adults for that matter, knew Neil Armstrong's story. The Korean War veteran by age twenty and native son of Wapakoneta, Ohio (pop. 9,830), who had gotten his pilot's license before his driver's license. If they knew what Armstrong had done, what his first footprint (left foot), on July 20, 1969, represented to Americans—and to the world.

My own dad, I explained to Phelan, was in Vietnam that day, on a C-130 headed back to Pleiku after escorting a prisoner to Long Bien jail in Saigon. He arrived under, of all things, a full moon that night at Camp Enari and could see two Cobra gunships strafing nearby Dragon Mountain, where a North Vietnamese Army unit had launched an attack. Armstrong's moon looked peaceful, but planet earth was not.

Decades later Dad said that as he watched red tracers streaming from the gunships and the white flashes of exploding rockets, "I realized how events could be so disconnected. We were risking our lives daily and the rest of the world was watching the moon landing on television. We wondered whether our efforts and sacrifices really had any meaning." While Sergeant (E-5) Weston and hundreds of thousands of other soldiers and Marines were in Vietnam, over a million Americans had congregated at Cape Kennedy in Florida to witness the launch of Apollo 11.

My dad's comments reminded me that the Vietnam-Iraq parallels, and home front/war front disconnects, were deeper, a lot deeper, than I had thought.

And America's moon landing narrative had found audiences worldwide, not only then but also to this day.

The July 1969 lunar journey—with only thirty seconds of fuel to spare in the Eagle module—took place eight years after President John F. Kennedy had challenged the nation to help get American astronauts there, before the Soviets did. A huge mission accomplished, you might say. And what were Astronaut Armstrong's words after placing the American flag on the moon? "It has a stark beauty all its own. It's like much of the high desert of the United States. It's different, but it's very pretty out here."

Perhaps like the high deserts of California, outside Twentynine Palms.

Perhaps like the high deserts of Utah, outside Topaz.

The New York Times ran a giant headline above three large photos:

MEN WALK ON MOON
ASTRONAUTS LAND ON PLAIN;
COLLECT ROCKS, PLANT FLAG

Voice From Moon: 'Eagle Has Landed'

A Powdery Surface Is Closely Explored

The *Times* story began with a transcript of the transmissions between the astronauts in space and Houston: "Houston, Tranquility Base here. The Eagle has landed."

(The astronauts dutifully filled out a customs declaration dated July 24, 1969, and marked their flight number as "Apollo 11." They listed their departure from "Moon" and declared their "cargo" as "Moon Rock and Moon Dust samples.")

Phelan and I bemoaned how it seemed the U.S. could not do "big things" anymore—to maintain let alone expand a space program, which was canceled in 2011. And win wars, for that matter. We chuckled, awkwardly, about how a Russian spacecraft is now required to act as an orbital taxi. With U.S. taxpayers footing the almost half-a-billion-dollar bill in order for American astronauts—only six seats allowed, mind you—to get to the International Space Station. And back.

At least, I thought to myself, NASA was in the dream business again, looking to space well beyond the moon, beyond Mars even, backed by science and engineering—and billions of dollars. It had announced a new program: a solar-powered spacecraft in development that would take astronauts into deep space, well beyond earth's orbit, possibly back around the moon and even all the way to Mars.

Its name?

Orion, with the first crewed launch date planned for 2021—a mission, at last, that matched Ray Bradbury's books, Ray Bradbury's imagination, Ray Bradbury's dreams.

I finished a third cup of black coffee as the sun was setting. Phelan concluded by saying a group of SEALs he considered friends had encouraged him to help out other service members, particularly one branch he knew I was closest to more than the rest.

"They told me I should help Marines because these wars have been unconventional. The SEALs said Marines have been the ones doing the hardest kind of fighting."

His comment made me think of an email a Marine friend had sent in response to the tsunami of SEAL memoirs and movies. He had been an infantry company commander in Fallujah, earning that rarest of wartime street credibility in U.S. military circles. The Marine wrote to me explaining how one of his platoon commanders saw a Naval Academy grad buddy-turned-SEAL at Camp Fallujah. They compared daily missions, with the SEAL "incredulously" saying, "You guys actually live out there?" (Out there being the rest of Anbar province.) The lieutenant said it seemed his special operator friend believed "that all Marines did was haul ass out of Camp Fallujah and break things, like SEALs did, then go back and work out." My friend said he remembered the SEAL-Marine dynamic himself: "We watched SEALs in Ramadi in 2007–2008 when shooting everything that moved was no longer required, and they did not adjust well to the complexity."

My friend went on to add another point on night raids: "We learned the best breaching tool is a key." He would know. He served in the most violent and dangerous locations in both wars. And unlike for most in-and-out Special Operations Forces, these places were the full-time home for Marine infantry units (as well as for me) during deployments, not drop-by single missions. If tribes wanted revenge after SEAL operations went bad, as they sometimes did—civilians shot, for example— well, we became the targets. The subsequent proliferation of roadside bombs and attacks killed more U.S. troops, on top of the Iraqi and Afghan noncombatant dead. This was a tragic and hard cycle to break once under way. It had a dark wartime momentum all its own.

The multi-deployment Marine infantry officer put the dilemma this way: "I've raided a lot of houses, and detained a lot of dudes, and we never had to shoot anyone. Doesn't mean there aren't dudes who shoot at raiders, but I think when you know you have to walk or drive by the next day, you balance your immediate risks to your force protection during the raid with the risks over the term of the deployment. When you just need to stay safe long enough to exfil [exfiltrate from a hostile environment], your incentives are understandably, but incorrectly, biased to minimize your risks in the short term—at the expense of us poor helmet heads."

I kept this part of the much less well known SEAL narrative to myself while encouraging Phelan to reach out to top Marine leaders I knew in Washington and California, as well as to the Mammoth Mountain–based disabled veterans coordinator. He said he would. I was grateful SEALs had urged him to help Marines. Phelan then walked over to a shelf behind his desk. From a stack of hardcovers, all with the same title, he handed me a book and urged me to read it: *The World America Made* by Robert Kagan.

The title reminded me of one of Phelan's most appealing business principles, all listed on his company's website: "We must continually remind ourselves of our limitations and dedicate ourselves to the avoidance of hubris. If our methodologies are valid and our people are talented, hubris is one of the only things that can make us fail."

. . .

I eventually sent the rest of the Neil Armstrong moon landing story to Jamshid in Afghanistan—an example of American soft power resonating decades later.

Before the astronauts' launch into space, Armstrong's younger brother, Dean, recounted how Neil slipped him a piece of paper during a late night game of Risk after their kids were in bed. Neil said, "Read that." "And I did," Dean recalled in the documentary *First Man on the Moon*. "And on that piece of paper there was 'that's one small step for a man, one giant leap for mankind.'

"He [Neil] says, 'What do you think about that?'" I said, 'Fabulous.'"

According to NASA, Neil Armstrong's footprints on the "Sea of Tranquility," 238,900 miles above earth, will remain on the moon "for a million years" because "there is no wind to blow them away."

Mission control in Houston at the time remarked to the earth-bound astronauts, "We'd like to say, from all of us and all the countries in . . . in the entire world, we think that you've done a magnificent job up there today." Armstrong's reply after spending two and a half hours on the moon: "Thank you . . . couldn't have enjoyed it as much as we did."

The Apollo 11's crew took a plaque with them and left it on the chalky and still lunar surface: "Here men from the planet Earth first set foot upon the Moon, July 1969, AD. We came in peace for all mankind."

An enduring American story.

It took Jamshid to remind me of that.

And to remind me of President Kennedy's words in 1962: "We choose to go to the moon. We choose to go to the moon in this decade and do other things, not because they are easy, but because they are hard."

Hard . . . like fighting wars . . . and winning wars, though troops and I could only imagine what that felt like, having ourselves been stuck in two seemingly endless American conflicts.

I continued my trip. It was time to return to Texas—to visit Dallas, a world apart though within the same state as Menard and the cemetery there. Where Marine Captain Christopher Alaniz was buried, next to his mother.

Libraries allow children to ask questions about the world and find the answers. And the wonderful thing is that once a child learns to use a library, the doors to learning are always open.

LAURA BUSH

The Library

One of the books SEAL Team Six found in Osama bin Laden's compound in Pakistan, the night they killed him on May 2, 2011, was *Imperial Hubris*, an account of the George W. Bush administration in the run-up to the Iraq War. It was just one of several in English in the terrorist leader's small personal library. Other titles? *The Rise and Fall of the Great Powers* by Paul Kennedy, Bob Woodward's *Obama's Wars*, a copy of the 9/11 Commission Report, among various other reading material, such as: *The Best Democracy Money Can Buy; Secrets of the Federal Reserve; Christianity and Islam in Spain, 756–1031; Guerilla Air Defense: Antiaircraft Weapons and Techniques for Guerilla Forces;* Project MKULTRA, the CIA's program of research in behavioral modification (a Senate report); *The U.S. and Vietnam, 1787–1941;* and, reportedly, a lot of porn.

Receiving repeated emails in broken English from Iraqi friends about the deteriorating security situation in Iraq made me think it was finally time to spend the day in Dallas, the site of another and much bigger library. Though hesitant, I had to go. And so I bought an airline ticket, packed a carry-on bag, rented a car, and headed to the Lone Star State a second time. My destination was the campus of Southern Methodist University, adjacent to a busy freeway and towering dark blue glass Merrill Lynch building, just off exit 3, which had a prominent road sign near it: George W. Bush Presidential Center.

Never before had I visited the official library and museum complex of a former U.S. president. For many reasons, however, I believed this one, this self-scripted political shrine, should be my first. I would rather have been at Lincoln's in Springfield, Illinois; Truman's in Independence, Missouri; Eisenhower's in Abilene, Kansas; Clinton's in Little Rock, Arkansas; Reagan's in Simi Valley, California; or, for that matter, the library of President George Herbert Walker Bush, the elder (the wiser?), in College Station, Texas.

I wondered how one ex–commander in chief more than the others told his story—and, specifically, how this famous Texan told the Iraq story. How a president of the United States of America conveyed his own war story beyond past service in the Texas Air National Guard, as a stateside pilot in the 147th Fighter Interceptor Group during the Vietnam War. George W. Bush had, after all, started the war in Iraq, never insisting his national security team debate the pros and cons of preemptive war in the White House Situation Room. The only time I had met him occurred over a decade earlier, in New York City, minutes before he stood at the United Nations podium in front of the world, challenging Saddam Hussein to hand over his alleged stockpiles of weapons of mass destruction.

That was September 2002, six months before the "shock and awe" Iraq invasion. Somehow since then I had survived seven consecutive years of the wrong war he launched in Iraq and the right war he turned the nation away from in Afghanistan. Too many of my Iraqi, Afghan, and American friends had not survived. It was they—their sacrifices, memories of them—who formed the basis of my own war story and motivation to write, and to be in Dallas, notebook in hand.

These uncomfortable thoughts stayed with me as I passed through the front doors of his library. Yet I walked into the main foyer trying hard to keep an open if still skeptical mind. Before long, a silver-haired Steel Magnolia (think Barbara Bush blunt, in a good way) basically ordered me to start my self-tour in a specific wing on the ground floor of the Texas limestone, dark redbrick, bunker-like, and near-200,000-square-foot building with clean lines surrounded by native wildflowers. I knew when to follow orders. She said I could take pictures, as long as the flash was off. I promised it would be.

When I got there, just past a cavernous central area called Freedom Hall, one of the first voices I heard in an audio recording in the low-lit and largely empty room was Condoleezza Rice's, the Stanford academic, national security adviser, secretary of state, and my prior top boss. She had awarded me (certificate signed, then mailed) a State Department Medal for Heroism for serving between 2004 and 2007 in Fallujah with Marines. I appreciated the gesture, but never felt heroic or deserving of this medal—a real one, engraved sterling silver, inserted in a small case even—in a war I believed to be a strategic disaster for the country I represented. The glass-framed certificate with her signature on it and the medal remained in the bottom of one of my big, black, padlocked footlockers.

This State Department award only brought into sharp relief all of the past tragedies for Marines and countless U.S. troops—and which continued to be a present-day, ongoing tragedy for millions of Iraqis. They deserved far more recognition than I ever did. Iraqis who died, almost always violently, and whose families never got death certificates, let alone awards honoring the courage of a dead father or a dead husband or a dead brother. Or brave mothers, and there were a lot of them. Everyone always knew the cause of death. Terrorist bullets or bombs ended their bravery, their public service, in an instant. Kamal, Hamza, Najm, Sami, Khudairi, Abbas . . . among so many, many more.

Sounding professorial (she teaches a ten-week seminar at Stanford U. titled "Challenges and Dilemmas in American Foreign Policy"—too bad Khost U. and Baghdad U. students cannot enroll), Dr. Rice was describing President George W. Bush's surprise visit to Anbar province on Labor Day in September 2007. No U.S. president, Republican Bush or Democrat Obama, would ever manage to land in Iraq except in secrecy, for a few hours only and almost always at night, amid Secret Service paranoia. No "Victory Day" celebration.

On the wall in the darkened exhibit area, I watched video footage showing the commander in chief in a room full of Marines and Iraqis at Al Asad, a military base in the middle of Iraq's western desert, the province I had called home across three Iraqi winters. He was there to meet with the United States' new Sunni tribal partners, several of whom I recognized. Rice narrated this still misunderstood and mythologized Petraeus-to-the-rescue moment in self-congratulatory words. Needless to say, few if anyone in Washington ever credited the Iraqis first, or sometimes at all.

As I stood there, I kept hearing echoes of Rice's "we don't want the smoking gun to be a mushroom cloud" pronouncement in the run-up to the Iraq invasion. The reality? No WMD found. No matter how hard George W. Bush looked in the Oval Office. And no public *mea culpa* from her for getting it all deadly wrong—museum visitors would not hear the details of that part of the Iraq War story in this well-orchestrated and well-edited history room.

During his 2007 visit to the Marine base, President Bush told assembled U.S. service members: "You see Sunnis, who once fought side by side with Al Qaeda against coalition troops, now fighting side by side with coalition troops against Al Qaeda. Anbar is a huge province. It was once written off as lost. It is now one of the safest places in Iraq." Those self-assured words were not in the video either. Before long, it would be clear to Americans and the world, including those who had lost family members in the war, that Anbar was anything but "one of the safest places" in the country.

Iraq was imploding. Iraqis killed by the dozens, sometimes daily.

Proceeding to walk around the corner, I saw the paintings, the reason I was told to start the tour in this section. The former president-turned-painter's portraits of world leaders were introduced in big block lettering on a scarlet wall.

THE ART OF LEADERSHIP: A PRESIDENT'S PERSONAL DIPLOMACY

It included a self-portrait: gray hair, blue suit, white shirt, blue-striped tie. Among the others I stopped to view in more detail was that of Prime Minister Tony Blair, below which the museum had placed a gift Mr. Blair had presented Bush: a copy of *Never Give In! The Best of Winston Churchill's Speeches* selected and edited by his grandson. On the title page, Blair had inscribed: "To George, My ally and my friend" dated 17 July 2003. Neither of them, president or prime minister, struck me as particularly Churchillian. Churchill had helped end a global war, not start a heedless, needless one.

I walked by other hanging portraits, one of them Chinese president Jiang Zemin, near a photo of Bush driving China's Communist Party leader in his F-250 truck on his Crawford ranch. A green-and-purple-robed President Hamid Karzai, dour-faced with dark ovals under both eyes. And a portrait of Vladimir Putin, skeletal and tight-lipped, whose eyes, at least in Bush's rendition, did not appear very soulful, more reptilian than anything. I saw others on the wall as well: the Dalai Lama; German chancellor Angela Merkel—her cell phone surely and inexcusably tapped by us in those days; the Saudi crown prince in white and gold headdress; and the face of a bespectacled, unshaven man with sagging jowls, almost frowning. It was Nouri al-Maliki, Iraq's sectarian prime minister—our, and even more so Iran's, Man in Baghdad.

Brushstrokes, I thought, must serve as some kind of therapy for the former president, as many had speculated. One self-portrait, much commented upon, showed Bush's slightly hunched back in the shower and, within a small round mirror to the left, the former commander in chief's disembodied face. It has a disjointed and unnatural quality to it. A Picasso quote came to mind: "Who sees the human face correctly? The photographer, the mirror, or the painter?" I thought to myself—*perhaps it is the writer or the poet.* And what about the face of war? I read the former president had painted many cats and dogs, but no U.S. soldiers among the hundreds of thousands of troops he once commanded and ordered to two war fronts.

Portraits of America's WIA or of the people whose countries the U.S. had invaded probably would require a different kind of reckoning, more personal, as the subject gazed back into the eyes of the artist.

In the Bush exhibit, two quotes were prominently displayed amid the portraiture.

That's what the people of our respective countries expect. They expect people to work out differences in a constructive way. They expect leaders to seize opportunities for the benefit of their respective peoples. And the spirit is very strong to work together.

George W. Bush
March 14, 2007

In order to work together to make difficult decisions—decisions
of war and peace, decisions of security, decisions of trade—
you've got to have somebody to talk to that tells you straight up
what's on their mind.

George W. Bush
May 16, 2006

As the son of a fifth-grade school teacher, I noticed the former first
lady had her own part of the museum as well, in a section titled "Laura
W. Bush: Teacher and Librarian." It featured a black-and-white photo
of her from 1970, smiling, when she was known as Laura Welch, a
fourth-grade teacher at John F. Kennedy School in Houston. She would
have liked Abbas, I thought, the English teacher in Fallujah. (After he
was killed, a Marine friend emailed me to say, "I often thought of him
as a good English teacher, who probably would have liked to discuss
Dickens if the war were not going on.") And she would have liked the
students in Khost, I am sure, especially that one Afghan girl—the top
student—as well as Commander Erika Sauer. Much to her credit, Laura
Bush in the past had brought much needed public attention to the
importance of ongoing U.S. support for girls education in Afghanistan.

I also noticed the Bush Library and Museum had online resources
for teachers, with one lesson plan titled "Analyzing Historical Objects."
It stressed the importance of "provenance, authenticity and reliability."

I walked a few meters more under the watchful eyes of another
guide, into a room marked "September 2001" with a follow-on headline ". . . And then there came a day of fire." This was the room, the
part of the library/museum, that had brought me to Texas. Right away,
the self-designated chaperone approached me as if on cue as I scanned,
360 degrees, what lay ahead. All that President Bush had decided to put
on display concerning the seismic event that had not only changed the
trajectory of his presidency, but also our nation and many others—lives
and futures counted in the tens of millions.

The guide came up to my side.

"The only thing missing is the bull horn. They asked us to loan it
to the new 9/11 museum in New York City."

She really wanted to start a conversation.

"What brings you here?"

"Oh, I'm into history. I majored in it in college. This is the first presidential library I've been to."

"A lot of thought went into this part. You can touch that if you'd like," motioning to her right.

She had noticed I was looking at a column of twisted burnt orange metal marked "C-11" from Ground Zero in New York.

I put my fingers on it and felt worse, not better.

"We also encourage visitors to leave a 9/11 message on the computer here."

I sat down at the terminal she escorted me to, with a photo above it showing President Bush on the telephone, gazing out of a window, in what looked to be Air Force One somewhere at 30,000 feet. Close to his picture was an invitation to museum visitors:

"Share your memories from . . . 9/11."

I took them up on the offer.

After entering required information, name, place of residence, and so on, the screen opened up.

What would be my message?

I thought for a minute, as the helpful but nosy matriarch-of-the-museum stood over my shoulder. I waited until she moved on to assist another visitor in the room. And then I typed and hit enter. A new screen automatically flashed. "Thank you for submitting your 9/11 memory. We value your story and want to share it with other visitors. Your story will be available for public viewing after our staff have reviewed it."

That was the kicker. I knew then my message would be filtered out by diligent and loyal staff members. I had left a simple one. I listed names. American and even more Iraqi names followed by a concluding line that ended with "and for the hundreds of thousands of others dead." My words felt right. My words felt honest. My words felt necessary. It was the Thursday before Memorial Day Weekend. I believed I had the right to name names—names few knew from wars already forgotten by most back home.

Venturing deeper into the room, I noticed a cabinet devoted to Iraq, near a sign on the wall that read "Defending Freedom." It included the deck of fifty-two Iraqi "Most Wanted" playing cards, Saddam Hussein's "9mm Glock model 18C Automatic Pistol"—and a Hussein "Wanted" poster, announcing a $25 million reward for "any information leading to the arrest or proof of death of Saddam Hussein." It also housed an Iraqi election ballot. I recalled how I had given many of mine to a Marine friend from Hickory, North Carolina, who framed the ballots for many Gold Star families across America.

About midway through the tour, a new guide suggested I go over to the "Decision Points Theater" computer simulation. She said it helped visitors understand how difficult being president was, the hard choices faced by Bush during his eight years in the Oval Office. There were only four of us seated in the *Star Trek* bridge–like semicircular room. On a large blue screen, a computer counted down the minutes until we could "vote for your scenario experience" from the following four options:

> Threat of Saddam Hussein
> Hurricane Katrina
> The Surge
> Financial Crisis

Without hesitation, I chose "Threat of Saddam Hussein." Two narrators appeared, one of them White House chief of staff Andrew Card, a Massachusetts-born transplant to Texas for a time, Life Scout, and former member of the White House Iraq Group chaired by Karl Rove.

Card's September 2002 comment in an interview with *The New York Times*—"From a marketing point of view, you don't launch a new product in August"—soon gained notoriety. That "product" being war, the invasion of Iraq. Our digital narrators said a "majority" in the simulation had picked the Hurricane Katrina role-play scenario. I turned to my left and asked the two people next to me what they had selected. "We didn't choose the hurricane." One of them, a woman in a wheelchair, added, "I'm from Florida. I don't want to hear about Katrina!"

That made three of us, out of the four . . . a majority . . . who had *not* picked Katrina. Iraq would not be explored that day. Any day?

I left the room and asked the guide about the Iraq simulation and what people thought about the decision to invade.

She looked uneasy.

"Most visitors agree with the Iraq decision, but they don't about the financial crisis."

I did not pursue either subject, though I was tempted to tell her about the time Fallujah's reconstruction committee leaders had sarcastically volunteered to help repair the devastation in New Orleans, given the amount of experience they had in rebuilding a destroyed city. And how Mississippi National Guardsmen deployed in southern Iraq had requested emergency leave from Marine Major General Stephen Johnson to return home to the flooded Gulf Coast. To do what they could to save their family properties.

Back in the main hall, I delayed a bit in order to view several large cabinets, prominently arranged on both sides of the building's front desk, containing "Gifts to the American People" from around the world. Europe and Russia. The Americas. And so on. But there was one also marked "Gifts *from* the American People." That collection, more than the others, grabbed my attention right away. The former president and first lady must have had hundreds and hundreds of gifts to choose from for this particular, and most important in my view, display case.

Peering through the glass, I saw that the Bushes had selected mostly martial items: a "silver saber with gold detailing, engraved U.S.M.A. Given to President Bush in honor of his 2002 commencement address to the United States Military Academy"; an artillery shell casing "given by an Air Force lieutenant general commemorating a successful operation"; a "Marigold carnival glass serving bowl, inscribed with the phrase 'Good Luck'"; a "handcrafted, silver-tone belt buckle with gold trim reading, 'George W. Bush January 20, 2001'"; a "stainless steel and pewter sword engraved with 'United States Air Force Academy'"; a "limited edition Pfaltzgraff platter with words inspired by President Bush's September 20, 2001, address to a joint Session of Congress, during which he described the nation's resilience in the war on terror, saying: 'We will not tire, we will not falter, and we will not fail'"; and an "eagle sculpture on marble base with engraved plaque."

But it was two other gifts situated side by side that gutted me: a sculpted metal dog bowl and seven KIA/MIA memorial bracelets from the families of U.S. service members. A bright spotlight above outlined paw prints and "B-a-r-n-e-y" spelled out, the name of the Bush family's beloved black Scottish terrier. The light caused the bracelets to glint, as if rightly forcing eyes that way above all the other items. If the Bush library had any ghosts, they would be at this spot. One bracelet had the name of a Marine killed in Fallujah on March 27, 2007:

SSgt Marcus "Ski" Golczynski (30, of Lewisburg, Tennessee, pop. 11,121).

A Marine who died a month after I had left.

Listed as "Item 7" in the cabinet, the museum label read: "Memorial bracelets. Family members of captured and killed service members gave President Bush these tokens of remembrance." Perhaps a loaded gift with hidden meaning in a time of an unnecessary war, and I could only hope none of them saw how the bracelets were placed next to Barney's handmade tribute, labeled "Steel dog bowl with paw-shaped feet."

When a Marine friend of mine who had served in Iraq and Afghanistan saw the picture I had taken of the bracelets and adjacent Barney bowl, he said, "I about threw up." Like me, he had lost friends in Iraq. The infantry officer also had Marines under his direct command killed by snipers and IEDs. All who fell in Anbar by following orders and the strategies, some of which failed, that I helped devise with the generals and colonels.

On my way out of the GWB Presidential Center, I stopped in the gift shop. Signed copies of President Bush's memoir, *Decision Points*, were priced at $200 and "limited" to five per customer. The shelf was full of them.

Inscribed copies of the Karl Rove book *Courage and Consequence*— which sounds like a war book but is definitely not—cost $30. Thirty bucks too many. (In April 2015, Rove lectured an Iraq veteran and student, former private and medic Ryan Henowitz, about war. At a public forum at the University of Connecticut in Storrs, Henowitz asked Rove to "apologize" to veterans and Iraqi civilians for the invasion and the tremendous cost in lives. "I saw my friends torn apart and Iraqi children screaming for their parents as indiscriminate shrapnel scarred them and us in ways that we will never know. We were exposed to more questions about life and death than any twenty-year-old should have. These scars stay with me and other veterans who are now one of the highest demographics who commit suicide." The student went on to say, "Can you take responsibility and apologize for your decision to send a generation to lose their humanity and deal with the horrors of war which you have never had the courage to face? Will you apologize to the millions of fathers and mothers who lost their children on both sides of this useless war?" Instead of an apology or any acknowledgment of the human cost of the Iraq invasion, Henowitz got from Rove a steamroll of defiant words—"Removing Saddam Hussein from power was right. He had thumbed his nose at the international community . . . the United Nations had passed fourteen resolutions . . . fourteen times he gave the finger to the United Nations . . . And he was a state sponsor of terrorism," along with a choice "but I appreciate your service" kicker. As if the two of them had equal experience, and standing, on such matters. And as if no one would remember that the person who had given the biggest finger the most times to the United Nations and the international community in the run-up to the Iraq War was Karl Christian Rove himself. I know because I was there. The god-awful gall of it all.)

Laura Bush, who holds a master's degree in library science and was a librarian at Dawson Elementary in Austin, also had her own recommended reading lists, in the past remarking: "As long as we have books, we are not alone" and "Libraries offer, for free, the wisdom of the ages—and sages—and, simply put, there's something for everyone inside."

The former first lady, who had cofounded in 2001 the National Book Festival held annually in Washington, listed her "Family Favorites," including *Little House on the Prairie*, *Little Women*, *Old Yeller*, and *Winnie-the-Pooh*. For adults, she recommended nine books, among them Toni Morrison's *Beloved*, Willa Cather's *My Antonia* and *Death Comes to the Archbishop*, and *Ship of Fools: The Collected Stories of Katherine Anne Porter*.

Crowding the rest of the shelves were thick memoirs, multiple copies of Dick Cheney's *In My Time: A Personal and Political Memoir*, Condoleezza Rice's *No Higher Honor: A Memoir of My Years in Washington*, Donald Rumsfeld's *Known and Unknown: A Memoir*, each with the author's prominent picture filling the cover: Cheney standing in a dark suit astride a regal red carpet; Rice smiling and wearing a large and luminescent white pearl necklace; Rumsfeld in jeans and a fleece vest leaning against a rustic log fence. All of these authors looked very comfortable indeed. (Cheney has written two more books, one with his cardiologist, titled *Heart: An American Medical Odyssey*, and another coauthored with his daughter, titled *Exceptional: Why the World Needs a Powerful America*. The former vice president dedicated his latest writing

"To the men and women of the United States Armed Forces, defenders of liberty, sustainers of freedom.")

I also noticed another book at the gift shop, *A Patriot's History of the United States: From Columbus's Great Discovery to the War on Terror.*

"War on Terror," an invented phrase meaning war without end.

An attendant asked if I wanted to buy anything. I said no thanks, but that I liked Laura Bush's recommended reading list—Cather, Morrison, and Porter, as well as *Old Yeller.*

On the shelves, I did not see any books by Colin Powell, whom Bush had nicknamed "The World's Greatest Hero."

Despite my jarring tour, I wished George W. Bush and Laura Bush well. Unlike Dick Cheney, Bush had remained noticeably quiet as Iraq imploded. In this regard he was more the statesman, as many Americans expect presidents (and vice presidents) will be, not only during their time in office but also in the unscripted years that follow. George W. Bush had also offered important words to reduce divisions. In April 2002, he said, "America rejects bigotry. We reject every act of hatred against people of Arab background or Muslim faith. . . . Every faith is practiced and protected here, because we are one country."

In a fundamental way, though, the need for wartime accountability about an unnecessary war trumped my instinct to give President Bush too much of a break. Iraqis warranted, by far, the most empathy. In my mind, they always would. Always should. I felt the same about our troops and their families. The decision to invade Iraq affected millions of lives, with many hundreds of thousands now dead, and more injured. Whole nations. Entire hometowns left to grieve the deaths of their young, and survivors forced to flee the growing violence, if lucky enough to get far enough away from it soon enough. American hometowns devastated, others in allied countries, but also countless and unknown ones across Iraq and Afghanistan.

Washington could not even—or chose not to—get many of the most deserving of our collaborators, those who somehow survived, Special Immigrant Visas to come to the United States despite documented and mounting threats directed toward them and their families. If not for one former USAID official named Kirk Johnson, who had started his own Schindler-like list for Iraqis, far fewer would have been saved. (He later authored an important but far too under-read account and accounting of this un-American travesty, titled, appropriately, *To Be a Friend Is Fatal.*) That also amounted to a topic left unaddressed in this presidential museum: All Those We Left Behind.

And so I made a point before leaving the museum to record with a picture the handwritten "Iraqi Sovereignty Note" passed by National Security Adviser Rice to President Bush on June 28, 2004. Prominently displayed, the note reads:

> Mr President,
> Iraq is sovereign. Letter
> was passed from Bremer at
> 10:26 AM Iraq time.
>
> Condi

Over which the commander in chief had written in thick black ink:

> Let Freedom Reign!

Of course it was the U.S. invasion and subsequent occupation of Iraq that had made the country *not* sovereign in the first place—and where terror now reigned.

The same day President Bush's dog Barney died, which he noted with a heartfelt Facebook page update on February 1, 2013, news headlines read, "Chaos and Violence Continue, Protests Take Place Across Iraq" and "Al-Qaeda Front Calls to Arms" with photos showing the biggest anti-Maliki protests centered near Fallujah. An AP wire story noted 178 Iraqis were killed the prior month in bombings and shootings.

And the U.K.'s *Guardian* newspaper featured a story that day as well, under the headline: "U.S. Military Struggling to Stop Suicide Epidemic Among War Veterans."

The war that goes on—for some.

There's no such thing as a crowded battlefield. Battlefields are lonely places.

GENERAL ALFRED M. GRAY
29TH MARINE COMMANDANT

A Museum of War

It felt right to be making these visits over Memorial Day Weekend.
What began as Decoration Day after the Civil War had become much
bigger than an annual calendar marker for one terrible conflict, North
vs. South, American vs. American. While the tradition of leaving flowers at gravesites continued, I knew there were other ways to remember and honor America's war casualties. Many of the most affecting
examples could be found in museums, which chronicle some of the least
well-known story lines of warfare. One such place located in northern
Virginia details the contributions of those who almost always are sent
in first to any fight: U.S. Marines.

The same military branch charged with protecting U.S. embassies and State Department personnel worldwide. As American diplomat Karen Aguilar said in 1991 when the U.S. embassy in Mogadishu,
Somalia, was threatened by a violent crowd: "They told our perimeter
guard to open up [the embassy] or 'we'll blow you away,' and then they
looked up and saw the Marines on the roof with these really big guns,

and they said in Somali, 'Igaralli ahow'—which means, 'Excuse me, I didn't mean it, my mistake.'" (The embassy was later evacuated in a dangerous mission by Marine helos, two CH-53 Super Stallions. A number of other nations' diplomats who were bunkered alongside U.S. diplomats in the compound were also rescued.)

After departing Dallas, I landed in Washington, D.C., where my Marine friend Mark, nicknamed "Brick," introduced me to his two children for the first time, a kindergartner and a third-grader. I had already met Mark's spirited Australian-born wife, his exact opposite: a self-described hippie and yoga expert, known to change her hair color on a regular basis. She had some of the best insights into Marines of anyone I knew. They had scheduled a family field trip to the Marine Corps Museum near Quantico, Virginia, that holiday weekend, before the family was to go camping in Maryland. Mark decided to bring his son along even though his wife had to stay back home with their sick daughter.

It was my third visit to the museum, a place I felt comfortable in, unlike the Bush Library and Museum. After spending almost four years alongside Marines in Anbar and Helmand, I knew well their way of war—how they managed their own heroic story line and media messaging. U.S. Army General John Abizaid, during his regular Fallujah stops as boss of Central Command (CENTCOM), used to joke about the latest Marine success story being shamelessly and aggressively promoted back home to Congress and, more important, to the American people.

"Semper Fi" had attained its own special place in U.S. military history and lexicon even before a museum was built to reinforce the USMC saga. Marines' "core values" defined as Honor, Courage, Commitment, with recruiting commercials that featured Marines in precisely tailored uniforms with shiny swords—and figurative dragon/monster slaying abilities in the digitized 1990s version ("more than a trial by fire, it is a rite of passage").

Not to mention the silent drill team, standing in a row at attention, in scenic locales coast to coast, from urban Manhattan, mountainous Colorado, a red sandstone mesa, all the way to a fog-shrouded Golden Gate Bridge. All of this effective spin based on Marine traditions unmatched by other service branches. "The Few, the Proud" are indeed cocky, always have been, I suppose—but with good reason and in a way the United States of America will always need in a dangerous world. They remain Uncle Sam's expeditionary force, America's modern-day legions expert in one primary mission: warfare, a subject top Marines take courses in at their graduate-level School of Advanced Warfighting.

Even so, I knew Marines were not just muscled robots only set to kill mode when need be. In Fallujah, I had seen how some of the toughest Marines cried when buddies died or showed visible torment when Iraqi civilians were caught in the crossfire.

Upon entering the museum, one cannot help but notice the wheelchairs first. They are lined up in a row at the entrance. Each has an imprint of the Marine Corps symbol: a big red, gold, and white Eagle, Globe, and Anchor. I have observed corporals pushing and escorting other corporals, their onetime battle buddies. It is an amazing thing to witness. A reminder just how young most Marines are. The youngest, still teens, reminded me more of Boy Scouts—granted, a lot tougher version than the ones I knew in my childhood.

While the Bush presidential museum charges an entrance fee, the National Museum of the Marine Corps, Marine Corps Heritage Center does not. Jutting out of immense green foliage, the triangular building resembles a slanted steel and glass pyramid, designed to evoke Marines raising the flag over Iwo Jima on Mount Suribachi.

As one guide told me: "They sent the architects to Iwo Jima, and said walk the beaches. They sent them to Europe's battlefields, and said here's where thousands of Marines died. They sent them to Korea and Vietnam too. Their job was to make a museum that fit the level of sacrifice and unique traditions of the United States of America's Marine Corps."

On full display before me I could see just how much architects had succeeded in doing that. There are war museums—and then there are war museums. The Marines' set a new standard. In its halls, the biggest battles of prior conflicts are reenacted and accompanied by video, audio, and interviews of all ranks.

Open every day except Christmas, museum sections explore each part of USMC lore in visceral detail: "Born in the American Revolution," "To the Shores of Tripoli," "Barbary Wars," "The War of 1812," "The Seminole War," "Swamp Action," "Pacific Expeditions," "The Civil War," "John Brown's Body" (with the secretary of the navy saying, "Send all the available Marines at Head Quarters . . . to Harper's

Ferry ... which is endangered by a riotous outbreak"), "Confeder-
ate Marines," "The Battle of New Orleans," "With Lincoln at Get-
tysburg" (his Marine aide, First Lieutenant Henry Clay Cochrane,
writing, "In [Lincoln's] simple wisdom and eloquence, something had
been said which would live forever"), "The Spanish-American War,"
"Philippine Insurrection," "The Boxer Rebellion," "Latin American
Interventions," "Cuba," and perhaps the most famous: World War I's
Belleau Wood; World War II's Guadalcanal, Tarawa, Peleliu, and Iwo
Jima ("the caves," "the beach assault"); Korea's Inchon and the Frozen
Chosin; Vietnam's Hue City ... and a section that resonated with me
perhaps more than all the rest, "Guerilla Warfare." (The first gallery
also, incidentally, contains a virtual firing range within the "Making
Marines" part of the tour.)

When visiting, I have always paused at the Marine account of not
leaving allies behind. Particularly since we had left so many behind in
Iraq and Afghanistan. The museum recounts "Operation New Arrivals" in 1975, designed to help fleeing Vietnamese establish new homes
in America. It describes how the USMC base at Camp Pendleton,
California, served as one of four "national welcome centers" where
"Marines erected berthing, dining, and recreational facilities, just as
tens of thousands of refugees began arriving. By November, more than
50,000 Vietnamese (38 percent of them children) had found a temporary home at Camp Pendleton, en route to permanent relocation
throughout the U.S."

For Iraqis and Afghans, the message could be summed up as:
Stay out.

The first female Marines are also showcased. The museum displays
a letter home, written in 1918, by Private Martha L. Wilchinski: "I
hear some people are giving us nicknames. . . . Anybody that calls me
anything but 'Marine' is going to hear from me."

I would have liked to have met this Marine.

But what about the wars in Iraq and Afghanistan?

In contrast to the established museum wings packed with twentieth-
century war memorabilia and poignant firsthand accounts from World
War I, World War II, Korea, and Vietnam, the 9/11 wars section has not
yet been built. Countless Marines enter the immense central hall to see
how USMC historians have recorded "their" wars in Iraq and Afghanistan. They leave disappointed, for in one small corner, a few enlarged

color photographs have been placed on display boards, the kind you see in traveling roadshow exhibitions. And that is it. One side is titled "The Liberation of Fallujah 10 Years Ago." Another side, "Afghanistan." And a summary of "American Support for Free Elections."

Every time I visit, I realize how hard a job the museum curators have ahead of them. And yet there is a telling preview of what will surely come, as troops begin to record more of their stories from the 9/11 wars. Australian photojournalist Stephen Dupont, for example, collected handwritten notes by a group of Marines based in Helmand. He had been embedded with a weapons platoon there, in the remote outpost in southernmost Afghanistan named Khan Neshin, a forlorn stretch of desert toward the Pakistan border that Larry and I had visited several times. Dupont took black-and-white photos of each Marine and asked them to write down on a piece of paper an answer to one question:

"Why am I a Marine?"

Displayed along the wall one Marine's words, a sergeant's, stood out most to me. He looked about my age, prematurely war-wrinkled around the eyes, and reminded me of Jean-Claude Van Damme. He answered the question in self-edited plain script, an author of authenticity:

> I've been doing this for long enough that I'm not sure I remember anymore. I love the Marine Corps, but talking about it seems a little like discussing a personal, intimate and deeply dysfunctional relationship. It's tumultuous, it's hard, and I don't always feel that things are going very well, but in the end it's rewarding in [a] way that nothing else could be. Besides, it's loving the Corps that is hard, loving Marines is easy.
> Sgt Ingels, John A.
> Line Sgt Mortar Section
> "Death Dealers"
> "THE OLD MAN"

After three years in Fallujah and a year in Helmand living with the USMC, I also felt like an old man, having seen death dealt to many Marines, the dreaded battlefield Ace of Spades. And to the Iraqis and Afghans as well, who died in the greatest numbers around me—they too fell "to my left and to my right" as assassins' bullets found the bravest among us and among them.

As Mark and I left the museum to go to a McDonald's on base for lunch, we did not dwell on the long list of Marine battles. Amid past great Marine heroics, we had lived the most recent losses. Instead, I asked my Marine friend questions I always asked infantry guys I had worked with in both wars and knew well, well enough to ask: "Do you want your son to be a Marine?"

I got the answer I usually heard.

"No.

"But if he wants to join, I'll support him."

Reticence and pride in equal measure.

"And your daughter?"

"Hell, no."

And I knew why on both counts.

Unnecessary Iraq and necessary Afghanistan had been endless wars fought by the few on behalf of the many, only to be forgotten during them, not just after the conflicts were said to be over by the politicians in Washington.

Mark elaborated later on in an email.

It is a really important and interesting question. One I've talked about with a few Marine friends over the years over a few beers. I think that this is a deep question actually, and therefore my "real" answer is deeper than just a simple "no" though that's partially right.

Once talking with a friend who had served in Saqlawiyah and then later in Fallujah, he recounted a fucked up story and I recounted a fucked up story. He said something to the effect of "now do you want Sam to one day have stories like this?" Sam had just been born, so of course I said, "hell no."

But there is more to it too, deep down in places we Marines don't talk about at parties. I'd of course be a bit proud if Sam or Chloe joined the Marines, and I kid them about it all the time. Neither of them wants to so far, and Sam doesn't play dress-up like a Marine or want a Marine haircut or any of that. But I'd love if they did, and be absolutely afraid if they did. And were killed or injured in a war that I'd be to blame for leading them in that way.

Their decision to join must be completely theirs, and if I

think it is to make me proud or impress me I'd tell them hell no. This is a decision that must be made personally, you can't do it for someone else, like if you read *Fortunate Son* by Chesty Puller's son. It didn't work out for him.

Make sense?

Mark concluded his message by adding:

I love the Marine Corps and I don't bear it any grudge for all the f'ed up things that have happened. They never promised me anything better, and I am as much to blame as anyone else. I do have some arthritis in my back and thinning hair, but I'm in good shape all things considered.

I also recognize that the consequences of our individual choices were much more significant than we understood at the time, like when I joined. My father understood this when I enlisted in the reserves in college. He had done four years in the Air Force from 1960–64, but he knew from Vietnam that such possibilities existed. He made it clear to me that even in peacetime, even in the Reserves, that joining was no joke.

The easiest way to avoid all this is to hope your kids just find something different and safer to do. At the same time they may never have the same type of friendships and appreciation for what they have if they didn't join.

I actually hope they choose some line of work that offers similar life experiences without the individual risk of trolling for IEDs and snipers, like the State Department, FBI, CIA, or an NGO.

Just not my kind of State Department career, I thought.

Construction of the Marine Corps Museum's newest wings (a $100 million expansion), with exhibits dedicated to the wars in Iraq and Afghanistan and other operations post-Vietnam, began in 2015—sacrosanct architecture measured most fundamentally in lives lost. The KIA, as well as the WIA. According to a press release, the new exhibit will include: an oil-soaked Marine Corps flag from Desert Storm; election ballots from Iraq (almost assuredly the very ones I had sequestered in Fallujah in 2005); gear worn by female Marines during Operation Iraqi Freedom and Operation Enduring Freedom; and the rifle carried by Navy Cross recipient Sergeant Rafael Peralta. Born in Mexico City, he joined the Marine Corps after receiving his green card and became a citizen while in the service. Peralta died in Fallujah on November 15, 2004, age twenty-five, after being shot multiple times and, reportedly, by placing his body on top of an insurgent-thrown hand grenade, an action that saved other Marines' lives.

Everywhere I went the ballots followed, which was both an honor and a most difficult reminder of all the sacrifice, Iraqi and American.

Until the new wings are constructed, museum curators have placed a simple card within a temporary small exhibit covering Iraq. It is titled "They Gave All."

The tribute reads:

On March 21, 2003, four Marines from Marine Medium Helicopter Squadron 268, aboard a CH-46 Sea Knight helicopter, were killed in a crash. They were among the first U.S. personnel killed in Operation Iraqi Freedom.

By the time the last Marine team left Iraq in October 2011, 1,022 Marines had died, and 8,626 had been wounded in action.

. . . Four of the earliest Angels in the Iraq War . . .

After making multiple visits to the Marine Corps Museum, I had gained a deeper understanding of war and war's toll. USMC martial history seen through Marine eyes, with the backdrop being the almost 250-year history of America at war dating from 1765—when colonists were the insurgents—to the present day. These museum tours prompted a recurring question. It was straightforward enough, although one not for any U.S. Marine, museum curator, or American historian for that matter to answer.

I had been in both Iraq and Afghanistan long enough to know the local people had seen us doing some good, even acting at our best at times. They had also seen our worst instincts and behavior. Amid the girls schools we had built, there was Abu Ghraib and Bagram. Amid

Marines' usually disciplined restraint in night raids, there were occasional black ops and other missions during which civilians were killed, and women and children left shaking and forced to face the walls, hands tied, in dark corners. And so on. "Mistakes"—but much more than that overused and scapegoating-kind-of word—that cost more Iraqi and Afghan lives than our own. Along with our generosity and partnering came tragedies and a nonchalant detachment among too many on our side toward Iraqi and Afghan suffering. We redeployed home. But for them, the wars continued to be fought in their cities, villages, and neighborhoods.

Al Qaeda followed us into Iraq.

The Islamic State arrived after we left.

The Taliban are stronger today than in 2002.

The people of Iraq and Afghanistan should have the last word about the successes and failures of U.S. efforts in their countries. Some of the "iconic artifacts" (to use Marine Museum terminology) they might choose to highlight would probably surprise us. Perhaps election ballots next to orange jumpsuits? U.S. taxpayer–bought science textbooks next to Guantánamo detainee diaries?

Visuals to go along with the varied war stories they would want their children and grandchildren to know, retell, and remember.

The bad. The good.

Nick's Home

I continued on from Quantico to Colorado to visit a two-mile-high town called Leadville.

The mountains have served as a welcome escape for many, I think, and for me, for sure. The thin oxygen of high terrain had long been in my blood. Mountains, natural geographic fortresses, whether Afghanistan's Hindu Kush or the American West's Rocky Mountains. In the Mosquito Range in central Colorado, there is a location named Weston Pass. I feel at home when hiking there. As I am sure the Afghans in Khost's Qalandar District, mountain people, would as well if they ever had the chance. It sits at 11,921 feet. I understood why John Denver (born Henry John Deutchendorf, Jr.) had changed his name and relocated below 14,000-foot peaks to write his best music. At such heights, life's lows never seem quite as low, reminding me what a war-worn and war-wise Marine veteran from California once told me as we traded stories in another mountain setting. Following his war, Vietnam, he relocated to the Sierras, he said, for solitude, adding, "I was finally ready after a few years to return to civilization. My wife sure was too."

Upon arriving in Denver, I made my way up the eastern flank of the Rockies, where I noticed patches of dead or dying trees along I-70. Just like those forests I saw in Khost's Qalandar District that might have saved my life because I noticed them when meeting with Afghanistan's own mountain men. Halfway into my drive, I turned onto a scenic byway off the interstate. A blue metal sign was posted at the start of it, which read: "Fallen Heroes Highway, Dedicated to LCPL Nicklas Palmer, USMC." The two-lane road begins near Copper Mountain Ski Resort and is the site of an annual motorcycle ride in honor of this fallen native son, a Marine, who was killed in Fallujah.

Unlike so many other places across the West, the trees surrounding Nick Palmer's hometown of Leadville had not died. I found the resilient foliage reassuring. The winters are cold enough, the elevation high enough, the peaks white enough, to kill bark beetle infestations. The weather-toughened pines, populating thick forests, remain green year-round, apart from when snow drifts surround them below weighted branches.

I never met Nick Palmer, but he was the reason I was in Colorado. I attended his memorial at the end of 2006 in Fallujah. A terrorist sniper killed Nick almost a year after Lance Corporal Ryan McCurdy had been shot just outside the CMOC.

Nick was nineteen, Ryan twenty.

The Palmer family asked me to join the town's veterans memorial service. Less than a year earlier, a local community leader had introduced me to Brad and Rochelle Palmer after hearing about Denver-based Marines and our plan to hold a "war reunion" there.

At the time, Nick's parents invited me into their home to see Nick's room. To sit at the kitchen table and on the living room couch to hear Nick's story, including before Nick joined the Marines, before Nick went to war.

Brad said to me, "I just don't want my son to be forgotten." And that, in a fundamental way, was why I was in Leadville. Not to forget. Fallujah tied this family to me in a way none of us ever would have wanted.

And so I went and listened. I had seen magazine photos of bedrooms of the fallen, but was unsure how I would feel actually walking into one. Knowing what I knew about the successive failures in American war policy and my own role in them as a longtime U.S. official in Iraq and Afghanistan.

After entering their welcoming light yellow home with green trim, first built on the hillside in Leadville to house silver miners a century earlier, we walked into the kitchen. Across the road, fittingly, sits the National Mining Hall of Fame and Museum. The Palmers began to narrate as still grieving parents what they had collected and displayed to memorialize their son. Many old items prominently featured from his childhood, alongside new ones. Gifts, some anonymous.

On a living room wall, they had Nick's formal Marine uniform and an American flag, folded below, in a lighted wooden case.

Brad, a Montana native and bear of a man with a raspy voice who supervised the Lake County public works department (no ice pile too big to clear by sunrise), held up a snow globe. It contained Nick's picture. While a tough-talking Westerner, of the Rocky Mountain variety I knew so well, he was always the first to tear up on the topic of their youngest son.

He described how he and Rochelle first thought the knock on the door was three Jehovah's Witnesses—until both parents saw the Marines standing on their porch in uniform. "Then we went numb."

We walked past the gun safe, a massive black steel lockbox the size of a refrigerator, to a poster on the wall: "United States Marine Corps Silent Drill Platoon." Brad proudly related how he had his snow-removal team plow the roads so that the famous platoon could film footage with Mount Massive in the frame. The now iconic video in military circles shows the practice-perfect, picture-perfect Marines throwing swords in precise fashion in ultra-Americana settings coast to coast, from a lighthouse in a foggy Maine to the Golden Gate Bridge in a foggy San Francisco Bay. This conversation with Nick's parents reminded me how the recruiting commercial's baritone narrator declares:

"There are those who dedicate themselves to a sense of honor.

To a life of courage. And a commitment to something greater than themselves.

They have always defended this nation. And each other.

They still do.

The Few. The Proud. The Marines."

The Continental Divide had been one stop, the Marine Silent Drill

Platoon's favorite, according to what many of them told Brad. After watching a YouTube clip of the scenic compilation, I was tempted to contact a platoon of Marine generals and urge they put this commercial back on the air. Older Americans needed to see it again. Younger Americans needed to see it for the first time.

A bit farther along in the Palmer home, I saw a watercolor painting of Nick and his older brother, Dustin, a Navy veteran. Another gift.

Rochelle, also a Montana native, said she worked in the county recorder's office and only had to walk a few blocks to the office five days a week. Leadville winters, however, were "getting old," she added. Particularly after a recent major snowfall, two-plus-feet deep, which collapsed a roof on Harrison Avenue. A quiet woman, she insisted I eat some pizza from the fridge and handed me a copy of the book *Final Salute: A Story of Unfinished Lives*. Written by onetime Colorado resident and Pulitzer Prize–winning journalist Jim Sheeler, it chronicles several KIA, their families, and one Marine Casualty Assistance Calls Officer named Major Beck—charged with making official death notifications. I told her I would get a copy for myself, while thinking these pages would not be easy ones for me to turn.

Brad motioned to me to sit next to him as he opened a file on his computer containing Nick's last photos from Fallujah. They had been on his flash drive, part of the personal belongings shipped home after his death. But first he showed me a set of pictures of Nick's casket being lowered and transferred to a hearse at Denver International Airport below a silver-bodied American Airlines jet. Snow had begun to fall. It was night. A Marine honor guard stood at attention. Vacationers showing up to ski took a different exit.

Vail, Telluride, Snowmass, Steamboat . . . all popular wintertime vacation destinations far removed from a place like Fallujah, or Leadville for that matter. I wanted to tell Brad that before Iraq and Afghanistan I used to hit the slopes a lot more often. But again I kept to myself how the big guns and explosives used by ski patrols for avalanche control reminded me of the 155mm howitzers at Camp Fallujah, unforgettable wartime audio.

In town, on the county football field Christmas week, Leadville residents and students had stamped down foot-high snow to read: "Honor NP."

Nick's personal photo archive from Fallujah showed his daily routine and personality, and included: several buddies giving the middle finger salute to the camera; a dust-covered red and yellow sign that read "Welcome to Camp Fallujah, Iraq" (the same sign I had taken photos of in 2004); Marines building defensive perimeters next to HESCO barriers; a self-portrait, arms folded with a serious look; another of Nick wearing his sweat- and dirt-encrusted helmet, goggles atop, while seated in a Humvee. Clearly this Marine was no deskbound Fobbit.

The final set of photos were not of Iraq but instead showed Leadville's Veterans Memorial, a construction project Brad had helped spearhead. A flag flew at half-staff, a small boy walking forward, the son of Nick's older brother, Dustin.

Moving up the staircase, the Palmers continued to narrate personal stories. How Nick used to play football. Camp almost every weekend he could in the summer near Turquoise Lake. Hang out on Main Street, looking to see who was new in town. And after deciding to enlist in the Marine Corps, stuffing a backpack full of heavy rocks and running for miles at two-mile-high elevation, no less, for pre-boot-camp training.

Two pictures in pencil had been sent to them and hung on another wall. One featured Nick in his desert tan digital camouflage uniform, the other of a kneeling Marine, titled "Never Forget," in front of Old Glory, rifle, helmet, and boots.

Once we reached Nick's childhood bedroom, which the Palmers had since made their own, they pointed out a quilt in browns, reds, and blues. In the center was a gold star, with the following dedication:

In Memory of LCpl Nicklas J. Palmer, 1987–2006, made by the TQL Quilt Guild, Leadville, Colorado

They went to the dresser and pulled out several more quilts donated by Americans across the country. I had never seen so much carefully stitched material in one place.

As we walked downstairs, family photos hung along the wall: one when both parents had no gray hair, another one of the newlywed couple in spoof Wild West attire, and Dustin and Nick in grade school. Little boys. Big smiles. By evening, Brad and Rochelle Palmer offered me a drink as we watched an hour-long video of the town memorial service held for Nick at the local high school. They said they had not watched it in years. I soon saw why.

Throughout that day, in his home, at the kitchen table, on the living room couch, the full loss hit me. Only nineteen years, then gone. No more camping. No more fishing. No more dragging main. No more Marine Corps. No son or daughter to call his own. I almost wished they had not hit play on the video recording. I saw in each of them another version of the face of war, and just as pained as those I had witnessed on Iraqis, Afghans, and Marines.

Despite being mostly a teetotaler when it comes to hard liquor, I think I drank more whiskey that night than I ever had. And I might have had even more than Oscar Wilde did when he visited town in 1882. In his travel memoir, *Impressions of America*, the British dandy recounted the story of having dinner with Leadville miners, where he was "lowered in a rickety bucket in which it was impossible to be graceful" into a silver mine in order to have "supper" . . . "the first course being whiskey, the second whiskey and the third whiskey." But this was not an evening for Wilde-like wit and levity among deserving imbibers.

That night, Nick's parents cried the entire time. Their son had been killed in Fallujah seven and a half years earlier.

To understand Nick and the Palmers, you have to understand the place they call home. It is geographically and historically unique, a mostly out-of-the-way place to seek out—and to return to. It has got character and has always been full of Western characters, one of the settings for Wallace Stegner's *Angle of Repose*.

Their scrappy Colorado hometown ranks as the highest incorporated municipality in America, also known as Cloud City. Many made their fortunes in the area, including the Guggenheims. Horace Tabor built a famed opera house, the only one at the time between St. Louis and San Francisco. The "unsinkable" Molly Brown got married at the Annunciation Church, and ex-dentist Doc Holliday took up residency despite recurring pneumonia made worse by Leadville weather. And there is a mine called Resurrection not far from the city's biggest steeple, outlined by Mount Elbert and Mount Massive, Colorado's two tallest peaks.

But the nineteenth-century town legacy is not all riches. The Lake County Public Health Agency posts flyers at the local library today that read, "Our goal is to have every child checked for lead." The notice specifies children ages one to six and pregnant and nursing moms and includes an incentive: "$25.00 Safeway Gift Certificate given."

During the mining boom in the 1880s, well-dressed Easterners used to try to summit the mountains, some still in petticoats and in top hats. Now the mountains are filled with fitness freaks who hike, climb, bike, and run in a locale not far from Camp Hale, the original winter training ground for the 10th Mountain Division. A total of 992 of the Hale-trained "ski troopers" died, and another 4,000 were wounded, while fighting German forces in northern Italy. A number of the surviving veterans, carrying only their skis again and not rifles strapped to their backs, returned to Colorado after World War II and helped found some of the state's world-famous ski resorts.

The town today is most famous for the Leadville 100—a 100-mile race for ultramarathoners across craggy peaks and steep mountainsides. Mount Hope is the midway turnaround point. On the other side of the mountains is situated the pricey resort community and part-time home to many commuting billionaires and millionaires: Aspen. Where fleets of Learjets park dozens deep and each summer an Ideas Festival is convened among the nation's mighty and moneyed elites. In recent years, various VIP panels have been organized to discuss the wars in Iraq and Afghanistan, usually featuring invitation-only think tank staff, current and former senior government officials, generals, veterans-turned-authors, and cable television anchors. One Ideas Festival episode in particular, given Nick's story, represented the obvious disconnect between those who debate war and those who go to war.

In summer 2012 in Aspen, Dr. Stephen Cambone, PhD, the former intelligence head in Donald Rumsfeld's Pentagon, described Iraq as "one of the great strategic decisions of the first half of the twenty-first century, if it proves not to be the greatest." While not in attendance myself, I received a text at the time from someone in the audience during the exchange, and asked right away whether anyone had challenged the ridiculousness of Cambone's statement.

"No one," came the reply.

After leaving the wars and the State Department, I had attended a similar Aspen panel that included the topic of Iraq. A friend managed to get me a visitor pass and said I should drive my truck into the ski town and check out the festival. Feeling a bit guilty, I offered to pay fifty bucks for the pass. A fair price, I thought, until an organizer who had waived the fee said entrance passes cost thousands of dollars. I kept my fifty bucks but also got to keep the pass. The speakers included my old boss, ex-director of national intelligence and ambassador to Iraq John Negroponte, former California congresswoman Jane Harman—the onetime leading member of the House Intelligence Committee—as well as the British ambassador to the U.S. During the Q&A session no one, surprisingly, raised their hand for some time, so I finally asked a question of my own—about the failure of Washington politicians pre-invasion to read the Iraq WMD reports.

Negroponte cautioned against "relitigating" the past, citing progress in Iraq. But had America yet litigated the Iraq War in the first instance? I did not think so. War, I believed, was a worthy subject of a lot of litigation—and relitigation. Harman said she was not aware of which reports I might have been referring to. But the former congresswoman did state she had challenged Deputy Secretary of Defense Paul Wolfowitz in a phone call . . . before voting to authorize the Iraq War.

Rather than reengage the two VIP panelists I made one more comment, saying in my view that Iraq was a "political failure more than an intelligence failure." Harman nodded but stayed silent, as did Ambassador Negroponte. Their silence felt a lot like a cop-out. I wondered how they deal with their own mirror moments—both had long and distinguished records as public servants—as violence in Iraq got worse and stayed that way, on top of the tragic pattern of veteran suicides. While in Iraq, I had seen firsthand how the war exhausted Negroponte as he tried to referee between warring sectarian factions. I respected his efforts, pursued in the best traditions of the U.S. Foreign Service.

Not many senior diplomats or famous politicians or Silicon Valley entrepreneurs or Hollywood directors, however, ventured to the other side of Independence Pass. Ore mines, not ski lifts. Jeeps, not jets. Burgers, not brie. Beer, not Chardonnay. And lots of lead . . . not platinum. I wish they had. I think they would like Leadville.

The last time I had been in Colorado was for a "war reunion" of sorts. About forty veterans ate, drank, and reminisced at that gathering, also held in Leadville. The group, which included members of my family, had traveled from California, South Carolina, Utah, other parts of Colorado, Connecticut, North Carolina, Virginia, Florida, and even as far away as the Dominican Republic. Beer washed down cheeseburgers at the Silver Dollar Saloon, meters away from where a tuberculosis-stricken Doc Holliday shot his last outlaw.

Our discussions over that weekend focused on stories from the Marines' combat tours in Anbar or Helmand. Captains, corporals, sergeants, colonels, and even a two-star commanding general took part.

One of the Marines, James Cathcart, said he wanted to talk to me about my time in Fallujah, not about the unfolding events in Syria. I said sure. It seemed he had something specific in mind. A half-laidback, half-intense native of San Luis Obispo, California, he and his girlfriend had relocated to Colorado for the hunting and hiking, and to get away from people. A young Grizzly Adams, you could say. For much of the year, they had lived in a modified trailer on a wide sagebrush plain outside the town of Hartsel, just down the road from Leadville.

The last night of the reunion, Katie said James and I should talk. He asked if I had time and added, "We could go sit in my truck, where it's more private."

It was a wet night as another thunderstorm moved over nearby ridgelines. The Colorado Rockies had received near-record rainfall that summer, a soggy and Hemingway-esque weather pattern for sure. ("I'm not afraid of the rain. I am not afraid of the rain. Oh, oh God, I wish I wasn't.") As we sat in his big Ford F-350 with the heater on, I listened to James describe how hard his tours had been, from the first round of fighting in Fallujah in spring 2004 to his return in 2005, when the "Lionesses" were killed after a suicide bomber rammed their convoy. We both had been in the city at the time. We both knew some of the female Marines killed. We both could not forget the tragedy. (James would later recount to a *New York Times* reporter, as he did with me, how it was his platoon that had been sent to the scene that day, after the massive explosion: "I wanted to get with that girl, and then the next day I was seeing pieces of her all over the side of the road.")

I then offered my own confession. One I rarely conveyed to anyone, even in my own extended family.

"There is one decision, one day I'd take back because of what happened January 26, 2005. I was the one, James, who sent those thirty Marines and a Corpsman on that election mission in the middle of the night. General Dunford, when he was at Division, argued the opposite. I should have agreed with him.

"A day doesn't go by that I don't think about what happened, all their deaths."

James looked at me stunned, while smoking his third or fourth cigarette—being sure to blow the smoke out of the driver's side window.

"Wow, no way. You are the only person other than Marines who has ever said they remembered what happened on that date."

I could not hold back now, so I told him how we at Camp Fallujah had decided to send Marines across the province in preparation for Iraq's Election Day. Our rationale. Our logic. Our decision. *My decision*, after General Hejlik had turned to me for the final call, a decision that led to the nighttime mission during which the CH-53 helicopter crashed, killing thirty-one, the oldest not yet thirty-five years old and most still in their teens and twenties.

James lifted his shirt to show me a large tattoo on his side.

Next to a Marine rifle, with a helmet on top, above a map of Iraq:

Mourad Ragimov, 1/26/05 RIP
"Greater love hath no man than this,
that a man lay down his life for his friends"
—John 15:13

For the next several hours, through a lot of rain and even more cigarette smoke, we talked about Iraq and his friend Mourad, who had been on the helo that crashed that night. I said I was sorry. Repeatedly.

"James, if there is one decision on one day from over there that I could take back, it'd be that one."

"Your job, Kael, was to unfuck things for the State Department. Hard to do that in a place like Iraq after we invaded."

"I knew the Sunnis in Anbar would boycott that election," I said.

"Have you ever considered visiting with the family members?" James asked.

"Not sure I'd know what to say to them."

"Well, it might give you the chance to be forgiven. Mourad's family might want to talk to you."

"If you think it'll help them, let me know. I'd be a bit nervous, I bet. Actually, really nervous."

"I think you should."

The regret and sadness in me still ran deep, and always would. I was not sure either of us felt better by morning. Some personal war archives, I have learned, stay padlocked tightly and for a lot longer than others. Still, I promised James I would get back to Colorado and visit Hartsel. He wanted to continue our discussion.

Almost a year later, I kept my promise. Hartsel, pop. 825, is the geographic center of the state and is known as "the Heart of Colorado."

James offered to show me around, tell me more about Mourad. I met the locals who gathered at the only café/bar in a town without a stoplight. We sat under a mounted five-point elk head, not far from a stuffed raccoon, and tin signs that read "No Dancin' on the bar with spurs on." Nearby, a white board had the following local ads written under the heading "Check this out! . . . Horse and hayrides, private fishing, horseback weddings." As James drank beer and I poured black coffee, he described how their friendship got started. They were both computer nerds. Liked listening to Janis Joplin and Jimi Hendrix.

He recounted how Mourad's family had emigrated to the U.S. when he was two years old after fleeing the civil war in Azerbaijan.

"After 9/11, he said this is my country now. I need to go."

James had joined the Marines at age seventeen, needed his parents' consent. His mom said no, but his dad, a musician, reminded her, "This is the only thing James has pushed."

He enlisted.

Mourad soon followed, telling James, "If reincarnation is true, I'm a reincarnated Marine from Vietnam." They both cut their "California hippie hair." And while James was based at Twentynine Palms, Mourad went off to boot camp.

Soon after the helicopter crash near Ar Rutbah, James received a call from Mourad's younger sister, Shayla. After telling him about his best friend's death—they were very close siblings—he said she had only one more thing to say.

"Good luck with that Marine thing," and hung up.

James said Mourad's mother was "devastated and she still is."

The last two at the bar, we opted to crash in James's Colorado winter-proofed van (since the last time we saw each other in Leadville, he'd been forced to sell his Ford truck). It had a black-and-white bumper sticker on the back window, half in English and half in Arabic. "Stay

back 100 meters or you will be shot. OPERATION IRAQ / ENDUR-
ING FREEDOM." With pot legal in Colorado, James had brought
some with him. I admitted, while feeling embarrassed in a way, that I
had never smoked a joint before. He said it helped with sleep and some
veterans claimed it was good for PTSD. James vouched for it, enough
peer pressure for me. And so for the first time in my life, and very likely
the only time, I inhaled. And slept for eight hours uninterrupted.

The next morning, Memorial Day, I woke up on the floor of the
van with frost on the windows. Above me peered George W. Bush. But
I was not imagining it. James had a bobble-head doll of the president
affixed halfway up the passenger side of the van. I bobbled the bobble-
headed president a few times as I got ready to make my way to Leadville, my fourth trip there in two years.

Before leaving Hartsel, however, I told James he was right. After
thinking about it, I agreed I should be open to meeting some of the
families, if that is what they wanted and had any questions I might be
able to answer.

"Okay, I'll help arrange that with Mourad's family in San Diego. I
think his younger sister will definitely want to talk to you. She wants to
know what really happened that night."

"So do I," he added. "I heard it was a sandstorm."

As we scraped frost from the windshield, James asked me if I had
heard his 9/11 story.

"No, what happened?"

"It was my birthday if you can believe it," he said.

"Really?"

"On September 11, every year, I celebrate my birthday. But in 2001,
it was a hell of a lot different.

"My mom comes in and wakes me up in SLO [San Luis Obispo].
She tells me 'we're under attack' and to turn on the TV in my room.
That's when we saw the second plane hit.

"We watched, stunned. After a while, Mom said, 'Oh yeah, happy
birthday.'"

"Not quite like being born on the Fourth of July, is it?" I said.

On the drive from Hartsel I shared the road with only a few vehicles:
a truck pulling an empty livestock trailer, a camper that looked to be

guided by some semi-lost European tourists, and a few Subarus with bike racks. After getting more coffee, I arrived at the memorial site next to the local cemetery, where several hundred residents had gathered. The Memorial Day event lasted about an hour, under sunny skies. The grounds looked their best. Harley-Davidson motorcycles, three rows deep, were parked on one side. A towering Marine staff sergeant, last name Buck, who had served with Nick Palmer and had been close when he was shot and killed, described Nick's service in Iraq and the model Marine he had become after leaving Colorado. Bagpipes and Taps played, as a few blue jays flew near. I stayed in the back of the crowd.

In Washington, D.C., earlier that morning, President Obama and leading government officials had visited Arlington National Cemetery, the usual tradition. The Leadville gathering, in contrast, symbolized all the American families in far-flung communities. Those who watched their sons and daughters sent to faraway war zones and then, once back home, laid them to rest close to high schools, baseball parks, and Rotary Clubs, whether within inner-city projects or McMansioned suburbs.

While Nick had grown up in Leadville, he was interred in Great Falls, Montana. Where the Palmer family roots run deepest, where he was born and began school at Riverdale Elementary before moving to Colorado.

One day perhaps a commander in chief will turn her or his attention—and thereby the nation's attention—westward. Landing in Air Force One and motorcading to honor our buried KIA in a small place, far from the Potomac River and the marbled capital of Washington, D.C. I hope so. As in past conflicts, most of America's Iraq and Afghanistan war dead are not buried at Arlington, near the Tomb of the Unknown.

They are buried back home.

They are buried in their hometowns.

I deliberately did not read anything about the Vietnam War because I felt the politics of the war eclipsed what happened to the veterans. The politics were irrelevant to what this memorial was.

MAYA LIN

The Mall of America

My visits to Leadville, the Marine museum outside Quantico, and the George W. Bush library in Dallas prompted mixed feelings alongside painful reminders—about war in general and the wars in Iraq and Afghanistan in particular. By the time I redeployed home, these conflicts had comprised eighty-four months, almost 20 percent of my life and consuming most of my thirties. A co-worker had predicted (when I was in my twenties and she was in her forties) that this stretch of a decade would be "the best years" of my life.

Looking back, I suppose I could only view them as my red years, my most unforgettable years, but not in a sentimental kind of way. Leonard Delbert Philo, Corporal, United States Marine Corps, had put it well a century earlier during World War I when he wrote home about his war: "The forgetting part is impossible." Before he entered the deep and silenced ranks of America's KIA.

With so much on my mind, so much remembering going on, the National Mall in Washington was a natural spot to be on a Memorial Day

Weekend. A vast rectangular grassy area designed for reflection—no less the Reflecting Pool prominently featured within it—amid other sculpted reminders of loss. A nineteen-foot Abraham Lincoln, seated in his chair and head tilted slightly downward, personifies the pervading mood. The greatest wartime president's somber stone visage, carved in Georgia white marble, faces Capitol Hill and the nation's other war monuments. None of which memorializes the U.S. Civil War. The war Lincoln ended, leaving as many as 750,000 Northerners, Southerners—all Americans—dead.

The historic 146-acre National Mall was the same location where, months earlier, politicians had celebrated a U.S. government shutdown, with sequestration of taxpayer funds to follow. A Marine friend in Denver told me these shenanigans in Washington led to new restrictions on Corps-wide travel budgets, limiting his ability to see wounded veterans in Montana and Utah. They would have to wait. Like thousands of other service members affected by elected official malfeasance, they had no other option. These events coincided with polls showing Congress's popularity at all-time lows. As well as updated statistics revealing the number of veterans serving in the House and Senate had dwindled to a small minority, where argumentative lawyers dominate. The Greatest Generation, including those who had returned from war to serve again in the U.S. capital, had long since reached retirement age. And with them, I sensed, went a lot of wisdom too.

In the other Mall of America—as in the largest shopping mall in America (over 500 stores, 4.87 million square feet), located in Bloomington, Minnesota—there is a moving 9/11 tribute. Next to an escalator and Nordstrom Court, a metal statue resembling a door with stars on it honors a native Minnesota son. Tom Burnett, Jr., a father of three daughters, boarded United Flight 93 and decided to be one of the passengers who charged the cockpit, telling his wife, a former flight attendant, in a final call about the plan and urging her not to worry. My brother-in-law's uncle from Northern California died in that crash when the San Francisco–bound United Airlines jet, colored silver and blue, plowed at a 35-degree angle, almost upside down, into green fields in Pennsylvania. His wedding ring was eventually found and returned to his widowed spouse living on the west coast. The impact site, a smoldering, blackened pile of earth, metal, and human remains, resembled a crumpled phoenix.

The artist and sculptor of the statue in the Mall of America, Patrick D. Wilson, described his intent in casting the bronze work, which symbolizes a cockpit door. "This sculpture remembers a moment of decision. It is the intersection of strength in a moment of crisis. The connections between those on Flight 93, their families and loved ones, their lives and their country, generated in them the courage and the ability to act." I wondered how many shoppers stopped there, maybe even explained to children and teens what the art piece represented, what the day, September 11, 2001, meant for the nation and for many more nations overseas. And I wondered how many Americans visited the field in Shanksville, Pennsylvania. It too is a National Memorial.

I was waiting in line with hundreds of others in the center of Washington, D.C. Many of us, it seemed, wanted to begin our visit in the same place—the Maya Lin–designed Vietnam tribute.

I remembered how Vietnam had been introduced into my childhood. How war had been introduced to me—introduced by my father.

Like so many of them, my dad did not talk much about it, never applied for VA benefits or joined the local VFW chapter. But once in a while he would pull out an old slide projector on Sunday afternoons and set it up in our dark, cluttered 1970s-era basement with its vinyl wood paneling, gray carpet scraps, and used furniture from Grandpa's store colored in striped greens and browns. A white popcorn-like spackled ceiling encrusted with silver sparkles and, undoubtedly, healthy levels of asbestos, served as our impromptu theater's roof. As I grew up, these home matinees functioned as my only view into his generation's defining war.

His generation's Wrong, Long War, which he always called " 'Nam."

Dad clicked through his 'Nam pictures: a school-bus-sized, dual rotor Chinook helicopter dropping off heavy bundles of razor wire, and even a translucent-yellow coiled bamboo viper, which slithered into the tent housing dad's platoon. The poisonous snake did not last long in the company of grunts. Vietnam's jungle canopies formed the backdrop to dozens of canvas tents aligned in rows and at right angles, reminding me of Camp Leatherneck in Helmand. In none of the images did I see fear. Or chaos. Or death. Or war's occasional triumphs, whether personal or national, but I knew my dad, a U.S. Army infantry sergeant, had experienced all of this after leaving boot camp in Fort Ord, California. The West Coast base, long since closed, once boasted a recruit roll call including Jimi Hendrix, Clint Eastwood, Jerry Garcia, and sergeant-turned-defense-secretary Chuck Hagel.

Decades later, standing at the Vietnam Veterans Memorial, I recalled the tales Dad shared about his buddies. There were slides of a soldier awkwardly seated on a makeshift wooden toilet in the middle of the dense jungle, snaking vines twisted into layered curtains. I pictured the gregarious First Sergeant Porter, attested to be "hard-nosed but with a heart of gold." My father described another soldier named Eddie who engaged in sign language performances during foot patrols, a private missing the conversations back home with parents who were both deaf and mute. Hands once used to communicate with his mom and dad at the kitchen table were used to throw grenades and disarm trip wires, Eddie's new war zone vocabulary.

These men comprised the most memorable part of Dad's war, he said. In addition to when Miss America 1969, a trampoline champion, and other beauty queens with beehive hairdos showed up to meet the troops at long lunch tables covered with Meadow Gold milk cartons and ashtrays. He shared tent space, rations, and rotated point duty while on patrol with these fellow soldiers. Dad knew some whose names were etched on the subterranean black monument Wall, which I now stood in front of—part of the over 58,000 inscribed there.

As a kid, I never asked him how they died. Nor have I since.

Amid the tourists and veterans of all ages lined up along the Vietnam Memorial Wall—492 feet long and the only one in black marble amid all the white marble along the National Mall—I saw certain names, ones that had not been forgotten decades later. Family members had left notes, flowers, photos, poems, and lots of flags. While walking behind a gray-haired older man with a ponytail, his hands held by a woman wearing a pink T-shirt, I chronicled what I saw that day. His vest read, "United States Submarine Veterans." I thought it fitting that a veteran, who had spent his military career under the sea, was now back on land but walking below ground level to honor the fallen.

There were so many MIA signs along the wall that I lost count. Such as for SP5 Carl A. Palen, USA, MIA 1/3/71 in South Vietnam, whose information card read at the bottom, "His family still waits for answers!" It made me think that death notifications during wartime might, in some ways, be easier to receive than "Missing in Action" ambiguity. No military family, like my own, wanted either. We had firsthand experience about how unsettling such notifications, or ones perceived on the verge of being made, could be.

My Uncle Chad, my mother's baby brother, enlisted right after high school, serving in Vietnam as a sergeant with the elite Special Forces Green Berets. My aunt still tears up describing the time she and the rest of the family thought he had been killed. We all remember the story, a shared multigenerational bond. It began when a Red Cross ambulance drove up near Grandpa's store on Main Street in their four-street town of Milford, Utah. Only the day before, they had read an Associated Press wire report that Chad's location in the Thong Duc Corridor had been overrun by Vietcong. His mission was to train Vietnamese army units deep in the jungles so U.S. troops could transfer security responsibilities and return home. The same exit strategy we would attempt to repeat forty years later in Iraq and Afghanistan.

As my grandpa waited for the Red Cross staff to knock on his store door, he saw them pass by and enter the lone Chinese restaurant in town for lunch. Our family eventually learned that Chad had survived the attack, albeit narrowly. He suffered a sucking chest wound and shrapnel lodged in most of his backside, sharp pieces that surface today, four decades later. My aunt's dream of continuing to be a dental assistant in glamorous Hollywood, California, changed overnight. Both moved back to its polar opposite, to a place called Beaver, in Beaver County, Utah, near the town of Minersville, for good.

Uncle Chad, also known as Sergeant Chad W. Johnson, 5th Special Forces Group (Airborne), did keep his Green Beret business card with him. The small card listed his impressive job qualifications as one of Uncle Sam's premier fighters, a "Soldier of Fortune Specializing in Civil Wars, philanthropist, hero of the oppressed, casual hero, and world traveler" and a founding member of the "Far Eastern Indochina Special Forces and Jungle Fighters Association, LTD."

I later gave one of these well-worn business cards to a gung-ho Green Beret team leader in the middle of Marjah, Afghanistan, after Larry Nicholson and I joined his unit on a foot patrol through the area's ubiquitous purple poppy fields. He smiled as he read how his work, like my uncle's work decades earlier, had changed little. They shared the danger and sense of humor that is a hallmark of tough men assigned tough missions. Times change—but not much.

A bit farther along the Vietnam Wall was taped a tribute to the crew of a "helicopter ambulance" from the 54th Medical Detachment. It said Dustoff 19 had been shot down while on an operation on October 18, 1968, near Chu Lai, killing all four crew members. These KIA reminded me of all the dustoff crews in Iraq and Afghanistan, who flew under fire to pick up wounded troops amid bullets and even rocket-propelled grenades.

One such team on a mission to aid a badly wounded British soldier in a Pave Hawk helicopter, call sign Pedro 66, went down in Sangin in June 2010 after being hit in the tail rotor by a Taliban RPG. The crash killed Michael P. Flores (31, of San Antonio, Texas, pop. 1,409,000), Benjamin D. White (24, of Erwin, Tennessee, pop. 6,097), David C. Smith (26, of Eight Mile, Alabama, pop. 12,749), and Joel C. Gentz (25, of Grass Lake, Michigan, pop. 1,169). Pilot David A. Wisniewski, nicknamed "Wiz" (31, of Moville, Iowa, pop. 1,629), died of his wounds at Bethesda Hospital, not long after Larry and I visited him.

If any category of pilots and crew deserved a Combat Action Ribbon, it was they. The U.S. Air Force pushed for a medal for drone operators, deployed stateside. If approved, it would have been rated higher in precedence when worn on a uniform than the Bronze Star and Purple Heart. After much controversy within the U.S. military and veterans community, especially its infantry ranks, including many vocal Fallujah- and Helmand-tested Marines I know, the designation was placed under Pentagon review and eventually dropped.

Echoes of past wars continued along my walk. Toward the end of the long black wall, I saw a remarkable memorial that belonged in its own category:

In memory . . . PFC Dan Bullock, Youngest American To Die in Vietnam War, Killed In Action June 7, 1969. At Age 15

The Goldsboro, North Carolina–born Marine had altered his birth certificate so he could enlist. He arrived in Vietnam on May 18, 1969—the same year my father deployed. PFC Bullock was killed by small arms fire twenty days later, not even old enough to drive—that is, if he had been back home and not having volunteered to go to war. This young African American Marine clearly did not have "other priorities," as multi-deferment Dick Cheney once put it as to why he missed his generation's war. Bullock, a vivid contrast in comparison, made his nation's war, his generation's war, *his* priority. Now that is a patriot.

Another family had left bags of popcorn, perhaps their dead brother's, cousin's, uncle's, or father's favorite snack.

I saw a cake with white frosting and red lettering.

"Happy Birthday Dad"

Just before leaving the Vietnam Memorial, I noticed a collection of recent color photos, including one of a Marine, clearly not from the 1960s or 1970s. My gut turned. I knew this Marine had to have been killed in Iraq or Afghanistan. Perhaps his friends or family placed their special items here because Vietnam was the closest war memorial—another unnecessary war—to leave a remembrance.

His name was Lance Corporal Swain.

Only later would I read online tributes about how the Kokomo, Indiana, native had been killed by small arms fire in Fallujah, November 15, 2004—five days after I first entered the city, on the Marine Corps' birthday. He was twenty years old and the third native of Kokomo (pop. 56,895) to die in Iraq. I recalled all too clearly how Fallujah in those days boomed and shook and smelled, filled with packs of dogs and packs of Marines eyeing each other amid leveled neighborhoods and abandoned streets, both sides inhaling the scent of the dead and the dying.

I decided it was time to head to the next memorial, for the Korean War. In front of me stood several tattooed men, looking to be in their mid-fifties and sixties, each wearing leather jackets with "Leathernecks, New York" printed in big gold and red lettering. In the middle, the USMC's Eagle, Globe, and Anchor symbol. If Korea was considered America's "Forgotten War" . . . how was it memorialized? In dramatic if understated fashion, I soon saw.

While approaching the monument, the first thing I noticed were the life-sized metal statues of soldiers spread out in a platoon-like formation amid a garden-like setting, with bushes covering their patrol area. In uniform, they have heads turned in all directions, rifles at the ready or slung over their backs. All wear capes, as if deflecting the rain from pouring skies. *Rain . . . yet again*, I thought, that most foreboding of weather phenomena in Hemingway's *A Farewell to Arms*. Troops probably got way too much of it in Korea (and in World War II's European battlefields, not to mention during the "island hopping" military campaigns in the Pacific), while Marines and I never got enough in Iraq's or Afghanistan's deserts. To their right was another reflective wall, but instead of names, it contained images of faces of all kinds of U.S. service members. Below one panel, I saw four placards for four men still listed as MIA.

But it was one statue that I gravitated toward from the get-go. He looked hunchbacked. When I got closer I realized he was a "comms guy"—holding a radio and with box-like communications equipment strapped to his back. The statue reminded me of all the Marines who had held the same job. In Fallujah, the joke (really an un-joke) was that Dragunov-wielding insurgent snipers preferred to hit the guy who had the antennae poking above his head. And whenever I was near one of them, the thought crossed my mind how tempting a civilian target, weapon-less and usually in jeans or khakis, standing nearby might be as well. Attending memorial after memorial at remote outposts reinforced how war remains the ultimate equalizer. Death dealt out in extreme fashion and without prejudice, with more than one ace of spades in the Reaper's deck.

Near a pool of water, and under the U.S. flag, the Korean War Memorial pays tribute to other nations that comprised the full United Nations force. Etched in worn-out stone are tallies for both categories of the missing: U.S. and U.N. Another for captured or wounded, followed by blocks with the names of individual countries, such as the Netherlands, Norway, and so on. This war, I could tell, represented a real coalition of the willing, unlike the politically manufactured one we said we had in Iraq. Some had called it the "Coalition of the Bullied and Bribed."

In Afghanistan, Afghans used to remind me that "over forty" countries were there to help. Unilateralism in warfare rarely works out very well. I found generals to be among the most pro-U.N. and pro-coalition allies in either war, particularly Marine commanding generals. On battlefields, it feels good, and is safer, to have more friends around regardless of the differences in uniforms, accents, and training. A joke in Afghanistan was that ISAF—the abbreviation for the International Security Assistance Force—stood for I Saw Americans Fighting. Untrue. The British suffered their own painful KIA losses (453), as did the Canadians (158), French (88), Italians (53), Poles (44), Danes (43), Aussies (41), Spaniards (35), Georgians (29), Dutch (25), Romanians (23), Turks (14), Czechs (10), New Zealanders (10), and Norwegians (10), as well as many other nations.

War coalitions aside—the better and much longer U.S. diplomatic tradition—there is a glaring architectural absence on the National Mall for a war between the "Allied Powers" and the "Central Powers" that ended a century ago. To this day, no World War I Memorial has been built to honor the estimated 4.7 million Americans who served and 116,500 who died. A small circular District of Columbia War Memorial with twelve columns commemorates only D.C.-area veterans, the 26,000 who served and 499 who died, in the "Great War" between 1917 and 1918. Missouri-born Frank Buckles, the last surviving American veteran of World War I, sat on a committee pushing for a memorial on the National Mall for all who served in the war—his war. Buckles, nicknamed "Pershing's Last Patriot," died in 2011 at age 110.

July 28, 2014, marked the 100th anniversary of the war's beginning, when Austria-Hungary declared war against Serbia. That Great War among the Great Powers . . . called at the time "the war to end war" . . . proved to be anything but—and clearly did not bring about an end to the ultimate human tragedy that is warfare.

Moving up the National Mall toward the towering Washington Monument, I made my way to the last stop. Unbelievably, America's World War II Memorial took fifty-nine years after the ticker-tape parades in Manhattan and smaller ones across American towns to be constructed. It dwarfs in size the Vietnam Veterans Memorial and Korean War Memorial. In the middle are two large fountains, surrounded on each end by stone pillars with the names of each state listed under black metal wreaths. Along the memorial's elongated stone edges, architects have featured quotations, such as President Franklin D. Roosevelt's "a date which will live in infamy" remarks after the bombing of Pearl Harbor on December 7, 1941. Another pays tribute to the Battle of Midway, citing the words of author Walter Lord: "They had no right to win, yet they did . . ."

Equally moving to me are the words of President Harry S. Truman. He paid respect to the sacrifices of U.S. troops, an important given, but also those of the Allied nations in World War II. "The heroism of our own troops . . . was matched by that of the armed forces of the nations that fought by our side. . . . They absorbed the blows. . . . And they shared to the full in the ultimate destruction of the enemy."

And I particularly liked reading a nearby tribute from FDR, which only served to highlight how connected Americans had been, could be, in a time of war. Roosevelt thanked his fellow citizens this way. "They have given their sons to the military services. They have stoked the furnaces and hurried the factory wheels. They have made the planes and welded the tanks, riveted the ships and rolled the shells."

FDR's words are closely followed by another commemoration, in honor of women who self-deployed in effect while still at home—Rosie the Riveter and thousands like her. "Women who stepped up were measured as citizens of the Nation, not as women. . . . This was a people's war, and everyone was in it."

Norman Rockwell paid his own tribute in his own art. His rendition of a riveting Rosie appeared on the cover of *The Saturday Evening Post*. Rockwell's version looks like she would have made a great Marine—with Popeye-like forearms and a proud "Don't mess with me" tilt to her curly red-haired head.

A people's war. The home front was engaged. Citizens cared and showed it.

I suppose this was how wars were won. A nation at war sharing sacrifice, not just a country at war sharing nonchalance.

It was hard to imagine that degree of mobilization. That kind of citizen participation while the United States of America was at war. It felt so undoable these days. The only time it seemed Americans had any sense of what was going on in Iraq and Afghanistan came from nightly newscasts—more bombs, more blood—or perhaps most common, while transiting an airport. When a Marine or soldier passed by in some terminal, did one say, "Thank you for your service?" Stay silent and look away?

Once, at Denver International, I saw a small group of Marines in civilian clothes. They can be spotted right away—the distinctive haircuts and precise bearing the biggest giveaway, along with wolf-pack-like movement. Two had massive wounds, mostly healed, but which left tremendous scarring. One Marine sat in a wheelchair, missing his legs below the knees. A big part of me preferred not to look them in the eye. And admit to myself that U.S. war policy, which I had a role in shaping and an even bigger role in implementing with military leaders on the ground, rarely matched the sacrifice—their sacrifice. I felt as if an apology was due each of them, of the deepest kind, even if conveyed informally at an airport near a food cart and magazine shop. They never got one.

While I too was guilty of this civilian-military disconnect after I returned home, sometimes I opted to approach service members in a passenger terminal and, yes, thanked them for their service. This usually led to a longer conversation about where he or she had been deployed, or was headed back to, and where I had served in my State Department roles. As we compared our time "in the sandbox," I occasionally would say I somehow survived seven consecutive years in Iraq and Afghanistan. More often, I said little or nothing further, acting as if I had only a basic sense of war-zone geography.

But I had my reasons. I was a former policy guy who knew too much because of my job functions—the interagency debates often driven by egos, not wisdom, the officious memos full of preachy talking points to Iraqis and Afghans, and the self-serving excuses when we got it wrong. I also knew too much about how the politicians and White House war cabinets had failed them, how much I had failed thirty-one of them in particular.

During such conversations with veterans, I rarely brought up how many times I was shot at, RPG'ed, or mortared across those seven years. I was not brave. I was lucky. I was very lucky.

Surviving certain experiences refocuses priorities, even while I never reminisced about these sharp reminders of my friends' and my own mortality, all adrenaline memories across both wars, all unwanted war stories, all now a blur, looking back across those years: roadway ambushes, including the complex attack (RPGs, small arms fire, command-detonated IED) on Christmas Day in 2006; another on MSR Bronze (a major supply route) in Anbar when multiple mortars landed between nearby date palms as I watched AK rounds kick up dirt outside my Humvee and a lackadaisical, annoying fly circle between my knees (its persistent buzz bothering me more than the other, louder sounds that day) and the Marine seated in front of me; white-fire trails well past midnight of RPGs sailing over my convoy between Camp Fallujah and Baghdad, and the dents from bullet impacts on our Humvees' studded metal armor casing; seeing a Marine a few meters away enjoying winter sunshine outside the CMOC in downtown Fallujah just before getting hit in the middle of his chest with a sniper round—saved by his body armor, only to then watch him grab the cheap plastic chair he was sitting on and running with it in the opposite direction, cartoon-like; the many sneaky, deadly snipers on both sides in and around Fallujah—one side killed Iraqi teens, the other side killed American teens; big IED explosions in Anbar that only got bigger in Sabari, including the giant one that killed Fassal and Qadir and split their SUV and spread their remains in front of us along a rocky gray riverbed; the suicide car bomb attack outside Chapman in Khost that sprayed what was left of the bomber on trees; another rocket attack on base that scattered shrapnel just behind our chow hall, and numerous others that led to us hibernating for hours and hours inside concrete bunkers below the starry and drone-filled skies above Pashtunistan; the very accurate (bullets hitting a thick mud wall about three to four feet to my left) Taliban machine gunner in Marjah—my very warm and very red ski jacket serving as his target on that very cold and very scary day; an RPG streaking overhead along Marjah's main street as a squad of reporters (from *The Wall Street Journal* and *The Washington Post* among them) hit the turf, I took a knee, and only Larry remained standing as a platoon of Marines returned fire, unleashing a horizontal curtain of lead, just above our heads; Russian-made Dishka rounds impacting next to us inside a small radius below Now Zad's Dahaneh Pass; mortars falling at Caferetta as I watched Helmand governor Mangal raise the Afghan flag—a memorable COIN disconnect; CH-53 evasive maneuvers to avoid small arms fire from the ground—plus a few bonus brownouts when landing at Fiddler's Green and at Khan Neshin; bumpy V-22 Osprey airspace de-confliction issues with a C-17 (a lot bigger aircraft) at 4,000–5,000 feet; and the C-130J near-crash, saved by a few seconds and by a few feet, on a cross-windy night above Camp Leatherneck, leading Marines to scatter on the tarmac below us, all certain that our aircraft was about to smash into them. And it almost did.

I have tried to repress even more incidents like these from Fallujah, Sadr City, Khost, and Helmand. The more you experience war, I believe, the raw version at least, the less you tend to want to talk about it, but perhaps the more you tend to remember it. And for a long time for me even the less you want to write about it.

The other people and their stories remain the most unforgettable and important part of "my wars": diplomats, aid workers, and troops in USMC, U.S. Army, and allied uniforms, and especially the Iraqis and Afghans who wore dishdashas or burkas or had Pakols or turbans on their heads.

They are the subjects I prefer to bring up in conversations.

They are the subjects I prefer to write about.

Of them all, I am indebted to one tribe the most, and always will be. The Semper Fi one. The Marine tribe that protected me. The Marine tribe that almost got me killed.

My tribe.

After leaving the National Mall, I received an email from Mark. Since visiting the Marine museum together, he had thought about how our wars, the ones in Iraq and Afghanistan, might be memorialized.

Mark wrote:

> I thought about a memorial, but man that shit is too deep for me. I'm ambivalent to it, as long as it doesn't mention the words "Iraqi Freedom or Enduring Freedom." Possibly some of the greatest and most Orwellian euphemisms of all time, and on that note, it could say:
> Some fought for vengeance,
> Some fought to protect their homeland,
> They all fought for each other,
> Despite the name, only the politicians mentioned "freedom."

Well put and from someone who would know—having been in both wars' toughest places. I wondered whether Americans remembered that hundreds of thousands of U.S. troops had been deployed to Iraq and Afghanistan to fight wars officially named by the U.S. government as *Operation Iraqi Freedom* and *Operation Enduring Freedom*. How would our nation, our fellow citizens, choose to remember the longest war in U.S. history, the one in Afghanistan, and the unnecessary war in Iraq?

It seemed that question would not be answered soon. But when it is, and discussion begins, any architect or commission will be challenged to capture just how hollow these wars have been for such a narrow part of the U.S. population, deployed over and over and over, with some troops doing five or six tours of duty, or more. And at a time when Iraq and Afghanistan continue to be a violent home for tens of millions of Iraqis and Afghans—countless lives ended and psyches ruined.

America's first commander in chief and one of its first veterans, George Washington—"the American Cincinnatus"—once said on the matter of war: "My first wish is to see this plague to mankind banished from off the Earth."

President Washington's "first wish" was contained in a letter the man—a citizen who famously would not be a king—wrote from his home in Mount Vernon to Dr. Humphreys dated July 25, 1785:

> My first wish is to see this plague to mankind banished from off the Earth, and the sons and Daughters of this world employed in more pleasing and innocent amusements, than in preparing implements and exercising them for the destruction of mankind: rather than quarrel about territory let the poor, the needy and oppressed of the Earth, and those who want Land, resort to the fertile plains of our western country, the second land of Promise, and there dwell in peace, fulfilling the first and great commandment.

What will a future president, who dedicates the Iraq War and Afghanistan War Memorial, or Memorials, want recorded as both testament and epitaph? And when will that commander in chief, Republican or Democrat, lead an essential national discussion: just what exactly should be carved and conveyed in stone, above or below ground, somewhere along the National Mall, honoring those who were at war for so many years on behalf of so many others after September 11, 2001?

Many veterans want that dialogue among citizens to begin and so do I.

The British already have their memorial, honoring their troops' sacrifice in Afghanistan. Located at Britain's National Arboretum, it incorporates a two-foot-high cross made of brass shell casings from Camp Bastion, now the desert home to some Afghan soldiers and many vacant buildings.

Meanwhile, as we wait for our official memorial or memorials for the Iraq and Afghanistan wars to be debated and decided (the Commemorative Works Act stipulates a full decade must pass before a design can be funded and built: "Commemorative works to a war or similar major military conflict may not be authorized until at least 10 years after the officially designated end of such war or conflict"), thousands of U.S. veterans and their families have already gone online.

They are memorializing the wars in their own words, in their own way—writing digital tributes to the "fallen heroes" they knew so well and mourn to this day.

They are not waiting for new marble monuments in the nation's capital.

They are not waiting for the politicians.

Count all the crosses and count all the tears,
These are the losses and sad souvenirs.

ENNIO MORRICONE
"THE STORY OF A SOLDIER"

EPILOGUE

New York City

It had been over a decade since I last lived in New York City. Yet I knew I would get back to Manhattan and, once there, perhaps find some closure—if that were possible. Since that day when the two great towers fell, I wanted, I needed, to see the city's rebuilt skyline.

In addition to Colorado's white peaks and Utah's red canyons, New York's streets under starless skies seemed to be the best place to begin to move forward after my seven years away at war. I had an idea of where to go, really, the only place to go.

To Ground Zero.

So I went about contacting friends who lived in the city. One of them, Jason Brezler, the Brooklyn-based Marine reservist and NYC fireman I had first met in Fallujah and later in Now Zad, said he would join me at the recently opened 9/11 Memorial. Jason, a Brooklyner before and after his deployments to Iraq and Afghanistan, was also seeking some closure.

Passing through the turnstiles, I waited for the next green number 4 express subway. Hundreds of New Yorkers crowded the platform on either side of me. It felt odd that thirteen-plus years later construction at Ground Zero was still under way. The first transcontinental railroad took six years to complete between 1863 and 1869 . . . all one thousand nine hundred steel miles of it. The massive Hoover Dam less than five years to construct, ahead of schedule . . . and millions of dollars under budget. Even America's historic man-to-the-moon project required less time than rebuilding Ground Zero.

I recalled seeing in 1999 a newlywed couple celebrating on the observation deck of the World Trade Center. I had gone there one weekend when I worked at the U.S. Mission to the United Nations. While posing for the official photographer and dozens of gawking visitors, the smiling brunette in white and her crew-cut husband in black had their backs to Midtown and the 102-story Empire State Building. The bride held roses.

In those days I often visited the site, not as a tourist but as a New York transplant. These were buildings that enabled views as long and as wide as those I missed so much back in the Rocky Mountains. Ear-popping elevation. Seeing the Statue of Liberty from so high up reinforced the immense scale of the Twin Towers. At such a distance and height, America's 150-foot Lady Liberty—her corroding copper and bronze skin cloaked over a century in what Italians call "noble rust"—looked like a plastic green army soldier. The kind my brothers and I used to play with inside the sandbox in our backyard.

Jason texted me saying he was running late just as I exited the Fulton Street subway stop. It was lunchtime as I began to make my way to the 9/11 Memorial via Liberty Street. The sweet smoky smell of shawarma from a curbside stand reminded me of the kebabs in Fallujah and Sadr City. While navigating the crowds, I recalled how it was afternoon Central European Time when a U.S. embassy co-worker in the Netherlands said, "You've got to come see this." I arrived in his office a few minutes before the second plane struck the second tower.

For the next three days, I held a flashlight at night in front of the embassy compound in The Hague. Hundreds of Dutch citizens day after day signed a "Dear USA" condolence book, inscribing names like de Groot, Krikke, Linden, and Lodder. They brought fresh-cut tulips, daisies, roses, and more to the front gates. Amsterdam's rebellious towheaded, nose-pierced, and tattooed teens visited as well. The flowers from area garden markets piled against our protective iron gates, with reds, yellows, blues, violets, and orange, the Dutch national color, contrasting with wet streets and leaden skies, as Holland's rain mixed with Holland's tears.

Dutch children left laminated pictures scrawled in crayon of the New York City skyline with airplanes drawn in waxy dark colors overhead.

The French paper *Le Monde* declared in a headline, "We Are All Americans."

Vladimir Putin called the attacks "barbaric" and promised cooperation.

Known for the quality of its doctors, Cuba offered medical assistance.

At a soccer match in Iran, fans observed a moment of silence.

And for the first time in its history, NATO invoked Article 5 of its treaty—the "self-defense" clause—that an attack on one member was considered an attack on all.

Citizens from seventy-eight countries died on that day in New York, Washington, D.C., and Pennsylvania, 372 foreign nationals in total.

For most of that week, I stayed at the embassy, with only the U.S. Marine guards on duty evenings into mornings. I showered in the basement and slept on a hard couch. The first night, the day of the attacks, I recall taking a call on the main switchboard from an elderly American woman in the neighborhood. She said she had lived in Holland for decades. The Marine guard at "Post One" preferred that I handle "all these afraid Americans" because he did not know what to tell them. Neither did I, I admitted. Living alone, she said in her English-Dutch accent that she needed to hear the voice of another American that night.

"What happens now?" she asked.

"I have no idea."

In truth, I had an idea, but did not want to tell her. I believed there would be more terror. And war.

These flashbacks were like a filmstrip of memories playing before my eyes. I began to feel the beginnings of a letting go. A shift toward a future not so dominated by the wars that had consumed so much of my past, so much of me, and so many of my friends. But a past all the same that would not be, could not be, and should not be forgotten either.

Jason had yet to arrive. Having now made my way to the front of the 9/11 Memorial, I walked around the grounds amid clumps of bus-deposited tourists. People huddled below leafy trees carefully selected for the site. Some saplings had been transported from forests in Pennsylvania and Washington, D.C. Around 400 swamp white oaks were planted because of their hardiness and leaf color and because they can live for three centuries. Overhead, planes zoomed by on a regular basis, landing at one of New York's three airports. Their silhouettes reflected off the sheer glass walls of the six-sided 1,776-foot angular Freedom Tower at One World Trade Center. The buzz was a bit unsettling to my ears, probably for others too, a repeat of how the first of the hijacked planes sounded in video footage recorded by New Yorkers—the one-way whine of a Boeing 767's jet engines running on max power and flying way too low.

At the site, cranes moved masses of corrugated metal above orange-clad construction workers with jackhammers in their hands. A large square fountain mirroring the foundation of one of the towers, dug deep into the ground, is bordered along the top with the names of 9/11 dead. I noticed a set of panels with the heading "Flight 11" and saw the name "Betty Ong"—one of the flight attendants who had updated American Airlines staff about the hijacking as it was under way. I could not help but think of a chief pilot, who, in summer 2003, said to me that he wanted his commercial airline, American, to be the first to land in Baghdad following the Iraq invasion. Of course it never happened. Three months after our conversation just outside his plane's cockpit, insurgents put a surface-to-air missile through the left wing of a DHL A-300 jet over Iraq's capital. (Though Iraqi Airlines did announce in 2013 new passenger service from Baghdad to three Chinese cities, in addition to their regular flights to Tehran's Imam Khomeini International Airport.)

Farther down, the names of victims from the first attack on the World Trade Center were listed, when explosives had been packed into the parking garage below, detonating February 26, 1993—a year I was old enough to vote and be drafted, if there ever were to be a military draft again. Perhaps we should not have been that naive. Perhaps we could only have been that naive. The towers for so long seemed indestructible, after all, and back then no one had heard of Osama bin Laden, let alone Fallujah or Khost or Sadr City or Helmand.

Some engraved names etched in stone around cascading fountains had roses placed in them. A white rose for Lesley Anne Thomas: 105th floor, North Tower, married, age forty, Australian, husband rushed to the World Trade Center as the building fell, her remains have yet to be identified. And a red rose for Kenneth Joseph Tarantino: married father of a three-year-old, with another child due December 24, 2001, known as the "cute sub" at Bayonne High School in New Jersey.

All of the hundreds and hundreds of other names as well.

Jason arrived just as the sun began to move behind thickening clouds that seemed to be flowing in from the west, hiding the sunshine. Rain had not been forecast. We linked up and I gave him his discounted ticket as a military veteran. After going through metal detectors, we entered the memorial. In the main glass-enclosed hall, an imposing steel column stands, reminding me of the smaller version housed in the George W. Bush Presidential Library and Museum in Dallas. A sign said it was the "last column" removed from the site, in 2002. Along a nearby wall was a photo of lower Manhattan from the morning of September 11, before the exploding planes had changed the city's topography forever. Not a cloud in the sky above a glassy New York Harbor.

A big map outlined what soon followed, with four separate clock times listed, individual minutes, seconds of smoke and fire and death that would lead to a decade and a half of war, and counting:

8:45 a.m.

9:03 a.m.

9:37 a.m.

10:03 a.m.

We continued, saying little. I noticed the 9/11 Memorial was not that crowded despite the bustle outside. I wondered how many New Yorkers visited. Or how many might never. Audio recordings in several languages were spliced together of individuals, global citizens, remembering where they were when they heard the news. Their partial sentences flashed slideshow-like on black walls in a darkened room, displayed in white lettering and merged into a shifting puzzle of words.

"All the people were watching silently," "I was very sad and we prayed," "Beautiful day," "I was in Lagos," "Working in Lelystad," "in

Wien," "when," "on fire," "My friend said, 'no, no this is a big plane.' I said, 'What do you mean?'" "Look, look what's happening in New York City."

We moved on to a cavernous chamber. The scale is immense, the mood somber, the lighting low. Jason motioned me toward the "Survivors' Stairs"—a remnant along with an unobstructed elevator that had enabled hundreds to escape.

A huge quotation from Virgil lined one blue-tiled wall:

No day shall erase you from the memory of time.

We walked past other items on display, including a massive elevator motor, its metal cords twisted like giant octopus tentacles, and the jagged remains of a towering antennae array. All six broadcast engineers overseeing the television equipment died, five on the 110th floor, one on the 104th.

And then Jason unexpectedly ran into some friends, other firemen from various firehouses in the city. They had gathered next to a fire truck, Ladder 3. Burnt and bent, it still retained its bright red colors, with yellow and white stripes. According to the museum information display, its crew reached the 35th floor of the North Tower by 9:21 a.m. The captain in charge made a final radio transmission: "Three truck, and we are still heading up."

All eleven members of the fire company died in the building's collapse at 10:28 a.m.

Suddenly, I felt very out of place. NYC firemen had lost 343 colleagues from seventy-five firehouses that day. Although I was not part of their tribe, they nonetheless welcomed me over. Jason introduced me as a guy who had spent more time in the wars than anyone—not something I felt particularly proud about, given how many Americans had not survived Iraq and Afghanistan, some dying within days of arriving or within days of leaving. Some dying in helicopter crashes. I explained to the firemen Jason's dangerous and never-ending Marine Civil Affairs work in Fallujah and Helmand—as challenging as infantry tours in its own way, but without the glory. They asked me to take a few pictures of the group, which I did.

One of them provided a succinct assessment of the 9/11 Memorial. "They did a good job. It took me a long time to get back here."

"I agree," I replied. "It took me a while to get back to New York."

Our last stop came in a narrow corridor at the end of the memorial. It outlines part of the North Tower's foundation, angled iron and concrete. Throughout our visit, I never saw President Bush's "the people who knocked these buildings down will hear all of us soon" bullhorn on loan from his presidential library.

And that was okay.

After leaving the museum, we made our way to a subway stop that would get us to Brooklyn, to meet up with another Marine friend turned New Yorker. (A Kansas native and former infantry company commander who had been shot at a lot by insurgents in Anbar and Helmand and awarded a Silver Star, but never mentioned it.) While walking, I noticed on the pavement that names were etched in narrow concrete slabs. Not far from the famed red "LOVE" sculpture, one set jumped out at me right away.

SEPTEMBER 10, 1963 ★ ZAHIR SHAH AND HOMAIRA KING AND QUEEN OF AFGHANISTAN

The same Afghan king who had sent his tax collector, unsuccessfully, to Qalandar District in Khost. I could not imagine what the odds must have been for me to walk over that exact spot. I was probably the only person in a long while asking pedestrians to stop for a moment so I could take a picture of it. I later read that Afghanistan's royal couple had visited the U.S. in 1963 on an official trip, meeting President Kennedy in Washington as well as traveling to New York. Soon after their return to Afghanistan, Kennedy was assassinated in Dallas on November 22.

The U.S. embassy in Kabul transmitted a condolence message to First Lady Jacqueline Kennedy, dated November 23.

```
WE WERE GRIEVOUSLY SHOCKED TO HEAR OF THE TRAGIC
LOSS OF YOUR ILLUSTRIOUS HUSBAND THE LATE PRESIDENT
[STOP] THIS TRAGEDY TO YOU AND TO THE AMERICAN
PEOPLE IS FELT BY US ALL THE MORE PERSONALLY AFTER
OUR CLOSE ACQUAINTANCE WITH DURING OUR RECENT
VISIT TO WASHINGTON [STOP] WE CAN ONLY CONVEY TO
YOU AND THE KENNEDY FAMILY OUR DEEP AND SINCERE
SYMPATHY IN THESE SAD TIMES
    MOHAMMAD ZAHER AND HOMAIRA
```

This last king of Afghanistan had, at age nineteen, witnessed his own father's assassination. Shot to death three decades earlier in Kabul—at a high school graduation ceremony.

I had one more day in New York before returning west. I decided to "hike" Broadway, from 110th Street on the Upper West Side and make my way toward Penn Station. I always liked to walk and ride that part of the city when I lived amid Manhattan's maze of streets, having brought my taxi-yellow mountain bike with me back then. This most urban of concrete trails borders the northwest edge of Central Park and continues in the direction of Grand Central and Penn Station for about 75 blocks.

Walking south, I passed all kinds of churches, an Apple computer store, cafés with couples smiling. Faces reflecting diverse hues and accents. I recalled telling madrassa students in Khost that if they were to stroll the streets of New York, they would pass mosques and an Islamic Cultural Center not far from a Hindu temple, Catholic and Protestant churches, Jewish synagogues, a Mormon meetinghouse, and various atheist societies—and with a lot of dive bars in between. In Iraq, I used to try to convince Fallujah friends they would understand the magnetism of New York City most clearly when experienced at Christmastime:

When the smell of cut pine, for once, is more dominant, at least for a while, than exhaust fumes.

When rhythmic street dancers, dressed as Santa elves, click their heels with bells attached to their shoes below an Empire State Building casting shadows amid blinking green and red light.

When snowdrifts muffle and soften the loud and brash city and prompt residents to throw snowballs, and some to ski, Telemark-style, in Central Park.

And when visiting the Metropolitan Museum of Art does not require a long wait, leaving plenty of time to see, among other works, Winslow Homer's *Veteran in a New Field*. Painted in 1865 at the end of the American Civil War, it shows a Union veteran, scythe in hand, harvesting golden wheat under a blue sky. Homer understood war, its aftermath, and America.

Winslow Homer understood American resilience.

As a young man the painter had spent time along the front lines of the Civil War, sketchbook in hand—a witness to war, a survivor of war, a chronicler of war.

But I also felt sad and gutted while walking along Broadway. The Manhattan cityscape, a local population of millions fully rebounding many years after 9/11, brought to mind the devastated cityscapes and people of Iraq and ongoing human hardships in Afghanistan, with violence now extending into Syria, Yemen, Tunisia, Egypt, and beyond— eventually to Paris, *La Ville Lumière*, or the City of Light . . . the City of the Enlightenment.

I had had plans to return to Fallujah and Khost, but they never got very far. These places were now almost more dangerous than when I lived there with U.S. troops, and in the case of Anbar even more dangerous. Iraqi and Afghan friends had invited me back, implored me, to visit if only for a few days. To help show, I imagine, that we Americans had not forgotten them.

Had we ever really known them?

I had.

But terrorists increasingly controlled Anbar province, as Fallujah fell, again, this time to the vicious ISIS, an expanding Islamic State. They released video footage from a hovering drone showing the City of Mosques, now with black flags over it—my Iraqi hometown. The BBC reported that Ar Rutbah, close to where the Marine helo had crashed nine years earlier, had fallen as well ("Iraq Crisis: Rutba Latest Western Town to Fall to ISIS").

The last email I received from a close Iraqi friend, Saad, whom I had first met in Fallujah a decade earlier, said it all. He concluded his message with five words: "Ohh it is so bad."

Saad had fled the city with his wife and kids to northern Iraq. His youngest brother, not yet a teenager, had been killed in Fallujah. He attached a picture: Saad and his four young children seated on the cement floor of a cinder block building. My friend looked like an old man. And I felt like one.

Waleed, now a father and who had somehow survived the U.S. and Al Qaeda era in Anbar, emailed a concise summary of his current life in Iraq: "Things here still the same, ultimate chaos . . . everything here get destroyed." TV news networks ran the same headline—"Iraq in Chaos." NPR described the situation in Fallujah this way: "Barrel

Bomb Attacks Devastate Iraqi Families." Dropped by the Iraqi government, mind you. American F-18s launched from an aircraft carrier named for President George H. W. Bush as "unmanned aerial vehicles" were guided from an Air Force base in the Nevada desert outside a fluorescent Las Vegas. Loads of U.S.-made Hellfire missiles and weaponry shipped to the Kurds as Iraq's political system imploded. And the sale of Predator drones approved for the first time to a non-NATO ally, the United Arab Emirates.

In Afghanistan, more violence on display as well: a suicide bomber who killed over fifty kids at a volleyball tournament. I thought of the students in Khost. Governor Jamal, a married father of six, assassinated in 2013, blown up while in a mosque in Logar province. Only weeks before, he had begun to help me try to get the sick mother of an Afghan friend admitted to a hospital in Kabul for kidney treatment. Attacks in Helmand as well: insurgents managed to infiltrate Camp Bastion, again, adjacent to Camp Leatherneck—once home to thousands of Marines and me. While another group detonated a massive car bomb in the provincial capital Lashkar Gah, which killed seven and wounded over forty.

And I read about how Afghan carpet weavers were now selling their newest "war rug" designs—images of U.S. drones, an update to the more common patterns I saw in Kabul featuring Soviet tanks and missiles. Rug dealers had named this latest category "American Weapon Red Rugs." Khost no longer had a U.S. military presence. Even the CIA said, publicly no less, they were pulling out. The only connection I could maintain came through the Internet, infrequent phone calls, and occasional TV news updates, usually when more Iraqis or Afghans had died in some violent way.

In Iraq, more weeks passed with more tragedies. Another newspaper headline that read "Thousands of Iraqis Flee as Islamic State Gains in Sunni Heartland." Some Anbaris described by the reporter as leaving homes in Ramadi with their possessions in wheelbarrows. A tribal sheikh declaring: "People are practically dying of fear." In the north, the main library in Mosul ransacked, its books destroyed by terrorists. An AP story detailed how ISIS broke locks and took approximately 2,000 books "including children's stories, poetry, philosophy . . . sports, health, culture and science," loading them onto pickup trucks to be burned—a nightmarish version of *Fahrenheit 451*. Iraqi antiquities demolished by sledgehammer and with explosives. There would be worse: an eighty-three-year-old Syrian archaeologist beheaded in the ancient city of Palmyra. The same terrorists posted videos showing Iraqi truck drivers stopped on the side of dusty highways and quizzed about their religion. If they were deemed to be Shia, as Bassam and my teamster friends overwhelmingly were, they got bullets to the head. And only more death: a massive truck bomb in Sadr City's Jamilla market, where I had once walked with U.S. soldiers, that killed more than fifty and wounded over 200. With Reuters reporting a "witness at the site saw fruit and vegetables mixed with blood and body remains littering the blast crater."

Time magazine ran the headline, "Who Lost Fallujah?"

While a three-star general and Iraq veteran, not named Larry Nicholson, emailed me after seeing American Humvees and MRAPs being driven on Iraqi streets by Islamic State terrorists to say, "Number one lesson learned from Anbar. . . . If you are going to go somewhere to support the people and gain their confidence and you are not going to stay, don't go."

In Washington, the government ramped up arms shipments as senior officials, in echoes of Vietnam, referred to enemy body counts. My old employer, the State Department, approved the sale of 175 full-track M1A1 Abrams tanks to the Iraqi government—and then piles of antitank missiles to target American hardware that had fallen into terrorist hands. The Pentagon, in its own Fiscal Year 2015 budget, requested funding for the Iraqi army: 198 sniper rifles, priced at $8,500 each ($1,683,000); 261 M2 .50 cal machine guns ($2,216,673); 342 12-gauge riot shotguns ($80,370); 45,000 units of body armor ($90,000,000); 12,000 grenades ($551,160); among dozens of other "Overseas Contingency Operations" requests, for a total tally of just over $1.6 billion. The item that stood out most to me: $18.5 million "to support an initial Anbari force of tribal fighters." Our attempt to reawaken the so-called Awakening. Sunni friends in Anbar, however, had emailed me that it was mostly too late for that. Our Ben Franklins had lost their luster.

Almost as a footnote, Washington policy makers said they had prioritized $200 million in aid for displaced Iraqi civilians. I wondered when Saad and his family, or Waleed and his children, among thousands of other Iraqi families in similarly bad—or worse—conditions, would benefit from these U.S. tax dollars dedicated to humanitarian relief. The much larger sums allocated for Made-in-the-USA weaponry had already been fast-tracked, with even more war-making hardware through U.S. loans under discussion. Perhaps Iraq's prime minister would strike an interest-free deal with the U.S. Treasury—he had already approached Tehran and Moscow for more arms. On top of the estimated $26 billion previously provided by the U.S. in military-related aid to Baghdad according to the Special Investigator General for Iraq Reconstruction.

Along with this billion-and-a-half-plus dollars in new guns-over-butter transfers, hundreds of U.S. military "advisers" soon returned to Baghdad and other locations in Iraq, over 3,000 in total, including a new contingent of Marines. They had been ordered back to Anbar in support of the revised American military effort in Mesopotamia—and ordered to stay inside the wire as part of a new "lily pad" basing strategy. I had a hard time imagining lily pads, even iron ones with airstrips, in Anbar. The new fight updated and renamed Inherent Resolve. Meanwhile in Afghanistan, troop numbers dropped as President Obama, the 2009 Nobel Peace Prize laureate, declared he was bringing the war there to a "responsible end." Withdrawal deadlines were extended and Taliban attacks continued. America's latest and unanticipated effort in the Hindu Kush was given a new name as well: Operation Resolute Support, preceded by Operation Freedom's Sentinel.

America and Americans back at war.

Resolved. Resolute. Sentinels for Freedom.

I suppose. I guess that is what we had to tell the world—and tell ourselves. Tell the Iraqis. Tell the Afghans. But all that convincing by a still overstretched superpower, expressed in grand words, did not necessarily make it so.

And there was the sudden loss of Ambassador Richard C. Holbrooke, my would-be mentor and Big American who had done Big Things for the United States of America. In late 2010, the special representative for Afghanistan and Pakistan suffered an aortic dissection while briefing Secretary of State Hillary Clinton in her office, dying soon after. I flew east to Washington for his memorial at the Kennedy Center and sat, alone, at the very back of the grand hall.

That day Bill Clinton remembered Holbrooke this way: "I loved the guy because he could 'do.' Doing in diplomacy saves lives."

More unnecessary wars, like Iraq, prevented. John Adams, America's second commander in chief, once said: "Great is the guilt of an unnecessary war."

After the Iraq invasion—the Iraq fiasco and its bipartisan complicity—if the denizens of any city in the world should have had a guilty conscience it was those very politicians and policy makers who still called Washington, D.C., home.

But they did not. Many only seemed to want more war.

It took me about an hour and a half to traverse the Upper West Side along Broadway because I walked slowly. I knew it would be a while before I would get back to Manhattan—and as a onetime New Yorker I always missed Gotham most when farthest away from it. Upon arriving at Penn Station, I got on a bus to JFK Airport.

After takeoff, as the plane gained altitude, I could see rivers, farmland, hills, cities, and towns between cloud banks. Within these anonymous communities, gravesites marked the buried dead of hundreds and hundreds of U.S. service members killed in Iraq and Afghanistan. And before them, hundreds of thousands of veterans laid to rest from earlier wars. They all were now back home, where there are no tombs of the unknown—including three Marines: Brian D. Bland of Newcastle, Wyoming; Nathan A. Schubert, of Cherokee, Iowa; and Paul C. (Christopher) Alaniz, of Menard, Texas.

Where on Memorial Day, many mayors, coaches, teachers, and clergy offer remarks and eulogies for the KIA. Or mourn veterans who, once back home, commit suicide in garages, childhood bedrooms, backyards, near a local church, along a county dirt road, or close to a mountain campfire, as onetime school buddies, girlfriends, boyfriends all gather, somber.

SEALs and Delta Team members in the Special Operations Forces community are not immune either—experiencing the highest rate ever of suicides in their own elite ranks. Admiral William McRaven commenting in 2014: "And this year, I am afraid, we are on a path to break [that record]. My soldiers have been fighting now for twelve, thirteen years in hard combat. Hard combat. And anybody that has spent time in this war has been changed by it. It's that simple."

Parents across America left to weep, like Nick Palmer's did in front of me in Leadville, Colorado, not to mention nameless Iraqi and Afghan ones.

War catching up. War victimizing all.

For most of the trip, I listened on auto-replay to the newest addition in my iTunes collection. Maestro Morricone's lyrical *Once Upon a Time in America*.

Once upon a time in America . . . and *once upon a time in Iraq and Afghanistan* . . . as well, I thought—three nations, three peoples, with intersecting, if all too tragic, story lines. Story lines with a common link:

War

Morricone's music helped me get through it all. Helped me reconnect with the American West of my youth, and with America itself.

Midflight in economy class I opened my passport, around the time I observed a flight attendant block the front aisle with a food cart so the pilot could use the first-class cabin bathroom—and so no one could rush the cockpit. When traveling, domestic or international, I realized most how much I missed carrying my old diplomatic passport, colored black. Not because of the immunity it afforded or the special status it conveyed. But because of the official U.S. government job I once had and worked very hard to be good at for a very long time, before the wars and during them.

I still believed there was no greater honor, or challenge, than representing the United States of America—particularly in a time of war.

Flipping through my passport's selectively scripted patriotic pages, I noted the various quotations inside, all the tributes to our "American" character. The idealistic words I read and the images I saw were not about an American empire, military or economic, but rather an America that could still inspire. No pictures of American tanks or banks, but instead statements of long-held American values and ideas:

The Declaration of Independence with its "unalienable rights . . . life, liberty and the pursuit of happiness."

Martin Luther King's dream speech . . . "May God grant that America will be true to her dream."

John F. Kennedy's "Pay any price, bear any burden" promise.

Herbert Lehman's "It is immigrants who brought to this land the skills of their hands and brains to make it a beacon of opportunity and hope for all men."

Harry Emerson Fosdick's "Democracy is based upon the conviction that there are extraordinary possibilities in ordinary people."

Jessamyn West on the transcontinental railroad: "A big iron needle stitching the country together."

Horace Greeley's "Go West, young man, and grow up with the country."

Dwight D. Eisenhower's "Whatever America hopes to bring to pass in the world must first come to pass in the heart of America."

And the images, between passport covers, that accompanied the prose?

A sailing ship. Buffalo herds. Saguaro cactuses. A wheatfield. Grizzly bear and a totem pole. The Statue of Liberty. Mount Rushmore. Independence Hall.

A steam engine locomotive.

The Tetons.

And perhaps the most moving U.S. passport image of all, at least to me, printed on the inside back cover?

A view of earth from the moon.

It symbolized an America that did big things, and not just on behalf of Americans. The America that Jamshid, the Afghan medical student, saw when he gazed up at the moon from Jalalabad, reflecting on the death of Neil Armstrong—all the way from the easternmost edge of Afghanistan. Apollo 8 astronaut William Anders, who took the iconic photo "Earthrise" ("Oh, my God, look at that picture over there! There's the Earth coming up. Wow, is that pretty"), reminded us all of the real discovery that day in space: "We came all this way to explore the moon, and the most important thing is that we discovered the Earth."

I put my blue passport back in the front pocket of my blue jeans. And for the first time in a long while, I began to feel better. I began to feel more at ease, back in my own country at last—returning west, heading home. These quotations, these images, I thought, represent the more enduring part of the American Experience, the American Story. The true Spirit of America.

What we stand for. The things we need to remind ourselves of—opportunity, responsibility, rights, dreams, to be shared—amid the uncelebrated and dark chapters worth recalling: the Sedition Act of

1798 ("seditious writings" banned, such as criticism of the president), and the Sedition Act of 1918 (in effect a loyalty test "when the United States is in war"); slavery (*Plessy v. Ferguson*, separate deemed equal, and the KKK and Jim Crow laws that followed, well before the Voting Rights Act passed); treatment of Native Americans (more than one Trail of Tears and Indian reservations that now number over 300 across the U.S.); Japanese American internment camps (handmade signs that read "I am an American" on Northern California storefronts as the War Relocation Authority forced tens of thousands of families to move, Supreme Court–approved in a 6–3 ruling—and never overturned—to remote locations like Topaz, surrounded by barbed wire and guard towers, where camp schoolchildren each morning continued to recite the Pledge of Allegiance ". . . with liberty and justice . . ."); and Vietnam, as many as half a million Vietnamese civilians dead and over 58,000 Americans, among too many other examples.

All cracks in the mirror of America.

Still, these "better angel" themes featured between passport covers are—aren't they?—the dominant positive American traditions we need to remind Iraqis and Afghans and others of as well. These model qualities of ours to counter America's newest faults and failings after September 11, 2001—torture, rendition, black sites, Abu Ghraib, Bagram, Guantánamo, "signature" drone strikes (based on patterns of behavior, not solid intelligence), warrantless wiretapping—a policy that preceded, not followed, public debate about it—and more. Only then might our wrongs begin to be set right. Only after U.S. citizens take a hard look in the mirror and live up to the ideals printed within United States of America passports. The Patriot Act of 2001, for example, signed into law forty-five days after 9/11 replaced by the Freedom Act of 2015. A lot of fear replaced by a degree of reason after fourteen years.

A Guantánamo prisoner-turned-author, Mohamedou Ould Slahi, perhaps put it best in his book, *Guantánamo Diary*. Writing behind bars in Cuba, Slahi challenges Americans by asking the key question: "So has the American democracy passed the test it was subjected to with the 2001 terrorist attacks?"

Have we?

I would add:

What do we see in the mirror as a country still at war?

Only the things we can feel good about and would prefer to see?

Or ugly, uncomfortable things too?

Even un-American actions?

And what do Iraqis, Afghans, and the rest of the world now see in us?

Who we are.

Who are we:

I had a couple of hours left on my westbound flight from New York. The pilots were chasing remaining daylight at almost 500 miles per hour. In the window, I saw a reflection, a hazy one, of my own face. In the Plexiglas, I recognized other faces as well—more distinct ones. Abbas, Kamal, and Hamza of Fallujah and Khost's Dilawar of Yakubi, Fassal and Qadir, and Governor Arsala Jamal, as well as Ryan's, Trevor's, Rick's, and Bill's. Faces young and old. Iraqi. Afghan. American. All of them died violently and all of them died too soon.

And there was the meeting over dinner with family members who had lost their twenty-one-year-old son and brother, Lance Corporal Mourad Ragimov, in the helicopter crash outside Ar Rutbah. One of the 31 Angels whose personal motto, which he shared with those closest to him, was "Everything matters and nothing matters." At San Diego's Tomcat Bar & Grill, his younger sister had the most questions for me that night about what happened that other night in Iraq a decade earlier—the most difficult kind for her to ask and for me to answer.

I also thought of Arif's emails. How Dilawar's brothers in Khost wanted to meet with me. Even if I could, what would I say to them? In some mud-brick compound in the foothills near the Pakistan border perhaps: "I will never forget what we did to your brother. And my country should not either. I am so sorry."

Maybe I would then tell them—more like confess to them, to Dilawar's whole family—something further: The United States of America had invented the torturous words "enhanced interrogation techniques" to mask unconscionable and un-American policies. Words to confuse the conscience. And then had too easily moved on to other matters without any reckoning, political, legal, or otherwise.

But I was imagining such a discussion. Dilawar's story was already forgotten, although *The New York Times* and a television documentary team had done their part in detailing his violent and unforgivable death. Would American schools and textbooks ever teach his story? At least the *Times* also had, finally, begun to call torture, well, torture in its pages.

By the time we landed, I knew the sun would be setting over the California coast and Twentynine Palms. The wind would be blowing strong, as it usually does, moving the massive turbines that dot the land, row after row, not far from the main gates of the sprawling military base. It was there, years earlier, in the isolated desert community U.S. Marines and their families call home, that I first saw a certain billboard along a two-lane stretch of road across from the town's Motel 6.

FREE Reconstructive Surgery for Battle-Scarred Warriors of the Iraq and Afghanistan Wars: Shrapnel Removal. Scar Revision. Laser for Facial Sandblast.

It was also there, on that day, I decided to write—to write a war book.

The words, the images, had stayed with me. As had thoughts of Marines and soldiers who needed these medical procedures. And all the Iraqis and Afghans who never would have the opportunity. No Veterans Administration hospitals or Operation Mend for them.

And I remembered how, beyond the billboard, westward past Coyote Valley Road and Joshua Tree National Park, when the air is still, the wind farm between Twentynine Palms and Palm Springs resembles a rolling field of bent white crosses—a reminder of real cemeteries.

Where the dead are buried, and where, on Memorial Day or on any day, so many of us have things to say and things to leave behind.

After War

The real war will never get in the books.

WALT WHITMAN

A Soldier's War Journal

A Soldier's Mirror Test

Vietnam War veteran Tim O'Brien has written: "A thing may happen and be a total lie; another thing may not happen and be truer than the truth." As well as: "I want you to feel what I felt. I want you to know why story-truth is truer sometimes than happening-truth." And: "Can the foot soldier teach anything important about war, merely for having been there? I think not. He can tell war stories."

Like O'Brien, Baylen Orr is a former U.S. Army infantryman, a veteran of America's most recent and longest conflicts. He enlisted and deployed to Sadr City, a sprawling Baghdad neighborhood home to millions of Iraqis, mostly poor Shia. In late 2013, Baylen sent me an email after I had been invited by his college to discuss my experiences in Iraq and Afghanistan. Since then we have stayed in touch.

Baylen's journal entries, excerpted below and juxtaposed with more recent commentary provided by him (in italics), comprise a stand-alone firsthand account of the Iraq War as it happened. While Baylen does not view himself as a writer, I consider his depiction of war to be among the most authentic I have read. Personal. Evocative. Visceral. Honest. (A quote from E. L. Doctorow, who also served in the U.S. Army, comes to mind: "The reason we need writers is because we need witnesses." And another, from Svetlana Alexievich, the most recent Nobel Laureate in literature and tribune of the common people—after Chernobyl, during war—who tells their stories, who records their truths: "I love the lone human voice . . . I am drawn to that small space called a human being . . . a single individual. In reality, that is where everything happens.")

This account is Baylen's war in Baylen's words. His voice, unfiltered. His words, unedited. His reckoning, unavoidable.

His mirror test.

A foot soldier, Baylen writes about trying to shoot and kill an Iraqi kid running to retrieve a rocket-propelled grenade and the consequences that followed. It is not a Hollywood or fictionalized account. He describes the effects of an IED blast of molten metal, which badly wounded his friends, and how the smell inside the eviscerated vehicle reminded him of his uncle's meatpacking plant. He conveys what it felt like then, and now, for him. War as he lived it—what Tim O'Brien calls "happening-truth"—and lives it still.

His forever war.

Like so many others, Baylen's story is an important one and a real one, most of which will never be published.

Some writers write about war because they can. Some writers write about war because they feel they should. Some people write about war because they must. Baylen's Sadr City journal reflects that last category:

The truth about war.

Baylen, who is studying Arabic and Middle Eastern history and culture through the GI Bill (while also working thirty hours per week), writes:

Not that its important, but this first entry shows how the average grunt had no idea as to what the hell was going on. In your Sadr City part, you ask the commander what the killed soldier's mission was. I'll bet if you would have asked the soldier yourself, he probably wouldn't have been able to tell you anymore than "fixing a shit pipe," not knowing why, or even the greater picture. America's fighters are usually kept in the dark. Perhaps we function better that way. We had no idea why we were putting walls up. Route Aeros runs north/south and intersects with route gold (Jamilla street). Route Gold was the southern border of our sector, and route predators (aka, The Thunder Run, named after the constant IED's. haha) was our eastern border. The grammar and spelling in my entries is awful. I think it's because of how tired we always were and how I just didn't care.

22 March 08 1241

Man, were to I start. I guess, we were supposed to be doing some normal patrols, you know, go pick up chow. As we were doing it we had a frago that told us to go back to commando bar, pack for loyalty for a week, and support the delta plt. in the t-wall emplacenment operations on Aeros. The first night was not bad, just long. Me and Ayers were placing them in with the cranes. While roberts was our security element. Its a long operation. With 10 trucks full of 6 foot tall t-barriers. But, I guess they wanted to close off Sadr city.

Anyways, last night, was crazy. Me and ayers were placing them in. I had told Roberts to bring it in closer and had him move to our left. I had him go check some things out to see if there was better cover over there. (Because we had a power station right behind us, but it was comming to and end) He went over there, and after a couple minutes I went to go check on him. To our surprise, thre was a completely new avenue of approach. It was road that had bee blocked off by at 7 feet tall burm. So, I placed him there and checked on him then went back to work.

It hadnt been but five minutes later there were a couple pop shots. the second I heard those shots I started running toward boberts. As I was running over there he returned fire, several bursts. And right as I got to the burm I hit the ground and some rounds went right over our heads. I will never forget that image, looking through my NOD's a tracer went right by where I was, right as I hit the ground. I watched the bullet strike a courtyard gate. We grabbed our breath and started trying to assess where the fire came from. I tolled Ayers I was going to stay there, while they continued construction. It hadnt been a long time later when more shots were fired. We returned fire on a tall building to our 1 o'clock. Several 240's and a .50 went rocking too. After that barrage Halcrow, and Sgt. Simmons got there. They reinforced the burm as I went to go fix halcrows NODs, and get some water and check the sectors of the nearby trucks. I also made sure the other trucks new were it was comming from. During that second barrage, I just remember seeing some muzzle flashes, blazing them, engaging, and all the sudden all the dirt in the world kicked up in front of us. These guys are not bad shots at all. They were getting close.

All this happened right as we were almost done, so it wasnt bad. But we are going out again tonight, and the next, and the next. So, we will see how things go on from here on out. But anyways, Im going to go find something to eat and what not. Cant wait for another night.

After we started on the walls, things just got nuts all over the place. Some of the most intense fighting was the immediate weeks after the wall started being put up.

25 March 08 2231

Well, its been a long couple days. After doing another night mission on Aeros putting up barriers, we came back to Commando Bar to switch out with the rest of the plt. The other two nights were uneventful, with the exception of several pop shots towards Delta Co. And they didnt fire back . . . pansies.

Anyways, so we came back and have been doing a lot of guard. On our day shift, it was crazy. A 60mm hit 50 meters aways from me and storrs at the ECP. And then 10 minutes later we had some rounds wizz past us. Several feet away.

But also, today has been crazy everywhere else. Everwhere in Iraq to I guess. The IP were in a constant fire fight all day long . . . like, seriously, all day long. Just on predators. Constant Machine gun fire and small arms all day. Every Fire Base got hit but ours. Which is interesting, because everyone was gone on the Aeros missions. So we have been running on a skeloten crew the past several days, up until a couple hours ago. But everyone is back now. They decided to wait a couple days before finishing the barriers. Cause I guess Aerostat saw 8 machine guns being placed in today. I say we go get them.

Anyways, so its been a crazy day. The Sigacts is off the board. Its been a crazy day in Iraq. Maybe tomorow will be worse. Who knows. We will be on guard for the next day and a half, so it will be a good time to rest.

30 March 08 0715

Im not sure where to start. Lets just say that I went to sleep yesterday afternoon, but it was the only sleep I had got since my last journal entry.

Somewhere, the nxt day, our Fire Base was under attack. Twice. We recieved a lot of indirect. We had one WIA. One of the National Guard engineers. He recieved shrpanal in hi leg and it blew out both his ear drums. I think I killed a guy on that guard shift too.

The National Guard had sent a few people to build us some bathrooms so we wouldn't have to keep shitting in a bucket and burning it with JP8 while stirring it with a long stick. They were working on the project when we received indirect, and one was hit while the other two ran inside panicked. A fellow team leader in my platoon, Sgt. Ayers with a private (cant remember his name) ran out of our bunker when they learned of the wounded National Guard dude lying outside by himself wounded from the mortar impact. They ran out while our small firebase was under mortar fire to bring him back in. They never received recognition.

Then, we ended up going to a building several hundred meters away. One thats just on predators. And set up an OP there for several nights. And just got back yesterday afternoon. But half the plt. is still there. While we were there we got in several fire fights. The D. co. plt that was there before us killed like 6 dudes. And we were watching an RPG that they had dropped all night. In the morning, they got it. This guy ran out there do fast and picked it up I felt ashamed. Me and grant were watching it and we ened up missing. And he got away. I learned something from that though. T better fin a position that I can shoot from. The second floor would have been better.

And we had several small fire fights through out the day. Roberts almost ran out of ammo.

Anyways, Its been long, and Im still tired. And we havent had a resupply for 5 days now. So, no one has ate, or hardly slept for a long time. So Im going to cater my hunger by sleeping more.

We had been using the RPG as bait to try and lure an enemy fighter into our trap. It worked, as a young kid cautiously approached it, obviously knowing that we were watching it, and sprinted for it and grabbed it and got away. We shot several times (he was only about 50 meters away) and missed, inexcusably. I never wrote this in my original journal entrée, but about 30 minutes later, a supporting element suffered a KIA from an RPG attack across the street, and from the same building that the insurgent had ran into for cover. And that is something that myself, and Grant live with for the rest of our lives.

31 March 08 0652

Yesterday was also a crazy day. When we wole up we went on a normal patrol through 738. Everybody there was going about there normal buisness despite the violence in Iraq. I spoke with a guy who spoke well english. He told me that Beladyiate was safe but everywhere else in Iraq was crazy. Yeserday afternoon we ended up going on a raid. My squad was the main effort. It was a company size mission. Delta had outer cordon and my plt. cleared the building. we took fire as soon as we got to the gate. It was a huge coutyar wall. We stared taking small arms fire and we all got out of the truck. We umped out to find little to no cover. All 9 of us were trying to get as low as we could behind a 1 foot tall burm. As bullets were wizzing past our head. I was yelling at the MWRAP to ram the gate in, And finally they did after what seemed forever. We were all in that building quick. Me and simmonsen were the first ones in. We cleared the imdiate court yard and second squad set up local support by fire while we rushed to the compound. It was very easy to clear. It was a contruction site that was empty, one guy that we took down, and a bunch of open doors, and big empty rooms. We cleared the building in under two minutes easily.

Then we started looking for the cache, which we didnt find. Eventually we left. And when we left we hit an IED that had been placed after we got the the OBJ. Once we hit the IED, we took a seondary exfil rout. No one was seriously hurt. But one guy in D. Co. was pretty bruised up I guess.

Anyways, we are supposed to be going on another raid tonight, in retalliation of all the violence. So, Im going to get some things done for the day because you never know what you have to end up doing.

Here is part of an entry taken just before the wall project. Forbes, Levi, and Coapland were all part of our companies Mortar Team. Forbes was my first roommate and basically my older brother. He suffered two compound femoral fractures and lost part of his left hand. Coapland lost a testicle, sight in one eye, hearing in one hear, lost a few fingers, and suffered various shrapnel wounds but was the only cognitive person in the truck after the EFP strike. "c's" or "c" was the nickname of a guy in our company. Where it reads: ' "c's" "Under the Influence" stickers' is referring to some personal stickers that he had made, and distributed like candy amongst the company earlier. Levi lost both legs above the knee, and the use of one of his arms. Later we learned that 19-year-old PFC Coapland secured tourniquets on both Levi and Forbes. He used all the tourniquets that he had, and then removed his body armor (while under mild small arms fire) in order to create a makeshift tourniquet to secure on Levi. We later learned that Levi and Forbes were saved by his efforts until the medic was able to get there. He would later be denied a metal for valor.

When we got there the vehicle was messed up. The entire front was just blown to peices. There was motor oil everywhere. The truck had been hit, gone out of control, slid like 75 meters onto, and across the median, and slammed into the curb. When we got to the site me and george were called to come get all the sensitives out of it. As we were waslking up I remember them pulling out an M4 with one of "c's" "Under the Influence" stickers. I imediately knew it was my good friend Forbes weapon. I just felt . . . an internal sigh. Is the best way to describe it. We started cleaning out the truck of all sensitive items and it was just blown to hell. The entire truck was just messed up. There was blood everwhere. Blood, and chunks of meat were al over the place. What it reminded me of was uncle quinns meat plant n monticello. The smell, was just like it.

Coapland got out and started working on Forbes imediately. He didnt know it yet, but he had lost several fingers and couldnt get the tourniquet on tight enough. So he made a makeshift one out of the rip cord from his IBA. He then went and stared working on Levi. He was trying so hard to work on Levi but because his fingers were gone he was having trouble getting the tourniquetes on tight enough. Once the medic got over there he had to force coapland off of Levi to work on him. Coapland was so resistant, he just wanted to help get levi better. Finally, Doc told Coapland that if he wanted to help, to just hold his aid bag.

Baylen would also recount another moment that had stayed with him since leaving Sadr City and Iraq. A story about a U.S. soldier, an old Iraqi man, his grandson, and a cat, the day they all met:

I had a soldier, a real philosophical bastard, you know, one of those types. Excellent fighter, hard worker, and great Infantryman, but thought about things too much. Anyways, after a patrol he told me about something that he had learned. We had been out, and while we were stopped for a minute and pulling security, he watched an old man who was sitting on the curb, playing with his grandson and a cat. He looked at this old man, and the old man looked at him. So he smiled and waved, and the old man smiled and waved back. My soldier took out a camera and snapped a picture of the old man, his grandson, and this cat, and then we moved on. Anyways, he told me something that has stuck with me ever since. He said that he realized that we humans are all way more similar than we often realize. We all want to be happy, and we all want the best things for our loved ones and family, and want them to have better lives and opportunities than we have had.

Baylen concluded,

It's amazing how we all forget that we all have those things, which are the most important things, in common.

31 Angels

On January 26, 2005, at 1:20 a.m., thirty U.S. Marines and a Navy
Corpsman died in a helicopter crash in western Iraq's Anbar province,
near Ar Rutbah. Marines reported the incident to U.S. military headquarters in Baghdad. At 10 a.m. local time, Marines confirmed thirty-
one KIA. In their report, the Marine Aircraft Wing included a Google
map insert. It showed the exact location where the helo went down,
adjacent to Wadi Hawran—the only known geographic marker in the
desolate area. They listed the GPS grid location as FS 1676 6225.

Here is how the crash was communicated and recorded in real time:

3D MAW CH-53 CRASH EAST OF CAMP KV, IVO AR RUTBAH:

31 USMC NBD

AT 0120C, ROTARY-WING FRAGGER INFORMED BY KV AIR
CONTROL THAT SAMPSON 22 (CH-53E) IS DOWN 15.5 NM
NE OF KOREAN VILLAGE (FS 13689 62848), IVO AR RUTBAH.
SAMPSON 21 (DASH-1) WILL LAND AT KV AND ATTEMPT TO
RELAUNCH WITH TYCOON 53 TO LOCATION. UNKNOWN
AT THIS TIME WHETHER AIRCRAFT HAS CRASHED OR
EXECUTED PRECAUTIONARY EMERGENCY LANDING.

AT APPROXIMATELY 0120C, CAMP KV AIR BOSS RECEIVED
WORD THAT (1) OF THE HELOS REPORTED THAT THE SECOND
AIRCRAFT WENT DOWN. THE FIRST HELO PROCEEDED TO
CAMP KV DUE TO LIMITED FUEL SUPPLY. UPON ARRIVAL AT
CAMP KV, THE PILOT STATED THAT THE AIRCRAFT WERE
3KM WEST OF THE CRASH SITE (37S FS 13689 62848) WHEN

THEY ENTERED AN AREA OF LIMITED VISIBILITY.

AT 0148C, KV REPORTS VISIBILITY OF ½ MILE. TYCOON 53 UNABLE TO LAUNCH.

AT 0151C, KV MMT REPORTS SAMPSON 22 HAS CRASHED.

AT 0153C, PROFANE 55 FLIGHT DIRECTED TO LAST REPORTED LOCATION OF SAMPSON 22. WILL NEED TO CONDUCT FWAR PRIOR.

AT 0205C, KV AIRBOSS REPORTS THAT 31ST MEU GROUND UNIT `RANGER` IVO AL RUTBAH IS ENROUTE TO LOCATION.

AT 0215C, PROFANE 55 FLT COMPLETE FWAR. INBOUND TO CRASH SITE.

AT 0230C, RANGER ON SCENE ATT. CRASH CONFIRMED. ADDITIONAL GROUND UNIT (TF-NAHA QRF) ENROUTE FROM KV.

AT 0250C, TF-NAHA (GROUND QRF) ON SCENE AT THIS TIME. REPORTS UPDATED GRID FOR CRASH SITE (FS 1676 6225).

AT 0255C, TF NAHA QRF REPORTS (18) CONFIRMED KILLED AND NO SIGN OF SURVIVORS. CONTINUES TO SEARCH CRASH SITE. TOTAL # OF KIA IS PENDING RECOVERY OPS AT CRASH SITE. ID OF DECEASED AND UNIT IS PENDING NOTIFICATION OF NOK. CAUSE OF CRASH IS TBD. MORE TO FOLLOW. UPDATE: REPORTED NUMBER OF PAX ON BOARD: 27X PASSENGERS, 4X CREW MEMBERS.

UPDATE 260810C JAN 05: AT 260050C JAN 05, (1) TF NAHA SECTION OF CH-53`S ENROUTE FROM CAMP TQ TO CAMP KV TRANSPORTED MARINES FROM COMPANY C/1/3 5KM NW OF AR RUTBAH (37S FS 167 622).

UPDATE 261000C JAN 05: CONFIRMED (31) KIA

That tragic day represents the deadliest single incident for U.S. troops in the Iraq War and the Afghanistan War. A devastating toll for families and communities: thirty-one KIA, thirty-one next-of-kin notifications delivered at doorsteps across America.

As the State Department representative in Fallujah, I made the decision that resulted in the Marines' fatal mission, as described in the chapter "Helo Down." Then Brigadier General Joseph Dunford, now the chairman of the Joint Chiefs of Staff, had wisely advocated an opposite position. I should have deferred to him and the 1st Marine Division staff officers who were dispatched to Fallujah from Ramadi to make their case, but I did not. Dunford was right. I was wrong.

I promised myself that upon returning to the United States from Iraq, I would visit all thirty-one gravesites. That list so far includes hometown cemeteries in Newcastle, Wyoming; Cherokee, Iowa; Menard, Texas; Merrimack, New Hampshire; and San Diego, California. There remain many more of these quiet places to spend some time, marked by headstones above buried Marines.

Over Memorial Day Weekend 2014 in the two-mile-high Colorado mountains, I met up with former USMC Private First Class and Fallujah veteran James Cathcart. Growing up in California, he was a close friend of Mourad Ragimov, one of the 31 Angels. Years earlier, James had persuaded Mourad to enlist. Once he learned of Mourad's death, James got a black-ink tattoo on his left side, which read, *Mourad Ragimov KIA 1/26/05*. At the only bar in sparse and spartan Hartsel, Colorado, he asked me again why I chose not to visit the family members of these thirty-one KIA.

"Aren't you giving up the chance to be forgiven?"

His question prompted a vague nonanswer. I would not know what to say to them, I thought. Parents. Sisters. Brothers. Grandparents. Children. Spouses. It seemed easier, better, to speak a few words to the dead rather than face the living. (I describe our conversation in the chapter "Nick's Home.")

But James had a point. I changed my mind.

When I visited Marine Mourad Ragimov's gravesite at Fort Rosecrans National Cemetery in Point Loma County, just outside San Diego, his best friend, James, stood with me—just over a decade from the date of the helicopter crash. The seaside cemetery is located on a scenic bluff of deep greens and has a sweeping view westward of the

Pacific Ocean of deep blues, a horizon divided by tombstones of white, row after row after row.

We also spent time in Southern California with one of Mourad's best friends, his younger sister, and father, but not his mother. James said that would be "too hard" on her—as well as for him and, he added, probably for me.

How and when the nation decides to officially honor service members' sacrifices in the 9/11 wars remains unclear. Friends and family members of those killed in Iraq and Afghanistan have not waited to share memories and stories about their wartime losses. They have gone online. On one website in particular, fallenheroesmemorial.com, the personal tributes continue to be posted, year after year. Parents, Marine buddies, high school friends, nephews, sisters, concerned strangers, grandparents, and others leave comments, all available for public viewing. It is in this way the casualty statistics of war become human. Each name represents a real story. Each name, real pain.

Real loss.

Below are some of those written in memory of the 31 Angels who were killed in the helicopter crash in Anbar province on January 26, 2005. They include a series of comments from Beverly Johnson, the mother of Marine Staff Sergeant Brian Bland, who is buried in Newcastle, Wyoming.

Brian's was the first hometown and local cemetery I visited after coming home from the wars. Four years later, in summer 2015, I returned to the Cowboy State. Having added nearly 45,000 miles to my truck by then and losing half an inch of tire tread, I checked in, once again, at the Sundowner Motel. The town's Pizza Hut, where Brian worked as a teen to save money for his first motorcycle, was undergoing remodeling. Perkins Tavern on Main Street promised the "best bloody Marys in the Black Hills." Other signs advertised "coveralls patched" and "boots & shoes stretched & repaired" and a quilt shop. All local businesses located not far from a towering oil refinery, just west of the high school ("Home of the Dogies") and BNSF rail lines transporting coal. Three times in two days I stopped my Tacoma to wait until a rumbling blur of railroad cars had passed, reminding me of my own grandfather's Union Pacific trains that crossed the West's deserts and mountains all the way to Los Angeles.

At the Beaux-Arts facade of the century-old Weston County Courthouse in Newcastle, the county's granite war memorial proclaims "In Honor of These Our Heroic Dead" below a pavilion roof that reads "In Memory of Those Who Gave Their Lives for Home and Country." After a list of names marking sacrifices in World War I (nine dead), World War II (twenty-five dead), Korean Conflict (two dead), Vietnam Conflict (two dead), "Brian D. Bland" is listed under "War on Terror."

The same morning I visited Brian's gravesite a second time under a gray canvas of clouds splotched crimson, I woke to news that the U.S. government had reached a deal with Iran on its nuclear program.

Another war avoided? Perhaps. Most of the veterans I knew hoped so, as did I.

As the war in Iraq went on . . . A *Washington Post* headline that day read: "Iraq Launches Offensive Against Islamic State Strongholds in Anbar."

After eating a breakfast sandwich at Donna's Main Street Diner, and with Fallujah and Rutbah still on my mind, I left Newcastle heading toward Buffalo, Wyoming, and the Montana state line. Along the winding route, I came across a local radio program on the FM dial called *Cowboy Swap*. It began around the time I rejoined a part of I-25 renamed "Wyoming Vietnam Veterans Welcome Home Highway." The flat terrain turned more hilly amid alfalfa fields dotted with a few oil derricks as an animated pair of on-air hosts highlighted what was on offer that week: "a size seven used" cowboy hat, "an old truck," 168 pounds of frozen beef ("all for 707 dollars"), a superglide fifth-wheel hitch, antique saws, used sleeping bags. One listener requested help finding a lost Red Heeler (aka, an Australian cattle dog) named Willy "who ran away after being kicked by a horse." Another Wyomian sought "fencing posts and supplies."

But a particular caller's voice and words resonated most with me. A fiftysomething-year-old-sounding man rang in toward the end of the program, as I imagined Brian Bland might have done himself had he survived the war.

This Wyoming cowboy speaking on *Cowboy Swap* that day said he wanted to invite neighbors to "a big party" to celebrate his mom's birthday. He sounded like a good son. As Brian had been, I could tell, based on what his own mother, Beverly, had written about him online, year after year, as well as what others had to say about him:

A good friend. A good BBQ chef. A good uncle. A good nephew. And a very good Marine Drill Instructor.

A Marine—a good man—killed in Iraq, among so many, many others, brought back to life, in a way at least, and for a time at least. Brian remembered.

And 30 more Angels remembered.

BRIAN D. BLAND
NEWCASTLE, WYOMING

"10 years ago today you left us. Although you are gone from us physically, you will always live on the the hearts of those who love and respect you Son. I miss your face and that beautiful smile!!!!" *Beverly Johnson of Sheridan, Wy*

"Love and miss you. Always you are in my heart and in my daily thoughts." *Beverly Johnson of Sheridan, Wy*

"Miss your beautiful smile every day!!! I think of the wonderful man you were and the one you could be today! You are in my heart always!!!!" *Mom of Sheridan, Wy*

"I miss you so much!!!! There are days like I have had lately that I could use a phone call from you!!! I am so proud of you." *Mom of Sheridan, wy*

"'Happy Birthday' Today you would be 34 years old and I miss you very much!!! Love you!" *Beverly Johnson (Mom) of Sheridan, Wy*

"Hello, My Boy!!! I know you are in a good place but I miss you more and more everyday. You are with me and always will be, but I miss seeing your smile :) Here's to remembering all of those who have served their country for no other reason than that of making the world a better place!!!" *Mom of Sheridan, Wy USA*

"Hey baby boy! Happy 33rd birthday. I miss you and love you very much!" *Mom of Sheridan, Wy*

"Son, its been 6 years and not a day goes by that I don't remember that smile and the wonderful man you became. From the day you were born that smile grew with you everyday but it always stayed the same no matter what you had to go through. No mom could be more proud!! I love you and miss you always." *Beverly Johnson of Sheridan, Wy*

"Today is the day we remember all that you and your brothers sacrificed for this great country!!! Thank you!" *Beverly Johnson of Sheridan, Wy*

"I learn so much about Brian on this website. How many lives he touched in his too short life. He was a wonderful boy and man. I think of him everyday and remember the little boy with a big smile who grew into the handsome man with that same smile. Thank you all for keeping his memory alive. He is just as close to me today as he was then and in my heart always. He is missed dearly by me (his mom) and the rest of his family." *Beverly Johnson of Sheridan, Wy*

"There they are again. Thank you for making sure Brian and all his brothers are remembered. I love this web site!!! Brian we are missing you this year and always." *Mom of Sheridan, Wy*

"I am wondering what happened to all of the beautiful messages. I come here often to read all of the wonderful things people have to say about Brian now they are all gone. What happened? I really hope they are not gone for good. I guess maybe I will have to just start things over. I miss you Brian, more than anyone can imagine. Merry Christmas, My Angel, My Hero, My Son!!!" *Beverly Johnson of Sheridan, Wyoming*

"You are on my mind so much right now. I wish you were here to see how happy Americans are today. They got the big target, Bin Laden this week. It's taken them almost ten years Brian, but no one has forgotten all the sacrifices that have been made in the last years from the 9/11 victims & the soldiers and their families. It's a great victory Brian but so much loss and tragedy to have in between. We miss you dearly Brian! Madison and Gabe were so excited and talking about you all night when they heard the news that the USA got the #1 target. Still so proud of you Brian. God Bless!!" *Hidie of Sheridan, WY*

"Brian, I think about you every day. You will always be remembered for ever. It still seems like you will knock on the door when I am home for lunch and walk in. I think of you often this time of year with deer season and remember the time you and Scott shot a buck and brought it up to the yard and hadn't field dressed it yet, that might have been one of your first deer. God bless all our veterans!!" *uncle Dean of newcastle, wy.*

"Heh Brian . . . I just got off the phone with Bender . . . We're triying to make plans to come out and see you. There isn't a day that goes by that we don't think about you. Me and Rob are talking about paying a visit in June or Sept. Rob might be going to OKI in June. We talked about possible dates that wouldn't conflict with Rob's deploying. All I know is we are both set on wanting to see your final resting place . . . We love you brother..Semper Fi!!!" *Nick of VA*

"As it nears yet another year passed, I'm reminded of Brian, a good friend and true warrior. He would give you the shirt off his back, and he made the ultimate sacrifice for our country. I know now that time is not going to heal this wound. I still get the feeling he's going to show up at my doorstep with a bag of steaks whenever I have a barbeque. He was a great cook, and I always breathed a sigh of relief when he showed up to take over the grill! It's a much different Iraq and much safer world now, and Brian helped make that possible. I often bump into a mutual friend of Brian's and we share fond memories of him. Speaking for my fellow Marines, myself, and my family, we miss you Brian and we will never forget you." *GySgt Jim Hall of Fallujah, Iraq*

"Brian, I have tried to leave messages here before but just couldn't do it. Finally I am able to. I will never forget all the great times we had in IULC and our snowballs chance in hell of meeting in Al Asad that fateful day. From our times at the Stampede in Temecula, getting you and everyone else home from there every weekend, and the tequila injected chocolates (shots) we had before we parted ways for the last time. You are greatly missed my brother. Fate has a hell of a way sometimes. That flight of 53's were supposed to have flown my platoon out to the Syrian border that day but bad weather canceled those plans. It's not fair that you and the rest of your Marines left us way too soon, and I think about how things would have turned out if we had taken that flight. You're in my thoughts every day buddy. I know that your family, friends, Kerry, and your Marines miss you and think of you often too. It was a real pleasure to have known you and I am privledged to have been your friend. I hope that I can earn a place up there with you one day. Until then, keep a cold one for me bro. Semper Fi" *SSgt Soltis, Drill Instructor, of MCRD San Diego*

"As I left my last class today I noticed a whole quad full of tiny white crosses, on each was the rank, name, age, unit, and death of each military member to die in Iraq. I couldn't wade through them all long enough to find Ssgt Bland, especially after running into two of my brothers who died. Gone but not forgotten." *Lcpl Hight, Kymball L. of Grand Junction, CO*

"When I met SSgt Bland, he was Sgt Bland as I was a recruit Plt. 3095 India Company. Out of the five Drill Instructors who trained us, I looked up to SSgt Bland the most. SSgt Bland pushed me harder than any of the other DI's did and I am better for that. I found out of his death while at a bar (I was trained correctly) celebrating my unit's safe return from Iraq. I think that night was the first night in a very long time that I can remember crying. It is my personal belief that he was and will always be, the greatest Marine to ever walk the face of the earth. I got out of the Marine Corps in June of this year, although that chapter of my life is over, I will always be forever in debt to SSgt Bland, he turned me into a man." *Cpl David W. Martin E Co 2/8 Wpns Plt of Great Bend, PA*

"I knew SSGT Bland as SGT Bland, Drill Insturctor of Plt 3095, India Compnay. He was one of my DIs and he was an excellent example of what I should strive for to be a Marine. I was also part of 1st Platoon, A Company, 3rd LAR, that secured the crash site that horrible night. I walked through the crash looking for suvivors. I found out later that one of my Drill Instructors had been in that helo that crashed. SEMPER FI!" *Cpl Kyle Martin of West Lafayette, IN*

"My son, Cpl. Richard A. Gilbert, Jr., went down on the helicopter with SSgt. Bland. They will always be brothers in arms. My thoughts and prayers are with your family." *Helen Gilbert of Dayton, Ohio*

"My thoughts and prayers are with all of Brians family. We share your grief as we lost a grandson 1/13/05 and had his funeral on his 20th birthday 1/22/05. I hope you can find comfort in the great memories you have. We thank you and Brian for all you have done to further freedom." *Dianna of Woonsocket SD*

———

PAUL CHRISTOPHER ALANIZ
MENARD, TEXAS

"From being my baseball coach when I was a kid at Miller High School, to running in to each other at Pensacola and again on duty at the Boxer, 29 Palms, or Iraq you were always someone I looked up to as a big brother figure and the kind of man I hope I have become today Sir. God Bless." *Chris F. of Cedar Creek, TX*

———

JONATHAN E. ETTERLING
WHEELERSBURG, OHIO

"Jon: I will never forget that sweet little boy that picked me the bouquet of wildflowers the first time you met me. Thank you for being so brave you will be missed always. . . ." *Kim Etterling of Roanoke, Va*

MICHAEL W. FINKE, JR.
HURON, OHIO

"Mike and I would talk time to time in the hallways about our experiences in the Corps, and I'd even catch'em at family gatherings in San Diego every once in a while. Funny story: Battalion formation run (everyone loves those!) Finke, then still with Lima Co's H.Q. Plt., was runnin in the trail end of the formation (as that was the designated spot for us short guys). I was called upon to lead my platoon with a running cadence. Naturally I chose a colorful cadence, one that I can't fully disclose at this time, but it went something like this: "F. I. N. K. E.! Finke is kinky and so are we!" . . . he turned around and laughed as he got a kick out of that. We went on float as a part of the 13th MEUSOC on the USS Duluth in Aug, 2000 (I believe he was re-assigned to 3rd Plt). We'd bump into each other from time to time and check on how the other was doin, how our families were back home. We were in the Seychelles, just off the coast of Madagascar, when the USS Cole got hit. So together we were a part of Operation Determined Response and escorted the Fed's to and from our ship to the Cole. We hit Thailand twice on the trip, 5 days out and 5 days commin back in where we'd occasionally see each other. Just like most of my friends, I got out almost as soon as we got back in early 2001. I honestly can't say I remember the last time I saw Cpl. Finke, only to say that he did leave an impression on me that he was truly one of the good guys with a good heart . . . a good soul. I remember when his cousin, Lisa, had told us of his passing in Iraq. Now, up until that moment, I had not personally known anyone that had made the ultimate sacrifice. But all that changed after we got the phone call from Lisa, he had just been cleared to go home too and was only a couple weeks away. Mike, I wish I could say that I would have been as brave as you buddy. God Bless you Marine. Semper Fi." *Formerly Sgt. Rick Roberts/ 1st Plt/ Lima Co./ 3rd BLT 1st Marines of Huntington Beach, CA USA*

TRAVIS J. FULLER
GRANVILLE, MASSACHUSETTS

"sir you led me in and out of battles since the first day we knew each other we hung out as officer and enlisted should not and i idolized you. you comforted my family without telling me and you walked me through many har times you also saved my life as you promised you would, i was getting on that bird untill you told me to go on the other one..i will never forget you semper fi john dugan" *john dugan of new york city*

TIMOTHY M. GIBSON
MERRIMACK, NEW HAMPSHIRE

"Hey Tim, I know i didn't get to know you very well, and I never will now ... But I loved you and respected you. I keep your memorial card on my dresser and every day I see it, I wish i had been there to actually be your cousin and go fishing, play ball, wrestle, everything we should have been able to do, but never can now. I miss you man, and I'll never forget you" *Jake Parker of Conesus, New York*

RICHARD A. GILBERT, JR.
MONTGOMERY, OHIO

"Hey Kiddo, it been 5yrs, I still find myself wondering, telling the story, i remember you and Uncle Rick coming to the house before you left, than hearing the updates as to what you where going through over there, and then the news came, i watched this family fall, like it took a sucker punch, but u know the Irish, right back up again,standing proud 'for you' we miss you and think of you daily, i look at it like this, you could'nt protect all of us from here so you moved on to a place that you could, i will never forget" *Vincy of Beavercreek ohio*

LYLE L. GORDON

MIDLOTHIAN, TEXAS

"Lyle was a warrior long before he joined the Marines. Those that grew up with him know this to be true. He was a great mixture of warrior and compassionate friend. I find it to be an honor to have grown up with Lyle. He will NEVER be forgotten. As a Police Officer in Dallas I ran a license plate late one night on a busy highway. The plate came back to Lyles dad, Dickey. Knowing Dickey wouldn't be out that late I stopped the car. The driver was Lyles younger brother, Boyd. It was the most pleasant traffic stop I've ever had. I think Lyle would have laughed at me pulling his little brother over. No tickets. . . . Just a short conversation. Boyd still looked like Lyle. I could help but tear up as I walked back to my patrol car. I can't help but think about Lyle and how hard he hit people, me included, during our high school football days. Lol . . . God, what a warrior he was. God Bless the Gordon family and those that served with him. You guys are all hero's to me." *Hud Hartson of Midlothian, Tx*

––––––––

KYLE J. GRIMES

NORTHAMPTON, PENNSYLVANIA

"Gone from my touch, but never my mind. Gone from my sight but never my heart. Kyle it's almost been 3 years since you left me and it has taken me this long to even get enough courage to leave a message. There isn't a day that goes by that I don't think about you and the last phone call you made. I keep trying to make sense of everything in my head but I just keep going around in circles. If I could do it all over again I would tell you how much I loved you instead of waiting until you came back home like we said we would. I have fallen in love with your entire family and am blessed to have them in my life. You were and will always be my HERO. I will love you forever Cpl Kyle 'Danger' Grimes" *Chandra Steenhoek of Sacramento, CA*

TONY L. HERNANDEZ
CANYON LAKE, TEXAS

"It has been only a few months since we lost four of our own. I remember walking into the squadron area, and knowing, from the stillness in the air, that something was wrong. The news hit us all like a wall. I thought I would be strong when I heard about the accident, then I asked who was on the flight . . . once I heard Tony was on that flight I began trying to believe that it was a mistake. I just saw Tony, he wasn't missing or in some crash. They must be mistaken, I kept thinking to myself, but the more I looked around I realized it was true, and the tears were uncontrollable. It sank in that I would never see him again. Tony will always be remembered as the guy who makes people feel good no matter what the situation. I'm happy that I had the opportunity to be friends with Tony, and I'm sure everyone who knew Tony felt the same. I am truely blessed to have known him at all, and I regret not letting him know what a good friend he was to me. He will always be remembered. I send my deepest condolences to his family and friends who also suffer in the loss of a truely dedicated and outstanding Marine. The passengers of Tiger 60 will always be remembered. The memory will keep them with us forever. May we never forget the sacrifices they have made to give us the freedom some people take for granted." *M. N. Rodriguez, Sgt USMC of San Diego, Ca MCAS Miramar*

BRIAN C. HOPPER
WYNNE, ARKANSAS

"I remember when we were little kids running around bare-foot and playing all over the place. Brian you are missed." *Ashley of Wynne, Arkansas*

JOHN D. HOUSE
SIMI VALLEY, CALIFORNIA

"House! Man we all had great times back on the boat . . . Westpac 02'. I remember asking you about the tattoo on your hand . . .

or SgtMaj Benford catching us with our hands in our pockets! Remember when I cut my finger off? You held it in place while that lousy doctor sewed it back on. Now, it can hold the ring that's on it. Cheers, brother." *Sgt. Pascual, USMC of Tampa, Florida*

———

SAEED JAFARKHANI-TORSHIZI, JR.
FORT WORTH, TEXAS

"Freedom for everyone in everywhere. God bless my American cousin who created the eternal power in our heart, and a great honor for his nation (Iran / US) The next generations will remember him (and all American brave soldiera) as a truly liberators. As nowadays we remember Amrican liberators in 2nd world war. Jr., You will be alive in our hearts for ever. Dear Rani, accept our deepest condole. God bless Iran, God bless USA XXXXXXX@ yahoo.com" *Alireza of Tehran / Iran*

———

STEPHEN P. JOHNSON
COVINA, CALIFORNIA

"Hi, johnson it was hard for me in the marines. because i'ave aleays been different in my thinking than most thanks for not judging me and for giving me humor when i needed it." *I 3/3 marine*

———

SEAN P. KELLY
GLOUCESTER, NEW JERSEY

"Hey man, Sean Ryan from A 1/3 here, you and I also went to bootcamp together and were in the same platoon. Thought about the day when I saw you in your burgundy Ford F-150 with your wife and kid in the barracks parking lot on K-bay after our first deployment. I still see you with all kinds of dip stuck in your teeth. You made history my man, I'll take your memory with me all my days. Semper Fi - Sean" *Sean Ryan of New York*

DEXTER S. KIMBLE
HOUSTON, TEXAS

"Dexter, I know it's been a long time bro. I think of you constantly. It's been quite a few years since you and I shared a meal on the mess deck. Man, you could eat like nobodies business. I'm retired now. I couldn't take it anymore. I miss you so much. I wish i could've been with you. I don't know. I made it to 24 years. I made it to MSgt. But, for some reason, it just wasn't the same without you around. I'm so sorry that your wife and kids can't enjoy you being there. I hate it more than anything. I'm sure nobody will ever know how much I miss you. I love you bro. I think about you all the time. You were such a good friend. I'm sorry I picked on you about how much you would eat at chow time. I know it was because you worked so hard. You gave so much and asked so little. You never complained. You would always just laugh it off . . . no matter the challenge or how bad it got. You were an inspiration to me and to your marines. You were my friend. I will always love you and I will always carry our memories with me every day for the rest of my life. God bless you Dexter." *Jeff of Grayson, GA*

ALLAN KLEIN
CLINTON TOWNSHIP, MICHIGAN

"Losing my brother was the worst thing to have happened in my life. The only thing I can take any comfort in is Al had become the person he always wanted to be, a U.S. Marine. My condolences to all who have lost someone in wartime and my deepest respects and honor go out to all who have served and to those still serving. God's speed." *Kurt Klein of Puerto de Santa Maria, Spain*

TIMOTHY A. KNIGHT
BROOKLYN, OHIO

"Tim, It has been 5 years today, That you left us. We all miss you so much. I will never forget when Robin E. called me on the phone and told me. I was fresh out of the military myself and everyone told me you were overseas in iraq. Tim there isn't a day that i dont think of you man ... You were a very good friend of mine in high school. I also got to chill with you in hawaii. Great Times. Well just wanted to let you know that i love ya man and no you can't have my bud light. Love ya and miss ya..but will never forget ya" *Michael Browning of Brooklyn, Ohio*

––––––

FRED L. MACIEL
SPRING, TEXAS

"I will always love you and miss you! Wow there are so many things to say and I just don't know where to start. We had every-thing planned out and we almost made it, but I guess God had other plans for you. I still don't believe it and I don't know if I ever will be able to accept it. It's so hard! I don't have any idea how I'm going to get through it this time, but I'm going to try to handle things the way you would want me to handle them. I hope you know you meant the world to me, I would have done anything for you ... I would have even let you buy a big screen before our bed. I'm very proud of you for what you've done. I know you were happy and died doing what you wanted to do and with tons of honor. I will never forget you and the memories we share. Take good care of Shannon for me. I know I'll be with y'all again one day, but until then help me, your family, and your friends get through this. You will ALWAYS have a very very special place in my heart, and I will NEVER forget you. I love you with all my heart. You still are and always will be my fiancee. I will miss you horribly. Love always your fiancee, Jamie Daugherty" *Jamie Daugherty of Spring, Texas*

––––––

JAMES L. MOORE
ROSEBURG, OREGON

"UNCLE JAMES I LOVE AND MISS YOU SO VERY MUCH, YOU ARE ALWAYS ON MY MIND AND FOREVER IN MY HEART. I WILL NEVER EVER FORGET YOU. I HOPE TO MEET YOU AGAIN SO WE CAN TALK LIKE OLD TIMES AND YOU CAN TELL ME YOUR THOUGHTS OF HOW I TURNED OUT IN THIS WORLD" *Ariana Housel of Glide, Oregon*

NATHANIEL K. MOORE
CHAMPAIGN, ILLINOIS

"S/F, brother. See you in valhalla."

———————

MOURAD RAGIMOV
SAN DIEGO, CALIFORNIA

"Mr. and Mrs. Ragimov, Unfortunately we've never have had a chance to meet, but we share something in common. Our son Lance Cpl. Richard 'Ricky' P. Slocum was killed in Iraq on October 24, 2004. He was a machine gunner on the turret of a Humvee which overturned while on a night patrol near Abu Gharib approx. two weeks after arriving in Kuwait. I believe our boys met in boot camp in San Diego and went to MOS training together at Camp Pendleton training on the 50 caliber machine guns. They became friends and were very close prior to deployment to Iraq. My wife Kay and I had the privilege of meeting and talking to Mourad on a several occasions when the boys would stay at our home in Saugus on the weekend while in weapons training at Camp Pendleton. They would get here on a Friday evening and return on Sunday afternoon. We just wanted to let you know that Mourad was a fine young man and you should be very proud of him. He will be remembered as a hero. We know—as only parents who have lost a child can know—how deep and devastating your pain is. We cry with you, and pray God will comfort you and in time bring you some semblance of peace. We have a picture of the boys while in weapons training at Camp Pendleton on our refrigerator and would like to send you a copy. I hope you can access this site or that you have friends that can print this out so you can contact us. If you would like to talk, please e-mail us you contact information to xxxxxx@hotmail.com. God Bless your family, Bob, Kay Slocum and Family" *Bob Slocum of Saugus, CA*

RHONALD D. RAIRDAN
SAN ANTONIO, TEXAS

"Dane, Rest in Peace. Not forgotten. All my 1/3 brothers in Fallujah. Navy EOD will never forget." *Pete of San Diego*

HECTOR RAMOS
AURORA, ILLINOIS

"Hector and I met in the 3rd grade at Archbishop Romero Catholic School in Aurora, since day one, he was known as 'Moe,' because his hair looked like Moe from the Three Stooges. Of course Hector didnt mind it, instead when people asked him what his name was, he would say 'Moe' It was hilarious! As we grew up and went through junior high together, he eventually cut his hair, but that still didnt take from the name, nor from who Hector was. When we had lunch, he would make up the weirdest things! He would mix anything and everything he could get his hands on, and eat/drink it! As gross as we thought it to be then, now all we can do is laugh..Hector also had a tendency to make a fist, cup it under his chin and say 'Daaaah!' That would ALWAYS get us going because we didnt know where in the world he got that from, it was just him. In junior high, Hector LOVED Mankind from WWF, he would carry a sock with him and call it 'Mr. Socko' just like in wrestling. Monday night was Hector's favorite at that time because the whole class would come to my house and watch WWF. You knew the show had started once you saw Hector jumping off the couches or making himself fall. It was too funny (although at the time, my mom didnt think so ;))! People thought he was clumsy, but WE knew he wasnt, he just was out to make everyone laugh, and 99% of the time he achieved that. Come 8th grade graduation, we were all closer than ever! Once highschool came around, a lot of us went our seperate ways, however myself and a couple of others, including Hector, went to East Aurora H.S. He and I still talked and hung out, more so our senior year. We had Driver's Ed. together along with Teresita, an old friend of ours, good times in there. We were also in DECA together, and some days when we had half day, we would pick up food and go to his house w/ Jessica, his girlfriend, and Jenny. Good Times! Many of us who went to Romero together kind of grew apart, until now. Hector was always the peacemaker of the class, and who wouldve known he would STILL be going at it, getting people to 'reunite' and become friends once again. We love you Hector Ramos, and we will always miss you! Love you 'Hec-Dork' A.K.A 'Moe' - 'Jaz-fus'" *Jazmin Nunez and ALL your friends from Romero of Aurora, IL /U.S.*

GAEL SAINTVIL
ORANGE, FLORIDA

"My son Sgt. Michael Finke was on board the helicopter with Gael. My condolences to his family, as I share in the pain of losing one so loved. We are forever united through the sacrifices that our young men made. Thank you and God Bless." *Sally Rapp of Westlake, Ohio*

NATHAN A. SCHUBERT
CHEROKEE, IOWA

"Dear family of Nathan Shubert, Hi my name is Gabriel Sauceda and i was Shuberts fire team leader from 02-04. He was an outstanding Marine and never gave me any problems. Its been a year since shuberts passing and there not a day that goes by that i dont think of him or the other marines that i was in charge of. (Spence, Gilbert, And Kelley) I was with Shubert in the Phillippines and he was a guy that kept everyone motivated we'd have to stand 8 hr posts and shubert would say a joke or sing Tim Mcraw to keep everyones hopes high he was that kind of Marine. I want to tell Shubert and the other Marines that i cant wait to guard the gates of heaven with you guys I love you guys and i miss you guys so much. Semper Fi Charlie corps." *Sgt Gabriel "tito" Sauceda of Madera, Ca tito24@xxxxxxx*

DARRELL J. SCHUMANN
HAMPTON, VIRGINIA

"I too was driving, with my mind on 'important' things—when I came up behind the pick-up truck with a painted tailgate - Memorial in Honor of Marine Lance Corporal Darrell J. Schumann. Thank you for remembering (and reminding) us all of those who risk (and sometimes lose) their lives for our freedom, may we do our best not to take it for granted. As a veteran, military brat and spouse of a military member - I am truly sorry for your loss." *Susan M. of Hampton, VA*

DUSTIN M. SHUMNEY
VALLEJO, CALIFORNIA

"julie, this is david apple. I served with your husband in the first platoon he commanded, before the war. when we were on ship in and out of the persian gulf.. I was stuck on ship with him for months on end..lol. I have so much to say.. I have pictures of him chasing sheep off the road in greece, I still remember the advice he gave me that I will carry forever in my heart and in my mind. I struggled for years with the deaths of my friends in Iraq, until one night on memorial day weekend, dustin came to me in a dream, i told him how bad I wished I could bring them all back and he very loving and symphathetcally told me, that we could never do that, I awoke crying harder than I have ever cried, my wife was shocked to see this unfolding. but I coud still feel his presence. I have been able to to go on with less pain ever since that night. I think about you and your kids ever single day and tell people about him all the time. my wife has heard his name more than most of my current friends.. I was shocked to see this on facebook I have been thinking of how to reach you." *David Apple of stigler ok*

MATTHEW R. SMITH
WEST VALLEY CITY, UTAH

"As the weekend after thanksgiving 2010 comes to a close I think of all the things I am greatful for, I think also of the sacrifices of others. I would like to wish you and your family a happy and peiceful holiday season. I miss Matt!" *Steve Rasmussen of magna utah*

JOSEPH B. SPENCE
SCOTTS VALLEY, CALIFORNIA

"I miss you Joey." *Mom of Lakeport, CA*

MICHAEL L. STARR, JR.
BALTIMORE, MARYLAND

"My name is Jennifer Sagner & I am Michael big sister. I wanted to thank everyone for all your prayers & support. It has been about 6 years since my brother's death & I would like to say it gets better with time but it does not I miss him more & more as the days go on. There are no words to describe the hurt & pain that I face without Mike. It is very sad that my son will grow up not really knowing what a wonderful uncle he has. I tell my son everyday that his uncle Mike is a wonderful man, but it's not the same. . . . I wish my son could have had more time with his uncle Mike . . . my son was a baby when Mike past away. I would like to talk to anyone who knew my brother, I can be reach at XXX-XXX-2718 thank you." *jennifer sagner of perry hall, md*

Source: www.fallenheroesmemorial.com

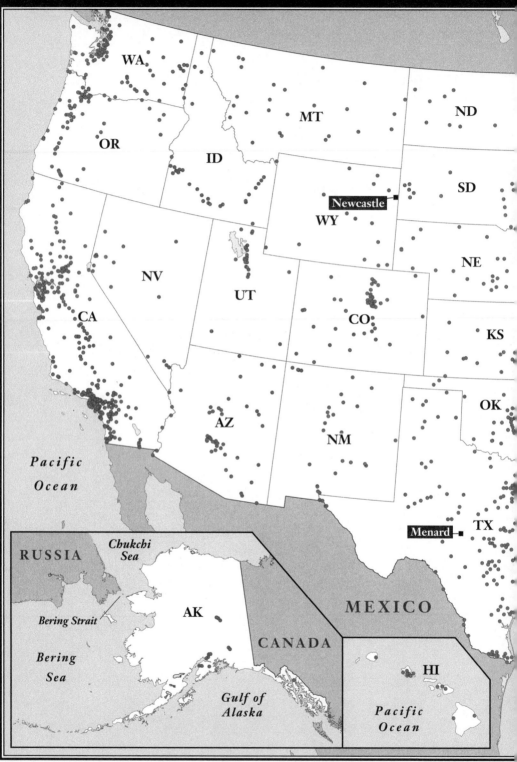

HOMETOWNS OF U.S. SERVICE MEMBERS

WA

OR

MT

ND

ID

SD

Newcastle

WY

NE

NV

UT

CO

KS

CA

OK

AZ

NM

TX

Pacific
Ocean

Menard

Chukchi
Sea

RUSSIA

Bering Strait

AK

MEXICO

CANADA

Bering
Sea

Gulf of
Alaska

HI

Pacific
Ocean

KILLED IN IRAQ AND AFGHANISTAN

CANADA

0   200 Kilometers

0   200 Miles

Lake Superior

Lake Michigan

Lake Huron

Lake Ontario

Lake Erie

MN

WI

MI

Cherokee

IA

IL

IN

OH

MO

KY

WV

VA

TN

AR

MS

AL

GA

LA

NC

SC

FL

NH

VT

ME

NY

MA

RI

CT

NJ

PA

DC

DE

MD

Arlington
Nat'l Cemetery

Atlantic
Ocean

Gulf of Mexico

BAHAMAS

CUBA

Estimated Iraqi Dead: 200,000+
                          600,000–1,000,000+*
Estimated Afghan Dead: 86,000+
Total American Dead: 6,970+

(Figures as of 2015)

SOURCE: BROWN UNIVERSITY "COST OF WAR" (WATSON INSTITUTE)

*MASSACHUSETTS INSTITUTE OF TECHNOLOGY (CENTER FOR INTERNATIONAL STUDIES)

لو لم أكن مِلِكاً لكُنتُ مُعلماً

If I was not a king I would have been a teacher.

FAISAL BIN ABDULAZIZ

Author's Note

I am sure my twelfth-grade English teacher, Mr. "Rocky" Baldwin of Mountain View High, never wanted any of his students to experience war, though he said reading about the subject remained essential. After all, wars have always been part of the American story. If any of us did go off to a war zone on behalf of our country, I believe he would want us to write about it.

Years later, I befriended another teacher, this time in the middle of the Iraq War. Mr. Abbas, introduced in this book, taught English to Fallujah's youth and collected literature. He had begun to translate English texts into Arabic so that Iraqis could read—indeed, hear—American voices. I had given him John Irving's *A Prayer for Owen Meany*, among other books, to add to his growing collection and small home library along with *Inside 9-11: What Really Happened*, a chronicle he said he was especially motivated to translate. We both noted the irony.

I discovered Afghans made good teachers as well. Madrassa students showed two handshakes were better than one. The tribal elders in Qalandar District hated, like me, to see trees die, and they knew the symbolic value of an axe hanging on a mud wall. Message: foreign armies beware. I also will never forget the ex-Taliban leader, Mullah Sardar, his first impression, his lasting impression. The same goes for Habib and Zahirullah, who left the Taliban ranks to build better lives and perhaps a less violent Afghanistan.

It is in this context, one of remembrance and responsibility, based on my many years in America's longest wars and after some needed distance from events, that I wrote *The Mirror Test*. Throughout the writing process, I kept teachers and students foremost in mind—at all levels, high schools to colleges, military academies, Marine Schools of Infantry, Expeditionary Warfare, and Advanced Warfighting, as well as the State Department's own Foreign Service Institute. This book should be read as a reflection of what goes on in U.S. classrooms. And in similar settings in faraway places, including in the schools we built (and often rebuilt) in Iraq and Afghanistan.

The Afghan girl in Khost province I write about particularly comes to mind. We Americans could leave her country, this "top student" said, but only after she graduated from college. More than a request, hers was a plea. So, too, come to mind memories of how I used to quiz Afghanistan's youth about the "two most important jobs" anywhere, in every country, whether a nation was at war or at peace. That most crucial of relationships: the one between teacher and student. I believed it then, as the son of a fifth-grade schoolteacher, and I believe it even more so now.

A related reminder from Iraq: amid rampant sectarian killing, the acting university president in Baghdad told me he never closed the classroom doors. Baghdad University stayed open for all, Shia and Sunni alike, despite dozens of faculty members shot dead and some students kidnapped and tortured by drill bit. No medals awarded for this kind of courage and leadership, quiet and sustained and far removed from any headlines.

I have included on my website unclassified State Department cables I wrote detailing these interactions in Iraq, as well as similar ones in Afghanistan. The perspectives of these Iraqi and Afghan students are worth reading, worth hearing, in their own words. One example: a young Iraqi proudly declared to me during a classroom visit that he was Baghdad U.'s "Neocon Scholar" (poor kid).

Other students at home, in the United States, made these pages better. They asked good questions, lots of them, about America at war. I have seen how those at Marine Corps University, Utah State, the University of Utah, Lewis & Clark College, the University of Arizona, Princeton, and the University of California, San Diego, share qualities with their counterparts at Baghdad University and Khost University. Each cared enough to listen to someone else's stories—my own and, more important, the Iraqi and Afghan ones I witnessed.

I welcome more campus visits, more discussions.

And I remain thankful to everyone who has read *The Mirror Test* and perhaps even recommended it to others. Dialogue about these wars should be ongoing and proportionate to the stakes and the sacrifices on all sides. Future contributions from more authors, including those written by Iraqis and Afghans, will follow. Let's all look forward to their accounts—the mirrors they might place before readers, the mirrors they should place before the United States.

Teacher Abbas did not survive America's war in Iraq. The same day I departed Fallujah his body fell to the ground outside his home in Iraq's City of Mosques. Abbas's death left his family grieving beneath broken minarets under an iron sky.

If my dead friend Abbas had lived, he could have added many more books to his shelves, including the one he planned to write himself. I would have urged him to title his book, simply,

Mu'alem Al-Ingleeziya

The English Teacher

Sources

David McCullough has said: "I write about real people, and in telling their stories, I'm not free to play around with facts or make things up. And again and again come vivid reminders that the truth often is not only stranger than fiction, but far more remarkable as a story."

My time as a U.S. State Department official across seven years in Iraq and Afghanistan, 2003–2010, serves as the basis for *The Mirror Test*. This book is, in fact, about real people. Real stories. People and stories based on my personal experiences, the content of detailed notes I took (boxes full of lime green Marine-issued notebooks) and official diplomatic cables I wrote (dozens later WikiLeaked). I also sent home numerous audiotapes, over 180, to my family throughout the same period, which captured the wars as they happened. Various excerpts, including those tied to specific book sections, can be found on my website:

www.jkweston.com

The site, updated regularly, contains additional information beyond what is detailed in this book—more on the people and places I have introduced, more stories from Iraqis, Afghans, Americans.

I encourage readers, particularly students and teachers, to visit my website. It has been designed to expand and deepen the reading experience, to help close the gap between "us" and "them." More empathy might mean fewer wars. More mirror tests among more engaged citizens leading to more public debate on matters of war and peace.

Except for a few photos otherwise noted, the rest of the images in the book comprise my own. Pictures taken by me across the years I lived in Iraq and Afghanistan.

They are reflections, reckonings—a collage of both wars.

A postscript: Any errors in these pages, and I am sure there are some, and any misremembering of events, comprise my failings alone, as the author—despite concerted efforts, including numerous calls and conversations with Marines and soldiers, State Department colleagues, Iraqis, and Afghans, cross-referencing dozens of notebooks and dozens of audiotapes, and fact-checking by editors.

Acknowledgments

In a letter to his father ("Dear Pop . . ."), dated February 14, 1945, William Styron wrote: "Now the crux of the situation lies in the fact that, to the writer, war is a gigantic, inexorable, relentlessly terrible panorama, which, although at every hand fraught with mists of beauty and pathos, swirls about him so swiftly and chaotically that he is unable to find a tongue to utter his thoughts. And after the war, if he has extracted himself from the whole mess with a sound mind and body, he is usually so terribly cynical and embittered that those golden words turn to dust."

Styron Jr., a Marine, writing at age nineteen from Parris Island (the storied boot camp for east coast and southern state USMC recruits), makes a good if wordy point. Amid the "mists of beauty and pathos" of war, I had a lot of support in not becoming too cynical or embittered after my seven years in Iraq and Afghanistan—to find my tongue after war and get this book started. Reshaped and reworked, then edited, and edited some more, until at last: done.

It was a joint effort.

Authors, I believe, need not be stingy with their acknowledgments, but rather a bit wordy, indeed, particularly when thanking others for help in surviving two wars, and the after, and in finishing a six-hundred-plus-page brick of a book. I am grateful to many people, foremost the three groups to whom this book is dedicated.

Among Iraqis: the country's truck drivers and Fallujans especially, they and others who stood with us to collaborate in the worst days, the hardest days, the most dangerous days. Those who survived our invasion and all that followed—and those who did not. Some of their stories are detailed here, but far from enough. Iraqis remain the bravest in a war they did not ask for.

A war that goes on.

Afghans in Khost and Helmand: interpreters, including Arif and Farid, whose calm demeanors were welcome in such un-calm settings; madrassa and college students; mullahs; "reformed" Taliban; and a governor now gone. We ventured into their mountains and deserts as strangers. Some of us left as friends. In a harsh but beautiful land, Afghans remain a proud and persevering people who have known war for decades. The United States and other allies should endure as well and not abandon Afghanistan. It remains a right war.

U.S. Marines: the strongest tribe, for sure, and also filled with some of the wisest men and women I have known. Generals, corporals, sergeants, colonels, and company commanders, who had to become America's diplomats, and aid workers, and not just fighters in uniform. You and your families deserve the gratitude of the nation.

In the State Department, my first tribe, and USAID, thanks to Rebecca F. (committed diplomat, "Hey, let's go to Cuba" travel partner, and master chef), Amb. Robert F. (a pro, whether out among the people of Iraq and Syria or in interagency conference rooms full of officious people), Amb. Alex L. (who fought Ebola on behalf of the U.S. government as well), Amb. Karl E., Mike R., Gail L., Amb. Ron N., Lane B., Lina M., James S., Larissa M., Amb. Pat K., Valerie F., Frank R., Allison A., Amb. Henry E., Ashley B. and Rosemarie P. (RCH, RIP), Virginia B., Gustavo D., Howie S., the late Andrew H., Suki C., Lorraine K., Emma G., Sheila T., Marc C., Daria D., Amb. John N., Amb. Jim J., Seth C., Amb. Nancy S., Alex (of the USMC too), and Goranka H., Amb. James C., Amb. Mark M., and to the USUN and Security Council team, who taught me early on how the business of State is done right. Likewise for our bench of expeditionary diplomats and aid workers—they deployed to both wars, with words (and some USG cash) and wit as their weapons. Colleagues who served in Anbar, Khost, Baghdad, and Helmand made good partners and good counterinsurgents.

For U.N.-based diplomats from around the world who shared thoughtful advice, particularly before the U.S. invasion of Iraq, in the North Delegates Lounge and over lunch in Midtown. We should have listened.

I am also grateful to the journalists and writers and photographers who deployed to the wars as well. They risked their lives in order to make sure the stories got told. Jane A. (who defines wartime endurance), Rich O. (who has been around several of the toughest war zone blocks), Rajiv C. (who stayed on the job in Helmand after his helicopter fishtailed and almost crashed), Quil L. (who, stateside now, is keeping attention focused on veterans issues), Linsey A., Peter V.A. (Will B., too), Dexter F., Soraya S.N., Bing W., Anand G., Ned P., Tim A., Carlotta G., Pamela C., Thanassis C., Anne B., Adam E., Tom B., Josh S., Vanessa G., Sebastian J., Roger C., Rachel M., Jack F., Tony P., George P., Tyler H., Dan L., Thomas G. N., Alissa R., Ernesto L., Chris C., Michael G., Matt A., among others, including Jim Dao, at *The New York Times*, who first reported on the "mirror test" in an article he wrote about disfigured veterans.

And in memory of: Marie Colvin (a modern-day Martha Gellhorn, whose Vietnam War dispatches appeared in *Ladies Home Journal* . . . imagine that), who asked us some of the best and hardest questions in Helmand; the incomparable Anthony Shadid; Tim Hetherington; and the Iraqi and Afghan journalists, hundreds, who have been killed on the job, like one of Fallujah's own reporters and a friend, Ibraheem.

I also owe Tina B. and Lucas W. They reached out at a time when I had a few war stories to tell after coming home, then gave me a platform to do it—and a paid one at that. And Sir Harold Evans, whose *The American Century* (also a Knopf book) captivated many of us two decades ago, for his conscience-driven leadership while at Random House. Few know that Sir H. helped publish the downwinders story, my family's storyline and too many other families' story as well. He gave voice to those who survived and some who died in the irradiated desert valleys of the American West.

My literary agent, Katherine Flynn, and the team at Kneerim & Williams—you read the early writing, when it needed the most work, and still said yes. Thank you. And to Kirk Johnson, who called me in a forest in Colorado from a forest in Montana to make the first introduction. You, more than anyone, did not forget our friends in need "over there." You and your list saved lives. Read his book, and hear more Iraqi voices.

At Alfred A. Knopf and Penguin Random House, led by the singular

Sonny Mehta, I owe a long line of people at this great and giving publishing house I am fortunate to call home. My editor, Tim O'Connell, first and most of all—a patient, precise, and passionate advocate, he shared every word, every page, making it come together. I would award him a medal for heroic editing if I could. And the rest of the Knopf and Vintage team, who include: Andrew Ridker, a fiction guy (a Roth enthusiast), who provided thoughtful recommendations on this nonfiction book; Mark Chiusano, a valued second set of eyes and ears across early drafts; Oliver Munday, whose jacket design is as strong and distinctive as it is simple; Chip Kidd, for his work on earlier versions of the cover art; Jon Segal, for encouraging words in the beginning and throughout; Victoria Pearson, a conscientious and accommodating production editor ... through all 200,000+ words and her essential sticky notes and paper-clipped pages; Soonyoung Kwon, who orchestrated so well the book design and photo insert; Janet Stark, Kris Koscheski, Gabriela Joglar, Darlene Sterling, and Stan Bush of Penguin Random House audio for guiding me through the narration; Fred Chase, my cutting (in all the right and welcome ways) copy editor; Benjamin Hamilton and Bert Yaeger, two excellent freelance proofreaders; LuAnn Walther; Kathy Hourigan; Christine Chunn; Erinn Hartman; Ryan Smernoff; Katie Schoder; Danielle Plafsky; and Lisa Montebello, and to many others whose patience and expertise and effort made *The Mirror Test* a better book, made it a Borzoi book.

Happy 100th, Knopf—here's to another 100 years, at least.

I remain grateful to Colin Wood and Nick McDonell, key early facilitators, and Ben L., the first champion of this book and its title, Jonathan K., Mike B., Barry H., Brandon P., Clive P., Peter O., and Dan S. on the other coast, in Berkeley. All of them make lasting books.

Overseas, Hanna R. S., in Oslo, a good friend and good editor with pitch-perfect Norwegian ears for American words, and the Cambridge crew from way back when. I miss our long dinners and even longer debates before the wars. I miss that more peaceful era before September 11, 2001. Our many conversations then inform these many pages now. Jai C., an early believer from Brazil, thank you. And to polyglot reader J. Gabriel B. T., whose day of birth coincides with thirty Marines and a Navy Corpsman's day of death, gracias and merci.

Gideon B., Richard L. J., and Carolyn M. of Helmandshire and Marinestan: allies in the middle of a war, and welcome SOS civilian reinforcements when surrounded by Marines in a place called Camp Leatherneck. With each of you stationed at our HQ, we Yanks were much better able to carry on. The same goes for Hugh P., Lindy C., Lt. Gen. Tim R., and Brig. Greville B. and others across the U.K.-led PRT and U.K. Army ranks. British troop sacrifice was significant throughout the province. We were fortunate to call you friends alongside our Estonian, Bahraini, Georgian, and Danish allies.

On the home front: Jody O. H., Matt O. H., Sean B. (Rocky and Freeze too), thank you for reminding me that dogs remain best friends, at war and after war. At Spirit of America: Jim H., Isaac E., Matt V., and team, as well to John P. and Amy P., Chris T. and Marcella F. And to Operation Mend's Ron K. and Dana K. and everyone in Los Angeles, MDs and staff and donors, who have done so much without being asked, and are now working with The Warrior Care Network to assist veterans and their families with medical issues related to post-traumatic stress and traumatic brain injuries. Interested individuals should contact Operation Mend for more information (www.operationmend.ucla.edu). The same goes for the Mammoth Mountain team in the Sierras, led by the indomitable Kathy Copeland and others of Disabled Sports Eastern Sierra. Their affiliated nonprofit has plans underway for an alpine National Wounded Warrior Center, an initiative worth supporting (www.disabledsportseasternsierra.org/national-wounded-warrior-center).

Special thanks to Baylen Orr: who shared his own story, his own words, unstudied writing that is some of the best in this book—some of the best, I believe, in any war book about Iraq and Afghanistan for that matter. His journal is an echo of journals from earlier wars. More voices like his are out there, in out-of-the-way towns, inner cities, suburbs, farms, campuses, reservations, and places in between. I trust that agents, editors, and publishers will seek them out.

James Cathcart and Katie: for Colorado and California quality time and pushing me on key parts of this book, when it would have been easier for you to stay silent.

Deep gratitude to Nick Palmer's family of Leadville, Mourad Ragimov's family of San Diego and his cousin Tamara in Chicago, Nathan Krissoff's family of Rancho Sante Fe, California, and Daniel Wyatt's family of Racine, Wisconsin, whose time and hospitality and honesty gave this book its soul in a way that only Gold Star families can.

May future policy match future sacrifice.

Back east, Margaret Childers (keeper of *The Riddle of the Sands*), Millie M., Hannah R., Maj-B. D., Mike E., and Ameer F., whose company and conversation always matched the good food. Thank you for encouraging me on the book over the years. You are the kind of readers I wrote for, and will continue to write for.

Out west, the stoic and independent Westons (Brad, Linda, Linley and Mike, Craig and Kari and Kyle)—my time in the wars meant less time being a more present and more decent son, brother, and uncle to Ian, Jack, Ella, and Lauren and now the new twins, Grace and Audrey. (Ella, yes, your uncle's book is finally done . . .) To Dad, uncles Chad and Ron, and bro-in-law Mike: your service in Vietnam and the Gulf War, along with grandpa Warren's and great uncle Harold's in World War II, set the family standard. I also owe my parents for supporting my decision to leave a well-paid government job, with great benefits, to almost qualifying for the earned income tax credit as a writer, now with no benefits but a well-used MacBook Pro. Kyle, my twin brother, acted not only as the first and last editor of this book but also as its best editor. He spent nearly as much time on it as I did.

Thanks also to Mary (a writer) and Mike (a reader) and Ed, Greg, Ian, Dianne, Betty, Stan, Jan, and Linda, Stone Mountain neighbors, residing under Zion National Park's red canyons, and to other friends lucky enough to live two miles up in Colorado's white peaks, who include the Leadville bunch (the mayor, Marcia M., the Blands, and more). They enthusiastically hosted a bunch of Iraq and Afghanistan veterans in town one summer and, I expect, will do so again before long. Readers: go visit historic Leadville and spend some money there (Aspen already has plenty). You will want to return.

Gratitude to a couple of professors and an English teacher: John Francis at the U., a mentor and friend, and Jeannie Johnson at USU, both of whom continue to educate and inspire the next generation of troops, aid workers, and diplomats; and Mr. Baldwin, who not only assigned me to read my first war book, but also said something a quarter of a century ago about my early and awkward writing in high school that stuck. Thank you.

To two Italians too: Ennio Morricone, for the music, and the late Sergio Leone, for the movies—for their lyrical and cinematic takes on the Great American West, a place my family and I have long called home.

And Ken Burns, America's Longest Wars deserve as great a chronicler and storyteller as he has been for America's Civil War (and America's national parks).

And there are more, specifically:

To "Calamity" Adamson and teams, who had one of the most trying jobs in the USMC, Mortuary Affairs. We will work together, I hope, to convey your story in the next book.

Elliot Ackerman, friend, fellow Fallujah survivor, and author, whose writing will continue to add to the discussion for years to come, and not just about matters of war.

Mark "Brick" Broekhuizen, Colin McNease, Ryan Sparks, George Saenz, Zach Martin, Chris Hastings, Ben "Hog" Wild, Adam Landsee, Scott Winslow, Rye Barcott, Greg Workman, Matt Frazier, Brian McLean, Dave Lapan, Brad Fultz, Mark Bradford, Todd Bowers, Andy Terrell, Lu Lobello, Nate Fick, Adam Panzarino, Andrew Exum, Michael Haft, Harrison Suarez, Eddy Dvorak, Dave Adams, Erika Sauer, Aaron Gulick, Tom Roth (and the rest of the Khost PRT crew), Ed Howell, LJ Defrancisci, Jodie Sweezey, Dave Morgan, Al "Top" Blankenship (and the rest of the Fallujah CMOC crew), Doug Whimpey, Jay Bargeron, Rip Miles, Bill Mullen, Brandon Barnes, Chris Johnson, Derik Graybeal, Scott Cuomo, Ryan Brannon, Abe Sipe, Bill Pelletier, and Jason Brezler, all of whom saw the worst in Iraq and Afghanistan and still retained the best qualities and professionalism of the U.S. Armed Forces. Our nation, not just the Corps, lost a lot—as Iraqis and Afghans could attest—when Major Brezler was asked to leave its uniformed ranks.

(LCpl) Scott Dempsey, a Marine, aid worker, and future Buffalo, New York, leader. Thanks for the help in Fallujah and after.

SSgt Dean Sanchez, a Denverite and doer still getting things done for wounded warriors across the Rocky Mountain West, part of a nationwide team backed up by Deloitte, key sponsor of the Warrior Games. And thank you to one of its D.C.-based employees, Linnea Gavrilis, who (along with the Caerus team—Dave, Phil, Erin, and Sam) welcomed me into the private sector after leaving Helmand and the State Department.

I am grateful to SSgt Reece Lodder, a Seattle-based Marine, Afghanistan veteran, and talented USMC combat correspondent and writer, who helped cross-check this book from an NCO's perspective.

He also took the photo that went viral of the Marine, Jarrett Hatley, taking a nap after a patrol under a Washington Redskins blanket next to his IED dog, Blue, a golden Lab.

And to Pat Carroll: without your comradery and transcript-quality notes covering repeated CMOC meetings in the middle of Fallujah, this book would be a lot less alive; Carter Malkasian, an Honorary Marine in my eyes: may your serious books on serious matters continue to fill shelves, including when you and A. & A. relocate back to California one day—until then, the chairman and the commandant are lucky to have you so close at the Pentagon; and Dave Meadows, aka Abu Yusef, the favorite Marine among Fallujans, you made the city safer for all of us. (Your triumphant farewell speech, among the faithful in Iraq's City of Mosques, was only missing one part . . .)

To my fellow tentmates in southern Afghanistan: SgtMaj Ernest Hoopii, Chief Preston McLaughlin, Deputy Slam Amland, and Command Master Chief Frank Johnson—apart from Hoop's Old Spice splashes fumigating our shared space every morning (doubling as my alarm clock), you were good roommates. And to the rest of the 2nd MEB, you were good teammates.

Marines Mike Killion, Eric Mellinger, Bill McCullough, Ed Yarnell, Randy Newman, Jeff Rule, Scott Pierce, Curtis Lee, Jerry Fischer: the super-glue during the escalation, and Bruce Hemp, the glue after the brigade's redeployment.

The Nicholson clan: Larry, Debbie and sons and daughters-in-law. U.S. policy makers asked much of your family, along with all the other military families, after September 11, 2001. You saluted, deployment after deployment after deployment. One day, our troops just may get a commander in chief who served in uniform in wartime and who could relate. It has been a while. It has been too long.

And not least, thank you to Aaron Mankin and Tony Porta: they and other Operation Mend patients and their families show the rest of us a true definition of courage and resilience.

Finally, I want to acknowledge the service and tell the story of a soldier I never met in a war I never experienced: PFC Tommie Cole in the Vietnam War. He appeared on the cover of the February 11, 1966, issue of *Life* magazine. The searing black-and-white photo by Henri

Huet, headlined "The War Goes On," shows Cole (a "Richmonder at An Thai") cradling the bandaged head of a soldier in Vietnam, and whose own head is wrapped as well, almost entirely covering both eyes. The wounded men, one lying down, the other, Tommie, kneeling, were photographed in a muddy trench dug into a jungle turned battlefield as rain continued to fall.

Inside there are more photos and more captions: "On with War and 'Operation Masher'" . . . "As Bullets Rip into a Paddy" . . . "Then a Pause in the Enemy's Trench Won at a Cost" . . . concluding with Huet's photo spread of "A Medic—Calm and Dedicated." (The next story in the same *Life* issue, incidentally, being "Right Down on the Moon." It includes grainy photos of the lunar surface from the 218-pound Soviet lander, Luna 9, an unmanned spacecraft. Three years later Apollo 11 would take men to the moon, on behalf of mankind.)

But Tommie Cole's story did not end there, as a medic in Vietnam, saving many lives, American and Vietnamese.

After coming home, he disappeared.

A May 15, 2000, article in the *Richmond Times-Dispatch* explains:

Thomas Cole "was left with the Richmond welfare department by his parents when he was 4 or 5 years old and lived with several families in the Richmond area," according to a yellowed wartime news clip.

Tommie Cole, who apparently attended John Marshall High School for a time, lived with Sidney and Vera Skinner for a year before enlisting in the Army in November 1964. "He has been like a son to us," Sidney Skinner, a Goochland County prison guard, said 14 months later.

The Skinners, who had two grown sons, Charles and Thomas, were an older couple then, according to former neighbors. Dozens of calls could not determine their whereabouts, or if they are still alive.

The 18-year-old had long been interested in medicine, and had dreamed of being a physical therapist. He became a medic with the Army's 1st Cavalry Division, 7th Cavalry Regiment, 2nd Battalion, A Company.

On Jan. 30, 1966, he was in the mud and the blood "in a shell-pocked no-man's land" called An Thai, a central lowlands village that was part of the North Vietnamese first line of defense, according to an account written by war correspondent Bob Poos.

Snipers firing automatic rifles ripped into the infantry-men. Mortar shells shook the ground. The battleground soon "looked like the photographs of the beachhead at Iwo Jima," wrote Poos.

"Medic Thomas Cole, himself wounded in the head, helped tend the wounded, sprawled in the mud of the trench. He was nearly blinded by the bandage wrapped around his head."

"But Cole kept going, answering the call of a wounded man here, a dying man there. Cole spent an hour in mouth-to-mouth resuscitation trying to revive one terribly wounded soldier. The man died."

Then he began working on the villagers. "A baby barely a year old had been hit by shrapnel in the abdomen, arms and legs." The baby's mother had been hit in the face.

There was little that Cole or any of the other medics could do for the wounded child. "As the day passed into night, and the rain grew heavier, the baby began whimpering, then died."

Little by little, the battle was won. Napalm fell like rain from hell. Soldiers hid behind graves in a cemetery as they picked off the snipers. With the second day's dawning came stillness. "In the village a rooster crowed and hens pecked in the mud," Poos wrote. "A pig rooted through empty C-ration cans."

Six months later, two weeks before he was due to ship out stateside, Cole (with a deep scar on his cheek) volunteered for a mission in Nha Trang. Again he heard bullets whistling and the screams for medics. He ran to help a fallen sergeant.

"I felt something hit me and spin me around," he told a combat correspondent, "and the next thing I knew my face was hitting the gravel." His left arm was shattered. Another bullet ripped into his left thigh. The article said Cole's mother was living in Pittsburg, Kan. Poos, now 69 and living in Alexandria, lost track of Tommie Cole, but he'll never forget him.

"He was really doing a yeoman's job," he said. "He was saving a lot of lives. Sharp kid. A real good kid."

Poos also will never forget that two-day firefight. "I thought we were all going to be killed."

John Setelin of Glen Allen, who fought with the 7th Cavalry at An Thai, said he wished he knew where Cole was. "He patched a whole bunch of us up."

"Several of the medics in the 7th Cav have made a hobby out of looking for him," said Joseph Galloway, a UPI war correspondent in Vietnam and co-author of "We Were Soldiers Once, and Young." "A whole bunch of us have been looking for Tommie Cole for years . . . It's just like he fell off the face of the Earth," Galloway said.

"Just where the hell is Tommie Cole? He's an American hero. We're hoping he's alive somewhere, and living good. If we just knew that, that would be enough."

Tommie Cole's story, an unfinished story about a real American hero, should be known and shared. It mirrors the sacrifices of troops in Iraq and Afghanistan and embodies the human costs of conflict endured by the Iraqi and Afghan people.

Lessons that still apply half a century later, when a great nation started another wrong war.

Do you regret your journey? No . . . but I'm a little tired.

The Seventh Seal, 1957

One lived with a mask until one thought the face fitted it. Then suddenly one day another face looks out of the mirror and the mirror cracks.

WALLACE STEGNER

Wisdom begins at the end.

DANIEL WEBSTER

A NOTE ABOUT THE AUTHOR

John Kael Weston represented the United States for over a decade as a State Department official. Washington acknowledged his multiyear work in Fallujah with Marines by awarding him one of its highest honors, the Secretary of State's Medal for Heroism.

A NOTE ON THE TYPE

This book was set in Janson, a typeface thought to have been made by the Dutchman Anton Janson, a practicing typefounder in Leipzig during the years 1668–1687, but it has been conclusively demonstrated that these types are actually the work of the Hungarian Nicholas Kis (1650–1702).

Composed by North Market Street Graphics,
Lancaster, Pennsylvania

Printed and bound by Berryville Graphics,
Berryville, Virginia

Designed by Soonyoung Kwon